BLACK MAGIC, WITCHCRAFT AND OCCULTISM

Black magic, occult practices and witchcraft still evoke huge curiosity, interest and amazement in the minds of people. Although witchcraft in Europe has been a widely studied phenomenon, black magic and occult are not yet a popular theme of academic research, even though India is known as a land of magic, *tantra* and occult. The Indian State of Assam was historically feared as the land of Kamrup-Kamakhya, black magic, witchcraft and occultic practices. It was where different Tantric cults as well as other occult practices thrived. The Khasi Hills are known for the practice of snake vampire worship. The village of Mayong is the village, where magic and occult is still practiced as a living tradition. This book is one of the rarest collections, where such practices are researched, recorded and academically analyzed. It is one of those collections where studies of all three practices of Black Magic, Witchcraft and Occult are combined in one single book.

Sajal Nag is currently a Senior Professor and Head, Department of History and Dean, School of Social Sciences, Assam University, Silchar. He is the author of *The Beleaguered Nation: Making and Unmaking of the Assamese Nationality* (Manohar: 2016); and *Contesting Marginality: Ethnicity, Insurgency and Sub Nationalism in North East India* (Manohar: 2002); among others.

Black Magic, Witchcraft and Occultism

Secret Cultural Practices in India

Edited by

SAJAL NAG

MANOHAR
2022

Routledge
Taylor & Francis Group
LONDON AND NEW YORK

First published 2023
by Routledge
4 Park Square, Milton Park, Abingdon, Oxon OX14 4RN

and by Routledge
605 Third Avenue, New York, NY 10158

Routledge is an imprint of the Taylor & Francis Group, an informa business

British Library Cataloguing-in-Publication Data
A catalogue record for this book is available from the British Library

ISBN: 9781032522500 (hbk)
ISBN: 9781032522517 (ebk)
ISBN: 9781003405764 (ebk)

DOI: 10.4324/9781003405764

Typeset in Adobe Garamond 11/13
by Kohli Print, Delhi 110051

MANOHAR

The idea and inspiration of the theme of this book came from my teacher and mentor

PROFESSOR IMDAD HUSSEIN

Retired Professor of History, North Eastern Hill University, Shillong

This book is dedicated to him

Contents

PART IV: WITCHCRAFT AND WITCH HUNTING

List of Illustrations

Preface

While Assam was known as the land of black magic, rest of the north-east was known for occults and widespread practice of witchcraft. Yet very little study has been made to examine such prevailing ideas, practises and culture. With this aim in view this volume was planned. Since it was difficult to get articles on the subject, an international seminar was organized. The outcome of the seminar is this volume. Some relevant articles which were not presented in the seminar are also included to make the volume viable. Since the volume is a pioneer project, the objective is to inspire and enthuse scholars to come out with more research on the subject of black magic, witchcraft and occult practices in not just north-east India but rest of India as well. If it succeeds in the objective, the untiring efforts to bring out this volume would be justified.

Silchar SAJAL NAG
21 March 2022

Introduction

SAJAL NAG

The present State of Assam was 'famed in Hindu traditions as the land of magic and witchcraft'.[1] It was known as a place of black magic, witchcraft and occult practices. It was indeed a land of Tantra, Tantric Buddhism, Tantric Hinduism, Yogini Tantra and other occult practices. Its earlier name Kamrupa which 'is better known to Hindu India as a land of magic and witchcraft with its famous Tantric shrine Kamakhya with which it is frequently associated together (Kamrupa-Kamakhya)'.[2] The land is dotted with temples and ancient structures of mysticism, eroticism and Tantra. Its adherents base their observances on the tantras, a series of religious works in which the various ceremonies, prayers and incantations are prescribed in a dialogue between Siva and his wife Parvati. The fundamental idea is the worship of the female principle, of procreative power of nature as manifested by personified desire. It is a religion of bloody sacrifices from which even human beings were not exempt. In the *Kalika Purana*, it is said that a man without blemish is the most acceptable sacrifice that can be offered and the manner in which the victim is to be dealt with is laid down in great detail. When the new temple of Kamakhya was opened the occasion was celebrated by the immolation of no less than a hundred and forty men, whose heads were offered to the Goddess on salvers made of copper. Similar sacrifices were also offered to various aboriginal deities.[3]

While Kamrupa region has its origin in the legend of Kamadeva, Kamakhya is built as one of the fifty-two *pithas*, where according to Puranic stories, the reproductive organ of Sati had fallen when her dead body was cut into in many pieces by God Vishnu to prevent the desperate Shiva from devastation of the universe. 'According to the *Kalika Purana*, the genital organ of Sati fell here when her dead body was carried hither and thither in frantic sorrow by her husband Siva. The mountain represented the body of Siva himself and when Sati's genital organ fell on it, the mountain turned blue. The goddess herself is called Kamakhya.'[4] The same author also feels that originally the region was known for its Saivite practices and the female cult was a practice of the aboriginals who were preponderant in the region. In fact, Kamakhya was a goddess probably of the matriarchal tribes like the Khasis and Garos.[5] The Goddess cult was legitimized by the state only to save the Saivite tradition. That Kamakhya was a Khasi Goddess is recognized by the Khasi tribe themselves. According to their claim, Kamakhya was a derivation of the word *Ka Meikha* referring to their Mother Goddess and the temple was a site of pilgrimage for the Khasis even until the nineteenth century before the absolute takeover of their religion by Christianity. In fact, the worship of *yoni* (genital) in Kamakhya is considered quite un-Aryan and a tribal practice by non-followers: '. . . the temple is unique from other temples of the Devi in different parts of India in that it enshrines no image of the Goddess. Within the temple there is a cave in a corner of which stands a block of stone on which the symbol of a *Yoni* has been sculptured. The stone is kept from the oozing of a natural spring within the cave.'[6] In fact, in a year, three days in the month of May-June the doors of the temple are kept shut and no one is allowed to enter. These three days are called Ambubachi which are claimed as the days of menstruation of the Devi. These three days are also celebrated outside the door of the temple as a big fair where worshippers of the Mother Goddess come from all over India and camp in the temple vicinity. Such celebration adds to the mystic and magical aura of the temple and province. The cult spread to other parts of north-east India like Jaintia Hills and Tripura among others. In all these places a Mother Goddess is worshipped and sacrifices of animal and even human beings were regularly made.[7] There are many other forms practised around the temple which are considered magic and sorcery. It is said that 'While mundane Tantra as *louika* is mostly comprised of magical rituals and incantations with its aim to get *siddhi*, eight great successes, the super-mundane Tantra, *lokottara, aim* for non-reversible bliss. Both kinds of *siddhi* and *sādhya*, either at the mundane or at a higher spiritual level, are still within the realm of desire and *pravritti-mārga*, difference being what kind of pleasure one looks for, mundane and carnal or spiritual and refined. On the one hand, Mother Goddess Kāmākhyā is Kāmesvarī, the blue and the mysterious Goddess of love-sex and power and on the other hand she is the Great Goddess, who in her transcendental and religious position can bestow liberation from the bindings of desire and of Kāma.[8] All these established Assam as a land of Tantra and Tantric practises. Recently the Tantric form of practice has been sought to be understood in modern concepts of power and transgression.

> Tantra in Assam centres around the release and harnessing of power—the dangerous, awesome power that lies on the margins of the physical and social universe. On the religious level, Tantra harnesses the dangerous power of the Goddess—Shakti or Kamakhya—the terrible, violent female who alone can conquer the forces of impurity in the universe. On the social and geographic level, it harnesses the dangerous power of tribal peoples on the margins of Hindu India. On the ritual level, it harnesses the power of violent practices like sacrifice, specifically the beheading of animals considered impure by traditional Vedic standards. And on the political level, it harnesses the dangerous power of kingship—the power of rule, warfare, and the necessary violence that comes with the office of the king.[9]

The province was earlier known as Pragjyotishpur marking it out to be centre of astrological practices. While historians have no issue on the etymology of the word Pragjyotishpur they offered different explanations for the name. One of them wrote:

> It is significant that to the immediate east of the town of Gauhati there is a temple on the crest of a hill known as Citrachala and the temple is dedicated to Navagraha or the nine planets (essential for any astrological study). It is probable that this temple is the origin of the name Pragjyotishpura . . . the Citracala or Arvak hill where the *navagraha* or nine planets are worshipped is one of the many sacred places mentioned in the *Kalika Purana*. The place is not given any prominence in the *Purana* or in local traditions to lend a name to a whole province. The association of Assam to magic and incantation seems to be covered by the term Kamarupa and not Pragjyotisha.[10]

Historian Edward Gait translated it as the City of Eastern Astrology.[11] 'The name is interesting in connection with the reputation which the country has always held as a land of magic and incantation and with the view that it was in Assam that the Tantric form of Hinduism originated'.[12] Historians have established that the province was called by different names during different historical periods. Its earliest name was of course Pragjyotishpur. Another version states the Kamrupa and Prgajyotishpur were alternative names of the same province.[13] However, it is by the name Prgajyotishpur that it is referred to in the epics *Ramayana* and *Mahabharata* and the *Puranas*.[14] True to its name not just the plainsmen who practised astrology, even the tribals had their own interpretation of stars and planets and accordingly developed their own astronomy.[15] The most familiar constellations for example in Assam are those of Orion and the Pleiades, which are visible throughout the cold weather when the sky is clear. The Miri tribe of Assam appear to regard these constellations as representing a young man or men pursuing girls across the sky. Another familiar constellation in north-east India is that of the milky way. This constellation is visible early in the cold weather, it is generally associated with the cleavage between the end of the rains and the beginning of the cold weather by tribes. As far as sun and the moon are concerned there is a good deal more uniformity. Both the entities are assigned gender. The respective genders of the sun and moon vary from community to community. The eclipses of the sun and moon have always troubled the tribes. There seem to be quite different ideas about eclipse among the inhabitants of the region. The next phenomenon in my list is the rainbow which excited people in very many ways. Earthquakes cannot strictly be called astronomical phenomena but the notion of earthquakes as caused by ghosts seems to be linked to that of the responsibility of a god under the earth by the Kachha Naga story. Other tribes view it differently.[16]

Talking of Tantra, magic, occult and sorcery brings the question of *mantras*, sacred chanting for invoking good spirits/gods/goddesses or propitiating evils. The *mantras* are also chanted for other purposes as well, both spiritual and material. The *mantras* are known as *bej-bejali, jora phooka, tontro-montro*. The religious and ritual dimension of *mantras* is contextualized and used in much more practical, immediate and almost clinical purposes by these practitioners of these practises. Clients would come with a problem, the practitioner would listen, diagnose and give a remedy, using *mantras* to interpret and resolve the problem. *Mantras* chanted on everyday things like rice, sugar, water, a thread, an amulet, a fruit, a pot, could make them into potent objects capable of immediate action on someone or something. The results could be both benevolent and malevolent depending on the intention. *Mantras* are a combination of potent words, syllables and assorted sound units with a specific pronunciation and intonation. It is said that the right *mantra*, spoken by the right person in the right manner generates a power, which can be either positive or negative. This power can in turn be harnessed and channelled by the practitioner for various purposes—divination, healing illnesses, causing illnesses, solving life problems and causing life problems.[17]

Medieval text and chronicles have testified the existence of many such beliefs about Assam. One of them is that if anybody visited it, they were converted into sheep by sheer magic, and hence, they would never be allowed to return to their native place. The Mughal invaders too felt the same way, 'As no one who entered this country ever returned and the manners of its natives were never made known to any outsiders, the people of Hindustan used to call the inhabitants of Assam sorcerers and magicians and consider them standing outside human species. They say whoever enters this country is overcome by its charms and never comes out of it.'[18] The fame of Assam as a land of magic and occult had preceded and coloured the advancement and defeat of the Muslim power in the neighbouring Bengal who invaded or planned to penetrate into Assam. The practice of magic and incantation which prevailed in Assam attracted the attention of the Persian chroniclers of the sixteenth and seventeenth centuries. The *Ain-i-Akbari* and *Fathiya-i-Ibriyah* contain reference of Assamese magical rites. The author of the *Baharistan-i-Ghaibi* written by Allauddin Ishfani alias Mirza Nathan, a Mughal general who had accompanied the Mughal army during the Ahom Mughal conflict in the early part of the seventeenth century dwells at length on the practices in the Khuntaghat *paragana* in the present Goalpara district and narrates how the people resorted to such practices to influence the course of war. The *Alamgir-namah* states that whoever came to this country lost his way and could not go back. Mayong and Pragjyotishpura (ancient name of present-day Assam) find place in several mytho-logical epics including *Mahabharata*. Chief Ghatotkacha of Kachari Kingdom took part in 'The Great Battle of *Mahabharata*' with his magical powers. Reference of such practice is found in the *Baharistan-i-Ghaibi*. He stated 'Muhammad Zaman Tabrizi who was appointed as a *Karori* (revenue officer) in the *pargana* of Khuntaghat (which falls in the present Goalpara and is a Rabha dominated area) was a victim of such witchcraft. The incident has been stated as follows—

> Muhammad Zaman was a hot tempered man and he began to oppress the *ryots* and seize their beautiful girls and boys. This place is notorious for magic and sorcery. Thus, if a man takes by force a fowl from a *ryot* and the *ryot* comes to the judge for redress, and if that person is refused justice then the complainant by means of his magic and sorcery could make the accused produce the voice of a fowl from inside his stomach, and thus proves the falsity of the protestations of the accused, if a bailiff of the judge stayed at a village in connection with the work of the *Dihidar* or the *Pattadar* (the tenure holder or the revenue farmer) and if in a state of drunkenness, he demanded fish with violence in the evening or midnight when no fish was available, and persisted on his demand by torturing the *ryots*, then they would bring some leaves of mango tree or another tree whose name reads like *lahsura* and breathe on this leaves some words of magic or sorcery. These leaves would forthwith turn into a kind of snail fish. When these fish were cooked by him in a state of drunkenness, they turned into blood. As soon as they were eaten by the baiiiff, he died.[19]

Even Muhammad Zaman was so bewitched by some person, that for two or three days he used to produce sounds of beast like dogs cats or other animals of that class, following which he died.[20] Even Guru Nanak the founder of Sikhism had fallen prey to the magical charms of Assam. Legend has it that, when Guru Nanak visited Kamarupa in the late sixteenth century, the country was governed, according to Sikh accounts by a woman called Nur Shah. There is no evidence to corroborate the account. The name of the queen sounds quite Perso-Arabic, which also seems scarcely possible that any region of the neighbourhood of Kamarupa was hardly governed by a Muslim woman. However, the general belief was that Kamarupa was a land of sorcery and magic which was woven into the story. Nur Shah was however, known in the folklore as a famous witch mentioned in the *Janamsakhi.* Nur Shah and her women were said to have approached the Guru and his follower Mardana and tried cast the power of their magic spells. Since it did not work, the women began to sing and dance which also did not have any impact on the Guru. Following this they brought pearls, diamonds, gold, silver, coral and such invaluable items from the state treasury and placed them before him. When this too failed, Nur Shah and her women fell at the feet of the Guru who gave them the message of the Holy Name and advised them to renounce magic. The Guru, then, left Kamarupa by the Brahmaputra River and came back to Puri in Orissa.[21]

A similar corroboration of the fear of the practice of magic and sorcery was found in the records of medieval invaders from the west. 'In 1337 Mohammed Shah Governer of Bengal sent 100,000 horseman well equipped to Assam, but the whole army perished in that land of witchcraft and not a trace of it was left. He sent a second army to avenge the former disaster but when they came to Bengal they would go no farther and the plan had to be given up'.[22] When Mughal general Raja Ram Singh was ordered by Aurangzeb to take an army to Assam and subdue the Ahoms in 1667, he picked up the assignment with trepidation. He didn't fear the Ahom military might, but was afraid of Assam's fearsome reputation as a land of black magic. Mayong, a village some 40 km from Guwahati, was the deemed capital of the occult. Ram Singh took along the ninth Sikh Guru Teg Bahadur to ward off evil. Teg Bahadur inadvertently introduced the Sikh faith in Assam, but couldn't save the Mughal generalissimo from defeat. As stated by Macauliffe during their visit to Dhubri, Guru Tegh Bahadur advised all the soldiers of Ram Singh to 'bring five shields full of earth to raise, in memory of the founder of the Sikh Religion, a mound which could be seen at a great distance'.[23] This mound is the famed 'Gurdwara Tegh Bahadur Sahibji' of Dhubri. As the legends go, a group of women, expert in sorcery or black art, under the guidance of a washerwoman known as Netai, were sent to do their best to frighten away both Guru Tegh Bahadur and Raja Ram Singh. On the other side of the Brahmaputra River, opposite Dhubri, where Guru Tegh Bahadur had already camped, these women, began their magical skill of destruction. These women violently threw a 26 ft long stone, which came across the sky like an object thrown at a target. The stone hit the ground adjacent to the camp of Guru Tegh Bahadur. The stone hit the ground so forcefully that almost half of the stone went into the ground and the remaining part lying out of the ground. Even today the remaining half of the stone is lying in the same position, which is known as the Netai Dhubuni Ghat.[24] Then the women threw a tree which dropped down near the camp of Guru Tegh Bahadur. But the magical skill of those women failed to do any harm to either Guru Tegh Bahadur or his companions. At last the women admitted the truth of Guru Tegh Bahadur's superior powers. Ikhtiyaruddin Yuzbuk Tughril Khan, a sultan of Bengal invaded Assam in 1256-7 and perished with his army there. The Mughals were routed in the Battle of Saraighat in 1671 and Ram Singh did a hasty retreat. He was lucky; a few others before him did not come back alive. *Alamgir Nama* of Mirza Muhammad Kazim, a chronicler of the first ten years of Emperor Aurangzeb's reign, while talking about an invasion by Muhammad Shah in 1332 with one lakh horsemen, says, 'The whole army perished in that land of witchcraft, and not a trace was left'. Mention has been made in the *Tarikh-i-Aasham* that anybody who came to this country, never returned unless death overtook him. That is why an outsider did not know very much about Assam and its people. The people of Hindustan describe the inhabitants of this land as magicians and consider them as beings out of the pale of human race. They believe that this land is a land of magic, which prevents them from returning home.

The present Kamarupa district of Assam was an ancient kingdom too. Early Kamarupa was known in northern India to be associated with magical practices. The *Kalika Purana* and the *Charyapadas* provide most of the evidence relating to the existence of Tantric practices in early Kamarupa. There are references to such practices in medieval Assamese literature as well. These references to Buddha and Baudhamata in various Vaisnavite scriptures certainly point to the existence of Buddhist Tantric practices in the fifteenth and sixteenth centuries in Assam. According to the *Haft Izlim*, there was in Kamarupa a class of persons called the *Bhogis* who were voluntary victims of a Goddess named Ai who dwelt in a cave; from the time when they announced that the Goddess had called them, they were treated as privileged persons. They were allowed to do whatever they liked and every woman was at their command, but when the annual festival came round they were killed. Magic also held an important place in the estimate of the people and in the *Ain-i-Akbari* they were accused, among other practices, of divination by the examination of a child cut out of a body of pregnant woman who has gone her full terms.[25] This was an example of the occult practices prevalent in the province. The prevalence of night worshippers (Ratikhowa) who indulged in magico-religious practices is also documented in literature. According to historian K.L. Baruah 'the *Ratikhowa* or *purnadharia* sect of Assam, which continued till recent times, had its origin undoubtedly in the system which was evidently a mixture of Tantric Buddhism and tribal customs'. The medieval Assamese society in which a large section of the people were going through the process of de-tribalization due to extension of advanced plough agriculture and expansion of Hinduism, provided enough space for the development of nocturnal cults. In tribal and primitive worldview, natural productivity was equated with human productivity and as such the ritual association of sexual union with agriculture is universal. The importance of sexual union prevalent among different sections of the people in the *Ratikhowa pratha* must also have carried with them some of their pristine and tribal beliefs. Assam is also the habitat of myriad tribal communities. Among many of these communities like the Bodos, Dimasas, Deuris, Tiwas, Kukis, Lushais, Nagas there is widespread practice of witchcraft. They believe that evil spirits are responsible for all sufferings of men like disease, death, pain and trauma. They also believe certain human beings often acquire these evil powers and cause disease and death to fellow men. These persons are then targeted and eliminated by calling them witches. Often women are the targets of such labels who are then brutally murdered. The Khasis practice *thlen* or snake worship in which worshippers claim to receive material benefits. The practice is dreadful and sends shiver and panic among the ordinary Khasis:

The legend of U Thlen, or Thlen, is a living one and to this day people talk about this man-eating, blood-sucking serpent as they would talk of the plague, cancer, tuberculosis and any other killer disease. That is what this monster represents now; the cause of a kind of deadly illness where a person loses his natural colour, grows thin and weak, with a strange bloatedness about his face and belly. They say the keepers of this creature and the killers in their employment, whose business is the hunting of men for their blood, are still very active in some parts of the Khasi Hills.[26]

Among the myriad tribes who inhabit the region, one common occult practice is that of witchcraft and witch-hunting. There has been a 'prevalence of witches' in Assam for a long time now. All pre-mughal texts and Mughal accounts talk about the 'magical' land of Assam where a woman can transform a man to a goat. According to Assam State Legal Service Authority, 'witch hunting' in Assam involved branding a woman as a witch or *daini*, mostly based on declaration by an *ojha* or *bez* (quack). This usually happens when villagers approach the village *ojha* with a chronic ailment and the *ojha* identifies a woman to be the source of the ailment and is branded as a *daini* or witch. The woman identified as a *daini* is dragged out and subjected to inhuman torture in the form of beating, burying alive, paraded naked or even raped. If the victim manages to survive, she is ostracized from the village and is dispossessed of her property. Sometimes the village leaders impose a heavy fine on the family of the woman in order to relieve her of her misdeeds towards her fellow villagers.[27] But witch-hunting is not confined to indigenous tribes only. It is widely prevalent among the indentured labour migrants who have settled in various tea gardens in Assam. One of the largest community of these migrants are the Santhals. Within the Santhals cosmology centrality is accorded to their belief in *dains/dans/chudails* (witches) or *bongas* (spirits). It is said that 'There is no genuine Santal who does not believe in witches'.[28] It is posited within the belief that human beings can be intimate with and control evil spirits. Both men and woman can, within this system cause harm and even kill their kin as well as their fellow villagers. As women are considered ritually inferior within society, any visible sign of them being in close contact with the *bongas* could lead them to be perceived as a witch and persecuted. Ritual specialists belonging to certain Hindu castes would generally play the role of an exorcist, which is a pointer to the hybrid cultural evolution, rendering women marginalized and the sole gender identified as keeper of evil. It is to be noted at this point of this discourse that neither the Santhal nor the Bhil have words for 'witch' in their own languages.[29] But witchcraft is not associated with evil only, it is often used for faith healing too. The Nepalese of Sikkim have belief in faith healing, the rational being the belief in God as a supreme power. The *shamans* or priests as faith/spiritual healer were perpetuators of religion. The same was true of the Mizos, Nagas and other tribes, who healed diseases by propitiating evil spirits where the village priests/exorcists arranged elaborate ceremonies to propitiate the spirits which brought illness to particular persons. There were even beliefs that certain agents carry diseases with them. The Mizo tribe for example were terrified of white Christian missionaries, who they believed were the carrier of smallpox and, therefore, migrated to new villages to avoid contact with these missionaries who pursued them. But Christianization did not rid these societies of certain occult practises. There are a number of obscure and occult cults that emerged in these recently Christianized societies. These cults were given the name of Satanic cults by their people. Satanic cults and practices developed in recent times in the four states of Mizoram, Manipur, Nagaland and Meghalaya among the Christian population. It could be traced to the growth of this group and proposed that these cults were set up as a resistant movement against the church and missionaries.[30] Magic was not performed only culturally. It was used politically. The attribution of magical power to the religious leaders as well as the medieval rulers was quite common.

Magical attributes of saints impacted upon the society to bring about social cohesion. A number of saints and millenarian prophets had appeared in north-east India who were declared to have magical powers. Dimasa prophet Sambhudhan, Naga prophets Jadonang and Guidilu were all attributed with massive supernatural powers. The numerous Sufi saints who appeared in north-east India also claimed to have magical powers.

Among some other tribes totemism was also practised. Certain persons were believed to have the power to transform themselves in some animal form like tiger, cat, bear, dog and so on at night and go on a prowl. All such secret cultural practices are gradually dying out with modernization and state strictures against them. With Christianization, a number of tribes have desisted from such practices. Similarly, the religion of the Chutiyas was a curious one where various occult practices existed.

> They worshipped various forms of Kali with the aid not of Brahmins but of their tribal priest or Deoris. The favourite form in which they worshipped this deity was that *Kesai Khati* 'the eater of raw flesh' to whom human sacrifice was offered. After their subjugation by the Ahom, the *Deoris* were permitted to continue their ghastly rites; but they were usually given for the purpose, a criminal who had been sentenced to capital punishment. Failing them, the victims were taken from a particular clan, which in return was accorded certain privileges. The person selected was fed sumptuously until he was in sufficiently plum condition to suit the supposed taste of the goddess, and he was then decapitated at the Copper temple at Saidya or at some other shrine of the tribe. Human sacrifices were also formerly offered by the Tipperas, Kacharis, Koches, Jaintias and other Assam tribes and it is thus easy to see how they came to regarded favourably by the Tantric sect of Hinduism, which is believed to have had its origin in this corner of India.[31]

In a bizarre example of occult practice a young boy was sacrificed to Goddess Kamakhya to celebrate a victory. This was the time when Bali Narayan, the brother of Parikshit, who had just been defeated by the Mughal Sultan *Muhammedans*, took shelter with the Ahom king Pratap Singh in 1615. Enraged by the murder, Sheikh Qasim, the Governor of Bengal decided on a punitive expedition and sent Sayyid Ali, an imperial officer along with Sayyid Abu Bakr and Sattrajit, the son of a zamindar near Dhaka, and Akhek Gohain. The invaders reached Koliabor. But the invasion failed in the face of a determined counter by the Ahoms.[32] The Ahoms then expressed their gratitude to the Goddess Kamakhya for their victory by sacrificing the prisoner Sattrajits's young son to the Goddess. The heads of the slain were then piled up in heaps.[33] A curious practice of animal sacrifice was also in vogue in the Siva temples of the province. On the occasion of Siva Chaturdasi festival castrated goats were strangled to death in the precincts of the temples. The flesh is then cooked and a huge feast is held at night in the temples. An exception occurs in the Kamakhya hill, where a castrated goat is decapitated on the same occasion.[34] In the same temple the dance of the *Devadasis* was also quite a scary and erotic.

> Thus the free use of wine, women and flesh scriptureally enjoined as accompaniment to varied modes of Siva worship in an atmosphere of infinite varieties of aboriginal sexual relationship promised an easy deliverance which excited the wrath of Yama [god of death] and led on to the expulsion from Saivite temples of the four orders of Aryanised people.[35]

The growth and development of Tantric and Vamachari practices in early medieval Assam have been widely discussed by several scholars. The strong presence of Tantric practices in the fifteenth and sixteenth centuries in Assam can be inferred from the fact that the *Yogini Tantra* was composed in the latter half of sixteenth century. The absence of Tantric literature in medieval Assamese literature can be explained by the fact that the Neo-Vaishnavite movement ushered in the development of Assamese language and literature and the Tantric handed tradition followed by sections of the lower caste people that remained on the fringes continued through oral traditions in the succeeding period. The secret orgiastic practices remained secret among the different communities and the reason of their failure to emerge as organized cults can be explained in terms of overwhelming presence of the *Satra* institutions in the Brahmaputra Valley. In the seventeenth century, there were at least 1280 state-recognized *satras* in Assam. These *Satra* institutions played the most important part in legitimizing and popularizing the Hindu caste norms and practices. In an article published in 1851, Captain E.T. Dalton reported that, 'There are in the Kamrup district, one hundred and ninety five *Shotros* subordinate to that of Barpetah. I do not know how many there may be in other districts'. The proliferation of secret orgiastic congregational ceremonies in the seventeenth and eighteenth-century Assamese society should be studied in relation to the social outlook of the hierarchical caste society. The critical study of the oral sources of these sects apparently show that some of the rituals and practices express the idea of rural protest and resistance against the hegemonic Brahmanical social codes and ethics. The making of the social ideology of the medieval Assamese society with its patriarchal and hierarchical caste rules posed challenges to the tribal egalitarian ethos of the newly Hinduized groups and also to the various Tantric beliefs and rituals which were on the fringes of contemporary society. These secret night ceremonies and rituals provided the space for the continuation of such traditions and these got a fresh lease of life in the nocturnal ceremonies. Followers of these practices declared their rituals to be outside the Vedic norms and asked fellow participants to resist the upper-caste social codes and norms and thus this resistance finds expression in the secret selective gatherings.

The remnants of the magical practices are still active in a village called Mayong. There are several stories pertaining to the name Mayong, a few say that it is the land of illusions or *maya*, therefore the name Mayong originates from this aspect. There is also a legend associated with the name, it is said that they are sacred parts of Goddess Shakti, hence the older generation called it as Maa-R-Ongo (parts of the Goddess), and later on it became Mayong. Mayong was once called the Land of Black Magic, it is said that during the medieval period in India, the ancient Mayong kingdom occupied a very important place in magic. It remained the Indian capital of black magic and witchcraft. Mayong is the famed ancient place where sorcery and magic was practised in the past and is still practised today. The village of Mayong can be found around 40 km away from Guwahati, and is next to Probitora Wildlife Sanctuary. Shrouded in myths and stories, it is said that almost every family here has scriptures and manuscripts that have been passed down from to ancient times. While some families have hidden them skilfully, others have burned them for fear of the magical knowledge falling into the wrong hands. Legend has it that the people here can cure illness using *mantras* and can even turn leaves into fish. An example of the place and its magical practices was provided by an author

> Imagine yourself a guest in any one of the numerous households of Mayong. You have come unannounced, but your host is unperturbed. He is least anxious about what to serve you at lunch of rice and *kawai* fish curry. The rice has

already been cooked, but the fish curry is nowhere in sight. The host goes to the backyard, collects a few leaves from the mango tree and the *khoeowah* tree, washes the leaves as if those were live *kawaiu* fish and puts them in the frying pan. He asks you to watch very carefully. And just in front of your eyes, lo and behold, you find that the leaves are not leaves; in fact these have transformed themselves into jumping *kawai* fish and were sizzling in the frying pan. You partake your lunch of rice and mango leaves, sorry, *kawai* fish, and return happily to your home and hearth. This is one magical feat-to transform leaves of the mango and 'Khorowah' tree into live *kawai* fish that almost every other household of Mayong can boast of. The total bewilder-ment of the whole feat would take anyone's breath away! This is illusionary magic, which conjures the manifestation of *kawai* fish out of mango leaves. Mayong still boasts of many more magicians. In this age of globalization the honored magicians know how difficult it is for them to keep their art alive. There is for instance one Ramdhan Das, who possesses immense skills of a magician. He had studied in Rajamayong Higher Secondary School and was a student of Sri. Akbar Ali, a respected teacher of that locality. Sri Akbar Ali takes pride in extolling the virtues of his 'magician' student. One extraordinary feat Sri Ramdhan Das can still perform is to get the *pyol* (*peerah,* a flat stool) stuck to your bottom and making it impossible for you to get up from the pyol on the ground. This particular magical feat was one amongst the many such magic performed by the Mayong *bej* in the ancient times.

This present volume includes articles to explore various aspects of the occult practices like black magic and witchcraft in north-east India. It tries to record, analyse and study these practices before they die out absolutely. The theme includes History of Tantricism, Tantric Buddhism, and Shakti cults, black magical practices, witchcraft among the hill and plain tribes, current practices, performance of occultism, Mayong and its magical antecedents, Khasi practices of *thlen*, totemsim, concept of tigerman, bearman, cat women and so on practised by various communities.

NOTES

1. Edward Gait, *A History of Assam*, LBS Publication, Guwahati, original pub 1905, rpt. 1984, p. viii.
2. Bani Kanta Kakati, *The Mother Goddess Kamakhya*, Publication Board, Government of Assam, Guwahati, rpt. 2004, p. 1.

3. Edward Gait, *A History of Assam*, LBS Publication, Guwahati, original pub 1905, rpt. 1984, p. 58.
4. Bani Kanta Kakati, *The Mother Goddess Kamakhya*, Publication Board, Government of Assam, Guwahati, rpt. 2004, p. 34.
5. Ibid., p. 16 & 40.
6. Ibid., p. 34.
7. Ibid., pp. 62-3.
8. Archana Barua, 'Elements of Magic, Esoterism and Religion in Shaktism and Tantrism in the light of the Shakti Pitha Kamakhya', Paper presented in an international seminar on Black Magic, Witchcraft and Occult Practices in North Eastern India, in Assam University, Silchar 5-6 November 2014. Included in this volume.
9. Hugh B. Urban, 'The Path of Power: Impunity, Kingship and Sacrifice in Assamese Tantra', in *Journal of the American Academy of Religion,* vol. 69, no. 4 (December 2001), pp. 777-816.
10. K.L. Barua, *Early History of Kamrupa*, LBS, Gauhati, p. 13.
11. Edward Gait, *A History of Assam*, LBS Publication, Guwahati, original pub 1905, rpt. 1984, p. 15.
12. Ibid., p. 15.
13. Bani Kanta Kakati, *The Mother Goddess Kamakhya*, Publication Board, Government of Assam, Guwahati, rpt. 2004, p. 1
14. Ibid., p. 1.
15. J.H. Hutton, 'Some Astronomical Beliefs in Assam', *Folklore*, vol. 36, no. 2 (30 June 1925), pp. 113-31.
16. Ibid.
17. Vandana Goswami, 'Bej Bejali in the Assamese Socio-cultural Context', Paper presented in an international seminar on Black Magic, Witchcraft and Occult Practices in North Eastern India, in Assam University, Silchar 5-6 November 2014. Included in this volume.
18. Shihabuddin Talish, *Tarikh e Asham*, cited in Edward Gait, *A History of Assam*, LBS Publication, Guwahati, original pub 1905, rpt. 1984, p. 148.
19. Mirza Nathan, *Baharistan-i-Ghaibi*, tr. M.I. Borah, vol. l, para 306, p. 273.
20. Ibid., vol. I, para 307; p. 274.
21. Max Arthur Macauliffe, *The Sikh Religion*, vol. 1, pp. 73-82 cited in Maheshwar Neog, *Religions of the North East: Studies in the Formal Religions of North Eastern India*, Publication Board, Government of Assam, Guwahati, 2008, p. 185

22. Edward Gait, *A History of Assam*, LBS Publication, Gauhati, original pub 1905, rpt. 1984, p. 37.
23. Max Arthur Macauliffe, *The Sikh Religion*, vols. 3-4, 1909, Cambridge University Press, Cambridge, 1909, p. 355.
24. This stone of Netai Dhubuni Ghat of Dhubri is lying even today in the same position. It is said by people that a British officer tried to ruin the stone, but he failed in his attempt, because blood exuded out of it.
25. Edward Gait, *A History of Assam*, LBS Publication, Guwahati, original pub 1905, rpt. 1984, p. 58.
26. Kynpham Sing Nongkynrih, 'U Thlen: The Man-eating Serpent,' in *India International Centre Quarterly*, vol. 32, no. 2/3, Where the Sun Rises When Shadows Fall: The North-east (MONSOON-WINTER 2005), pp. 33-8.
27. Suryasikha Pathak, 'The Prevalence of Witches and the Gender Question', Paper presented in an international seminar on Black Magic, Witchcraft and Occult Practices in North Eastern India, in Assam University, Silchar 5-6 November 2014.
28. Olympia Kurmi & Sarah Hilaly, 'Witchcraft Practices in the Plantations of Upper Assam: A Case of the Santhals', Paper presented in an international seminar on Black Magic, Witchcraft and Occult Practices in North Eastern India, in Assam University, Silchar 5-6 November 2014. Included in this volume.
29. Ibid.
30. Phoibi L. Tuolor, 'Satanic Cult in Northeast India', paper presented in an international seminar on Black Magic, Witchcraft and Occult Practices in North Eastern India, in Assam University, Silchar 5-6 November 2014. Included in this volume.
31. Edward Gait, *A History of Assam*, LBS Publication, Guwahati, original pub 1905, rpt. 1984, p. 43.
32. Ibid., p. 107.
33. Ibid., p. 108.
34. Bani Kanta Kakati, *The Mother Goddess Kamakhya*, Publication Board, Government of Assam, Guwahati, rpt. 2004, p. 31
35. Ibid., p. 32.

PART I
TANTRA AND ESOTERISM

CHAPTER 1

Vaishnavite Occult Practices in Medieval Assamese Society: A History of Acceptance and Defiance

CHANDAN KUMAR SARMA

abadi swarupe ochina swarupe
sajao bandhu sabar maj
amar banhu sabe ji aharma achare
chario vedare baj

(In known and unknown form we arrange a meeting of the likeminded; whatever route or religion we prefer to follow is outside the Vedic system.)

In the medieval Assamese society, especially in the eighteenth century, one sees the emergence of Vaishnavite occult practices among certain sections of the communities and the newly Hinduized sections of the people. Though these secret occult practices have been studied by some scholars, most of the studies are related with the enumeration of the cultural practices and the oral literature associated with them. These secret nocturnal practices have not been studied as a resistant ideology, which provided the space to question and contest the hegemony of privileged caste ideology and ritual. This article is an attempt to understand the origin and development of the secret orgiastic practices popularly known as the *Ratikhowa* or *Rati Sewa* (ceremony held at night) as part of 'populart culture' and 'popular religion' in the context of the social ideology of medieval Assamese society. In these magico-religious practices, one sees the synthesis of Vaishnavism, tribal fertility rites and debased Tantric-Buddhist practrices, and these remained on the fringes of the medieval Assamese society. Such practices developed in different parts of the Brahmaputra Valley and their continuance in the twentieth century is reported from different parts of Assam such as Goalpara, Sonitpur, Mangaldoi and the upper Assam districts. Medieval Assamese sources contain only stray references to the existence of such magico-religious practices. Most of the literature related to these beliefs and rituals are in oral form and though some oral literature were codified in subsequent times, it is very difficult to determine the exact time of their composition. A critical study of the rich oral traditions associated with these secret practices provides us enough opportunity to understand the complex process of Hinduization and the resistance to the social ideology of the emerging caste society in Assam. According to Sekhar Bandopadhay:

> The hierarchical ideology of caste has been most vigorously contested in the realm of 'popular' religion, which is often defined through 'a process of exclusion' as the 'other' religion. It is discursively positioned in an oppositional relationship to the established religion of the elite, which is supposed to represent the classical tradition, legitimated by the ancient tests. This ascription of an essential residual character to popular religion is the result of an unconscious acceptance of the elitist stereotyping of certain practices and beliefs as 'popular' or not confirming to the accepted ethical and moral standards or epistemological norms of the elite. . . . In its wider sense, popular religion means quite simply the religion of the vast mass of people; popular in the sense of its 'widely favoured', and it incorporates also its 'narrower uses', that of religion as an 'oppositional form'.[1]

The practice of secret nocturnal ceremonies among certain sections of Assamese people can be seen as a religion in the oppositional form, opposed to the dominant and hegemonic ideology of a caste society. Popular religion reflected the social protest of the subordinated classes against their social superiors and the ideology of domination. These esoteric practices reflect the resistant ideology of the deprived castes and the newly Hinduized indigenous communities against the ideology of a hierarchical caste-based society, which was popularized and imposed through the neo-Vaishnavite tradition in the medieval Assamese society. Popular religion, through the process of creative appropriation, gradually develops a subversive edge against the ideology of domination.[2] Natalie Davis has argued that people are always passive recipients of the values of their social superiors; they also adapt and redefine them in their own way.[3] The emergence of occult practices within the Vaishnavite fold among certain sections of the people can be seen in the context of the process of Hinduization and the consequent resistance to the ideology of a caste-based society and social norms. Though these deprived castes and the indigenous communities were initiated to the Mahapuriusia fold and gradually brought within the larger Hindu social framework, they brought in some deviant social behaviour, which was against the dominant social order. The practice of such deviant ritual and ceremonies could not pose any meaningful challenge to the hierarchical caste-based society and such resistant behaviour remained largely on the fringes of the society.

Though the popular religion and practices provided a space outside the control of the upper castes and the elite for interrogating and contesting the hegemonic ideology of a hierarchical caste-based society, the popular religions themselves could not provide an enduring alternative to the hegemonic ideology. According to Partha Chatterjee, the failure of the popular religions to construct an alternative universal to the dominant *dharma* was the mark of their subalternity.[4] In the late medieval period in Bengal, there was a large-scale proliferation of heterodox sects among the lower sections of the population and they posed a challenge to the orthodox social ideology. According to Ramakanta Chakravarty, after the gradual incorporation of the Chaitanya movement, which was largely committed to social equality, into the orthodox Hindu order, there emerged at least fifty-six Vaishnavite and semi-Vaishnavite heterodox sects in Bengal which became popular, specially among the lower sections of the society.[5] In medieval Assamese society also, the deviant social practices emerged within the neo-Vaishnavite fold and these were confined mainly to the newly Hinduized and deprived sections of society. Though there are a number of instances of secret nocturnal rituals and practices in Assam, these failed to emerge as organized heterodox cults or formal sects as it happened in Bengal.

I

The secret esoteric sects in medieval Assamese society have been studied by some historians in the context of the Moamaria rebellion and such studies are confined mainly to whether the rebels participated in such night congregations or not. References to the participation of Moamoria rebels in secret occult practices are available in the *Tungkbungia Burani, Satsory Asom Buranjio* and *Asomor Padya Buranji.*[6] This association of Moamoria rebels with the *Ratikhowa* sect is explained as a 'pernicious campaign of vilification' by some scholars. Description of the ceremonies of these sects is also available in the *Assam Burunji* by H.D. Phukan[7] and the *Burunji Vivek Ratna* by Maniram Dewan.[8] In these references the sect is referred to as *Ritia, Aritia,* etc. It was called *Aritia* as its rituals are not sanctioned by the traditional upper caste social laws and customs. The followers of these sects indulge in nocturnal feast, music, dance, drinking and sexual orgies. The followers of these practices worship Krishna and Shiva through *bamachari* or left handed practices and *pancha makara*[9] elements are essential ingredients associated with the secret ceremonies. Different scholars have tried to analyse the role of these secret nocturnal sects in the Moamoria rebellion that shook the foundation of the Ahom administration in the latter part of the eighteenth century. Some scholars deny the participation of the Moamoria rebels in occult practices totally and the association of the rebels with these sects is explained as a derogatory campaign by the royal chroniclers.

In the Ahom chronicles, there are references to the secret cult of nocturnal worshippers and one such reference is related to the conspiracy hatched by one Panimua against Purnananda Borgohain.[10] The chief of the cult was reported to be one Gajala Mahanta. Pani-mua could enlist the support of neighboring villages in the conspiracy against the Ahom royalty but they were dealt with severely by the royal troops. Panimua was executed and Gajala Mahanta, mentioned as a Brahmana, by the *Tungkhungia Buranji* was exiled, Gajala Mahanta's actual name was Sunandadeva and he was the abbot of the Katanipara Satra. Though he was mentioned in the *Tungkungia Buranji* as a Brahmin, actually he was not a Brahmin by caste.[11]

Maheswar Neog stated that the rebellious Moamorias did not perform any esoteric occult practices in the course of the revolt. According to him, this reference to the Moamoria rebels performing occult practices is an example of the

> [P]ernicious campaign of vilification, to which *Kala Sangbarti* in general and the Moamorias in particular were subjected. . . . The Satras that have been popularly associated with night worshipping of varied shades of practices were all connected with another *Kala Sanghati* Satra that was pitched in battle against the Moamorias behind the royalist front.[12]

In spite of prejudices against the Moamoria rebels in the royal chronicles, the performance of night worshipping by the rebellious masses cannot be denied. One of the terms used for these night congregations in the Ahom chronicles is *bor asuric mel* (diabolical assembly), and this term carries the echo of anti-royalism which was increasingly being pronounced in the course of the Moamaria revolt. It should be noted that in the course of the rebellion, a large number of common people participated in it irrespective of their caste, ethnic and *satra* affiliations.[13] These secret nocturnal sessions were forums for fomenting discontent and hatching conspiracies. These occult sessions must have helped the rebels in enlisting the support of the common folk, as these practices carried with them some magico-religious traits inherited from their tribal past. These congregational sessions were highly egalitarian in character, as casteist taboos in terms of food and religion were completely forbidden in the ceremonies. These congregational egalitarian occult practices were practised to express and enlist the solidarity of the common folk in the rebellion. According to Amalendu Guha,

> . . . during the phase of armed struggle, the peasant society, a tribe caste continuum, therefore, solicited its spiritual inspiration and nourishment no longer from the classic form of neo-Vaishnavism but from the age old magico-religious cult of night worshippers, an admixture of tribal fertility rites and debased tantricism long drivern under ground. (T)hus there was a vigorous revival of the cult in the eighteenth century.[14]
>
> It gave expression to the urge for an escape from the rigours of the caste society into the millennium of primitive communism cherished in the subconscious mind.[15]

The participation of women in the Moamoria revolt was unprecedented and in this case the role of these nocturnal congregations, which provided central positions to women in the rituals, may also be investigated. Further writes to Guha, 'Through ceremonal participation in this bacchanalia, which was supposed to cast a pro-tective spell around and rejuvenate the participants, the Moamaria rebels were believed to have acquired the fighting acumen.'[16] These occult practices were the result of the synthesis of the earlier trend of *brahmachari* practices which probably continued among the less-privileged sections of the society, especially the Kaivartas with the modes of social resistance of the newly Hinduized converts from Ahom, Matak, Moran and other tribal and semi-tribal groups against the norms and socio-religious codes of the hierarchical caste divided society. Guha interpreted the emergence of such practices among certain sections of the newly Hinduized people in terms of the influences of Aniruddha Deva whom he considers to be 'unmistakably influenced' by Sahajia Tantricism. Guha writes that:

> Literary evidences and subsequent events suggest that Aniruddha Deva, the founder of the Moamoria cult was unmistakably influenced by the sahajia tantricism of his day. He blended magic and miracles with the egalitarian content of neo-Vaisnavism and was said to have conceded to tribal ways of life in the matter of food habits, caste and man-woman relations (*anna-yoni-visara*).[17]

This interpretation of Guha that Aniruddha Deva, the founder of the Moamoria Satra, was influenced by the Sahajia Tantricism cannot be corroborated by historical documents, and that he was liberal in gender relations is also not based on any historical sources. The *Kali Sanghati* Satra founded by Gopala Deva and his apostles. Aniruddha Deva and Yadumani Deva were instrumental in bringing large sections of the deprived castes, Kaivartas, Morans and others within the Mahapurusia fold.[18] Due to its liberal and relaxed outlook, this *Sanghati* had to face much ridicule and censure from the other *Sanghatis*. Brahmanical outlook could not get a foothold in this *Sanghati* and this certainly encouraged the deprived castes and the other tribes to be initiated into this fold.[19] Some writers alleged that Gopal Ata introduced the cult of night worshipping into the Vaishnavite fold. This explanation is also not supported by any historical sources. This impression might have begun as he was the founder of the *Kala Sanghati* which initiated the process of bringing a large section of the people in upper Assam within the Mahapurusia fold and as certain sections of these newly Hinduized people retained some of their earlier tribal ritual and practices. Moreover, it should also be taken into account that this secret sect and its practices were not confined to certain sections of the *Kala Sanghati* alone and followers of other *sanghatis* were also associated with the secret nocturnal practices.[20]

II

The existence of the unorthodox practices in the medieval Assamese society can be traced from the writings of a number of Vaishnavite preceptors, as they had to face a lot of resistance and hostility from the followers of these groups in the propagation of neo-Vaishnavite texts. Shankara Deva's writings contain stray references to his contempt regarding such practices with Shakta tantric rituals. 'They are libertine by nature and tempted by worldly affairs. In the hope of attaining heaven, they gladly dissect ganders and goats, perform various gory deeds, worship various deities and after their virtues are spent out, they again go to hell' (*Bhagavata* 1/34). 'They hold vain discourses on the scriptures that speak of the worship of wine, women and meat. They are all great fools. They do not worship god and will rot in hell' (*Nimi-navasiddha sambada* v. 335) in the *Namaghosa,* Madhava Deva refers to this class of worshippers in the following way: 'There are persons who putting on the cloak of Vaishnavism roam about transgressing the path drawn by the Vedas'. They indiscriminately indulge in enjoyment of sex and palate and thus put *Kirtana Ghosa,* Shankara Deva mentions that the Buddha incarnated only to destroy the path of *Vedas* and made people spellbound with *vamachara shastra* (v. 12). He describes the followers of such practices as *pachanda* and warns the people to get rid of their evil propaganda. Ram Saraswati, disciple of Shankara Deva has also referred to such tantric practices in his *Vyasasrama* 'the common folk will be fallen due to sinful deeds and Brahmana will propagate Buddhist scriptures'.[21] In the *Vansi Gopaldevar Charitra* written by Ramananda there is reference to such Buddhist persons who harassed Vansi Gopaldeva several times. It is also stated that due to his unflinching commitment to Vaishnavite ideology and his persuasion these heterodox believers ultimately became initiated in the Mahapurusia fold.[22]

These references to Buddha and Bauddhamata in various Vaishnavite scriptures certainly point to the existence of Buddhist tantric practices in the fifteenth and sixteenth centuries in Assam. According to K.L. Baruah 'The *Ratikhowa* or *Purnadharia* sect of Assam which continued till recent times had its origin undoubtedly in the system which was evidently a mixture of tantric Buddhism and tribal customs.'[23] The growth and development of tantric and *bamachari* practices in early and early medieval Assam have been widely discussed by several scholars.[24] The *Kalika Purana* and the *Yogini Tantra* provide most of the evidences relating to the existence of left-handed tantirc practices. The strong presence of tantric practices in the fifteenth and sixteenth centuries in Assam can be inferred from the fact that the *Yogini Tantra* was composed in the latter half of the sixteenth century. Even if tantric practices are mentioned as stray references in the contemporary Vaishnavite literature, the continuity of tantric thought and practices in that period can be inferred from the very composition of the *Yogini Tantra* in that period. The absence of tantric literature in medieval Assamese literature can be explained by the fact that the neo-Vaishnavite movement which ushered in the development of Assamese language and literature was totally against such practices and the tantric left-handed tradition, followed by sections of the underprivileged caste people, continued through oral traditions in the succeeding period.

There are polemical discussions relating to the origin of Vaishnavite occult practices in the medieval Assam. It is believed among the certain sections that Ram Deva was the first Gosain to propagate the cult of night worshipping in upper Assam through his disciples. Ram Deva was the son of Sudarsana Deva and the eldest grandson of Saru Krisna Deva, the founder of the Chaliha Barighar Satra. The third and the youngest son of Saru Krishna Deva, popularly known as Sunanda Deva, founded the Katanipar Satra. In a number of oral mystical songs known as *yuguta visara* songs used by the followers of this sect there are references to the names of Sunanda Deva and Ram Deva as their preachers.[25] Though the followers of this Satra deny these two abbots as preacher of this cult, the repeated reference to their preaching of this sect in a number of oral songs popular among the followers of the nocturnal cult clearly show that they were important preachers and propagators of these practices.

The introduction of these secret esoteric practices of night worship within the Mahapurusia fold can be explained in terms of gradual incorporation of the followers of these ancient practices within this fold. The process of Hinduization of the indigenous communities through the Mahapurusia tradition in the medieval period did not lead to a total change in the life and practices of these groups and they retained much of their tradition, lifestyle and practices. The diversity in the nomenclature and its varied practices in different parts of Assam clearly suggest that the resurfacing and growth of this secret orgiastic cult within the Vaishnavite fold cannot be ascribed to one or two preceptors. Some other sects of the night worshippers are known as *Batibhagia, Chari Karania, Digambaria, Karantipatia, Madhupuria, Purna Bhagia,* etc., and these sects have their presence in different areas of upper Assam. In Sonitpur and Mongoldoi districts some sects performing such nocturnal sessions are known as *Puthimechia, Thakura Kheli* and *Bara Khelia.* Most of the followeres of these sects are from the Bej or Vaidya community. The oral devotional songs of these sects are popularly known as *Chia Geet.*[26] The origin of these nocturnal practices is spuriously ascribed to Shankara Deva and Madha Deva and their names may have been incorporated in the devotional songs of night worshippers to gain legitimacy among the wider sections of the people. Through the process of 'creative appropriation', at the popular level, the people assimilated deviant social and religious rituals and customs within the larger Mahapurusia cultural and religious idiom. The oral literarture associated with the secret sects continue the fervour and flavour of the Vaishnavite culture. It also demonstrates the level of religious syncretism at the popular level. The rituals and practices of these nocturnal cults demonstrate assimilation of divserse trends and streams, such as

Vaishnavism, Tantric Shaivism, Vajrayani Buddhism, primitive tribal rituals, Nathism and Bengali Sahajia Vaishnavism. The impact of Shaivism and tribal rituals are dominant in the Borasewa sect of the night worshippers and this sect is present among some communities of the Mongoloid group such Ahoms, Morans and Mishings. Only upgraded *Bhakats* are allowed to attend the nocturnal sessions. One special *Bhakat* named as *eknami Bhakat* is selected to conduct the ceremonies and he is accepted as the Lord Shiva and he is helped in the rituals by the *dokani* and the *sevaki,* who are selected from the women participants. The *pancha makaras* are essential ingredients in the rituals. In early Assam, Shiva worship was mixed with varied forms of tantric rituals. According to S.K. Bhuyan, 'In the *Kalika Purana* and in the *Yogini Tantra* Shiva appears more often as a Vairava than as a normal god, and therefore, *bamachara* practices could be legitimately held in Shaiva temples.'[27] These currents which remained on the fringes of the society resurfaced among some sections of the population due to mixing them with the primitive tribal practices of the newly Hinduized sections of the people. According to some scholars the *kaivarta* community came under the influence of tantric Buddhism in the early medieval period and even after their initiation to Vaishnavite Hinduism in the later period, they must have retained some of the earlier practices.

Some references to the secret practices of such sects will make it clear that these practices were the result of social and cultural assimilation and elements from diverse sources were blended in the making of such esoteric sects. Among the *Gopidhara* and the *Gopikhela* sects, the role the Radha-Krishna cult played, was central one in the ceremonies. In the practices of these sects the chief among the *Bhakatas* was considered the manifestation of Krishna and one woman was selected to play the role of Radha. The followers of these sects adored the couple as the primordial deities of Brindavan.[28] All the elements of *pancha makara* are essential in the rituals of the sect. Thr rituals can be compared with the *Kumari Puja* still prevalent in the temple of Kamakhya. According to S.N. Sarma, there may be an impact of the Kisori Bhaja sect in these rituals and this Sahajia Vaishnavite tradition probably entered Assam in the eighteenth century along with the musicians, artists and religious persons imported by King Rudra Singha.[29] The Sahajia tradition 'discarded brahmanical rituals, deplored the intellectualism of the learned theological debates, shunned the strict disciplines of orthodox Hinduism and preferred instead to follow nature (*sahajia*)'.[30] In the texts of the Sahajia Vaishnavites such, as *Rativilasa Paddhati, Sahajia Upasana Tattva,* men and women are accepted as the representatives of the two streams of love and described respectively as *rasa* and *rati* or *kama* and *madana.*[31] All forms of tantric teachings insist on the symbclical union of the male and female principle—the efficient and material cause of creation. An impact of such principles and ideas are also present in diverse sects of night worshippers in Assam.

In the *Dangaria Sewa* ceremony tribal and village deities are worshiped through *bamachari* practices.[32] The village deities are classified as Thalasai, Jalasai and Burha Dangaria. The names seem to suggest that the Thalasai deity resides on dry land and his permanent abode is believed to be the forest. The Jalasai deity is generally associated with the Kaivarta community. Burba Dangaria is worshipped in expectation of recovery from diseases and natural calamity and this practice is generally confined to certain sections of the Ahom community.

The Nath Panthis could also influence the occult practices in medieval Assamese society. In Bengal and Assam the Nath Panthis are known as the Yogi community. Nathism is highly syncretic in character and its main tenets and concepts were influences by contemporary Shaiva, Vaishnava, Shakta and Buddhist tantras. Nathism was associated with the less-privileged sections of the society and it was anti-Brahmanical in character.[33] The strong anti-Brahmanical outlook expressed in the oral literature of these occult sects and its prevalence among certain sections of the less-privileged class may be due to the influence of the Nath Panthis, who had a strong presence in certain areas of Assam.

III

Neo-Vaishnavite abbots (especially in the later period) and the sections of privileged upper caste of the society, in spite of their professed loyalty to the tenets of Shankara Deva, were highly reluctant to yield in the sphere of caste rules and practices. The social ideology of medieval Assamese society, in spite of the neo-Vaishanvite movement and its liberal outlook, was patriarchal in character and in course of time, the privileged caste Hindu norms and codes emerged as the model to be emulated by the poorer orders. Ramakanta Chakravarty in the case of appropriation of the Vaish-navite movement in Bengal by the privileged caste ideology in course of time stated that,

> The social aim of the Vaishnava movement was deflected from the removal of caste distinctions towards the establishment of social and ritual parity between the Vaishnava and the brahmana, Vaishnavism was projected as a form of neo Brahmanism, the aim of which was to revitalize the moribund Hindu society by lending substance to a neo-brahmanical order, nurtured in bhakti ecstasy and, therefore, purer than the orthodox *smarta* order. The Vaishnava was described as the new brahmanas.[34]

In course of time, the neo-Vaishnavite movement in Assam also lost its original ethos of social and caste equality and the various Satras situated in different parts of Assam emerged as the institutions, which promoted and sustained the ideology of a hierarchical caste- based society. In this respect, the role of the various Bengal Brahmins brought by the Ahom kings may be also be re-examined, as they were pioneers in propagating and popularizing the *smarta purna* tradition in Assam in the eighteenth century. Raj Mohan Nath in his *Background of Assamese Culture* explains the impact of the social and religious ideology popularized in Assam by the Parbatia Gosain Krishnaram Bhattacharya, who was brought to Assam by Rudra Singha.

> Since the time of Sena kings, Bengal had developed rigid hierarchical caste divisions and these got further impetus from the codes of Ragunandan. In Assam, Krishna Ram Bhattacharya was instrumental in introducing and enforcing the same rigid social code.

Nath very clearly states that,

> Krishna Ram came from this country (Bengal) and without considering for a moment the past history the social framework of Assam, started to introduce the suicidal customs of the country of his origin, by virtue of the power

and position he had luckily gained in this country . . . [h]e and his progeny always retained an unbroken social connection with Bengal.[35]

In certain aspects his ideology and its subsequent acceptance by the sections of the privileged castes among the people led to the unmaking of the neo-Vaishnavite ideology in the long run. The hereditary private secretary of Siva Singha, who was a Daivajna by caste was removed from the respected post due to the insistence of the Parbatia Gosain, as he thought that a person belonging to the Daivajna caste should not be on such a post. This caste was not very well placed in the social hierarchy in the medieval Bengali society.

The idea of a non-brahmin being a religious preceptor even as a Vaishnava, was declared definitely repugnant, and the brahmin Goswamis became so encouraged by the idea that they cut off all connections with the non-brahmin Goswamis and began to disown even Sankaradeva. A move was to trace the initiation of Damodar Deva to Sri Chaintanya of Bengal; for Chaitanya Deva was a brahmin. Even in the matter of daily socio-religious observances Krishna Ram wanted to introduce the Raghunandanian code prevalent in Bengal, without taking into consideration that Assam had for centuries been ruled by Hindu kings, who had their subject ruled by . . . certain codes suited to the country.[36]

It should be noted that this introduction of rigid caste norms and ideology by the *Parbatia Gosain* were not only confined to the Brahmins and the *sakta* cult propagated by them, but soon these became the social ideology to be followed even by followers of all the *sanghatis* of the neo-Vaishnavite movement except the *Kala Sanghati* order.

The process of Hinduization and subsequent castification of different ethnic tribal groups in the medieval period, occurred through the Shaivite Shakta tradition and this process was further accelerated by the Mahapurusia tradition, especially by the *Kala Sanghati* order in upper Assam. 'The Siva Sakta tradition was acceped by the diverse communities because of their perceived continuity between their own ancestral tribal religion and the one they were adopting and adapting.'[37] The Mahapurusia tradition, at the same time did not compel them to depart completely from their communitarian way of life. But this process of Hinduization and exposure to the hierarchical caste-based society of the diverse ethnic group also developed a certain resistance to the casteist norms and practices. Despite the exposure and initiation of these groups to Hinduism, they maintained some of their original beliefs and rituals. Though the social, religious and food habits of the privileged cast were alien to their way of life, in due course of time these casteist codes emerged as the established and dominant norms to be emulated by them. The process of Sankritization among the newly Hinduized groups demanded a gradual conformity to the norms and practices of the sections of the privileged castes of the people. This process of Hinduization of the indigenous tribal communities by the Vaishnavite *gurus* continued throughout the nineteenth century. The census of India report of 1891 enumerates the system of Hinduization of the indigenous population like the Kacharis and the Lalungs through the Mahapurusia tradition in Nowgong district.[38]

This exposure to the hierarchical caste-based society and to the ideology of domination certainly created problems to their sense of tribal equality and to their social customs and rituals. These occult practices and rituals provided some avenues for these communities to retain some of their past practices in a different way and also to resist and interrogate the upper caste idea of purity and pollution. It may be noted that the section of Ahoms, who have resisted to conform to the casteist norms and regulations and have retained some of their practices are known as *bhitarpakia* Ahoms. Different historians have considered the presence of such non-Aryan religious cults and rituals in the medieval Assamese society as a sign of religious syncretism and assimilation. But most of the writings on medieval Assamese society have failed to analyse the conflict and resistance to the processes of Sanskritization and imposition of patriarchal and Brahmanical codes among the newly Hinduized groups of people properly. The oral literature of these sects clearly point out the resistance to the hegemonic Brahmanical social order and the castiest discriminations. The oral songs associated with such heterodox sects, which are integral to the rich oral folk tradition of Assam can help one to reconstruct the complex and conflict ridden trajectory of social and cultural history of Assam. It should be noted that the mention of opposition to the introduction of casteist social and ethical codes among the different sections of society is absent in the contemporary literature of Assam. In this context it should be emphasized that the literature of medieval Assamese society was influenced by the hegemonic Brahmanical social ideology and even the followers of the Mahapurusia tradition failed to get rid of the hierarchical caste-based ideology. The opposition and resistenace to the caste-based ideology prevalent among the deprived castes and the newly Hinduized groups are represented in the oral folk tradition and this tradition provided the space to offer a critique of the hegemonic Brahmanical outlook which was not available in the literary tradition of the medieval Assamese society. According to W. Scott, 'History and social science because they are written by an intelligentsia using written records that are also created largely by literate officials, is simply not well-equipped to uncover the silent and anonymous form of class struggle that typify the peasantry'.[39]

Similarly, social conflicts and opposition to the privilged caste normative codes of conduct imposed in the society in general can be discerned mainly through the oral traditions as literary traditions convey mostly the ethos of the social elite. The language used in the oral devotional songs associated with the secret nocturnal sessions were composed in enigmatic and coded language and only those initiated into the nocturnal sessions could make out their original meanings.[40] The use of such enigmatic language was also present among the Bauls of Bengal who belonged to the Sahajia Vaishnava tradition. The Bauls also seriously interrogated the orthodox social order and the caste hierarchy. 'They not only overturned the epistemological world of Hinduism; they challenged seriously the notions of purity and the behavioural norms of established Hindu society.'[41] This unorthodox attitude of the Bauls was vehemently criticized by the privileged caste sections. According to Bandopadhyay,

> (t)his opposition from the social establishment that drove the Bauls into their well-developed web of secrecy: their songs were written in an enigmatic *sandhya bhasa* or secrecy: their songs were written in an enigmatic *sandhya bhasa* or a language that was open to various interpretations, and there *guhya sadhana* or secret spiritual practices were only performed in the privacy of their *akhras* away from the eyes of the uninitiated.[42]

The use of ambivalent language in the oral songs associated with the nocturnal sessions in Assam can also be explained in terms of avoidance of direct confrontation with the established religious and social order and to continue the practices surreptitiously. In spite of the presence of hundreds of Satras, the secret ceremonies of these sects were performed in the home of one of the senior initiators and its specific place was known as *sachang* and the Satras were not formally associated with such rituals.

However, in some of the oral songs of these sects, their anti-Vedic traditions and outlook and aversion to caste regulations is celarly reflected.[43]

Abadi swarupe ochina swarupe
Sajao bandhu sabar maj,
Amar banhu sabe ji aharma achare
Chario vedare baj.

(In known and unknown form, we arrange a meeting of the like-minded; whatever route or religion, we prefer to follows outside the Vedic system.)

Abil Ramdev gribar kaje
sajale grihar kaj,
Krishnai rup dhari ji dharma achare
Dharma chari vedar baj.

(Ramdev arrived to arrange the residence and did so; in the guise of Krishna whatever route or religion he follows, it is outside the Vedic tradition.)

Protest against the imposition of Brahmanical code of conduct and the resistance to the upper castes rules and regulations are also reflected in clear and unambiguous terms in some of the oral verses of these sects.[44]

Acharna pravartan sape pheti gome,
Ihak acara tanbe.

(The introduction of upper castes' behavioural codes can be compared with snakes and reptiles; and it is difficult to conform to such codes.)

vaikunthar para guruye matile
ki kara bharastar lok

acharan pravartan sajat namarile
duarie nidie bat

(The Guru or preceptor asks the people of the world about their well being from heaven; He reminds that if the establishment of [privileged castes'] behavioural norms were not demolished, no one would enter heaven.)

IV

One of the most important aspects of the tantric *bamachari* practices that emerged in the early medieval period in different parts of India is the centrality of women in the rituals. In the *ratikhowa pratha* of varied groups in Assam, womenfolk play an equal part in all the rituals along with the menfolk. According to N.N. Bhattacharya,

> Of the existing modes of tantric worship the *bamachari* is so important that the terms have become synonymous with the tantra itself. The conception of *dakshinachara* as opposed to *bamachara* seems to be a latter development and it is possible that the first word of the expression *bamachara* is not *bama* meaning left but *bama* meaning women.[45]

The importance of women in the rituals and the production process in the early period can be understood in the context of the immediate socio-economic environment. Bhattacharya stated that,

> The leading part played by women in religious life, their identification with the mother goddess, the symbolism of varied concepts and relations as ascribed to women, extravagant praises showered on them, insistence on the cult of sex and the female organ as the sole seat of all happiness, the unction of women as priestesses or shamans, the idea of the superiority of the goddesses over the gods, the concept of the supreme being as a female principle must have a social basis.[46]

The medieval Assamese society in which a large section of the people were going through the process of de-tribalization due to the extension of advanced plough agriculture and the spread of Hinduism, provided enough space for the development of nocturnal cults and fertility rites. In tribal and primitive world view, natural productivity was equalled with human productivity and as such the ritual association of sexual union with agriculture is universal. The importance of sexual union prevalent among different sections of the people in the *ratikhowa partha* must also have carried with them some of their pristine and tribal beliefs.[47]

Through the neo-vaishnavite movement was associated with the idea of equality and liberal outlook in the sphere of caste system in the initial period, yet it always promoted patriarchal values among its followers. The story of Sati Radhika[48] enumerated in the *charit puthis* and mentioned in the oral folk tradition demonstrates the segregation of women and imposition of patriarchal values among the women from the underprivileged caste. In the lower stratum of the society, womenfolk played a very important part in the daily walks of life and patriarchal values in terms of widow-remarriage, equal participation in the production process, etc., had lesser impact on their life. Through the story of Sati Radhika, the concept of a *sati* or chaste woman, who fully conforms to the injunctions of the *Dhammashastras* was popularized among the less-privileged sections of the society and Sati Radhika was projected as the model of a chaste woman to be emulated by the womenfolk in general. In the tribal social set up and tribal economy, womenfolk played a larger role and in the religious sphere also women were more privileged which is absent in the caste-based societies. In the medieval Assamese society, there was a continuous attempt to popularize the patriarchal values both by the Brahmanical and the neo-Vaishnavite traditions. Some of the preceptors of the neo-Vaishnavite movement have portrayed the womenfolk as lesser human beings and unworthy of trust in their works.[49] Bhakti literature in medieval Assam also equated women in many references with the shudras, yavanas and people of low birth.[50] In one of the references relating to women, the *Katha Guru Charit* mentions that so long as everything is provided to a wife, she is faithful and good, but as soon as she does not get her desires, she begins to disregard her husband and acts in a way, whereby the position of the husband is jeopardized.[51]

One of the most important aspects related to the vast amount of literature in Assamese language, produced by the neo-Vaishnavite movement is that there is hardly any work written by any woman.

Though there are stray references to educated women in the medieval Assamese society, generally women and the lower castes were prohibited from being instructed in the culture of the alphabet. Moreover, the literary tradition enunciated and sustained this ideology in the medieval Assamese society. The striking absence of women as active agents in the contemporary religious discourse can explained in terms of the emerging patriarchal values popularized and sanctioned by the Brahmanical land and the neo-Vaishnavite traditions. Neo-Vaishnavite ideology was quite Brahmanical about the perception of women. The oral folklore on the contrary provides a contrasting picture, where one finds the women-folk contesting and interrogating patriarchal values. The oral domain presented the women with the necessary space, where they could interrogate the prevailing set up and at the same time emerge as active agents in the popular cultures and the popular religious practices. The vast amount of oral literature associated with the popular religious and occult practices apparently show this contrasting picture. A careful reading of these devotional songs makes it clear that most of them were composed by the womenfolk. The process of Hinduization of the different tribal communities in the medieval period resulted in a gradual popularization of patriarchal values among them. In the case of the Tiwas in middle Assam, which came under the process of Hinduization, there was a transformation towards patrilineal society from a matrilineal one. The gradual emergence of patrilineal values among the newly Hinduized tribal groups resulted in a transformation in their attitude towards the womenfolk and the rights and liberties enjoyed by them in earlier period were substantially reduced under the changed circumstances.

But this 'attempt to introduce the patriarchal Hindu code among the predominately tribal population is persistently counteracted by the pressures of tribal society working against the hierarchical caste-dominated structure of Hindu society and [aspiration] towards greater democratization in attitudes and observances.'[52] Casteist taboos and the idea of purity and pollution in terms of menstruating women were interrogated and contested in the secret night congregations practised by these newly Hinduized groups. Among the practitioners of the Gopidhara and the Gopikhela sects of the night worshippers, the menstruating women *Bhakats* are held in high esteem and they are not treated as polluting agents. It should be mentioned that 'the deeply ingrained dread of impurity and unholiness and the terms attached to the taboo on menstruating women is not to be found in the primitive and original form of the concept'.[53] In primitive religion menstrual blood was visualized as having regenerative power. 'In the tantras also menstrual blood has been regarded as so sacred that it is prescribed as an offering to the great god Siva and his consort Devi.'[54] This practice demands a comparison with the Brahmanical and neo-Vaishnavite treatment of menstruating women in general. In Barpeta Kirtan Ghar, women are not allowed in *en masse* lest some menstruating women pollute the holy shrine. Hinduization of the tribal communities in the medieval period also demanded conformity to such gender-biased codes.

V

Much of the indigenous communities in medieval Assam were in the process of de-tribalization due to the process of extension of wet rice cultivation and Hinduization and their tribal egalitarian ethos and rituals along with gender sensitivity must have crept into these occult congregational sessions. The histories of Hinduization of the different ethic communities show the emergence of a syncretic and multi-dimensional religious culture in the medieval period. The incorporation of the different tribal groups within the Maha-purusia fold resulted in the growth of rich and varied forms of religious cultures within the neo-Vaishnavite fold. The critical study of these subcultures provides the instances of resistance and defiance against the ideology of the hierarchical caste society and the process of Hinduization of the indigenous tribal groups in Assam is not without conflict, as it is made out to be in certain writings.[55] Thus the emergence and proliferation of the medieval caste-based society cannot be explained in terms of a simple narrative of assimilation of Aryan and non-Aryan traditions. Most of the indigenous communities in spite of the process of Hinduization retained some of their beliefs and practices and refused to conform fully to the casteist codes and regulations on commensality. During the period of this study most of these communities such as Ahoms, Morans, Mataks, Chutias, etc., remained suspended between a tribe and a caste. The *khel* system of organising the population and the related production system introduced by the Ahom administration provided the institutional mechanism with the help of which these indigenous groups could maintain some of their communitarian way of life and socio religious practices. Though these groups lost their own languages and ultimately accepted and contributed towards the development of Assamese language due to the process of acculturation, yet they retained some of their distinct identities and this helped them in asserting in the modern period as ethnic communities as against caste identities in spite of being fully Hinduized.

The secret orgiastic practices remained as secret practices among the different communities and the reason of their failure to emerge as organized cults can be explained in terms of the overwhelming presence of the Satra institutions in the Brahmaputra Valley. In the seventeenth century, there were at least 1,280 state recognized Satras in Assam. These Satras played the most important part in legitimizing and popularizing the Hindu caste norms and practices. In an article published in 1851, Capt. E.T. Dalton reported, 'There are, in the Kamrup district, one hundred and ninety-five Shatros subordinate to that of Barpetah. I do not know how many there may be in other districts.'[56]

The proliferation of secret orgiastic congregational ceremonies in the seventeenth- and eighteenth-century Assamese society should be studied in relation to the social ideology of medieval Assamese society. The making of the social ideology of medieval Assamese society with its patriarchal and hierarchical caste rules posed challenges to the tribal egalitarian ethos of the newly Hinduized groups and also to the various tantric beliefs and rituals which were on the fringe of the contemporary society. These secret night ceremonies and rituals provided the space for the continuation of such traditions and these got a fresh lease of life in the nocturnal ceremonies. The followers of these practices declared their religious rituals to be outside the Vedic norms and asked fellow participants to resist the social codes and norms of the upper castes and thus this resistance finds expression in the secret gatherings. According to Raymond Williams, 'In every society there is space for alternative and oppositional views, which are tolerated and accommodated as they do not, at least not openly challenge the fundamentals of the effective and dominant culture'.[57] The secret nocturnal sects with their deviant social behaviour could assert their place in the larger social space of the Assamese society although in the long run they lost the sharp edge of resistance and were accommodated within the dominant social ideology.

NOTES

1. Sekhar Bandyopadhay, *Caste, Culture and Hegemony*, Delhi: Sage, 2004, pp. 77-8.
2. Ibid., p. 78.
3. Ibid., 2004. p. 78.
4. Partha Chatterjee, 'Caste and Subaltern Consciousness', in Ranajit Guha (ed). *Subaltern Studies* VI, Delhi: Oxford University Press, 1989, p. 185.
5. R. Chakravarty, *Vaishnavism in Bengal*, Calcutta: CSSS, 1985, pp. 348-50.
6. *Tungkhungia Buruanji*, ed. S.K. Bhuyan, *Tungkhungiya Buruanji*, 2nd edition, Guwahati: Spectrum, 1964, pp. 169-99, *Asamar Padya Buranji*, ed. S.K. Bhuyan, *Satsari Asam Buranji*, 2nd print, Guwahati: Lawyers, 1964, p. 101.
7. Holiram Dhekial Phukan, *Assam Buranji*, Guwahati: APB, 1962, pp. 96-7.
8. Maniram Dewan, *Buranji Vivek Ratna*, ed. N. Saikia, Dibrugarh: Dibrugarh University, 2002, pp. 207-8.
9. *Pancha-makara* or five elements means *madya* (wine), *mamsa* (meat) *matsya* (fish), *mudra* (cooked or ripe food), and *maithuna* (sexual intercourse).
10. *Tungkhungia Buruanji*, ed. S.K. Bhuyan, *Tungkhungiya Buruanji*, 2nd edition, Guwahati: Spectrum, 1964, pp. 169-99, *Asamar Padya Buranji*, ed. S.K. Bhuyan, *Satsari Asam Buranji*, 2nd print, Guwahati: APB, 1964, pp. 169, 199.
11. N.N. Dutta, *Obscure Religious Practices*, Calcutta: Punthi Pustak, 1990, p. 99.

12. M. Neog, *Socio-political Events in Assam Leading to the Militancy of the Moamaria Vaisharavas*, Calcutta: CSSS, 1982, p. 71.
13. S.L. Baruah, *Last Days of the Ahom Monarchy*, New Delhi: Munshiram Manoharlal, 1984, pp. 60 ff.
14. Amalendu Guha, *Medieval and Early Colonial Assam*, Calcutta: K.P. Bagchi, 1992, pp. 124-5.
15. Ibid., p. 125.
16. Ibid., p. 126.
17. Ibid., p. 127.
18. S.L. Baruah (ed.), *The Life and Teachings of Sri Sri Aniduddha Deva*, Dibrugarh: Dibrugarh University, 2003.
19. Maniram Dewan, *Buranji Vivek Ratna*, ed. N. Saikia, Dibrugarh: Dibrugarh Univesity, 2002, pp. 73-4.
20. N.N. Dutta, *Obscure Religious Practices*, Calcutta: Punthi Pustak, 1990, pp. 80-9.
21. Ibid., p. 81.
22. S.N. Sarma, *The Neo Vaisnavite Movement and The Satra Institution of Assam*, Guwahati: Lawyers, 1999, p. 193.
23. K.L. Baruah, *Early History of Kamrupa*, 2nd edition, Shillong: Author, 1933, rpt., Gauhati, 1996, p. 203.
24. For the growth and development of Tantricism in early Assam See B. Kakati, *The Mother Goddess Kamakhya*, Guwahati: Lawyers, 1948.
25. *Rahasya thanare rahasya bhakati*
    rasika sakale gai
    Kaise Sri Ramdeve suna bandhu sabe
    Ei ras Sankare gai
    (It is the secret esoteric devotional worship performed at a secret place. It is sung by the female devotees after taking the *geet*. This cult is preached by Ramdeva, listen o' friends; Sankar sings this *bhakti rasa*.)
    Koise Sunanda Deve suna bandhu sabe
    Diya sachangate thai
    (So said Sunandadeva, hear friends, give a place in the *sachang* that is the assembly of the devotees.) Quoted in P. Gogoi, *Tai Ahom Religion and Customs*, Guwahati: APB, 1976, pp. 47-8.
26. A good collection of the *chia geets* are compiled in N.P. Bordoloi, *Gopan Sadhana Rati Sew*, Dhemaji: Author, 2004.
27. B. Kakati, *The Mother Goddess Kamakhya*, Guwahati: APB, 1948, p. 20.
28. N. Dutta, *Obscure Religious Practices*, Calcutta: Punthi Pustak, 1990, pp. 104-15.

29. S.N. Sarma, *The Neo Vaisnavite Movement and The Satra Institution of Assam*, Guwahati: Lawyers, 1999, p. 194.
30. Sekhar Bandyopadhyay, *Caste, Culture and Hegemony*, Delhi: Sage, 2004, p. 84.
31. N.N. Bhattacharya, *History of Tantric Religion*, New Delhi: Manohar, 1999, p. 279.
32. It should be pointed out that throughout the centuries some of the rituals and practices have undergone various changes. At present the rituals of *Dangaria Sewa* and *Bura Sewa* have lots of diversities and in most of the places such practices are without fertility rites. But the existence of fertility rights within these practices in certain areas is reported by N.N. Dutta. See N.N. Dutta, *Obscure Religious Practices*, Calcutta: Punthi Pustak, 1990, pp. 104-15, 125-30.
33. N.N. Bhattacharya, op. cit., 1999, pp. 265-69.
34. R. Chakravarty, *Vaishnavism in Bengal*, Calcutta: CSSS, p. 302.
35. R.M. Nath, *Background of Assamese Culture*, Shillong: A.K. Nath, 1948, pp. 145-6.
36. Ibid., pp. 145-6.
37. V. Nandi and V. Raman, *The Long Transition: The Koch Rajbangshis of North Eastern India, in From Tribe to Caste*, ed. D. Nathan, Shimla: IIAS, 1997, pp. 452-3.
38. *Census of India 1891 Assam*: vol. 1, chapter X: Caste, tribe, etc.
39. James C. Scott, *Weapons of the Weak: Eveready Day Forms of Peasant Resistance*, Yale University Press, New Heaven & London, 1985, pp. 36-7.
40. N.C. Sarma in his Introduction to N.P. Bordoloi, *Gopan Sadhana Ratikhowa*, Dhemaji: Author, 2004.
41. Sekhar Bandyopadhyay, *Caste, Culture and Hegemony*, Delhi: Sage, 2004, p. 88.
42. Ibid., p. 88.
43. N.P. Bordoloi, *Gopan Sadhana Rati Sew*, Dhemaji: Author 2004, pp. 74-80.
44. Ibid.
45. N.N. Bhattacharya, op. cit., 1999, p. 279.
46. Ibid., 1999, p. 115.
47. 'It must be remembered that these acts of ceremonial license are not mere indulgences, but they express a reverential attitude towards the forces of regeneration and fertility in man and nature, the forces on which the very existence of society and culture depends'. Malinowski, *Magic, Science and Religions*, quoted in *Tradition to Modernity*, Sivanath Barman, Bhabani Book, Guwahati, 2013, p. 37.

48. M. Neog, (ed.) Guru Charita Katha, Gauhati University, 1986, p. 138.
49. For the position of women in the medieval Assamese society see, J.G. Nath's 'Social Attitudes Towards Women in Medieval Assam' in S.L. Barua (ed.), *Status of Women in Assam*, New Delhi: Munshiram Manoharlal, 1992, pp. 9-16.
50. Ibid.
51. Ibid., p. 10.
52. A. Mahanta, 'Women, Religion and Science in the Non Tribal societies of Assam' in S.L. Barua (ed.) *Status of Women in Assam*, New Delhi: Munshiram Manoharlal, 1992, p. 95.
53. N.N. Bhattacharya, op. cit., 1999, p. 136.
54. Ibid.
55. 'Aryanisation of Assam came slowly but steadily without any trace of conflict and misunderstanding'. Cf. Bangagobinda Parampanthi, 'Aryanisation and Assimilation of Assam', in Udayan Misra (ed.), *Nation Building and Development in North East India*, Guwahati: Purbanchal Prakash, p. 112.
56. Capt. E.T. Dalton, 'Notes on the Mahapurusia: A Sect of Vaishnavas of Assam' published in *Journal of Asiatic Society*, 1851, Annexure in 'Asomar Samaj Itibasat Neava Vaishnavbad' by A. Raychoudhury.
57. Raymond Williams, 'Base and Superstructure in Marxist Cultural Theory', quoted in Sekhar Bandyopadhyay, *Caste, Culture and Hegemony*, Delhi: Sage, 2004, p. 79.

CHAPTER 2

Kecāikhātī, Eater of Raw Flesh: A Profile of the Multifaceted Goddess in the North-East

JAE-EUN SHIN

One of the most famous goddesses worshipped in the north-east and one of the first to receive attention from British colonial officer-scholars in the 1800s, is the Goddess Kecāikhātī, eater of raw flesh, and her history should have been well-chronicled. This is, however, not the case. She has been mentioned only in relation to human sacrifice or represented as a typical bloodthirsty tribal goddess in many works on the north-east.[1] This article will look at the hitherto little known history of Kecāikhātī in the period between the eleventh and nineteenth centuries and will then attempt to contribute towards a better understanding of her multiple identities created by different social groups with their own intentions.

THE GODDESS OF THE EASTERN LIMIT OF KĀMARŪPA

The shrine of Kecāikhātī has always been referred to as the Tāmreśvarī Temple in later times because it was covered with a roof of beaten sheets of copper. The temple formerly stood at lat. 27° 56', long; 96° 21' near Paya in Arunachal Pradesh, about 8 km away from Tebangkhunti on the Sadiya-Teju route.[2] On the basis of the inscription of Śaka 1364 (AD 1442) found in the temple, which was first noticed in *The Annual Report on the Indian Epigraphy*, 1957-8, p. 56 (No. B 386), the goddess was identified as Digaravāsinī. The name is, for Sircar, no doubt the same as or mistaken for that of Dikkaravāsinī, residing on Dikkara, the eastern frontier of early medieval Brahmaputra Valley where the kingdom Kāmarūpa flourished.[3] According to the eleventh-century *Kālikāpurāṇa* (51.76-7), Kāmarūpa is triangular in shape and also one hundred *yojanas* in length from the Karatoyā to the Dikkara and thirty *yojanas* in breadth from the north to the south. It is black in colour and interspersed with innumerable hills and hundreds of rivers.[4] Here, the dwelling place of Dikkaravāsinī is deemed as the eastern limit of Kāmarūpa. This supposition is further supported by a reference in the sixteenth-century *Yogi-nītantra* (1.11.16-7), describing the eastern end of Kāmarūpa as the abode of Dikkaravāsinī.[5] However, her precise location, Dikkara, is still uncertain: some scholars locate it at Sadiya,[6] while others locate it at modern Dikrang near Sadiya and sometimes beside the Dikṣunadī which is identified with the modern Dikhu falling in the Brahmaputra near Sivasagar in Assam.[7]

In any case, the area in which Dikkaravāsinī resided seems to have remained on the fringes of sedentary society, and was scarcely absorbed in the Brahmanical social set up by the thirteenth century. This view is corroborated by the distribution of material evidence: while a growing number of inscriptions between the fifth and twelfth centuries in the lower Brahmaputra Valley indicate steady progress of the Brahmanical culture. Their woeful paucity in the upper valley, especially in the two contiguous districts of Sivasagar and Dibrugarh, shows that this process progressed at a much slower pace. The extant ruins of the pre-thirteenth-century temple structure are conspicuous by their absence in these districts. As Guha rightly argued, the social conditions of early Assam are assumed to have remained uneven in two parts of the Brahmaputra Valley. The Nagajari-Khanikargaon, Negheriting and Deopani finds only suggest that the Indo-Aryan thrust reached eastward up to Jorhat district south of the Brahmaputra.[8] Such different social conditions are well reflected in the spatial perception of Kāmarūpa represented in the Naraka story of the *Kālikāpurāṇa.* Naraka, the legendary progenitor of Kāmarūpa, drove away the Kirātas, or forest tribes of the region, up to the abode of Dikkaravāsinī, when he established his kingdom following the instructions of Viṣṇu.[9] It indicates that the worship of Dikkaravāsinī was already in practice among local communities before the conquest of Naraka, and her place belonged to the realm of the Kirātas, a vast area of the upper Brahmaputra Valley. That was in sharp contrast to the lower valley, especially the area of the present city of Guwahati and its environs, which was the dwelling-place of Kāmākhyā (*kāmākhyā-nilaya*), many Brahmins well-versed in the *Vedas* and *Śāstras*, and people in the *varṇa* order.[10] Despite being recognized as one of the seven goddesses of renowned Śākta *pīṭhas*, her trajectory seemed different from that of Kāmākhyā due to the far-off location.[11]

In view of the above, Dikkaravāsinī the eastern frontier of Kāmarūpa was, in all likelihood, a tribal goddess though her name had a Sanskrit tinge. The *Kālikāpurāṇa* (80.64b-5a) claims that the goddess is called Dikkaravāsinī because she resides on the sun and Viṣṇu, both are youthfull (*dikkara*), but it is a preposterous philological interpretation. Her tribal character is well represented in her terrible form called Tīkṣṇakāntā or Fiery Mistress, having a black complexion, a pot belly, a braid of matted hair (*ekajaṭā*), and ferociousness. In this form, she is famed as the Goddess Ugratārā. Dikkaravāsinī has her other form called Lalitakāntā or Charming Mistress, but she is always worshipped in the former attribute by votaries.[12] Moreover, she is worshipped with a sacred circle (*maṇḍala*), spells (*mantras*), eight door-keepers (*dvārapālas*), and six *yoginīs*. The sacrificial vessels, ritual object and others, and also the place and seat prescribed in the *Uttaratantra*, should all be used for worshipping the Goddess Dikkaravāsinī in both her Tīkṣṇakāntā and Lalitakāntā forms.[13]

It is important to note that Dikkaravāsinī in the form of Tīkṣṇakāntā was compared to Ugratārā or Fierce Tārā, one of the most powerful goddesses in the Vajrayāna pantheon. It leads some scholars to the strong suspicion that Dikkaravāsinī was of Buddhist origin,[14] but that is not very convincing. As has been argued elsewhere, a number of ferocious goddesses were gradually adopted from Vajrayāna to Śākta Purāṇic and Tantric traditions of eastern India in the eleventh to thirteenth centuries. The terrifying forms of Tārā were identified with Kālī or other fearsome goddesses of the Brahmanical pantheon. For example, Ugratārā, found at the

Ugratārā Temple in Uzan Bazar, Guwahati, is quite different from any of her known Buddhist images. It rather represents the fierce Goddess Cāmuṇḍā, who has an emaciated belly, sunken eyes and a corpse as per vehicle (*vāhana*). This adaptation inevitably involved a conscious modification through which Buddhist attributes of the goddess were removed or reinterpreted, and different features were superimposed upon her.[15] Ugratārā depicted in the *Kālikāpurāṇa* (61.63b-8) is not associated with Akṣobhya, one of the five Dhyānī-Buddhas, but has Śaiva traits such as a wreath of shaven human heads, a snake necklace, a tiger skin, bone ornaments, etc.

A close affinity between Śiva and Ugratārā is also emphasized in another story of the same text (81.1-23), in which she is said to be Vāmā, the goddess worshipped in the left-hand path (*vāmācāra*), among *mlecchas*. The term '*mleccha*' has been used to describe the people, who do not conform to the usual Brahmanical norm such as foreigners or people living beyond a sedentary society. Similarly, *vāmācāra* has been regarded as unconventional, revolting or indecent practices by Brahmanical traditions because their rites usually contain five esoteric elements (*pañcamakāras*), viz., liquor, meat, fish, a gesture or seal, sexual intercourse. These practices were often associated with the lower social strata, including tribal communities. Considering that, the goddess Tīkṣṇakāntā, the ferocious form of Dikkaravāsinī, was not of Buddhist origin, though compared to Ugratārā. Rather she had a strong local affiliation. It is laid down in the *Yoginītantra* (2.9.10) that the local rites and practices and also rules of drink are not to be transgressed.

The offerings made to the Goddess Dikkaravāsinī demonstrate her non-Brahmanical character even more clearly. According to the *Kālikāpurāṇa* (80.49b-51), she in the form of Tīkṣṇakāntā specially relished strong spirituous liquor among drinks, human flesh among all sacrifices, sweetmeat (*modaka*), coconut, meat curry and sugar cane. It talks about sacrifices including those of human beings who were generally offered to Tīkṣṇakāntā. The aim of sacrifices was to accomplish worldly goals, such as killing one's enemy, bring prosperity to one, having long life, wealth, fame and destroying the innumerable obstacles in one's way. This transgressive practice is given canonical sanction in the *Kālikāpurāṇa*. Chapter 67 in the book, titled Rudhirādhyāya or Chapter of Blood, gives a long descriptive list of sacrificial objects for the Goddesses Caṇḍikā and Bhirava, including birds, tortoises, alligators, fish, nine species of deer, buffaloes, big lizards, bulls, he-goats, mongoose, boars, rhinoceros, antelopes, Śarabhas (a fabulous beast with eight feet), lions, panthers, men and blood drawn from one's own body.[17] Among them the best sacrifice was that of human beings. Therefore, the goddess would be pleased for full one thousand years when a man was sacrificed, and for one hundred thousand years when three men were sacrificed.[18]

As Urban pointed out, this rather motley list of victims was drawn less from a traditional Vedic rite than from a wide array of local traditions and the many jungle animals sacrificed by diverse indigenous people of the hills in the north-east.[19] Tribal rituals and customs exerted a strong influence on the framing of rules of sacrifice, and brahmins of the region admitted it by saying that Śiva himself created animals for the sake of being sacrificed. Killing for sacrifice is not murder.[20] Such open recognition to sacrifice notwithstanding, brahmins themselves tried to keep a strict distance from its actual execution. They were supposed to follow the injunction that a brahmin should never offer a lion or tiger or man and also the blood from his body and spirituous liquor to the Goddess Durgā. If a brahmin sacrificed either a lion or tiger or man, he would go to hell and live for a short period in this world suffering misery and misfortune. If a brahmin offered blood drawn from his own body, he became guilty of killing another brahmin.[21] Needless to say, brahmins should not be the victims of sacrifice, and those who have already been given to brahmins should not be sacrificed.[22] These references lead one to assume that the sacrificial ritual for Dikkaravāsinī in the form of Tīkṣṇakāntā was presided over by non-Brahmanical priests such as the Deoris among the Chutiyas in later times. Moreover, no inscriptional evidence of royal donation to the Dikkaravāsinī Temple by any Kāmarūpa rulers casts strong doubt on the presence of brāhmaṇas on that sacred place in the pre-thirteenth century. Considering the description of her seat given by the *Kālikāpurāṇa*, even the existence of a permanent temple structure is uncertain. It is said that the holy stream of Sītagaṅgā, which is identified as the River Dikhu by Sircar, flowed by the side of Dikkaravāsinī, and she lived in the seat located on the ground and was occasionally submerged under the water.[23]

THE TUTELARY GODDESS OF THE CHUTIYAS

The period from the thirteenth to the sixteenth centuries saw a new phase in the history of the north-east, characterized by the arrival, growth and consolidation of a new power, the Ahoms, and the establishment of many local powers—the Chutiyas, Kamatas, Dimsa-Kacharis, Koches, Jayantias, etc. Among them a great deal of importance is given to the Chutiyas in connection with worship of the Goddess Kecāikhātī, mentioned as Digaravāsinī (i.e. Dikkaravāsinī) in their inscriptions and later known as Tāmreśvarī. The Chutiyas belonged to the Bodos, a linguistic group of the Brahmaputra Valley, speaking Tibeto-Burman languages and having different cognate groups within them.[24] They seem to have assumed political power in the Sadiya area in upper Assam and the contiguous area falling within Arunachal Pradesh at some point of time before the entry of the Ahoms there-in.[25] However, the first confrontation between the Ahoms and the Chutiyas as a political power was recorded in some Assamese chronicles such as the *Deodhai Assam Buranji* only during the reign of King Sutupha (1369-76), about hundred years after the death of the first Ahom ruler, King Sukapha (1228-68). It is more likely that, if there was any Chutiya state, it was of little significance till the second half of the fourteenth century.[26] Besides, the earliest known inscription of the Chutiyas comes from that period. The Dhenukhana copper plate inscription of 1314 śaka (AD 1392) records, for instance, that King Nandin (or Nandi), a great hero of many virtues, was the lord of Sadhayāpurī (*sadhayāpurīśa*), and his son was Satyanārāyaṇa. Sadhayāpurī is probably the same as Sadhiyā or Sadiya of later times.[27] It was the political centre of the Chutiyas.

The aforementioned inscription on the Tāmreśvarī Temple near Paya, about 40 km east of Sadiya, is dated to 1364 Śaka (AD 1442) and written in five lines in the Bengali-Assamese character of

Sanskrit prose. It records that through the grace of Śiva's feet, the doubly illustrious Muktādharmanārāyaṇa, who was the son of the *vṛddharājan*, effected the construction of the wall of the doubly illustrious Digaravāsinī (i.e. Dikkaravāsinī) in bricks, etc., on the date quoted above. Here *vṛddharājan*, the old king, mentioned without disclosing his personal name, as the father of Muktādharmanārāyaṇa, seems to suggest that the prince was administrating the state during the old age of his father.[28] Neog considers that Muktādharmanārāyaṇa was Lakṣmīnārāyaṇa, the son of Satyanārāyaṇa, on the basis of the records of another inscription. In this case, the old king was perhaps Satyanārāyaṇa, the son of Nandin, the lord of Sadiya. According to the Barmurtiyabil copper plate inscription dated to 1313 Śaka (AD 1392), Muktādharmanārāyaṇa was a valorous king and was much given to the worship of the goddess.[29]

Given these two inscriptional records, the temple of Dikkaravāsinī seemed to be built, or rebuilt if there had been any earlier construction on the site, in the period between the end of the fourteenth century and the former half of the fifteenth centuries, possibly in the reign of King Muktādharmanārāyaṇa of the Chutiyas. This temple is now completely in ruins, and we can-not help depending on the accounts of modern explorers for a picture of the temple and its features. Dalton mentions in his short note on the Chutiyas of Upper Assam in 1848 that the *Tāmar Ghar* or copper temple was lately visited by Captain Vetch, probably in 1841-2. He says:

> It is described [by Vetch] as a small stone building, nearly square, built without cement, the stones joined by iron pins not clamped. The roof was of copper, but it has fallen in and now lies there. The interior is 8 feet square. The whole is enclosed within a brick wall 130 feet by 200. Near the grand entrance in the western wall is a small stone tripod.[30]

Major (later Col.) S.F. Hanny of Bengal Army visited the shrine at a slightly later time, around 1848, which he calls Tamaseree Mai or copper temple, on the right bank of the little stream, Dol or Dewul panee. By citing the report of Francis Hamilton, he calls the goddess of the temple 'the eastern Kāmākhyā'. Further details of its structure are given as follows:

The dimensions of the interior is a square of 8 feet, the walls being about 4.5 feet thick, excepting in front, where there are two recesses on each side of the door, which is formed of three entire blocks of stone. The outer line of wall therefore encloses a square of about 17 feet. . . . [The temple was] covered over with sheets of beaten copper, laced together through copper loops fastened on the edges of the different sheets; as the groins, however, are not above 5 or 6 feet long, the roof must have been rather flat; a carved vase-shaped block, now lying in the river, in all probability formed the centre of the dome.[31]

Hanny adds the comment that the style of architecture is ancient, but the present temple was rebuilt in the middle of the fifteenth century with the materials of an earlier construction.[32]

Judging from these two accounts, Tāmreśvarī, another popular name of the Goddess Kecāikhātī, is probably derived from a unique feature of her temple roofed with copper (Skt. *tāmra*; local pronunciation *tāmar*). The reason why they covered the temple with copper sheets remains obscure; it might have been chosen for protecting the building from heavy rains which often cause damages, or showing the bloodthirsty nature of the goddess by red colour of the metal. Bloch, on the other hand, points to the fact that very often the first part of similar compound names of Indian deities enshrined in a temple contains the name of the person who puts up such particular deities. He further suggests that the name of Tāmreśvarī in all probability originally meant simply 'the Īśvarī, or Durgā, put up by Tāmra'.[33] Neog supports this view by identifying Tāmra as one of the seven sons of Naraka on the basis of a reference in the *Bhāgavatapurāṇa*. For him, the Tāmreśvarī Temple may have been set up by this very Tāmra, and this was the point up to which the aboriginal Kirātas were expelled by Naraka.[34] I find both the arguments less convincing on two points. First, it is rare to find goddesses named after their donors, though it is not uncommon for Śiva and Viṣṇu in early medieval South and Southeast Asia.[35] In many cases, goddesses are named after localities or specific geographical features like mountains, rivers, caves, etc., because the locale of worship and its attributes are the most important aspects of goddess cults, especially on a popular level. Second, Tāmra is not the son of Naraka but that of Mura, a demon (*asura*) having five heads. His heads were cut-off by Kṛṣṇa, and his seven sons including Tāmra were put to death by Garuḍa in charge of the outskirts of the city of Prāgjyotiṣa.[36] The connection between the Tāmreśvarī Temple and the son of Naraka, therefore, cannot be established. Notwithstanding that, the opinion expressed by Neog leads one to consider an important aspect of goddess cults in north-east India which had long been associated with demonic kings.

For instance, the Goddess Kāmākhyā is well-known for her close association with Narakāsura or demon Naraka. As a son of the Earth and Viṣṇu in his Varāha incarnation, he had been the central figure in the fabricated genealogy of Kāmarūpa and the constant source of political authority of three ruling families, the Varmans, Mlecchas, and Pālas, from the seventh to the twelfth century.[37] The royal genealogy beginning with Naraka is not found in the inscriptional records of the post-twelfth century. Nevertheless, it does not mean that the tradition of a demon ancestor of ruling families faded away in the north-east. According to the Dhenukhana inscription (AD 1392), Satyanārāyaṇa, a son of King Nandin who was the lord of Sadhayāpurī (i.e. Sadiya), had his origin in the womb of Daivakī, Nandin's wife, forming part of the lineage of the enemy of the gods (*suraripu-vaṃśāṃśa-bhūto*).[38] As mentioned earlier, Muktā-dharmanārāyaṇa, who constructed the wall of Tāmreśvarī (*alias* Kecāikhātī, Dikkaravāsinī) Temple or the temple itself in AD 1442, was probably a son of Satyanārāyaṇa belonging to the lineage of the enemy of the gods. Neog interprets this lineage as the *asura* dynasty.[39]

The reason for his demonic lineage is not explained explicitly in the inscription. Also, it is not yet known whether this lineage had some connection with demon Naraka of the previous tradition.[40] It is, however, plausible that ruling powers of indigenous origin, often represented as descendants of demons in the pre-modern north-east, achieved political legitimacy and influence through the royal devotion to tutelary goddesses and patronage to their temples. The Kāmarūpa rulers initiated this process between the ninth and eleventh centuries, which proceeded in the fifteenth century under the Chutiya kings and still later under the Dimasa-Kachari kings around the eighteenth century. The Goddesses Kāmākhyā,

Tāmreśvarī and Raṇacaṇḍī attained their exalted positions in different places and time through this process. It can be seen clearly that the sphere of influence of the goddess cults associated with political powers extended from the nuclear area of the early state of the lower Brahmaputra Valley to its periphery such as eastern Sadiya and southern Cachar Hill where so-called secondary states emerged. It was a continual, ongoing process. But it is by no means a repetition of the same exercise because the agents for each goddess cult consisted of a specific social group and the way they interacted with ruling powers differed in each case.

THE GODDESS SERVED BY THE DEORIS, TRIBAL PRIESTS

In the case of Tāmreśvarī Temple, the goddess was served by the Deoris, the representatives of the priestly class among the Chutiyas. They were permitted to continue their religious service to her including human sacrifice even after their subjugation by the Ahoms in 1523.[41] In Brown's study of the Deoris, they were presumed to have preserved the language, religion, and customs which had come down to them with comparatively little change from a period anterior to the Ahom period. They drank strong liquor and ate all kinds of flesh except beef. There were four different kinds of priests of whom each was attached to a particular division (*khel*), viz., the Bar Deori (Deori Dema) and the Saru Deori (Deori Surba); the Bar Bharali and the Saru Bharali. It was the duty of the two Bharalis to collect the dues of the temple and to provide animals for sacrifice. The two Deoris performed the sacrifice; they alone entered the temple and sung hymns, which were scarcely understood by the common people. The Deoris had a great reputation among ordinary Assamese for working black magic. They were believed to be able to make their enemies die mysteriously of a wasting disease, or resorted to in cases of loss of cattle and undetected robberies.[42]

Though the Deoris were well-known for their sacrificial ritual for the Goddess Tāmreśvarī, they also served as priests at the other two temples. The first one was *Girasi-gira* or the Old Ones, called *Bura-buri* in Assamese, always spoken of as a wedded pair and worshipped by the Dibongia *khel*. Their original temple was on the Kundil River. The second one was Pishadema or the Elder Son, called Boliya-hemata in Assamese, and worshipped by the Tengapania *khel*. His temple was on the Tengapani River. The Goddess Tāmreśvarī was called Pishasi or the Daughter and also known as Tameshari Mai or mother of copper temple and Kechakhati or eater of raw flesh. Her temple was somewhere around Chunpura on the Brahmaputra. She was worshipped by the Borgaya *khel*.[43] It is interesting to note that Tāmreśvarī was considered to be a member of the family of deities. She was the daughter of Girasi-gira and the younger sister of Pishadema, even while renowned as an independent goddess with her own identity. Pishasi, another name of Tāmreśvarī, may have been derived from Piśācī (female Piśāca), a flesh eating demon in Hindu mythology. This name retains the original features of Tāmreśvarī such as demanding human sacrifice and eating raw flesh, and is no other than Kecāikhātī.

According to the myths on the subject, human sacrifice was originally a propitiation for the introduction of sin into the world, offered by the daughter to the old ones, viz., Pishasi to Girasi-gira. However, in effect, it become a sacrifice to her on behalf of the whole nation.[44] Such a shift added a political dimension to the religious practice, closely tied to power, warfare, and royalty.[45] As Beane pointed out, 'the sacrificial cults had royal patronage, and sacrifices were demanded of the most royal officials. . . . [T]he occasion tended to coincide with calamities such as war or for obtaining wealth.'[46] The *Kālikāpurāṇa* already made it clear that royal members and courtiers could offer human sacrifice, but it needed the permission of the king.

> Princes, ministers, counsellors and *sauptikas* (persons engaged in nocturnal adventure or combat) may offer human sacrifice for the purpose of attaining prosperity and wealth. If one offers a human being without permission of the reigning king, he will find great misfortune. During an invasion or war, one may perform human sacrifice at will, but only a royal person [may do so], and no one else.[47]

A similar injunction is also found in second chapter of the *Tikha Kalpa*, a manuscript found in Manipur State Library. It is said that human sacrifices [to the goddess living on the golden mountain] were to be made, after the royal consent had been obtained, on the occurrence of public calamities, such as war, or for the purpose of obtaining great wealth.[48] The Ahom kings, too, are said to have the exclusive right to perform human sacrifice. The four chief Deoris thus had to make an annual visit to the Ahom court in order to demand and obtain the sanction of the king for their annual sacrifice of human beings. They were treated with much respect by the Ahom kings on that occasion. It is said that when any Hindu Gosain (the leaders of neo-Vaiṣṇava order) appeared before the Ahom king, the latter remained seated, while the Gosain put the garland on his neck and gave blessing; but when the four chief Deoris made an annual visit to the court, the king rose and stood before them to receive their salutation.[49] It shows the distinctive identity and important position of the Deoris as the only priests who actually carried out such a dangerous ritual for the king. They were even exempted from compulsory labour service and provided with guards and slaves in the same way as the leaders of neo-Vaiṣṇava institutions (*satras*) or brahmins of established Hindu temples. The copper plate inscriptions mentioning land grants to some Deoris were still extant at the end of the nineteenth century, although their whereabouts are unknown to us.[50]

The Deoris offered human sacrifices to the goddess on certain special occasions including their annual performance, and also to avert special calamities such as cholera, small pox, and drought.[51] According to some *Buranjis*, people even offered sacrifices of one hundred men to Āi (Mother Goddess) of Sadiya for extending the life of King Pratāpa Siṁha (*alias* Susenghpa, 1603-41) in the last moments of his life.[52] Here, Āi of Sadiya is probably the Goddess Kecāikhātī of the Tāmreśvarī Temple. But it is not easy to know precisely who the victims of that sacrifice were. In Dalton's report, the victims to be immolated should be of pure caste and perfect form, the slightest blemish or mutation rendering them unfit to be offered to the goddess. Brahmins and members of the royal family were exempted as a privilege. Doms, Haris, Musalmans, and women were excluded as unfit.[53] The *Tikha Kalpa* takes a similar view on the selection of victims:

A brahmin or a woman should never be sacrificed. Neither should one sacrifice his own body, as then he will be guilty of the sin of suicide. A brother, a father, a son, a wife's brother, a sister's son, a maternal uncle, none of these should be sacrificed; nor anyone who is acquainted with the Vedas, or has renounced the world, or is a student, or belongs to the royal family. An enemy, a sick person, a eunuch, one who is infirm or has defects or scars should not be offered.[54]

These instructions, though canonical in character, show that the selection of victims for human sacrifice was carefully made on the basis of caste hierarchy, gender, religion, physical feature, etc. They seemed to be far more elaborate than the ones given by the *Kālikāpurāṇa* of the eleventh century.[55] In the latter part of the Ahom period, victims were usually chosen from among criminals who were to be executed. When none such were obtainable, a particular section of population or *khel,* known as the Baruāli *khel,* was called upon to produce one, in return for which certain privileges were granted to the members of the *khel,* such as being exempted from payment of ferry and market duties.[56] Gait provides further details of this custom.

On a woman of the *khel* becoming pregnant, the astrologers were called on to say whether the child would be a boy or a girl, and if they predicted that it would be a boy, the mother was carefully looked after, and the child was anointed, as soon as it was born, with a paste made of tamarind and *mātikalāi* (*Phaseolus radiatus,* mung bean). When a sacrifice was thought necessary, volunteers were called for, and some person usually came forward of his own accord; if not, a victim was taken by force. In either case, the victim was shaved, anointed with the paste of tamarind and *mātikalāi,* and decked with gold and silver ornaments. He was then conducted before the image of goddess, when he prostrated himself, and was promptly decapitated by the Bar Deori or the high priest. The body was left on the spot until the following morning, when it was removed. Victims were taken only from amongst the juvenile male members of the clan; on attaining full age, they became exempt, and were allowed to marry and settle down.[57]

These rituals continued till the late eighteenth century. But in 1794 in the reign of King Gaurīnātha Siṁha (*alias* Suhitpangpha, 1789-95), Sadiya was taken by the Khāmtis who had migrated from Upper Burma some fifty or sixty years back. Their chief arrogated to himself the title of Sadiyā-khowā Gohāin, the officer appointed by the Ahoms since the early sixteenth century to administer the area ruled by the Chutiyas. Human sacrifices in the temple of Kecāikhātī seem to have ceased to be performed from this time.[58] For the Deoris, this institution was abolished by King Gaurīnātha Siṁha himself; who also, being unable to protect them from the Mishmis and other tribes, removed them to the Majuli. Despite that, their strong beliefs in the effect of human sacrifice remained unchanged. The Deoris have remarked to Brown that 'from the abolition of this sacrifice, the Ahom kingdom began to go from bad to worse'.[59]

THE GODDESS AND NEW IDENTITY CONSTRUCTION OF THE CHUTIYAS

Meanwhile, there has been an interesting change in perception of the Goddess Kecāikhātī, especially in connection with a new identity of the Chutiyas. According to the chronicle found in 1850, the Chutiyas traced their descent from Birpal (Skt. Vīrapāla), a chief belonging to the lineage of Bhīṣmaka.[60] Bhīṣmaka was a legendary king whose daughter, Rukmiṇī, was married to Kṛṣṇa. Though he was known as the ruler of Vidarbha kingdom located in the south of the Vindhya range in the epics and *Purāṇas*, he has gained much popularity in the areas around Sadiya. The name of Kuṇḍina, the capital of Bhīṣmaka, is supposed to survive in that of the Kundil River at Sadiya.[61] The ruins of two forts in Lohit district of Arunachal Pradesh are said to be the remains of his city, viz., Bhīṣmakanagara.[62] Some scholars, thus, claimed the ancient presence of Bhīṣmaka's kingdom in the Sadiya area,[63] but there is no conclusive evidence to support that. The earliest one found on the site is an inscribed brick with the name of Śrīśrī-Lakṣmīnārāyaṇa of the early fifteenth century, who constructed the wall of the Tāmreśvarī Temple in AD 1442.[64]

The prominence of Bhīṣmaka can be attributed to the *Rukmiṇī-haraṇa*, the well-known poem composed by Śaṅkaradeva. He interwove the two versions of story of the abduction of Rukmiṇī by Kṛṣṇa, as given in the *Harivaṁśa* II, chapters 59-60 and the *Bhāgavatapurāṇa*, 10, chapters 52-4, and incorporated distinct regional features in the poem. To the original tale he added scenes of common domestic life, which transformed the Purāṇic story into a narrative of popular experience. Rukmiṇī's family was represented as a prototype of Assamese Hindu family in the poem, and King Bhīṣmaka was recast as an ideal father and a devout Vaiṣṇava.[65] Considering the wide popularity of the poem among the people, it is quite probable that the legendary places associated with Bhīṣmaka were reproduced in the local landscape of the Sadiya area at a later time, possibly in the seventeenth century. The neo-Vaiṣṇava movement seemed to play a significant role in transplantation of the Bhīṣmaka legend into the area around Sadiya. Further, this reproduction led to conscious identity construction of some tribal groups including the Chutiyas and the Idu Mishmis of the Dibang Valley. They claimd to be the descendants of Bhīṣmaka and considerd Bhīṣmakanagara as the sacred heritage symbolizing their past glory.[66]

Eventually, Bhīṣmaka was represented as the king who authorized the right of the Chutiyas' to serve the Goddess Kecāikhātī as priests in her temple. According to a popular local story, Kecāikhātī assumed the form of a stone image and lay in the Dibang River in order to reveal her identity to the people. King Bhīṣmaka wanted to lift this image and install it in a temple, but his men failed to do it. Thereupon, the king announced that one who could lift the image, individually or collectively, would be given the right to officiate as priests in the Tāmreśvarī Temple. Many people attempted to do it, but on their failure four Chutiyas having purified mind and soul were able to lift the image and install it in the Tāmreśvarī Temple.[67] This story illuatrates an important change in the Kecāikhātī cult of the Chutiyas, from aniconic worship to iconic adoration. It was a part of the gradual process of Brahmanization of a tribal group, which replaces indigenous practices progressively with mainstream traditions. In fact, the expansion of brahmin settlements and diffusion of their influence were seen in the areas ruled by the Chutiyas from the end of the fourteenth century, albeit on a very limited scale.[68] Dalton's report said that some brahmins of the areas moved the Ahom kings to send one of their members to the temple of Kecāikhātī to superintend the rites. The Deoris would not admit for a long time the brahmin or alter their ceremonies according to their instructions. Finally, they consented to introduce some innovations, but continued with their own customs and rites, declining the brahmin's assistance or interference; he was, however, allowed to perform a *pūja* of his own during the season of the sacrifice.[69]

This shows how the Deoris tried to keep their religious hegemony over other social groups, probably including brahmins of the areas, while accepting adoration of sacred images that was of the upmost importance in Brahmanical mode of worship. Interestingly, the person who authorized the priesthood of the Deoris of the Tāmreśvarī Temple in the aforementioned story was not the Ahom ruler, the overlord of the Chutiyas, but Bhīṣmaka, the king of the ancient kingdom of Vidarbha, renowned as one of the cultural centres since the *Mahābhārata.* He was moreover the father-in-law of Kṛṣṇa, who became one of the most significant deities in the north-east after the sixteenth century. The close tie forged between King Bhīṣmaka and the Deoris is not based on any historical facts, but nevertheless it discreetly connects the wider world of the Epic and the local centre of the goddes worship.

This is further emphasized by another popular story about construction of the temple by a Chutiya king. It is said that the Goddess Kecāikhātī revealed herself before a king who was the descendant of Bhīṣmaka. She told him she would be his devotee only on the condition that he could erect a temple with a copper roof in one single night before the first cock's crow in the morning. In the case of the king's failure to do it, their role would be reversed and the king would have to be her devotee. The king worked all night, building a temple with a copper roof, and then, just before its completion, the goddess caused a magical cock to crow. The king had to leave the work unfinished and become the devotee of the goddess.[70] A similar story is also told of Naraka, except in this case the king wanted the Goddess Kāmākhyā as his bride and constructed the incomplete staircase of the Kāmākhyā Temple.[71] The Chutiyas seemed to remake this well-known story of Naraka and Kāmākhyā for explaining the origin of the Tāmreśvarī Temple. In their version, the temple was built by a king descended from

Bhīṣmaka. This king, whose name was not mentioned in the story, was possibly Birpal, the supposed progenitor of Chutiya kingdom, belonging to the lineage of Bhīṣmaka. Scholars ascribed the Chutiya chronicle beginning with Birpal to the early nineteenth century, perhaps written by some members of the Chutiya aristocracy as an attempt to legitimize their claim over a part of Assam during the establishment of the Matak kingdom in 1805, or after 1826 when the East India Company annexed the region.[72] The lineage narrative of Birpal links the peripheral power with established ones endowed with all appropriate royal qualities and locates it within the ambit of the Epic-Purāṇic world of the mainstream tradition. Looking at this, the above story appears to be made at a much later time despite its antiquarian taste. The nexus between the goddess and the king with sacred genealogy and its antiquity are not a given fact but an imagined reality. A significant point to remember is that it is part of a long religious process which has been ongoing since the twelfth century when the image of Goddess Kāmākhyā and King Naraka was made in the lower Brahmaputra Valley.

THE AFTERLIFE OF THE GODDESS

Kecāikhātī still enjoyed her fame in the nineteenth century although the human sacrifice to her ceased during the reign of King Gaurīnātha Siṁha (1780-95). Francis Hamilton in his report on the survey of eastern India in 1808-14, refers to three important pilgrimage centres of Assam, including the Kāmākhyā Temple at Nilachala, a temple (its name not defined) at Kaliyabar now in Nagaon, and the Dikkaravāsinī Temple at Sadiya.[73] Dalton also said in 1848 that the copper temple of the goddess was respected by and had its votaries among all the hill tribes in the vicinity, as well as by the Ahom and Hindu population of Assam. It was also visited by pilgrims, who brought offerings from regions far more remote, perhaps from Tibet and China, as well as from other parts of India.[74]

When Bloch visited the site in 1905, however, the temple was nothing more than a heap of broken stones past all repairs with only a part of the wall standing; a huge tree growing over the debris. He identified the two figures on the lintels on the door in the northern wall as images of Mahādeva posing as Dvārapāla. On the east of the boundary wall he found some ruins of brick and stone buildings, amongst which he could make out three statues of Hindu deities: Sūrya, Kālī dancing on Śiva and the third probably represented Sarasvatī, if the indistinct object, which she held in her right hand was a musical instrument. Among other interesting archaeological finds on the site was a line of tiles, about three feet apart from each other, carved on the inner sides of the walls, except the eastern one. These carvings represented figures of men, animals, birds, flowers, and geometrical figures without any religious bearing. The style was that of semi-tribal kind, as in the carvings at Dimapur and other places of Assam. Remarkable among these were the Durgā image with the maneless lion, often found in Assamese painting.[75] It has not yet been possible to date these images accurately, since none of stylistic features were scrutinized. But in view of the fact that Durgā *pūjā* with the earthen image of the goddess was first introduced to the Ahoms by King Pratāpa Siṁha in the middle of the seventeenth century,[76] these images including Durgā can be assigned to the eighteenth century.

In the 1950s, Debala Mitra explored the place and wrote a short report suggesting that the temple was originally a *caturāyatana* having four shrines or cells.[77] However, the temple site and structure are now reported to be untraceable, probably because of the great earthquake of 1950.[78] In my observation in 2012, it was found that the Tāmreśvarī Temple located in Sadiya town at present is a recent construction of not more than fifty years old. The local people still consider the Goddess Kecāikhātī as a daughter of the Old Ones called Bura-buri in Assamese or Girasi-gira in Deori language. They offer buffalo sacrifice to her at this new Tāmreśvarī Temple every three years, and a Deori who comes from a specific family performs the sacrificial ritual.

Some other goddesses with similar names and attributes are still worshiped by different communities in different parts of the region.[79] For instance, Kāchakāntī (or Kāncakāntī) has been a renowned goddess of the Kacharis whose shrine is now at Udharbond near Silchar in Cachar district. According to a local legend,

King Kṛṣṇacandra (1773-1813) had a dream in 1806 and then constructed a temple for worshipping Kāchakāntī, one of the terrifying forms of Śakti. The royal preceptor pandit Sonaram Sarma on hearing the description of Kāchakāntī from the king made a four-armed golden image and installed it in a temple inside a deep forest near present Udharbond.[80] Some scholars identify Kāchakāntī of Cachar with Kecāikhātī of Sadiya, based on the assumption that when the Kacharis were in the upper Brahmaputra Valley Kecāikhātī was their tutelary deity.[81] The Kāchakāntī Temple of Cachar was also one of the principal places where human sacrifices were offered. The ceremony was performed by a family of brahmin residents at Udharbond, who were known as Deshmukhiyas. The practice is said to have been put a stop to during the reign of King Kṛṣṇacandra around 1818, in consequence of a brahmin having narrowly escaped being sacrificed by mistake.[82] The possible association between Kecāikhātī of Sadiya and Kāchakāntī of Cachar, though based on very limited historical evidence, throws light on a proliferation of goddess cults in the process of tribal state formation of the north-east. It does not mean a unilinear development but a continuous adoption from the past and retrospective redefinition from the present.

To sum up, among a number of powerful goddesses worshipped in the north-east, Kecāikhātī was infamous for eating raw flesh as the name shows. Her cult spot, later known as the Tāmreśvarī Temple near Sadiya, was almost always described as the most notorious place of human sacrifice in the reports of British colonial officer-scholars in the nineteenth century. They repeatedly identified the practice of human sacrifice associated with Kecāikhātī as one of the clearest signs of 'degenerate Hinduism' or of the barbaric characters of 'impure tribes' in the region. Sometimes, they claimed that a wily and bigoted brahmin may have made it a price for the liberty of proselytism to his creed.[83] Even some Indian scholars tend to internalize such a negative image of the goddess coming down from colonial sources. However, the history of Kecāikhātī over a prolonged period from the early medieval times to the present rather shows her multiple identities represented in various names such as Dikkaravāsinī, Tīkṣṇakāntā, Ugratārā, Lalitakāntā,

Tāmreśvarī, Pishasi (Piśācī?), Kāchakāntī and so on. Her attributes and nature have neither been static nor monolithic, since different social groups with their own interests, including tribal priests, kings, brahmin and local people, participated in the making of the goddess. Brahmanization of tribal custom and resistance to Brahmanical dominance over tribal worship appear to go against each other, yet the one does not necessarily negate the other. The Kecāikhātī cult is indeed remarkable as a site of constant and subtle negotiation between those two processes which has characterized the religious traditions of the north-east.

NOTES

1. Neog's article may serve as the most useful introduction to the Goddess Kecāikhātī , see M. Neog, 'Goddess Tāmreśvarī and Blood Sacrifices', in idem, *Religion of the North-East: Studies in the Formal Religions of North-Eastern India*, Delhi: Munshiram Manoharlal, 1984, pp. 109-72. For a brief reference to the Goddess, see K.L. Barua, *Early History of Kamarūpa: From the Earliest Times to the End of the Sixteenth Century*, Gauhati: Lawyers Book Stall, 1933 (1966 repr.), p. 183; B. Kakati, *The Mother Goddess Kamakhya*, Guwahati: Publication Board Assam, 1948 (2003 repr.), pp. 55-63; S.N. Sharma, *A Socio-Economic and Cultural History of Medieval Assam,* AD *1200-1800*, Guwahati: Bina Library, 1989, p. 97; N.N. Bhattacharyya, *Religious Culture of North-Eastern India*, New Delhi: Manohar, 1995, pp. 102-7; N.R. Mishra, *Kamakhya: A Socio-Cultural Study*, New Delhi: D.K. Printworld, 2004, pp. 5, 18; Hugh B. Urban, *The Power of Tantra: Religion, Sexuality and the Politics of South Asian Studies*, New York: I.B. Tauris, 2010, p. 97; Mary Storm, *Head and Heart: Valour and Self-Sacrifice in the Art of India*, New Delhi: Routledge, 2013, p. 80.
2. D.C. Sircar, 'Prāgjyotisha-Kāmarūpa', in H.K. Barpujari (ed.), *The Comprehensive History of Assam*, vol. 1, Guwahati: Publication Board Assam, 2007 (3rd edn.), p. 64.
3. D.C. Sircar, 'Pāyā Tāmreśvarī (Dikkaravāsinī) Temple Inscription of Muktādharmanārāyaṇa, Śaka 1364 (AD 1442)', in idem, *Some Epigraphical Records of the Medieval Period from Eastern India*, New Delhi: Abhinav, 1979, p. 3.
4. Biswanarayan Shastri (ed. and tr.), *Kālikāpurāṇa*, Delhi: Nag Publisher, 1991-2.

5. Biswanarayan Shastri (ed.), *Yoginītantra,* Delhi: Bharatiya Vidya Prakashan, 1982.
6. P.C. Choudhury, *The History of the Civilization of the People of Assam to the Twelfth Century,* Guwahati and Delhi: Spectrum, 1959 (1987 repr.), p. 420.
7. D.C. Sircar, *The Śākta Pīṭhas,* Delhi: Motilal Banarsidass, 1948 (1998, 2nd edn.), p. 17, fn. 3; D.C. Sircar, *Studies in the Geography of Ancient and Medieval India,* Delhi: Motilal Banarsidass, 1971 (2nd edn.), p. 163.
8. Amalendu Guha, 'Pre-Ahom Roots and the Medieval State in Assam: A Reply', *Social Scientist,* vol. 12, no. 6, 1984, June, pp. 71-2.
9. *Kālikāpurāṇa,* 38. 113-27.
10. *Kālikāpurāṇa,* 38. 128-30. As to the spatial extent and perception of Kāmarūpa, see Jae-Eun Shin, 'Region Formed and Imagined: Reconsidering Temporal, Spatial and Social Context of Kāmarūpa', in Lipokmar Dzuvichu and Manjeet Baruah (eds.), *Modern Practices in North East India: History, Culture, Representation,* London and Routledge, 2018, pp. 40-1.
11. For the seven Śākta *Pīṭhas,* see *Kālikāpurāṇa,* 18. 41-50; for the trajectory of the Goddess Kāmākhyā, see Jae-Eun Shin, 'Yoni, Yoginīs and Mahāvidyās: Feminine Divinities from Early Medieval Kāmarūpa to Medieval Koch Behar', *Studies in History,* vol. 26, issue 1, 2010, pp. 1-29.
12. *Kālikāpurāṇa,* 80. 37-9a.
13. Ibid., 80. 40-5.
14. B. Kakati, *The Mother Goddess Kamakhya,* p. 60; M. Neog, 'Goddess Tāmreśvarī and Blood Sacrifices', p. 110.
15. Jae-Eun Shin, *Change, Continuity and Complexity: The Mahāvidyās in East Indian Śākta Traditions,* London: Routledge; New Delhi: Manohar, 2018, pp. 123-5.
16. C. Chakravarti, *Tantras: Studies on Their Religion and Literature,* Calcutta: Punthi Pustak, 1972 (repr.), p. 55; N.N. Bhattacharyya, *History of the Tantric Religion,* New Delhi: Manohar, 1999 (2nd edn.), p. 316.
17. *Kālikāpurāṇa,* 67.3-5a.
18. Ibid., 67.18.
19. Hugh B. Urban, *The Power of Tantra,* p. 63.
20. *Kālikāpurāṇa,* 67.39.
21. Ibid., 67.48b-50.
22. Ibid., 67.101-2.
23. Ibid., 80.32b-4a.
24. R.C. Buragohain, 'A Note of the Morans, the Borahis and the Chutiyas', in H.K. Barpujari (ed.), *The Comprehensive History of Assam,* vol. 2, Guwahati: Publication Board Assam, 2003 (2nd. edn.), p. 61.

25. M. Momin, 'Socio-Economic Linkages in Decline of Prāgjyotiṣa-Kāmarūpa', in Fozail Ahmad Qadri (ed.), *Society and Economy in North-East India*, vol. 2, New Delhi: Regency, p. 44. Ney Elias, on the basis of an old Assamese chronicle found in the possession of a Burmese king, stated that when the Ahoms migrated to the Brahmaputra Valley, it was inhabited by three tribes, the Chutiyas, Morans and Borahis, of which the Chutiyas was the ruling group and thirty three Chutiya kings had ruled in succession before the foundation of the Ahom kingdom in the early thirteenth century under the leadership of Sukapha (1228-68). See Ney Elias, *Introductory Sketch of the History of the Shans in Upper Burma and Western Yunnan*, Calcutta: Foreign Department Press, 1876, p. 61. Based on this, some scholars tried to trace the history of the Chutiyas back to the middle of the seventh century. See S.L. Baruah, *A Comprehensive History of Assam*, New Delhi: Munshiram Manoharlal, 2002, p. 184. Yet no convincing evidence, both archaeological and textual, asserts such an early presence of the Chutiya kingdom. The inscriptions of Kāmarūpa between the seventh and twelfth centuries provide no reference to Sadiya and the names of people inhabiting the area.
26. D. Nath, 'State Formation in the Peripheral Areas: A Study of the Chutiya Kingdom of the Brahmaputra Valley', in J.B. Bhattacharjee and D.R. Syiemlieh (eds.), *Early State in North East India*, New Delhi: Regency Publications, 2013, pp. 24-5.
27. M. Neog, 'Lights on a Ruling Dynasty of Arunachal Pradesh in the Fourteenth and Fifteenth Centuries', in idem (ed.), *Prāchya-śāsanāvalī: An Anthology of Royal Charters, etc. Inscribed on Stone, Copper, etc., of Kāmarūpa, Assam (Saumāra), Koch-Behar, etc., from 1205 AD to 1847 AD*, Guwahati: Publication Board, Assam, 1974 (2008 repr.), p. 94, ll.8-10; p. 218.
28. D.C. Sircar, 'Pāyā Tāmreśvarī (Dikkaravāsinī) Temple Inscription', p. 2.
29. M. Neog, 'Lights on a Ruling Dynasty of Arunachal Pradesh', p. 216.
30. E.T. Dalton, 'Notes on the Chutiyas of Upper Assam', 1848, manuscript printed in W.B. Brown, *An Outline Grammar of the Deori Chutiya Language (Spoken in Upper Assam)*, Shillong: The Assam Secretariat Printing Office, 1895, p. 76.
31. S.F. Hanny, 'Notes on Ancient Temples and Other Remains in the Vicinity of Suddyah, Upper Assam', *Journal of the Asiatic Society of Bengal*, vol. 17, pt. 1, 1848, pp. 465-6.
32. Ibid., pp. 466-7.
33. T. Bloch, *Report of an Archaeological Tour in Assam in January and February*, Shillong: Assam Secretariat Office, 1905, p. 25.
34. M. Neog, 'Goddess Tāmreśvarī and Blood Sacrifices', p. 115.

35. For some examples of Śaiva and Vaiṛṣṇava temples in which images of their chosen god were installed, animated, and named after the donor kings, see A. Sanderson, 'The Śaiva Age: The Rise and Dominance of Śaivism during the Early Medieval Period', in S. Einoo (ed.), *Genesis and Development of Tantrism*, Tokyo: Institute of Oriental Culture, 2009, pp. 60, 274.
36. C.L. Goswami and M.A. Shastri (ed. and tr.), *Bhāgavatapurāṇa*, Gorakhpur: Gita Press, 1971, 10.59. 6-19.
37. As to Naraka and his relationship with Kāmākhyā, the tutelary Goddess, see Jae-Eun Shin, *Change, Continuity and Complexity*, pp. 256-9. For Naraka in the political genealogy of Kāmarūpa, see Jae-Eun Shin, 'Changing Dynasties, Enduring Genealogy: A Critical Study on the Political Legitimation in Early Medieval Kāmarūpa', *Journal of Ancient Indian History*, vol. 27, 2011, pp. 173-87.
38. M. Neog (ed.), *Prācya-śāsanāvalī*, p. 94, ll.10-12.
39. M. Neog, 'Lights on a Ruling Dynasty of Arunachal Pradesh', p. 212.
40. The socio-historical implication of this issue is beyond the scope of this article. For further discussion, see Jae-Eun Shin, 'Descending from Demons, Ascending to Kshatriyas: Genealogical Claims and Political Process in Pre-modern Northeast India, the Chutiyas and the Dimasas', *The Indian Economic & Social History Review*, vol. 57, issue 1, 2020, pp. 49-75.
41. In 1523, Ahom King Suhungmung, *alias* Dihingia Raja (1497-1539), conquered the Chutiyas and annexed their kingdom to his state. A new officer of state, known as the Sadiyā Khowa Gohāin, was appointed to administer the area ruled by the Chutiyas. See E.A. Gait, *A History of Assam*, Guwahati: Spectrum, 1905 (2011 repr.), p. 88.
42. W.B. Brown, *An Outline Grammar of the Deori Chutiya Language*, pp. iii-v.
43. Ibid., p. iv.
44. Ibid., p. vii. On the other hand, Dalton reported in 1848 that a yearly human sacrifice was offered at these three temples. See E.T. Dalton, 'Notes on the Chutiyas of Upper Assam', p. 75.
45. For more details on human sacrifice and kingship in the region, see Hugh B. Urban, *The Power of Tantra*, pp. 88-98.
46. Wendell C. Beane, *Myths, Cult and Symbols in Śākta Hinduism: A Study of the Indian Mother Goddess*, Leiden: E.J.Brill, 1977, p. 59.
47. *Kālikāpurāṇa* 67. 116-17.
48. Cited in E.A. Gait, 'Human Sacrifices in Ancient Assam', *Journal of the Asiatic Society of Bengal*, vol. 67, pt. 3, 1898, p. 62. The *Tikha Kalpa* deals with the mode of worshipping Kālī or Tārā including human and other sacrifices. For a brief introduction of the *Tikha Kalpa*, E.A. Gait, *Report on*

the Progress of Historical Research in Assam, Shillong: the Assam Secretariat Press, 1897, p. 25.

49. W.B. Brown, *An Outline Grammar of the Deori Chutiya Language,* pp. vi-vii.
50. For the privileges of the Deoris received from the Ahom kings, see ibid., p. vi.
51. E.A. Gait, 'Human Sacrifices in Ancient Assam', p. 58.
52. Kasinath Tamuli-Phukan, *Āśām Burañji,* p. 35; Gunabhiram Barua, *Āśām Burañji,* p. 105, cited in M. Neog, 'Goddess Tāmreśvarī and Blood Sacrifices', p. 112.
53. E.T. Dalton, 'Notes on the Chutiyas of Upper Assam', p. 76.
54. Cited in E.A. Gait, 'Human Sacrifices in Ancient Assam', pp. 62-3.
55. According to the *Kālikāpurāṇa* (67.101-2), brāhmaṇas, caṇḍālas, and princes should not be sacrificed. But the sons of the enemy kings, who are captured in battle, could be offered.
56. E.A. Gait, *A History of Assam,* p. 88; E.A. Gait, 'Human Sacrifices in Ancient Assam', p. 58; E.T. Dalton, 'Notes on the Chutiyas of Upper Assam', p. 76 .
57. E.A. Gait, 'Human Sacrifices in Ancient Assam', p. 58
58. *Assam District Gazetteers,* vol. 11: *The Sadiya Frontier Tract Gazetteer,* pt. 1, Shillong: Assam Secretariat Press, 1928, p. 17; E.A. Gait, *A History of Assam,* p. 214.
59. W.B. Brown, *An Outline Grammar of the Deori Chutiya Language,* p. vii.
60. It was found in the possession of some Chutiyas by William Robinson and published in Assamese in the *Orunodoi,* December, 1850. It has been reproduced in E.A. Gait's *Report on the Progress of Historical Research in Assam,* pp. 18-19 and in the *Deodhai Asam Buranji,* 1932 and the *Satsari Asam Buranji,* 1960, both compiled and edited by S.K. Bhuyan.
61. E.A. Gait, *A History of Assam,* pp.15-16.
62. For more details on the sites, see Sukanya Sharma, *A Sourcebook of Archaeology of the Himalayan Region: Arunachal Pradesh,* Kolkata: A Centre for Archaeological Studies & Training, Eastern India, 2014, pp. 77-80.
63. See P.C. Choudhury, *The History of the Civilization of the People of Assam to the Twelfth Century,* p. 236; D. Sarma (ed.), *Kāmarūpaśāsanāvalī,* Gauhati: Publication Board Assam, 1981, p. 73.
64. M. Neog, 'Lights on a Ruling Dynasty of Arunachal Pradesh', p. 216.
65. For the *Rukmiṇī-haraṇa,* see M. Neog, *Śaṅkaradeva and His Times: Early History of the Vaiṣṇava Faith and Movement in Assam:* Delhi: Motilal Banarsidass, 1985, pp. 177-8; B.K. Barua, 'Śaṅkaradeva: His Poetical Works', in Banikanta Kakati (ed.), *Aspects of Early Assamese Literature,* Gauhati: Gauhati University, 1953, pp. 88-90.

66. For the Bhīṣmaka legend and tribal groups, see Amrendra Kr. Thakur, 'Pre-modern Accommodation of Differences and Modern Innovations: Religion and Society of Arunachal Pradesh', in Tripathy and S. Dutta (eds.), *Religious History of Arunachal Pradesh*, New Delhi: Gyan Publishing House, 2008, pp. 345-6.
67. The story is reported in N.N. Bhattacharyya, *Religious Culture of North-Eastern India*, p. 103.
68. There are only two inscriptional records on this matter: the Dhenukhana plate (AD 1392) mentions that Satyanārāyaṇa gifted 600 *puṭis* of land in the village Ludumimari to the son of the brahmin Nārāyaṇa; and Pratyakṣanārāyaṇa made another such gift of 600 *puṭis* in the village Vyaghramari, and Yaśanārāyaṇa (or Yamanārāyaṇa) still another gift of 200 *puṭis* to the son of Bhārgava among *brahmins*. See M. Neog, *Prācya-śāsanāvalī*, p. 94, ll. 13-6; p. 96, ll. 34-6. The Ghilamara plate of Lakṣmīnārāyaṇa (AD 1401) records his donation of 200 *puṭis* of land in the village Bakhana to the *brahmin* Ravideva, the son of Hari who was a devotee of Vāsudeva. See Ibid., p. 97, ll. 8-12.
69. E.T. Dalton, 'Notes on the Chutiyas of Upper Assam', p. 76.
70. The story is reported in N.N. Bhattacharyya, *Religious Culture of North-Eastern India*, p. 104.
71. For details of this story, see N.R. Mishra, *Kamakhya: A Socio-Cultural Study*, p. 147.
72. D. Nath, 'State Formation in the Peripheral Areas: A Study of the Chutiya Kingdom of the Brahmaputra Valley', p. 29.
73. S.K. Bhuyan, *An Account of Assam: First Compiled in 1807-1814 by Francis Hamilton*, Gauhati: Department of Historical and Antiquarian Studies, 1963, p. 57.
74. E.T. Dalton, 'Notes on the Chutiyas of Upper Assam', p. 77.
75. T. Bloch, *Report of an Archaeological Tour in Assam in January and February*, Shillong: Assam Secretariat Office, 1905, pp. 92-4, cited in M. Neog, 'Goddess Tāmreśvarī and Blood Sacrifices', pp. 113-14. See also *Annual Report of Archaeological Survey of India 1904-05*, Calcutta: Superintendent Government Printing, India, 1908, pp. 7-8.
76. For the early Ahom kings who adopted Brahmanical traditions, see L. Gogoi, *The Buranjis: Historical Literature of Assam*, New Delhi: Omsons, 1986, pp. 256-61.
77. D.C. Sircar, 'Pāyā Tāmreśvarī (Dikkaravāsinī) Temple Inscription', p. 4.
78. *Census of India 2011: Arunachal Pradesh*, Series 13, Part XII-A, Arunachal Pradesh: Directorate of Census Operations, 2011, p. 52.
79. It is reported that there was a temple of Kecāikhātī in North Lakhimpur,

though its historical connection with the Kecāikhātī temple in Sadiya has not yet been examined. See N.N. Bhattacharyya, *Religious Culture of North-Eastern India*, p. 103.

80. Gouri Sen, 'Life in the Kachari Kingdom at Khaspur', unpublished PhD thesis submitted to the University of Gauhati, 1994, p. 117.
81. S.K. Bhuyan (ed.), *Kachari Buranji,* Gauhati: The Government of Assam in Department of Historical and Antiquarian Studies, 1951, p. vi; J.B. Bhattacharjee, 'The Kachari (Dimasa) State Formation', in H.K. Barpujari (ed.), *The Comprehensive History of Assam*, vol. 2, Guwahati, Publication Board Assam, 2003 (2nd edn.), p. 393.
82. E.A. Gait, 'Human Sacrifices in Ancient Assam', p. 57; Gouri Sen, 'Life in the Kachari Kingdom at Khaspur', p. 120.
83. S.F. Hanny, 'Notes on Ancient Temples and Other Remains in the Vicinity of Suddyah, Upper Assam', p. 463.

CHAPTER 3

Witchcraft, Sorcery and Tantricism in the Khasi Pnar Society

HERMINA B. LAKIANG

Before engaging in the socio-historical and conceptual case study of witchcraft, sorcery and tantiricism in the Khasi Pnar society it is required to look at some historical conjectures on Western societies by Lynn Thorndike (*History of Magic and Experimental Science in the Middle Ages*, 8 vols., New York, 1923-58) and Jules Michelet (*Satanism and Witchcraft*, New York, 1965) where they postulate that witchcraft was a product of the misery of the fourteenth century with its black death and the Hundred Years War, among other misfortunes.[1] H.C. Lea (*The History of the Inquisition in the Middle Ages*, New York, 1888, *Materials Towards a History of Witchcraft*, New York, 1957), his disciple G.L. Burr (*Narratives of the Witchcraft Cases*, New York 1914, *Life and Selection*, N.Y., Ithaca, 1943) and A.D. White (*A History of Warfare of Science with Theology*, New York, 1897) assume witchcraft to be due to church, due to widespread superstition, due to the manipulation of the common people by casuists and quibblers and because of the general oppression of the few going hand in hand with the submission and fear of the many.[2] The most perceptive and philosophical modern French Historian, L. Febvre (*Sorcellerie; sotisse ou revolution mentale, Annales, economics, societies civilization*, 1948) proposed that 'the mind of one age is not necessarily subject to the same rules of the mind of another'. Many of the suggestions offered as explanations are valuable, but hardly adequate.[3] The anthropological studies that shed the most light upon witchcraft were pioneered by Bronislaw Malinowski (*Magic, Science and Religion and Other Essays*, New York, 1954) and were continued by Evans-Pritchard (*Witchcraft, Oracles and Magic Among the Azande,* Oxford, 1937) and their students and successors,[4] by taking the African, the Oceanian and the English societies as case studies. The excerpts of these two anthropological works can be found in Max Marwick edition *Witchcraft and Sorcery,* Penguin Education, 1970.[5] Some sociological readings are also included in this edition,[6] which are used in the study of the Khasi Pnar Society. It must be pointed out that historical works have been done by N.N. Bhattacharya, on the Indian belief in tantricism[7] and on the religious culture of north-eastern India.[8] Through careful examination of these works done on tantricism, like the work of C. Chakravarti,[9] a materialistic approach to tantricism found in D.P. Chattopadhyaya's *Lokayata*[10] and S. Kapur's study,[11] it is discovered that Tantricism is one of the belief systems of Hinduism relating mainly to the fertility cult involving the sexual union of the male and female principles including the practice of magic-witchcraft and sorcery, which involves rites, rituals, *mantras,* medicine, charms, amulet, etc., used to attain ones's desire for boon and at the same time to destroy one's enemy.[12] But none of these works finds any reference to the Khasi Pnar society except vaguely in N.N. Bhattacharya's *Religious Culture of North-Eastern India.*[13] No conceptual historical works has ever been done in this regard except a stray mention here and there about the mystical belief in witchcraft like *U thlen* and *ka taro* and the belief in tantricism. Most information about witchcraft, sorcery and tantricism in the Khasi Pnar context can be gleaned from books on religion, society and folklore. This article is a result of one particular article by H.H. Mohrmen, 'The Khasi Pnar Beliefs in Curse and Witchcraft'[14] and a work in vernacular which is a critical narrative by R.M. Mukhim, *Ki Maraw ka Jingngeit Bieit*[15] in which she narrates the Khasi Pnar superstitious belief in *U thlen, ka taro, U noingaiksuid* and *ka bih.*

It must be mentioned at the onset that there are two kinds of magic, white magic and black magic. White magic constitutes the rites and rituals of all religious, which are engaged by the believers for boons, blessings and at the same time for protection from one's enemy or from evil with the help of the gods and goddesses. Black magic on the other hand is the degenerated form of rites and rituals used to get one's desire for materials gain or venegeance at the expense of harming fwellow human beings. It is generally given the term of witchcraft and sorcery and is being associated with demons and seeks to control even the gods as in the case of 'left' tantricism. White magic is used as a counter-reaction to the practice of witchcraft in any society including the Khasi Pnar society. Tantricism is also viewed by some as a degenerated belief and practice system of a person of lowly socio-religious status. At the same time, even within tantricism itself, the belief and practices are classified into the right and the left (*vamacharya*) paths, i.e. positive and negative aspects respectively. Its positive aspect deals with inner visualization of the sexual union of Shiva and Shakti. The creative power of this union is applied to the cosmos itself, and specially the elements of the earth.[16] Through this act of procreation of humans (representing gods and goddesses) it is believed that it will bring forth the productivity and fertility of the earth necessary for agriculture.[17] In fact, this kind of magic is performed in different parts of the world. On the negative side, when the *sadhaka* acquires *siddhis* he sometimes chooses to use it in 'black art' or witchcraft to harm others for monetary gain or vengeance, forgetting the great goal of worldly detachment.[18] The 'left' *sadhaka* indulges in the actual physical pleasure of meat, drink and women. In fact, the witches of the Western world are also accused of this same indulgence in partaking of meat and sexual ritual involving nude participants.[19] In this light, the study of witchcraft and sorcery is conducted in link with tantricism or to be specific with the degenerated form of it, as a result of which even human sacrifice was made, even in Jaintia Hills in Nartiang before the colonial period. Thus the question of whether the *Pnars* really practised this gory sacrifice after their Hinduization, if there was no such traditional belief and practice prior to the coming of tantricism among them is hoped to be answered by the Khasoi Pnar belief in the existence of human sacrifice done 'directly' to the *thlen* and 'indirectly' to the *taro* to gain wealth and prosperity in all aspects of life.

H.H. Mphrmen began with the incident in Mawlai, where the

people stood up against a supposedly *thlen* keeper and a similar incident that had happened in Mowtrychiah village in Jaintia Hills (alleged *taro* keeper).[20] The writer also talked about a personal incident, where he was supposedly a victim of the evil eye (*Ka She Sabuit or Sakai*) and suffering from constipation. His father performed a certain magic ritual by taking a pinch of lime and rubbed it on a betel leaf. Then he chanted some *mantras* and spat on the lime three times. Then he took a little of that lime on the forefinger to make a tick mark on his forehead, moved towards his tummy, unbuttoned his shirt and then drew a huge circle on his stomach and finished it with another lime tick on his big toe. After that, he drew another circle on the betel leaf with a cross inside the circle and then placed the lime sketched pan leaf inside the circle and then placed it on the nearest crossroad. He also mentioned about the damage of the houses and the owners who were alleged to be *thlen* keeper and *taro* keeper, who were also ostracized. Families were detested by the village according to him because they were in possession of the power of black magic or witchcraft and could cast an evil spell (*Ai Ksuid*) on their enemies. In Jaintia Hills, they avoid mixing with certain families as they are accused of casting a spell (*ai bih* in Khasi and *ea kymbad* in Pnar) on somebody having food and the victim would fall sick. People' suffering from *Kymbad, Jymbich I Bih* lost their teeth unnaturally, also suffered from neck pain. Even throat cancer was attributed to *Kymbad I Ka Bih.* Families who are alleged keepers of *Kymbad I ka Bioh* are forbidden from taking part in the preparation of a community feast for fear that those who partake might suffer. The family is, however, not forbidden from joining the feast, but people would avoid sitting next to them or opposite them. He also differentiates between the Pnar and the Khasi belief in *nongaiksuid.* In the Khasi context certain families are alleged to possess the power of black magic (*nongaiksuid*), because they can cast a spell on their enemies to make them fall sick. In the Pnar context, if any person wished to cast a spell on his/her enemies, he would seek the help of a shaman (*Ksoh Stad I Pa Stad*) and pay him to do the job. It is believed that the shaman can do a variety of things to make the enemy suffer, similar to voodoo.[21]

Mohrmen's article providers some valuable information about witchcraft and some valuable insight in it but he did not give a clear definition of it and also completely failed to mention its relation to sorcery. First, witchcraft and sorcery are inter-linked, there is a difference between the two. While witchcraft is psychic, sorcery is practical. Second, though he mentioned the existence of the evil eye in the Pnar society and described the episode of the 'transference of evil into inanimate object' as a remedy of the sickness as a result of the evil eye, he was unable to give it a definition which is found in J.G. Frazer's work, *The Golden Bough.*[22] He seems to mix up between *Bih I Kymbad* and the evil eye in the event of any feasts amongst the Khasi Pnars. Avoiding of inter-dining with certain people takes place in case of the evil eye, which is a psychic ability causing stomach problems to those who eat near them or sit opposite to them and eye them while they have the food. It should be noted that *Bih I Kymbad* is a practical form of magic which is sorcery which the accused administers through his finger tips to the food (the 'poison' of *ka bih* resides supposedly in their nails). In this case they are forbidden to take part in preparation of the food in any feasts but not in inter-dining. He also states that, when the Pnar resorted to witchcraft, they engage the help of a shaman. It is again an error to say this on his part as witchcraft is a psychic ability which is inherent in a person. At the same time, shamanism as understood by its definition and explanation is in fact a form of healing and knowing about certain confusing facts of life in relation to a personal experience by employing mystical means.[23] So a person who resorts to *Ai-ksuid* (sorcery) or cursing others especially enemies to inflict misfortunes like sickness and death, engage the help of a sorcerer not a Shaman. It is necessary to quote the definition of witchcraft and sorcery as defined by Evans-Pritchard. . .

> a witch performs no rite, utters no spell and possesses no medicines. An act of witchcraft is a psychic act . . . sorcerers may do them ill by performing magic rites with bad medicines.[24]

Hence, this article is going to examine the existence of witchcraft and sorcery in the Khasi Pnar society according to the definition of E.E. Evans-Pritchard in a historical and conceptual perspective. From the time of the emergence of the traditional religion in the Pnar society, witchcraft existed side-by-side with religion. In actuality the first *syiem* of the Pnars, U Long Chyllong was deposed by his nephew U Synriang as the common people accused him (the former) of association with witchcraft and sorcery. The tarnished image of U Long Cyllong, enabled Synriang later to win the trust of the people at large who looked up to him since the days of his youth as their promising leader. This incident, mentioned in the Jaintia collection of myths and legends,[25] proves that allegation of wizardry sometime might be used as an instrumental technique by persons to manipulate the social structure to their own advantage.[26] Max Marwick is of the opinion that witchcraft is a social strain gauge resulting from a strained relationship in the society '. . . reflecting in part the fact that the accusation of sorcery is often involved in a younger man's bid for leadership'[27] is also worth considering.

This incident also pointed one important fact, that in the study of witchcraft and sorcery in the Khasi Pnar society, social structure must be taken into consideration. In order to understand, this it is felt that the postulation of Monica H. Wilson in her paper, 'Witch Beliefs and Social Structure', whose case study involved two African societies Nyakyusa of Tanganyita and the Pondo of South Africa, is needed to cite here as an example. Among the Nyakyusa, witchcraft accusation was usually amongst neighbours as they have a close relationship, in which social friction is most likely to occur as feasts were usually given to their neighbours, while the Pondo live-in close relation to their relatives. So, according to the Pondo any pressure in came from their ancestors, they believed even in that having to kill their cattle for the customary practice of providing feasts to their relatives.[28] So, in this light the Khasi Pnar case needed to be examined. This called for the attention to the social structure of the Pnar before the emergence of *syiemship* amongst them. The leader of the group was a headman, U Lakriah, who was also at the same time a mediator (or priest) between the people and God, looking after their socio-religious, economic and political welfare.[29] But, he functioned through a 'dorbar', constituted of all the members of the group. During this time it seems that no clan gained any importance over the rest. When he was too old to carry on the task, he decided to appoint a *syiem* to take over. Through the act of divination he selected the Chyllong clan. U Long Chyllong, the eldest of the family of four siblings was preferred as the *syiem*. He was endowed with the responsibility of retaining the customary laws which were given religious sanction.[30] He was expected to deal equally with all his subjects. But, he showed partiality to the rich, neglecting the plight of the less fortunate 'neighbours' which fermented resentment in the latter. So he was alleged to be the lover of witchcraft. It seems that even during this point of time the people associated prosperity and power with some mystical power. So the allegation of witchcraft started amongst neighbours in the society, the poor against the prosperous one, as in the case of the African tribe, Nyakyusa. This was also reflected in the Navaho saying, 'He's a witch. That's why he has lots of sheep, horses and cattle, and beads of all kinds, and all kinds of skins'. He had everything, and because of that everyone knew him and was afraid of him.[31]

Another related incident must be narrated here. The mother of the younger bidder to power Ka Lysan Chyllong was cast away by her brother U Long chyllong as a result of the 'virgin birth' of her son, U Synriang. Her brother accused her of indecent behaviour, Later the *durbar* of the people realized that it was a 'diving' pregnancy (getting information about this from a shaman), they sought her forgiveness and reinstated her. When her son was of age, it was seen that the uncle was depicted in the traditional sources as a *syiem* whose arrogance grew by the day. He went against the custom of the time by issuing an order regarding the community hunting expedition (*Beh Kpong*) of the Pnars, that the first one to shoot an arrow at an encircled deer should be the privilege of the *syiem* only. But Synriang defied this order and shot the deer first. When Long Cyllong confronted him asking him who he was, his answer was that he was the *syiem*. The tension broke and, 'mystical battle' started between the two, each having his own following later According to the legend a real battle broke out between them where Long Chyllong was defeated by Synriang. Long Chyllong, Sin

Chylloing and Rah Chyllong were then exiled and portrayed as dishonoured persons who associated with witchcraft and sorcery.[32] Thus in the Khasi Pnar society only tainted persons turn to witchcraft and sorcery. This is remarkably similar to the Indian belief in general that tantricism is the refuge of those, who have fallen from the Vedic way of life.[33] With the study of this, it is realized that accusation of witchcraft was used as a 'political weapon'.[34] Through strong negative public opinion that was formed against U Long Chyllong. Synriang won the favour of the people and was installed. The social structure of the Khasi Pnar society is matrilineal and that, through strong negative public opinion that was formed against U Long Chyllong, Synriang won the favour of the people and was installed. It must be noted here that the social structure of the Khasi Pnar society is matrilineal and that the *syiemship* is passed on from an uncle to a nephew in a selected clan (chosen for *syiemship*) naturally, when the uncle has aged or is dead. It is difficult, therefore, not to come to the conclusion that the sequence of related events could not have come about had the accusation which was made not been made in the idiom of wizardry.[35]

That a person's reputation and positive public opinion can be ruined by accusing him of anti socio-religious behaviour was proved true in the medieval period when the Pnar underwent steady Hinduization. During this period one Jaintia Raja, whose name was not mentioned in the traditional source, a contemporary of the legendary Sajar Nagli Chadap no longer pleased his subjects because he had accepted Hindu socio-religious beliefs and began practising polygamy, even desiring to make Sajar Nagli Chadap's daughter one of his wives. As a consequence of this, the people under Sajar Nagli Chadap rebelled against him. This action of his also made the people accuse him of practices like taking the milk of a young mother and using babies as cushion while sleeping.[36]

One social structure of the Khasi Pnar that is of utmost importance in studying witchcraft and sorcery is its tribal egalitarian and cooperative base. But with the coming of the concept of private property, a clan went and settled on the best land, staking their claim on it and became known as the original or founding clan.[37] In such a society, a well-do-do person or family is expected to be benevolent and share the wealth or possessions (like providing a feast for instance) with his relatives or neighbours. In such a situation, a person or family claims to be in possession of witchcraft or sorcery like *Ka Taro or Ka Kymbad* to keep their wealth from being drained away by their neighbours, which makes the Khasi Pnar case unique.[38] This usually happened when rich, generous persons or families lent a hand to their neighbours in need, they went unpaid for their efforts and debts were not cleared by those concerned.[39] Such frequent occurrences could hurt the generosity of the spirits.

The belief in the evil eye and the adherence to 'the transference of evil' into an inanimate object also points to the social relation among the Khasi Pnares. It shows that in their society close relations exist not only among family but among neighbours as well. The occurrence of feasts among the people takes place not only in the family but in the neighbourhood too. These gatherings brought in the fear of being the victim of the evil eye which caused constipation and other stomach problem. So a person who is suspected of being the culprit of having the evil eye is discouraged to sit nearby or in the opposite direction. A person who is accused of this witchcraft is usually a neighbour, who is not socially liked.

Even though witchcraft and sorcery had already existed in the Khasi Pnar society, the allegation became predominant with the coming of British colonialism. In fact, hearsay from the wife and children of an indigenous Welsh Church minister pointed that even missionaries had to believe in *thlen* and take part in chasing away *nongshohnoh* (one who beats to death and throws away the body).[40] This was the result of the emergence of the struggle for power between the noble founding clan or *ki jaid bakkaru* and the small clan i.e., (the commoners). This was the result of the prosperity of the commoner clans as a result of their success in trade. They were considered a threat to the position of the founding clan (noble clan). To clarify the fact that allegation of witchcraft and sorcery is a result of class struggle Cecile a Mawlong has written:

That tension and social conflict had emerged in the society as trade developed is brought out in the endearing Khasi folktale of *U Thlen.* It is held that worship of this evil spirit is often the reason for murders carried out by man called *Nongshohnoh* (one who beats to death) with no apparent motive. The *Thlen* is said to take many forms but seem to be especially partial to the snake form. The *Thlen* which attaches itself to wealth and property must be propitrated with human blood by its keepers in return for material wealth. Persons and families suspected of keeping the spirit is socially ostracized. Fear of this spirit is so stong that it survives to this day in many parts of the Khasi Hills. The only way that its keepers can redeem themselves in society is by discarding the practise which could be appropriated by the *Syiem* on whom there were not taboo restrictions for such an action as he had the sanction of custom. Among the Jaintias similar belief exists in the form of the *Taroh* superstition.[41]

The significance of the *Thlen* and *Taroh* superstitions lies in the fact that, they are a clear index of social tensions that had emerged in society in response to the demands of new social relations as distribution of economic power changed. This is inferred from the fact that persons and families accused of harbouring such spirits were more often than not traders and business folk. The *thlen* superstition is also a reflection of how dominant groups of Khasi society sought to manipulate ideology to safeguard their interests. These interests were probably linked with the control of profits from trade particularly Khasi iron which going by British report and accounts appears to have been substantial.[42]

In the post-colonial period, the accusation of witchcraft is less but belief in the existence of sorcery is stronger than ever. Evidence of the allegation of witchcraft as a political weapon is proved truer by the occurrence of the allegation of witchcraft against families coming from the founding clan or big clan (*kmaikur*). It seems that the *khian kur* (small clan) uses the same weapon that the noble clan has used against them during the colonical period, i.e. the allegation of witchcraft to snatch away socio-political power from them as at present some of them are richer and more educated than some members of the founding clans. The weapon is thus, a two-edged weapon and is as useful in securing the retention of power in the face of a challenge as in securing the advantage of a person seeking to challenge the established power.[43] A close observation of the Khasi Pnar society as a member and witness in the society ('Even in the same society there are as we all know differences between what informants tell us and what, when we are fortunate enough to have the opportunity, we see actually happening')[44] shows that till now belief in sorcery is strong in any strain that occurs amongst relatives or neighbours since sorcery is a practical form of magic as rationalized by the modern people, which involves the use of 'bad medicines'[45] against one's enemies.

As both men and women are members of any society, it is necessary to look into the position of women in the Khasi Pnar matrilineal society in response to witchcraft, sorcery and tantricism. The three traditional sayings of the Khasi clarify the social staus of the three significant members of the Khasi Pnar family, 'the mother gives life', 'the uncle who can' (all in all) and 'the father gives stature'. In such a background, it will be interesting to note that the demons like the *taro* were given a feminine gender and the *thlen* a masculine one. In the case of the *tari* superstition the female members of the alleged family are believed to possess the psychic power to harm the neighbours, if they are thought to hurt the sentiments of the *tari* owners. If the mother connects with the *taro,* to gain wealth, her daughters automatically inherits it though the *taro* resides permanently with the youngest daughter (according to the line of inheritance). The son of such a family on the other hand, is never heard of practising this psychic act of witchcraft even though he is a part of the suspicion that falls on the family, as he manages the family affairs (as a brother and an uncle). The psychic acts of witchcraft in practising *kymbad/jymbieh, ka bih* (poisoning) and *ka ske* (the evil eye) are also attributed to the female members excluding the male members of the accused family. While in the act of propitiating the *thlen*, where human blood is needed, murders are carried out by the male members, the female performs the rituals of blood offering to the *thlen.* Regarding this particular act of witchcraft, the male members of the suspicious family are more feared than the females. The psychic ability of the Pnar woman is extended to shamanism also. In the sphere of practical magic, i.e. sorcery, the practitioners are always men (*leh stad/ ai ksuid*). So the fact that the woman gives birth (life) endows her with supernatural power and psychic ability in comparison to men while in practical and physical world (the one who can on the whole and the one who gives stature) the men are more powerful. Thus, in the Khasi Pnar society the allegation of witchcraft and sorcery reflects its matrilineal social structure and the gender relations within it.

In accordance to what has been studied, it is found that in every transitional phase in the Khasi Pnar society, witchcraft comes forth to serve the purpose of allaying the insecurities consequent upon the break-up of any social order of the day. In order to have a clear picture of witchcraft and sorcery in the Khasi Pnar society, one needs to examine its relation to social structure, social relations, social function as a social strain outlet and its function as political weapon; and also to its equivalent tantricims. It is safe to conclude that tantricism has existed in every society including the Khasi Pnar society. According to those in favour of it, it has its sanction even in the *Vedas*,[46] while according to Chakravarti it is universal in character and is based in primitive beliefs.[47] It, thus, paves the way for the future adherence to tantric Hindu beliefs especially among the Pnars of Jaintia Hills.

This subject matter is taken up with the intention that it will serve the purpose for further in depth study by a social historian, who is aware of the anthropological theory.[48] This is considered necessary because though witchcraft, sorcery and tantricism can be flicked off as mere 'superstitions', they are real to those who believe in them in any cultures in societies. Every society has its own culture, which shapes its world view and 'culture is the sum total of the labours of the gifted minds which the group accepts through the action of social selection'.[49] If the culture has demons, then the witch functions with the aid of demons.[50] As in the case of the Khasi Pnar culture, where the *taro* and the *thlen* are both demons, it is also the objective to bring the readers to notice that accusation of witchcraft and sorcery like *U Thlen, Ka Taro, Ai-Ksuid,* Evil Eye (*Ka Sabuit/Ka ske*) and 'the transference of evil; and *ka Bih/Kymbad/Hymbieh* provide a short lived explanation or strain-outlet of any unlikable, unsettling situations that occur in the society leading to further aggravation of the ugly social strains and tensions, which has disrupted the relation amongst relatives, family and the society at large. Herein rests the problem because cultural trait and belief already shape the human mind, which acts like an already programmed computer in obedience to an input of values and assumptions. However, at various times there emerge creative, pioneering minds, a genius, who upsets the currents and proposes new circuits, new values and processes so that progress ensues. A historical approach to understanding superstitions and practices in a society is perhaps a big step in the path of this progress.

NOTES

1. Mark Gradubard, *Witchcaraft and the Nature of Man*, Boston Way Lanham: University Press of America, USA, 1984, p. 270.
2. Ibid.
3. Ibid., pp. 270-1.
4. Ibid., pp. 242-3, 270.
5. Max Marwick (ed), *Witchcraft and Sorcery*, Great Britain: Penguin Educations, 1970, rpt. 1975, pp. 210-16.
6. Ibid., pp. 201-369.
7. N.N. Bhattacharya, *History of the Tantras Religion*, New Delhi: Manohar, 1992.
8. N.N. Bhattacharya, *Religious Culture of North Eastern India*, New Delhi: Manohar, 1995.
9. C. Chakravarti, *Tantras, Stdues on their Religion and Literature*, Calcutta: Punthi Pustak, 1963, rpt., 1972.
10. D.P. Chattapadhyaya, *Lakayata*, Delhi: People Publishing House, 1959, pp. 269-325.
11. S. Kapur, *Witchcraft in Western India*, Bombay: Orient Longman Ltd., 1983, pp. 58-80.
12. Margaret Stutley, *Ancient Indian Magic and Folkore, As Introduction*, London and Henley: Routledghe and Kegan Paul, 1980, pp. 1-6.
13. N.N. Bhattacharya, op. cit.
14. N.H. Mohrmen, 'The Khasi Pnar Beliefs in Witchcraft and Curse', *The Shillong Time*, vol. no. 53, issue no. 322.
15. R.M. Mukhim, *Ki Marw Ka Jingngeit Bieit*, Shillong: Ri Khasi Press, 1982.
16. S. Kapur, *Witchcraft in Western India*, Bombay: Orient Longman Ltd., 1983, pp. 60-8.
17. D.P. Chattopadhyaya, *Lokayatra*, Delhi: People Publishing House, 1959, pp. 269-325.
18. S. Kapur, *Witchcraft in Western India*, Delhi: People Publishing House, 1959, pp. 56-8.

19. Ibid., p. 73.
20. H.H. Mohrmen, 'The Khasi Pnar Beliefs in Witchcraft', vol. no. 53, issue no. 322, p. 6.
21. Ibid.
22. J.G. Frazer, *The Golden Bough,* London, 1922, pp. 706-98.
23. Comparative study based on Richard Cavendish et al., *Man, Myth and Magic, Encyclopedia of Mythology, Religion, and the Unknown*, New York: Marshall Cavendish Corporation, 1995, pp. 2350-3.
24. A.D.J. Macfarlane, 'Definition of Witchcraft', in Max Marwick et al., *Witchcraft, and Sorcery*, op. cit., p. 41.
25. Ka Khynroo-Khyllood committee Sein-Raij Jowai, *U. Tree-Kirot ha U Niawwasa,* Khnroo-Khyllood Committee, Sein-Raj, Jowai, 1992, pp. 40-62.
26. J.R. Crawford, 'The Consequences of Allegation', in Max Marwick et al., *Witchcraft and Sorcery*, op. cit., p. 305.
27. Ibid., Max Marwick, 'Witchcraft as a Social Strain—Gauge', in Max Marwick, et al., *Witchcraft and Sorcery*, p. 286.
28. Ibid., Monica H. Wilson, 'Witch-Beliefs and Social Structure', in Max Marwick et al., *Witchcraft and Sorcery*, pp. 255-60.
29. Ka Khynroo-Khyllood Committee, *Sein-Raij, Jowai, U Tre-Kirot ha U Niaw-Wasa*, op. cit., pp. 28-39.
30. Ibid., pp. 40-1.
31. Clyde Kluchohn, 'Navaho Witchcraft', in Max Marwick et al., *Witchcraft and Sorcery*, op. cit., 1970, p. 236.
32. Ka Khynroo-Khyllood Committee, *Sein Raij, Jowai, U Tre-Kirot ha U Niaw—Wasa*, op. cit., pp. 40-62.
33. N.N. Bhattacharya, *History of the Tantric Religion*, op. cit., p. 3.
34. Op. cit., Max Marwick, et al., *Witchcraft and Sorcery*, Great Britain: Penguin Education, 1970, pp. 144, 371, 192-4, 210-31, 234-5, 305, 318, 317-18.
35. J.R. Crawford, 'The Consequences of Allegation', in Max Marwick et al., *Witchcraft and Sorcery*, op. cit., p. 305.
36. Donbok. T. Laloo, *Riheh*, Shillong: The Author 1991, pp. 3-4.
37. S.N. Lamare, *The Jaintias Studies in Society and Change*, New Delhi: Regency Publication, 2005, p. 35.
38. R.M. Mukhim, *Ki Mraw ka Jingngeitbieit*, op. cit., p. 20.
39. Ibid.
40. Interview with C.M. Lyngdoh, the daughter of (Late) Rev. Mania Lyngdoh, Shillong, 14 September 2007.
41. Jaintia Hills in M. Mumin & C.A. Mawlong (ed.), *Society and Economy in North-East India*, vol. 1, pp. 47-8.

42. Ibid., p. 48.
43. J.R. Crawford, 'The Consequences of Allegation', in Max Marwick et al., *Witchcraft and Sorcery*, op. cit., p. 318.
44. Max Marwick's article 'Witchcraft as a Social Strain—Gauge', in Max Marwick et al., *Witchcraft and Sorcery*, op. cit., p. 283.
45. A.D.J. Macfarlane 'Definitions of Witchcraft', in Max Marwick et al., *Witchcraft and Sorcery*, op. cit., p. 41.
46. C. Chakravarti, *Tantras, Studies on their Religion and Literature*, op. cit., p. 11.
47. Ibid., pp. 7-9.
48. Monica H. Wilson, 'Witch-Beliefs and Social Structure', in Max Marwick et al., *Witchcraft and Sorcery*, op. cit., p. 2062.
49. Mark Graubard, *Witchcraft and the Nature of Man*, op. cit., p. 238.
50. Ibid., p. 240.

CHAPTER 4

Magic, Religion and Mother Goddess Kamakhya: Esoteric Practices in Assam[1]

ARCHANA BARUA

In the overall religious mosaic of this vast country called India, religion has played its significant role in a manner that from Kashmir to Kanyakumari, from Gandhara to Kamarupa, the Indian psyche has comfortably adopted the most accommodating and harmonious attitude to life and its mysteries. There is a harmonious co-existence between the profane and the sacred, the human and the divine, to such an extent that religion has become a way of life-style and a pattern of thought. As Cramb puts it: 'India is not only the Italy of Asia; it is not only the land of romance, of art and beauty. It is in religion earth's central shrine. India is religion.'[2] In this overall religious mosaic each region has contributed its own distinctive share, thus keeping room for a kind of creative dialogue between the text and its sub-texts. Assam has enriched this religious tradition with the pure Vaishnavism of Sankaradeva, its cult of Eka Sharana Naama Dharma, religion of absolute surrender to the One. And interestingly enough, Assam also remains the land that has contributed immensely to the magico-religious cults of the *tantrikas*, the prime centre of Matsyendranath and Gorakhnath, the Tantric Siddhas, whose descendants and followers came to be known as the kanphata yogis. Perhaps, the most important figure for the early development of both Hindu and Buddhist Tantra in South Asia, Matsyendranath has received his esoteric knowledge in Kamarupa while living among the many powerful female *yoginis* who dwelt here. Among their four *pithas*, *Kamrupa-Kamakhya* is prominent. As per Tibet's *Pang Sam Jon Zen* book, Sarah or Rahulbhadra was born of a Brahmin and a dakini in eastern Assam in a place called Ranjni, a place identified as Rani in Nowgaon district of Assam.

SACRED AND SECRET RITUALS IN THE YONI-PIṬHA KAMAKHYA

At a time when the ancient land Pragjyotishapur came to be known as Kāmarūpa, with its centrality of one of the most venerated Shakti shrines in medieval India, the Devipitha Kamakhya, the Devi here becomes completely transformed into the eroticized form of *yoni* of Sati or Parvati, the Goddess who fulfils all desires at Nilachala, her permanent abode in which, like a sixteen-year old (*sodasi*), still passionately in love, Sati as Kamakhya waits for her beloved husband Siva for fulfilling her sexual desires, and also to bless her devotees. According to the *Kalika Purana*, the genital organ of Sati fell here when her dead body was carried hither and thither in frantic sorrow by her husband Siva. The *yoni* (pudendum), no sooner had it fallen on the hill, turned into stone, and Siva himself finding no corpse on his shoulder, sat down and became a stone.

Inside the temple, there is a cave and in the cave stands a block of stone resembling *yoni* and the block of stone has always been kept moist from the oozing of a natural spring within the cave. The *Kalika Purana*, a work composed in ninth century AD in ancient Assam for glorifying Kamakhya, gives a description of Manobhava Guha. It says, 'Inside the cave there exists a very lovely pudendum on the stone which is 12 *angulas* (9 cm) in width and 20 *angulas* (16 cm) in length gradually narrowing and sloping. It is reddish in colour like vermillion and saffron. On that female organ the amorous Goddess Kamakhya, the primordial force resides in five different forms. The Goddess is supposed to have her annual period in the month of *Ashadha* (June-July) for three days, there after the summer crop is planted in Assam. A comparison is drawn between human female becoming pregnant after menstruation and the mother earth getting heavy with crops after divine menstruation in Ambubasi festival. *Yoni-puja*, or womb worship is the cornerstone of Kamakhya worship. The red colour closely associated with Goddess worship is the red seed or menstrual blood that flows out of the body of a fertile woman, who is not carrying a child. Metaphorically, the womb represents *prakriti*, (nature), the material world, full of fragrances and fluids that can take various forms. This is the world of death and fear and life and love; it is the world of desires and passions and ambitions and attachments. Shiva, the hermit, shuns both, the literal as well as metaphorical aspect of the Goddess.'[3] At Nilachala, Shiva who takes the form of Bhairava, inadvertently becomes the guardian of the Goddess.

The cave is called *Manobhava Guha* (the cave of Cupid) because, according to mythology, this was created by or belonged to Kama. 'The name *manobhava* itself is comparatively new, which means Madana or Kamadeva (*eros*) Guha and it is originated from Tantra. *Manobhava* is in the *lajja* seed syllable *hrim*.'[4] Scholars note the phases and layers of the temple's early associations that do not rule out early association of the shrine with some primitive group.

Thus, the *Kalika Purana* explains the origin of *yonimandala* located inside the temple on the Nilachala, and identifies the hill both as a graveyard and a scene of the secret love-tryst of the Goddess. This narrative makes Nilachala both a graveyard and a place of Shiva Parvati's amorous pastime. It is this graveyard motif which provides the occasion for Banikanta Kakati to speculate on the deity's Khasi connection. In an attempt to substantiate a folk origin of the Goddess or an origin independent of Sati's limb story, Kakati draws attention to the lack of mention of Kamarupa-Kamakhya as a *pitha* in the *Devi Bhagavata*.The folk origin of Goddess Kamakhya is also reaffirmed by the fact that neither the Umachal Rock Inscription of 500 AD (which is situated so near it), nor the travel records of Hiuen T'sang made any mention of the shrine.[5]

THE BLUE GODDESS AND TANTRIC RITUALS IN THE YONI-PITHA KAMAKHYA

As Devi Kamakhya, the blue Goddess of the Tantras, dwells on the blue mountain Nilachala, Siva also becomes blue here. 'Among the Bhairavas, the Nilachala Bhairava on the Nilachala and the

Mahabhairava of Tezpur became the most famous ones and magnificent temples came to be built in their honour. One of the principal idols inside the main temple, identified as Kameshvara Mahadeva, is actually a statue of Bhairava.'[6] To quote Pranav Jyoti Deka: 'In Nilacala, we have Hinduized Buddhist Tantras. Statues found here do not carry an image of Dhyani-Buddha on or near their head. The transformation of the Goddess took place from Chinnamunda Vajrayogini to Vajravārāhī, then to Vajravairochani and ultimately to Kamesvari Kamakhya, but Hetuka-Bhairava is the only link where the essence did not altar with the change of goddesses.'[7] The seed incantation of the Tantra for the Goddess Kamakhya are addressed to Vajrayogini, Varavārahi and Vajravairochani, who later became closely associated with the Shakti in the form of Chinnamasta and Bauddha Chinnamunda.

These two parallel Tantras came up only in the nineteenth century. Gradually, Chinnamasta merged with Bouddha Goddess Shveta Kurukulla and Hindu Rati, Goddess of sex, and a new Goddess Sodasi emerged, who is the progenitress of medieval and post-medieval *Yoni* cult. If it is assumed it took roughly one hundred years to modify the Chinnamasta cult to Kameshvari-Kamakhya cult, the cult could not come up before late tenth or early eleventh century. One has to remember that in India, Vajravarahi statues are the first deity showing *vaga mudra*, i.e., exposing her sex organ to view'.[8]

'Ash adorned Shiva', the patron deity of the previous king Kumara Bhaskarvarma, who once declared that he would not bow his head before nay one except 'ash adorned Shiva', was of the form Jyotirlinga Lingeshvara; subsequently the white Svāttika Shiva was replaced by the royal, red form of Shiva, the Kāmesvara Shiva at a time when the Mahā Gauri concept came up from unification of Visnumāyā and Durga. Deka submits: 'The Shiva was no more "the ash adorned Shiva" (Lingaraja) but became Kameshvara, who though was still smeared with ash, is to be propitiated with red flowers and kum-kuma (saffron, an item of luxury). Kāmesvara is a *rājasika* (royal) Shiva, while Lingaraja is *sāttvika* and Bhairava is the Tantric form of Shiva'.[9] Kāmesvara Mahadeva replacing Lingaraja resurrection of *madana* (eros), acceptance of one form of Tara as Shveta

Kurukulla Tara (equivalent to Rati) shows that society has become a fertile ground for seeds of Kameshvari-Kamakhya cult, where Kameshvari is the Goddess of desire and Kāmākhyā is the deity of cessation of all desires.'[10]

During the rule of the Varman dynasty, types of Shiva proliferated in Kamarupa as Rudreshvara, Siddheshvava, Kedareshvara, Ishana and many local Shivas as Harupeshvara, Hatupeshvara, etc. As the Tantric branches of Hinduism gained strength, the *tamasika* or *tāntrika* Shiva, the blue Shiva Bhairava came into force. Tāntric rituals specially associated with the cult of power and harnessing of it in all its forms, dangerously leaning toward transgression of normal laws of purity and impurity and redefining it, to an extent that *Tantra* and also *Yoni-Tantra* remained specially attractive to many kings and rulers and the royal, in the context of Assam.'[11] Originally constructed in the eighth century during the Pāla dynasty in Kamarupa, renovated by Cila Rai and King Naranarayana is the present temple of Kamakhya as the ancient Kamarupa temple was destroyed in natural calamity and the 'templeless Goddess' was brought to 'new roofless one', the roof of which was later provided in 1565 AD renovated by Koch king Naranarayana and his general Cila Rai'.[12] One also finds that a divine lineage to the Koch royal-dynasty was acknowledged during that time by the Brahmanical order. 'Certain late Medieval Tantras and other works dealing with Shaiva and Shakta cults (e.g. *Ānandamangala*, Vangavasi edn. p. 78) represent Shiva as an ardent lover of Koch girls. This trait is not found in earlier works, no doubt resulted from the identification of Siva with a tribal deity of the Koch people after their Hinduization in the medieval period. . . .'[13]

'Thus, we find that different ethnic elements contributed towards the development of esoteric *sadhana* in India; the proto-Australoids contributing *sadhana* with wine and flesh; the Homo-Alpinus (?) an erotic form of *sadhana*; and the Mongoloids, the *sadhana* with wine, flesh and women. *Matsya*, or fish which was added later on with this worship is interesting for custom shows that fish is offered to in the *bhoga* or daily meal of the Devi in Bengal only. The *Mahanirvanatantra* 'recommends three species of fish for sacrifice which are found especially in Bengal, while *mudra* or fried rice is a favourite food primarily in eastern India, and these might have been added when the practice spread to Bengal.'[14]

MAGICAL AND RELIGIOUS ELEMENTS IN THE YONI PITHA KAMAKHYA

The cult flourished also with royal patronage in various forms till it finally led to confrontation with traditional priesthood of the temples in general, represented by Vashishtha, the Goddess, 'heart-broken' at the unkindness shown, disappeared as per Vashishtha's curse against the whole *Yoni-mandali.*[15] In her second phase of re-appearance in the shrine, she is none other than the strong Goddess Camunda and Kālī who can be propitiated with sacrifices and with blood. Strong goddesses like Chamunda, have been portrayed as 'extreme in its violence and eroticism'. Decapitated at the copper temple at Sadiya, or at some other shrine of the tribe, human sacrifices were also formerly offered by the Tipperas, Kacharis, Koches, Jaintias, and other Assam tribes.[16]

There was this period of the Devi's disappearance from the shrine as per the curse of the traditional priest of the Hinduized Goddess Tara as Kali and Chamunda and in her second phase of appearance Kamakhya became indisguishable from these strong Hindu goddesses that also justified sacrifices being offered to her. In this phase of her re-appearance the Devi remained completely indistinguishable not only from some other strong Hinduized goddesses of the Hindu pantheon like Chandi and Chamunda and Kali, but also other local strong goddesses like Kechaikhati, Ugratara and others.

RE-VISITING BOUNDARIES BETWEEN MAGIC, ESOTERISM AND RELIGION

How can these two opposite aspects of the Devi be combined in a harmonious manner? Krishnaram Nyayabagish, the preceptor of the Ahom king, Shiva Simha, better known in the history of Assam as the Parbatiya Gosain, was a well-known Shakta theologian of his time. A native of Nadia, Bengal, he was the last philosopher of eminence to offer an explanation on the 'composite character of the Goddess Kamakhya-Kamesvari.' 'She will put on red clothes and red and yellow flower garlands and bestow sexual pleasure to her devotees. During the war and danger, she will throw away her clothes and flowers and will take *khadga* (sword) in her hands to protect her devotees and will take revenge.' (*Sri Sri Kamakhya Tirtha*, M. Bhattacharya, p. 15). 'According to Krishnaram Nyayabagish the Goddess has two forms, the erotic one when she seats on the red lotus (*sodasi*) and the destroyer-cum-preserver form when she stands on the lion, (Durga Katyayani) or sits on the dead body (Candi Cāmunda).'[17] Deka comments:

The duality did not work with the Assamese psyche. . . .' Goddess *Kāmākhyā* remained benefactress and protectress,

> that is the role Goddess Kāmākhyā is playing for the last 500 years. In the minds of a large section of the people of Assam, irrespective of creed and language, Kāmākhyā is the mother and they generally approach her either to work for a boon or when in distress. In dire distress, people may offer her a goat or even a buffalo as a sacrifice. That is primarily a primitive a *quid pro quo* policy.[18]

But 'she is not a blood thirsty Goddess. She is a three faceted Goddess synthesized from the Hindu Sakti Tantra and Buddhist Anuttra Tantra or Vajratantrapath. She protects her devotees by destroying the enemies as Shakti, bestows prosperity on them as Lakshmi, can grant emancipation from the cycle of rebirth as Vajrayogini, also sexual pleasure as Vajravairocāni.[19] She remains a bitter sweet combination of Buddhist klesha as suffering and Hindu ānanda. She is both Kāmeswari, kāmaisvari, the goddess of desire, and the expiration of all the desires, and Kāmākhyā-kamma= khyaya.

While mundane Tantra as *Laukika* is mostly comprised of magical rituals and incantations with its aim to get *siddhi*, eight great successes, the super-mundane Tantra, *lokottara*, aim for non-reversible bliss. Both kinds of *siddhi* and *sadhya*, either at the mundane or at a higher spiritual level, are still within the realm of desire and *pravritti-mārga*, the difference being what kind of pleasure one looks for, mundane and carnal or spiritual and refined. On the one hand, Mother Goddess Kāmākhyā is Kameshvari, the blue and the mysterious Goddess of love-sex-and power and on the other hand she is the Great Goddess, who in her transcendental and religious position can bestow liberation from the bindings of desire and of Kāma. 'How does Kamakhya-Kameshvari, a Shakti Goddess, assure her devotees release from the cycle of rebirth, which generally does not fall in the domain of a Shakti deity?' Deka wonders.[20] Can the Goddess in the Shakti and the *Agama* scripture bestow salvation or can simply fulfil desires of the devotees, not taking them to a desireless state?

For this the Goddess had to imbibe the Kamakhya aspect, a blend of *pravritti* and *nivritti* in one, and finally she remains a combination of all these aspects in these various aspects; Scholars submit: 'Hindu Tantra borrowed the goal of emancipation from rebirth from Bauddha Tantra, and Bauddha Tantra, in turn, adopted the concept of visualization (*dhyana*) and to merge with the deity, from the Hindu Tantra.'[21] In order to understand the mystery of this mysterious combination of the magical with the religious, of desire and power and bondage in the level of *triguna prakriti* and the ability to bestow on her devotees the *mantra* of rising above that very bondage by rising above the mundaneness of the mundane, Mother Goddess Kāmākhyā remains a bitter sweet combination of Bauddha *klesha* as suffering and Hindu *ananda*, she is both Kameshvari, kama = isvari, the Goddess of desire, and the expiration of all the desires, and Kāmākhyā—*kamma* = *khyaya*.'[22] She is a three-faceted Goddess synthesized from the Hindu Shakti Tantra and Bauddha Anuttara Tantra or Vajra Tantra path. She protects her devotees by destroying the enemies as Shakti, best prosperity as Lakshmi, can grant emancipation from the cycle of rebirth as Vajrayogini, also sexual pleasure as Vajravairocani'.[23]

Balabhadra the earth-tiller, and Bhumi the Earth-mother, remained dominating myth of the agrarian cult and Kāmākhyā cult added the sex-based cult to this agriculture centric fertile land of Kāmarūpa. Assam underwent another form of Vaishnavite reform movement in the time of mahapurusha Sankara Deva and his neo-Vaishnavite followers, that centred round agricultural God

Vishnu-Krshna, Krishna is depicted here as the sun rather than Tantra based Radha centric moon of Sri Chaitanya sect, with more focus on Buddha-Mahavira centric 'non-violence' and glorification of family centric virtues of *dasya* and *vatsalya.* Being accommodative and flexible in her position, the Goddess in the *Yoni-Pitha* already opened herself for change in the basic key concepts that defined her belief systems when the two major scriptures, the *Kalika Purana* (*KP*) and the *Yogini Tantra* (*YT*) put divergent interpretations about the *yoni* circle as a symbol of sex, and as a symbol of creation. The *Yogini Tantra* modified the eroticised form of the Goddess with focus on creativity of the 'eros' than its sex centric newness. The *Yogini Tantra* has also recorded certain local customs prevalent in different parts of ancient Assam, and the Goddess in the *Yogini Tantra* also adopted the most catholic attitude not only to local and regional cults and practices, but also toward accommodating the other as a foreigner, allowing them flexibility on codes of conduct and rituals in its un-Hindu like attitudes and practices. Rather, she herself sought to imbibe some such 'different' norms in her own persona! It also simplified religion with its catholicity. In the myth of the *Yogini Tantra,* there is nothing to show that the *yoni* circle or Kamakhya had any connection with Durga or Parvati the etymology of *KP* refers to a later fable based on imported ideas. As Mother Goddess, she definitely absorbs all previous forms of worships in her.

Now at this juncture of the neo-Vaishnavite reform movement, Mother Goddess Kamakhya concentrated more on her motherly love despite retaining the centrality of the eros centric *Yoni-Cult* in its Hindu-Buddhist forms. This neo-Vaishnava cult has become the second most influential cult on the modern Nilachala hills and influencing profoundly the Kalika-Kamakhya-Kamesvari cult. To quote Deka, 'Benediction in Kāmākhyā nowadays ends with words like 'Hari-bol' (invoke the name of Hari/Vishnu). Animal sacrifice is no more a festive occasion. It is done virtually-surreptitiously behind walls as if it is the fulfilment of an indecent private contract between the gods and the devotees'.[24]

NOTES

1. A revised version of the article was subsequently published in an academic journal. This is the original version presented in the seminar organized in Assam University, Silchar in 2015.
2. Bhagavan Das, *The Essential Unity of All Religions,* Theosophical Publishing House, Adyar, Madras, 1940.
3. Rajib Sarma, *Sri Sri Kamkhya Temple: A Socio Religious Perspective* (Online) http://www.jaimaa.org/articles/sri-sri-kamakhya-temple-a-socio-religious-perspective/(retrieved on July 2014).
4. Pranav Jyoti Deka *Nilachala Kamakhya: Her Story and Tantra,* Guwahati, Pranabjyoti Deka, 2004, p. 14.
5. Kali Prasad Goswami *Kamakhya Temple,* A.P.H. Publishing Corporation, Guwahati, 1998.
6. Pranav Jyoti, Deka, *Nilachala Kamakhya: Her Story and Tantra,* Guwahati, Pranabjyoti Deka, 2004 , p. 14.
7. Ibid., p. 92.
8. Ibid.
9. Ibid., p. 9.
10. Ibid.
11. Ibid.
12. Ibid., p. 14.
13. Ibid.
14. Sudhakar Chattopadhyaya, *Reflections on the Tantras,* Motilal Banarasidas, Delhi, 1990, p. 59.
15. Not against Kāmākhyā as such, but the whole set up there and its Tantras and rituals and its 'new ness' and secretiveness as such which differed from the already accepted Hinduised Buddhist Goddess worships, including Hinduised Goddess Tārā as Kālī.
16. E.Gait, quoted in Sudhakar Chattopadhyaya, *Reflections on the Tantras,* p. 60.
17. Quoted in Pranav Jyoti Deka, *Nilachala Kamakhya: Her Story and Tantra,* Guwahati, 2004, pp. 20-1.
18. Pranav Jyoti Deka, *Nilachala Kamakhya: Her Story and Tantra* , Guwahati, Pranabjyoti Deka, 2004, p. 98.
19. Ibid., p. 43.
20. Ibid.
21. Ibid.
22. Ibid., p. 40.
23. Ibid.
24. Ibid.

REFERENCES

Bhattacharya, Benoytos, *Introduction to Buddhist Esoterism*, 2nd edn., Varanasi: Chowkhamba Sanskrit Series Office, 1964.

Deka, Pranav Jyoti, *Nīlācala Kāmākhyā: Her History and Tantra*, Guwahati: Pranav Jyoti Deka, 2004.

Dold, Patricia A., 'Reimagining Religious History through Women's Song Performance at the Kāmākhyā Temple Site', in *Re-Imagining South Asian Religions*, ed. Pashaura Singh and Michael Howly, pp. 115-54, Leiden: Brill, 2013.

Goswami, Kali Prasad, *Kāmākhyā Temple*, Guwahati: A.P.H. Publishing Corp, 1998.

McGee, Mike. 'Matsyendranath and Gorakhnath are Revealed', volesoft.com/ 20 11/01/29/matsyendranath-and-gorakhnath/.

Urban, Hugh, 'The Path of Power: Impurity, Kingship, and Sacrifice in Assamese Tantra', *Journal of the American Academy of Religion*, 69, no. 4, 2001, pp. 777-816. http://dx.doi.org/10.1093/jaarel/69.4.777

Wilson, H.H., tr., *The Vishnu Purana: A System of Hindu Mythology and Tradition*, Calcutta: Punthi Pustak.

PART II
PRACTICES OF OCCULT

CHAPTER 5

Some Astronomical Beliefs in the North-East and other Parts of India*

J.H. HUTTON

There is no part of the world in which, there is so striking a diversity of tribes and tongues as in Assam. In the administered portion of the Naga Hills alone there are eleven different languages, not to mention dialects often so diverse that one village cannot understand that of its neighbours. The other districts of Assam are not quite so heterogeneous as that, but that is a fair type of the province as a whole.

Along with this diversity in language, there is a similar diversity in customs and beliefs, and it is the purpose of this article to review some of the views held by different tribes regarding a few astronomical phenomena, so as to see, how far they are traceable to some common origin or, are beliefs held independently by the tribes that hold them in order to explain familiar but mysterious experience. Some instances of similar beliefs in other areas outside Assam are also pointed out. The tribes dealt with, extend from the north of the Assam province, where it merges with Tibet, to the south, where the Lushei Hills reach down almost to Arakan and the Bay of Bengal.

The most familiar constellations that can be seen in Assam are those of Orion and the Pleiades, which are visible throughout the cold weather when the sky is clear. The Miris of the north bank of the Brahmaputra regard these constellations as representing a young man or men (Orion's belt) pursuing girls (the Pleiades) across the

*Reproduced from *Folklore*, vol. 36, no. 2 (30 June 1925), pp. 113-31.

sky.[1] The Sema Nagas also regard the Pleiades as girls, but girls who were caught and killed in a raid.[2]

On the other hand, they regard Orion's belt as the Rooftree Carriers,[3] as do the Angamis,[4] an idea that seems to recur among the Abors on the north bank of the Brahmaputra, as the Galong Abors call it *karig-ipe*, 'the star roof-tree', though the Pasi, Padam, and Minyon Abors speak of it as a 'quiver and arrows'.[5] The Lhota Nagas again describe it as three men searching for lost cattle. As for the Pleiades, the Angamis regard them as men, who were killed while digging out rats, and the Thado speak of them as seven brothers who had only one cloth between them and had to cover themselves with it at the same time. Others speak of it as a hen and her chickens, and the Khasi as the Hen-man. The Thado describe the belt of Orion as a kind of rat which digs a very straight deep hole at first, and then turns off at right angles, this part being represented by Orion's sword. The Lushei associate Orion with the square of Pegasus, and regard the whole as representing a game prevalent in Assam played with the big flat beans of the creeper *entada scandens*. There is, therefore, very little uniformity as regards Orion and the Pleiades among the Assam tribes, though the idea of the roof-tree appears in two places among tribes widely separated and with very different customs and language.

Another obvious and familiar constellation visible in Assam is that of the milky way. This constellation is visible early in the cold weather and it is generally associated with the transition between the end of the rains and the beginning of the cold weather. The Lushei call it Thla Sikkong (the way of winter), and the Abors 'The cold weather guide'; the Miri too call it 'Winter and summer boundary,' and the Ao Naga the 'cold-weather-rains-divider'. With the Chang Nagas it has the same association, and its appearance in the cold weather is welcomed with joy indicating that the rains are over. The Angamis too regard its appearance as indicative of fine weather, though they speak of it as 'pfiu's water channel', which is also the name given to the Barak River, which, like the milky way, runs from north to south. The Sema Nagas, on the other hand, speak of it as the 'soul river'.

In the case of Venus, no two tribes seem to agree on the subject, though several have names which are picturesque enough. The Angami call the evening star 'the thief watcher', as it shines at the time thieves and housebreakers are busy, while the Abors call it 'fish eye' and say the fish do not feed till it sets, or 'fish-blink', because it looks this way and that to avoid the net of the sun, or the 'moon's nurse' (Abors employ small children to carry their infants for them), while they call the morning star *ru-pun* (Blossom of Dawn). The Semas apparently recognize the identity of these two aspects of Venus, but one is doubtful whether most tribes do. Except for the Semas, the ones mentioned have, at any rate, different names for the two appearances, and the Lushei definitely regard the morning star as a girl and the evening star as a chieftain, who, they say, meet in the zenith and marry.

When one comes to the sun and the moon one finds a good deal more uniformity. There seems to be no worship of the sun or moon at all, though they are called on to witness oaths, 'since they see all that takes place', as a Naga put it. On the other hand, the Chang Nagas, like the Aos, attribute virtue to the rising sun. They are also careful to observe the place where the sun rises, marking it by the alignment of some familiar tree or post in the village against the peaks on the horizon, and there are also amongst the Angamis certain persons who observe the sun and note the day on which it turns back from its northern course, and J.E. Tanquist said that a man of Kohima named Sitsalie, who made such observations, assured him that the sun had not of late years risen at quite so northerly a point on the horizon as it used to do in the days of his youth. He also said that the method of co-relating the solar to the lunar year, which the Angami, like the Chang Nagas, do by the insertion of an intercalary month, is done by guesswork. The Terhengi festival begins on the 16th day of the twelfth lunar month. When this festival, which celebrates the completion of the harvest, seems to fall much too early, an extra month is thrown in 'only after much wrangling in which the whole village takes part'. The Cherama clan of Kohimna village observe a calendar different to the other six clans, apparently regulating it by observations of the sun, while the others have the lunar system.

The respective genders of the sun and moon vary. According to the Galong Abor they are both neuter and a sort of *objets d'art.* The Lhota Naga is more explicit, and describes the sun as a flaming plate of hard metal, the size of the ground on which a basket of seed is sown.[6] The Pasi, Minyon, and Padam Abor, as also the Miri and apparently the Mishmi, regard the sun as male and the moon as female, which, for some reason seems very natural and proper allocation of gender, though the Aka regards them both as masculine. On the other hand, many, if not, most of the Assam hill tribes, including the Dafla,[7] the Khasi, and nearly all the Naga tribes, regard the moon as the male and the sun as female.

Underlying both views of the genders of the sun and moon, there is a story of an interchange of functions between them which links together the two views and shows how the one may have arisen from the other. The bare outline of this tradition is that the moon performed the functions of the sun, and a great deal more vigorously than the sun does now, but something being thrown in his face, his heat was abated and he was reduced to the inferior function of lighting the night. This tradition of the interchange of functions appears in a more or less garbled form throughout the various accounts of the luminaries. For example, the Miri state that the marks on the moon are caused by human dung thrown at her by another deity in a quarrel. The Mishmi state that the sun and moon were husband and wife. The moon demanded a share of the heat of the sun, who got angry at her importunities, saying he had to keep it all for his children, the mankind, and threw the moon down into a pond, the mud of which still clings to her face. As a result of this she is afraid to venture out by day and waits till the sun has gone behind the hills.[8]

The Rangpang Nagas of the Patkoi have a story which links these versions to the other ones. At first, the sun and moon were sister and brother, and the moon told his sister of some herbs which would turn to meat when cooked, enjoining strict secrecy. She, however, told the monkey, who went round and told everyone else. The moon was angry and abused the sun, who took it to heart and relieved his feelings by drying up everything on earth and killing all things with excessive heat, but, when a dry branch from a dead tree fell on the moon and killed him too, the sun herself died of grief and ultimately the two were re-born with the sexes reversed.[9] This inversion of the sexes, however, does not form part of the usual Naga story, which is content with saying that on account of his excessive heat a man threw ashes or cow dung in the moon's face, and told him to shine at night only, when it was cooler, instructing the sun, who till then had lit the night, to shine in the day, as she was less harmful. The Angamis add a point, which indirectly recalls the Mishmi version in saying that the sun, being womanly, is afraid to go out at night, which the male moon did not fear to do. The story about the basis of the interchange of functions also appears partly in the Khasi view that the moon falls in love monthly with his wife's mother, who throws ashes in his face,[10] and more clearly in the version recorded by Col. Gurdon,[11] in which the ashes reduce the moon's heat, which was previously as strong as the sun's. The Garo story[12] likewise records an interchange of functions of a very similar description. So, too, the Thado Kuki record that the moon and sun had their functions interchanged, though the mountains visible on the moon's surface are described by them and by some Ao Nagas, as a tree,[13] and not, as by the Semas,[14] Lhotas[15] and most Aos,[16] dung, nor, as by the Khasi, ashes. This tree which the Thado see is no doubt the same tree as that which the Rangpang Nagas, as already noted, regard as having fallen on the moon and killed him. The Angamis regard the markings on the moon, which they say is as big as a field, as a giant nettle-tree.

When one turns to the eclipses of the sun and moon, there seem to be two different ideas. The prevailing notion is the familiar idea that the sun is eaten up by a monster of some sort. With the Sema and the Ao Naga it is a tiger that eats up the orb. According to the Kabui Nagas,[17] the Manipuris, and the Lushei[18] it is a dog. According to the Singpho it is a frog[19] and according to the Khasi[20] it is a toad or frog. One has seen in a Konyak Naga *morung* a carving representing a frog eating the moon, though one could obtain no further information as to its significance. According to the Miri, it is a demon that eats the moon and they call him Raghon. The Aka call him Tsipzebhu, and describe him as a god who quarrels with the orb and tries to eat him. The Dafla have a more circumstantial version, which strikes one as combining the notion of the orb being devoured with the idea that it is obscured by its passage through a building. They relate that the god Tammui built a house on the spot crossed by the moon from east to west just after his creation. Tammui asked the moon to make a diversion, but the moon insisted on cutting her path straight through Tammui's house, on which they quarrelled. Tammui shot an arrow at the moon's right eye, and ate him up slowly. The moon passed on, however, and out through Tammui's body. Later the sun, following the moon, took the same path, and Tammui ate her up too. This he contrived to do to both orbs from time to time, and it is a portent of disaster to mortals. The other idea of the cause of eclipses is found in an ingenious notion of the Angami that it is due to the eclipsed orb having to repay to the other one a loan of borrowed light. This idea does not occur elsewhere in Assam, though it seems, perhaps, to have influenced Mishmi ideas, seeing that, as already stated, they ascribe the marks on the moon to mud that stuck to her when he threw her into the pond because she begged him for a share of his heat. Parhelia are regarded as portents of disaster by the Sema,[21] the Ao, and the Manipuri.[22]

The next phenomenon to be considered is the rainbow. As to this one has not been able to obtain much information about beliefs in Assam, but among the Naga tribes it appears to be regarded as the heavenly bridge used by the spirits in the sky in their communications with the earth. At any rate the Semas call it *Kungumi phuku*, which can be translated as 'Sky spirit's leg', but which could equally mean 'Sky spirit's bridge', and that, in the light of the parallels to be adduced shortly, is what one is convinced it does mean. Moreover, they say that the spot at which it touches earth is one at which some offering has been made in the fields to the sky spirits, while if it touched the earth at any village a noted warrior of that village would die, his spirit, passing up the rainbow to the sky. This, too, is the point of putting imitation rainbows on the graves of great men in the Ao and Chang areas, though Mills said he could obtain no specific reason for it among the Aos and the Changs asked, they would not say more than that it was the custom. Among the Angamis also, they say it is the path of a god, and regard it as fatal to approach the foot of the rainbow. It is, perhaps, the same idea which made the Meithei of Manipur see the rainbow form about the head of his Raja,[23] though the old Kuki idea of the rainbow as the lips of God spread to drink, picturesque as it is, seems little to the point.[24] Among the Angami, Sema, and Ao Nagas, the rainbow must not be pointed at, lest the finger wither.

Earthquakes cannot strictly be called astronomical phenomena, but one has taken the liberty of including them in this article. Here again, the beliefs fall into more than one category, some tribes associating them with the ghosts of the dead, others again with the subterranean movements of a great serpent, and others with a god of the lower world. Thus, the Dafia regard earthquakes as caused by the spirits of the dead clearing the jungle from their path on their way to the underworld. When there is an earthquake the Dafla stands up, fearing that if he remains seated disease will attack him. The Memi division of the Angami Nagas regard earthquakes as caused by the souls of the dead men throwing their spears at Pirhe, or Pekujikhe,[25] who is the guardian of the world of the dead, and wrestling with him,[26] while one was told, rather vaguely, by a Khasi that the Khasis ascribe them to war somewhere or other, possibly the same idea.

This notion of earthquakes as caused by ghosts seems to be linked to that of the responsibility of a god under the earth by the Kachha Naga story given by Soppitt,[27] in which a dead king going to paradise married the daughter of the god. A struggle took place in consequence of the dead king's attempt to set himself up as his father-in-law's equal, and the king, having been defeated by the aid of his wife, who tied his feet together with her hair, was imprisoned in the centre of the earth, from where his struggles to free himself, are felt by men as earthquakes. In a Kabui Naga version of the same story, the wife snatches a lock of her husband's hair and throws it in the fire, thus causing him to be worsted,[28] as Samson by Delilah. The other Kabui account of earthquakes given by Hodson[29] is that a deity under the earth named Bangla-ong sent a grasshopper to bring him fire from above. This grasshopper reported that men were all dead. The deity shook the earth to see if they were alive, so, when an earthquake takes place, they say, 'We are alive'. This is virtually identical with the story of the Akas on the lower Himalayan slopes, who accuse the mole-cricket of burrowing down into the earth, and telling the God Phumbadega the same lie with the same results. The Singpho (or Kachin) have apparently the same story, substituting a beetle for the cricket.[30] Among the Semas, earthquakes are attributed to spirits shaking the earth to find out how the crops are going and its general purport. This is usually followed by a poor harvest, the reason for which is to be found in the Ao practice (reported by Mr. Mills) of holding the basket of cooked rice steady during an earthquake in order that the rice spirit may not be frightened away. The Lhota Naga, likewise, hold the meat rack over the fire and the bin with the daily rice supply steady.[31]

No doubt the same fear of the spirit of the rice, etc., being frightened away by the earthquake is present, when the Manipuris call 'Fish! Rice!'[32] as there are tremors, perhaps, not as suggested by Hodson[33] in order that the spirit shaking the earth may hear and desist, but addressing the fish and rice to keep the soul of them from being frightened away, just as those attending on a dying Naga keep calling his name into his ear, as they also do when a man faints, to cause the soul to return to the body, a view which is possibly supported by the consideration that, in the case of the Lhota at any rate, the cause of the earthquake is not exactly the deliberate act of a god, but the movement of a great serpent coiled round the world, a legend shared in Assam by the Abor in the north and the Lushei in the south; so the Thado Kuki too attribute earthquakes to this serpent's succeeding in biting his own tail. The Ao legend, however, is that an anthropomorphic being called Ningtangr holds up the post that supports the sky, and when he gets hungry and leaves his post to pluck certain leaves to eat, the post shakes and there is an earthquake.[34] The Garo legend recorded by Playfair[35] also refuses to fall into line with any other known Assam legend. It is that the earth is square and slung on a rope, or supported by a leg, at each corner. In the former case, a squirrel gnawing the rope, in the latter a mouse moving up the leg, causes the earth to shake. The Khasis tap their children's backs during an earthquake and say 'grow quickly', but one has been unable to obtain any explanation of this.

So much for the beliefs within Assam. One can now turn to their parallels insofar as one can able to locate them outside that province, and begin as earlier with Orion and the Pleiades. The Miri legend of youth pursuing maidens is apparently linked to a Hindu tale of Bengal. This would not be unnatural, as the Miris have of late been considerably influenced by Hinduism. The same idea, however, is found among the Karens, who regard the three stars on Orion's belt daughters of the Pleiades who are seized and forced to become wives.[36] The only other external parallel one can offer is the Khasi name of 'the Hen-man' for the Pleiades. This, Hooker points out,[37] is distinctly reminiscent of the Italian name for that constellation, 'the Chickens', and he might have gone further and added that the Lincolnshire term was 'hen and chickens', though one is unable to quote any specific authority for this. Probably it is the twinkling elusive aspect of the individual stars of that constellation which suggests the sudden erratic movements of little chickens. There is, however, a curious parallel between the Naga and the Greek in the matter of the number of the Pleiades. Whereas the Angami, like the Mech tribe, see seven stars in the constellation, the Sema see only six, but state that there used to be seven once, just like the Greeks, who stated that there had been seven but the seventh star, Sterope, had become invisible because of shame, so that only six could be seen.[38] The Milky Way is interpreted as the division of the seasons somewhere in East Africa. Turning to the sun and moon, one finds the ascription of a masculine gender to the moon and a feminine one to the sun widespread outside Assam. The Semang of Malay consider the sun female.[39] The Oraons of Chota Nagpur see the moon as masculine[40] and so do the Fijians;[41] as also some of the early Scandinavians,[42] while the moon is looked upon as masculine and the sun feminine in west Germany; so also the Eskimo, who appear to follow the Khasi in ascribing to the moon an illicit desire for the sun, in this case his sister, who throws soot instead of ashes in his face.[43] This story brings one back again to the interchange of functions between the moon and the sun, on account of the great heat thoughtlessly if not maliciously radiated by the former. There seems to be an echo of the Mishmi version in the Santhal story of the sun and moon recorded by Bompas,[44] though, as with the Mishmi, they consider the sun masculine. The Nicobarese have the story of the interchange of functions[45] and the Malays have a tradition which suggests it.[46] The Igorot of the Philippines clearly though the same way[47] as Lumawig turned one of two suns into a moon for the benefit of mankind.

The dung or ashes of the Naga version becomes a hare elsewhere—(there are no hares in the Naga Hills). In Sri Lanka it is a hare which is thrown (by Buddha) at the moon,[48] as also in Mexico,[49] while the hare is associated with the moon in Burma and Japan, as well as apparently in parts of Africa. In Melanesia, however, where again there are presumably no hares, the thing thrown is a yam mash[50] or hot leaves.[51] The underlying idea is, however, the same throughout. The orb of day was much too hot and so he had his face daubed and his functions exchanged with those of the orb of the night. Moreover, the idea seems hardly of a kind to originate independently in many different places. On the other hand, the description of the objects seen in the moon's face as a tree, which has been here noted among the Thado Kuki and the Angami, Rangpang and some Ao Nagas in Assam, appears to be the sort of idea that might easily arise simultaneously in different parts of the world with no connection at all. One cannot, therefore, attach much importance to the fact that the Polynesians also regard the markings on the moon's surface as a tree.[52] It is worth noting in this connection, that a remarkable coincidence seems to exist between the Maori story of a man in the moon and a Scandinavian version, that in both versions the victim seems to have been fetching water by night at the time of his abduction. In the Maori version the water fetcher climbed a tree to escape the moon when the tree fell on to the moon's surface with the climber. Can the introduction of water be traceable to something suggested by the vivid reflection of the moon so often seen in that element? If so, it seems suggestive again of the Mishmi theory of the moon having got her face muddy by being thrown into a pond. Further, the tree stories seem linked up with the interchange of function stories related to the Palaung view of the fierce heat of the moon as intercepted and kept from damaging the earth by the banyan trees growing on the moon's face.[53]

Turning to the reason behind eclipses, the Angami notion that an eclipse takes place when the orb is repaying a loan of borrowed light or heat, seems possibly to be present in a garbled form among the Munda of Chota Nagpur, who state that the eclipse is caused by the orb being surrounded by the emissaries of God, dunning the orb for the debt of the Mundas,[54] though why there should be debts due between the orb and mankind and of what sort they are, is not stated. Whether the idea is to be found anywhere else or not one does not know, but the idea of the orb being devoured is common enough. In China,[55] Siam,[56] and among the Subanos of the Philippines,[57] and the Semang of the Malay Peninsula[58] it is a dragon that devours it.

In Manchuria,[59] in China again,[60] and among the Karens of Burma[61] it is a dog, as in some parts of Assam, while the idea that it is a spirit that devours the orb spreads from Hindustan[62] through the Malay Peninsula, where it is held by the Besisi,[63] Mantra,[64] and the Negrito Sakai,[65] to Polynesia,[66] and the same idea seems to have extended to Italy, where Livy[67] writes to frighten the spirit into letting the moon go, exactly as is done in the Assam hills. Perhaps, the real key to this explanation of eclipses is in the Palaung view of the sun, the moon, and the dark orb which crosses them, as the three heavenly orbs, originally brothers, who fought over their food.[68] While on the subject of the moon, one may refer in passing to the fact that the growth of plants in Assam, as all over the world, is considered to vary with the phases of the moon. This, however, would again seem to be merely the result of common observation of a natural process, since the latest researches into the germination of plants seem to show that polarized light, like that of the moon, hastens the dissolution of starch grains and so aids the germination of seed. Indeed, it seems just conceivable that the theories of the one time excessive heat of the moon may have been falsely deduced from some actual knowledge of the conduciveness of lunar light to germination. This idea seems less extravagant when one realizes that the Chinese practised or practise it as an ordinary method of testing in court the legitimacy of offspring a coalescence of blood test[69] of the same sort as one recently suggested for that purpose as a result of the most modern investigations of the human blood.

As some Assam tribes mentioned, the Chinese regard parhelia as portents of evil.[70] One should also perhaps notice in passing the Naga theory of successive layers of sky worlds. This view is held by the Ao[71] and by the Lhota Nagas[72] and it is also held by the Chinese[73] and by some Polynesians.[74] One is, of course, familiar with the expression 'Seventh Heaven', but the Chinese and Polynesians agree in making it ten.

As regards the rainbow, as mentioned, it appeared to be regarded by Nagas as the 'Bridge of the spirits'. This is probably a widespread idea. It is found in the Andamans, where it is regarded as the bridge by which the dead visit their friends on earth[75] and the same idea appears to be held among the Dusun of Borneo.[76] In the Society Islands the Heavenly Twins descended from the sky to earth on the rainbow,[77] which is likewise familiar to us in classical mythology as the path of Iris, the messenger of the gods. Similarly in Teutonic mythology the rainbow appears as the bridge of the gods to heaven,[78] and also of the dead.[79] It is, no doubt, this aspect of the rainbow as the path of spirits that causes it to be forbidden to point a finger at it. The spread of this taboo seems much the same as that of the belief that the rainbow is the path of the spirits. One finds it forbidden in Germany (Brunswick), and China,[80] among the Karen of Burma[81] and the Dusun of Borneo[82] in the last two cases the penalty being a lost or withered finger as with the Nagas, and also among the Lifuans of the Loyalty Islands,[83] where the penalty is the death of the offender's mother.

In the case of earthquakes the explanations given in Assam seem to have no particular relation to those elsewhere, unless the one which ascribes it to the movements of a great serpent encircling the earth is to be connected with the great serpent Mitgard of Scandinavian mythology, which does not seem impossible. The results ascribed to an earthquake all over Assam do, however, reappear in the Loyalty Islands, where again earthquakes lead to short crops, but not, as one is told, owing to the flight of the frightened rice spirit, but the actual abstraction of the yam roots by the spirit below who shakes the ground in the process.[84]

The question now arises as to whether any conclusion can be drawn from the rather heterogeneous information collected in this article. At any rate one or two facts seem to emerge. As regards the constellations, there seems to be little cohesion or identity of ideas among the various Assam tribes and such ideas as exist seem to have comparatively little connection with the ideas of other people.

It is further obvious, that those ideas which show the most cohesion and the clearest trace of a wide distribution are ideas about the sun, the moon, and the rainbow, which are more or less constant phenomena, whereas the constellations are invisible for half the year and consequently, except in certain localities, are not phenomena of ordinary and frequent experience. Considering the isolation of the Assam tribes, until quite recent years, one is perhaps justified in ascribing the former group of ideas to some pre-migratory origin, the latter ideas with regard to less perceptible or less obvious phenomena having been developed by different groups for themselves at a later date. Whether these pre-migratory ideas are Caucasian or Mongolian in origin, one does not knows for sure. Both stocks are credited with having contributed to the racial composition of Assam, Indonesia and the Pacific, as well as of Northern Europe. One school would perhaps attribute these ideas regarding the sun and moon to gold-seekers from Egypt, and one can conceive of the degradation of the moon to an inferior position being interpreted as the survival of a tradition of the overthrow of a lunar by a solar race, but the fact that the sun is so often the female seems to militate against this, and one does not find either idea particularly convincing, and must be content to leave the question as it is for the present, awaiting the collection of additional data.

NOTES

1. Communicated by E. Bardalai, as is the subsequent information, as to Miri beliefs.
2. J.H. Hutton, *The Sema Nagas*, p. 251.
3. Ibid.

4. J.H. Hutton, *The Angami Nagas*, p. 412.
5. Communicated by R.C.R. Cumming, as also is the other information as to the Abors given below.
6. J.P. Mills, *The Lhota Nagas*, p. 172.
7. Communicated by Capt. Nevill, as are other particulars as to the Aka and Dafla.
8. Communicated by T.P.M. O'Callaghan, who provided the other information regarding the Mishmi as well.
9. Communicated by R.N. De.
10. Sir J.D. Hooker, *Himalayan Journals*, vol. II. p. 278.
11. P.R.T. Gurdon, *The Khasis*, p. 172. Cf. K.U. Rafy, *Folk-Tales of the Khasis*, p. 18.
12. A. Playfair, *The Garos*, p. 85.
13. J.P. Mills, *The Lhota Nagas*, p. 172.
14. J.H. Hutton, *The Sema Nagas*, p. 250.
15. Communicated by Mills.
16. T.C. Hodson, *The Naga Tribes of Manipur*, p. 124; Ibid., The Meitheis, p. 121.
17. J. Shakespear, *The Lushei Kuki Clans*, p. 184. But a Lushei told the author that it was the spirit of a Chin chief.
18. O. Hanson, *The Kachins*, p. 119.
19. K.U. Rafy, op. cit. p., 17, where '*U Hynroh*', translated as 'toad', may equally well mean 'frog'.
20. J.H. Hutton, *The Sema Nagas*, pp. 226, 252.
21. Communicated by Mills.
22. T.C. Hodson, *The Meitheis*, p. 121.
23. Ibid.
24. J. Shakespear, op. cit., p. 184, and he adds that the rainbow is also regarded as simply God's 'Glory'.
25. Cf. Sir G.A. Grierson, *Linguistic Survey of India*, III.ii, p. 461.
26. J. Shakespear, in Appendix II to *The Angami Nagas*, p. 341.
27. C.A. Soppitt, *Short Account of the Kachha Naga (Empgo) Tribe*, p. 16.
28. T.C. Hodson, *The Naga Tribes of Manipur*, p. 128
29. Loc. cit.
30. O. Hanson, op. cit., p. 120
31. J.P. Mills, *The Lhota Nagas*, p. 172.
32. J.M'Culloch, *Statistical Account of Munnipore*, p. 3.
33. T.C. Hodson, *The Meitheis*, p. III.
34. Communicated by J.P. Mills.
35. A. Playfair, *The Garos*, p. 88.

36. H.I. Marshall, *The Karen People of Burma*, p. 53.
37. Loc. cit.
38. W. Smith, *Smaller Classical Dictionary*, s.v. 'Pleiades'.
39. W.W. Skeat and C.O. Blagden, *The Pagan Tribes of the Malay Peninsula*, vol. ii. p. 202.
40. *Man in India*, vol. I, p. 303 (December 1921).
41. J.G. Frazer, *The Belief in Immortality etc.*, vol. I, p. 67.
42. N. Kershaw, *Stories and Ballads of the Far Past*, pp. 25, 223 n.
43. Peschel, quoted by Skeat and Blagden, op. cit., vol. II, 203 n.
44. C.H. Bompas, *Folklore of the Santal Parganas*, pp. 402 et seq.
45. *The Indian Antiquary*, August 1921.
46. F. Ratzel, *History of Mankind*, vol. I, p. 478.
47. A.E. Jenks, *The Bontoc Igorot*, p. 216.
48. *The Statesman*, 12 September 1923.
49. *Man*, vol. XVIII,(1918), p. 169.
50. R.H. Codrington, *The Melanesians*, p. 348.
51. E. Hadfield, *Among the Natives of the Loyalty Group*, p. 232.
52. W. Ellis, *Polynesian Researches*, vol. III, p. 171.
53. L. Milne, *The Home of an Eastern Clan*, p. 365.
54. Sarat Chandra Roy, *The Mundas and their Country*, p. 489.
55. G. Tradescant Lay, *The Chinese as they are*, p. 199.
56. La Loubere, *Royaume de Siam*, tom. I, p. 523.
57. F. H. Sawyer, *The Inhabitants of the Philippines*, p. 359.
58. W.W. Skeat and C.O. Blagden, op. cit., vol. II, p. 203.
59. J.G. Frazer, op. cit., vol. I, p. 460.
60. S. Kidd, *China*, p. 301.
61. H.I. Marshall, op. cit., pp. 231, 289.
62. F. Bernier, *Lettre & M. de la Mothe le Vayer.*
63. W.W. Skeat and C.O. Blagden, op. cit., vol. II, p. 298.
64. Ibid., p. 319.
65. J.H.N. Evans, *Studies in Religion etc. in British N. Borneo and the Malay Peninsula*, p. 208.
66. W. Ellis, op. cit., vol. III, p. 171.
67. Cf. Pliny, *Nat. Hist.*, II, XII.
68. L. Milne, op. cit., p. 365.
69. S. Kidd, op. cit., p. 303.
70. N.B. Dennys, *The Folk-Lore of China*, p. 120.
71. Communicated by J.P. Mills.
72. J.P. Mills, op. cit., p. 172
73. S. Kidd, op. cit., p. 158.

74. W. Ellis, op. cit., vol. III, p. 169.
75. A.R. Brown, *The Andaman Islanders.*
76. J.H.N. Evans, op. cit., pp. 51 et. seq.
77. Sir J.G. Frazer, op. cit., vol. II, p. 267, and cf. p. 269.
78. J.S. Stallybrass, *Teutonic Mythology*, vol. II, p. 731.
79. Ibid., p. 733.
80. Ibid., pp. 732-3.
81. H.I. Marshall, op. cit., p. 228.
82. J.H.N. Evans, op. cit., p. 15.
83. E. Hadfield, op. cit., p. 113.
84. Ibid., pp. 48, 113.

CHAPTER 6

Remnants of Spiritual/Faith Healing System among the Lepcha and Limbu Communities in Sikkim

MAHENDRA PRASAD GURUNG &
E.K. SANTHA

INTRODUCTION

Modernity and scientific advancements have not been able to uproot the age-old customs, practices and supernatural beliefs from the minds of the people completely. It is true that the relevance of traditional practices, have decreased to a large extent, among the communities; but the 'secret chambers' are still active. It is a fact that rich traditional knowledge is intertwined with these customs, beliefs and practices, which are either undervalued, understudied or on the verge of extinction along with the fading away and dilution of these practices; hence this article is not an attempt to scorn at these practices but to analyse their relevance among these communities in the present-day context. This article looks into the spiritual/faith healing system, the practice of exorcism and other shamanistic practices among the Lepcha and Limbu communities in Sikkim.

As this article deals with the shamanistic principles of two ethnic communities in Sikkim, it is pertinent to define shamanism at the outset. The *Encyclopedia of World Beliefs, Practices, and Culture* defines shamans as, 'intercessors who diagnose and treat afflictions that trouble their clients using ritual practices incorporating a mastery over spirits'.[1] Shamanists have strong belief in the spirits and the evil powers that trouble people; one of the reasons, they imply is that it is the human beings that knowingly or unknowingly cause the imbalance; the disrespect and disturbances is caused to the spirits due to human activities. The shamans, it is believed, have the power to communicate with the spirits and they can propitiate the spirits by offering prayers, chanting and through animal sacrifices.

While one largely agrees with the definition of the shaman by Shirley Kurz Jones that, 'a shaman is a person who at his/her will can enter into a non-ordinary psychic state (in which he either his soul undertake a journey to the spirit world or he become possessed by a spirit) in order to make contact with the spirit world on behalf of the members of the community'.[2] As far as the *bongthing* and *mun* of the Lepcha community and the Limboo shamanistic priests are concerned, they have a large role to play among their communities, They have mastered the power over spirits—good or evil—'who at their will can introduce these spirits into themselves and use their power over the spirits in their own interests, particularly helping other people who suffer from the spirit. . . .'[4] carry out enormous rites and rituals other than exorcism and they are also the medicine men of the community.

The Shamans were known by different names like *phedangma*, *samba*, *yeba*, *yema*, *satteyhangma*, *bongthing* and *mun*; but their work is the same. The common thread is that they all carry out animal sacrifice to propitiate the spirits, they connect with supernatural beings such as ghosts, spirits and demons and their activities are supposed to be transcendental. They are healers (main medicine men) and they have the power to forecast the future.

BONGTHING AND MUN: SHAMAN, AMONG THE LEPCHA COMMUNITY IN SIKKIM

Lepchas are an indigenous community in Sikkim. The Lepchas call themselves *rong kup* (children of snowy peak) or *rum kup* (children of God)[4] and the Kanchenjunga peak is their presiding deity. The Tibetans and Bhutanese call them *rong pa* which means ravine (narrow valley) folk. Lepcha in Parbatiya dialect (a dialect of Nepal) means unintelligible, (inarticulate) speakers—*lap* = speech and *cha* = unintelligible which originally had a derogatory connotation. No authoritative/authentic history of Lepchas is available. The Lepcha folklores, especially the oral tradition are the main source of information.[5]

The primitive religion of Lepchas was of pagan type (not a part of any established religion). Lepchas paganism encompasses a diverse community with some groups concentrating on specific traditions, practices or elements, such as nature, witchcraft traditions or certain gods. To be precise, the Lepchas were shamanistic until they came under the influence of Buddhism (more precisely, Lamaism) in the seventeenth century thanks to the exodus of Tibetan Buddhists to Sikkim. Even after the conversion to Lamaism, Lepchas did not get rid of shamanistic practices.

Lepchas who live amazingly close to nature, have numerous *rums* (gods) whose abode is huge trees or rocks or most difficult and inaccessible places. They perform numerous rituals and rites to propitiate these supernatural forces. The popular belief is that if they fail to please the *rums,* then they will turn into *mung,* evil spirits and will show their wrath on the people. The gods and goddesses mingle with their day-to-day life and its hardships. Hunting in the deep forests have made them vulnerable to the attacks of wild animals; so they perform the *mutrum* ceremony to please the hunting god. They please the fertility God called Sakyuo Sakyuorum who looks after all seasonal crops and vegetables through the medium—*bongthing,* the spiritual healer, to have a good harvest; there are ceremonies to prevent accidental death, suicides, ceremonies to please Run Si Mung who worries children and make them cry at night and so on.

Spiritual healers—*bongthing* (always a male) and *mun* (may be from either sex)—are indispensable part of Lepcha life from birth to death. The origin of these spiritual healers is yet to be ascertained; but the position is mostly hereditary. The legendary The Kong-Tek (*bongthing*) and his wife Nye-Kong-Nal (*mun*) were mentioned in the royal chronicles connected to the origin of the Bhutia dynasty in Sikkim. This is assumed to be in the first half of the fifteenth century.[6] In the primitive religion of the Lepchas, the role of *bongthing* and *mun* were very important as a shaman (spiritualist), a medicine person and exorciser. People believed that the *bongthing* had the power of prop and grant boons.

From birth to death, Lepcha life is enamoured with numerous ceremonies and *bongthing* and *mun* carry out these ceremonies as mediums between the people and a large number of supernatural powers—gods and goddesses.

> The services of the *Mun* are continuously necessary in the life of every Lepcha. They must always be present at birth, at marriage they are the only essential priests, and at the death of laymen their roles is more emotional than the Lamas. Throughout the life, they are necessary for cleansing from supernatural danger, for blessing and solemnizing different undertakings, and above all, for expelling devils.[7]

Though both of them are healers, only *mun* can conduct the death ceremony. It is an elaborate one. The three day long and strenuous journey of a soul (*A-Pil*) to Kanchenjunga for final rest is assisted by a *mun.* Before reaching the destination, the belief is that nobody from the village should meet the soul, as it would be hanging around the favourite places of the deceased. The soul would enter the *mun* and through the medium it will disclose his/her unfulfilled desires, unpaid debts and unfinished tasks and so on in the full view of the relatives and villagers. The *mun* will promise the deceased that she would see to it that these will be taken care. Then the *mun* would instruct the soul to the ancestors whose abode is somewhere in the mystic Kanchenjunga. The *mun* also conducts the ceremonies related to birth. It is basically a thanksgiving function where everyone from the village is invited. The birth god *Tang Bong Rum* is invoked on the occasion; beaten rice, chicken, ginger, dry bird meat and dry fish are offered for the safety and for the bright future of the child. If a boy child is born after three or four girl children in the family, an ox is sacrificed. At the end of the ceremony, the spiritual leader would put a drop of *chi* on the tongue of the new born baby.

The *mun* also exorcise the evil spirits, who possess unfortunate victims. The *mun* identify the supernatural spirit, which possess the victim and contact the spirit through performing rituals. He/

she exorcises the evil spirit by pleasing it through offerings and animal sacrifice. Interestingly, apart from ceremonies for appeasing the supernatural beings, there is a ceremony called *Thorsu* to please the quarrel gods (*Soo Maang*—enemy of speech, *Ge Maang*—enemy of thought, *Thor Mang*—enemy of action) to prevent ill-will and maintain harmony in the community.

SPIRITUAL HEALERS AMONG THE LIMBOO COMMUNITY IN SIKKIM

Limboo, an ethnic tribe in Sikkim has a very distinct tradition, ritual, belief and way of life. It is believed that Limboos lived in Sikkim even before the arrival of Tibetan Lamas in Sikkim and the subsequent commencement of Namgyal Dynasty in AD 1642. They had been living not only in Sikkim but the land they called 'Limbuwan' covering parts of the present Nepal, Sikkim and West Bengal. '. . . the land mass lying in between the Arun River in the west to the Tista River in the east, prior to the establishment of Namgyal Dynasty in Sikkim was known as Limbuwan (the land of Limboos).[8]

The Limboos 'have a distinct religion of their own which is known as *yuma samyo* (*samyo* = religion)'. They believed in a female Goddess named 'Tagera Ningwaphuma'. 'Literally, Tagera Ningwaphuma means the primordial mother goddess and she is believed to be omnipotent, omniscient, omnipresent, infinite and eternal and is also worshipped in her earthly form as a household deity—*Yuma Sam* (spirit of Yuma)—*Samyo* means religion that is *Yuma Samyo* means Yuma religion or Yumaism.'[10] They have a unique way of preserving and passing their history to their children with the practice of Mundum. '. . . they have a long tradition of narrating or reciting Mundums and performing rituals and observing ceremonies in their own distinctive ways. Mundum is a legend, a folk-lore, prehistoric accounts, sermons and moral or philosophical exhortations in poetic language. It is a scripture living in oral tradition.'[10]

One of the distinct and unique practices of the Limboo that brings them into discussion here is the practice of shamanism like the Lepchas. The Limboo believes in gods, as well as the evil forces and they have several myths connected to it. The popular belief is that, 'the supreme goddess Tagara Ningwaphuma gave away various ways or sources of secured knowledge and scripture to the eight wise leaders', 'these religious resource persons were expert in the practice of ritual exorcism to get rid of the invading evil spirits as the illness were believed to be the result of possession by evil forces or not observing the propitiatory rites duly and properly'.[11]

J.R. Subba, himself a Limboo, described the belief among his community and the rationale behind the practice:

> Limboos believe that God is almighty and a benevolent deity who does good for the people irrespective of whether he is worshipped or not. The trouble is with the evil spirits who hover around and are responsible for diseases, accidents, etc. These evil spirits are to be regularly appeased so that they may not cause harm to the people. Whenever there is any disease, accident or an indication of bad omen, the particular evil spirits responsible for the same, are traced out by the Shamanistic Priests through the performance of magico-religious rites who appease these spirits by uttering incantations and sacrificing fowl and other animals and offering Cha-thi to them. The Limboos believe that the soul cannot die, it leaves a body to visit the land of the dead (probably heaven) or 'Khema Yongsong Phanbhey' (probably hell) according to its work in this world where too it again comes back.[12]

In the Yumaism of the Limboos, there are different spiritual leaders known as: Phedangma, Samba, Yeba, Yema and Sattey-hangma, and together they are also called 'Limboo shamanistic priests'.

> These are resource persons of Limboo culture, tradition and oral literature. They are religious preachers, conveyers of traditional messages from generation to generation, perpetuators of age old values and belief system, healers of illness, diseases and personality disorders in their own unique way of diagnosis and treatment. They are also astrologers, foretellers and performers of various rituals for the welfare of the households.[14]

As in the Limboo belief 'phedangma', a priest performs the rituals of the dead. During the process the priest helps the soul of the dead for returning to the source; means the origin of the soul the forefathers at Sangram Pedang Den in the village of the ancestors of the dead. During the process of rituals of dead, the *phedangma* conveys the message to soul of dead in this way,

You have done nothing wrong, this is the way of life and death. One who comes to this physical consciousness with the body in the temporal world has to go like this only. Now, you are shedding your physical consciousness or the body here in this temporal world and leaving with the spiritual consciousness and joining your origin or your forefathers at Sangram Pedang Den in the village of your ancestors. This is for the last time you are being fed by your family members and close relatives in this physical word. Now onwards, they will not be able to feed you. You will not be dining together now onwards. They will not be with you; you have to travel with us in the soul journey in the Akashic field to Sam Yukna Den. Please take the food, drinks etc. offered by your family members, relatives etc. now. After this you will be leaving etc. . . .[14]

CONCLUSION

Modernity, of course, has brought down the intensity of these rituals and rites, but these are still very much part of the lives of these communities. Since the villages were electrified, the roads were laid, educational facilities were increased and communication between other communities were made possible, the relevance of some of the gods and spirits have faded away from the lives; so has the intensity of some of the ceremonies. However, their life is dominated by ancient beliefs and customs. For instance, the Lepchas in the Dzongu Reserve, the protective area of Lepchas in the Kanchenjunga Bio Reserve, visit the *bongthing* or *mun* first when they get unwell. They are still the primitive medicine persons. They visit a doctor only on the advice of the spiritual healer. Likewise, before the first seasonal planting (cultivation), the spiritual leaders still carry out the rituals to please the fertility gods to have a good harvest.

On the religious front, those who converted to Lamaism, practise a mixed religion of both Lamaism and shamanism. The Lamas are part of most of the ceremonies; however the ceremonies are initiated by the *bongthing* or *mun* before the lamas conduct the *poojas.* Lamas do not take part in the animal sacrifices which is an exclusive domain of the *mun.*

The most significant aspect is the traditional knowledge of these spiritual persons in herbal medicines and there is all probability that this rich oral tradition and knowledge may disappear along with the traditional practices of the spiritual healers. Hence, protecting these traditions, custom and beliefs while refraining from the redundant rituals, is much needed.

Shamanism is an oral tradition and the initiation to these customs and transfer of traditional knowledge from one generation to another used to take place through oral transmission. It was a long process that took years. As modernity began to claim the areas of tradition, believes and customs, these are facing extination. In the recent times not many are coming forward to learn them, even the practice of worshipping patrilineal gods is gradually vanishing from the tribe.

NOTES

1. Mariko N. Walter & Eva Jane Neumann Fridman, *Shamanism: An Encyclopedia of World Beliefs, Practices, and Culture*, vol. II, California: ABC-CLIO Inc., p. 767.
2. John T. Hitchcock, *Spirit Possessions in Nepal Himalayas*, chapter by Shirley Kurz Jone, Delhi: Vikas Publishing House, 1996, p. 16.
3. Ibid.
4. Yishely Doma, *Legend of Lepchas: Folk Tales from Sikkim*, Sikkim, 2010.
5. It is said that they originally migrated from the Assam-Burmese border around thirteenth century but there is no authentic proof. They speak Tibeto-Burman Language. Lepcha Alphabet was invented in the seventeenth century and the grammar was written by General Mainwaring in 1876.
6. The legend about the origin of the Namgyal Dyansty in Sikkim is that on the advice of the Lamas from Sakya Monastery, Kye-Bumsa (son of Guru Tashi of 25 lineage of Mynak House of Kham, Eastern Tibet who migrated to Sikkim) travelled to meet Lepcha leader The-Kong -Tek Bongthing). The legend says that he met with The-Kong-Tek and his wife Nye-Kong-Nal (*mun*) and the chief blessed that Kye-Bumsa would have three sons and also predicted that his descendants would become the future rulers of Sikkim. They established their friendship by swearing blood brotherhood in an elaborative ceremony.
7. Geoffrey Gore, *The Lepchas of Sikkim*, New Delhi: Gyan Publishing House, 1996, p. 380.

8. J.R. Subba, *The Limboos of the Eastern Himalayas; with special reference to Sikkim*, New Delhi: Ambica Printers, 1999.
9. Ibid., p. 321.
10. Ibid., p. 303.
11. Ibid., p. 309.
12. Ibid., p. 308.
13. Ibid., p. 308.
14. Ibid., p. 24.

CHAPTER 7

Leopard-Men in the Naga Hills

J.H. HUTTON

Speaking of leopard-men, it should first of all be made clear that the word 'leopard' is usually the animal associated with Naga lycanthropists. The tiger, however, is similarly, as well as one or perhaps more of the smaller wild cats. For all of these animals there is a generic term in most Naga languages, and when a Sema Naga, for instance, speaks of *angshu* he may mean a leopard or a tiger, between which he makes no clear distinction, or even a smaller animal such as a clouded leopard, a caracal, or the golden cat. The same applies to the word *tekhu* used by the Angami Naga. On the other hand, the Chang Nagas have different words, and refer to a tiger as *saonyu*, the leopard as *khonkhii* and a civet cat as *khii*.

All Naga tribes seem to regard the ultimate ancestry of man and the tiger (or leopard) as very intimately linked. The Angamis relate that in the beginning the first spirit, the first tiger and the first man, were three sons of one mother, but whereas the man and the spirit looked after their mother with the greatest tenderness, the tiger was always snarling around the house giving trouble. Moreover, he had his food raw, while the man ate his cooked, and the spirit his smoke-dried. At last the mother got tired of family squabbles, so put up a mark in the jungle and told the man and the tiger to run to it, the one that touched it first, would be allowed to live in villages, and the other to live in the forest and jungle. By an arrangement between the spirit and the man, the former shot an arrow at the mark while the other two were racing, and the man cried out that he had touched it. The tiger arrived while it still trembled from the impact of the arrow, and being deceived, went away angry to live in the jungle.

After this the man sent the cat to ask the tiger, when he killed a deer, to leave him a leg on the village wall, in virtue of their brotherhood. The cat got the message wrong and told the tiger to leave the entire deer he had killed, which started hostility between the man and the tiger. This story is found in a more or less identical form among the Angami, Sema, Lhota, and Rengma Naga tribes, the Sema making the tiger search for the corpse of his dead mother to eat it.

Man and the tiger are, however, still regarded as brothers, and if an Angami kills a tiger he says 'the gods have killed a tiger in the jungle' and never 'I have killed a tiger', while the priest of the village proclaims a day of abstention from work 'on account of the death of an elder brother'.

After killing a tiger or leopard the Angami wedges the mouth open with a stick and puts the head into running water, so that if the animal tries to tell the spirits the name of the man who killed him, all that can be heard is an inarticulate gurgling in the water. The Sema puts a stone, as well as a wedge, into the mouth to prevent the tiger lying in wait for him after death and devouring him on his way to the abode of the dead, while he also becomes entitled to wear a collar of boar's tusks, the insignia of a successful warrior, as though he had killed a man.

Among some tribes whole clans are associated with the tiger, thus among the Changs the whole Hagiyang Sept of the Chongpu clan is in some vague way intimately connected with tigers (not in this case with leopards) and is apparently of lycanthropic tendencies. At the same time it is taboo for all true Changs to touch tigers at all, far more to combine, as men of other tribes do, to hunt them. If a Chang meets a tiger in the jungle, he will warn it to get out of the way before throwing a spear or shooting at it. Should he kill one he is under a taboo for thirty days, and treats the head in the same way as an Angami, putting it with its mouth wedged open under falling water.

The Chang will eat leopard flesh, but not of course that of the tiger. The Sema will eat neither, the Angami both—but it must be cooked outside the house.

When it comes to the practice of lycanthropy one finds that the Angami Nagas, though believing that the practice exists and can be acquired, do not indulge in it themselves. Like other tribes they believe in a village far to the east peopled solely by lycanthropists, a belief, which is, perhaps, based on the claims of some clan like the Choingpu-Hagiyang of the Changs, in which all members of the community are believed to possess this faculty of taking the form of a tiger or other forms in a greater or less degree. But the Angami also believe in the existence of a spring, said to be by some, of blood, or of reddish coloured water. Whosoever drinks from it, is supposed to become a lycanthropist. They believe that the people of the neighbourhood know and shun this spring, but that the danger is greater for strangers. Moreover, when the children of that neighbourhood are peevish, it is customary, they say, to dip a blade of thatching-grass into the spring and give it to the child to suck. It stops his wailings, but he grows up a were-tiger. The Angami, however, does not practise lycanthropy himself, and the only Angami villages in which persons who do practise it, are those on the borders of the Sema country, where a large part of the population is Sema by origin. The Sema is an inveterate lycanthropist, and it is in that tribe that specific examples are the easiest to come by.

Both the Angami and Sema agree in believing that, there is no actual transformation of the body of the lycanthropist into a leopard. What he seems to do is to project his soul into a particular animal with which his human body also, thus, becomes very intimately associated. A leopard which is, thus, the recipient (from time to time) of a human soul may be recognized by having five claws on each foot, and is called by the *a.ngaini mavi* (which might mean 'real man') and *angshu amiki* by the Semas, an expression which will be referred to again. I have myself seen a leopard with dew-claws (making five instead of the usual four) killed in a Rengma village, and at once asserted to be the recipient of a lycanthropist's projected soul. Incidentally, I have seen, and followed in the soft bed of the Dayang River the tracks of a freak tiger, which had apparently five toes on its forelegs.

The lycanthropic spring, in which the Angami believe, is sometimes said to be located in the Sema country, but the Semas give an entirely different account of the way in which they acquire the lycanthropic habit.

The theory and symptoms are clear and recognizable and perhaps, differ from most lycanthropists in other parts of the world. The Sema undergoes no physical transformation whatever. The 'possession', if one may term it so, is not ordinarily induced by any external aid, but comes on at the bidding of spirits, which may not be gain said, and under whose influence the man possessed, loses his own volition entirely. The faculty can, however, be acquired by very close and intimate association with some lycanthropist, sleeping in the same bed with him eating from the same dish with him and never leaving his side for a considerable period. Two months is said to be the shortest time, in which the faculty can be acquired in this way. It can also be acquired, according to some, by being fed by a lycanthropist with chicken flesh and ginger, which is given in successive collections of six, five, and three pieces of each together on crossed pieces of plantain leaf. It is dangerous, too, to have food or drink that a lycanthropist has left unfinished, as the habit may thus be unwittingly acquired. The animal, whose body[1] the lycanthropist makes use of, though sometimes the tiger proper (*abolangshu*), is usually a leopard and is known as *angshu amiki*, a word which is said to be derived from the verb *kemiki*, meaning to wander alone in the jungle for days together, since men who do this are most liable to be possessed. It may be observed, however, that the root *miki-* also means 'to bite'.[2] Cowardly and worthless men, if they acquire the habit, make use of the body of a red cat (*angshu akinu*, probably = *Felis aurata*, the golden cat). The habit is very far from desired. No one wants to be possessed by the habit and it is, on the contrary, feared as a source of danger and a great weariness to the flesh.

The soul usually enters the leopard during sleep and returns to the human body with daylight, but it may remain in the leopard for several days at a time, in which case the human body, though conscious, is lethargic. It (i.e. the human body) goes to the fields and follows the usual routine of life, but is not able to communicate intelligibly, or at any rate intelligently, with other persons until the possession expires for the time being. The soul, however, is more or less conscious of its experiences in leopard form and can, to some extent, remember and relate them when it has returned to its human consciousness. During sleep, the soul is the leopard with its full faculties, but when the human body is wide awake, the soul is only semi-consciously, if at all, aware of its doings as a leopard, unless under the influence of some violent emotion experienced by the leopard.

The possession is accompanied by very severe pains and swellings in the knees, elbows and small of the back in the human body, both during and during the course of the possession. These pains are said to be such as would result from far and continuous marching or from remaining long periods in an unaccustomed position. During sleep at the time of possession, the limbs move convulsively, as the legs of a dog move when, it is dreaming. A were-leopard of the Tizu Valley, in a paroxysm at such a time, bit one of his wife's breasts off. When the leopard is being hunted by men, the human body behaves like a lunatic, leaping and throwing itself about in its efforts to escape. Under these circumstances, the relatives of the were-leopard feed him up with ginger as fast as possible in order to make him more active, so that the leopard-body, on which his life depends, may have the agility to escape its pursuers.

Were-leopards are particularly liable to possession between the expiry of the old and the rising of the new moon. Those possessed are liable to a special sort of disease, which is believed to attack tigers and leopards generally, but no human beings except were-leopards. When the leopard is wounded, corresponding wounds appear on the human body of the were-leopard, usually in the form of boils, and when the leopard is killed the human body also dies. It is, however, apparently possible for the soul to throw off the possession permanently as old age approaches. The father of Inato, Chief of Lumitsami, got rid of the habit by touching the flesh of a leopard. The village had killed one and he carried the head home. After that, he explained, he could no longer associate with the leopard kind. It is generally held, and doubtless not without some substratum of truth, that a man under the influence of the possession can be quieted by being fed with chicken dung. Probably this produces nausea.

Possession is not confined to men. Women, also become were-leopards and are far more destructive as such than men are. Men, who have taken heads are most dangerous, and are believed to kill as many men as leopards or tigers as they have done as warriors.

The actions of the leopard's body and of the human body of the were-leopard are closely associated. As has been noticed, if the human limbs are confined the leopard's freedom of action is restricted and troublesome were-leopards are said to be sometimes destroyed in this way.

On one occasion, the elders of a large Ao village (Ungma) came for permission to tie up a certain man in the village, while they hunted a leopard which had been giving a great deal of trouble. The man, in question, who was, by the way, a Christian convert, also appeared to protest against the action of the village elders. He said that he was very sorry that he was a were-leopard; be did not want to be one, and it was not his fault, but seeing that he was one, he supposed that his leopard body must kill to eat, and if it did not, both the leopard and he himself would die. He said that if he were tied up the leopard would certainly be killed and he would die. To tie him up and hunt the leopard was, he said, sheer murder. In the end permission was given by the elders to tie the man up and hunt the leopard, but told them that if the man died as a result of their killing the leopard, whoever had speared the leopard would of course be tried, and no doubt hanged, for murder, and the elders committed for abetment of the same. At this, the elders refused un-animously to take advantage of my permission to tie up the man. I was sorry for this, though I had foreseen it, as it would have been an interesting experiment.

One's information regarding were-leopards was obtained directly either from were-leopards themselves or their relatives, friends, and chiefs. Unfortunately, I have not so far succeeded in seeing a man actually at the moment of possession. I have had the marks of wounds shown by men who claim that they were the result of wounds inflicted on their leopard bodies. Kiyezu of Nikoto, now Chief of Kiyezu-Nagami, who used to be a were-leopard in his youth, can show the marks on the front and the back of his leg above the knee where he had been shot, as a leopard, long ago by a sepoy of the Military Police outpost at Wokha with a Martini rifle. The marks, in corresponding positions on the front and back of the thigh, looked like marks caused by bad boils. Zukiya of Kolhopu village showed me fairly fresh marks around his waist, which he said were two months old, and caused by shot which had hit his leopard body, and the marks looked as though they might have been caused by a shot. Ghokwi, the Chief of Zukiya's village, said that Zukiya was in the habit of pointing out the remains of pigs and dogs killed by him in leopard form, so that their owners might gather up what remained. He said that, he had a quarrel with his own brother, one of whose pigs he had killed and eaten by accident. Ghokwi mentioned the names of various people whose animals Zukiya had killed and eaten.[3] Sakhuto, Chief of K-huivi, showed a wound on his back, which was quite fresh on 1 March 1913, which he said was the result of someone having shot at him when he was in leopard form a few days before. The wound in the human body does not, under such circumstances, appear at once. It affects the same place in the human body as the original wound did the leopard, but takes several days to appear.

In March, 1919, an Angami interpreter, Resopu of Cheswezuma, at that time working with me in the camp, wounded a large tiger near Melomi. Three or four days later, the Head Interpreter of the Deputy-Commissioner's staff, a very well known, highly intelligent and reliable man, Nihu of Kohima, happened to meet a sick Sema road *muharrir*, Saiyi of Zumethi, being carried home. The man, who was employed near Melomi, complained of having had an accident, but on being pressed several times for details, admitted that he had no external injury that could be seen, but was suffering from the effects of the wounds inflicted by Resopu on his tiger form, having very severe pains in his neck or shoulder and abdomen and being haunted by the horrid smell of rotting flesh.

I have personally known a large number of Semas who are, or claim to be, were-leopards or were-tigers. The Headman of Chipoketami is one; Chekiye, Chief of Aichi-Sagami, is another; Inaho, Chief of Melahomi, a man of great physical strength and endurance, is perhaps the most notorious. Gwovishe of Tsukohomi and his daughter Sukheli were only known to me by repute, Gwovishe's son Chekiye of Lukammi more intimately. Kusheli of Litsammi, a second woman were-leopard, has her home inside the frontier, and has a most unenviable reputation. The Sakhuto above-mentioned died on 19 July 1916, as a result of the leopard which was occupied by his projected soul[4] having been shot by Sakhalu on 30 June that year. It was reported to the writer on 4 July that, Sakhalu had shot a were-leopard, but it was then believed to be identical with one Khozhumo of Kukishe, and it was expected that he would die when the news reached him, as the death of the man concerned does not actually take place till he hears that his leopard body has been killed. It was, however, Sakhuto who claimed the leopard, who had the honour of dying to prove his claim. The son of Yemithi of Lizotomi, whose leopard-cat body was killed at Sagami, heard the news as he was returning to his village and died on the spot for no known reason—a curious example of the power of the Sema mind over the Sema body.

Both Inato of Lumitsami and Inaho of Melahomi related to me independently how, when they were going up together from Pusumni to Lotesami, Inato managed to persuade Inaho to show his tiger form. The latter lingered for a moment behind, and suddenly a huge tiger jumped out on the path in front of Inato with a roar and an angry waving of his tail. In a flash, Inato had raised his gun, but the tiger-Inaho jumped in time to avoid the shot, and disappeared. Since this Inaho has had an excellent excuse for refusing to show his tiger form to anyone at all.

It is also told of Kusheli of Litsammi that she cured her husband of making sceptical and impertinent references to her lycanthropic peregrinations by appearing before him in leopard form. His name is Yemunga, and he was returning from a business deal in Chatongbung when suddenly he saw a leopard blocking his path. Guessing it was his wife, he laughed at it and told it to go away. It went on and blocked the path a little further ahead. This time, he threatened to spear it, and it slid off into the jungle, only to reappear behind him unexpectedly with a sudden growl. This frightened him, and he ran home as fast as he could, the leopard pursuing till near the village, where it disappeared. When he entered his house his wife at once started to mock him, asking why he was perspiring so and whether he had seen a leopard.

The Sema were-tiger, or reputed were-tiger, with whom I was best acquainted was Chekiye, Chief of Lukammi and a son of the famous Chief Gwovishe of Tsukohomi. He would never admit to me that he was a lycanthropist, but none of his Sema acquaintances ever doubted that his reputation was well deserved.[5] He came nearest to admitting to me that he was a were-tiger on the occasion of a tiger hunt in which I took part at Mokokchung on 29 March 1916. Ungma village ringed some tigers—there were certainly two full-grown animals and two three-quarter—grown cubs present. The old tiger himself broke out early in the beat, mauling a man on his way; shortly after that Chekiye turned up, armed with a spear, but no shield. The tigress broke near him and came within a few feet of him, bit and mauled his next-door neighbour and went in again. Chekiye, when remonstrated with for having stood quietly by and not having speared the animal, said: 'I did not like to spear her as I thought she was probably a friend of mine'. After the beat, he stated that the tigress killed was a woman of Murromi, a transfrontier village in unexplored country where all the population are said to be were-tigers. He also explained that the tiger in the beat was really far more frightened than even the hunters themselves, which is probably true enough and shrewdly observed that the use of the tail, which is stiffened up and out behind and swayed at the end from side-to-side, is to make the grass wave behind the moving tiger, so that the position of the tiger's body is mistaken and the aim disturbed accordingly, an observation which seems to be at least true of the result of the waving tail. It was reported that he claimed in private to be identical with the tiger that first escaped, but he would not admit this to me, and there was indeed another and more likely candidate to this rather doubtful honour. This was an Ao named Imtong-lippa of Changki. While this beat was going on three miles away, he was behaving like a lunatic in the house of one of the hospital servants at Mokochung. During his possession, he identified himself with one of the tigers being hunted and stated that one of them was wounded and speared; that he himself was hit with a stick (the Ao method of beating entailed the throwing of sticks and stones and abuse incessantly to make the tiger come out). He laid a rolled mat to represent a fence and six times leapt across it. He ate ginger and drank a whole bamboo *chunga* (about a bucketful) of water, after which he said that he had escaped with two other tigers after crossing a stream and was hiding in a hole, but that one tigress, a trans-frontier woman, had been speared in the side (in point of fact she was speared in the neck) and had been left behind and would die. (We shot the tigress in the end.) He said there were four tigers surrounded. Chekiye said six. Actually, four were seen, two grown and two half- or three-quarters grown. There might have been others, but it is not very likely. Some sixteen cattle had been killed in two days. I got this account after returning from the beat, on the same day, from an eye-witness of Imtonglippa's exhibition, which was watched by a large number of men.

I have given these details as they show the Naga beliefs on the subject clearly. Of course, among the Semas the idea of what one might describe as the projectability of the soul is very pronounced. It is a common thing for a sick person to ascribe his sickness to the absence of his soul from his body, and under such circumstances he takes food and drink and goes to the field or any other places where he thinks his soul has got left behind and summons it, calling it, of course, by his own name. When it has arrived he comes slowly home, bringing his soul behind him. A case once came up before me for adjudication in which an old man named Nikiye, who had been ill for some time, went to the fields to call his soul. It came, and he was climbing slowly back to the village occasionally calling 'Nikiye, Nikiye!' over his shoulder to make sure that the truant soul was following. Unfortunately, a personal enemy had observed him, and lay in wait in the bush by the path with a thick stick. As the old man tottered by he sprang from his ambush with a yell, and brought down his stick with a thud on the path immediately behind Nikiye's heels. The frightened soul fled and the old fellow himself died of the loss of it two days later. To avoid losing the soul a Sema, who makes a temporary shelter away from home, always burns it on leaving it, lest his soul, having taken a fancy to it, should stray back there by itself.

To return to lycanthropy in particular, the practice described, as distinct from the belief, seems particularly associated in Assam with the immigration from the north-west—that is, from the direction of Nepal and Tibet. The Changs probably have an admixture of Singpho blood, and the Singphos are known to have come from that direction; so, too, the Kacharis who, like the Changs, have a clan of tiger men, and call it the *Mosa-aroi*, and the Meches who have a corresponding clan called *Masha-aroi*, which also goes into mourning for the death of a tiger—both came from the north of the Brahmaputra. Among the Garos also, the practice is found, and they too came from the same direction. On the other hand, the Khasis, who seem to belong to a different stock—perhaps, to the Kol-Mon-Annam race and have come from the east—say they believe in the existence of tiger men, but appear to have absorbed the idea from the Garos, who are their neighbours and do not have it as an indigenous idea, neither belief that they indulge in, nor the practice itself. The Angami, who does not practise lycanthropy, seem to have immigrated into the Naga Hills from the south-east and are intimately connected with the Bontoc and Igorot of Luzon in the Philippines. In other ways, however, particularly in language, the Sema is connected with the Angami, though on the other hand there are points of culture which keep suggesting a connection between the Sema and the Garo. One of them is the use of Y-shaped posts to celebrate feasts given to the village, similar wooden posts being used by the Garo, though he is at present entirely isolated from the Sema, while the Kachari ruins at Dimapur contain the same bifurcated monuments in stone. Perhaps, the explanation is that the present Sema tribe is the result of the amalgamation of a small Angami element which has imposed itself upon another stock, a process which the Sema tribe itself is still carrying on with regard to its neighbours to the east at a very rapid rate, a Sema chief or adventurer grafting himself and a few followers on to a Sangtam or Yachungr village; this in a generation or less becomes entirely Sema in language and polity, though no doubt retaining its former beliefs and certainly retaining much of its former ceremonial events.

The theory that this form of lycanthropy comes from a northern source is perhaps supported by the fact that the form which the belief takes in Burma and Malay, as well as in the plains of India, seems to turn on an actual metamorphosis of the body. Grant-Brown, writing in 1911 about the Tamans, a tribe of Chinese origin in the Upper Chindwin Valley, notes that they transform themselves into tigers by making water and then, rolling naked on the earth they have wetted.

A nearer approach to the Naga belief appears to exist in Malay, but here again actual metamorphosis seems to be essential to that form of lycanthropy. O'May, writing in *Folklore* in 1910 (vol. XXI, p. 371) says that in Burma and Sumatra an ordinary man may turn into a tiger in the evening without any fuss, and he goes on to describe a Malay game of turning into a civet cat, in which a boy is actually hypnotized and caused to behave like a civet cat, becoming (as the Naga were-leopard does) much exhausted when the trance is over. So, too, Skeat mentions the case of one Haji Abdallah caught naked in a tiger trap in Korinchi state in Sumatra (*Malay Magic*, pp. 160-3), while Messrs. Skeat and Blagden note that the were-tigers of the Malay Peninsula (most unlike the Nagas, here) cannot be shot in their metamorphosed condition (*Pagan Races of the Malay Peninsula*, p. 227).

Skeat also records the inverse of the Naga case, in the process by which a possession of the human body by a tiger spirit is invoked to cast out another and less powerful possessing spirit (*Malay Magic*, p. 436), and similarly (p. 455), the induction of a monkey spirit into a girl who, while thus possessed, is capable of the most remarkable climbing feats.

In all these cases, however, the practice differs from that of the Nagas in that either metamorphosis takes place, or it is the animal spirit which possesses the human body, not the other way round. For with the Naga were-leopard the soul is merely projected into the body of the animal, while no metamorphosis of the human, body takes place nor is any sort of hypnotism employed—unless, indeed, it be self-hypnotism, and involuntary at that.

Sir James Frazer (*G.B.*, vol. XI, p. 196) gives instances from Asia of the location of the external soul in animals for the purposes of ensuring its safety or for enhancing the power of the magician. Neither of these two motives appears to influence the Naga were-wolf in any way. It is recognized on all hands that the practice is a dangerous one, and it is said to be rapidly decreasing owing to the increased number of guns in the district, which make it still more dangerous than it was. Lycanthropy is not practised by wizards, as were-tigers are, as far as I know, invariably ordinary men who do not claim to have supernatural powers of any sort. The nearest parallels seem to come from Africa, and Sir James Frazer mentions several beliefs from Nigeria, which resemble the Naga belief pretty closely. One other point may be added. In some cases, lycanthropy among Nagas seems to be hereditary, or perhaps, rather one should say that a tendency towards it may be inherited, as in the case of many diseases; and indeed Baring-Gould[6] described lycanthropy as a disease, associating it in this respect with the mania for cattle-maiming and with a morbid desire to devour human corpses. I have met with cases of both of these in the Naga Hills, the latter, however, being regarded by the Nagas themselves as symptomatic of extreme insanity; whereas the former is, like lycanthropy, merely a vice which is liable to be very troublesome to the neighbours of those that practise it.[7]

Note on Ao Naga belief as to a certain form of relationship between men and leopards. One Longrizibba of Yongimsen village was haunted by a leopard, which very frequently came at night and slept outside his house close to that place by the wall nearest which Longrizibba himself was sleeping inside. Whenever the leopard came, Longrizibba fell into a deep sleep and could not be aroused by his wife, even though he had previously sharpened his spear with a view to killing the animal. Then he took to sleeping on the platform at the back of his house, when the leopard took to sleeping underneath. On one occasion water was poured on to it, but without discouraging it.

After this and other efforts to get rid of it, Longrizibba induced the leopard to leave him alone by the sacrifice of a dog. This took place in 1919, when I was on leave, and my attention was drawn to the case by Mills, Sub-Divisional Officer of Mokokchung, one of whose interpreters saw the leopard outside the house at night.

Apparently such associations of men with leopards are, according to the Ao tribe, fairly frequent. The relations between the man and the leopard are normally quite friendly and mutually harmless until on an appointed day, they are brought to an end by the leopards devouring the man.

If the haunting is caused by some ceremonial fault on the man's part, it can be ended by a ceremony, which includes the surrender of a cloth, a dao sling and a piece of the man's own hair. If, however, the relationship dates from a man's infancy and has no cause that can be specified, he is unable to break it off.

A mountain with twin-peaks is pointed out by Ao as a meeting place of tiger-men. The practice of surrendering to the leopard a piece of the haunted man's hair is paralleled in the Chang tribe by the practice, when a man loses himself in the forest, of cutting off a little hair and putting it in the fork of a tree for the rock python which is believed to have caused him to lose himself. After this the lost man is able to find his way home. Semas cut a piece off the fringe of their cloth instead of their hair under similar conditions.

NOTES

1. This article is reprinted from *The Journal of the Royal Anthropological Institute of Great Britain and Ireland*, vol. 50 (January-June 1920), pp. 41-51.
2. Incidentally, it also means 'to tell lies'.
3. According to some a were-leopard who kills cattle may be found in the morning to have bits of their flesh sticking to his teeth.
4. A The Sema word is *aghongu*, which primarily = 'shadow', but is used normally in Sema eschatology for the soul of a dead person.
5. He was, however, once caught out in a pure and demonstrable romance by one of my Sema interpreters.
6. *Book of Were-Wolves.*
7. Professor Elliot Smith tells me that Egyptian boys practise lycanthropy in association with the forms of the common cat. A bibliography on the subject of lycanthropy will be found at the end of McLennan's article in the ninth edition of the *Encyclopedia Britannica*, but it relates almost entirely to the European races.

CHAPTER 8

U Thlen—The Snake Vampire: Belief and Practice among the Khasi

TEJIMALA GURUNG NAG

In Meghalaya, several incidents of killing, including the burning down of property in the Khasi Hills of so-called *mensohnohs* or persons said to be practising human sacrifice to the snake serpent called *U thlen* is reported by the media at recurrent intervals. On 5 March 1999, in Mawlai locality (in Shillong), a mob burnt two people—Soben Kurbah and Phrosimai Ryntathiang on the suspicion of being keepers of the mythical vampire snake. Such murderous incidents were reported again on 17 June 2007 in Mawbsein village. On 27 April 2011 again at Mawlai, in Shillong, a mob burnt the house of suspected *thlen* keepers.[1] On 7 October 2011, three men were reported to have been lynched at Sohra (Cherrapunjee) by villagers on the suspicion of being *nongshohnoh*—a term for people hired by certain *kur* or family who offer human sacrifices to *U thlen.* On 23 April 2013, a four thousand strong mob hailing from various villages within Sawymper area torched the house of a prominent businessman Tremlin Nongsiej of Mawryngkang village in East Khasi Hills on the charge that, he was a *menshohnoh* as confessed by his hired *nongshohnoh.* Nineteen people were arrested.[2] In August 2013, three members of a family who were accused of being *menshohnoh* at Smit village near Shillong were killed.[3] Such incidents frequently make media headlines in the Khasi Hills of Meghalaya. Interestingly, among a tribe where the majority are Christians, the belief in the prevalence of snake worship and human sacrifice to it has been a recurrent source of crime and violence among the Khasi and people are legitimately frightened. They are fearful of either being accused of being snake worshippers or becoming their victims.

What is interesting is that such instances of killing were reported by British authorities even more than hundred years back in Khasi Hills during the colonial period.

> There have been two or three murders in the neighbourhood of Shillong this year suspected to have been connected with the superstition of *Rithlen* . . . there are persistent rumours of *thlen* murders in the neighbourhood of Shillong which the district official do not hear of and which the Khasi police will not report.[4]
>
> It has been brought to my notice that some of the Khasis in this district are in a state of great panic as they are afraid of being murdered by *Nongshohnohs.*[5]

What is important is the fact that the belief in *thlen* worship, which dates back to the distant past continued to be prevalent during the colonial period and has survived to the post-colonial period. In the meantime the Khasi as a community has grown from a conglomeration of village communities to a conscious nationality, gone through a process of modernization, Christianization and as a global community.

THE LEGEND OF SNAKE VAMPIRE

The legend of the snake vampire—*U thlen* among the Khasi, is part of Khasi lore and history. There is a strong belief prevalent among the Khasi of the existence of a serpent named *U thlen* requiring appeasement by human sacrifice, who is worshipped by certain Khasi *kur* (clan) or family. Periodically, *U thlen* is appeased with human blood of the Khasis and the snake in turn, bestows wealth and prosperity on the family that nurtures it. The family that worships *U thlen* in the hope of acquiring wealth, are called *menshohnoh*, and the persons hired by the family to capture human beings for the sacrifice to *U thlen* are called *nongshohnoh* (literally 'the beater'). Notorious for being branded for practising *U thlen*, worship have been the clans of Kharkongor, Kharasawian, Kurbah, Marbaniang, etc.[6] These clans, because of their business and wealth have been associated with the *U thlen* stigma and were greatly feared and avoided by most others even in marriages. It is believed that *U thlen* is still kept in some homes in the Khasi Hills. Even in modern Khasi society, mysterious deaths and disappearances are attributed to *U nongshohnoh*.

COLONIAL RECORD OF THE PRACTICE

The widespread belief in *U thlen* worship, and of its practice in Khasi Hills was reported by the British. While the British administrators recorded it as a matter of law and order and acts of crime, the colonial ethnographers recorded it as a matter of their religio-cultural practice, which evoked immense academic curiosity. Historical record of *U thlen* practice also comes from writings of the missionaries. Both, however, used the prevalence of the widespread belief to depict the tribe as sorcerers and savages. It also provided them with the opportunity to show the Khasi as demon worshippers in need of civilization and a higher religion like Christianity. A Catholic missionary noted:

> Here, as everywhere else, when the true faith does not spread its light, superstition grows apace with all its appalling consequences. Here, as in the Baptist's time, it is necessary to lay the axe at the root of the tree of evil and superstition, and replace it with true faith in God. Thus a wide field of activity lies open to the missionary in Assam.[7]

Despite the abhorrence of the practice by the Christian missionaries and even after the conversion of many Khasis to Christianity, the belief in the practice of *U thlen* continues to this day and remains a source of great turbulence in the society, which is going through a process of modernization, globalization and liberalization.

In a monograph a colonial official cited a case that took place in the capital town of Shillong:

> A Mohammedan servant, not long ago in Shillong, fell a victim to the charms of a Khasi girl, and went to live with her. He told the following story to one of his fellow servants, which may be set down here to show that the *Thlen* superstition is by no means dying out. In the course of his married life, he came to know that the mother of his Khasi wife kept in the house what he

called a *bhut* (devil). He asked his wife many, many times to allow him to see the *bhut,* but she was obdurate; however, after a long time, and after extracting many promises from him not to tell, she confided to him the secret, and took him to the corner of the house, and showed him a little box in which was coiled a tiny snake, like the hair spring of a watch. She passed her hands over it, and it grew in size, till at last it became a huge cobra, with hood erected. The husband, terrified, begged his wife to lay the spirit. She passed her hands down its body, and it gradually shrank within its box.[8]

Further he stated that:

It may be stated that the greater number of the Khasis, especially in certain Syiemships, viz. Cherra, Nongkrem and Mylliem still regard the *thlen,* and the persons who are thought to keep *thlens,* with the very greatest awe, and they will not utter even the names of the latter for fear some ill may befall them. The superstition is probably of very ancient origin and it is possible that the Khasi sacrifices to the *thlen* demon may be connected with the primeval serpent worship.[9]

The above statement was made by P.R.T. Gurdon in his monograph on the Khasis. The monograph formed part of a series on the important tribes and castes of Assam, commissioned by the then Chief Commissioner of Assam Sir Bampfylde Fuller. Gurdon, who was also Superintendent of Ethnography in Assam and editor of the whole series, was closely acquainted with the Khasi having also served as Deputy Commissioner of the district. In the early twentieth century, he mentioned how murders in the Khasi hills have been attributed to *thlen* sacrifice. To quote him:

Many families in these hills are known, or suspected to be keepers of a *thlen,* and are dreaded or avoided in consequence. This superstition is deep rooted amongst this people, and even nowadays, in places like Shillong or Cherrapunjee, Khasis are afraid to walk alone after dark, for fear of being attacked by a *nongshohnoh.* In order to drive away the *thlen* from a house or family all the money, ornaments and property of that house must be thrown away, as in the case with persons possessed by the demon *Ka Taroh,* in the Jaintia hills. None dare touch any of the property; for fear that the *thlen* should follow it. It is believed that a *thlen* can never enter the *Syiems* or chiefs clan, or the *syiems* house; it follows therefore, that the property of the *thlen* keeper can be appropriated by the *Syiem.*[10]

ORAL TRADITION OF THE ORIGIN

The oral tradition of the origin of *U thlen* connected it with the Khasi religion and cultural practice itself:

Legend had it that long ago there lived an important deity, *U 'Lei Mawlong*, near Sohra (Cherrapunjee). He had a daughter, *Ka Kmat Kharai*, who resided in the crags and trenches, and was a strong and wilful child. She had the power to assume any identity she wished and very often would assume the persons of a comely woman and mingle freely with mankind. *Ka Kmat Kharai* was admired all over the *blei* world and many deities sought her hand in marriage. She was, however, besotted by *U Lei Umwai* and wanted to marry him. Her father *U Lei Mawlong* strongly disapproved of this match. This so angered the young goddess that, by way of retaliation, she encouraged the attentions of strange and undesirable lovers and eventually became pregnant. She fled from her home, fearing the wrath of her father and put herself under the protection of her maternal uncle, who lived in the Pomdoloi cave. There, she gave birth to a hideous monster, who had the likeness of a snake and the characteristics of a vampire and became known as *U Thlen*.

In the make believe world of the Khasis, there was regular intercourse between the *Bleis* and mankind. Mankind were privileged to attend the *Iew-blei* the fair of the *Bleis*—at *Lynghing-khongkhen*, the way to which passed the Pomdoloi cave. *Ka Kmat Kharai* would assume various forms, entice, waylay and kill many people, whenever *U Thlen* had to be fed. The common mode by which people were lured to their doom was through *Ka Kmat Kharai*, who approached them in the form of a woman merchant and dazzled them with brilliancy of the jewellery she offered for sale.

Mankind sought divinations and offered sacrifices to the gods for the ending of these atrocities, upon which a *durbar* of the *Bleis* was called. *U Lei Mawlong* overruled the *durbar*, declaring that no authority could deprive the *Bleis*, or the demons, of any power they possessed be it for good or for evil, but to mitigate the distress of mankind the number of people to be devoured was restricted to half the number of captives. If *U Thlen* captured two victims, one was to be released, if he captured ten, five were to be released. However, this agreement helped but little to allay the sufferings of mankind. Mankind again sought divination and took counsel together and it was made evident that the only one who could help them successfully was *U Suidnoh* (the fleeting demon), who haunted the forest of *Lait-ryngew* to the north of Sohra. Known for his fugacity, he consented to help. His only condition was that man should first seek the formal blessing of a *blei* and a *syiem* before he set to work. The people agreed to go to *Lei Shillong* and *Syiem Syrmoh* both of whom willingly gave their support and benediction.

U Suidnoh at first went and befriended *U Thlen's* family, *Ka Kmat Kharai* and her uncle. Then he, very cunningly, offered to be the procurer of *U Thlen's* food. *Ka Kmat Kharai* was most relieved and readily agreed. *U Suidnoh* with the full cooperation of man managed to get fat pigs and goats whenever the need arose. Through a big crack above the cave where *U Thlen* resided he would shout, 'cousin, here is a young, succulent one for you. Open your mouth so that you may devour it', and then he would shove the hapless animal down. The *Thlen*, too sluggish and dissipated to even open his eyes leave alone move, got very easily tricked in this way. Unlike his mother, *U Thlen* could not take any form he liked but he could increase and decrease his size, whenever he wished.

After a while, however the procuring of fat animals became an ordeal. The people met again to seek a solution. *U Suidnoh* suggested they should also ask the famous giant, *U Ramhah* for his assistance. The giant, to show his usefulness and strength, agreed to make a pair of tongs in his smelting house to destroy *U Thlen*. When this was done and on the appointed day, *U Ramhah*, went to *U Thlen's* cave. From the same crack, where the food was usually delivered, *U Suidnoh* called out, 'Cousin, dear cousin, open your mouth, I have yet another delicious dish for you'. It was then that *U Ramhah* thrust the red-hot giant tongs into his open mouth. The vampire groaned and howled most horribly and shook and convulsed with such force that the earth trembled for many miles around. When the sound of tremor subsided, the people cried with joy for they found *U Thlen* had truly been killed. They, then, dragged him out of the cave and chopped him into pieces. Everybody was summoned from all over the hills to be part of the macabre last rites. They believed that if they neglected to do so, the particular family would be afflicted with some misfortune.

There was a woman there, however, whose son had failed to turn up. She was worried and apprehensive that bad luck would befall her family, and took a piece for her son and hid it in her bag. When she reached home she put it in a pot and covered it. When her son returned he brought news of many misfortunes which he had met that day, which loss he attributed to his neglect of the important feast. His mother was most upset, for the family had always been tradesmen and she did not want her son to take to the plough. However, when the son went to take the meat from the vessel there was only a tiny live snake wriggling about. The little snake began to beseech not to kill him. He said he was *U Thlen*, come back to life, and that he was there by the decrees of the *Bleis* to bring them great wealth and prosperity.

Greatly tempted and without thinking of the consequences the mother and son agreed to let the *Thlen* to live, harbouring it in secret. When *U Thlen* had fully regained his vitality, he demanded human sacrifices from them. Gradually *U Thlen* cast his sway over other families also, and as his devotees increased he reproduced himself mysteriously, so now there arose many *Thlens*.[11]

The story of *thlen* was recorded by the British in their official accounts which do not vary much from the oral narrative which is of course much more detailed and nuanced. The following brief account of the tradition appeared in the *Assam Gazette*, in August 1882:

There was once in a cave near Cherra a gigantic *thlen* who committed great havoc among men and animals. At last, one man bolder than his fellows took with a herd of goats, and set himself down by the cave and offered them one by one to the *thlen*. By degrees the monster became friendly, and learnt to open his mouth at a word from the man, to receive the lump of flesh which was then thrown in. When confidence was thoroughly established the man acting under the advice of a god called *U Suidnoh* having heated a lump of iron red hot in a furnace, induced the snake at the usual signal to open his mouth, and then threw in the red hot lump and so killed him. He proceeded to cut up the body, and sent pieces in every direction, with orders that the people were to eat them. Wherever the order was obeyed, the country became free of the *thlen,* but one small piece remained and from this sprang a multitude of *thlens*, which infest the residents of Cherra and its neighbourhood. When a *thlen* takes up its abode in a family there is no means of getting rid of it, though it occasionally leaves of its own accord, and often follows family property that is given away or sold. The *thlen* attaches itself to property, and brings prosperity and wealth to the owners, but on the condition that it is supplied with blood. Its craving comes on at uncertain intervals, and manifests itself by sickness, by misadventure, or by increasing poverty befalling the family that owns the property. It can only be appeased by the murder of a human being.[12]

CHRISTIAN MISSION AND MISSIONARY PERSPECTIVE

Christian Mission reports and missionaries too who visited the Khasi Hills noticed the belief prevalent of the so called 'demon' worship among the people. A missionary historian wrote:

The Khasis have no idols or temples. A number of 'house-gods'—spirits who make their abode in gourds in the people's houses are believed in very generally and sacrifices are offered to them on every occasion of importance. The most dreaded of this class of demons is *U Thlen.* In form, it is supposed to resemble a small serpent. The *Thlen* possess power to confer great riches upon the family with whom it dwells; but it imperiously demands to be fed with human blood. For a season, it may be satisfied with a kind of human hair or a small piece of man's garment, but blood must ultimately obtained. Having strangled or clubbed his victims to death the murderer cuts off his eyebrows, nostrils, lips and finger nails which together with his blood are presented as an oblation to the demon.[13]

The missionaries too traced the origin of the practice from the old Khasi legend:

The tradition regarding the *Thlen* is briefly as follows: in a cave near Cherrapoonjee, a gigantic snake, *U Thlen* had taken up its abode and committed great havoc among both Khasis and Plains people, who were obliged to pass that way to the market. A great durbar was held to devise some means of slaying the monster. One man U Suidnoh, renowned for his courage was urged by the durbar to make friends with the *Thlen*; so he took with him a herd of goats and having set himself down near the cave, he offered them one by one to the great devourer. In time, the *Thlen* became very friendly with *Suidnoh* and at the word of command would open its mouth to receive the lump of flesh which he threw in. Having thus secured the serpent's confidence *U Suidnoh* built a smelting house and having heated a lump of iron red hot in the furnace, he carried it with a pair to tongs to the cave and as soon as the serpent opened its mouth to receive its daily quota of flesh, *U Suidnoh* threw the red hot iron down its throat and thus killed the monster. A great durbar was again held to decide what to do with the body and it was resolved that the Khasis should eat one half and the Plains people the other half. The plains people being very numerous ate their half entirely leaving not a scrap behind; for this reason there are no *Thlen* in the plain. The Khasis being fewer in number were unable to consume their entire portion and from the little pieces which they left, the *Thlen* species became repropagated on the Hills. The belief in the *Thlen* and its power is very strong in many parts of the country to this day.[14]

The name of the cave where the gigantic serpent resided was Pomdalai, near the waterfall of Noh Kalikai. According to a second version an old woman belonging to Mauphu village, west of

Cherrapunji forgot to eat her share and thus the *thlen* 'grew again and lives among them to this day'.[15] Where the *Thlen* has made its home, good fortune and wealth accrued to the family. This creature was carefully preserved in a safe place and kept secret by the families who possessed it (called *nongri-thlen*) and was only seen by the family of the owner It was also maintained by some that the *thlen* had the power to change into a cat, a cock or a stone and live in any of these forms with his owner.[16]

VARIANTS OF THE *THLEN* STORY

There are many variants of the *thlen* narrative. The following was given by Gurdon:

In the olden days there was a market in the village of Langhiang Kongkhen and there was a bridge sacred to the gods there. All the children of men used to frequent that heavenly market. They used to pass by Rangjirteh, where there is a cave which was tenanted by a gigantic 'thlen' (Rangjirteh was popular in those days for marketing lump iron to Sylhet). When they went to that market, as soon as they arrived at Rangjirteh they were swallowed up by the 'thlen'. . . . When many people had been devoured, and when they saw that all the children of men would be destroyed, whether they were Khasis or plains people, they held a great durbar at Sunnai market to which both Khasi and plains people came. . . . After they had deliberated for a long time they decided to adopt the following plan. In the grove that is close to Laitryngew, which is called 'the grove of U Suidnoh,' there was a man called 'U Suidnoh'. They counseled together to get 'U Suidnoh' to make friends with the 'thlen'. This Suidnoh was a courageous man who did not care for any one. The people advised U Suidnoh that he should go and give the 'thlen' flesh every day, either goat, pigs, or cattle. After he had done this for some time, the 'thlen' became tame, and became a friend of U Suidnoh. When both of them became very intimate thus, the children of men advised U Suidnoh to build a smelting house. So he had one built and in it made a piece of iron red-hot, and, holding it with a pair of tongs, be took it to the 'thlen'. When he arrived, he said to the 'thlen', 'Open your mouth, brother-in-law, here is some flesh.'[17] As soon as he opened his mouth, he threw the red-hot iron down his throat. The monster 'Thlen' struggled and wriggled so violently in its death agony that the earth shook as if there had been an earthquake. . . . They then . . . convened a durbar to decide about eating him. In the durbar they came to the following understanding i.e. that the Khasis should eat half, and the plains people half (of the body). After they had come to this decision, they went to take him out of the cave, and lifted him on to a rock. They then cut the *thlen's* carcase into pieces. The plains people from the East being more numerous ate up their share entirely not leaving anything—for this reason there are no '*Thlens*' in the plains; but the Khasis from the West, being fewer in numbers, could not eat up the whole of their share and they left a little of it. Thus because they did not eat it all, the *Thlen* has remained with them. U Suidnoh gained for himself fame and honour, which he enjoys up to the present day.[18]

THE REALITY OF PRACTICE

The practice and ritual involved in sacrifice of the victims have come from British and Christian missionaries According to Gurdon, the *U nongsohnoh*:

Before he sets out on his unholy mission, he drinks a special kind of liquor called *ka 'iad tang-shi-snem* (literally liquor which has been kept for a year). This liquor, it is thought, gives the murderer courage and the power of selecting suitable victims for the *thlen.* The *nongshohnoh*, then, sets out armed with a short club, with which to slay the victim; for it is forebidden to kill a victim on these occasions with any weapon made of iron. He also takes the pair of silver scissors, a silver lancet to pierce the inside of the nostrils of the deceased, and a small bamboo or cylinder to receive the blood drawn there from. The *nongshohnoh* also provides himself with rice called *U khawtyndep* i.e. rice mixed with turmeric after certain incantations have taken place. He throws a little of this rice over his intended victim, the effect of which is to stupefy the latter, who then falls an easy prey to the *nongshohnoh.* It is not, however, always possible to kill the victim outright for various reasons, and then the *nongshohnoh* resorts to the following subterfuge: he cuts off a little of the hair or the hem of the garment, of a victim, and offers these up to the *thlen* . . . who soon falls ill, and gradually wastes away and dies. The *nongshohnoh* also sometimes contents himself with merely throwing stones at the victim, or with knocking at the door of his house at night, and then returns home, and , after invoking the *thlen,* informs the master that he has tried his best to secure him a prey, but has been unsuccessful. This is thought to appease the *thlen* for a time. . . . It soon manifests his displeasure for the failure of his keepers to supply him with human blood, by causing one of the latter's family to fall sick. The *thlen* has the power of reducing himself to the size of a thread, which renders it convenient for the *nong-ri thlen*, or the *thlen* keeper, to place him for safety in an earthen pot, or in a basket which is kept in some secure place in the house. When the time for making an offering to the *thlen* comes, an hour is selected, generally at dead of night, costly cloths are spread on the floor of the house of the *thlen* keeper, all the doors are opened, and a brass plate is laid on the ground in which is deposited the blood, or the hair, or a piece of the cloth of the victim. All the family then gathers round, and an elderly member commences to beat a small drum, and invokes the *thlen* saying, '*koknikokpa* (oh, maternal uncle, father), come out, here is some food for you, we have done everything we could to satisfy you, and now we have been successful; give us the blessing, that we may attain health and prosperity'. The *thlen* then crawls out from its hiding place and commences to expand, and when it has attained its full serpent shape, it comes near the plate and remains expectant. The spirit of the victim then appears, and stands on the plate, laughing. The *thlen* begins to swallow the figure, commencing at its feet, the victim laughing the while. By degrees the whole figure is disposed of by the boa constrictor. If the spirit be that of a person from whom the hair, or a piece of his or her cloth, has been cut, directly the *thlen* has swallowed the spirit, the person expires.[19]

According to the Salvatorian missionary C. Becker, in case of illness, some non-Christians sought to recover their health by seeking the protection of the *thlen.* This was done by giving to the owners some of their belongings with money or food.[20] The following detail of narration[21] was given by a former *thlen* owner of his experiences to Father Corbinto Bonheim, who had worked for many years in Cherrapunjee. When a *thlen* keeper wanted to be rid of the *thlen* called *pyndud noh ia u thlen* the family had to part with their entire property. This involved a ceremony performed by the priest of the village and with the cooperation of members designated by the *syiem.* Houses and furniture had to be burnt, the valuables disposed off, even their clothes. Since the *thlen* was popularly believed to be connected with the property, no one dared to take anything disposed including the fields. Objects of value could be taken only by the *syiem* as the *thlen* could not enter the *syiem's* house. The former *thlen* owner was given clothes; rice, and was helped to build a hut to begin a new life. Becker stated:

> As late as 1908, a Thlen worshipper at Cherrapunjee parted with his entire property. He owned among other things, large orange gardens. No one among the pagans would dare buy those gardens or take the fruit from them.[22]

Becker referred to the 'deep fear' of the *nongshohnohs* among the Khasis. This was specially to be seen in the *himas* of Cherra, Mylliem and Nongkrem. People avoided the *thlen* keepers and 'did not even dare to pronounce their name for fear of being afflicted'. A woman in Cherra believed to be *thlen* worshipper, as noted by Becker had a house built of stone and roofed with metal sheets in contrast with the neighbouring Khasi huts. On way to faraway markets, the Khasi always went in groups. When they had to go to larger markets, which were some days away from their villages, they only went to specified ones where they had friends on the way and with whom they could spend the night.[23] The missionaries were inconvenienced too. Even though only one coolie was needed for carrying their load, the missionaries had to engage and pay for two-the reason cited would be the Khasi fear of *nongshonohs.* Also, the missionary noted:

> At certain times, when the 'Thlen-worshippers' are particularly active, we ourselves have to keep guard over our orphanages for fear of the children being abducted. Some attempts of this nature have been made. For several nights the servant at our mission station at Laitkynsew had an exciting time keeping guard over the mission house while the Father was away. The killers tried to get him into their power. He was lucky indeed to escape.[24]

Becker further informed that to kill a *nongshonoh* was not considered a crime. However, a fine of 5 rupees along with a pig had to be paid to the *Syiem.* In 1909, one *nongshonoh* who was apprehended in the act of killing at Nongrem village had his nose mutiliated as punishment. The houses of 'convicted' *thlen* keepers were burnt. Sometimes, lynching of the *thlen* keepers also happened.[25] Instances of killings in official reports were ascribed to the *thlen* belief. In most cases the guilty could not be found and punished due to lack of witnesses. Becker, while mentioning of an incident of killing about 10 miles from Shillong in the year 1890, noted that the villagers did not dare to give information out of fear of incurring the wrath of *thlen.*[26]

Another belief associated with the practice was only people of sound mind and good health were to be sacrificed to *U thlen*; and the victim should not be killed and hit from behind on the head.[27]

When a person is ailing and grows sick due to *U thlen*, he/she could be cured only if a *syiem* belonging to the *syiem* clan took a sword that was blunt and heated it in the fire and then burnt a little bit of hair of the person who had been suffering.[28]

CHARACTERIZING THE OCCULT

The practice of *thlen* worship was characterized as demon worship and human sacrifice. Characterizing the tribal religion, American Baptist missionaries like P.H. Moore in 1886 had remarked: '. . . all these hill people were demon worshipers; but each tribe has its own demons and its own ceremonies, preserved in pristine purity or largely modified by their environment'.[29]

The religion of Khasi was frequently described as animism or spirit worship in which the worship of demons or evil spirits was repeatedly emphasized. As far as the religious faith of the tribes was concerned, it was repeatedly emphasized that their religion was: 'a crude form of demonology. Its main principle consists in the endeavour to propitiate evil spirits by the offering of sacrifices'.[30]

These spirits were said to reside in caves, jungles, mountains, large rocks and stones, trees and rivers; and sickness, or misfortune were always attributed to the wrath of the demons, which could only be appeased by the offering of appropriate sacrifices.[31] The colonial report characterized *thlen* worship as a form of human sacrifice which was also connected with their religion. Referring to human sacrifice in Assam, Edward Gait stated: 'A peculiar form of sacrifice was and still is, in vogue amongst the Khasis, but this is based on purely non-Hindu superstitions, whereas amongst the other tribes mentioned, the custom seems to be more or less closely connected with the rites enjoined in the *Kalika Purana*'.[32]

A Resolution by the Chief Commissioner of Assam in the *Administrative Report of the Khasi and Jaintia Hills District for the year 1881-82* dealt with the *thlen* belief characterized as human sacrifices prevalent amongst the Khasi:

> Of the cases tried this year, were three murders of singular atrocity, two of them committed on inoffensive old women, and one on a boy; in none of them was any adequate cause alleged, and at least two of them are believed to

> have been connected with the very remarkable superstition of the *Thlen*. . . . When a *Thlen* takes up its abode in a family, there is no means of getting rid of it, though it occasionally leaves of its own accord, and often follows property of the family when given away or sold. The *Thlen* attaches itself to wealth, and brings prosperity and wealth to the family, but on the condition that it is supplied with blood. Its craving comes on at uncertain intervals, and manifests itself by sickness among the family, by misadventure or increasing poverty. It can only be appeased by the murder of a human bring. The murderer takes the hair, the tips of the fingers, and a little blood from the nostrils, caught in a bamboo tube and offers these to the *Thlen*, The belief is that the demon then appears in the form of a snake and devours the body of the murdered person, which is materialized from the portions thus offered. After this, its craving is satisfied for a time, and the affairs of that house prosper. Many families in these hills are known or suspected to be *nong-ri-thlen*, or keepers of a *Thlen*, and are dreaded and avoided in consequence. Whenever a dead body is found with the marks above described on it (and particularly if it is killed with no wound, but by twisting the neck), it may be presumed with almost absolute certainty that the object of the murder was to appease a *Thlen*. This happened in one of the three instances referred to in the others these marks were not found, but in the absence of any other cause for the murder, it was more than probable that it was due to this dreadful superstition. In each of the three cases one or two persons (though perhaps not all the accomplices) were convicted; one man was hanged, and the rest were sentenced to transportation for life or for a terms of years.[33]

Some indigenous scholars[34] have opined that the *thlen* cult was an outgrowth of Hinduism and it had nothing to do with the original Khasi traditional religious faith and belief. It may be noted here that, in neighbouring Bengal, snake worship was widely practised. Especially, the worship of an anthropomorphic snake goddess called Manasa was very popular. She was also worshipped for prosperity by the trading community. Human sacrifice was however not unknown in the region. The Jaintia Raja who had adopted Hinduism practised human sacrifice to the Goddess Kali at Jaintiapur (at present in Sylhet, Bangladesh). In fact, one of the excuses given by the British for their annexation of Jaintiapur in 1835 was the sacrifice of three British subjects to the Goddess Kali by a subordinate chief of the Jaintia Raja. The Jaintias also formerly used to offer human sacrifice to the Kopili River, which the Jaintias worshipped as a Goddess. In the past, human sacrifice is also said to have been practised in *raid* Iapngar, *raid* Thaiang and other *raids* (cluster of villages) in Ri Bhoi area.[35] Besides belief in *U thlen* is not the only 'satanic worship' among the Khasis; there is also *ka taro ka shwar*, (black magic) *ka Bih*, (poison put in food for purpose of gaining wealth) *ka lasam, ka tympiam*, etc.

Historians studying the *thlen* legend have looked at it as providing insight into or reflecting historical developments.[36] In an attempt to understand the prevalence of the belief and practice theoretically, Rengsi asserts that the legend cannot be relegated as some witchcraft. It has to be understood as a dynamic aspect of the social process—when the Khasi tribal structure was giving way to the process of state formation. Society had reached a certain stage of affluence by engaging in trade and plunder with neighbouring Cachar and Sylhet and warriors had come to acquire significant position within their society. The *thlen* legend was used to facilitate the entry of *suidnoh* as *syiem* a position not existing in the clan-tribal system. He argues that 'As the office of Syiemship was created, apart from being alien to the original clan structure, it did not provide any real power or privilege as society, in so far as its laws were concerned, was intrinsically tribal and thus egalitarian in nature. Power still remained vested with the clan heads'.[37]

The *thlen* legend was twisted so that it remained a menace to be used as a system 'to exploit the people'.[38] The wealth derived particularly from trade was considered as elements of threat to the existing system and power of the warrior class. The legend of *U thlen* came to be used as a means to ensure that those who have gathered a lot of wealth and become powerful should be checked and put under control. The suspected *thlen*-keeper now 'had to relinquish all his belongings' to the *syiem's* family, since they were the only ones 'immune to the *thlen*'. Rengsi argues that that 'Feasts of Merit', which existed among the Mizo and Naga had 'served as useful channels or means by which surplus (produced or acquired) within the society may be dissipated in a very useful and functional way while at the same time keep up the competitive spirit between individuals'. It enabled people to elevate themselves in society without endangering the existing power structure. In the absence among the Khasis of an equivalent system like the 'Feasts of Merit' the Khasi society:

became one of hidden and disguised antagonistic, suspicions, and hostile elements with the Syiem ruling in tyranny with a decadent group of clanheads. There was total apathy in surplus production as condemnation, rather than reward, awaited the person who showed up sign of having wealth—a whole society waiting to point an accusing finger and stone him.[39]

Cecile Mawlong on a similar line links the *thlen* folk tale to the emerging tension and social conflict in society as trade developed.[40] Traditional sources have associated the emergence of the institution of *syiemship* in Khasi society with the struggle for power among the 'traditional elite' or leading families (*bakhraws*) over the control of vital resources and trade. From colonial records of the eighteenth century, it is evident that the Khasi traders or *nongkhai* were playing an important role even as middlemen in the trade with Sylhet, Cachar and Assam. Apparently in the Khasi-Jaintia society, the development of trade and coordination of trading activities played a crucial role in the rise of *syiemships*.[41] *Syiemship* arose to deal with crimes against authority particularly the violation of customs and tradition. Such acts included among others claiming the wealth of persons and families, who had accumulated it through wrongful means, such as propitiation and worship of the *thlen* spirit; imposition of fines, etc.[42] However, the *bakhraws* continued to wield their authority through the *Syiem's* council, the highest governing authority in the *hima* or state; which was dominated by them as *basans*, *lyngdohs*, *dolois*, etc. As she argues:

The significance of the *thlen* and *taroh* superstitions lies in the fact that they are a clear index of social tensions that had emerged in society, in response to the demands of new social relations, as distribution of economic power changed. This is inferred from the fact that persons and families accused of harbouring such spirits, were more often than not, traders and business folk. The *thlen* superstition is also a reflection of how dominant groups in Khasi society, sought to manipulate ideology to safeguard their interests. Their interests were probably linked with the control of profits from trade, particularly Khasi iron, which going by British reports and accounts appear to have been substantial.[43]

The *thlen* legend is certainly interwoven with some historical aspects and markers of change related to Khasi society during the pre-colonial period. Their interaction with the Ahom state in the north and particularly Bengal in the south, would certainly have led to the elaboration of their polity formation and diffusion of snake worship cults. This is indicated by references to markets, of iron, importance of trade, new social groups like traders, *syiems*, loan words such as *darbar*, etc. The territorialization of Khasi village settlements into larger *himas* necessitating emergence of the institution of *syiemship* and of new avenues of trade generating wealth were indicative of Khasi society undergoing political and economic change. The emergence of Khasi belief in *thlen* worship may be seen as their way to provide a rationale of their changing world or to deal with the breakdown of the traditional moral values, the lust for wealth, and anxiety of its members.

Historically, belief in magic and witchcraft and its practice has been widespread across societies. Anthropologists who have studied and analysed witchcraft beliefs have contributed to our understanding of it. They[44] have also looked at the functional aspects of the beliefs and practices that human needs (individual and social) are fulfilled. It is understood that magic and witchcraft are related to the human problem of control in cultures. Whereas magic may be either malevolent or beneficial, witchcraft is invariably evil. Pritchard in his classic ethnographic study of the Azande tribe in Africa referred to witchcraft as a belief in an innate, psychic ability of some people to harm others.[45] Evans Clyde Kluckhohn defined witchcraft as 'the influencing of events by super-natural techniques that are socially disapproved',[46] Witchcraft, magic and sorcery were strategies for people to understand or deal with bad luck, illness, injustice and other misfortunes that they cannot otherwise explain. Certain phenomena that do not seem to have 'natural causes' are explained in terms of witchcraft or sorcery. To the Azande, witchcraft provided a natural philosophy by which the relations between men and unfortunate events are explained.[47] Witchcraft belief also embraces a system of values which regulate human conduct. A person who is very successful is accused of witchcraft. In early and less stratified societies such accusations militate against any strong striving of success. Socially, it may also absorb latent hostilities through accusation and angers against witches. As for example among the Navajo, economic differences were believed to be related to witchcraft—those who had more wealth had gained it through witchcraft activities. The only way a person could refute such an accusation was to share his or her wealth with friends and relatives. Thus Kluckhohn hypothesized that the belief in witchcraft had the effect of equalizing the distribution of wealth and promoting harmony in the community.[48] Belief in witchcraft also has its dysfunctional aspects—it causes real fears and promote dangerous conflicts.[49]

The belief in the worship and practice of the *thlen* continues to be very much a part of the Khasi mind. Many Khasi, despite their conversion to Christianity, still harbour deep fear and suspicion in the existence of 'satanic' worship (*U thlen*) by some families. Instances of families being socially ostracized or driven out of their villages continue to be reported by the media. On this socially sensitive issue, even the Church has been silent.[50] As noted by many who can be considered to be part of Khasi intelligentsia, deep in their hearts the Khasi continue to be afraid of *U nongshohnoh*, and other 'demonic' practices. For this reason in every *jingiaseng* (church gathering) it is announced that 'These food stalls are recommended by the church as safe (meaning that people can eat without fear of *ka bih* or *ka lasam*).[51] As Rev. Lyndem Syiem has observed:

> . . . the *Thlen* is firmly embedded in our collective consciousness . . . religious intervention is often regarded as ineffective or at best mismatched. . . . Mission anthropologists concede that it is extremely difficult to wean people away from deeply rooted components of their traditional world view, especially demonic spirits which they fear, like *U Thlen*. . . . No matter how much mass awareness on the nonexistence or non-potency of the *Thlen*, people will stubbornly cling to the familiar fear they have held for centuries.[52]

NOTES

1. 'A Year of Superstitions and Lynch-mobs', *The Shillong Times*, 30 December 2013.
2. Fabian, 'Some Truths about U Nongshohnoh', *The Shillong Times*, 25 April 2013.

3. 'A Year of Superstitions and Lynch-mobs', *The Shillong Times*, 30 December 2013. The village council did not even allow the victims Yesly Mawthow (70), his son Entarsing Nongdhar (30) and Besly Mawthoh (65) to be buried at their village.
4. Assam Secretariat, Judicial Department 1916, Police A, February 1916, No. 25 G.E. Soames to Undersecretary, 10 September 1913, Assam State Archives.
5. Assam Secretariat, Judicial Department 1916, Police A, February 1916, No. 25, A.W. Dentith to Commissioner, 20 September 1913, Assam State Archives.
6. Vanlalruata Rengsi, '"Thlen" in Khasi Society', *Proceedings of the North East India History Association*, Doimukh Session, Shillong, 1994, p. 97.
7. C. Becker, *Early History of the Catholic Missions in Northeast India (1598-1890)*. Vendrame Institute, Sacred Heart College, Shillong, 1989, p. 86.
8. P.R.T. Gurdon, *The Khasis*, New Delhi: Akansha Publishing House, Reprint 2010 (first publication 1906), p. 101.
9. Ibid., pp. 101-2.
10. Ibid., pp. 101.
11. Bijoya Sawain *Khasi Myths, Legends and Folk tales*, Shillong, 2006, pp. 45-9, Moses Kharbitai, '"U Thlen": Myth, Socio-Cultural Belief and its impact on Modern Khasi Society' Unpublished seminar paper presented on Black Magic, Witchcraft and Occult Practice, Department of History, Assam University, Silchar 7-8 October 2014
12. *Assam Gazette*, 1882 in P. R.T. Gurdon, *The Khasis*, New Delhi: Akansha Publishing House, Reprint 2010 (first publication 1906), p. 98.
13. J.H Morris, *History of Welsh Calvinistic Methodist Foreign Mission to the end of 1904*, Liverpool, 1910, reprint, Delhi: Indus, 1996, pp. 65-6.
14. Ibid.
15. C. Becker, *Early History of the Catholic Missions in Northeast India (1598-1890)*, Shillong: Vendrame Institute, Sacred Heart College, 1989, p. 77.
16. Ibid.
17. P.R.T. Gurdon, *The Khasis*, New Delhi: Akansha Publishing House, Reprint 2010 (first publication 1906), pp. 173-6.
18. Ibid. Acording to Gurdon, the *syntengs* also have their *thlen* but he differs much from the Khasi *thlen*. The *syntengs* also believe that he is a kind of serpent, and there are some families and clans who keep him and worship him like a god and in exchange the *thlen* gives prosperity to the family. They sacrifice a pig to him; they do not propitiate him with human blood as the Khasis do.

19. P. R.T. Gurdon, *The Khasis*, New Delhi: Akansha Publishing House, Reprint 2010 (first publication 1906), pp. 99-101.
20. C. Becker, *Early History of the Catholic Missions in Northeast India (1598-1890)*, Shillong: Vendrame Institute, Sacred Heart College, 1989, p. 79.
21. Ibid., pp. 82-4.
22. Ibid., p. 82.
23. Ibid., p. 80.
24. Ibid., p. 80.
25. Ibid., p. 80.
26. Ibid., p. 86.
27. Magdalyne Syiemlieh and Naomi Carey Nonglait, 'Thlen in Khasi Society: Then and Now' in *The International Journal of Humanities & Social Studies* in vol. 2, issue 7, July 2014, pp. 191-7.
28. Ibid.
29. P.H. Moore, 'Need of a Native Ministry', in *Papers and Discussions of Jubilee Conference of the American Baptist Missionary Union*, held in Nowgong, 18-29 December, Gauhati, (1886) Reprint 1992, p.15.
30. J.H. Morris, *The History of the Western Calvinist Methodists: Foreign Mission, To The End of The Year 1904*, New Delhi: Indus Publishing Company, reprinted 1996 (First Published in 1910), p. 64.
31. Ibid.
32. Edward Gait, 'Note on Human Sacrifice in Assam', no. 2, G-5, 6 CB no. 1, pp. 55-79, Mizoram State Archives, subsequently published in Human Sacrifices in Ancient Assam', *Journal of the Asiatic Society of Bengal*, vol. LXVII, part III. no. I, 1898, pp. 64-5.
33. Edward Gait, 'Human Sacrifices in Ancient Assam', no. 2, G-5, 6 CB no. 1, pp. 55-79, Mizoram State Archives, subsequently published in *Journal of the Asiatic Society of Bengal*, vol. LXVII, part III, no. I, 1898, pp. 64-5.
34. Fabian, *Our Reporter*, Thursday, 25 April 2013; Barnes Mawrie, 'The cult of Nongshonoh', *The Shillong Times*, 28 August 2013.
35. Fabian Lyngdoh, *The Shillong Times*, Thursday, 25 April 2013.
36. Refer Vanlalruata Rengsi, 'Thlen in Khasi Society', *Proceedings of the North East India History Association*, Doimukh Session, Shillong, 1994, pp. 92-7; Cecile A. Mawlong, 'Megaliths and Social Formation in Khasi-Jaintia Hills', in Mignonette Momin and Cecile A. Mawlong (eds.), *Society and Economy in North-East India* , vol. 1, New Delhi: Regency Publications, 2004, pp. 35-56.
37. Vanlalruata Rengsi, 'Thlen' in Khasi Society', *Proceedings of the North East India History Association*, Doimukh Session, Shillong, 1994, p. 94.

38. Ibid.
39. Ibid., pp. 96-7.
40. Cecile A. Mawlong, 'Megaliths and Social Formation in Khasi-Jaintia Hills', in Mignonette Momin and Cecile A. Mawlong, (eds.), *Society and Economy in North-East India*, vol.1, New Delhi: Regency Publications, 2004, p. 47.
41. Ibid., p. 44.
42. Ibid., p. 47.
43. Ibid., p. 48.
44. Bronislaw Malinoswski, *Magic, Science and Religion, and Other Essays, Beacon Press, Boston,*1948; E.E. Evans-Pritchard, *Witchcraft, Oracles and Magic among the Azandes, 1937*, New York: Oxford University Press, 1976; A.R. Radcliffe-Brown, *Structure and Function in Primitive Society*, 1952; Emile Durkheim, *The Elementary Forms of The Religious* Life, London, 1915; Clifford Geertz, 'Religion As A Cultural Symbol' reprinted in William A, Lessa and Evon Z. Vogt (eds.), *Reader in Comparative Religion: An Anthropological Approach*, fourth edition, New York: Harper and Row, 1979, pp. 78-89, Clyde Kluckhohn, *Navaho Witchcraft*, Beacon Press, 1967.
45. E.E Evans-Pritchard, *Witchcraft, Oracles and Magic among the Azandes, 1937*, New York: Oxford University Press, 1976. p. 52.
46. Clyde Kluckhohn, *Navaho Witchcraft*, Beacon Press, 1967.
47. William A. Lessa and Evon Z. Vogt, *Reader in Comparative Religion: An Anthropological Approach*, fourth edition, New York: Harper and Row, 1979, pp. 362-6.
48. Clyde Kluckhohn, *Navaho Witchcraft*, Beacon Press, 1967.
49. A. Lessa and Evon Z. Vogt, *Reader in Comparative Religion: An Anthropological Approach*, fourth edition, New York: Harper and Row, 1979, p. 333.
50. Patricia Mukhim, 'Conspiracy of Silence', *The Shillong Times*, 14 October 2011.
51. Fabian Lyngdoh, *The Shillong Times*, Thursday, 25 April 2013.
52. Rev. Lyndam Syiem, 'Dealing with Obstinate World Views' *The Shillong Times*, 28 August 2013, http://www.theshillongtimes.com/2013/09/05/

CHAPTER 9

Chon Ritual and Head Hunting among the Kukis of North-East India

TINGNEILAM THANGEW

Kukis are one of the major tribal communities of north-east India who are known as one of the head hunting communities. While head hunting was undeniably a part of the Kuki culture, where the heads collected would be displayed outside the respective villages in the *Chon* ritual, the nature of head hunting among them was that when a head was obtained it became a part of the community, made part of important social rituals to establish prominent social status. Likewise, the obtained heads were also buried along with the dead body of an individual to accompany him in the *Mithikho* (resting place of the deceased). This article will highlight the importance of the *Chon* ritual mainly from secondary sources and give a basic understanding as to who the Kukis were, where they had their settlements, what were their beliefs and whether they still follow their ancestral traditions at present.

According to Lalmaunpuii Khiangte, head hunting among the Kukis prevailed, due to the claim on occupational land resulting in land feuds with the neighbouring tribes.[1] Among the co-existing tribes, head hunting was resorted to in order to retain lands keeping the contenders at bay. The method of attaining heads ranged from surprise attacks, done on the grounds of taking revenge. The origin of the tradition of head hunting among the Kukis is still unknown. But the custom of collecting heads of women seems to have originated among the Kukis of Tripura as narrated below.

In ancient times it was not a custom among them to cut-off the heads of the women whom they found in the habitations of their enemies. But it happened once that a woman asked another why she came so late to her business of sowing grain, the latter answered, that her husband was gone to battle, and that the necessity of preparing food and other things for him had occasioned her delay. This answer was overheard by a man at enemity with her husband. He was filled with resentment against her, considering that, as she prepared food for her husband for the purpose of sending him to battle against his tribe, so in general, if women were not to remain at home, their husbands could not be supplied with provision, and consequently could not make war with advantage. From that time it became a constant practice to cut-off the heads of the enemy's women; especially if they happened to be pregnant, and therefore confined to their houses. This barbarity was carried so far, that if a Kuki attacked the house of an enemy, and killed a woman with a child, so that he might bring two heads, he acquired honour and celebrity in his tribe, as the destroyer of two foes at once.[2]

So basically head hunting was an individual practice which set a trend among the hillmen's warfare. However Shakespeare firmly believed that the custom was originally invented by the Thado-Kuki. Whereas William Shaw assumed that he was only a slave hunter and taking of the heads was infused from the neighbouring tribes. This was like the way in which the Kukis borrowed the manufacture of guns and gunpowder from indigenous products through one of the neighbouring tribes, Shendoos.[3] The reasons for head hunting among the Kukis had four motives for:

(a) for revenge
(b) as a tradition of the primal Kuki
(c) or war trophy
(d) for soul matter.[4]

THEIR SETTLEMENTS

The ancestors of the Kukis had dwelled in almost extensive areas of north-east India. The Ahom government had practically no connection with the tribes in the Lushai hills, though there is evidence to show that they knew the Kukis through their envoys to Tripura, who preceded through the Lushai hills.[5] Traces of the Kukis inhabiting the Cachar or Silchar district is found in fragments in the form of accounts and theories as explained in the following paragraphs. The compound word Hailakandi by which the southern district of Assam is known derived its name from two words: Hallam (a Tripuri term for the Kukis) and Kandi (paddy field) meaning *Hallam* (and thus, *Haila-kandi*) means *Hallam ram* (land or territory) or land of the Hallam people.[6] Again, a theory suggest that the Kukis lived in different groups, in Hailakandi for example the region was inhabited by the Kukis named as *Halam* and according to the Kuki language *Hala* means God and *Kundi* means Almighty Siva. So, Hailakandi means the country of gods renamed as *Halpa-kundi* during Kachari kingdom and the present name Hailakandi during the British rule.[7] One theory suggest that:

> Hailakandi was originally a part of the Kuki kingdom i.e.'Hidmba Raja' may be explained by a linguistic derivation of the name itself. In Kuki Dialect 'Hala' means 'Isvara' and 'Kundi' means 'Param Purush Shiva' or 'Narayana'. So 'Hailakandi' means Kingdom of Lord Shiva or Narayana. Here it is important to note that the Kukis (who are referred as Kirates/Mlechhas in the epics) were originally Shiva worshippers.[7]

Interestingly, the *History of The Biates* by Ramdina Lalsim mentions the relations of the Kukis in Tripura. The king called as Vairengpa to the Biate tribe offered a *bala* (bangle), to the Biates, Sakecheps and Hrangkhols. After the presentation of the *bala*, some years later, the Vairengpa again offered a tiny idol of Hindu deity called Devi. Though the Hrangkhols and Sakachep accepted the gifts and one of the Hindu deities called Devi was included in their traditional pantheon of *Chung Pathen* (High God), they were afraid that their own God might be angry with them. They also feared reprisal from the King of Tripura who insisted on including Hindu gods in their pantheon. As a result, due to the fear of the wrath of the Vairengpa, the Biates finally left Tripura says the legends.[8] Archaeological evidences of the Biates settlements in North Cachar Hills is found in Kobak village.

The territory inhabited by the Kuki-Chin tribes extends from the Naga Hills in the north down into the Sandoway district of Mynamar in the south; from the Myittha River in the east, almost to the Bay of Bengal in the west.[9] Inhabiting such vast territories from time immemorial, it is safe to say the Kukis considered themselves to be safekeepers of the lands dwelled upon by them. Whenever wrongful killings was done, steps were taken to ensure that such incidents were curbed by exacting revenge, i.e. a life for a life and for the proof of the kills, heads were taken. This was the nature of revenge that the Kukis followed in order to retain territories and maintain their strongholds. Before the British came to the region the entire valleys adjacent to the hills were virtually under the control of the Poitoo Kukis over which the Tripperah Rajahs claimed authority in theory but the former were practically independent from its authority. They protected the whole valleys from all intrusions.[10] The character of revenge took shape in the North Cachar Hills in 1850 between the Kukis and the Nagas, when some Nagas had killed one Thado-Kuki Chief. The nature of vengeance was serious whereby the Thados, with 350 fighting men followed up, at which all the villagers fled for safety. The Naga Gangbura, being left alone, was killed by the Kuki.[11] Hence, the Kukis maintained their independence even during the time of the Ahom rule and continued to do so until the 'Anglo-Kuki War' (1917-19), when the Kukis were subjugated by the British. It was this belongingness and authority on the land which prompted the Kukis to take necessary measures to safeguard their ancestors' land, and one method to furnish their agenda was the method of head hunting.

In the borders of the Chittagong Hill Tracts, the Kukis are known by the name of Lushai. They extend in numberless hordes, north and north-east, until they reach Cachar on the one hand, and the frontiers of Mynamar on the other.[12] The peculiarity of the Kukis is that they have distinct differences in their languages, but can understand each other well unlike the Nagas. They are known to the Bengalis by the name of Kookie, and to the Burmese as the Lankhe. Thus, for an individual, who does not have prior knowledge about this community, it is but, natural to be confused. They are again further divided into clans and sub-clans. In terms of head hunting the Lushais were not far behind their neighbouring tribes. In fact, the term 'Lushai' has been of debate among the colonizers regarding the meaning. J. Shakespeare was of the opinion that 'Lushei' was a combination of 'lu', head, and 'shei', long. Earlier to him T.H. Lewin suggested that the name 'Lushai' was from '*lu*' (head) and '*sha*' (to cut). While Shakespeare believed that head hunting was practised originally by the Thado-Kuki, the Lushai-Kuki were raiders, who also did not hesitate to take heads as a proof of killing during the raids.

Some specific raids carried certain importance, when a great Chief or a Rajah died. The nature of these raids carried spiritual and social value in the sense that it was a way of projecting the significance of the late Chief, a kind of allegiance paid to him in the form of heads which would be buried along with him. Similarly, a head would mean an additional slave to serve him at the *Mithikho*, whereas a common individual have to hunt heads for on his own during war or as opportunity arose. The Kukis owned specific weapons exclusively for hunting and war; a small bow with poisoned arrows, a spear and a *dao*, or sword, a most destructive kind of heavy short sword. They did not attack their enemies openly in the day, but stole on them by night and having surrounded the place to be attacked, at the break of day, rushed in on every quarter and exterminated young and old, women and children indiscriminately. If they were completely successful, a few might be spared to be kept as slaves. Previous to setting out on a hostile incursion, they offered a pig as a sacrifice to the deity. If any one of the parties was slain by the enemy, the corpse was buried on the spot without burning, the customary ceremonies were dispensed with and neither relatives or friends lamented together on the occasion. If victorious, they brought home the heads of their enemies and on reaching their villages the warriors dressed out in their war attire had a dance, beat drums, played bamboo pipes and the instrument called *jhanjh*, after which the heads of their enemies were fastened to a pole and put up where three or four roads met together.

In a memoir on Sylhet, Cachar and other districts by the late Captain Fisher, formerly Superintendent of Cachar, that officer states . . . that the object of the Kuki inroads on the plains is not plunder, for which they have never been known to show any desire but they kill and carry away the heads of as many human beings as they can seize and have been known in one night to carry off fifty. These are used in certain ceremonies performed at the funerals of their Chiefs, and it is always after the death of one of their Rajahs that their incursions occur. As narrated by T.H. Lewin on getting the firsthand account of head hunting done by his housekeeper:

A young man, a Riang Tipperah, who lives in my house, was formerly a slave of Rutton Poia's (a Lhooshai Chief), and I have heard from him many accounts of raids made by his master. He used to accompany the Chief as the bearer of his weapons. His first raid was in 1860, made on the Bengallee inhabitants of Kundal in Tipperah. They fell upon the villagers at day-dawn, according to custom; and the Bengallee man, with one consent, ran away. The women, however, stood their ground, and abused their grim assailants vociferously for breaking into honest people's houses. The Lhoosai laughed at their shrilled tongues at first, but later it was found troublesome, and one young woman had to be caught down *pour encourager les autres*. The Chief confided to my boy's care two women, captives. All the prisoners were fastened together by a chord through the lobe of the ears, and the Lhoosai set out with their plunder on the return journey. Now, one of the captive women was young and not accustomed to walking; so after the first day's march her feet swelled, and she was unable to go further. The Chief, therefore, ordered that she should be speared. 'well,' said the narrator, 'I took the spear and went towards her, and Rutton Poia said, 'Do it neatly, I will look on,' for it was the first time I had ever speared anyone. When the girl saw me take the spear and come towards her she fell a—weeping, and caught my garments and my hands, and all my heart thumped, and I could not hurt her. It was pitiful! So the Chief began to laugh at me and said, 'o white-livered, and son of a female dog, when we return to the village, I will tell the young maidens of your courage;' so I shut my eyes and speared her. My stroke was ill-directed, and she did not die; so the Chief finished the work and he made me lick the spear. The blood of Bengallees is very salty. Since then I have not been afraid to spear anyone.[13]

The Lushais went a step further and indulged in mild cannibalism, i.e. eating a piece of liver of the first slain enemy, which is believed to give strength and courage to the heart.

The Kukis identified themselves as belonging to one tribe prior to their dispersion on the basis of two virtual facts, one being architecture and the other a possession of flute called *pheiphit*. The former concerns itself with the structure of the house built with particular features known to an individual belonging to Kuki community:

> The *pheiphit* is a bamboo flute without holes. One end of the flute is closed by its natural knob. The other end is scraped a little for the player to hold it easily between the lips while playing. It is interesting to note that a single flute produces only one tone. Though, different players play on separate flutes simultaneously yet they are able to produce a sort of harmony between the notes of the several flutes like in a modern mouth organ. At the most, seven to eight separate tones are simultaneously produced from the same number of flutes.[14]

In the context of rituals around the world, *Headhunting and the Body in Iron Age Europe* by Ian Armit portrays the various aspects of head hunting during Iron Age in Europe. Of this, the most interesting perspective was that of Richard Bradley, an anthropologist who firmly separates ritual from religion; two concepts that are frequently confused. Ritual acts need not be religious in character. Though, they may involve interactions with the supernatural, rituals may also be essentially secular, centring on communication primarily between performers and the audience. But ritual acts do, necessarily relate to one or more of the triad of religion, cosmology, and ideology. He was of the opinion that decapitation may be ritualized as a means of accommodating it within a religious, cosmological, or ideological framework. So ritualization in a way can justify use of violence for a simple desire for personal power, slaves, land or tribute and more or less involve taking of heads.[15] In the article, *Heady Business: Skulls, Heads and Decapitation in Neolithic Anatolia and Greece*, Lauren E. Talalay states that, trophy head-taking by Indonesian, Indian, and Malaysian head hunters, however, reifies ideals of masculine prowess, honour, pride, and heroism, and procuring heads during warfare was officially sanctioned by both the Romans and the Assyrians. However, the author is of the opinion that the head was viewed as a discursive element of the body it reflected and helped construct complex ideologies. Futhermore, he adds that the head's presence, absence, adornment, and modification in various contexts and guises were regularly used to affirm, deny, submerge or give voice to individual and collective powers or identities where fragmenting the body at the neck can connect rather to the concept of continuity and rebirth.[16] Anahit Yu Khudaverdyan in the article, *Ritual and ceremonial dismembering bones in a burials in Bronze and Iron centuries from Armenian Plateau* says that the most common and widely distributed war trophy was the human head and to acquire an enemy's head was the sign of utmost valour and humiliation to the defeated foes. While deposition of human skulls has been interpreted as evidence for a head hunting cult, the accumulated skulls were also believed to provide symbolic protection. Also, the human skulls were used to communicate with the deceased and were supposed to secure power to the succeeding generations too. Adding to taking heads, there were also other forms of humiliating the enemies such as scalping. On some occasions, scalping took two forms—mourning war and shame-aggression war. Mourning war was a mechanism developed to externalize grief and hostility and was a cooperative action, involving a war party. Male mourners organized a response to death and disease, and the party did not establish an individual target for their grief. The first member of the enemy clan or tribe they encountered was killed and the scalp of the victim was brought back to the village and rituals were performed.[17]

As far as perspectives were concerned, head hunting was assumed as one of the primitive practices of the tribes around the world:

> For early European colonialists, encountering previously unknown peoples and attempting to come to terms with alien cultural practices and values, head hunting was the epitome of savagery. Head hunting raids seldom obeyed the proper rules of military engagement. They were often ambushes or surprise attacks aimed at overpowering individuals or small groups with little hope of defending themselves. Victims were often women, children and the elderly, suggesting a rather ungallant approach to battle out of keeping with the ethos (if not the reality) of Western modes of war. In the absence of any real understanding of the cosmological background that so often structured head hunting practices, most saw the removal and display of heads as simple trophy taking—an abominable denigration of the dead.[18]

In the nineteenth and early twentieth centuries, images of head hunting were an inextricable part of popular ideas of tribal peoples around the fringes of the European colonial world. More recently, however, head hunting has been effectively written out of the ethnographies of many non-Western peoples. Not unnaturally, anthropologists wishing to avoid stigmatizing their subjects have downplayed or simply omitted those behaviours that seem to align too easily with the popular stereotype of the savage'. Phenomena such as head hunting, cannibalism, and human sacrifice, which were the staples of nineteenth- and early twentieth-century ethnographic writing, and which helped form a persistent and pervasive popular caricature of the primitive', have, thus, almost disappeared from view.[19]

Anthropologist Christoph von Furer-Haimendorf described the head hunting rituals of the Konyak Nagas as follows:

> Following the welcome of the returning headhunters by the village elders and other men of the community, the captured head was taken to an area outside the village, close to where the heads of ancestors were kept in their stone cists' or pillars. There the trophy was pelted with raw eggs to blind the kinsmen of the dead foe'. Rice beer was then poured into its mouth, accompanied by invocations to the victim's kin to come and surrender themselves to the victorious headhunters. After this initial ceremony, the head was taken into the village itself where there was period of dancing in front of the cult house or morung', and the headhunters were ritually washed. The head itself was tied to a log gong, which was beaten during the festivities. Later the head was placed on a post in front of the morung, accompanied by a further period of dancing. On the day after its arrival, the head was taken in procession by the men of the village, all bedecked in body paint and ceremonial costume, to a ritual area specified for the purpose, where a priest' (usually the senior descendant of the village founder) cut off parts of the ears and tongue and once again called on the victim's kinsmen. This part of the ceremony was accompanied by the sacrifice of a chicken and reading of its entrails. The head was then hung from a tree and, for a period of a day, no work was done and the village was given over to dancing and feasting. After a month had passed, a further feast was held, during which the head was taken down from its tree, given rice beer to drink', and deposited in the morung.[20]

However, there are certain exceptions, when it comes to keeping of the heads collected and they are not treated equally as based on how and why the skulls were accumulated. Such is the case of tribes found in Africa like the Kagoro, Attakka, Moroa, Katab and Kajji namely:

> Peoples of the same origin may fight each other —even different members of a single family will do that—but they never keep the heads of their victims as trophies of war, though they retain those of their enemies, and, even if taken during the actual fighting, they are given back to the dead man's relatives to be buried with the bodies on the declaration of peace. If this were not done, the ghosts of the victims would have to serve those of their slayers in the next world, and although such a condition of affairs would be most desirable in the case of war with an enemy, it is not considered good form to make one's own blood relations (or should I say spirits?) do such work. And in fact, it is quite possible that such a ghost would work harm rather than good to the slayer, since it, and only it, can worry any of its living relatives, a ghost of a stranger being harmless.[21]

Feuds were of common occurrence among the groups which sometimes took a toll on the relations between them. One incident describes the gravity of the situation:

> The people of Babban Gidda had a feast to which they invited a number of Gannawarri, and having made five of their guests drunk, they shut them up in a hut and killed them, the rest of the honoured guests managing to escape. The heads of the victims were then cut off, and were set up by the chief in his house as a memorial of the gallant deed.[22]

The tools used by the headhunters were as follows:

> The weapons of the head-hunters were (1) a wooden club, (2) a knife, (3) the bow and arrow, (4) the sling, (5) the spear for throwing or thrusting, and (6) the shield. The club might be a mere thick stick, or a knob-kerry, or it may be a heavy wide (flat surface) similar, as with the Kagoma, or a longer, narrower one of light wood as with the Ayu. The knife might be of the usual dagger shape, or the handle might be in the form of an oval ring, and it would be bought from a Hausa trader, or else made in their own towns by foreign blacksmiths. The bow was not strengthened in any way, being a piece of merely bent wood some three to five feet long, but a ring might be worn on the right thumb when drawing it, so as to give a better grip on the missile. The arrows had iron heads with flanges and were poisoned, the shafts being notched but not feathered, and usually about three feet in length, but Jigya used some 4 feet 8 inches against the last patrol. The Toffs used

wooden-pointed arrows, the tips of which broke off on touching the target; the object in both cases being of course to keep the poison-bearing material in contact with the flesh as long as possible. Fire arrows are unknown, and this was rather surprising, considering the fact that the burning of the enemy's town was one of the objects of every attacking force.[23]

The beliefs of Mithikho as perceived by the Kukis and Nagas of north-east India were similar to those of the Kagoro group, Africa. The group believed: 'that the ghosts of the victims must serve that of the slayer in the next world, every householder in addition inheriting in some way the benefits from the heads collected by his ancestors, as well as from those he himself obtained'.[24]

Furthermore, there is evidence to prove that, amongst many tribes, cannibalism arose out of a belief that eating a man caused his good qualities to pass into the body of the host, which was based on the idea that special foods had special effects on the body, and then on the brain and nerves, carried a little further. So brave enemies were eagerly sought out, and the more gallant the foe, the more certain was he of providing a 'joint of black brother' for his captors, if he were unlucky enough to be taken prisoner. Or again, the victim might be one famed for his magical powers, or remarkable in some other way above his fellows.[25]

Philippine Scholar Renato Rosaldo his discusses *Ilongot Headhunting, 1881-1974: A Study in Society and History* written by the politics of head hunting in the following points:

- The taking of a human life with a view towards cleansing the participants of the contaminating burdens of their own lives. Once cleansed through participation in a successful raid, the men were said to become 'light' in weight, 'quick' of step, and 'red' in complexion.
- Head hunting made an individual eligible to wear red hornbill earrings mostly to gain the admiration of young women and to be able to answer back when other men taunted. 'Others will scorn you if you marry without taking a head'. But it was not obligatory for Ilongot men to take a head before marriage, a misconception widespread in Philippine ethnography and popular culture.
- Taking of a human head initiated the young man, a first major

step from his childhood and youth, centred in his family to marriage. Head hunting and marriage were the two critical moments in a period conceived of as the only significant rupture in the otherwise continuous course of the life cycle. Celebrated in ritual, story, song, and oratory, this change in social status was culturally elaborated to a greater extent than any other throughout the Ilongot lifetime.

- Feuds between families, clans and groups resulting in revenge in the form of head hunting.

Regarding the challenges in documentation of the oral tradition of the Ilongot, in their stories of wandering in terror, people uniformly listed the names of every foraged item of food and where it was found; every brook crossed and every hill scaled; every spot where they stopped to rest or eat or sleep. Piling place name upon place name, people's sagas of 1945, as noted earlier, appeared initially to be as irrelevant for Ilongot ethnography as they were impossible.

HEAD HUNTING AND ITS PLACE IN THE CHON RITUAL

The evidence of head hunting among the Kukis is mentioned in one ritual of Chon performed by the Chongthu man named Thangpi.

A large trunk of the tree named *kheng-thing* with its branches left intact was erected on the outskirts of the village where the evil spirits were believed to be living in subduement. Except for the branches at the top, the ends of the other branches were chopped off. At each end of the pruned branches, the skulls of the killed enemies were kept transfixed.[26]

The second day Chon ritual known as *gam-va-sa-neh-ni-galan pehni* set apart for giving a feast to the warriors, who fought in the battles and also to the souls of the killed enemies.

On this day between sunrise and noon all the different kinds of animals were killed by Thangpi himself. After dressing the meat the *Bechas* packed the meat pieces into thirty-two bundles. A very strong kind of wine was prepared by the

Tuchas and was poured into thirty-two bronze jars. These thirty-two jars of wine and thirty-two packets of meat were taken to the outskirts of the village by the *Bechas* and the *Tuchas*. The party was accompanied by Thangpi along with his priest named Sanglhu and the warriors. At a place in the outskirts, the warriors were given a feast. The whole party consisted of thirty-two persons.[27]

THE WARRIORS DRESS

The warriors who presented to Thangpi the skulls of the enemies and of the wild animals had attired themselves in the following manner:

Each of them put over his shoulder like a baldric a shawl with its ends knotted over the breast. They also wore the feathers of the jungle crow and the *tuhpahs*, the quivers with arrows, the bracelets, the arm plates and carried with them the *sou* (very sharp and pointed spikes made from bamboo splits and dry bones. To escape from the enemies these spikes were planted on the path to work as deadly obstacles for the enemies). Besides, they had the armours and the shields.

All of them led by Thangpi marched in formation to the outskirts of the village. At the head of of the column, the great Thangpi stood. Behind him stood Sanglhu the priest. They were followed by the warriors. Singing the song of the brave they marched towards the village outskirts. They sang the following song:

Ka thange ka thange namtin
Khovai phei laija. Chong hi
Tu son ka thange. Ka jon ei choie
Nam cham pha bagl eichoi je
Chunin eichije aikep pha bang eichije

Translation:
I am famous, I am renowned amidst all the
People of the village. I am the descendant
of Chongthu and as such I am famous. My
father loves and praises me as he love and
praises a good two-edged sword. My mother
loves and praises me as she loves and praises
a *conch* shell.

After reaching the selected place in the outskirts of the village, all of them gathered round the ritualistic stone erected for casting hyp-notical spell on the evil spirits to prevent them from entering the village. All the persons stood encircling the *Khengthing* post and observed the warriors transfixing the skulls of the killed enemies (*gal-lu*) on the chopped out branches of the *Khengthing*. Looking at the transfixed skulls of the enemies Thangpi said the following words:

O my enemies! Come and have your food.
I have made a platform on the tree.
I am standing below with my sword in hand.

(Thangpi was inviting the spirits of the dead enemies to partake of the food he had placed on the platform constructed at half height of the *Khengthing*. This was actually a subtle warning given by Thangpi to the spirits of the enemies that he was on his guard with his sword below the *Khengthing*.)

He then said heroically:

I am the son of Chongthu.
Your grandfather Failed to vanquish
my grandfather. Your Father failed
to conquer my father and you
Were also unsuccessful in defeating me.

After saying that Thangpi slashed the surface of the ground with a stroke of his sword with great force. This action was immediately followed by singing of the victory song (*hanla*) and yells of the victory that echoed and re-echoed.[28]

It is important to note that the warriors, who had failed to kill enemies and wild elephants, were not allowed to participate in the singing of the victory songs called *hanla* songs. In the Chon ritual the process of performing ritual was done usually seven times but in *Sha-Ai* it was done three times which was less compared to Chon.[29] The former ritual demanded everything to be done seven times. Seven *mithuns* were to be killed and everything else must be in multiples of seven. So rigorous was the Chon ritual that in a generation only two or one individual was able to perform it. In my opinion more than the Chon ritual itself the *Sha-Ai* ceremony was of utmost importance since the latter prepared the grounds for the former to take place. The origin of *Sha-Ai* was said to have began when an individual had slain animals more than his requirement. So, for the friends of the slain animals to prevent revenge on the hunter, a particular ceremony was performed. There the remains of the hunted animals, and in most cases tigers, were buried on the outskirts of the village and a tiger's replica was made. A song was sung by the individuals dressed in women's attire, which was suppose to mock the slain tiger. The song is as follows:

Nangin lamsah najot leh,
Ken lamlhang jot ingting.
Nang meipum, nang tin, nang ha;
Chu imacha hipontin.
Ka meipum thonda hen lang,
Ka kap leh nathin nalung tongkha henlang.
Tengle, napun lah eijou lou,
Napan lah kappa joulou.
Nangin lah kei neijou lou;
Nalung kachop a kachop khop jou,
Navai kachop a kachop khoplou.

Translation:

If you walk the upward path,
I will take the lower path.
Your guns, your nails, your teeth;
It is of no use then.
May my gun not lose its aim,
If I shoot it goes through your liver and your heart.
Then, your master could not defeat me
Your master could not defeat my master.
You could not defeat me.
I could easily jump above your heart,
Your length is not enough for me to jump over.

After this song, a stone was erected with chants for the tiger's kin to read lest they happen to take revenge on the village, while passing by. It was believed that, if the tiger's allies witnessed this ritual, it further dissuaded them from attacking the village. In course of time, there must have been a scarcity of animals due to excessive hunting. Conversion to Christianity also made the Kukis stop using the chants during rituals, as it was considered an abomination by the missionaries. Till the 1960s, Thonghao Kholhou and Tongsai Haolai of Vattop Leikeh perfomed *Sha-Ai* and *Chang-Ai* respectively.[30] There is no mention of women warriors participating in head hunting.

With the coming of the colonial government to the Kuki territories, the people went through a gradual change, their rituals too were considered an abomination with the coming of the Christian missionaries. Thus, head hunting was controlled and curbed both by the colonial government and the Christian missionaries to achieve their respective propaganda, i.e. control the 'wild' tribes. Decline of head hunting made the Kukis more approachable by the colonizers. It impacted the oral tradition of memorizing their ancestors' name not mandatory since it was used during rituals and head hunting. The modern era has ensured the Kukis better living conditions in exchange of the genealogy of their ancestors which was learned with much jest by the youngsters in earlier days.

NOTES

1. Lalmuanpui Khiangte, 'Moving Community: An investigation into the Migration and Non-settlement of the Kuki in North Eastern India (colonial period)'. Unpublished PhD thesis, Assam University, 2010, Silchar, p. 90.
2. John, Rawlins,'On the Manners, Religion, and Laws of the Cucis, or Mountaineers of Tipra', *Asiatic Researches* (vol. II, 5th edn.), p. 188.
3. T.H., Lewin, *Wild Races of South-eastern India*, WM H. Allen & CO., 1870, first edn. Reprint 2018, p. 283.
4. Lalmuanpui Khiangte, 'Moving Community: An investigation into the Migration and Non-settlement of the Kuki in North Eastern India (Colonial Period)'. Unpublished PhD thesis, Department of History, Assam University, 2010, Silchar, p. 90.
5. S.L., Baruah, *A Comprehensive History of Assam*, Munshiram Manoharlal Publishers, New Delhi, 2013 (5th rpt.), p. 379.

6. Jangkhomang Guite, 'Raja Lalsuhkla: Legendary king of the Kukis in Hallamram', *Souvenir: The 1st Barak Valley Chavang Kut*, 2012, p. 28.
7. Amalendu Nag, ' Urban Self- Government and Town Development (a case study of Hailakandi town)'. Unpublished PhD Thesis, Department of Sociology, Assam University, 2004, Silchar, p. 35.
8. Ramdina,Lalsim, *History of the Biates: One of the Oldest Hill Tribes of Assam*, first edition, Assam Institute of Research for Tribals and Scheduled Castes, Guwahati, 2013, pp. 56-7.
9. G.A. Grierson, 'Specimen of Kuki-Chin', *Linguistic Survey of India*, published by the Superintendent of Government Printing, India, Calcutta. 1904, p. 1.
10. Jangkhomang Guite, 'Raja Lalsuhkla: Legendary king of the Kukis in Hallamram', *Souvenir: The 1st Barak Valley Chavang Kut*, 2012, p. 28.
11. A.J. Moffat Mills, 'Jenkins letter to Moffat Mills', *Reports on Assam*, Govt. of Assam Calcutta, 1854, rpt., Assam Publication Board, Gauhati, 1984, preface, p. CXXXVIII.
12. T.H. Lewin, *Wild Races of South-eastern India*, WM H. Allen & CO., 1870, first edn. reprint 2018, p. 246.
13. Ibid., pp. 267-8.
14. Tarun Goswami, *Kuki Life and Lore*, first edition, Haflong: North Cachar Hills District Council, 1985, p. 268.
15. Ian Armit, *Headhunting and the Body in Iron Age Europe*; Cambridge University Press, New York, 2012, p. 14.
16. Lauren Talalay, 'Heady Business: Skulls, Heads, and Decapitation in Neolithic Anatolia and Greece', *Journal of Mediterranean Archaeology*, December 2004, DOI: 10.1558/jmea.17.2.139.65540, p. 139.
17. Anahit Yu, 'Khudaverdyan, Ritual and Ceremonial dismembering Bones in a burials in Bronze and Iron centuries from Armenian Plateau', *Journal of Antropologija*, no. 2 (14), April 2018, pp. 163-95.
18. Ian Armit, *Headhunting and the Body in Iron Age Europe*, Cambridge University Press, New York, 2012, p. 48.
19. Ibid., p. 48.
20. Ibid., p. 54-5.
21. A.J.N. Tremearne, *The Tailed Headhunters of Nigeria: An Account of an Officials Seven Years Experiences in the Northern Nigerian Pagan Belt, and a Description of the Manners, Habits and Customs of the Native Tribes*, Seeley, Service. London, 1912, p. 95.
22. Ibid., p. 154.
23. Ibid., p. 157.
24. Ibid., p. 180.

25. Ibid., p. 181.
26. Tarun Goswami, *Kuki Life and Lore*, first edition, Haflong: North Cachar Hills District Council, 1985, p. 269.
27. Ibid., pp. 270-1.
28. Ibid., p. 472.
29. See William Shaw, *Notes on the Thadou Kukis*, published on behalf of the Government of Assam, Shillong, 1928,
30. Moungpao Thangew interviewed by Tingneilam Thangew, 25 October 2020, Songpijang, N.C. Hills.

CHAPTER 10

Human Sacrifice in Assam*

EDWARD GAIT

The existence in Assam of the practice of offering human sacrifices in ancient times has often been mentioned; but, so far as I am aware, no detailed account has ever been given of the extent to which the practice prevailed and the manner in which such sacrifices were carried out. The tribes amongst whom the practice is known to have been common, are the Koches, Kacharis, Chutiyas, Tipperas and the people of Jaintia. A peculiar form of sacrifice was and still is, in vogue amongst the Khasis, but this is based on purely non-Hindu superstitions, whereas amongst the other tribes mentioned, the custom seems to be more or less closely connected with the rites enjoined in the *Kalaika Purana.*

HUMAN SACRIFICES AMONGST THE KOCHES

The prevalence of the custom of offering human sacrifices amongst the Koches is known from a statement in the *Vamsavali* of Raja Lakshmi Narayana Konar, of which a fairly full summary was given in my article on the Koch Kings of Kamarupa, which was published in *Journal of the Asiatic Society of Bengal* (vol. LXII, pt. I, p. 268). It is stated in this *Vamcavali* that, when Raja Nara Narayana rebuilt the temnple of Kamakhya in AD 1565, he celebrated the occasion by the sacrifice of no less than a hundred and forty men, whose heads he offered to the goddess on salvers made of copper. It

*Reprinted from *Journal of Asiatic Society of Bengal,* vol. 61, pt. III, 1898, pp. 56-65.

is not stated there how the victims were obtained for the sacrifice, but it appears from the *Halt Iqlim* that on some occasions at least persons were found willing to come forward as voluntary victims. Such persons were known as *Bhogis*, and from the time when they announced that the goddess had called them, they were treated as privileged persons. They were allowed to do whatevery they liked, and every woman was at their command, until the annual festival came round, when they were sacrificed to the goddess.

AMONGST THE KACHARIES

In Cachar, there is a legend that Raja Nirbhar Narayana, the forty-fifth Kachari king was a very pious man according to the traditional list of kings. One day, while meditating in the temple, he heard a voice, which said that, if he could go to the river next morning at daybreak and catch hold of whatever he might find there fearlessly, he would obtain the object of his worship in living form. On proceedings to the river, the king saw a poisonous snake swimming towards him; he caught hold of it, whereon it twisted round his arm, and the king being alarmed tried to shake it off. On this the snake changed into a sword, and the king took it to the temple, where he lamented the loss, which he had sustained through his fears. Soon he heard a voice, which told him that, owing to his timidity, the object of his worship had assumed the form of a sword; he was told to name it 'Rana Chandi', to worship it regularly, and to offer human sacrifices to it annually. To this origin is ascribed the practice which undoubtedly prevailed of offering human sacrifices in the Kachari Raj. The victims were Hindus of any caste other than Brahmanas, who were kidnapped for the purpose from places outside the Hidamba Raj. The practices said to have been put a stop to in the reign of Raja Gobinda Chandra, in consequence of a Brahman having narrowly escaped being sacrificed by mistake.

AMONGST THE CHUTIYAS

From a very early period, the practice of offering human sacrifices was common amongst the Chutiyas, the pre-Ahom rulers of

Upper Assam, whose priests or Deoris were in the habit of offering human sacrifices at the Copper Temple at Sadiya and elsewhere, the object of their worship being Durga under the name of Kesai Khati, the eater of raw human flesh.

These sacrifices were offered on certain stated occasions and also to avert special calamities, such as cholera, small-pox, and droughts. Kamakhya is one of the three deities to whom the offering human sacrifices is enjoined in the *Kalika Purana.* The name of the Goddess is there given as mother, and she was said to reside in a cave. The same story is told as accounting for the partial discontinuance of the practice of offering human sacrifice in Jaintia. Dalton, who gives a very full account of this revolting practice amongst the Chutiyas, conjectures that the sacrifices were originally offered to some aboriginal deity and that it was only when the influence of Hinduism began to be felt that, the name was changed to Durga. In support of this view, he points to the fact that the officiating priests were members of a Mongolian tribe and not Brahmans. But this argument may easily be pressed too far. We known that all the lower castes are ministered to by caste, and may not be true, Brahmans and the same mingle easily be the case amongst the Chutiyas, it is only in comparatively recent years. That the Chutiyas and Ahoms have in large numbers embraced orthodox Hinduism and placed themselves under the protection of Gohains, but it is now known that the beliefs which they professes prior to this formal conversion, were very largely of a Hindu character. This subject, however, is one which requires separate treatment. After the subjugation of the Chutiyas by the Ahoms, the Deoris, were still permitted to continue their ghastly rites, but they were usually given as victims criminals who had been sentenced to capital punishment. When none such were obtainable, a particular section of the population or Khel (known as the Baruali Khel) was called upon to produce one, in return for which certain privileges were granted to the members of the Khel. On a woman of the Khel becoming pregnant, the astrologers were called on to say whether the child would be a boy or a girl, and if they predicted that it would be a boy, the mother was carefully looked after, and the child was anointed, as soon as it was born, with a paste made of tamarind and *matikalai* (*Phaseolus radiates*). When a sacrifice was thought necessary, volunteers were called for, and some person usually came forward of his own accord, if not, a victim was taken by force. In either case, the victim was shaved, anointed with the paste of tamarind and *matikalai*, and decked with gold and silver ornaments. He was then conducted before the image of the goddess, when he prostrated himself, and was promptly decapitated by the Bar Deroi or High Priest. The body was left on the spot until the following morning, when it was removed. Victims were taken only from amongst the juvenile male members of the clan; on attaining full age they became exempt and were allowed to marry and settle down. According to Dalton, it was necessary that the victims to be immolated should be of pure caste and in perfect form, the slightest blemish or mutilation rendering them unfit to be offered to the goddess. Brahmans and members of the royal family were exempted as a privilege; Doms, Haris, Musalmans, and women were excluded.

For some time preceding the sacrifice, the victim to be immolated was detained at the temple, where he was fed sumptuously, till in sufficiently plump condition to suit the supposed taste of the Gucant. On the appointed day, he was led forth, magnificently attired and decorated with gold and silver ornaments, to be shown to the multitude that assembled on the occasion, then withdrawn and led by a private path trodden only by the officiating priests and their victims to the brink of a deep pit, where he was divested of his fineries and decapitated, so that the body fell into the pit. The head was added to a heap of ghastly skulls that were piled in view of the shrine.

AMONGST THE TIPPERAS

As regards the Tipperas, the information is more scanty. Several references are, however, made to human sacrifices in the Rajmala or chronicles of the kings of Tippera. It is related there that Deva Manikya, who reigned from AD 1522 to 1535, offered up some slaves as a sacrifice to 'the fourteen gods', but the sacrifice was not accepted, and the chief priest announced that Mahadeva had ordered the sacrifice of the best commanders of the army. Deva Manikya obeyed and gave up his eight best commanders to be immolated. His successor, Vijaya Manikya (AD 1535 to 1583), it is said on two occasions defeated the Musalmans, and offered the Pathans and 'others', who had been taken prisoners as sacrifices to 'the fourteen gods'.

AMONGST THE JAINTIA

In the case of Jaintia, a very full account of the practice has been sent by Babu Girish Chanda Dasa, Assistant Settlement Officer. It appears that human sacrifices were offered annually on the Sandhi day in the month of *Ashvin* (*shukla paksha*) at the sacred *pitha* in the Faljur pargana. They were also occasionally offered at the shrine of Jainteshwari at Nijpat, the capital of the country. As stated in the Haft Iqlim to have been the case in Koch Bihar, so also in Jaintia, persons frequently came forward voluntarily as victims. This they generally did, by appearing before the Raja on the last day of *Shravan* and declaring that the Goddess had called them. After due enquiry, if the would-be victim or Bhoge Khaora were deemed suitable, it was customary for the Raja to present him with a golden anklet and to give him permission to live, as he chose and to do whatever he pleased, compensation for any damage done by him being paid from the royal treasury. But his enjoyment of these privileges was very short. On the *navami* day of the Durga Puja, the Bhoge Kharoa, after bathing and purifying himself, was dressed in new attire, daubed with red sandalwood and vermilion, and bedecked with garlands. Thus arrayed, the victim sat on a raised dais in front of the goddess and spent some time in meditation (*japa*) and in uttering *mantras*. Having done this, he made a sign with his finger, and the executioner forthwith cut-off his head, which was placed before the Goddess on a golden plate. The lungs were cooked and eaten by such Kadra *yogis* as were present, and it is said that the royal family partook of a small quantity of rice cooked in the blood of the victim. The ceremony was usually witnessed by large crowds of spectators from all parts of the Jaintia Parganas.

Sometimes, the supply of voluntary victims fell short or victims were needed for some special sacrifice promised in the event of some desired occurrence, such as the birth of a son, coming to pass. On such occasions, emissaries were sent to kidnap strangers from outside the Jaintia Raj, and it was this which eventually led to the annexation of the country by the British. In 1821, an attempt was made to kidnap a native of Sylhet proper and while the agents employed were punished, the Raja was warned not to allow such an atrocity to occur again, Eleven years later, however, four British subjects were kidnapped in the Nowgong district and taken to Jaintia Chieftains. Three of them were actually sacrificed, but the fourth escaped and reported the matter to the authorities. The Raja of Jaintia was called on to deliver up the culprits, but he failed to do so, and his dominions were in consequence annexed in 1835.

The origin of human sacrifices amongst the Khasis is fully explained in the following extract from a Resolution by the Chief Commissioner of Assam on the Administration Report of the Khasi and Jaintia Hills district for the year 1881-2:

Among the cases tried this year, were three murders of singular atrocity, two of them committed on influensive old women, and one on a boy; in none of them was any adequate cause alleged, and at least two of them are believed to have been connected with the very remarkable superstition of the *Thlen.* Tradition is that there was once in a cave near Cherrapunji a gigantic snake, or *Thlen,* who committed great havoc among men and animals. At last, one man, bolder than his fellows, took with him a herd of goats, and set himself down by the cave and offered them one by one to the *Thlen.* By degrees the monster became friendly, and learnt to open his mouth, at a word from the man, to receive the lump of flesh, which was then thrown in. When confidence was thoroughly established, the man heated a lump of iron red hot in a furnace, induced the snake, at the usual signal, to open his mouth, and then threw in the red hot lump, and so killed him. He then cut up the body and sent pieces in every direction, with orders that the people were to eat them. Wherever the order was obeyed, the country became free of the *Thlen*; but one small piece remained which no one would eat, and from this sprang a multitude of *Thlen,* which infest the residents of Cherrapunji and its neighbourhood (including Shillong). When a *Thlen* take up its abode in a family, there is no means of getting rid of it, though it occasionally leaves of its own accord, and often follows property of the family when given away or sold. The *Thlen* attaches itself to wealth, and brings prosperity and wealth to the family, but on the condition that it is supplied with blood. Its craving comes on at uncertain intervals, and manifests itself by sickness among the family, by misadventure or increasing poverty. It can only be appeased by the murder of a human bring. The murderer takes the hair, the tips of the fingers, and a little blood from the nostrils, caught in a bamboo tube and offers these to the *Thlen.* The belief is that the demon then appears in the form of a snake and devours the body of the murdered person, which is materialized from the portions, thus offered. After this, its craving is satisfied for a time, and the affairs of that house prosper. Many families in these hills are known or suspected to be *R-thlen,* or keepers of a *Thlen,* and are dreaded and avoided in consequence. Whenever a dead body is found with the marks above described on it (and particularly if it is killed with no wound, but by twisting the neck), it may be presumed with almost absolute certainty that the object of the murder was to appease a *Thlen.* This happened in one of the three instances referred to in the others these marks were not found, but in the absence of any other cause for the murder, it was more than probable that it was due to this dreadful superstition. In each of the three cases one or two persons (though perhaps not all the accomplices), were convicted; one man was hanged, and the rest were sentenced to transportation for life or for a terms of years.

CONCLUSION

The above is a summary of all that one has been able to gather regarding the custom of sacrificing human being in Assam, one has not referred to the taking of life for reasons other than sacrificial purposes, and so no reference has been made to the practice of head-hunting so common amongst many of the hill tribes, or to the old Ahom custom of slaughtering all prisoners taken in battle and making of their heads a chaplet of skulls. Neither, has it been attempted to discuss the subject of human sacrifices generally or to trace its origin, as these general questions have already been dealt with by more competent hands.

CHAPTER 11

Bej Bejali in the Assamese Socio-cultural Context

VANDANA GOSWAMI

Bej is a very common word in Assamese everyday parlance. A *bej* is a healer; but at the same time, the word invokes terror as the *bej* are seen to cause utmost harm. It is an ambivalent term, shrouded in mystery, the occult, as well as healing. The cultural category of *bej* and the practice associated with this concept, popularly called *bejali* is analysed in this article. An attempt has been to understand and anthropologically interpret a cultural practice, why it continues and what it says about the Assamese world view.

The paper is based on the author's doctoral dissertation research from Michigan State University conducted in the early 1990s and the doctoral thesis that came out of that research.[1] The study was funded by the American Institute of Indian Studies. It was a pioneering work, using ideas of medical anthropology in the specific cultural and geographical context of Assam. There was very little existing academic writing on the topic at that time. The author has since then moved on from anthropology to areas of education and pedagogy, and this research stayed as is. Hence the findings compiled here have not been presented before, except in the doctoral dissertation. The purpose of the paper is to disseminate the findings of the thesis to today's scholars as well as to highlight methodological learnings from the field experience. This paper should therefore be considered in the context of a historical development of an area of study in Assam that seems to be taking up a lot of interest at the present times. The perspectives presented here are a steppingstone for future researchers working on medical anthropology and issues of culture, religion, and healing in Assam. The resources referred to reflect the ideas of that era of anthropological thinking. It is up to the readerto take these insights to newer directions.

From this point onwards in the paper, the narrative will often move into the first person, the term 'author' replaced by the pronoun 'I'. Situating the author in research writing has been a part of anthropological tradition as seen in the works of Marcus and Fischer[2] as well as Clifford and Marcus.[3] This paper follows that tradition that emphasizes the juxtaposition of the ethnographer's subjective narrative with objective description.

The study was based on a combination of primary and secondary research. Primary data was obtained from observations and interviews. Cultural ideas of *bej* and *bejali* were elicited through discussions, in-depth interviews, and casual conversations with a range of informants from across Assam—lay people, practitioners, their clients, as well as scholars specializing in Assamese society and culture. Most of my practitioner informants allowed me into their sessions with clients, enabling me to observe practitioner client interactions as they went on. Secondary data was obtained from available books and textual material, that I got from various sources. The Department of Historical and Antiquarian Studies of Assam had a large collection of local level texts. All these provided valuable background to my observations and interviews.

At the onset, I want to clarify that I am not addressing issues of does *bejali* work or not. As I observed and talked to clients who came to consult these practitioners and sat through healing sessions, it was obvious that what I was witnessing was something that a lot of people from different walks of life believed in. I was trying to understand that belief system what this system is, why it make sense to the people who believed in it, and why it continues.

LESSONS ON THE DEFINITION OF DOMAINS

Assamese dictionaries define *bej* as a conventional physician (*chikitsak, vaidya*), as well as a faith healer, as someone one who treats (*chikitsa kore*) by incantations and medicines. But there are other references to *bej* and medicine as well. The Assamese-English dictionary *Chondrokanto Abhidhaan*[4] defines an *ojha* as a *bej*, who uses *mantras* to cure. Dhanantari is defined as a king who was an expert in medicine, while *vaidya* is defined as a *bej* or a physician. *Jyoti Anglo-Assamese Dictionary*[5] defines a healer as a *bej*, *vaidya*, physician, as well as a religious physician (*dhormiyo chikitsok*)—a person who deals with *jora phuka*, an *ojha*; their definition of healing, besides the conventional one of curing or getting rid of illnesses, also includes getting rid of enmity and antagonism (*birodh aadi mitua*), to remedy, redress, retaliate (*protikaar kora*), and/or to bring about good relations (*somil mil kora*).

This sense of blurred boundaries became apparent, when I reached the field and tried to identify my subject of analysis—people who did *bejali*. As a native Assamese speaker, I was aware that a practice, referred to as *bejali* and its practitioners, called *bej*, were a part of common discourse. However, when I talked to people everywhere—at social gatherings, market places, temples, friends, acquaintances, scholars and strangers, no one could tell me exactly who a *bej* was. The other related terms—*ojhas*, *sadhaks*, *dhanantaris*, *vaidyas*, all came in the way, creating confusion. The conceptualization of these terms was flexible, with overlapping definitions. I ran into in disagreements among both practitioners and lay people, when deciding who was to be termed what. The same person would be categorized as *bej* by one informant, and as a *sadhak* or a *dhanantari* by another. I was often referred to someone as *bej*, but those persons did not see themselves as such. Some were clearly offended by the label. When asked to explain why they were not a *bej*, or what exactly did they call themselves, they were often unable to give a specific answer. It was, however, apparent that many of these practitioners did not want to be called a *bej* because of the negative connotations of the term. Some said that they did some *bejali*, but were not *bej* as they did not practise it full-time. Several placed themselves in more than one category. It was clear that they were practising something—their large clientele was proof enough —but the boundaries were too hazy to allow any categorizations.

As I looked for a cultural category that was becoming more and more elusive, I faced the dilemma of being unable to identify a domain of analysis. At that moment of confusion, I took a methodological decision and started the inquiry process again but this time with a different question. I started asking what a *bej* did, instead of who or what a *bej* was. Instead of compartmentalizing people into categories, I started paying attention to what exactly was being practised. Suddenly, a whole new vista opened up in front of me. A common thread connecting all of these practitioners was the use of *mantras* and incantations (*jora phuka*). Once I changed the label of my field—asking about the power of *mantras* as opposed to the power of *bej/bejali*, an entire healing practice emerged, consisting of practitioners who did *tontro-montro* or *jora-phuka*. It was a practice consisting of individual healers who had learned the art from their *guru* or a range of *gurus*. And as each *guru* was different, and each practitioner often had multiple *gurus*, each healer too was different, bringing in a great deal of diversity to what each one did. But use of *mantras* was common to all of them; it was *mantras* that was chanted in the form of incantations, it was *mantras* that was the basis of any *jora-phuka* or *tontro-montro* activity.

Nobody could give an exact definition of what *tontro-montro* was, but the general idea presented was that it dealt with esoteric *mantras* which can make things happen. *Jora-phuka* connotes curing through chanting *mantras*, while waving a hand or a blade of grass in front of the person (*jora*) and blowing *mantras* (*phuka*) into a person or an object. But *bej* are not the only persons dealing with *mantras*. *Ojhas*, *dhanantaris*, *vaidyas*, all deal with *mantras*, and most are seen to do *tontro montro* and *jora-phuka* too. Hence, the confusion in labelling and semantics.

Anthropologically, this was a huge eye-opener to me on setting the domains of study. I had been focusing on terms picked up from everyday conversations and corroborated by the dictionary. I created a cultural category, which I expected my informants to confirm. I naively expected to find the field laid out for my scrutiny. The reality was much different. Even though, I had used local terms, I had still started with a priory categories of what those terms would imply and what my domain of study would be. It was only when I allowed my informants to interpret the category for me that my domain emerged—that underlying all these different conceptualizations and terminologies was the use of *mantras*. The ambiguity and its resolution showed me that cultural categories can be meaningful only when reinterpreted in local terms.

THE CULTURAL PRACTICE OF DOING *MANTRAS*

As my research progressed, the ambivalence that I started with cleared and a cultural practice emerged. The practice was played out as practitioner client interactions. The interactions came about in times of affliction, misfortunes and dilemmas suffered by the client, and could be roughly structured into divination, diagnosis, and remedy. I explored the practice of 'doing *mantras*' by focusing on three questions about it:

- What is the nature of this practice?
- What is the logic underlying this practice?
- How influential is this practice in dictating the thoughts and actions of cultural actors?

THE NATURE OF THE PRACTICE

Examining the nature of the practice, I found that doing *mantras* is a domain of culture that involves temporary associations between practitioners and clients. In this context, I define a practitioner as a person, who has the knowledge of doing *mantras* and one who uses this knowledge as a service to others. Clients are defined as the people who come to these practitioners to avail their services. The interaction between the practitioner and the client constitute the practice of *mantras*. The interaction is brought into play in times of problematic life situations. It helps in managing suffering—the experiential dimension of affliction, misfortune, dilemmas, and crisis. These interactions help people to understand why suffering occurs and how they can be dealt with or prevented. The key element in these interactions is the use of *mantras*. The interactions are generally structured in terms of divination of some sort, diagnoses of the problem emerging from the divination and the remedy. I am condensing the entire process in this paper, but the details can be found in the dissertation which is available freely on line.[6]

DIVINATION

Divination is the main diagnostic tool used to understand the nature of the clients' problem. Most practitioners, I talked to saw a distinction between normal illness (*enei bemar*), which a person can get for no particular reason (*enei hoi*), and illnesses having specific underlying causes, such as spirits (*bhoot*), bad winds (*hawa botah*), bad *mantras* (*ku-mantras*), startling (*sok-khowa*), and evil eye (*nojor loga* or *mukh loga*). Divination is used to find out the exact cause so that the appropriate remedy can be given. The term most commonly used to refer to divination is *basoni soa* (selecting by looking). Various kinds of divination are used, each practitioner having his favourite style. Some use only one form, while others use more than one, depending on suitability. Some of these divinations are done by the practitioner himself, and some through a medium. The mediums could be ordinary people with special capabilities or could be beings and forces (*shaktis*) that the practitioner had been able to harness and control through rigorous training (*sadhana*). Many practitioners claimed to have supernatural beings under their control who gave them special powers to diagnose and give reme-dies. A practitioner's *shakti* can also be in the form of objects like a bone or any other material made potent through his *sadhana*.

I have put in a few examples of divination techniques used here, but this is not exhaustive—each practitioner uses whatever technique works best for him depending on the circumstance. One practitioner asks his clients to pick up a few matches from a new matchbox while thinking of the problem. He, then takes those picked matches and throws them on the ground. The number of matches picked and the way they fall when thrown on the ground told him the cause of the problem (Figure 11.1). Another common form (*nokhot sowa*) involved chanting *mantras* on the nails of a medium, who could then make predictions based on what he 'saw' on his nails.

Figure 11.1: Divination with match sticks
(Photograph taken by author during fieldwork)

Mantras when chanted on a bowl of water (*panit sowa*), enables the practitioner to 'see' the cause of the trouble. Similarly, *mantras* chanted on grains of rice (*saul jora*), empty bowls (*baati jora*), hands (*hatot sowa*), pot (*tekeli jora*), stick (*bet jora*), cowrie shells (*kori di sowa*) are used to divine causes of problems. Several practitioners used astrological calculations to divine. One uses horary astrology (*prasna tantra*)—the calculations are based on the exact time an agitated client puts forth his question (such as, will I get well; will my daughter get married). The precise time the person's eagerness or agitation is articulated to the practitioner determines the course of action. Another practitioner also uses numbers, but his calculations are based on the first letter of the person's name, and a random number that cames to his head, which he says, is suggested by his *shakti*. The first letter tells him the person's astrological sign, and each astrological sign has a number. Using this number and the number his *shakti* has put in his head, he does some additions and subtractions (*jog-biyog*), and comes up with a final number. The final number is the number of the page in his text in which the *mantra* and the procedure for the remedy can be found.

There are as many divination techniques and variations of techniques as there are practitioners. All these methods are, however, a means to an end. They aid the practitioner in counselling clients and in answering their questions about the outcome of their situation. They are the chief means of diagnosing problems, based on which remedies are suggested.

DIAGNOSIS

No matter what form of divination used, the diagnosis followed similar patterns—someone's evil eye touching the person (*nojor loga*), bad *mantras* done by others (*kumantra*), bad planetary configuration (*grohor doxh*), normal illness (*enei bemar*). I observed two other causes that was diagnosed frequently and seen to belong exclusively to the domain of *tantro-montro.* One was startling (*sok khowa*), which occurs when a person gets startled by a sudden fear or surprise. Startling is caused by a sudden fright or shock, but can lead to other illnesses, including madness. The person becomes sickly, restless, delirious, unable to eat and sleep, constantly scared, cannot stay alone at home, has frequent fevers, and sometimes in children, a bloated stomach. There is a general idea among both clients and practitioners that *sok khowa* can be cured only through *jhora phuka* and not by a medical doctor. Another set of problems seen to be diagnosed and cured only via *tantro-montro* is when supernatural beings such as ghosts (*bhoote dhora*) and poltergeists (*bira loga*) start residing in a person or in someone's home. One reason *bej* and *ojhas* are feared is because they are seen to be able to inflict such supernatural beings on hapless victims. Though often used synonymously, there is usually a conceptual distinction between the two. *Biras* are seen to be owned by a *bej* or *ojha*, who deliberately inflicts them on people to cause harm. *Biras* can cause problems ranging from simple, mischievous acts, like things disappearing in front of people's eyes, or beds forcefully shaken at night, startling the sleeper, to causing conflicts, various kinds of illnesses, as well as madness in the family.

Ghosts (*bhoot*), though sometimes owned by people, are usually independent and may mischievously or accidentally inflict themselves on someone. They are often referred to as 'winds' (*hawa botah*) or a 'bad wind' (*beya hawa*), because they touch a person suddenly and unexpectedly, like a breeze. Such 'winds' can make a person ill or behave in uncharacteristic ways or go insane. Ghosts may, among others things, be attracted by or caught in the long, flowing hair of a woman, especially if she is out alone at noon or at night, or by a person who passes under a banyan tree late at night, or by a small child left alone outside the house. A menstruating woman is especially vulnerable to 'winds', and women in that condition are usually told not to go under large trees.

As I observed sessions and talked to clients, it became apparent that though the practitioners differed in their methods, clients came to them for relief from similar problems. The language of diagnosis used by both clients and practitioners also came from the same cultural world, so the remedies suggested made sense and seemed logical.

REMEDY

Once the problem is diagnosed, the remedies are also similar. Almost all remedies involve chanting and blowing, *jora-phuka*, in some form or the other. I am using the word *potentize* here to refer to the practice of infusing something with supernatural power through the use of mantras or any other means. *Jora* refers to potentizing something by chanting *mantras* into it while waving a hand, or a blade of grass, or some other item of supernatural power over it (Figure 11.2). *Phuka* refers to potentizing something by chanting *mantras* and then blowing the *mantras* into the object to be potentized. *Jora phuka* can be done directly on a person (Figure 11.3)—clients claim to get relief when *mantras* are chanted on and blown into the ailing parts of their body; on edible things like sugar, water, herbal concoctions, which are chanted on and prescribed like medicines to be ingested; or on non-ingested items like

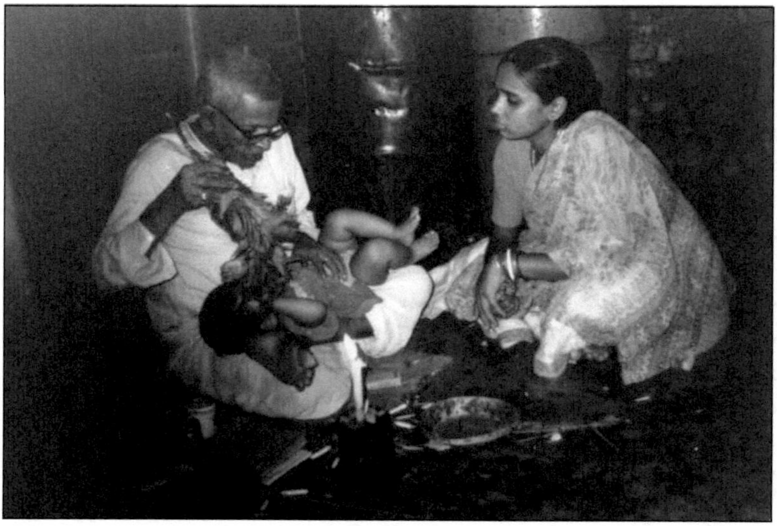

Figure 11.2: A child being chanted on for fever to subside
(Photograph taken by author during fieldwork)

Figure 11.3: *Mantras* chanted and blown into a client. The practitioner here was the Governor of Assam at that time. People of all walks of life flocked into his healing sessions at the Governor's Residence (Raj Bhavan).
(Photograph taken by author during fieldwork)

amulets, threads (*jaap*), seeds, rice, fruits and a range of other things to be worn or kept in the house. There are also sessions in the client's premises to get rid of evil spirits or *mantras* residing there.

The most common form of *jora-phuka* is *pani kota* (cutting water). The term gets its name from the procedure used to potentize the water. The practitioner chants *mantras* over a bowl of water, while making cutting motions over it with a blade of grass. 'Cutting' the water with the blade of grass enables the power of the *mantra* to go into the water. This 'cut' water, when mixed with normal water, potentizes that water. The client has to drink sips of this potent water and bathe with it. Rubbing this water into afflicted parts of the body is said to give relief. Cutting water is the most basic *bejali* technique with which all practitioners start their training. *Pani kota*, also called *pani jora*, is used ubiquitously and for a wide spectrum of problems—to counteract evil eye, bad *mantras*, startling, ghosts and spirits, illnesses etc. as well as for problems like a client's trees not producing fruits.

The term medicine (*aushad*) is often used for remedies. These are usually *mantras* chanted on some form of medium, which is to be ingested or be in contact with the person so as to get the power of the *mantra* into the person. Mediums range from fruits, sugar, honey, ginger, seeds, flowers to even harder substances like amulets and wax. The choice of the medium differs with the practitioners and with the power of the *mantra*. One practitioner told me that his diabetes 'medicine' is a *mantra* chanted on a small piece of lac to be worn as an amulet on the waist or arm. He said that, the medium used for this medicine was lac because the *mantra* was too powerful to be contained by a regular medium such as a copper amulet. His medium for sciatica pain is a bell metal plate (Figure 11.4). *Mantras* are chanted on the plate, and the client has to keep in the chanted-on plate in contact with his or her body for about an hour or so every day. One of his clients that I talked to claimed that the plate, along with chanted on water that she had to drink three times a day completely got rid of her chronic, excruciating pain. Another practitioner uses olive seeds as a medium for five illnesses—high and low blood pressure, diabetes, piles (haemorrhoids), 'head reeling', and tonsilitis. Though the medium is the same, each ailment

Figure 11.4: *Mantras* chanted on a bell metal plate for sciatica pain (Photograph taken by author during fieldwork)

required a different *mantra.* This same practitioner sticks seven date thorns into a raw banana in his popular cure for chronic stomach problems (Figure 11.5). As each thorn is stuck into the banana, a different *mantra* is chanted. The banana is then hung over the cooking stove of the client's kitchen. The practitioner's explanation is that stomach problems happen because the liver is enlarged. The raw banana mimics the liver of the sick person. As the banana shrinks in size from the heat of the stove, the *mantras* make the person's liver shrink too. This is a typical example of homeopathic magic that students of anthropology study. Several informants claimed that their own or their children's stomach problems were totally cured by this treatment.

A category of ailments frequently resorted to be cured by *mantras* are bites, stings and pricks. *Mantras* are seen to be very effective in curing snake bites, animal bites, stings and pricks from plants, insects and fish, or fishbone sticking to someone's gullet while eating fish. These reflect a ubiquitous part of Assamese everyday life. Snakes are rampart in the tropical landscape, as are insects like

Figure 11.5: Raw banana being chanted on for relief from stomach problems
(Photograph taken by author during fieldwork)

hornets and bees, plants like stinging nettles, and the staple of an Assamese diet—river fish, with its myriad bones that can get stuck in the throat while eating. An inexperienced cleaner can be pricked by the sharp protruding bones of common varieties of fish (*singi mas, magur mas*), while preparing it for cooking, which can be extremely painful. Caterpillar hair can cause intense itching, rashes, weals and even hives. These are common experiences, seen to be easily and often instantly cured by *mantras.* Usually, *mantras* are chanted on a bowl of water. Some clients claim to see the offending bone or thorn, or hair jump out of the body and go into the bowl. Others do not claim anything so spectacular—the welts and rashes gradually subside, bringing relief to the person. Though, most practitioners have *mantras* for pricks, stings and bites in their repertoire, not everyone has the knowledge of getting rid of snake venom. Snake bites are seen to belong to a different category from other bites. For these *mantras* to be efficacious, the practitioner needs to reach a certain level of competence (*siddhi*), and this level needs to be maintained through regular spiritual exercises. Such practitioners are sought after for their capability, and clients come to them from long distances or take them long distances to their homes.

Besides bodily ailments, medicines are given for a wide variety of life problems. Potentized sugar, to be mixed with regular household sugar is given to bring in good relations between family members, make children regular in their studies and obedient to their parents, or daughters-in-law obedient to their mothers-in-law. Potentized food items fed to a person can get that person infatuated or attracted to someone. Medicines inside a medium are often fed to a person, who has lost interest in life. Such a person is believed to have been fed something through someone's bad medicine, and hence a good medicine is needed to reverse the process.

Mantras chanted on rice grains, mustard or other seeds, raw bananas and a myriad other things are given to be kept inside the house, in kitchens, scattered over and under beds, or even buried under ground or under trees to protect from bad *mantras*, ghosts and poltergeist, and from evil eye. Iron nails are chanted on and buried in the four corners of a house to protect the family living there from illness, evil eye, bad *mantras* and misfortune. Chanted on rice or spice seeds like mustard, cumin, fenugreek, sprinkled around a house can bring in good tenants into a house that an owner is having trouble renting out. *Mantras* chanted into a wife's vermillion box can make her wayward husband come back to her after she starts wearing that vermillion on her forehead and in the parting of her hair.

Amulets (*tabeej* or *kabash*) are a very common forms of remedy. *Mantras* are chanted or written into pieces of paper, a flower, rice, or any other medium, stuffed into amulet shells, sealed and given to clients. These are instructed to be worn around the neck, waist, arm, kept in the home, in shop cash boxes, or wherever a solution is needed. Often, the thread on which the amulet is worn needs to be chanted on too. Empty amulet shells are available in the market, and are made in a range of materials—bell metal, brass, copper, silver, even gold. The nature of the *mantra* determine the material used for the amulet shell—it needs to be powerful enough to contain the *mantra* as well as porous enough to let the *mantra* do its job.

Sometimes, instead of an amulet, a thread is chanted on and a medium like a root, a piece of lac or other material that can hold the *mantra* is tied to it. Thread is a very common medium to hold the power of *mantras*. A very common remedy using thread that I saw over and over again is for the treatment for jaundice—a very common waterborne disease in Assam, usually caused by some form of hepatitis. The sick person has to wear a garland made of flowers and thread, which has *mantras* chanted on it. The garland starts as a small wreath to be worn around the head, but with each passing day it becomes longer and longer and gradually travels down the body. It reaches the feet when the illness has left the person. The person then stepps out of it and disposes it as per the instructions of the practitioner. Though, there are other remedies for jaundice using *mantras*, this is one of the most common. I have talked to people from all walks of life who have used this remedy, including highly educated ones, as well as the westernized Assamese.

The remedies, to be efficacious, need to be personalized to the person or persons on whom it has to take effect. *Bejali mantras* are always chanted in somebody's name. When the effect has be on an entire family, for instance to bring harmony in a conflict situation, each members' name needs to be chanted on. If two people need to be joined together in a marriage, or separated due to an unsuitable or illicit relationship, both their names are chanted on the *mantra*. A *mantra* directed specifically for a purpose are called *baans* (arrow), and the name is like the exact target the arrow needs to strike.

MANTRAS AS A PRACTICAL TOOL

Most of the time, when we think of *mantras*, we visualize something sacred and religious. This dimension of *mantras* has been extensively studied by indologists and other scholars, both Indian and western. In the practice of *bej bejali*, *jora-phuka*, *tontro-montro*, however, the religious and ritual dimension of *mantras* is re-contextualized and used in much more practical, immediate, and almost clinical purposes by its adherents. In this context, they can be said to be almost secular, the word 'secular' being used here to mean this-worldly, everyday concerns. Clients come with a problem, the practitioner listens, diagnoses and gives a remedy, using *mantras* to interpret and resolve the problem. *Mantras* chanted on everyday things like rice, sugar, water, a thread, an amulet, a fruit, a pot, make them into potent objects capable of immediate action on someone or something. The results could be benevolent or malevolent depending on the intention.

Mantras in this practical sense are seen to be a combination of potent words, syllables and assorted sound units with a specific pronunciation and intonation. I was repeatedly told that the right *mantra*, spoken by the right person, in the right manner, generates a power, which can be either positive or negative. This power can in turn be harnessed and channeled by the practitioner for various purposes—divination, healing illnesses, causing illnesses, solving life problems, and causing life problems.

This system of generating supernatural powers to solve practical problems is contextual, similar to a doctor-patient interaction. Clients seek a practitioner only in times of crisis, fear or worry. However, these situations went far beyond curing illnesses. *Mantras* were used to get rid of enmity and antagonism (*birodh aadi mitua*), to remedy, retaliate, redress (*protikar kora*) and/or to bring about good relations (*somil mil kora*). Once the situation is resolved one way or the other, the interaction is over. Unlike the supplicant stance of a temple priest, the *mantra* practitioner gives the impression of being in control of outcomes.

It is these practical purposes of *mantras* that my research explored. This quasi-religious dimension of *mantras* had not been studied much at that time. It was seen to be in the realm of the occult, of superstition (*ondho bisakh*), and hence, not worth academic time and interest. But as my research showed, both the religious and practical dimensions of *mantras* emerged as two divergent branches coming out of the same roots.

SOURCES OF PRACTICAL *MANTRAS*

Most of these practical *mantras* came from three major kinds of sources—the *Atharvaveda*, various Tantric texts, and local texts with *mantras* mostly in regional languages. The *Atharvaveda*, unlike the other three *Vedas*, consists largely of spells and incantations. Benjamin Walker[7] differentiates between two kinds of *mantras* in the *Atharvaveda*—*bheshajani*, which are of a medicinal, healing and peaceful nature, dealing with cures and herbs for treating fever, leprosy, jaundice, dropsy, and other diseases; prayers for successful childbirth, love spells, charms for fecundity, for the recovery of virility, hymns for the birth of sons, as well as chants for practical purposes like putting the household to sleep while the lover (or perhaps a thief) steals into the house at night. The other kind, *abhichara* are of a bewitching and malevolent nature, such as spells for producing diseases and bringing ill luck to enemies. There are spells that can make a woman remain a spinster, spells to destroy a man's virility, hymns to serpents, demons, and other dark forces.The *Atharvaveda* presents an entire pantheon of demons who bring about bodily distress as well as the *mantras* needed to expel these demons to cure the person.

As Kenneth Zysk shows,[8] this world view of the power of incantations is also seen in early texts of Ayurveda, where the healer chants *mantras*, often by waving or stroking certain plants over the patient, along with preparing and using medicines. The medicines too are often consecrated by the *mantras*. It appears that both Ayurveda and what I call the 'practice of *mantras*' had roots in the *Atharvaveda*, but at some point during its development, there was a doctrinal shift in Ayurveda from a magico-religious to a more 'rational' form.

In his study of *mantras* in ancient Ayurveda, Zysk[9] groups the use of *mantras* in early Ayurvedic texts into several categories:

i. the treatment of swellings, tumours, wounds, and sores (*sotha, vrana*)
ii. the treatment of poison (*visa*)
iii. the treatment of mental disorders (*unmatta, unmada, apasmara*)

iv. the treatment of fever (*jvara*)
v. the collection and preparation of certain medicines.

Though Ayurveda does not use *mantras* in these contexts any more, these categories, among others, were being used by most of the practitioners I talked to, along with the technique of *jora*—stroking some object like a blade of grass, a hand, or some other object over the patient.

In the Tantirc texts, the practical dimension of *mantras* can be seen in the performance of the Tantirc *satkarmas*, or the six acts by which a Tantric practitioner can have control over the universe.[10] These are:

- *Maron* (liquidation), the power to kill or maim by *mantras.*
- *Vasikaran* (subjugation), the power to infatuate, bewitch, cause one to be subservient and controlled by another.
- *Stambhan* (immobilization), the power to paralyze, stop someone in their tracks, stop other's actions, prevent the effects of other's actions even when they are already operating.
- *Ucchatan* (agitation, eradication), the power to torment one with pain, shame, or material discomfort, make enemies flee in shame and disgrace, remove an obstacle.
- *Vidvesan* (sowing dissension) power to separate friends, relatives, spouses, potential lovers, creating ill feeling between two parties.
- *Shanti* (pacification) the power to get rid of evil influences brought about by planets, spirits or other people's *mantras*, cure illnesses, bring peace and happiness.

These Six acts are performed through *mantras* and mystical diagrams called *yantras*—a combination seen to possess immense power, when directed by the right person in the right way. There are innumerable kinds of *mantras* and *yantras*, and each practitioner chooses, which one to use based on his own knowledge and his clients' needs. There is absolute agreement that a *guru's* guidance is needed to teach how to harness the strength of these instruments of power in the most effective and safe manner.

Besides these pan-Indian, purely Vedic or Tantric texts, various local level texts also exist, and are extensively used by both Tantric and non-Tantric practitioners. The *mantras* are mostly in regional languages, though sometimes mixed with Sanskrit words or *bija* (root) *mantras* that a practitioner may have been initiated by his *guru* with. At the time of my research, the literature on such texts was very scanty. In Assam, they are called by the generic term *bejali puthi* or simply *montro puthi*. These are unbound manuscripts, handwritten in an archaic form of Assamese, usually on bark (*saanchi paat*), or on pieces of paper (Figures 11.6 and 11.7). They are normally individual or family possessions. Most of the time, these are the texts used by the practitioner in his day-to-day practice, which he then passes on to his disciple or successor before he dies. Very few of these *puthis* have been published, as there is a fear that publication would lead to commercialization, which in turn will make the *mantras* lose their inherent power and efficacy.

Though, I make a distinction between these three sources, it, however, needs to be kept in mind that these are not clear-cut divisions. The history of the present form of *mantras* have been very eclectic, both in the context of source as well as in their use. Most of the practitioners I talked to use a combination of Vedic,

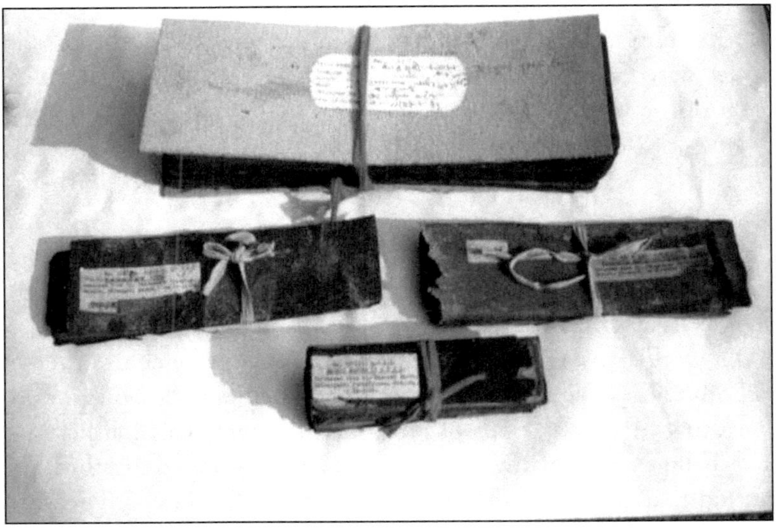

Figure 11.6: Local level texts
(Photograph taken by author during fieldwork)

Figure 11.7: Local level text
(Photograph taken by author during fieldwork)

Tantric and local *mantras*. More than the source it is the specific nature of these *mantras* which makes them distinctive. These are *mantras* used for practical purposes and are selected by the practitioner based on their immediate efficacy. These are usually not *mantras* for worship.

THE CULTURAL LOGIC OF *MANTRAS*

The analysis of the conversations between the practitioner and the clients, my own interviews with them and my discussions with people in Assam brought out several assumptions about reality and a world view that made these interactions make cultural sense to both parties. The general picture that emerges is that of a world consisting of various kinds of forces and dangers, which afflict human beings in various ways. There are supernatural beings lurking around that can inflict themselves on people; there are also people, who keep various supernatural beings to do their bidding, sometimes to harm others and sometimes to help people harmed by others. Others' words or envious thoughts are forces that can cause damage. There are beings or powers that can startle and frighten people and make them ill. Snakes and other creatures that can bite, sting or prick. Dangerous *mantras* can bring about affliction and misfortune to the victim and his or her entire family. There are also configurations of planets that can cause problems in people's lives. Besides these forces, the human body can also get periodically ill for no underlying reason. All these dangers that the world presents can be resolved in a culturally typical way—by *mantras.* The force of *mantras*, which can be used to cause suffering, can also be used to alleviate that suffering. Good *mantras*, when chanted into people's bodies or ingested, can help relieve affliction. They can be contained in amulets and worn on the body. They can also be contained in other mediums like mustard seeds or rice or water and kept around people's houses or premises to get rid of and prevent problematic situations. *Mantras* are, thus, seen as a source of power that can help people deal with affliction, misfortune and the experience of suffering. This is a cultural logic that makes sense to clients because it fits in with local notions of supernatural beings who have the power to make things happen.

CULTURAL CONCEPTIONS OF POWER

The cultural logic of resorting to *mantras* for problematic life situations makes sense to the clients because it addresses indigenous conceptualizations of power, or *shakti.* Susan Wadley's analysis of the two connotations of *shakti* in her studies of religion in northern India is especially useful in understanding the logic behind the practice of *mantras* in Assam.[11] Wadley found that conceptually, *shakti* 'implies the female energy of the universe, the energizing principle without which there would be no motion',[12] but it also means power in general. 'Shakti carries the concepts of strength, energy, and vigour; but the strength is based on spiritual force, not physical force'.[13] The idea of *Shakti* is bound with ideas of the supernatural. Wadley finds the notion of supernatural, as conceptualized by her informants, a complex one, and not easy to define. There is no bounded supernatural domain, and a supernatural being may be a god, a demon or a ghost. The basic characteristic of any supernatural being, whether good or bad is in the *shakti* they control or represent. Wadley states that as everything in the world embodies some power, everything in the universe is potentially a powerful being. She makes an analytical distinction between 'unmarked', or less marked deities and 'marked', or more marked deities. Unmarked deities are those which under all conditions are recognized as powerful beings, while marked deities are recognized as powerful beings only under some conditions in defined circumstances. Wadley uses the distinction between marked and unmarked not only in the context of deities, but also other power filled things, like wheat seeds, or a plough, which become powerful in particular ritual contexts. In the context of chanting *mantras*, this distinction helps in understanding why ordinary words and ordinary objects can be seen as potent item under particular circumstances—when infused with the power of *mantras* by a competent practitioner.

Wadley's analysis made absolute sense in the context of doing *mantras*. All the practitioners I met, talked of some kind of *shakti* behind their abilities. *Mantras* are thus seen as a source of power that can help people deal with adversity and calamities. This cultural understanding made resorting to *mantras* the logical outcomes for certain kinds of life problems.

CULTURAL DISPOSITIONS

The importance of understanding the logic behind people's actions is not new in Anthropology. Evans-Pritchard has looked at the cultural logic underlying Azande ideas of witchcraft.[14] Comaroff has emphasized the need to look at the logic behind medical systems.[15] The idea of cultural logic has been a key aspect of Pierre Bourdieu's influential body of ideas. Examining the schemes of thought, perception and action in terms of logical categories which make practices seem 'reasonable' or 'common sense', Bourdieu[16] demonstrates how pervasive, unconscious, unarticulated cultural logic influence people's behaviour. His conceptualization of habitus attributes a systematic character to 'habit' or 'custom', which incorporate many aspects of social life within one underlying logic.[17]

As he saw it, most behaviour is motivated by very general dispositions, which are totalized in any culture into a habitus. He defines habitus as a system of durable, transposable dispositions and central tendencies, which give rise to and guide the infinitely varied ways in which people respond to one another in a social setting. The habitus is the unifying principle of practices of different domains, and cultural practices make sense because of the habitus. It is the product of early childhood experiences, unconsciously inculcated through socialization and continually modified by the individual's encounter with the world.[18]

I have used a very simplified version of Bourdieu's extremely sophisticated analysis of society and social order to understand the context of doing *mantras*. I see the conjunction of his ideas of cultural logic, habitus and field as a means by which people rationalize their actions. Bourdieu indicates the notion of field to be the social and cultural arena in which specific cultural logic gets played out. Growing up in a particular milieu, certain ways of thinking, certain beliefs get ingrained in us so much so that they become 'common sense', and thus sensible, acceptable ways to act in particular circumstances. In the context of doing *mantras*, Bourdieu's conceptualization of habitus is helpful to a certain extent. Most of the clients operate on a tacit knowledge that *mantras* can do things. This knowledge has come through socialization, common phrases and everyday conversations. Children are often brought to practitioners for 'treatment' or accompany family members who come to seek their services. Most of the consultations are not private, but open to all present at that time. Hence, the practice becomes a part of the world view children grow up with. The practice makes sense because once this cultural knowledge and world-view is rationalized in a convincing manner in a person's mind, it becomes an unquestioned way of dealing with particular life situations.

Though I find Bourdieu's ideas very useful for my analysis of why the practice of *mantras* continues to make sense, his conceptualization of habitus seems to assume that people socialized in similar ways will have similar habitus, which in turn gets embodied within the actors, making them act in particular ways. This way of looking at cultural patterning appears to leave very little room for individual choice. They help in explaining why broader cultural frames emerge, but they do not say why, within the same cultural setting, people do not always follow the same logic.

This point came to my mind when, in talking to people about *bej bejali*, I was perturbed by a personal quandary. As an anthropologist studying my own society, I tried to understand why, in spite of growing up in the same cultural setting, these interactions were, in a sense, alien to me. I have been asked many a time whether I myself would resort to a practitioner in times of personal crisis, and my instinctual response had been a categorical 'no'. But at the same time, a lot of the ideas and cultural assumptions were familiar—the fear of someone's evil eye, wearing of amulets, or the role of planet configuration in determining outcomes were notions I knew well. These are also notions that I cannot emphatically say that I absolutely disregard. During my fieldwork in Assam, I encountered a broad spectrum of people who, though belonging to the same cultural milieu, were semi-believing; sceptical, but not disbelieving; or totally disbelieving of the practice of *mantras*. There were also people who believed in the power of *mantras* in certain contexts, but not in others. Some said they had heard of such practices, but had no idea what they entailed till they saw someone else's, or their own crisis get resolved by a practitioner. Now they are not very sure what to believe. The question that came to my mind was how was it possible to have these different mindsets coexist at different times in people from the same culture and going by Bourdieu's ideas, the same habitus. What made individual people's engagement with *mantras* so changeable and inconsistent?

CULTURAL SCHEMAS

I used Sherry Ortner's notion of cultural schemas as a theoretical framework to understand this shifting and contextual aspect of people's engagement with *mantras* for practical purposes. Cultural schemas are organized ways of interpreting and executing culturally typical relations or situations. These schemas shape human action in particular ways, endowing them with particular meanings, so that they unfold along more or less predictable lines. They are the symbolic frames through which people understand and respond to events.[19] Calling them key scenarios in her earlier paper, she says that 'key scenarios, by prescribing certain culturally effective courses of action, embody and rest upon certain assumptions about the nature of reality'.[20] For Ortner, cultural schemas are grounded in particular practices, and are the patterns or frames within which actors interpret and act upon their situation. They are found to be sensible, useful and logical ways of understanding reality.[21] Edward Schiefflien talks of a similar concept, which he calls a cultural scenario. He defines a cultural scenario as an event sequence, whereby a people repeatedly approach and interpret diverse situations and carry them to similar types of resolution. The situations themselves need not be similar; it is the similar manner in which they are interpreted, carried forward, and resolved that is important.[22] These works form part of a larger discussion in anthropology on the role of cultural structures in patterning human life. But for purposes of this analysis, I am only using the ideas of cultural schemas and scenarios to explain how diverse problems are defined, interpreted, and resolved in a similar culturally specific way, and why individual people connect with them only at certain situations and not others.

Schemas get into people's minds through stories—myths, legends, histories, folk-tales etc. As Ortner suggests, most of the time these cultural stories will be just a story, with little relevance to a person's life. But at particular moments in an actor's life, the stories seem to make sense of his or her circumstances and take on a new meaning. Not all stories make sense to all actors at the same time, nor will two actors necessarily have the same relationship to the schema. Actors have some amount of choice—they can take the schema or leave it. Linkages made with the schema are temporary and contextual. A key factor in the cultural schema is the human agent. The schema shapes human action in particular ways by suggesting culturally typical ways of interpretation and enactment. Human action, in turn, is critical in shaping the schema. However, different actors interpret the same schema in different ways, depending on socialization, family ideology, life circumstances and personality. This also makes the logic underlying these schemas very contextual—in certain contexts and situations they may make sense, at other times they may not.

I saw Ortner's ideas come to life in the context of *bej bejali*. A lot of my information on the practice of *bejali* and power of the *bej* came from stories—anecdotes, family legends, tales, even popular and folk songs recounting these stories. People would constantly narrate anecdotes of their own and other peoples' experiences. Even if one had not had any encounter with *bejali*, they had heard stories. And at particular crisis situations, stories and the circumstances connect, and the stories fit in with particular experiences. They then become something more than just a story—they help interpret what is going on, making a specific course of action the logical thing to do.

BEJ BEJALI AS INDIGENOUS COUNSELLING SYSTEMS

As I sat through practitioners' sessions and talked to clients about the problems they came for and their resolution, what was obvious was that practices such as these serve as indigenous counselling systems. A major role of the practitioners was to counsel and advice clients on a range of concerns, based on what they diagnose through divination. Clients seek advice for myriad dilemmas where they are unsure of what decision to take, the future outcome of a crisis, or how to handle a life quandary. Whether to stand for a forthcoming election or not, whether to accept a transfer to a new place, whether to get a child married at that particular period, whether to accept or reject a marriage alliance, where a missing person will be found, whether a cow or a piece of jewellery is stolen or lost, who has taken it, will it be found—the worries are endless. Practitioners are also taken to their client's premises to decipher why a family is having bad times, why someone's mill is not making profits, where to construct a new building or set up new machinery, or whether somebody has put something malevolent in their homes.

The practitioner's advice both gives direction to as well as validates clients' own thoughts and course of actions in understanding and coping in with these anxieties. These are coping mechanisms that help people deal with life's uncertainties. Whether the remedies work or not, they provide a means to make sense of problematic situations and often, provide peace of mind. A similar counselling role has been attributed to astrology,[23] which too people resort to in times of stress situations. Indigenous counselling systems and their role in maintaining mental health and well-being has a lot of research potential in the context of Assam.

COUNSELLING SESSIONS AS A WINDOW INTO A WORLD VIEW

The kind of problems people saw as afflictions to be counselled by a traditional practitioner also opens a window into the Assamese mind. I saw the areas of socio-cultural life that mattered enough for someone to seek redress—a daughter not getting married, a child not studying enough, illnesses, family quarrels, property disputes, men suddenly deciding to stop earning (a very common problem that I saw over and over), snake bites, in-law problems, gold or cow getting lost, trees or animals, which are the main source of income not thriving and a countless other issues that reflect everyday life. One practitioner had his most frequently used *mantras* and *yantras* pre-written on pieces of paper and kept in neatly labelled boxes to save time[24] (Figure 11.8). Whenever a client needed it, all he has to do is fill in the name of the person, chant the *mantra*, and put the piece of paper inside an amulet. For a cultural anthropologist, the analysis of materials such as these and the interactions associated with them provide an understanding of culturally important concerns and sources of distress that emerge from the socio-cultural setting.

These cultural windows brought out the meta-medical framework that several medical anthropology scholars have talked about. Illness and health are experiential situations and are not often differentiated from other life experiences.[25] Hence, the compartmentalization of medical anthropology to only issues of health and illness can be a distortion of what the reality is. Instead, there must be an interplay between medical anthropology and broader

Figure 11.8: *Mantras* and *yantras* pre-written on pieces of paper and kept in neatly labelled boxes to save time.[26] (Photograph taken by author during fieldwork)

issues of social inquiry. There was a growing sentiment at the time of this research that we are first social and cultural anthropologists, and hence, we need to look at social and cultural realities like misfortune, suffering, and affliction.[27] In Worsley's words, we are dealing, 'not with illness but with misfortune and the prevention of misfortune'.[28] Scheper-Hughes has a similar opinion when she says that 'ours must be an anthropology of affliction and not simply an anthropology of medicine'.[29]

These ideas all came together, when I started talking to people in the field, focusing on healing and *mantras* rather than an a priory category of *bej*. The term 'healing' went beyond just physical ailments—these practitioners did not cure just illnesses. Informants told me that people go through problems, dilemmas, maladies and conflicts all the time in life. These are often deliberately or accidently inflicted by others. Practitioners used *mantras* to identify and get rid of these problems, no matter what the nature or source of the problem is. They come to these practitioners to get help in coping with life problems, including illnesses. Through a combination of clinical and counselling sessions, they bring peace to a household made unstable by conflicts between the family members, restore marital harmony, help an unmarried person get married, a childless woman conceive, help secure a coveted promotion, get interfering in-laws out of the way, turn a person's mind away from an unsuitable liaison as well as help in securing a good outcome in marriage or property negotiations. Thus, the domain of 'doing *mantras*' is not confined to the context of health and illness. What these practitioners are dealing with can be termed as problematic life situations, misfortunes, or afflictions—of which, illness and health form one dimension.

Another insight into the local world view came about when analysing how a *mantra* was used. To illustrate, one client was reprimanded by a practitioner for asking for a 'remedy' that would make her son-in-law take her advice instead of his mother's. The practitioner refused to give her the remedy. A few days later this same practitioner willingly gave a mother-in-law a chanted-on packet of sugar to make her daughter-in-law listen to her and not to her parents.When I asked him about this discrimination, he said that the happiness of a family depends on a large part on the harmony between mother, son and daughter-in-law. In the previous occasion, his *mantra* would have broken that harmony, while the in second occasion, it would enhance it. Similar interpretations could be seen in deciding who is an unsuitable marriage partner for a child, what is a suitable job for a son that requires a *mantra* boost and what requires a *mantra* to thwart it. These and numerous such examples showed that the distinction is not really between a good *mantra* and a bad *mantra*, and by extension, between black and white magic that anthropologists often make. It is the purpose for which the *mantra* is used and the cultural construction of that purpose, that makes a *mantra* good or bad. It is from this perspective that the practitioners talked about the Tantric *satkarmas*. These are *mantras* of power to be used for the good of people, for protection against evil forces—there is nothing wrong in harming evil. The cultural construction of evil in this context would make a very interesting study for future scholars.

FINAL THOUGHTS

The terms *bej* and *bejali* have always been clouded in a sense of notoriety, mainly due to its association with a place in Assam called Mayong. Though a small village, once surrounded by dense forests and flooded rivers, Mayong earned itself the reputation of being synonymous with evil *mantras.* The word Mayong, even today, connotes greed, unscrupulous quackery, harmful deeds, and distrust. Both *bej* and *mantras* from Mayong region (*Mayongiya bej, Mayon-giya montro*) are feared all over the Assam. *Bej* are seen to wield immense power which they often use to deceive, and, if annoyed or angered, to deliberately hurt or destroy their victim.

A lot of discourse about *bej bejali* are conducted in the form of stories and legends about the fearsome *bej* of Mayong—most people I talked to had no personal contact with a *bej* from Mayong village or experience of the power of a *Mayongiya bej.* But the stories abound, bringing in dread and unease. Among other things, the *bej* from Mayong were supposedly experts in Mohini *mantras*—*mantras* used to infatuate others. Both men and women from Mayong could bewitch a person and keep him or her with them forever, at their beck and call. These *bej* supposedly also had the capacity to turn human beings into spirits, tigers, goats, or anything else they wanted to. They had *mantras* that could 'tie up' a person by inflicting intense pain or totally immobility. These *mantras* were supposed to be carefully transmitted within families and not taught to outsiders. All these tales and anecdotes add to the lore of Mayong. Perhaps the practitioners of Mayong had a hand in keeping this notoriety alive to advertise a particular kind of expertise. Because Mayong was so isolated, the mystique continued.

For the last few decades, however, Mayong is no longer remote and inaccessible. The forests of Mayong have been opened up to the public as Pobitora Wildlife Sanctuary, which has a high concentration of rhinoceros, along with dolphins, waterbirds, hornbills and other animals. Publicized by the government as a conservation success story, Pobitora is a tourism hotspot, close enough to Guwahati for day trips. The road to Pobitora goes through

Mayong, which has seen a transformation from a sleepy village to a tourism hub. It is almost as if Mayong has now reinvented itself with tourism-related activities, with its aura of magic becoming a part of that new *avatar*. There are *bejali* shows and demonstrations of rituals with magical outcome, as well as healing sessions to attract tourists. The scenic beauty of the area, a number of archaeological relics found nearby, all add to the charm of practitioners demonstrating their skills to visitors. The direction that the practice of *bejali* will take in this transition from notoriety to exotic tourism can open up new pathways for research.

I would like to end with one last point. The scope of my research did not include an in-depth study of local texts. Not much research has been done in these personal texts even in recent years. Since these are manuscripts that were owned by practitioners and each practitioner could modify these based on his experience and needs, they do not have the status of the classical texts. However, this I feel is an area that needs a lot of work as these *montro puthis* and *bejali puthis* are fast disappearing. Practitioners lament that the younger generation is not interested in the rigour needed to keep the practice alive—the effectiveness of the *mantras* depend on a lot of personal discipline. Besides, the *mantras* are said to be ineffective without a *guru* to teach the exact nuances and inflections that would give it its efficacy. Many practitioners have died without being able to pass down their knowledge to the next generation. A lot of the texts I was told, are now lost for posterity, because it is believed that if a person died without teaching his esoteric knowledge to a successor, then his *puthis* of potential power need to be immersed in a river and destroyed. Many texts have already been drowned in water, many of those that still survive are moth eaten and mouldy, due to lack of usage. Being made of bark and paper, they will not last indefinitely. These are pieces of Assamese cultural heritage, which need to be studied with due respect before they disappear forever.

NOTES

1. Vandana Goswami, *Potent Words, Potent Objects: 'Doing Mantras' in Assamese Everyday Life*, PhD Thesis, Michigan State University, East Lansing, Michigan, USA, 1994.
2. George E. Marcus and Michael M.J. Fisher, *Anthropology as Cultural Critique : An Experimental Moment in the Human Sciences*, University of Chicago Press, Chicago, 1986.
3. James Clifford and George E. Marcus (ed.), *Writing Culture: The Poetics and Politics of Ethnography*, University of California Press, 1986, republished by Oxford University Press, Delhi, 1990.
4. P. Gordon, Chandrakanta Abhidhan, *A Comprehensive Dictionary of the Assamese Language*, Assam Sahitya Sabha Jorhat, 1933, Guwahati University, 1962.
5. Pranavjyoti Deka, *Jyoti Anglo-Assamese Dictionary*, Hemkosh Printer, Guwahati, 1990.
6. Vandana Goswami, 'Potent Words, Potent Objects: 'Doing Mantras' in Assamese Everyday Life', PhD Thesis, Michigan State University, East Lansing, Michigan, USA, 1994.
7. Benjamin Walker, 'Hindu World: An Encyclopedic Survey of Hinduism, vols. 1 and 2', George Allen and Unwin, London, 1968.
8. Kenneth G. Zysk, 'Mantra in Ayurveda: A Study of the Use of Magico-Religious Speech in Ancient Indian Medicine', in Harvey P. Alper (ed.), *Understanding Mantras*, Motilal Banarsidass, Delhi, 1991, pp. 123-43.
9. Ibid.
10. Harvey P. Alper, 'A Working Bibliography for the Study of Mantras', in Harvey P. Alper (ed.), *Understanding Mantras*, Motilal Banarsidass, Delhi, 1991, p. 411.
11. Susan Snow Wadley, *Shakti: Power in the Conceptual Structure of Karimpur Religion*, University of Chicago Studies in Anthropology Series in Social, Cultural and Linguistic Anthropology, no. 2, Department of Anthropology, University of Chicago, Chicago, 1975. 'Power in Hindu Ideology and Practice', in Kenneth David (ed.), *The New Wind: Changing Identities in South Asia*, Mouton Publishers, The Hague, 1977.
12. Susan Snow Wadley, *Shakti: Power in the Conceptual Structure of Karimpur Religion*, University of Chicago Studies in Anthropology Series in Social, Cultural and Linguistic Anthropology, no. 2, Department of Anthropology, University of Chicago, Chicago, 1975, p. 55.
13. Ibid.

14. E.E. Evans-Pritchard, *Witchcraft, Oracles and Magic among the Azande*, Clarendon Press, Oxford, 1937.
15. Jean Comaroff, 'Healing and the Cultural Order: The Case of the Barolong boo Ratshidi of Southern Africa', *American Ethnologist*, 7(4), 1980, pp. 637-57.
16. Pierre Bourdieu, *The Logic of Practice*, Stanford University Press, Stanford 1990.
17. Pierre Bourdieu, *Outline of a Theory of Practice*, Cambridge University Press, Cambridge. 1977.
18. Ibid.
19. Sherry Ortner, 'On Key Symbols', *American Anthropologist*, 75, 1973, pp. 1338-46. 'Patterns of History: Cultural Schemas in the Foundings of Sherpa Religious Institutions', in Emiko Ohnuki-Tierney (ed), *Culture Through Time: Anthropological Approaches*, Stanford University Press, Stanford, 1990.
20. Sherry Ortner, 'On Key Symbols', *American Anthropologist*, 75, 1973, pp. 1338-46, 1342.
21. 'Patterns of History: Cultural Schemas in the Foundings of Sherpa Religious Institutions', in Emiko Ohnuki-Tierney (ed.), *Culture Through Time: Anthropological Approaches*, Stanford University Press, Stanford, 1990.
22. Edward Schieffelin, *The Sorrow of the Lonely and the Burning of the Dancers*, St. Martin's Press, New York, 1976.
23. Judy F. Pugh, 'Astrological Counselling in Contemporary India', *Culture, Medicine and Psychiatry*, 7:1-21, 1983. 'Concepts of Person and Situation in North Indian Counselling: The Case of Astrology', in E. Valentine Daniel and Judy F. Pugh (eds.), *South Asian Systems of Healing*, E.J. Brill, Leiden 1984.
24. There were 11 small, labelled boxes with pre-written *mantras* and diagrams (*yantras*) to put into amulets. The labels were—*kanna* (to stop a baby's incessant crying), *biye* (marriage), *vidya* (education), *gabondhini nozor* (to 'tie up a person's body as protection against evil eye), *groh* (planets), *jvar* (fever), *pohuta* (a kind of 'women's illness), *kola* (banana—women with menstrual problems are given chanted on bananas to eat for 21 days and an amulet to wear), *santaan* (children—amulet given as part of the treatment for childlessness), *bicched* (separate—break up unsuitable connections between people), *modhu* (honey—bring in good relations between conflicting people). Each of these amulets have their own ways of administration and disposal. The details are available in the original thesis (Reference 5 in this list).

25. Several scholars have contributed to this perspective that illness and health are life situations, and hence cannot be studied in isolation from other kinds of human experiences. Jean Comaroff, 'Healing and the Cultural Order: The Case of the Barolong boo Ratshidi of Southern Africa', *American Ethnologist*, 7(4), 1980, 637-57. Peter Worsley, 'Non-Western Medical Systems', *Annual Review of Anthropology*, 11, 1982, 315-48.
26. Judy F. Pugh, 'Astrological Counselling in Contemporary India', *Culture, Medicine and Psychiatry*, 7, 1983, pp. 1-21. Nancy Scheper-Hughes, 'Three Propositions for a Critically Applied Medical Anthropology', *Social Science and Medicine*, 30(2), 1990, pp. 189-97.
27. Some of the scholars who shared this view are:
Peter Worsley, 'Non-Western Medical Systems', *Annual Review of Anthropology*, 11, 1982, 315348. Robert A. Hahn, 'Rethinking "Illness" and "Disease"', in E. Valentine Daniel and Judy F. Pugh (eds.), *South Asian Systems of Healing*, E.J. Brill, Leiden 1984. Nancy Scheper-Hughes and M.M. Lock, 'The Mindful Body: A Prolegomenon to Future Work in Medical anthropology', *Medical Anthropology Quarterly*, 1(1), 1987, pp. 6-41. Nancy Scheper-Hughes, 'Three Propositions for a Critically Applied Medical Anthropology', *Social Science and Medicine*, 30(2), 1990, pp. 189-97.
28. Peter Worsley, 'Non-Western Medical Systems', *Annual Review of Anthropology*, 11, 1982, pp. 315-48, 327.
29. Nancy Scheper-Hughes, 'Three Propositions for a Critically Applied Medical Anthropology', *Social Science and Medicine*, 30(2), 1990, pp. 189-97, 196.

CHAPTER 12

Mayong: The Land of the Occult

ASSADUZZAMAN

Witchcraft and magic are the categories of beliefs and the system of knowledge used within societies. Magic, sometimes known as sorcery, is a very ancient art. Magic has been known in most societies for thousands of years. Over the ages, witches have been known variously as healers, gods, teachers, historians, priests and priestesses. It has been often stated that India is a land of magic, both supernatural and mundane. Hinduism is one of the few religions that has sacred texts like the *Vedas*, that discusses both white and black magic. The *Atharvaveda* deals with *mantras* that can be used for, both good and bad. The word *mantrik* in India literally means 'magician', since the *mantrik* usually known *mantras*, spells, and curses which can be used for or against forms of magic. In Tibet, a ritual dance by the Buddhist monks portrays an evil spirit from times which predate Buddhist beliefs and includes a Tibetan Buddhist priest. The dance is an attempt to drive out evil. The *shamans* of Sri Lanka treat maladies by the restoration of energy balance within the body. The magical art of *deng-shui* was developed by ancient Chinese cultures. Magic is seen as a social phenomenon, by sociologists, akin to religion and science, yet a distinct category. In practice, magic bears a strong resemblance to religion. Magic has a strictly ritualistic implication that implements forces and objects outside the realm of the gods and the supernatural being. To some, including the Greeks, magic was considered a 'proto-science'. The difference is that magic is more about the personal power of the individual and religion is about in the power of God. Magic is something that is passed down over generations to a specific group while religion is more broadly available to the community. In Britain, the 'Witchcraft Act' of 1735 established that people could not be punished for consorting with spirits, while would be magicians pretending to be able to invoke spirits could still be fined. Further, in England, a revival of interest in magic was heralded by the repeal of the last Witchcraft Act in 1951. Gerald Gardener published his first witchcraft-themed book, *Witchcraft Today*, in which he claimed to reveal the existence of a witch-cult that dated back to pre-Christian Europe.[1] No matter which place it originates in, magic is the power of the wishes. Sigmund Freud emphasizes that, what led primitive men to come up with magic was the power of wishes. Magic is sometimes known as sorcery. The practice is often influenced by ideas of religion, mysticism, occultism science and psychology. Although the entire state of Assam was once known for its magical practices, the part of the state which is known for the continuation of the tradition and practices is a small village called Mayong.

Mayong is only 58 km from Guwahati. Beside wildlife, archaeology, ethnical, pilgrimage, ecotourism, cultural, river tourism, this place is famous for magic and occult practices.[2] It is situated in Morigaon district in Assam in the southern bank of Brahmaputra and on the north bank of the River Kalong. It is strategically situated in the highest hill of the Morigaon and Nagaon district.[3]

Mayong, the very name itself holds a history and ever unsolved mystery. Though there are several stories about the origin of the name Mayong, it is said that it is the land of illusion or *maya.* The name Mayong originates from this concept of *maya.* It is also believed that Manipuris from the Maibong clan used to inhabit this area. The name Maibong became Mayong with time. Since Mayong is a hilly area, it is full of elephants, and in Manipuri language an elephant is called Mayong, hence some believe that this was how Mayong got its name. There is also a legend associated with the name, it is said that the sacred parts of Goddess Shakti had been preserved in this area. Hence, the older generation called it as *Maa-R-Ongo* (parts of the Goddess) and later on it became Mayong.[4] It is also said that the great Mayong kingdom originated from the days of Xuuyta Singha. There is a story, which said that this youth was very handsome and possessed all qualities of a king. He came across a few cowherds and when they asked him who he was, he replied that he was from Gorya Rajya or kingdom which in fact is from Maibong of Manipur. He said he had left his kingdom due to some unknown reason. After that, the native village recognized him as king and the complete ritual was done and the kingdom was established. Some others say that the Maibong kingdom was a part of the Koch Dynasty, and it was a Kochari kingdom, and they believed that all Kacharies belonged to the family of Ghatotkach the son of Bhima of *Mahabharata* and Hidimbesvari. It is indeed difficult to trace the history of Mayong, but it is known as a land of necromancy where scenic beauty and history is closely associated with ingredients of mythology as a topping.[5]

KAMARUPA THE LAND OF MAGIC

Kamarupa was known throughout the middle ages as a land of sorcery and magic. It is believed that the Tantric Buddhists are mainly responsible for the spread and development of the culture of witchcraft and magic. Babu Nandalal Dey has given us a clear account about how the Mahayana cult ultimately developed into Tantricism which further developed into mysticism and sorcery. K.L. Barua writes, 'It (Tantricism) ultimately spread into Kamarupa and established for itself a strong-hold in Kamakhya. The Kamarupa Kings, probably after Brahmapala, adopted Tantricism as their tenet and as a result of this patronage Kamakhya soon became a renowned centre of Tantric sacrifices, mysticism and sorcery'.[6] The *Katha-gurucarita* mentions two *Badhua tatakiyas* (Buddhist magicians) who used to cast evil spells on people, while Sankar Deva was living in Belaguri. The *Thakur-Carita* mentions a case in which a certain person was reprimanded by Chaturbhuja Thakur, the youngest grandson of Sankar Deva, for using a charmed cane to drive off evil spirits. The *Mayamara Satrar Vamsavali* describes, how Aniruddha Deva, the founder of the Moamoria sub-sect produced an illusory cobra in an empty pitcher by his magical power in order to prove the veracity of his statement before the Ahom king Khora Raja alias Chukhampha, A biographical work entitled *Adi Charit* confirms the existence of a book called *Dhatu-Tamraksari,* popularly known as *Kalpataru Sastra* in the custody of the Moamorias of the

Kalasamhati sect. According to the biography, the book originally belonged to the family of Sankara Deva. The story goes that Aniruddha, the founder of the Moamoria sect had stolen it. It was commonly believed that, Aniruddha could perform many wonderful feats with the help of the incantations and spells contained in the book. The monastery established by Aniruddha came to be known as Maya-Mara Satra, as he had killed a serpent by his magic powers.

There are varieties of magical practices—high and low manifest and subtle, divination and necromancy. There is also contagious magic and sympathetic magic. Magic, in its numerous forms still exists in Mayong. And, Mayong remains nestled amidst the sylvan surroundings of Morigaon, with the hills standing tall as sentinels to guard the secrets and spells of Mayong. Mayong has succeeded in savings its rich, ancient traditions of religio-magical and fold-magical past along with its progress and march into modernity. Magic and modernity have well merged in Mayong.

The *Tantras*, *Samhitas*, and the *Yamalas* are the main source of the *mantras* and spells with the help of which one can perform miraculous feats. The *Yogini Tantra* is a remarkable Tantric work. It mentions *mantras* called *svapna-vati, madhumati, padmavati* and *vasikarana*. It also states how and when these incantation are to be meditated, describing the supernatural feats one can perform with the help of these *mantras* after getting mastery over them. There are a number of manuscripts dealing with sorcery, magic and incantations. Of these works, one called *Kamaratna Tantra*, published by the Assam Government and edited by H.C. Goswami is noteworthy. This is a translation of the Sanskrit *Kamaratna Tantra* by Goraksanath. The manuscript describes, how by uttering incantations and applying other methods a man can be subdued. Charmed, made hostile, killed, freed from evils, etc., it also prescribes the methods to be adopted for the performance of the abovementioned feats in the form of medicines, *mantras* and *yantras* (talisman). Incantations are both in Assamese and the Sanskrit language. Another manuscript called *Mantra Aru Ausadh* (*Mantras and Medicines*) contains both *mantras* and medicines. Some of the *mantras* are for effecting joyous relationship between husband and wife. The others are meant for curing of fever, driving away of evil spirits and curing from the bites of rabid dogs. There is another interesting work called *Jvarjara Mantra Aru Birajara Mantra.* In contained incantations to conduct a *bira,* or/and evil spirit.

THE PRINCIPALITY OF MAYONG

Mayong was a principality from ancient times. Despite its absorption by various powers, it maintained its royal lineage and autonomy. The present king of Mayong is Tarini Singha Raja and he is said to be the direct descendant of a royal lineage, which goes back to AD 1616. He is a Koch-Rajbonshi. The Koches are a branch of the Tibeto-Burman people of a greater family called Indo-Mongoloid; therefore, they are akin to the Kacharis, the Tipperas, the Garos, the Rabhas, etc. The Sanskrit equivalent of Koch is Kuvaca and in the *Kalika Purana* and in the *Yogini Tantra,* they are referred to by this term. The present king is the fortieth in the line of descendants. He was crowned on 17 April. Sunday, 2005, *Raj Abhisheikh* was held on the third day of Bohag. The tenth king of Mayong was Sarachchya Sinha (1590-1625). It is said that he was able to exercise an immense power of his might. Mayong became a powerful kingdom during his reign. It was he who first initiated the custom of celebrating, the local festival of, Panchagossain. He was also the first royalty to have demarcated the boundary of the kingdom of Mayong. The present king is a nominal head today and has no royal power whatsoever but he is the most honoured and respected person of Mayong today. There were feudatory or dependent *rajahs* in ancient Assam. The name of the Mayong *rajah* finds a place of honour among the nine petty *rajahs* of Nohdooria. The nine petty Rajahs of Nohdooria of early Assam were:[7]

1. Morapooria Rajah
2. Balogoria Rajah
3. Two Panborria Rajahs
4. Laloong Rajah
5. Dhing Rajah
6. Gorokia Rajah and the
7. Mayong Rajah.

MAGICAL MAYONG

Once upon a time, magic was something which Assam famous was for. Not very far from Nagaon, in the district of Morigaon, is the place called Mayong. Mayong is the famed ancient place where sorcery and magic was practised in the past and this ancient art is still practised today.[8] Imagine yourself a guest in any one of the numerous households of Mayong. You came unannounced, but your host was unperturbed. He was the least anxious about what to serve you at lunch of rice and *kawai* fish curry. The rice has already been cooked, but the fish curry is nowhere in sight. The host goes to the backyard, collects a few leaves from the mango tree and the *khoeowah* tree, washes the leaves as if those were live *kawaiu* fish and puts them in the frying pan. He asks you to watch very carefully. And just in front of your eyes, lo and behold, you find that the leaves are not leaves; in fact these have transformed themselves to jumping *kawai* fish and were sizzling in the frying pan. You partake your lunch of rice and mango leaves, sorry, *kawai* fish, and return happily to your home and hearth. This is one magical feat to transform leaves of the mango and *khorowah* tree into live *kawai* fish that almost every other household of Mayong can boast of. The total bewilderment of the whole feat would take anyone's breath away! It is illusory magic, which conjures the manifestation of *kawai* fish out of mango leaves. Mayong still boasts of many more magicians. In this age of globalization the honoured magicians know how difficult it is for them to keep their art alive. There is, for instance, Sri Ramdhan Das, who possesses immense skills of a magician. He had studied in Rajamayong Higher Secondary School and was a student of Sri Akbar Ali, a respected teacher of that locality. Sri Akbar Ali takes pride in extolling the virtues of his 'magician' student. One extraordinary feat Sri Ramdhan Das can still perform is to get the *pyol* (a low stool) stuck to your bottom, making it impossible for you to get up from it the ground. This particular magical feat was one amongst many such performed by the Mayong *bej* in the ancient times.[9] Once upon a time, Mayong was a place full of wild animals. There was an abundance of tigers, rhinos and elephants to be found in Mayong. The Pobitora Wild Life Sanctuary is situated not very far from Mayong. Even today, it is not very surprising to come across a stray rhino amidst one's paddy fields. The *bej* or medicine men of Mayong knew how to tame a tiger, strange as it may seem to us today.[10] Through his magical feat, he could shift one particular tiger from one particular jungle to another part of the jungle; to keep a tiger confined within one particular part of the jungle was also one of his other extraordinary feats. The magical art of Mayong is passed down from mouth to mouth. These have not been written down. This oral history is a rich tapestry of magical knowledge which has been closely guarded all through the ages.

Mayong is considered to be the capital of black magic and witchcraft in India. Historically, entire Assam, earlier known as Pragjyotishpur (land of astrology) was known for its occult and magical practices which have dwindled in time. Mayong remains the only place where the occult is still practised in institutionalized form. The place can be called to be a community of occult practitioners. During its heyday, the magic of Mayong was feared so much that the word magic became synonymous with Mayong. It is not known exactly how magic entered this land. Still, the people of Mayong are true followers of those beliefs, it is said that centuries ago, a king of Nepal brought forth magic to the Brahmaputra Valley. He established a small kingdom and Rajamayong became its capital and the Burhamayong evolved as the firmament of radical Tantricism. Later through the glorious era of the Ahoms the magic of Mayong was diligently nurtured by the natives. Even today, the people of Mayong are true followers of those beliefs which they consider as god-gifted capability. For solving their day-to-day problems, they still depend on the magic and their indigenous herbs.[11] One can witness in Mayong rare tricks, which may look unnatural to modern men but are enough to shake one from within. Among many tricks like fortune telling via *cawries* (sea shells), palmistry, future projection through a piece of broken glass is unbelievable. There are practices to cure illness from a distance by cutting a handful of plants, while chanting some *mantra* makes one feel the power of magic. Perhaps, one of the most outstanding magic acts, which is still prescribed for curing back pain is the one through which is the village *bej* or the witch-doctor laminates the cure with magic chant in a copper dish to track the pain. When the pain originates, the plate gets stuck to the body and the pain disappears. The locals believe that this dish eats away the pain. The local witch doctor performs the magic, and if the person is really suffering from back pain, the copper dish becomes hot like fire and within seconds it gets scattered automatically. Then, for the remaining pain, if any, a new copper dish is put in place and the process begins again. Another common magic in Mayong is the recovery of a stolen item, which seem unbelievable but true. A metal bowl is used when the quack puts a flower, which starts moving by itself and it then move directly to the place where the stolen item is kept. Sounds really doubtful, but is true, however, only a handful of common magic is practised now. There are other *mantras* like *mohini mantra, bokhikaram mantra* too which are performed to create attraction between a male and a female. It is said that in the olden days magicians could actually move to wherever they wanted in minutes by the use of *uran mantra.* A few households at Raja-mayong and Burhamayong still possess some of the manuscripts and practise it in a milder from. The few who may be practising it are reluctant to reveal anything. The former governor of Assam, Loknath Mishra, was also a reputed Tantric who collected secrets of and *mantras* from Mayong. Even P.C. Sarkar, the famous magician, reported to have acknowledged his indebtedness to lessons learnt in Mayong for many of his performances.

According to legendary sources, during the Burmese invasion of Mayong, magicians cast a spell around the boundaries of the area and thus, prevented the Burmese from entering and plundering Mayong. Still now, many pilgrims and students of witchcraft migrate to Mayong to learn *tantra-mantra.* Though the country was filled with Hindu temples and Hindu immigrants from south India, the tides of Buddhism and Buddhist Tantricism with magical demonstration of supernatural power could not be stemmed and waves of missionaries flocked to this place from the neighbouring state Bengal.

The Buddhist Tantrics had now a stronghold on nearby Hojai and Ojal (Durjoya), which they called Ojjiana or Oddiana. They had other outposts in Goalpara districts where at Yogigtiopha, Pancharatna and Sree-Suryyapahar, they established regular religious centres.[12] There are also references that in ancient time, the incarcerated Buddhists from other parts of India found a safe shelter in this part of the country after being harassed by the Turks. They infiltrated through Bengal and settled in the hill areas. Though disorganized, they started propagation to the people, a form of religious idea made attractive with magical cures of diseases and other ailments. Thus they took religion more as a means of living than a mission. Already a hotbed of Shaktism and Buddhist Tantricism, this place became a seat for this debased from of a religion to germinate the seeds of what are now the secret societies of Rati-khown, Tamul-nukhown and Gopidhara. Newly-formed chiefs who were extremely zealous for culture on principle, but miserably poor to judge or assimilate it, found the mystic cult highly appealing. Something of the real old civilization mixed with the savage practice and sauced with supernatural magical demonstration of immediate practical benefit, made up a dish palatable to everybody who cared anything for religious order. There were stories developed to support the power of magic in Mayong and Kamarupa. It is said that it was the power of magic that in 1337, the 1,00,000 strong cavalry of the valiant of Bengal perished to a man in this land of witchcraft and when a second army was raised, not a single soul would step beyond the border of Bengal into this dreaded land of black art. Even as late as 1530, Guru Nanak, the founder of the valiant Sikh faith, had the bitter anguish of finding his brave Punjabi servant Mardana transformed into a lamb before his very eyes by a woman of this place, who could as well transform the young man again to his natural shape according to her personal and private needs. The faithful private secretary of the great religious preacher diligently recorded this sad incident in his memories, perhaps as a warning though without any effect to the followers of his great master against future entry of any of their progeny into this horrible place.[13]

GENESIS AND PRACTICES OF *TANTRA* AND *MANTRA*

In this connection, references may be made of the vast mass of writings in early Assamese known as *mantra*, which bear the district stamp of 'Vajrayana' tenets. These *mantra puthis* (books on magical charms) composed in mystical words and syllables contain magic formulas against snake bite, demons evil doers, etc., and various spells for healing of diseases and winning of good future and desired ends. Most of these *mantras* bear the impression of the Buddhist *Dharani Sutras.* Another notable change among the local residents of Raja-Mayong is transformation from the Nath cult and Shaktism to Vaishnavism. In the pre-Vaishnavite era, the people of Mayong were believers of the Nath cult and Shaktism. All the followers of the Nath cult gave up their faith with beliefs and practices and embraced Vaishnavism as preached by the Vaishnava *gurus*—Chaitanya Deva and Shankar Deva. As a result of this conversion, a lot of change took place in their beliefs and practices. The practice of animal sacrifice was almost totally abandoned. People believed that even human sacrifice took place in the past. As result of this, magical beliefs also dwindled to a great extent through they could not be totally abandoned.[14]

CHRONICLING OF THE OCCULT

The practice of magic and incantation which prevailed in Assam attracted the attention of the Persian chroniclers of the sixteenth and seventeenth century. The *Ain-i-Akbari* and *Fathiya-i-Ibriyah* contain references of Assamese magical rites. The author of the *Baharistan-i-Ghaibi* dwells at length on the practices in the Khuntaghat *pargana* in the present Goalpara district and narrates how the people resorted to such practices to influence the course of war. The *Alamgir-Namah* states that whoever came to this place, lost his way and could not go back. The *Alamgir Namah* states that Sultan Muhammad bin Tughlug invaded Kamrup (Kamata) then under Durlabh Narayan (1350-60). Manpower was the greater strength of any invading king. The huge army of 100,000 was well organized. But could organization stand in the face of wizardry? The *Alamgir Namah* states that the country of enchantment relegated this huge army to oblivion.[15]

It further states that to avenge this defeat, Muhammad bin Tughlug sent another expedition, but as the army arrived in Bengal, 'it was panic-stricken and shrank from the enterprise'. Mirza Nathan speaks of the practice of augury resorted to by the Ahoms before the commencement of any war. It was the custom of the Assamese that whenever they engaged in a war, they performed some sorcery a day prior to the battle. The way in which they practised sorcery, has been described by the writer of *Baharistan-i-Ghaibi.* Some magic objects were sent floating down the river towards the enemy's side. If it floated down towards the enemy's side they took it as a good omen. If it travelled upstream out of its own accord they took it as a foreboding something against them, considered it a sign of their defeat and did not go out to the battle.[16] When Ram Singha at the head of the Mughal army came to invade Assam, he brought with him the Sikh Guru Teg Bahadur and five Muslim *pirs* to undo the effects of the Kamrupi black art. The kings, nobles and the generals, in those days, took *kavacha,* i.e. an amulet or a talisman. It was believed that a soldier or a man with such a *kavacha* could not be killed by his enemies easily. In the *Darrang Rajvamsavali,* it is stated that King Nara Narayana and his brother Chila Rai received such *kavacha* from their teacher Brahmananda Sannyasi of Banaras. Deoraja, one of the Ahom princes had a powerful *yantra* (talisman) on the arm. Lachit Barphukan had a *brahma kavacha.* Badan Barphukan also had a powerful talisman.[17]

Assam was, thus, feared and looked upon with awe as the land of enchantment in the olden days. Even today, we are in awe of the *mayong bej* or the medicine men of Mayong, who possessed, along with his other magical powers, the uncanny power to turn human beings into lambs in the ancient times. In fact, the culture of witchcraft, magic and portioning is still in vogue in Assam, particularly in places like Kamakhya, Mayong, and the Cachar district.

THE *BEJ* OF MAYONG

Medicine men (*bej*) played an important role in treating different kinds of ailments, both mental and physical. There are such medicine men still in Mayong. The Mayong *bej* administer herbal medicines, and also treat many diseases by chanting spells and incantations. These *bej* are well-versed in a mass of spells and incantations for curing snake bites. The magical power of the *bej* of Mayong is endless.[18] He has the superhuman power to subdue a male person or to bring a woman under one's control or to put an end to the life of one's enemy. To do mischief to one's enemy, sometimes, the hair, nail or a piece of cloth used by the person are taken away secretly and buried under the earth. The Mayong *bej* knows how to find a stolen property or the culprit of any crime. *Sauka-chalowa, bati-cholowa* or *bachhari-chova* are some such tactics employed by these magiciens. Mischiefs to the health of a man are perpetrated by the *mantra* of *hera-dia* and *ban-mara.* There are even counter systems of *hera-dia* and *ban-mara. Ban-mara* seems to be an affair of injurious incantation. The system of *hera-dia,* employs the effigy of the enemy to cast a spell on him. Along with the utterance of incantation *karikas* (spits) are thrust into the body of the effigy. Many *bej* also domesticate an evil spirit called *biera* with whose help they become powerful enough to do harm to a man. The art of magic was not confined to Mayong alone. Magic was prevalent among other hill tribes as well. The remark made by Francis Hamilton in connection with the chief of the Dimaura territory deserves mention. He writes, 'In fact, he is a Garo chief and the recent occupant is supposed to know many powerful magic. On this account, he is very much respected and the Governor of the province carefully avoids giving him any manner of offence.' The system of determining the good or the evil by means of drawing lines and circles on the ground was known as *mangal cowa.* The Ahom foretellers used fowl-legs in calculating the future. They had a system of their own, probably derived from Burma or Thailand. This system is still prevalent in Mayong.

THE HISTORICAL ORIGIN OF THE *BEJ* OR *OJHA* OF MAYONG

Different tribal communities like the Karbis, Mikirs, Koch, Dimasas reside in Mayong today. The Garos came to Mayong after Independence. Most of the tribes have now been converted to Vaishnavism. The tribal people used to believe, and there are some who still believe, in innumerable lesser divinities or natural powers which are very often called, spirits, supernatural agents, *bhuts,* etc. These elements are believed to have exercised power to move nature, guide and control human action. Such faiths of the tribal people are the results of uncommon circumstances. Most of the tribal people, since time immemorial, lived in the midst of natural settings surrounded by hills, thick forests, rivers, streams, mountains, rocks and boulders of imposing character. These natural phenomena coupled with environment ecology, etc., had certainly influenced the evolution of their religious beliefs, as some wise men from amongst the masses of each tribe slowly emerged who began to interpret the various aspects and workings of nature in religious perspective and associate them with the happening in their day-to-day life.

Belief in spirits, ghosts and goblins were common during the times. These were known as *bhut, do't, yakh, bak, danah, kandha, daini, jigini, khetar* and *peret.* When a person did something which displeased any of these evil spirits or supernatural agencies, he was supposed to be possessed by that invisible being. The identification of a particular spirit possessing a person was generally done by the *bej* or *ojha* and the habitations of some of the spirits were also well marked. That the *yakh* generally haunted a cattle pen, the *kandha* moved in the cremation ground, the *bak* in the fishing pond, the *bhut* in a deserted cottage and the *buda dangariya* had his habitation in a banyan or a similar tree. The *Katha-Gurucarita* refers to a good number of *yakhs,* who lived at the outskirt of a marshy land near Barpeta and were forced to abandon the place due to constant congregational prayers conducted by Madhava Deva. It is stated that the Ahom king Pratapa Singha (1603-41) was frequently possessed by a spirit *deo* for which he was unwilling to abdicate the throne. Having appeased Mahadeva by constructing a temple he got rid of the spirit. Instances of such beliefs in the existence of supernatural beings are found scattered in medieval literature. The *bej* from the medieval period onwards was a man of great knowledge, who was put on a pedestal by the commoners. His magical powers remained unquestionable. The medicine men occupied a respected and honoured position in society. People were in awe of him. Gradually, however, due to rapid societal changes, the development in science and technology made this institution of the *bej* or *ojha* redundant. It was increasingly becoming difficult to convince the common people of the magical powers of the medicine men. It was, therefore, indeed heartening to find that here in this pocket of Morigaon, Mayong houses the most enchanting of all the medieval arts—the art and science of magic.

Many stories have been circulating all through the ages about the forefather of the magical art of Mayong. This wizardry of Mayong is its most fascinating feature. The inhabitants of Mayong are fond of recalling the Mikir Boora (old man) the Father of Magic of Mayong. Story has it that the Mikir Boora had been in Mayong for ages. It was whispered that he was as old as the hills of Mayong. People dared not look at his face. Then one fine day a person from far off Barpeta came to his household. The Mikir Boora took this man under his wing. This man from Barpeta entered into a matrimonial alliance with one of the kin of the Mikir Boora and very soon, he learned and mastered the art of magic from the Mikir Boora. After the death of the old man, he became the uncrowned magician of the next generation, the famed *mayongor bej*—the medicine man of Mayong.

Magical knowledge is passed on from one magician to another through families or apprenticeships. The information usually transferred consists of instructions on how to perform a variety of rituals, manipulate magical objects, or how to appeal to gods or other supernatural forces, as it is a valuable commodity to which each magician believes he has a right. In Mayong, strange as it may seem, every household can boast of having some magical powers inherited from the previous generation. The possession of magical knowledge of every single household of Mayong is indeed unique.

The *bej* of Mayong knows very well that only certain words and phrases or words spoken in a specific context are considered to have magical power. Mayong language, according to C.K. Ogden and I.A. Richards' (1923), categories of speech, is distinct from scientific language because it is emotive and converts words into symbols for emotions whereas in scientific language words are tied to specific meanings and refers to an objective external reality.[19] Magical language is, therefore, particularly adept at constructing metaphors that establish symbols and link magical rituals to the world.

INFLUENCES OF MAGICAL AND *MANTRA* PRACTICES ON THE SOCIETY

People believed that misfortune befell the evil doers through magic. They cited the example of the infertility problem and mental diseases of the children of some of the practitioners of magic. The new generation in this region does not advocate the practice of magic. Of course, they feel proud of their traditional rich heritage of magic.

The magical practices continue to exist as a part of folk medicine. Earlier the people of Raja-Mayong used to take help of a traditional practice of medicine for seeking remedy for a disease. In the event of a person suffering from pox, they would resort to '*Ainam* or *Devinam*' of any kind, *jorani* (divine water), *bhogsora* or *prashada*, etc. A physician also uses different *mantras* along with the use of traditional medicines. He accepts a sum of Rs 1.25 along with a pair of betel leaf and a betel nut. But, yet they choose to go to the doctor for his advice and treatment. Of course, in the initial stage of disease, they still use the magical practices in Raja-Mayong village for treatment.

The *bej* commands a considerable amount of respect in rural Assam. He is looked at with awe as he is believed to be adept in black magic also. But most of the *bejs* interviewed, reported ignorance of black magic. They claimed to profess only white magic. The *bej* believed that the practice of black brought misfortunes upon the *bej* himself and he had to suffer towards the end of his life. Moreover, his family also had to suffer the evil effects. It ruined not only his own life but the life of his descendents also. The possible misfortunes that might befall were madness, death of children, prolonged illness, etc. The *bej* was regarded by the local people as a specialist in folk medicine. The female counterpart is also known as the *bej*. It has been noticed that besides the specialist, the common people also have a nodding acquaintance with the common remedies.

MAGIC AS CURE

There is an opinion that folk medicine has popularity among the uneducated as well as the educated people in Assam, which is not totally devoid of truth. It has been observed that the unenlightened section of the inhabitants of Assam first try the indigenous methods of curing ailments by application of herbal medicine prescribed by the medicine man, magician-priest or sorcerer. Failure to cure maladies like child disease, child mortality and minor ailments persuades the victims to visit the holy places or temples of deities for propitiation of supernatural power and benevolent deities accompanied by divination and forecasts of oracles. The educated people on the contrary, first try the modern available means of curing acute diseases and maladies which overwhelm the afflicted persons. Finally, however, they take recourse to supernatural powers and agencies on their failure to get satisfactory result from allopathic, homeopathic or Ayurvedic medicine.

According to the prescription of the *bej* of Mayong, *japs* are worn as protection against evil spirits. Death and marriage in the family are two occasions on which *japs* are worn by the members of the family.[20] *Tabij* or *madali* is worn as protection against evil spirits, sorcery, snake bite, etc. It is a bundle of charmed objects put into a metal case, mostly of copper, and huge around the waist, neck, wrist or arm with a piece of string. Sometimes a *jap* is used for hanging. The charmed objects may be roots, steams, leafs, etc., of trees, nails, scales, hair, excreta, etc., of animals and a leaf or a piece of paper with a charm written on it. In a *madali* against snake bite, the root of *gumuni* (*Sensevieriaroxgurghiana*) is used. The object inserted into the small metal cylinder and mouth is sealed with wax or lac. For disease believed to occur out of natural causes empirical medicine and *mantras* are used extensively. There are *mantras* for almost every disease and normally the *mantra* is named after the name of the disease. *Jora-phuka* is the common Assamese term for incantation of the *mantra*. The word *Jora* means winnowing and *phuka* means blowing air from the mouth, in Assamese.

The performance of the *bej* while treating a patient with *mantras* has some time to do with lashing and blowing air. He takes a few *bihlongoni* plants (*Polygonumsp*) and lashes the patient while chanting the *mantra* over the patient. In some cases blowing of air is done thrice at the end of the *mantra*. This act is called *phuka*. The word *jara* also implies both the acts and is used more commonly. In some diseases, leaves of the castor (*Ricinuscomunis*) plant is used in lieu of *bhilongoni*. This method is applied in chanting a *mantra* over the patient. The act, *jora* is used in a wider sense to mean to charm also. In case of chanting, a *mantra* over medicines and other objects, only air is blown. In treating an upset stomach, ginger, water, etc., are charmed with *mantra.* In treating pains, the affected part is massaged with charmed mustard oil. Sometimes, the *bej* chants the *mantra*, while massaging the affected part with oil. Sprains, stiff neck, headache, toothache, and backache are treated in this way. For fracture and fissure of the bone, the *harjorowalata* (*Cissus uadrangalaris*) is tied to the affected part. Some of the *bej* make a paste of the ground *harjorowalata* and some other medicines and plaster the broken part.

Treatment of diseases believed to be caused by the wrath of gods, is normally done by propitiating the respective deities. No medicine is taken in small-pox, chicken-pox, measles and mumps. It is believed that taking medicine is like challenging the Goddess Shitala, popularly is known as Ai. The disease is always referred to in honorifics as *Ai sakal, Air phul* (*flower of Ai*), etc. The Goddess is propitiated with *Ai nam*, which is a variety of folk song, singing praises of the goddess. Offering of raw fruits, gram, green gram, flowers, etc., are made, while incense is burned. The singing of *Ai nam* and making of offerings are done by the woman folk on the third day of the occurring of the disease. If too many blisters erupt and burst, the patients are made to lie on plantain leaves. The patient is kept away from ritual impurities and cleanliness is maintained throughout the period of suffering. If any deformity occurs in the patient after cure, it is believed to be the result of displeasure of *Ai* in the propitiation. Mumps is called *Jodumoni Ai* or *pithakhowa.* A pie is made from powder rice and attached to the swelling until Jadumoni is cured completely. *Ai nam* is sung for mumps also. Sometimes, the patients are given a gold chain to wear. In the event of other epidemics, such as cholera and other misfortunes befalling the community, singing of devotional songs known as *nam* is conducted in the *namghar* (community prayer house) by the people. In some parts of lower Assam, a *puja* is offered to the god of the disease and the offerings are floated downstream on a plantain raft. This *puja* is known as the *bheldiya puja.*

In cases of disease resulting out of the wrath of any particular identified Hindu deity, which is found out through divination, offerings are made to the god concerned. Every deity is offered his favourite item in the manner prescribed through tradition. Some of the gods accept sacrifice of animals, while some accept only raw fruit. The favourite offering of the god Shiva is the hemp (*Cannabis sative*) while his wife Durga likes the sacrifice of animals. Offerings are made to gods as promised while doing *topolabandha* or *agkara*. Disease resulting out of non-fulfilment of this promise is treated by fulfilling the promise. In diseases resulting out of spirit possession, the *bej* resorts to exorcism. In exorcising the *bej* uses a *mantra*. There are different *mantras* for different spirits. The *bej* chants the *mantra*, which is to be pitted against the specific spirit. While chanting the *mantra*, he lashes the patients with *bhilongoni* (*Polygonumsp*) plant. The process is called *jara* in treating spirit possession. But in case of spirit possession, unlike other disease, the patient is beaten hard with the *bhilongoni*. The *bej* extracts a confession from the spirit in the patient. The *bej*, after chanting the *mantra* for sometime acts in a way as if he has overpowered the spirit in the patient. He, then, starts talking to the spirit and goes on asking him questions. The possessed person answers his questions as if he or she is the spirit and not his or her real self. Sometimes, the patient talks in a voice which is not his or her real voice. The *bej* tries to find out the identity of the spirit and drive it out. He coaxes the spirit to leave the patient. If it does not agree, he threatens it repeatedly. At last, the evil spirit leaves the patient and shows a sign of leaving by making a loud sound or breaking or shaking a branch or a tree, etc. The *bej* sometimes resorts to physical torture of the patient, if the spirit refuses to leave it. It is believed that any assault made on the patient hurts the spirit and not the patient.

This type of exorcising is done in case of possession by evil spirit. But when a god possesses a person he/she is not exorcised. In such cases the god is propitiated with sacrifices and sacramental offerings. The possessed is then given the status of the god that possesses it. It is not thought to be an ailment and no remedy is sought. After sometime the spirit or the god leaves the possessed and he or she leads a normal life. *Mukhbhanga* (breaking of the mouth): The remedy for Mukhlaga (*Flacherie, It is a bacterial disease caused by Streptococci, bacilus bacteria*) is *mukhbhanga*, which literally means the breaking of the mouth.

There are a few *mantras* for *Mukhbhanga. Mukhbhanga* is done in a number of ways with these *mantras.* In one method of *Mukhbhanga* the *bej* or *bejini* chants the *mantra* over a fire. While chanting the *mantra,* mustard seeds and dry chilies are thrown into the fire. It is believed the burnt chillies emit a strong smell, if the *mukhlaga* is of mild degree. In case of severe *mukhlaga,* it smell very little or no smells comes out at all. In another method, water or ginger is charmed with *mukhbhanga mantra.* The ginger or water is taken by the person suffering from *mukhlaga.* While charming, the ginger *mantra* is muttered and air blown over the pieces of ginger. But while charming water, a knife is taken to cut the surface of the water every now and then every while the *mantra* is chanted over it. Some *bej* prescribe only drinking of this water, while some prescribe drinking a portion of it and mixing the rest with water and taking a bath with it.

The process of *jora* with the *bhilingoni* plant is also another method of treatment of *mukhlaga.* Ailment arising out of sorcery is cured with counter sorcery. If it is caused by a *bira,* then it is expelled. Expelling of the *bira* is similar to expulsion of evil spirits. Sometimes the *bira* is believed to enter a person. This is not like spirit possession. The *bira* acts unnoticed by people and makes the person its refuge. In such cases, the person is exorcised and the *bira* is expelled. But the *bira* can act without entering a person also. In such cases the *bira* is expelled by overpowering it by *mantras.*[21] There are other forms of magical practices too by which peoples' sufferings, diseases, and misfortunes are countered. *Ban* is one of them. Literally, *ban* means an arrow (in Assamese and Bengali language). The belief is that an unseen enemy has thrown an arrow to cause distress to a person. The antidote to this is done by means of *bankata* and *banphirani,* as stated:

Bankata (*The cutting of the arrow*): Disease arising out of *ban* of the enemy is treated in two ways. In one, the *ban* is inactivated. This act is called *bankata* (cutting of the arrow), *mantras* are chanted to inactivate a *ban.* If some objects are believed to be buried as a part of the *ban,* the objects are found out through divination and inactivated with a *mantra* and disposed of by burning it or throwing it away.

Banphirani (*The throwing back of the arrow*): The other method of treating cases of *ban* is the *banphirani* (returning the arrow). In this method, the *ban* is not inactivated, but sent back to the person who had sent it. As a consequence, he suffers some effects which were the intended for the victim. This redirection of the *ban* is done with the help of *mantras*.

Treatment of maladies caused by animals: Maladies caused by animal agents are treated with *mantra* and medicine. For curing itching problems resulting from contact with a caterpillar people put lime marks on the ear lobes and wear *kal sosani* (fibre from plantain barks) around the neck. Apart from this, this practice of *jora* with *bihlongoni*, a *mantra* for inactivating the hair of the caterpillar is also there.

For curing the bite of rabid dogs, foxes, etc., an edible medicine made from herbs is given to the patient. The act of *jora* is also simultaneously carried out. Certain vegetables are forbidden for a person bitten by dogs or a fox. Two such vegetables are the *kantal urohi* (sword bean *Canavalia gladiate*) and *urohi* (country bean *Dolichos lablab*). Such a person is also forbidden to touch or even go under an *urohi* creeper.

The same method with different medicines and *mantras* is applied in cases of biting believed to be of the tiger, the spider, the centipede, the frog, the snake, the toad, etc. The snake bite is a serious affair and great mystery shrouds the treatment of snake bite by the *bej*. Snake bite is treated in many ways. The common people, as a first aid to snake bite, tie a strong knot just above the place where the snake has bitten. This is the done to prevent the snake venom from mixing with the blood. In the meantime somebody runs to the *bej* to fetch him. Sometime, the *bej* lands a strong slap on the cheek of this messenger. It is believed that some *bejs* can cure snake bite by merely slapping the messenger. The harder the slap, the quicker the cure. This slap is also believed to be *dharani dhara* that is arresting the poison. The *bej* comes and first he chants a *dharani dhara mantra* and then begins his cure. Some of the *bejs* suck the poison out with the mouth. Sometime they make an incision on the bite for sucking out the poison. It is also believed that some of the *bejs* bring the snake back with the power of the *mantra* and make it suck out the poison. Sometime a charmed stone is placed over the bite while on other occasions the bite is merely washed with charmed water. A portion of this charmed water is also orally administered.[22]

PRESERVATION OF OCCULT CULTURE

There is a museum near Mayong which has been established to preserve the occult culture of Mayong. The *Mantra Puthi* written in *Sachipat* are preserved in it. Besides other curios, the museum possesses another unique thing. These are cannon balls retrieved from Kajuulichookey. In the Battle of Saraighat, Lachit Borphukan had wrested Guwahati back from the Mughals. On 22 August 1667, a large army had sailed down the Brahmaputra. Fixing his base at Koliabar, Lachit had advanced towards Guwahati in two divisions. It was the south bank of the river. The Ahoms had stormed the forts of Kajali, Sonapur, Panikheti and Tatimara lying between the Kapili and Guwahati. These cannon balls are the remnants of a great war the brave Lachit Borphukan had fought. These cannon balls in the museum near Mayong vary in size, from little balls the size of ping-pong balls to those a little bigger than that. At Kajalichookey, there are still hundreds and thousands of these cannon balls buried deep in the earth. This is history and historical evidence of the great general Lachit Borphukan. A number of annual celebrations take place in Mayong. 'Panchagossain' is celebrated on the fourth, fifth, and sixth of Bohag (April) every year. This festival is in its 339th year today. The tenth king of Mayong, Sarachchya Sinha, had first started the custom of celebrating this festival. During the Zeth (May) month, *nagaria kirtan* is always held. There are numerous *thaans* (holy pedestals) in Mayong-Ganges *thaan;* where worshipping of Ganesh is performed at every Ganesh Chaturthi; Siva Thaan; Boori Aair Thaan, Bhagavati Thaan, where worshipping is done during the Aaahar and *Zeth* (May-July) months; Kachaikhaiti Thaan, etc. Worship of these gods and goddesses and the festivals associated with these celebration, have continued right from the olden days, with traditional gaiety and fanfare. The royal exchequer contributed generously for the organization of these festivals in the past. This royal generosity is still traditionally maintained by the present king of Mayong.

NOTES

1. Gerald Gardner, *Witchcraft Today*, Rider and Company, London, 1954.
2. Kamal Chandra Nath, *Mayonght Mantra: Sanskritir Sadhana*, Saidyasnata Prakashan, Morigaon, 2009, pp. 10-11.
3. Anshuman Das (ed.), *Morigaon Dapon*, Souvenir of 88th Annual conference Srimant Sankardev Sangha, Morigaon, 2019, pp. 15, 16; M. Goswami (ed.), *Nidanam: Dr. Braja Mahan Goswami Commemoration Volume: History of Medicine of Assam*, Jyoti Prakashan, Guwahati, 2012, p. 93.
4. Lokendra Hazarika, *Mayong Itihas*, Rodali Prakashan, Morigaon, 2011, p. 23; M. Goswami (ed.), *Nidanam: Dr. Braja Mahan Goswami Commemoration Volume: History of Medicine of Assam*, Jyoti Prakashan, Guwahati, 2012, p. 101.
5. Lokendra Hazarika, *Mayong Itihas*, Rodali Prakashan, Morigaon, 2011, p. 23; Kamal Chandra Nath, *Mayonght Mantra: Sanskritir Sadhana*, Saidyasnata Prakashan, Morigaon, 2009, p. 31.
6. K.L. Barua, *Early History of Kamrupa*, Author, Shillong, 1933, p. 23.
7. Lokendra Hazarika, *Mayongor Itihash*, Rodali Prakashan, Morigaon, 2011, pp. 106-7.
8. Romesh Chandra Nath, *Mayar Rajya Mayongor Kahini*, Morigaon, 2008.
9. Dipon Nath, *Mayongor Bej aru Romanchokar Gherjali*, Morigaon, 1990.
10. Ibid.
11. Kamal Chandra Nath, *Mayonght Mantra: Sanskritir Sadhana* , Saidyasnata Prakashan, Morigaon, 2009, pp. 18-19.
12. M. Goswami (ed.), *Nidanam: Dr. Braja Mahan Goswami Commemoration Volume: History of Medicine of Assam*, Jyoti Prakashan, Guwahati, 2012, p. 101.
13. Guneswar Deka, *Mantra Prahidh Mayong Aru Pabitara Itihas*, K.K. Konwar, Morigaon, 1995, p. 6.
14. Kamal Ch. Nath, *Mayonght Mantra-Sanskritir Sadhana*, Saidyasnata Prakashan, Morigaon, 2009, pp. 10, 11.
15. Nathan Mirza, *Baharistan-i-Ghaibi*, tr. M.I. Borah, vol. l, para 306, p. 273.
16. Ibid.
17. Ibid.
18. Dipon Nath, *Mayongor Bej aru Romanchokar Gherjali*, Morgaon, 1990 for details.
19. C.K. Ogden and I.A. Richards, *Meaning of Meaning*, 1923, English tr. H.B. Jovanaoavich, Harvest H.B.J. Book, Orlando, 1989.

20. M. Goswami, (ed.), *nidanam, Dr. Braja Mahan Goswami Commemoration Volume: History of Medicine of Assam*, Jyoti Prakashan, Guwahati, 2012, p. 93.
21. Ibid., p. 101.
22. Kamal Ch. Nath, *Mayonght Mantra-Sanskritir Sadhana*, Saidyasnata Prakashan, Morigaon, 2009, p. 31.

PART III

MAGIC, SUPERNATURALISM AND DIVINITY

CHAPTER 13

Magical Attributes: Some Glimpses from Medieval India

M. PARWEZ

Assam, located on the eastern fringes of Mughal India, seldom received close attention of the Mughal rulers. Though, there was some sort of trade and commerce, particularly supply of elephants and wood, the region was not well known. However, there were many invasions of the area. Most of the time, the invasion was repulsed or they withdrew due to the inhospitable climatic condition. Still some part of the kingdom remained under control of the Mughal state for a considerable time. Nevertheless the medieval chroniclers remained curious about the region which got reflected in their works. Except Shihabuddin Talish, who went there alongwith Mir Jumla's army and Mirza Nathan, who fought several wars in the region, none of the chroniclers had first hand information.

The medieval Indian chroniclers have rarely paid attention to the better half of the society. In their endeavours to describe different developments whether during Delhi Sultanate or Mughal India, they went on to describe conquests, annexations and policies useful for political purposes but ignored women's contribution in the society. Ziauddin Barani's magnum opus, *Tarikh-i-Firuzshahi* does not provide much information on women. However, there are some references to women, when Amir Khusrau describes women with spindles spinning yarn or Isami's bitterness about Razia Sultan reflected in his writings:

> That woman is better, who engages herself with the (spinning)
> Wheel (*Charkha*) all the time.

For a place of honour will make her lose her senses
Let cotton be her companion, sorrow her cup; and
Let the noise of spindle (*duk*) be her music[1]

Khusrau states that women should be involved in activities like spin-ning than becoming a sultan. However, his bitterness reflected his perception that by doing so, Razia Sultan had encroached into domain solely confined to men.[2] Most of the information on women during Delhi Sultanate comes from the texts related to Sufism, *bhakti* and Sikhism. However, the Mughal miniature paintings proved to be a mine of information on women, particularly about the women's labour. It depicts common men and women involved in different productive activities like cultivation, amusement, construction work, handling tools and implements, participation in the religious and secular ceremonies, etc. The accounts of European travellers also supplement one's understanding of women in the medieval society. The description of Jesuits, Thomas Roe, Bernier, Manucci, Ralph Fitch and the factory records provide some useful information on the subject.

The eastern frontiers often attracted attention of medieval rulers of Hindustan, especially the Mughal emperors, largely for economic reasons. The empire used to get elephants, timber and other produce from the eastern frontiers and this resource rich region got imperial attention which led to long long drawn warfares.[3]

One of the prominent state formations in the eastern frontiers of the Mughal empire was the Ahom state. Assam was ruled in the medieval period by Ahoms, who were a branch of the Shan/Tai race. The Shans were occupying the northern and eastern hill tracts of upper Burma and western Yunnan,[4] where they formed a group of states called Mung-mau or Pong. In AD 1228, the Ahom pressed by the Burmese in the Maulung district of upper Irrawadi, crossed the Patkai range and entered the eastern part of the Brahmaputra Valley and Sukapha was the chief of this marshall group of the Ahoms.[5] They had initially established themselves in the south-eastern corner of the Brahmaputra Valley after subjugating the Moran and Borahi tribes, who then got assimilated within the Ahom system.[6]

In the Brahmaputra Valley there were established state formations existing prior to 1228. The ancient kingdom of Kamrupa had disintegrated into a number of tribal and non-tribal polities.

The State of Kamrupa existed between the rivers Barnadi and Karotoya and in the east, there were two dominant states—Chutiya and Cachari and in the west there were a number of feudal chieftains called Bhuyan.[7] The political history of the Ahoms was, therefore, largely a struggle for the mastery between the new entrants, i.e., Ahoms and these state formations. The subsequent centuries were to witness intermittent conflict among the various powers and in this power struggle, the Ahoms, at the cost of already existing state formation, were successful in extending their domination.[8] Along with the political extension, the Ahoms kings also adopted a policy of systematic settling down of Ahom families in the newly conquered territories to strengthen their position. However, the main foundation on which the establishment of state, its function and domination rested on intervention of Ahoms in the production process, through which it strengthened state structure.[9] Since, 1206, the Ahom state was involved in large number of major conflicts with Bengal sultans and the Mughal rulers, which finally culminated in the battle of Itakhuli in 1682. Besides, they had constant warfare with other chieftains of the region. They faced existential threat from the mighty Mughal state and its immediate neighbour.

In this article, an attempt has been made to understand how chroniclers of the Mughal period have viewed Assam, particualarly Shihabuddin Talish, who had accompanied the invading army of Mir Jumla.

Ain-i-Akbari talks about Kamrupa (Kaonrup), where the inhabitants were good looking and addicted to sorcery.[10] It mentions strange stories about houses in which the pillars, walls and roofs were made of men compelled by the power of sorcery and criminals deserving death.[11] 'They also cut open a pregnant woman who had gone her full term of months and taking out the child, divine somewhat as to the future'.[12] Abul Fazl further remarks 'Bordering on this country (Bengal) are the dominions of the Rajah of Asham (Assam) whose great pomp and state are subjects of general report. When he dies, his principal attendants of both sexes voluntarily bury themselves alive in his grave'.[13] It indicates prevalence of a variant of *sati* customs though here the women were buried along with their husband. Shihabuddin Talish was the witness to excavation of such graves in Garhgaon, which were excavated in the presence of Mir Jumla. He writes, 'the noble and high ranking officers prepare funeral vaults for their dead and also put some utensils made of gold and silver, carpets dress materials and eatable items necessary for a period of several years inside it. They also put wives and servants of a dead person inside the crypt after having killed them'.[14] Our sources are silent as to whether all the queens or all the women of the king's *harem* were buried including women and slaves.

In the late seventeenth-century, Manucci the Italian traveller, also refers to Assam, He says:

> The city of, Kharganw (Kamrup) is very large and fine, inhabited by rich merchants—that is, according to the stories told me in Dhakah, when I passed through it. The natives of those lands take four wives. Here, the women are very lovely and they do all the work of the house, the men being indolent, except in war-time, when they all go forth to fight.[15]

Manucci further mentions about engraving of wives along with the Rajah to which Abul Fazl referred to earlier. He mentions,

> . . . Mir Jumlah, after occupying the place (Guergao or Kharganw), caused the tombs to be destroyed, which contained great treasures, it being the Assam custom to bury with the defunct the wealth that he possessed. It is the practice of the people that when the master of the house dies they bury with him all his wives, concubines, and servants that is, the tailors, washermen, barbers and others who serve in the deceased's house, setting them all on fire after binding their feet.[16]

Manucci's account suggests forceful burials of wives, concubines and others. The French traveller, Bernier too mentions Assam while discussing Mir Jumala. He says, 'It is a large and well-built city (Guerguon), very commercial, and celebrated for the beauty of its women'.[17]

A detailed account of Assam comes from Shihabuddin Talish, who accompanied Mir Jumla's army.[18] His account particularly focused on the period spanning from 1661 to 1663. Mir Jumla made deep inroads in Ahom Kingdom, and had captured the capital city Garhgaon for a considerable time. His style of narrative appears to be similar to Amir Khusrau, and is quite vivid and poetic. He has used verses liberally within the running text. However, he described the war and strategies adopted by the respective factions in detail, but as he was a keen observer, he also provided information on socio-economic, cultural environment as well as geography, climate, flora, fauna economic resources of the region. The assimilation of the Muslims, who came for conducting diplomatic relations, or as soldiers or prisoners were so complete, that rarely anyone went back to their original native place. Muslim settlers in Assam adopted dress and customs of the local inhabitants. He says:

> . . . As no one who entered this country (Assam) ever returned and the manner of its native were never made known to any outsiders the people of Hindustan used to call the inhabitants of Assam sorcerers and magicians and consider them as standing outside the human species. The saying is that whoever enters this country is overcome by its charms and never comes out of it.[19]

That sorcery played an important part in their life, is further described by Mirza Nathan. He informs us that, there was a custom among the Assamese that whenever they engaged in a war, they performed some sorceries a day previous to the battle. He said, '. . . they send some magic object floating down the river towards the enemy's side. If it floats down towards the enemy's side, they take it as a good omen. If it travels upstream out of its own accord, they take it as foreboding something against them and consider it as sign of their defeat and they do not go out to battle. According to that custom, they built one raft of plantain trees, which is well-known fruit of Hindustan, and performed *puja*, i.e worship of devils on it in the following manner. They sacrificed a black man, a dog, a cat, a pig, a monkey, a he goat and a pigeon, all black in colour. Their heads were collected together and placed on the raft along with many ripe banana, *pan*, betel nut, *chuiwa,* scents and rice paste, red yellow and green colours cotton seeds mustard seeds, gee and *sindur* (vermilion) and then the raft was pushed adrift.[20]

Talish further says,

The people of Hindustan describe the inhabitants of this land (Assam) as magicians and consider them as being out of pale of human race. They believe that this land is a land of magic and talisman. They say that whosoever goes to that country is charmed by magic, which prevents him from returning home.[21]

He further describes the region in details:

. . . the river Brahmputra situated in the north east of Bengal. The river Brahmputra flows through its middle from east to west. Its east-west wise length from Gowahati to Sadna (Sadia) is about 200 *Karoh Jarib*. Its north south wise breadth from the mountain (inhabitated by) . . . different tribes like Miri, Magami, Dafta and Landa (Naga?) to Naga hills is about a distance of 7-8 days of hill journey. The southern range of hills of this country consists of the Khasya (Khasi), Chachar (Cachar) and Kashmir (?) hills and adjoins the Naga hill in the east. The land lying to the northern side of the Brahmputra is known as Uttarkol and on the southern side, it is known as Dakhin Kol.

Mulla Darvesh Harvi, friend of Talish composed a verse on Assam.

The land of Aasham, which lies in the lap of China and Calthy.
It is a different world, where people and its geography are of different nature.
In this land, the humus becomes green without any external help.
The land of Aasham is totally cut-off from the main land like . . .
Its space is heart-rending like Fana (annihilation).
Its rivers like the thought of a wise person are very deep.

The rebels were sharp shooters, great warriors and equally quarrelsome, similar to the eyes of Taraz's beauties (a central Asian city famous for beauty). The people of this land are very dignified having superior qualities.[22]

The prosperity of the region was also testified by Talish when he observed: 'If this country was administered like the imperial dominion (Mughal), it is very likely that forty to forty-five lakhs of rupees would be collected from the revenue paid by the raiyats, the price of elephants caught in the jungles and other sources'.[23]

Similarly, he estimated an income of eight lakh of rupees from the region of Kuch-Behar provided it was governed as per imperial (Mughal) systems.[24] Talish also described the environmental settings of the countryside—right from the village of Kaliabor to the town of Kahargaon. Fruit trees encompass the surroundings, on both side of the road, there were high bamboo trees to provide shadow, besides having large varieties of fragrant flowering trees. He praises the agricultural fields, 'the agricultural fields and gardens are planted so systematically in the plains in this country that one can not see any depression ot elevation in the field'.[25] He found Uttarakhol was more cultivated and flourishing, but from habitation and strategic point of view the Dhakinkhol was preferred and therefore, the king of Assam always resided in the Dhakinkol.[26] The areas near the Brahmaputra River was fine for the invading army but the interiors were dangerous climatically as the region used to receive heavy rainfall for eight months and often even during four months of winter.[27] A keen observer like Talish described the health aspects, where he pointed out that the native people were not afflicted with deadly diseases like leprosy, elephantiasis, varicose veins, pharyngitis and other communicable diseases that were very common in Bengal.[28] However, jaundice was deadly for outsiders during summer than for the natives. About fruits, he mentioned those that were also growing in Bengal and Hindustan, but he was specific about those fruits and flowers which not found elsewhere in Hindustan. He says,

other varieties of flowers and fruits, both wild and cultivated, noticed in this country are not found in any part of Hindustan. The coconut and Neem trees are somewhat rare. But saplings of Pepper, *Sazaj* (*tezpat*) and various kinds lemon grow in abundance . . . pineapple found in abundance, is very juicy and tasty. There are three kind of sugarcane, black, red and yellow. Ginger are very big, soft and fibreless and have good flavor. *Panyal* a variety of *Amla*, is delicious and tasty. The chief crop of Aasham is paddy.[29]

Talish found a general scarcity of salt and they used to get some salt by burning banana trees into ashes. The ash was put in canvas bag and water was poured over it to filter salt.[30] While describing birds like duck, goose and fighting cocks and animal like the elephant, deer, stag, *nilgai*, ram and francolin, he described a contrivance he noticed in the capital city of Kahargaon. He writes,

. . . some cage like small but very strong structures supported by heavy wooden posts at the four corner, are constructed. It appears that these are used for different purposes. On enquiry it was found that there was some expert *Mahuts* of the Raja, who rubbed a particular herb on the body of a female elephant. Then she was carried to graze in the grazing grounds, where wild and *must* elephants live. As soon as the *must* elephant smelt that herb rubbed on the female elephant, it became uncontrollably mad and followed her. Then the Mahut skillfully brings back the female elephant to the cage like structure. The moment the *must* elephant enters the enclosures it is trapped to be trained and domesticated later on. The *Nawab* (Mir Jumala) tried his best find one of those expert in this art but he failed.[31]

He had seen musk deer which were very big as well as noticed different aromatic and heavy wood (*agaru*), which were found in large quantity in the hills of Namroop, Sadna and Lakhogarh. Animals like horse, donkey and camel were not seen in Assam and they wanted to see these animals again and again. He mentions that they were afraid of horses and if chanced to find horses they used to chop the legs of the animal immediately. If one horseman attack one hundred Assamese, they used to take flight throwing their arms.[32]

About arts and crafts, he observed that the Assamese were expert weavers of beautiful cloths of silk and velvet besides being good carpenters. Weapons like guns, matchlock, cannon, iron arrow head, long spears, bow (bamboo) and *dao* were known to native people and all able person had to participate in the battle. However, about twenty thousand young men formed the core of the fighting force, who always remained prepared for the wars.[33] Most of the time, they considered Tuesday night as auspicious for battle and raid. After capturing the capital city, he had observed the city and provided detailed description. Four doorways were constructed of mud and stone. From each gateways the distance to the king's palace was three *karoh*. A high, wide road leading to the palace was constructed having habitation on both sides. The city was fortified with cane field. But it seemed that the capital city was not planned properly.[34] A river Dikhow flowed near the palace. Inhabitants did not indulge in selling and buying food items which they used for their own consumption.[35] Though, there was a bazaar with *pan* leaves sellers.

The king's audience hall (*soolang*) was 120 cubit long and 30 cubit wide. It was supported by 66 wooden posts and every post was about four *zera* (104 cm) thick. The posts were beautifully carved as Talish says, '. . . there is no one in this universe, that can construct, design or decorate wooden houses like the people of Aasham'.[36] About twelve thousand men worked for one year to construct the palace. Besides, the king's palace there were other beautiful houses for the stay of the king. Bhukan also lived in beautiful and comfortable houses but those having matrimonial relations with the king got houses to live which were surrounded by gardens and ponds full of clean and sweet water.[37] The common people due to humidity did not sit or sleep on the ground but they used to prepare a *machan* (raised wooden plateform) and lived on it.

Talish also referred to belief about the divinity of Ahom Raja and termed the belief as corrupt and mystified, that one of the forefathers of this Raja (Jayadhawaj) was the sovereign ruler of the angels, and he descended from the sky on a golden ladder and he found the place so beautiful that he did not return to his abode.[38]

He describes Pran-Narayan, the ruler of Coochbehar as addicted to alcohol, and was always desirous to be in the company of beautiful and vivacious women. He lived in pleasure ignoring administration of his kingdom.[39] Then in a verse, he stated due to drunkenness many countries were ruined so one should beware of drinks as it has destroyed many kingdoms.[40] The *harem* of the king has been described as well planned and beautiful, full of gardens.[41] He says, 'The seed of beauty grows less on the face and physique of men and women of this country'.[42] According to him, Mir Junla strictly ordered that the honour and property of every subject whether present or absent must be protected. In case of defiance, he punished his own soldiers by passing an arrow through their nostril. Such protection encouraged the inhabitants who had fled, to return to their homes. A similar proclamation was also issued when Garhgaon was captured.[43] Regarding Bhutan, he remarked, that 'the Bhutia (ruler) was a healthy person and had a fair and pinkish complexion. . . . His only cloth was a white *lungi*, which did not cover his nudity properly. It is said that both male and female of this community wear the same type of cloth and behave in the same manner.'[44]

On 26 February 1662, the Simalgarh Fort was captured and

Mir Jumla encamped at Kaliabar. He issued a *farman* (separate) not to plunder the property and not to be cruel to the women and children of the local inhabitants[45] and it was so strictly enforced that during the stay of one year, none of the officers and army retainers could cast evil eyes on the property and honour of the women.[46]

Talish then proceeded to compose a verse indicating the pangs of army men desirous of meeting the charming women of Kaliabar and Assam.

If you are desirous of Kaba, then walk in the desert enthusiastically.
And do not become distressed, if the thorn of the deserts pricks you.[47]

The beautiful women hoping for union with their beloved were singing:

Be careful! when you pass through lane of my Ashiq.
Because even sidewall of his lane is notorious for breaking the heads.[48]

Talish observed that women of Miri and Majmi (Mishmi?) tribes inhabiting Uttarkol were more beautiful and attractive than the Assamese women.[49]

With regard to Raja Jayadhawaj Singha, he remarked that his wife did not give birth to a male child and deprived him of a successor due to his cruelty.[50] He gives his impression about the women of Assam. They have been described as beautiful, charming, having delicate body and black complexion. They also had long black hair, attractive hands and legs.[51]

They looked beautiful and charming from a distance but from near, they lacked grace and beauty.[52] He found aristocratic as well as common women roaming around freely without any cover in the *bazaar* and streets.[53]

The polygamy appears to be general practice as only a few persons had only two wives whereas majority of persons used to have four to five wives.[54] They also indulged in sell, purchase and even bartering their wives amongst themselves.[55]

Talish's description of Naga women indicate the tribal way of life however, he has praised their physical strength.[56] One also comes across political acumen of mother queen of Darrang (mother of

Makardhawaj), who ruled ably after the death of Raja of Darrang in establishing law and order, protected routes and showed compassion to subjects. She had requested Mir Jumla to restore the kingship of Darrang to the son of Makardhawaj and accordingly, a *farman* was issued.[57] Later on she was awarded two shawls and three clothes with gold and silk embroidery.[58]

Significantly, aristocratic Ahom women figured prominently as an instrument of diplomatic relation. There are large numbers of instances when royal women were sent to other kings as guarantee to peace agreement except the case of Ahom woman Mula Gabharu who fought to avenge the death of her husband.[59] When peace negotiation began with Mir Jumla, one of the conditions for peace agreement was to send one of the daughters of the Raja into the Mughal *harem*.[60] On 4 January 1663, when the agreement was signed one daughter of the Raja was given into the custody of Amarat Panah for escorting her to court.[61]

The two women leader of Moamaria rebels, Radha and Ruknimi also indicate the increasing role of women in political sphere.[62] Legends ascribed them hawing occult power and endeared the popular imagination for long.

Despite Assam's attempt to remain in isolation, the recurrent invasions brought the native into contact with outsiders. Some of the areas particularly, Kamrupa and Kuch Hajo remained in the control of invading armies for considerable time. During Mughal occupation of the regions, several Mughal administrative institutions were made operational like land revenue and collection of revenue in cash or kind. Subsequently, when the areas were freed, the altered system continued. This led to prevalence of two contradictory systems. This was one of the important cause for the eighteenth-century crisis in the Ahom state leading to British annexation in the early nineteenth century.

NOTES

1. Quoted in Irfan Habib, *Technology in Medieval India, c.650-1750*, New Delhi: Tulika, 2008, p. 41

2. Ibid.
3. Amalendu Guha, 'Medieval Economy of Assam', *The Cambridge Economic History of India*, vol. I, ed. Tapan Raychoudhury and Irfan Habib, Delhi: Orient Longman, rep., 1984, pp. 487-90. See also Irfan Habib, *The Atlas of the Mughal Empire*, Delhi: Oxford University Press, for economic products of eastern India.
4. Edward Gait, *A History of Assam*, Guwahati: LBS, 1997, p. 66.
5. Ibid., pp. 71-3.
6. Ibid., pp. 73-4.
7. Ibid.
8. Amalendu Guha, 'Medieval North-East India: Polity, Society and Economy 1200-1750AD', Occasional paper 19, Centre for Studies in Social Sciences, Calcutta, 1978, pp. 2-4.
9. Sajal Nag, 'The Socio-economic Base of Medieval Assam in the Light of the Asiatic Mode of Production', *NEHU Journal of Social Sciences and Humanities 1-1*, Shillong, 1998, pp. 32-8.
10. Abul Fazl, *Ain-i-Akbari* vol. II, tr. H.S. Jarrett, Low Price edn. Delhi, rep. 1997, pp. 130-1,where Abul Fazl describes the account of *suba* Bengal as part of the account of 12 *subas.*
11. Ibid.
12. Ibid., p. 131.
13. Ibid.
14. Shihabuddin Talish, *Fathiya Ibriya*, University Collection no.98 Maulana Azad Library, AMU, folio 38(b).
15. Niccolao Manucci, *Storia Do Mogor 1653-1708,* tr. William Irvine, vol. II, Delhi: Low Price Publisher, rep. 1990, p. 93.
16. Ibid., pp. 92-3, Khafi Khan, *Muntakhab-ul Lubab* also mentions about the practice.
17. Francois Bernier, *Travels in the Mughal Empire AD 1656-1668,* tr. Archibald Constable,New Delhi: Oriental Books Reprint, 1983, p. 172.
18. Shihabuddin Talish, *Fathiya Ibriya,* two manuscripts are preserved in Maulana Azad Library, AMU, Aligarh. One manuscript is in the Abdus Salam Collection, No. 307/77 having 118 folios and the other is in the University collection No. 98 containing 102 folios dated 1173 A.H. got 107 folios. I acknowledge the help provided by Dr. Abdus Salam Jilani STA Persian Language Department of History in reading and translating passages from original texts.
19. Shihabuddin Talish, *Fathiya Ibriya,* cited in Sajal Nag, *Roots of Ethnic Conflict:Nationality Question in North-East India*, Delhi: Manohar, 1990, pp. 19-20.

20. Mirza Narthan, *Baharistan-i Ghaybi*, vol. II, tr. M.I. Borah, Guwahati: DHAS, 1992, p. 487.
21. *Fathia Ibria*, AMU collection f. 21-24.
22. S. Talish, *Fathiya Ibriya* tr. Mazhar Asif, Guwahati: DHAS, 2009, pp. 46-7, Univesiry Collection M.A Library no. 98. see also Irfan Habib, *The Atlas of the Mughal Empire*, Oxford University Press, 1990.
23. S. Talish, *Fathiya Ibriya* tr. Mazhar Asif, Guwahati: DHAS, 2009, pp. 46-7, Talish, Univesity Collection M.A Library, M.A. Library Collection f. 66-7. Also cited in E. Gait, *A History of Assam*, Guwahati, 1997, p. 135.
24. Ibid., pp. 12-13.
25. Ibid., pp. 48-9.
26. Ibid., pp. 12-13.
27. Ibid.
28. Ibid., p. 49.
29. Ibid., pp. 50-1.
30. Ibid., pp. 12-13.
31. Ibid., pp. 50-1.
32. Ibid., p. 56.
33. Ibid., pp. 59-60.
34. Ibid., pp. 59-60.
35. Ibid., pp. 61-2.
36. Ibid.
37. Ibid.
38. Ibid., p. 54, see also *Ahom Buranji*, Eng. tr. G C Barua, Shillong, 1930 for detailed description.
39. Sihabuddin Talish, *Fathiya Ibriya* tr. Mazhar Asif, Guwahati: DHAS, 2009, pp. 61-2.
40. Ibid.
41. Ibid.
42. Ibid.
43. Ibid., pp. 13-14.
44. Ibid., pp. 14-15.
45. Ibid., pp. 31-2.
46. Ibid.
47. Ibid., p. 32.
48. Ibid.
49. Ibid., p. 52.
50. Ibid., p. 55.
51. Ibid., p. 56.
52. Ibid., pp. 61-2.

53. Sihabuddin Talish, University Collection, Maulana Azad Library, A.M.U., Aligarh, folio 36(a).
54. Ibid.
55. Ibid., folio 37(a), see also Sihabuddin Talish, *Fathiya Ibriya*, tr. Mazhar Asif, DHAS, Guwahati, 2009, p. 56.
56. Sihabuddin Talish,University Collection 98, Maulana Azad Library, AMU, Aligarh, folio-41(a). He has given reasons why the women covered only upper part and did not cover rest of the body.
57. Sihabuddin Tallish, University collection, 98, Maulana Azad Library, AMU, Aligarh, folio 68(b), Talish Mazhar Asif, op. cit., pp. 119-20.
58. Ibid.
59. Cf. S.K. Bhuyan, *The Military System in Medieval Assam*, Guwahati: Kamrup Anusandhan Samiti, 2010, pp. 32-4, for details of such exchange.
60. Ibid.
61. Sihabuddin Tallish, University collection, 98, Maulana Azad Library, AMU, Aligarh, folio 68(b), folio 70(a).
62. Amalendu Guha, cf. S.K. Bhuyan, *The Military System in Mediewal Assam,* Guwahati: Kamrupa Anu Sandhansamiti, 2010, pp. 32-4, for details of such exchange.

CHAPTER 14

The Divine Origin, but Not Right, of Khasi Kings

KYNPHAM SINS NONGKYNRIH

Naduh ki sngi ba rim ba jah,
Hangta ka trai ka jaid ka Spah:
Nangta ki ïeng ka Kñia ka Khriam,
Hangta ki seng ban long ka Niam:
Ka dei ka Ding ba rhem ha Dpei,
Nangta ki ïeng ban saiñ pyrthei. (Soso Tham)[1]

(Since the days ancient and lost,
There it rested their kinship their Wealth:
Then they raised their Rites their Rituals,
There they founded their Religion:
It was the Fire in the Hearth,
Then they raised their politics.)

Traditional Khasi democracy has been much spoken of—sometimes extolled in poetry or essays, sometimes vilified in the most insensitive terms. It seems that many of these adulators and vilifiers, however, have made their cases for, or against, traditional Khasi polity with little knowledge or understanding. Research-based analysis of the subject is what is needed at this point when many eyes are trained upon it.

As the quoted lines from Tham's *Ki Sngi ba Rim U Hynñiewtrep* may reveal, one has to draw on the oral tradition to realize that the communal smithy of the Hynñiew Treps, ancestors of the Khasi people, was the 'Fire in the Hearth' of the mother's house, where the uncles and fathers, that is, the lawmakers, had forged their social and economic systems, their religion and their political system.

It is not by accident that the poet had first mentioned the social, economic and religious systems before mentioning politics. This is in agreement with folk tradition, which maintains that the Khasis had evolved their political structure, as it survives today, much later, when the need to modify the then-existing set-up had been felt.

Before that, there was hardly any political structure. When Khasis migrated into these hills thousands of years ago, there were no *syiems* or 'kings'. They were led by a legendary leader known as Syiem Lakriah, who also featured in our creation myth, 'The Sacred Myth of Ki Hynñiew Trep'. But he was called a syiem because he was the leader. It was a title of respect, not to be understood in the sense that a syiem is understood now.

At that time, everything was very rudimentary. The Khasis organized themselves into groups of villages governed either by *ki basan*, 'the clan elders', or *ki lyngdoh*, 'the high priests'. It was only much later that they founded the *himas*, the democratic states, republican in nature, monarchical in form. For thousands of years before the birth of Christ, they had survived as provincial entities or *raijs*. Nobody knows when the first himas were established, but by the iron-manufacturing age, that is by 353 BC, it is definitely known from stories that the himas were already there. From the story of 'Ka Ïaw Shibidi', for instance, it is known for a fact that the State of Sutnga (which was later called the Jaiñtia Kingdom by the Bengalis, Ahoms and other non-Khasis) and the State of Shillong were already there before that time. And that means that the State of Madur Maskut was also already there since these three were among the very first democratic states to be established. In fact, it was said that they existed side-by-side until the fifteenth century AD. The State of Madur Maskut was right there between the states of Shillong and Sutnga. It had territories both in Ri Pnar and Ri Khynriam (Jaiñtia Hills and East Khasi Hills), as well as in Ri Bhoi (northern Khasi Hills), Assam and East Bengal. Also in existence by the iron-manufacturing age was the State of Sohra, which is mentioned in the ancient stories of *U thlen and ka likai.*

These three, the states of Shillong, Sutnga and Madur Maskut were supposed to be the very first to be established. Later, there were about 30 states spread over areas in western, southern and northern Ri Hynñiew Trep, or contemporary East Khasi Hills, West Khasi Hills and Ri Bhoi, and only one big one in eastern Ri Hynñiew Trep, or Ri Pnar. Before that, for thousands of years, Ri Hynñiew Trep had simply been organized into independent provinces governed by basan clan elders and lyngdoh high priests in Ri Khynriam, Ri Maram (West Khasi Hills) and Ri Bhoi; by provincial chiefs like *sirdars* in Ri War (southern Ri Hynñiew Trep, bordering East Bengal); and by *dolois* in Ri Pnar'.

Tham considered this aspect of his people's culture so important that he introduced it in the very first stanza of his book: 'How in ancient times the uncles, the fathers/had fashioned politics, had founded states'. These lines serve to arouse the curiosity of the reader, who would inevitably respond to them with his own question, 'How had the forefathers "fashioned politics" and "founded states"?' It has been seen how their politics had taken shape in the mother's house, but it is not till later in the poem (Section VIII) that the poet explains the political set up of his ancestors. He declares that it began *Haba ki wad hangno u Syiem* (When they sought, where was the King), who would be responsible for all.

Tham's line about the search for a king refers to the many legends about the emergence of the ruling 'Syiem' clan. The most famous of these is 'The Legend of Ka Pahsyntiew' considered to be the progenitress of the first kings of Shyllong. Before this, the areas around what is known now as the Shillong Peak, were all *ri raij*, 'community land', and *ri kur*, 'clan land', organized into seven separate provinces known as *Saw Kher Lai Lyngdoh* because four of the provinces (Raij Nongkseh, Raij Nongumlong—both in the south western periphery of Shillong—Raij Swer in the south and Raij Mawlieh-Mawshai or Raij San Shnong in the west) were under the control of *basan* clan elders and three (Raij Mylliem in the south, but north of Raij Swer, Raij Nongkrem in the eastern periphery of Shillong and Raij Nongbri in the south-east) were under the control of *lyngdoh* high priests.[2] The basan clan elders and *lyngdoh* high priests governed their provinces independently without any accountability to a central authority, for there was none.

And, because each of them was independent, it was inevitable for them to quarrel with each other over trade, land and boundary issues. Often these disputes, in the absence of a central authority to mediate and reconcile, led to mutually destructive wars. It was to end such divisive disputes and debilitating wars (that could only make them easy prey for foreign invaders), that the provinces finally decided to come together in a single state known as Hima Shillong, though when exactly that happened, nobody can say.

The new State of Shillong was to be governed by a syiem, who would not only conduct the day-to-day administration but who would also bind each of the provinces together under his direction. But who would this syiem, this 'king', be? Choosing one from among the founding clans of the state, *ki bakhraws*, 'the nobles', was impossible as each clan wanted to project its own member as the king. The elders were at their wits' end. What were they to do? How were they to solve the problem? It was at that time that the legend of *Ka Pahsyntiew*[3] emerged.

A long, long time ago, it was said that spirits haunted the forests on the hills around, what is now called Lum Shillong or Shillong Peak. The chief of these spirits dwelled on the highest and most thickly wooded hill. In those times, people of the villages surrounding the hills did not know much about rites and rituals. It was enough for them to pray to God, U Blei, morning and night. Although they knew about the hill spirits and were afraid to go anywhere near them, they did not think it necessary to make offerings to them. It was not till a village elder, a man of great wisdom and understanding of the mysteries of life had started making sacrifices to the chief of the spirits, that the villagers learned about propitiating and paying obeisance to more than the one supreme God that they knew.

The elder had learned the rites from the people of Sohra, who worshipped God through the mediation of certain spirits. He had seen how the people there prayed to U Mawlong Syiem, the guardian spirit of the villages around Sohra; he had watched the religious ceremonies performed for U Suidnoh, the god of health, at the sacred forest of Law Suidnoh in Laitryngew; and so, he too wanted his village to have its own guardian spirit. With that in mind, he taught the villagers how to pray to the chief spirit of the hills, whom he called Shulong, 'the self-begotten'. From that time onwards, the chief spirit became known as U Lei Shulong or U Lei Shyllong as he is known today. By and by, U Lei Shillong became the patron god of all the villages within the seven provinces of Saw Kher Lai Lyngdoh, and everyone began to pay homage to him.

That pleased U Lei Shillong so much that when he heard the people of Saw Kher Lai Lyngdoh praying to him to show them the way out of the impasse, they had found themselves in, he sent for his daughter and directed her to go and live among his human subjects. The nymph turned herself into a beautiful maiden and went to live in a cave called Krem Marai, near the village of Pomnakrai on the slopes of Lum Shyllong. It was a lonely spot. Only a few boys and girls went there once in a while, to graze their cattle and goats nearby. But it did not take the exploring children long to discover the beautiful woman sitting in the sun by the entrance to her cave. The sight of the strange and beautiful woman, sitting all alone in the middle of nowhere, struck terror into their hearts and they fled the scene to report the matter to their parents and elders.

Soon word of the mysterious woman at Krem Marai spread like wildfire to the four corners of Ri Hynñiew Trep. The people, who were quite superstitious in those days, began to avoid the place for fear of the strange woman whom they thought was some kind of spirit.

One man among them, however, was not afraid. His name was Sati Mylliemngap, an elder from the village of Bisi, respected for his wisdom and insight. The rumour about a beautiful woman alone in a cave in the wilderness inspired his adventurous spirit and he resolved, come what may, to visit her one day.

Sati set out for the cave on a splendid spring morning. Along the way, birds sang their love songs; wildflowers nameless, rainbow-hued, danced in the breeze; the scented air seemed to urge him on, as if to a predestined rendezvous.

Near the cave, he picked his way carefully through the undergrowth, now and then stopping to look for the maiden. Suddenly, there she was, sunning herself at the cave's entrance—just as the children had described. She had a little orchid in her hand, a *lamat ïong*, 'the black-eyed bloom'.

Sati's jaw dropped as he gazed in wonder at her strange loveliness. Her skin was fair and smooth as spring water. Her eyes were blue as the clear sky. Her long, flowing, brown hair cascaded down her back. And stranger still, she was not dressed like a Khasi girl at all! Her robe was a creamy yellow, of a cloth quite different from the silk spun by the villagers. She wore no *jaiñsem*, outer garment, which was quite unheard of for a local girl. As Sati stared at her, she caught sight of him and, with a little cry, disappeared inside the cave, which even bold Sati could not bring himself to enter.

But that was not the end of it. Sati stayed where he was, calling out to her: 'Dear Kong, why do you run from me . . . don't be afraid . . . I mean you no harm'.

When she did not come, he pleaded and coaxed her with gentle words of endearment: 'I'm an old man with neither strength nor inclination to harm you. I'm old enough to be your father; come talk to me ... all I want is to help you'.

Nothing worked however, and exhausted, he sat down for a while to think. It was not long before an idea struck him. He had noticed some wildflowers called *jalyngkteng* blooming some distance away. Since the maiden seemed to be quite fond of flowers, he quickly went to pick a handful and fashioned them into a bouquet, which he laid before the cave entrance. Then, he called out to her and said, 'I give up, I'm leaving, Kong, I'll not pester you again. But before I go, here are some flowers as a token of my goodwill. Please accept them. I'll put them here and go.'

That was exactly what he did. But having gone a little way, he doubled back by another path. He hid quietly by the side of the cave and waited. After a while, the shy maiden peeped out. She looked around to make sure the coast was clear and stooped to pick up the bouquet.

That was just what Sati had been waiting for. He ran up to her and overpowered her in one grasp, while all the time trying to calm her fears and crying, 'I mean you no harm . . . don't be afraid . . . I just want to know more about you. . .'

After a while, the woman calmed down a little.

Sati begged her forgiveness for playing such a trick on her. Once more, he told her that he did not mean to harm her, and that, on the contrary, he had only wanted to help her. He said the people in the villages had become very agitated and fearful, when they came to know about her stay in the cave. It was only to prevent anything untoward from happening that he had come, at the request of the council of elders, to find out more about her, and why and how she had come to dwell in those lonely backwoods.

Reassured by the gentle manner of her captor and convinced that she was talking to a true representative of the village council, the nymph revealed everything to a very astonished and reverential Sati. She told him how her father, happy with the people's unbounded faith in him, had sent her to be the progenitress of the Syiem clan, which would later become the ruling clan of the State of Shyllong. For the time being, however, she urged Sati not to disclose anything of all that except to the council of elders, which must also be sworn to secrecy.

The now elated Sati made his obeisance to her, and promising to do exactly as she had told him, took her home. At home, the nymph caused quite a sensation. People, neighbours, friends and relatives flocked to Sati's house to catch a glimpse of the strange woman. Sati introduced her to them as his adopted daughter, Ka Pahsyntiew, 'the one lured by flowers'. He chose the name, as the nymph had not wished to reveal her real name to anyone.

Meanwhile, the council of elders met, and on learning everything about the nymph from Sati, resolved to get her married to the most eligible bachelor in the land: the bravest, the strongest, the wisest and the most handsome youth they could find. After a long, hard quest they finally chose a youth from the Ri Bhoi village of Nongjri, a young man who came to be known later as Kongngor Nongjri, whom they brought to Bisi for the wedding, which was the biggest and the most memorable event of those times.

The moon was new, the moon was full. Time flew by and life for the couple slipped from one happy year to another. Pahsyntiew gave birth to a charming son, named U Naraiñ, and a beautiful daughter, named Ka Bamon Sari, who grew up to be strong, intelligent and noble hearted. They were the pride of the land, loved and respected by all. Kongngor, who doted on his divinely exquisite wife and who dedicated his entire life to the welfare of his family, thought their happiness could never end.

But then, one day, Pahsyntiew called her children to her. As they sat before her with their father, she said,

> My dear Kongngor, my beloved children, for so long I have hidden my true self from you, thinking only of your happiness. Now the time has come when I must go back to my own world. I am the daughter of U Lei Shillong, sent by my father to give the people of Saw Kher Lai Lyngdoh their own rulers. And rulers are what you, my children, shall be. I have done my duty and must return. Your father is a capable man, my dearests. I leave you with him with my blessing. . . .

Kongngor and his children were heartbroken. There was much crying and questioning, but since it was decreed that Pahsyntiew should return to her own kind, there was nothing anybody could do about it. With a pained heart and tearful eyes, Pahsyntiew blessed her children and left the house for her cave at Krem Marai and was never seen again.

Kongngor and his children grieved for her for a long time. But gradually, with the love and support of the people, they were able to overcome their sorrow. By and by, true to the words of Pahsyntiew, her eldest son, U Naraiñ Syiem, was made the king of the new state of Shyllong formed out of the provinces of Saw Kher Lai Lyngdoh. The new king ruled his people well. With the help of his *myntris*, 'the ministers' elected from among the founding clans, his state grew from strength to strength. In no time at all, it became one of the most powerful states in Ri Hynñiew Trep.

The people were greatly pleased with their syiem, and together they built the *ïingsad*, 'the ancestral house' of the Syiem clan, at Bisi. Here they performed all the ceremonies of the state, and here, in accordance with the customs of the land, lived the king's eldest sister, Ka Bamon Sari Syiem, as *ka syiemsad*, 'the queen mother', since her sons will later inherit the throne from their uncle.

But this is only one side of the story. The legend also points to the fact that Mylliemngap and some of the elders of the provinces of Saw Kher Lai Lyngdoh had brought the divinely beautiful and unusually fair-skinned young maiden from the plains of Sylhet east bengal, and had made her stay in the cave for a while. Then, they floated the story of a fairy living at the Krem Marai cave and made a great spectacle of her capture. This, they had to do because, as mentioned earlier, they were looking for someone who would lead their newly formed state as a syiem, their 'king'. But finding it impossible to choose such a man, who would have hitherto unheard-of powers over their lives, from any of the clans or villages without causing a rebellion, they, in their wisdom, had resorted to this stratagem. And in so doing, they had unwittingly propounded one of the earliest theories on the divine origin—but not right, as you shall see—of kings.

To bring their deception to its logical conclusion and to convince the people that she had returned to her father, the patron god of Shillong, they took her back to her own home in Sylhet.

Affirming this line of argument, R.T. Rymbai, in his essay, 'The Evolution of the Hynñiew Trep Polity',[4] discloses how the growing need to have a person who would run the day-to-day administration and preside regularly over the *dorbar hima* (council of state) had led to the invention of 'the institution of families and clans and the origin of titular heads of states called Syiems'. According to him, the syiems 'came not from the Bakhraw clans, the founding clans of the Hima, or from the indigenous clans constituting the citizenry called *u babun u balang* (the many the populace), in whose hands is vested the ultimate authority for the governance of the hima. As daylight comes after the dark night, we have the legend of Ka Pahsyntiew, a fairy queen emerging out of the cleft of a rock at Pomnakrai to found the dynasty of Ki Syiem Ka Hima Shillong, and the legend of Ka Li Dakha, a mermaid, who transformed herself into a beautiful maiden, to found the dynasty of Ki Syiem Sutnga', known later by non-Khasis as the Jaiñtia Rajas.

Li Dakha also founded the dynasties of Ki Syiemlieh (called 'Safed Rajas' by non-Khasis) and Ki Syiemïong ('Kala Rajas') of the states of Nongkhlaw, Maharam, Langrin, Nongspung and others in contemporary West Khasi Hills and Ri Bhoi District. The following is her story.[5]

In the nascent stage of its history, Ri Pnar was only organized into a group of provinces without king or state. Each province kept to itself under its own administrator, the doloi, who was elected from a particular clan by a *dorbar elaka*, 'the provincial council', comprising all eligible male representatives. The doloi was assisted by elders known as basans, *pators* and *sangots*, as well as by lyngdoh priests who were elected from each particular clan. The dolois ruled their provinces independently and consulted each other only in matters of trade. At that time in Ri Pnar, there were a total of 12 *dolois*. But soon, for very much the same reasons that had forced the provinces of Saw Kher Lai Lyngdoh to unite under the State of Shyllong, the dolois also decided to come together under one ruler. But finding it impossible to elect this leader from among themselves, their resolution to unite under one state and one ruler had to be put off for some time. It was then that the legend of Ka Li Dakha emerged.

At that time, there lived in a hamlet called Umwi, a very handsome man known as Luh Ryndi, sometimes also called Loh or Woh Ryndi. He lived alone, spending most of his time toiling in his field from morning till night. Like all other men in the hamlet, however, he was very fond of hunting and fishing and often indulged himself in these pastimes whenever he could.

One autumn morning, when the sky was blue and the sun was brilliant, Luh Ryndi took up his fishing rod and went striding off in the direction of a river called Waikhyrwi. At the river, he took his position by the side of a large pool and settled down for a daylong stint. Very soon he could feel something nibbling at the bait and tugging at the line. He took the strain and pulled. Dangling at the end of the hook was a sizeable fish. Catching it with one hand, he unhooked it, placed it inside the basket he had brought with him, and went back to fishing. After that, he went back to fishing. But strangely, although he tried till the sun sank below the western hills, he did not catch another fish.

When night came, Luh Ryndi returned to his hut with his fish, washed, made up the fire and cooked his meal. Then he took out the fish, put it inside a bamboo basket and left it dangling above the hearth to dry, meaning to boil it in the morning. But when morning came, in his hurry to prepare for his day's work, he forgot all about the fish. Eating a hurried breakfast, he gathered his tools about him, left for his field without a backward glance.

When he came back in the evening, he was in for a big surprise. As soon as he opened the door, the warmth of the room embraced him like a comforting companion. He could see the fire burning in the hearth. The room was neat and clean, as if it had been swept recently, and when he looked at his pots, his food had already been cooked. He began to experience an eerie sensation of an unknown woman's presence in the house. But he brushed that foolish thought aside and guessed it must have been one of his nieces who had come to keep house for him during the day. Thus thinking, he ate his food, which was exceptionally delicious that night, and went to sleep. But the following day the same story repeated itself.

Curious, he went to his sister's place to enquire if she had sent one of her daughters to his house that day and the previous one. The answer was no, she had not sent anyone to his house. That got him worried. Who was it, then, who had been keeping house for a lonely man like him? He could not think of any friend who would do something as inexplicable as visiting his hut and do the domestic chores for him while he was away. No, he said to himself, this will not do. I must find out, by any means, just exactly who had been at my place. Thinking about it, he suddenly hit upon a plan and, comforted by it, retired to bed.

The next morning Luh Ryndi got ready for work and went to his field as usual. But once out of sight of his house he doubled back by another route and proceeded until he reached the back of his hut, where he settled down to wait and watch through a hole in the wall. He had a long wait, but finally, towards cooking time in the afternoon, he saw, to his utter amazement, a stunningly beautiful woman emerging from the fish in the basket. He watched her for some time, gazing with wide-eyed wonder at the unusual fairness of her skin, the brilliance in her eyes and the midnight blackness of her hair which cascaded down to her heels. He knew, of course, who she was. She could only be one of those fairies called *puri*, and from the loveliness of her face and the snowy whiteness of her jaiñsem outer garment and her clothes, he guessed that she was a godly fairy or *puriblei*, and decided that there was nothing to fear from her. Even as he watched, he saw her sweep the floor, build up the fire in the hearth, clean the pots and prepare to cook the evening meal. But at that point, his patience ran out and he hastened into the house to confront her.

As soon as the creature saw him and realized that she had been outwitted, she dashed towards the fish, meaning to shelter in its scaly skin once again. But, surmising rightly, what she was about to do, Luh Ryndi jumped forward, snatched the fish from her grasp and threw it in the fire. Seeing her only means of escape destroyed, the strange maiden submitted herself to his powerful arms and listened to his eager questions: 'Who are you? Where did you come from? What do you want here?'

'I am the daughter of a river nymph', she said simply. I took a fancy to you as you sat fishing in the river alone. . . I have come to be your wife'.

Hearing this frank admission, Luh Ryndi stared at her, speechless. Presently, his face broke into a smile and he promised to return her love in full measure by marrying her as soon as he had introduced her to his relations. But first, she had to have a name. After briefly ruminating on the strange manner of his acquaintance with her, he decided to call her Ka Li Dakha, 'the one who came from a fish'.

After the introductions to his relatives were over and all the formalities had been completed, Luh Ryndi married Li Dakha in a grand ceremony that the dolois of Ri Pnar organised for him. Over the years they had three daughters whom they named Ka Rapungap, Ka Rapubon and Ka Rapunga (also known as Ka Ngap, Ka Bon and Ka Nga) and three sons, whom they named Shyngkhleiñ, Bania and Tetia-ksaw. By and by, the six children, being the scions of a nymph, grew up into exceptionally beautiful young men and women. The girls were especially adored by everyone and were constantly courted by the bravest and most handsome young men of the land. Consequently, when the time for their marriage came, the three had a very select band of admirers to choose from and naturally picked the best grooms in the field.

Having seen her children satisfactorily married off, Li Dakha determined to return to her pool. One day, while the family was sitting together, gathered around the hearth, she dropped her plan into their midst like a thunderbolt and said, 'My husband, dear children, it is time for me to return home. I can hear my mother and the others calling me back. From now on, you must learn to live without me'.

Stunned into silence, everyone could only gape at her in sheer disbelief. At length, Luh Ryndi roused himself and said, 'My dearest wife, what foolishness is this? What are you saying? Surely you cannot mean what you said?'

When she affirmed that she did mean what she said, the daughters joined in the general protest. 'Our beloved mother, how can you leave and render us orphans like this? Surely, you love us more than that! Forget this silly notion, stay on and let us be happy together'.

But despite many such earnest entreaties, and although they cried and pleaded with her for days, Li Dakha could not be persuaded to change her mind, for she argued that it was against the very nature of her being to stay on indefinitely in the land of mortals.

When Li Dakha had gone back to her magic realm, Luh Ryndi tried to lead a normal life once more. But he found that impossible. For him, it was as if the sun had suddenly set forever. He lost all zest for life and began to pine away till one day, finding the weight of sadness unbearable, and the longing in his heart unquenchable, he visited the pool with his fishing rod once again, in a desperate attempt to win back his beloved. And win back his beloved he did, but in a manner quite contrary to all his expectations. As he sat by the pool, toying with his rod, suddenly, a big fish took his bait and pulled him headlong into the murky waters.

Luh Ryndi was never seen or heard from again, but his children and their families prospered and grew in strength. Being the descendants of a supernatural creature, they were looked up to and loved by one and all. And this was like a God-send opportunity for the dolois, who were looking for a syiem to unite every one of their provinces under a single state. They sanctified a new Syiem clan for the children of Li Dakha and Luh Ryndi, made Shyngkhleiñ the first syiem of the State Sutnga and Ka Nga, the first syiemsad, she, being the youngest daughter.

In later years, the daughters of Li Dakha became the proud mothers of many sons and daughters, who spread throughout the land of the Hynñiew Treps. From Ka Ngap descended the clans of Phyrngap, Sutong, Pala, Huwa and Ïongrem among others. From Ka Bon came the Syiemlieh and Syiemïong clans, whose descendants later became the first kings of the states of Nongkhlaw, Maharam and Langrin, and from Ka Nga came the kings of the State Sutnga.

But as with Ka Pahsyntiew, the legend says that this too was a stratagem plotted by the *dolois* and Luh Ryndi. Luh had actually married an exceptionally beautiful Hindu girl from the Jaintapur Upazila, in East Bengal. When he brought her home, because her beauty was like that of a godly fairy, the *dolois*, with the approval of Luh, spread the story about a river nymph who had emerged from a fish. Later, to bring their deception to a logical conclusion, Li Dakha was supposed to have gone back to her pool in the river, followed afterwards by her husband. In reality, both of them reportedly went back to Jaintapur, one after the other, to live there for the rest of their lives.

Rymbai also narrated the divine origin of kings in many other states,[6] including that of Sohra. According to him,

> We have also the story of the legendary sow which gave birth to a handsome girl who founded the dynasty of Ki Syiem Ka Hima Malngiang [the kings of the State of Madur Maskut] which disintegrated sometime in the fifteenth century, whose syiems are found now in the state of Mawsynram. In the case of Ka Hima Sohra, when the Bakhraws were at a loss where to look for a syiem, there came a gentle woman of divine grace from nowhere who said that her progeny would be the syiems of their Hima.

Of course, there were states founded without such a divine king. In such a case, the founding clans had to go down to the plains of East Bengal or Assam and kidnap the first couple they could lay their hands on, so they could become the forebears of their ruling Syiem clan. This was exactly what happened in the State of Mawïang in West Khasi Hills, whose first king was actually the son of a Muslim woman.

It is partly because of these origin myths and legends that our ancestors, the Hynñiew Treps, attributed certain qualities to their kings. For instance, they called them *ki syiem ki blei*, 'the kings the gods'; *u syiem u kmie*, 'the king the mother'; and *u syiem u mraw*, 'the king the slave'. As a god (or at least a person with a supposedly divine origin), the king must be just and deliver equitable justice to all citizens regardless of their wealth and position in society. As a mother, the king must look after all his citizens with love and tender care. And as a slave, the king must work selflessly and untiringly for the welfare of one and all.

This is the kind of political wisdom that had made a poet like Tham sing the praises of the old Khasis, 'So they learned to forge their politics; So they learned to found a State'. They had discovered their first lesson in politics when they tried to find a 'king'. Having found him, they began organizing their provinces and villages into a 'state', which they vowed to protect at all costs. In this way, 'because their blood surges, Alive the Name the Glory stays' (Section VIII, 116-17). In other words, because of their patriotism, their states flourished and grew in name and glory.

On the subject of himas, S.S. Majaw[7] says:

As Soso Tham sees it, the politics of the Khasis is founded upon the formation of Himas. And the formation of Himas is founded upon religion, which in turn is founded upon the Covenant, that is, the agreement reached between u Hynñiew Trep and his Creator.

But what are these himas or states that form the basis of the politics of the Hynñiew Trep people, for which the poet experiences such a *hiraeth*?[8] Writing on Khasi democracy, Hipshon Roy states:

Their democratic system and way of life have carried them through the ages for thousands of years in their small republics. Hon'ble Freeman Thomas, Earl of Willingdon . . . during his visit to these hills as Viceroy and Governor-General of India had this to say: 'It is a proof of the stamina and virility and competence of your people that when greater Empires in the East and in the West have throughout the ages come and gone, you still maintain in your pleasant Hills the freedom of your small republics, based on your ancient ways and tenets of your race.[9]

Both Hipshon Roy and the Viceroy refer to the Khasi states as 'republics' implying a comparison between them and the Greek city states. Rymbai explains why:

The political organisation of Ki Hynñiewtrep is basically democratic where separate states, independent of one another, co-exist. Fundamentally they are all republican in nature, but monarchical in form. Tradition tells us that there used to be thirty States, each under a titular head called Syiem, twenty-nine of which were in Khasi Hills and one in [the present-day] Jaiñtia Hills . . . in Jaiñtia Hills originally there were twelve Dolois, independent of each other, but later chose one Syiem to be their titular head.[10]

Expounding further on the republican nature and formation of the Himas, he says:

The head of a Hima . . . is not invested with any power to act on his own authority. Power lies with the people, the head or ruler is an agent to implement the common will of the people. The people of a State are not subjects (raiyats) of the head of the State, they are its citizens called U Khun U Hajar. Power is distributed in a three-tier system. At the grassroots of the village level, there is the Rangbah Shnong (Village Headman) who, with the help of the council of elders of the village, administers all its affairs. Matters affecting the village on the whole are referred to the Dorbar Shnong (the Village Council), to which every adult male has a right to attend and participate. The headman is the first among equals. He is elected by the common will of the people [at the council].

A group of villages constitutes a Raij with a titular head called Syiem Raij. Like a Rangbah Shnong he has no authority to act on his own. He is assisted in his duties by a council of elders called Basans. He settles disputes between inhabitants of different villages of the Raij or of the inter-village disputes within the Raij. He is elected by the members of the clan from which alone a Syiem may be elected. All matters are disposed of by consensus of members-in-council. Matters affecting the Raij as a whole are referred to the Dorbar Raij to which every adult male of the Raij is entitled to attend and take part in its deliberations.

A number of Raijs constitutes a State, Hima. The number of Raijs varies according to the size of a Hima. The Syiem of a Hima is normally accepted by the Bakhraws (nobilities) if the members of the clan are unanimous in electing him; and he must not be otherwise ineligible by reasons of serious physical handicaps or moral turpitude. If the members of the Syiem clan or clans do not agree on one candidate only, the matter is referred to the nobilities, and should they also disagree, the choice is open to the male adults of the Hima.

According to Rymbai and Hipshon Roy, the republican nature of the Khasi political system derives its strength from the social structure of the society. In the social order, the Syiem clan (this also applies to the founding clans of a state) is not higher than any other clan since the Khasi society is strictly egalitarian. The difference is functional and merely relates to the parts they play in governance and administration. The king of a state is assisted in day-to-day administration by a council of ministers whose members are elected from the founding clans. In matters of ordinary administration, he carries out the people's consensus as conveyed to him through members of his council in session, and in matters of high importance affecting the state, as conveyed by the councillors in an open session of the council of state.

It is because of this republican nature of the Khasi states and the fundamental role of the people in matters of governance that it can be said with Tham:

U Syiem kam pher la dei 'u Maw';
Ka Hima kit u Rit u Khraw;
Bishar-khadar ryngkat bad ki;
Ha u ki ai ka Nar-bili:
Te kum u Tiew Myngngor Lyngsyun,
Kumta ka ïaid Dorbar pyllun. (Section VIII, 121-6)

(It matters not the King may be 'a Stone';
The State is borne by Small and Great;
Justice with them collectively;
To him the Fetters:
And so, rounded as Marigold,
It goes the Council of the State.)

The poet's understanding of the traditional political set-up is absolute. Since governance and the weighty issues of the state are dealt with together with the 'Great' ('Bakhraws', 'the nobles') and the 'Small' ('U Khun u Hajar', 'the citizens'), it does not really matter what kind of 'King' heads the state, as long as he is acceptable to one and all. What is all-important is the dorbar. The admiration of the poet for this dorbar is so great that he compares it to a marigold in full bloom. The comparison is not only because he is trying to describe the open air, circular seating arrangement of a Khasi council but also because of its majestic magnificence.

Tham is not the only one brimful of love and adoration for the democratic dorbar of the Khasis. Writing about it, Rymbai reveals;

This concept of Ki Hynñiew Trep about the role of their kings and the fact that power lies in the hands of the people, form the cornerstone of the democratic nature of their political organizations where the will of the people is expressed by consensus. . . . In their case, goodwill prevails throughout the deliberations, for or against, because each participant is guided and governed by the ruling spirit of the motto—*ïa kaba dei yn ïa bat, ïa kaba lait yn ïa bret* ('we shall keep what is right, reject what is wrong').[12]

It was this particular trait of the Khasi *dorbar* that impressed Netaji Subhas Chandra Bose into stating, in one of his speeches as the president of the Indian National Congress, 'that those who wanted to see true democracy in action must go to Khasi-Jaiñtia Hills and learn from the people out there its soul and spirit'.[11] Evidence of such high praise can also be found in the British official records relating to the proceedings of Nongkhlaw's council of state as it was discussing David Scott's request for permission to construct a road from Guwahati to Sylhet through Nongkhlaw's territories. According to Harry Inglis, a trader who was part of the English delegation,

The attendants came up the Hills, armed with swords, bows and quivers. The Rajah proceeded to explain the subject of the meeting and required the different orators to express their sentiments on the proposition of the British Government. The leading orator, on the part of the opposition, immediately commenced a long harangue in condemnation of the measure, expressed in a continuous flow of language accompanied with such animation of manner and appropriate gesticulation. This was replied to by an orator of the Rajah's party and in this way, the ball was kept rolling until evening. I was struck with astonishment at the order and decorum, which characterised these debates. No shouts of exultation, or indecent attempts to put down the orator of the opposite party [were made]. On the contrary, every speaker was fairly heard out. I have often witnessed the debates in St. Stephen's Chapel, but that of the Cossya parliament appeared to be conducted with more dignity of manner.[12]

This then is the politics of the Hynñiew Treps, ancestors of the Khasi people, and the formation of their states based on democratic values and republican principles that had drawn the highest commendation from the fittest representatives of the best cultures in the world, people like the Earl of Willingdon, and Netaji Subhas Chandra Bose. And this system founded since 'the days ancient and lost' is still practised today almost in its pristine form. For instance, the economic roles and functions of the king as established by our forefathers are followed even now. The king can collect tolls from markets and produce on the way to markets. He can impose fines and try criminal and civil cases for certain fees and see to the day-to-day administration, but he cannot impose taxes of any sort since the land and its resources belong to an individual, a clan, a village or a province and not to him.

The exception now, apart from the qualitative degeneration, is that the District Council has assumed to itself a constitutionally sanctioned supervisory role over and above the council of state, and no king can be appointed without its stamp of approval. This state of affairs has given rise to at least two conflicting demands—one, calling for the abolishment of the District Council and the restoration of these institutions to their former relevance and glory, though subservient to the state government, and the other calling for their replacement with the panchayati raj system.

NOTES

1. Soso Tham, *Ki Sngi ba Rim U Hynñiew Trep*, Primrose Gatphoh, 1976, All quotations relating to poetry are from this book.
2. Homiwell Lyngdoh, *Ki Syiem Khasi bad Synteng*, D.P. Reade Diengdoh, 1938.
3. Kynpham Sing Nongkynrih, 'The Legend of Ka Pahsyntiew', 'The Legend of Ka Li Dakha', *Around the Hearth: Khasi Legends*, Penguin, 2007, pp. 73-9.
4. R. Tokin, Rymbai, 'The Evolution of the Hynñiewtrep Polity', *Khanasamari—u Khun u Hajar ka Ri Hynñiewtrep*, ed. Sumar Sing Sawian, Apphira Publications, 1998, pp. xi-xxiii.
5. See n. 3 above, pp. 106-111.
6. See n. 4 above, p. xvi.
7. S. S. Majaw, *Ki Syrwet Jingshai*, S.S. Majaw, 1985.

8. Welsh word loosely translated as various forms of longing.
9. Roy, Hipshon, 'The Khasis'. *Where Lies the Soul of Our Race*, Hipshon Roy, 1982, p. 1.
10. See n. 4 above. After their occupation of the Khasi highlands, the British abolished seven states, which:
    they turned into British territories. They also downgraded eight of the states and placed them under lesser titular heads called Lyngdohs while five others were placed under still lesser heads called Sirdars. The British territories comprised 31 villages in present-day Khasi Hills and the whole of present-day Jaiñtia Hills. The territories in the Khasi Hills were placed under Sirdars while those in Jaiñtia Hills were placed under Dolois. But though the British interfered with the geographical aspect of Khasi himas, they did not tamper with their democratic structure.
11. As quoted by Rymbai, See n. 4 above, p. xvii.
12. As quoted by Rymbai, ibid., p. xviii, David Scott was the British political agent in north-east India.

CHAPTER 15

Supernatural Belief of the Kuki: A Case Study of Witchcraft and its Cures

D.L. HAOKIP

Edward Burnett Tylor defines 'religion' as supernatural. In this article, supernatural is divided into religion and superstition. Ceremonies to invoke *Chung Pathen* (God above) whose gender remain undefined could be termed religious and other beliefs associated with magical charms could be plainly termed as related to the supernatural or superstition (Gangte 1993). Witchcraft locally called *kaose* or *kao* by the Kuki, constituted one of the supernatural beliefs of the Kuki. Lhomi, (tigerman), demons, ghosts, or Thilha, the departed soul of human were also believed to be supernatural. The Kuki believed that there were human beings that possess the evil eye or spirits that could enter the human body and cause illnesses or suffering to the extent of death. Unlike other supernaturalism, witchcraft is a secret culture whose existence can be traced to times immemorial. But in the absence of contemporary records, it is difficult to give it a time bracket regarding its origin, even today.

The priestly charms of the Kuki suggest two types namely—*gamkaose*, that lived in the forest and *inkao*, these who inhabited human beings. Unfortunately, not many wrote about it or even gave a description of it for fear of being attacked by it or reasons not known. This belief is handed down from parents to children mostly and is still strong in the rural areas. In one's interaction with forty students of class I and II at Churachandpur in 2012, 99 per cent were aware of it. This shows that oral tradition normally handed down from the remote past with exaggeration and modification to draw the attention of younger generation is found very effective. The dark side of it is the division of society into *mitheng* (holy) and *miboh* (unholy or polluted). The holy section puts the blame for most of their sufferings, diseases, like stomach aches, heartburn, and skin allergy and even the cases of death on the unholy section of the society. The Kuki believed that if *kaose* which cannot be seen, touched or felt, licked someone with his or her tongue, the victim's skin started itching and their entry into one's body caused either heartburn, arthritis or stomach aches, etc. Now, was there any definition or description of *kaose* among the Kuki? Among the Kuki, the witch could be of any gender, but in English a witch is always a woman.[1] In the contemporary society it is called *kaose-mine*, meaning evil spirits, who eat men. But being a silent culture and tradition it will be difficult to answer without looking at the different segments of their tradition. This article argues that the origin of kaose among the Kuki of Manipur is rooted in practices of cannibalism and the existence of it until today could be due to lack of medical sciences, or infrastructure, fear of it's attack and lack of logical reasoning among them. The whole problem is that one will not come across a witch among the Kuki despite a strong indication of this belief.

To assess the origin of the Kuki and the traditional method of curing illnesses caused by it, the oral traditions related with it, and written accounts both in English and local dialects have been taken into account. The biggest problem one has to encounter in dealing with witchcraft among the rural population in general and among the Kuki in particular, is due to the absence of registration of the case at the concerned police station and courts. There is report of trial but being conventional, it is difficult to accesses such proceedings. According to Kathryn A. Edwards 'the 19th and 20th century folklorists compiled volumes of "legends" about such spirits and learned societies conducted censuses of apparitions, historians distanced themselves from the academic study of ghosts until the second half of the 20th century'.[2]

In his Notes on 'The Thadou Kuki', Shaw defines *kaose* 'as those people possessing the evil-eye and having magic powers of turning into animals at wish and killing people'.[3] T.S. Gangte's work, *The Kukis of Manipur* deals with the supernatural, rituals and ceremonies as a chapter and categorizes them into aerial (Chung Pathen) as benevolent and terrestrial deities like *Gamhoise, Inmunse, Joumi, Kulsamnu, Chomnu, Gamkao, Kaomei, Kaoseie*, as evil spirits and defines *kaose* as greedy spirits that can enter a person and convert the victim into a different personality, like changing his voice, behaviour, strength and can be released by giving it what it wants.[4] Among the Lushei Kuki (now Mizo), it is called *Khawhring*. Shakespeare traces its origin to the wild boar. He claims that a women who used its fat as hair oil acquired *Khawhring* and it got multiplied among the women who shared her *nam* (a plaited cane band for carrying loads) with the one who acquired it from wild boar for the first time.[5] The implication of it in the society and how people killed a person accused of possessing *Khawhringnei* is noted in this work. In his Monograph, *The Lushei Customs and Ceremonies*, Parry defines it as 'magic but of less deadly nature than *Dawi* that is frequently found among women'. He states that a *Khawhringnei* is a person, who possessed the evil eye and *Dawithiam* is an active wizard. He also asserted that the chiefs were never accused of being *Dawithiam* or *Khawhringnei* for they could turn one out from his village and confiscate his property.[6] In his work *Thempu Ho Thu* Lekhojam Haokips, accounted how it originated from a Mithun that can speak, and got multiplied among the Kuki from inter-marriage, and in different forms of social contact among them. His works also recount the rites and rituals to dispel the evil spirit from the body of the victims.[7] Tarun Goswami's *The Kuki Life and Lore* claims that Vanthang, believed to be the progenitor of Khongsai Kuki clans was an expert in witchcraft.[8] Melford E. Spiro's *Supernaturalism in Burma* deals with types of supernaturalism, ghosts, demons, illnesses caused by them and those who practised it. He claims that 'epistemologically witches are not different from ghosts, demons, and other spirits, and master witches who are skilled in deception, acts like a pious Buddhist, saying his beads, worshiping at Pagodas and so on'.[9]

Modern songs of 1980s, define *kaose* as cannibals. Based on this premise, one would like to incorporate some works both in English and local vernaculars, that mention cannibal practices. One of the songs sung by Jimmy Lamboi, contains the phrase *tulai nungah ho hi atamjo, kaose mine bang in achal sam atannun* meaning 'most of today's ladies cut their hair like a witch, who eat human flesh'.[10] Gerini's researches on Ptolemy's *Geography*, trace the practice of Cannibalism in Funan (Kamboya AD 245-50); eating lungs and liver of dead foes, in Cochin in China by Salang or Halang tribes, handing over of the assassin, Hwa-lu king Din to the populace to eat in Tonkin in the year 1811, the practice of cannibalism among the Wu-hu tribe of China, during AD 250-80. Famine brought about cannibalism in China, 204, 138 and 114 BC and the practice of it in Formosa, Java.[11] The practice of it among the Kachins, or Singphos (Chingphos) and Wab or Lawa also came to light at Fn. 2 of Gerini's work.[12] Local writer T. Haokip in his *Thusim Le Lakoila* (Legends and Poetry) mentions how, Telthang, Thanglun and Lunsong, a trio of hunters who set out to hunt wild games came across *kaosepu* (male evil possessor), who took shelter in a mythical cave, having the power to turn bones into a wild game and eat it raw.[13] Considering witches to be eaters of human flesh, it has one common character called Lhomi (Lho = tiger and Mi = men). In his *Thusim Thum*, Paokhohang Haokip, incorporated the story of Ahshijolneng, Galngam and Moltinchan. The three stories recount how they make friend with or encounter, a character half beast half man, namely Hangsai, Khalvompu, and also Lhomi, who practise cannibalism on and off.[14] Lhomi is also related to the Kuki legendary personality, like Ahshijolneng, Moltichan and also Lenchonghoi, who were known for their beauty and good moral character. Yet, a separate study on the supernatural beliefs of the Kuki awaits the attention and interference of academicians till now.

The Kuki belief in supernaturalism has had one commonality—witch and half-man half-beast, could transform from one form to another. But on deeper investigation, one comes to know that half- man or half-beast, locally called Lhomi, can transform into either tiger or man but in the case of *kaose*, it can transform itself into different forms, like insects, grasshoppers, snake, etc. But among the Nagas of the Nagaland, half-man half-beast would mean those people who can transform themselves into different forms as do *kaose*, among the Kuki. The Meitei appellate *Hingchabi* (raw flesh eater women) is also indicative of human flesh eater. The premise shows that the word *kaose* appears to be an address to the people who practise cannibalism. Even today, many people find difficulty in keeping up with the doctors or dietician's advice. Indeed, it is difficult to give up one's habit but stigmatizing the descendants of cannibal practitioner if any, would be a wrong way or an erroneous way of identifying. According to Kgatla, 'Witchcraft is seen as a manifestation of evil believed to come from a human source'.[15]

KAOSE IN THE ORAL TRADITIONS OF THE KUKIS

Mention of *kaose*, in the oral tradition of the Kuki is vaguely recorded. Narrative on the account of the migration of Shongthu from *Khul*[16] probably from a fortified village, a village towards the rugged mountain, claim how they felt themselves tormented by certain inexplicable spirits who they believed to have existed in the surrounding environment. This story claims that Santhu, a stranger was caught red handed in his attempt to steal the portion of meat locally called *Sachan,* the customary meat division or portion at the matrimonial ceremony of Thangpi and Seichin. Accusing him to have possessed *kao*, Shongthu had cut-off his head but he was brought alive by a flower based reptile *chilchite nupa*, and transformed into a wild gibbon *guldu.*[17] The informant whose name appears at endnotes categorically, stated that 'Santhu was a stranger, who attended the matrimonial alliance and ate raw flesh'. On a further query, he stated that 'Santhu was Kaose, for he had eaten raw flesh'. His version or notion indicates that a person, who ate raw flesh was considered possessor of *kao* by the other who ate cooked or boiled meat. Thus, this reminds one of the practice of cannibalism quoted and mentioned in the Chin Hills region in the early centuries of the Christian era. According to N.E. Parry, 'such tragic episode, warn them from taking the wild gibbon, but in course of time, against the advice and counsel, of parents and grandparents, their descendant consumed wild gibbons and acquired the dreaded evil spirits having the capability to cause harm to the flesh and souls of other normal human beings'. This version conveyed certain information. Local historians, claim the emergence of Shongthu between AD 900 and 950 on the basis of genealogical chronicles.[18] Considering the date of Shongthu migration as historical events, it can be stated that the belief on 'Kaose' can be dated much before the emergence of Shongthu.

The priestly charms to appease and/or terrorize *kaose* trace their origin to *mithun*. This version claims that the *kaose* could enter into the body of human beings after it was consumed. Paominlen Haokip opines that, the *mithun* was cursed by the evil spirits of the jungle *gammangte leh gamgilte* (spirits from the thick forest) but the failure of caution on the part of people against consumption of *kao* possessed animal that spoke like man resulted in the spirit to reside the inside human body.[19] If this is considered to be the first time Kukis contact with *kaose*, one cannot push back beyond twelfth or thirteenth century AD.[20] It contrasts sharply to the theory mentioned above, but indicates how the priests structured their charms though it had one thing in common—the origin of it from animals. *Vanthamjol* or heavenly space also appears to be the origin of spirits that can cause similar illness to mankind. The priest while chanting his charms, says, 'Thou had originated from heaven, come across thick cloud, red cloud, and take shelter on this tree, and cause harm to an innocent, who do not know that thou have resided on this tree and cut it'.[21] Attributing the origin of evil spirits from heaven is not a unique thing to a particular tribe but is a common phenomenon. Both the Jews and Christians trace the root of Satan to lesser spirits or angels that rebelled against God and were pushed down by the latter. According to Wikipedia encyclopedia, the oldest references to demonic possession are from the Sumerians, who believed that all diseases of the body and mind were caused by 'sickness demons' called *gidim* or *gid-dim*. The priest who practised exorcism in these nations was called *ashipu* (sorcerer) as opposed to an *asu* (physician). It is the spirits that shamanic cultures also believe in demon possession. Shamans performed exorcisms. In these cultures, diseases were often attributed to the presence of a vengeful spirits[22] (or loosely termed demons) in the body of the patient. In the Lushei Hill version, the concept of witchcraft first emerged from a woman who used the fat of an evil possessor, a wild boar as hair oil, and later transmitted it to people who subsequently came into contact with her in the form of hand shake, sharing the same dress, comb and cane basket and *nam*, a plaited cane fibred for carrying baskets.[23]

Another story narrated by Tonglam of Motbung, Sadar hills, claims that a legendary personality of the Kukis. Galngam was believed to have kept Doi-um (magic in gourd container) and Kao-um (Evil spirit kept in gourd container). In one of his visited to another village, he was left behind. He was put inside a stone by a woman who practised black magic in the village he had visited and out of helplessness, he collected the remnants of his own magic from his nail, putting all those together, he was able to make a hole in that stone with his fist, from where he conveyed a message to his wife to bring his magic and witchcraft containers, to unfold the magic done to him. His wife brought them to save him, but on her enquiry to locate the place where her husband was trapped, she was told that Galngam had died longtime back. She returned home and dropped those containers, in a river.[24] The story claims that the two gourd containers sang *galngam in doi-um anei heya heya heya he*. . . meaning 'Galngam has gourd magical containers Heya heya he. . .' Out of surprise, the Kom tribes collected the containers from the water and summoned all the differently abled persons from their village to break the magical gourd containers into pieces and watch for the result. Thus, 'they select differently able personality having visual problem of their village, as for them to die is better option. Against their expectation, all the differently abled persons were cured by the magic, containers. The blind could see and the lame could walk upright. The News of the miracle attracted the rest of the population, who came forward and broke the second gourd container, (witchcraft container). This version claims that the *kaose* spread out from the Kom tribe to all other Kuki in this way. The Kom tribe claims Shongthu/Chongthu as their progenitor. The above discussion shows that there are different stories for the origin of the same belief. But at what point of time the events mentioned above had taken place, is absent in their narration. The informers represent almost the entire hilly regions of

Manipur. Now, based on their community or geographical location, they narrated different stories relating it to the origin and evolution of *kaose*. This theory also holds some amount of reality with respect to rituals. The Kuki priest compels people who have problem's with their vision to hit or break a gourd after he chants his charms.

Their oral traditions were handed down by them in different forms—legends, folklores and charms. It conveys but one clue with regard to its origin and evolution. Santhu, a stranger, whose head was cut- off, could be a man, who practised cannibalism. But how did Shongthu who had identified him know that he was Kao? It shows that the notion of it was already with them. In other words, Santhu cannot be the first victim and or the originator of it. The other problem here is how the dead body transforms into gibbons. This simply shows how Shongthu and his subjects had encountered it and how people who despised, the counsel or advice of the seniors or Upas, becomes *kao* by killing and eating gibbons. Now, the story could be to induce one to obedience. It also hinted at protection of wildlife, particularly gibbons. The experience Shongthu and his men acquired from the new environment laid the foundation for some other rites and rituals as well. But those are not the concern here. The belief is deeply embedded in their culture. They believed that sharing of comb; hair-oil, and plaited canes, called *nam* and matrimonial alliance, etc., are the mode of acquiring it from possessors to non-possessors besides inheritance. If this version is considered as the origin and multiplication of it, one thing is certain. It is contiguous and by now everybody might possess *kao*. Sharing of comb, hair oil, handshake sharing dresses, salon, studying in the same school, etc., become a common practice with the advent of Christianity. Six senior citizens at Phailengkot were interviewed in 2012 and they traced the origin of it from travellers and a spring which suggest contiguity.[25] The Naga and Kuki believed that one who drank water from a specific spring, consumed by 'half-men, half-beast' could be transformed as beast in Naga Hills and Mani-pur. This also suggests contiguity.[26]

The word *gam-kaose* posed the belief on two types of *kao*. Forest *kao* are identified with flying objects that bore fire,[27] which seem to be men bearing traditional torchlight in the forest or in the village. Here one is concerned with those *kaose* who took abode in the village. Attribution of a tree locally called *Khengthing*, to be the abode of the *kao*, also made it more mysterious. One touch of it is enough to get skin allergy. But, it indicates the role of environment in shaping their notions on *kaose*.

WITCH HUNTING AND PUNISHMENT

Witch hunting is the most secret part of this belief among the Kuki. In brief, it can be said that identifying the villages, clans and personality secretly was important. If one looks at witch hunting in different parts of India and abroad, the kind of witch hunting that were practised can be called nominal, though the consequences can be felt in their customs, tradition and culture. According to Galtung, 'witch hunting is direct violence'.[28] Silvia Federici says that witch hunters are self-appointed persons who hunt women resulting to the murder of accused and confiscation of their properties.[29] In Europe, the absence of a trial of the witch by AD 1700 shows the decline of this belief.[30] Recently, the involvement of land mafias, who make use of superstition to grab the land and also rape before killing the so-called witch came to light in news reports.[31] It is found that most people strongly believed in witchcraft and the general perception is that it is the witchcraft practices that cause all kinds of suffering, sickness and deaths in the village.[32] The struggle between science and superstition has been a long standing one with each trying to overstep the other since centuries. A superstition is generally understood to be an irrational fear or reverence for something which cannot be examined or testified by science.[33] Superstition is associated with a wide range of phenomena, including magic, ritual, myth, and occult practices commonly prevalent in society and generally regarded as erroneous beliefs—irrational, primitive and based on inadequate information. K.S. Singh, former Director General of the Anthropological Survey of India opines that, the local people have larger view of shamanism (good and evil spirits), but the European influence on it began to get identified with black magic, white magic and witchcraft.[34] Rupak Bhattacharjee opines that despite the arrival of Muslim migrants and the spread of Christianity by American Missionaries it has not dispelled local superstitions.[35]

In Northern Ghana, female traders have been accused of gaining their wealth by turning souls into commodities.[36] She traces the influence of the European demonologies in Africa, likely reflecting on the influence of evangelization: associating it with night flights shape shifting, cannibalism, the causing of sterility in women, infant deaths, and the destruction of crops. In both cases, moreover, the 'witches' are predominantly older women, poor farmers, often living alone or women believed to be competing with men.[37] According to Soma Chaudhuri, 'explanations of intra-village micro-dynamics and conflicts, that went on before hunts provide clues to answer the questions around witch problems. Indeed, personal conflicts became manifest witchcraft accusations when individuals involved in the conflict underwent some unnatural illness leading to death'.[38] Village-level quarrels between the women to control household boundaries, feeding, child care, and other matters in the domestic sphere were associated with witchcraft.[39] The witch was typically seen as responsible for causing illness or death in small children, spouses, infants, or domestic animals. She had the power to interfere with nature. She was capable of causing barrenness, miscarriages, or deformed birth. Petty conflicts, usually between women, got transposed into a conspiracy of calculated attacks of a witch hunt against the accused witch.[40]

What happens to the victim, when he or she is attacks by *kaose*? The attack results in loss of memories, change of personalities, convulsions, fainting, vomiting, as if one were dying, and heartburn, drastic changes in vocal intonation and facial structure, superhuman strength and abnormality. They forced the *kao* to leave once for all by giving inhuman treatment of varied degree to the victim. The victim lay between life and death. The kind of treatment given needs to be highlighted here. They cover the person with a fishing net and use pliers or tongs to clip the victim's thumb or main toes. This is followed by interrogation to uncover, whose *kao* or spirit has been responsible for attacking them. If the victim sticks to his or her name, they upgrade the degree of torture, by saying 'we are not here to be fooled'. Tell the truth and we will release you from punishment. When the victim comes back to his senses, they say, the *kao* who attacked you is very clever, for it did not reveals its identity. The same is the case among the the Rabha, Hajong, Mishing, Bodo and the Adivasi community of Assam. The Assam tribals also covere the victim with hunting net and poked with a sharp object till he/she revealed the name of the witch.[41] Sometimes, when the victim whose memory is erased due to the reasons not mention here, can tell them the name of a person, whom he suspects to be a *kaose* possessor in the village or neighbouring village. This inhuman treatment is purposely given to identify the *kaose*. They believe that once the accused is identified, one can kill by changing the position he/she sleeps in his or her bed. The statement indicates murder of the accused in the past. Their belief gives one but a clue about the witch. They believed that the Kao possessor is asleep at his or her residence while his or her *kao* is inside the victim's body. Often the victims were possibly tortured to the extent of death. On the death of the victim, if the spies reported the death of the accused, the family members were humiliated to the extent of pulling down, his or her houses and immediately expelled from the village. The Tangkhuls do not allow him or her to walk proudly in their midst, to curtail their power.[42] In the Lushai hills, *boi* females were identified as 'possessed' by evil spirits.[43] It is believed that the anger on non-performance of sacrificial offerings the *kao* could take over the bodies of the non-sacrificer and consume human beings and livestock in the neighbourhood. Such accusations were tantamount to murder. When levelled against a deserted wife or 'orphans', who is not in a position to sacrifice animals for the recovery of the illness, the person often had to seek refuge at the chief's house. Unless the chief gave protection to them, corporeal death did not restore such a *boi* to personhood. For no family members dug the grave of such a person, feed the 'spirits' that caused death with flesh or fruits of the earth, or conducted the annual *rakhatla* ceremonies, the dead person's spirit remained excluded from the blissful condition to which skilled hunters, warriors and commoner were gathered (Pialral) or *mithikho* (hades). To be brief, witch hunting among the Kuki was very secret. First the accused evil possessor was identified by torturing him or her. On the advice of learned man (priest) the village council framed charges against him or her and expelled them from the village. The accused families had to bear the stigma wherever they settled. The implications were never taken into account and like a silent river this belief killed the moral of innocent and mostly poor family.

PROCEDURES OF CURING BY THE VILLAGE MEDICINE MAN

Usually, the victim's family engaged or called the priest to avert misfortune through a ritual or form of exorcism.[44] The ritual used to drive it off from the body of a man suggests that *kaose* lived in the village since it possessed *mithun*, (*selpao*) and from them went on to men.[45] The village priest performed the following rituals to avert or dispel its attack. *Nehboh* (throwing off edible items): the priest and kin of the sick person collected pieces of every edible item[46] and placed them on a mat and threw them away after he chanted his charms to appease the *kaose*. If, the victim did not recover after this ritual, the rite of *Sagojon* was performed to drive away *kaose*. Besides all the edible items, collected, they erected two posts on the road that led directly to the house of the sick. A bamboo container containing all the edible items and the sacrificial black chicken was tied to the stick placed over the two posts at the height of 8-9 ft. The priest asked the evil spirits to consume the displayed items. He pleaded with the spirits to release the sick immediately. Thereupon, the sick gradually became well. Otherwise, the last option was to perform *Khengsumlhah* (to trap the *kao* in a pit). They believed that this could kill *kao*. It was the highest and the most powerful rite performed in favour of the victim. Interestingly, the priest invited the *kaose* from different Kuki clans by chanting his charms and putting pieces of meat[47] in a pit prepared for the purpose. He let his attendant hit and kill in case spiders, grasshoppers and ants which entered the purposely dug pit.[48] The Kuki of Manipur believed that *kaose*[49] always came in the form of insects. Otherwise, they put an effigy of the *kaose* (human figurine) made of beewax inside a pit and struck with a wooden club. The effigy is permanently buried at the ritual spot. This ritual is similar to the magic practice among some tribes of Arunachal Pradesh. This is the art of capturing the soul of living and torturing him or her to die in course of time. This is an instance of black magic.

According to Aung-Thwin:

> Hindu-Buddhist notions of transmigration embedded in the doctrines of *karma* coexisted with the veneration of 'spirits' in many Southeast Asian societies precisely because there were always some deaths, which had not been 'fed' the appropriate libations by living kinsmen, and hence were believed to trouble the living. Women *boi* remained especially vulnerable not merely to charges of 'assault sorcery', but to charges of remaining hungry spirits roaming the forests on earth in multiple temporalities. The vestigial traces of such undignified deaths are encased in late twentieth-century tales, 'who' entwine captivity, food-production and freedom into a single narrative. Such as the one in which a mother spirit (*phungpuinu*), whose spirit children were killed and who, herself captured by men, had to buy her freedom by conjuring up implements that produced plentiful food for her captors. Without the ability to conjure food for them, and at death, remaining unfed by the living, female and male *boi* (Saibuanga, Liana and the woman Buangi) alike expressed to Fraser their fears of 'dying as a slave.

Rowlands' translation of 1903 put it; this god's invisibility was explained in terms of his being a spirit. Chatterjee opines it to be a watershed in the Christianization of the Lushai Hills that from 1907 onwards, the spirit that possessed was that of Jesus, the sacrificed son, the ritual lamb.[50]

THE IMPACT

The belief in witches was deeply embedded in their custom and culture. Here one would like to highlight the implication of it upon matri-monial alliance and also on the village polity. A marriage proposal needed a lengthy introduction including narrating genealogies from the remote past. This implied scanning of the parents and their ancestors. If one of the families fell under suspicion, it was rejected summarily. The in-depth investigation regarding marriage proposals to someone with a less known family background correlates such beliefs. Scanning of evil possessor before marriage proposals was found very intensive in the past. Such thorough investigations could be one factor why marrying maternal uncle's daughter is strongly prevalent even today. This avoids intensive scanning. But their gossip became secret and was ample reason to give stigma to an innocent. For, if the parent to parent relation was rough, stigmatization of an innocent youth could easily be made to happen. As far as the impact in the society was concerned, marriage as a social institution was one of the most affected one. Marriage proposals took place only after thorough scanning. Parents can force their sons and daughters to avoid loved ones on the ground of a mere suspicion. If a man married a girl, whose parents or ancestors were accused at one point of time, he is isolated from his relatives and friend circles silently. Thus, it shattered human minds and thence social bonds.

The belief also centred on the poor subjects of a villages belonging mainly to other clans. Only poor subjects, women and clans other than the Chief's clans are accused. The Chief and his relatives, his council members, and friend circles, were never accused of possessing the belief. This could be one of the reason why formation of new villages, and migrations were very common during the colonial period. The inter-clans conflicts among the Kukis during the colonial periods can not be isolated from this belief. When a village accused another village, of possessing it, inter-village war or feud was sure to follow. Tribal feuds of course flared up for other reasons as well. A village calling the other villagers *kaose* could not be ruled out.[51] Naturally, this notion of asserting oneself as holy and others unholy would have characterized the Kuki villages and many other tribes. Such beliefs would cultivate hatred, tensions, bad relations between villages and communities, thereby sowing the tendency of forming new identities, or separation from one another, leading to complication of dialects and cultural fabrics. The present scenarios of the tribal situations in Manipur have direct bearing on such an atmosphere. The language affinity among the tribes of the Chin Kuki and Mizo shows one foundation upon which division of rich cultural heritage took place. The Naga lives in large villages, but each village dialects is different from others in most of the cases. Thus, *kaose* as a supernatural belief would be a stumbling block to socio-economic development.

Indeed, most of the ancient communities of the world traced the origin of demonic or malevolent spirits to many mythical animals,[52] assuming that they existed. Women cutting hair straight on the forehead,[53] putting too much lipstick, or appear very fashionable; and people eating too much at odd hours; over consumption of red meat or raw meat were some of the characteristics of persons identified with *kaose.* In other words, these people were already supposed to be possessed by evil spirits in normal condition. They believed that these type of people having an odd status, position and character are often possessed by the evil spirit irrespective of clans or tribes. The belief in a large number of spirits, affected the economy and society in a very deep-rooted manner. A person, accused of possessing evil was given different treatment everywhere. As mentioned above, people who were not in a position to sacrifice animals or perform the requisite rituals were compelled to become the household slaves or *Boi* of the chief, with a status, almost similar to those of Sudras and other undefined or outcastes. The worst part of this belief was that if the possessor of evil or victim, if killed in corporal punishment, his or her soul remained unfed and not entitled to *mithikho* (heaven), a blissful place, where the soul of warriors, common men, and skill hunters were.[54] In the field surveyed, data gathered that indicated killing of the victim while driving out the demon or evil spirits, locally called *kaose* in many of the Kuki villages.

This belief caused a hurdle to colonial rule. R. Kapzinga said that it becomes a common problem to each and every household and to villages. For, a possessor of evil was not allowed to live with non-possessor during the colonial days. One had not heard expulsion and trial by the village authority for a number of decades but the present Kuki Society witnesses expulsion and trial in some villages.[55] Thus, the victim, who was innocent, became a refugee event in his/her own homestead, land and territory. The girl accused of it had to lost her beloved and parents had to part with their disobedient son or daughter who married the accused. The hatred that developed was partly responsible for the formation of many new villages as stated above. Inter-village feuds and cutting off communication between one village and another could be a big factor for the emergence of tonal differences among the Kuki. Language expression and pronunciation in due course, could lead to the growth of newer identities that stood against the formation of larger feudal states or territories than what they controlled. It narrowed their world view and contact with other ethnic groups would perhaps be another problem that stood against development. This was because the village chief and his kinsmen were never charged of it. In a discussion with J. Guite, the Sukte and Khongsai feuds that took place in the nineteenth century seemed to be the repercussion of such belief system. The conversion of the tribal to the Christianity also removed the position of the traditional priest, who found out the culprits or *kaose* who was behind it. The post-colonial society attempted to cure it, through prayer.[56]

CONCLUSION

This belief is very demanding. The rich can afford whereas the poor are reduced to the status of slaves in pre- and colonial days. The chief protected them from corporal punishments. However, the truth of it can be questioned here. Did the evil escaped from the possessor when the victim took refuge in the house of the chief? Was it a kind of recruitment processes for workforce; a tool for parents to control headstrong children, and/or a mind game to shatter the mind of helpless people; widow, orphan, etc. What happened when the chief took *boi* females for marriage? Didn't their son become an evil possessor? Such purposefully social constructs and bias operated in the society in the past for many years and is still persisting in the remote areas and among those with a weak mentality. This is due to the ignorance of the innocent people who are lacking basic knowledge in the field of sciences and social sciences. This belief is a social construct with the help of which the rich took advantage of the poor section. The above discussion shows that, this belief sowed the seed of hatred and disharmony secretly as it existed secretly in society. In due course of time, it became a silent killer, thereby disintegrating the social fabric. It became a big social barrier in the past and even today. As a belief system, they considered many of their neighbouring community as impure and thus become a barrier for them. The blames were mostly shifted to the women, the poor and stranger and also killed many in the process of healing or chasing out the spirits from the possessor. Thus, a study on it is related to ethnic groups, gender issue and also issues related to human rights. The theories of the origin of the *kaose*, among the Kuki do not hold validity to the concept of *kao* they believe now. The mode of transferring or acquiring it, was contiguous. For sharing of combs, hair oil, saloon, beauty parlor, taxi, buses, class rooms, etc., in the modern and post-modern ages, would have served as an agent for spreading it. The worst part is the possibility of people who do not believe in it but take advantage of the belief for vested interest. This is because people who strongly feared acquiring of it would avoid rape in the course of witch hunting and also gain from the property of the accused. Traditionally, the Kuki did not hold trial in the village court but identified the accused and the latter took precaution against them instead of ransacking their property. If a person was suspected to be a witch, they wisely planned and of course expelled them from the village. Perhaps, corrupting this belief system or taking advantage of it for vested interest needs were rampant. The absence of strong and vigilant laws to protect the victims were absence in the customary laws of the ethnic community.

NOTES

1. Gerald B. Gardener, *Witchcraft Today*, United Kingdom First Scan, 2002, p. 7.
2. Kathryn A. Edwards, *The History of Ghosts in Early Modern Europe: Recent Research and Future Trajectories* University of South Carolina, History Compass10/4, (2012): 10.1111/j.1478-0542.2012.00840.x pp. 353-66.
3. William Shaw *Notes on the Thadou Kuki*, Guwahati: Spectrum, reprint, 1997, p. 68.

4. T.S. Gangte, *The Kukis of Manipur*, New Delhi: Gyan Publishing House, 1993, pp. 161-2.
5. Shakespeare, *The Lushai Kuki Clans*, Aizawl: TRI, 1988 p. 111.
6. N.E. Parry, *The Lushei Custom and Ceremonies Award*, Aizawl: TRI reprint, 1988, p. 18.
7. Letkhojam Haokip, *Thempu Ho Thu*, Churachandpur, Tribal Research Institute, Imphal, 2000, pp. 47-52.
8. Tarun Goswami, *The Kuki Life and Lore*, North Cachar Hills, District Council, Halflong, Assam, 1985, p. 295.
9. Melford E. Spiro, *Burmese Supernaturalism*, New Jersey: University of Chicago, 1967, pp. 21, 23.
10. All India Radio Imphal Station, *Thadou Modern Song Section*, Date of Recording, 18 May 1982, cut I(one).
11. G.E. Gerini, *Researches on Ptolemy's Geography*, New Delhi: Oriental Reprint, 1974, pp. 827-8.
12. Ibid., p. 660 fn 2.
13. T. Haokip, *Thusim le Lakoila*, Imphal Manipur, 1998, pp. 2-3.
14. Paokhohang Haokip, *Thusim Thum*, Imphal 1998, pp. 45-50.
15. Kgatla, et al., *Crossing Witch Craft Barriers in South Africa: Exploring witchcraft accusation, Causes and Solutions*, SANP AD Research report, 2003, p. 5.
16. The word *Khun* or *khul* in Manipur still signifies villages. Perhaps the word *khun* is a corrupted word from *khul*. Khulkhun is name of a village belonging to caste or Loi near Leimakhong in Manipur.
17. Interview with Hemkhojang Haokip (90) of Kholmun village, Churachandpur on 24-5 October 2012.
18. The emergence of Shongthu from the Khul between AD 900 and 950 is calculated based on the generation that descended from him until the present.
19. M. Paominlen, 'They believed in Malevolent Spirit: In Kaose', in *North East India History Association 32nd Proceedings*, Agartala, 2011, p. 570.
20. William Shaw made a rough calculation on the birth of Thadou, Haokip and Kipgen to be around this century.
21. Letkhojam Haokip, *Thempu Ho Thu*, Churachandpur, 2000, p. 33.
22. Barbara Ambros Reviewed of: *Vengeful Spirits or Loving Spiritual Companions?: Changing Views of Animal Spirits in Contemporary Japan* Author(s): Source: *Asian Ethnology*, vol. 69, no. 1 (2010), pp. 35-6.
23. Shakespeare, *The Lushai Kuki Clans*, Aizawl: TRI, 1988 p. 110.
24. Interview with Tongkholam Singsit (90) of Motbung village Sadar Hills, Manipur on the 20 October, 2012, at his residence. He was born and

brought up at Jampi Village, Tamenglong district and migrated to Motbung in 1993 due to Naga Kuki conflicts.

25. Interview six senior citizens, on 20 October 2012 at Phailengkot village Sadar Hills.
26. D.L. Haokip, 'Mythical History: Lhomi (Half Tiger-Half Man)', in A. Koireng Singh et al., *Knowing Manipur from the Endogenous Perspective*, Imphal: Centre for Manipur Studies, vol. I, 2014, p. 25.
27. T.S. Gangte, *The Kukis of Manipur*, New Delhi: Gyan Publishing House, 1993, pp. 161-2.
28. J. Galtung, 'Cultural Violence', *Journal of Peace Research,* vol. 27, no. 3, 1990, pp.291-305.
29. Silvia Federici, Witch-Hunting, Globalization and Feminist Solidairity in Africa Today, New York, 2008, p. 1.
30. Jonathan Barry et al., *Witch Craft in Early Modern Europe*, Cambridge University Press, 1996, p. 12.
31. The Sentinel.com, Guwahti, 10 October 2014.
32. Rachana Shrestha, *Witch-Hunting: A Study of Cultural Violence against Women with Reference to Nepal and India*, The Hague: Institute of Social Studies, Graduate School of Development Studies, 2004, p. 33.
33. Joya Chakraborty and Anjuman Borah, 'Witch Hunting in Assam: Strategising Alternative Media for Women, Empowerment and Overcoming Supertition', *Journal of North East India Studies*, vol. 3(2), July-December 2013, p. 16.
34. The Sentinel.com, Guwahti, 10 October 2014.
35. Ibid.
36. Silvia Federici, *Witch-Hunting, Globalization and Feminist Solidairity in Africa Today*, New York, 2008, p. 8.
37. Ibid., p. 10.
38. Soma Chaudhuri, Women as Scapgoat: Witchcraft Accusations and Women as Targets in Tea Plantations of India, http://www.sagepublications.com p. 1219.
39. Ibid., p. 1220
40. Ibid.
41. Joya Chakraborty and Anjuman Borah, 'Witch hunting in Assam: Strategising Alternative Media for Women Empowerment and Overcoming Superstition', in *Journal of North East India Studies*, vol. 3(2), July-December 2013, pp. 15-24.
42. Ng. Mataisang, 'The Religious Life of the Naga Tribes of Manipur with special reference to the Tangkhuls', unpublished PhD Thesis, submitted to the Department of History Manipur University, 2002, p. 97.

43. Indrani Chatterje, 'Slaves, Souls and Subjects in a South Asian Borderland', Rutgers University, pp.15-16.
44. From Wikipedia, the free encyclopedia, accessed on 17 October 2012.
45. Letkhojam Haokip, *Thempu Ho Thu*, Churachandpur, 2000, p. 52.
46. They collect dried meat, fish, rice, chilli, salt, etc., and place on a mats. They put beneath and above the roadside after chanting the charms. The sick person spit his or her saliva over the ingredients and throws away by the roadside so for the evil spirits coming from different directions to collect and enjoy.
47. Holding the pieces of meat the priest randomly called the *kaose* from all the different clans of the Kukis. After mentioning one or two clans the priest would sing: *chonpi akijil te, hanpi akijil te; mi akim tai, juchih aneng e, saba aneng e; nang kalam me, tampi asu e, tamla asu e* which means 'People are now going to perform merit feast; everyone have arrived, all the rice-beer is ready, by now, pieces of meat are abundant, all dance, touch the front and back door of the house'.
48. The priests attendant make a 'log' similar to chilly grinder from 'Kheng-thing'.The priest aggrandizes the animal sacrifice, cuts its liver into several pieces to call forth the *kaose* that cause one's sickness. The priest's attendant then makes a pit in which the *log* or grinder could be posted. While calling *kaose* if spider or grasshopper enter the pits where pieces of meat is thrown in, the priest attendant or helper who holds *khengtum* the smooth log under his cloth/garment quickly places the log and hits vertically (*Thempu Ho Thu*, pp. 51-2).
49. The word *kaose* has close bearing with the Meitei word *hingchabi.* Among the Meiteis, this type of spirit is called *lamlai* forest or bad deities who harm to human beings by giving malafic effects.
50. Indrani Chatterje, *Slaves, Souls and Subjects in a South Asian Borderland*, Rutgers University, pp.15-16, p. 19.
51. When the writer of this paper went to another village for class II (two) standard competition Organized by Sadar Hills Autonomous District Council, in 1983, his aunty instructed him not to take any edible things in the public, to avoid the evil eye. She said 'all the villagers, where you are supposed to go for examination are *kaose.* Take care and do not eat any edible items in the public'. This advice still lingers in my mind.
52. Richard L. Dieterle, *Buffalo Spirits*, pp. 2-3.
53. All India Radio Imphal Station, Thadou Modern Song Section, Sung by Jangkholam one of the top singer Date of Recording, 18 May 1982, cut I (one).
54. Online Tribune, Chandigargh, India Jalhandar Edition 22 September 2012.

55. At K. Salbung village, Phailen and Pangshang of Churachandpur district, Manipur there is report of trial. At K. Salbung village authority trial there was a case related to a witch on 23 August 2014, 25 August 2014, 26 August 2014 and 29 August 2014 and the accused was forced to leave the village. The trial was preceded by personal conflicts between individuals.
56. The Kuki who are now Christian took the help of traditional priest belonging to the Valley, particularly the Meitei Maibas, whenever they felt they were attacked by witch or sorcerer. Maibas, traditional priest and sooth sayers are against the doctrine of Christianity. Church pastor or Christian leaders too look forward to healing ministry as alternative for the sick believed to be caused by witch.

CHAPTER 16

'White Magic' Practices of the Adivasis of Jungle Mahals: A Different World View

NIRMAL KUMAR MAHATO

This article seeks to shed light on the magic rituals, the botanical and pharmacological properties of folk medicines and psychic technique used by medicine men among the Adivasis[1] (Oraon, Munda, Kheria, Birhor, Santhal and Kurmi) of Jungle Mahals. On the nature of magic, social science contains two main traditions: Edward Burnett Tylor and James George Frazer observe that magic is superstition—an evolutionarily early stage of science, inadequate and misleading. According to Emile Durkheim, magic is immoral and anti-social. Here, religion solidifies the group, so magic is individualistic. Both traditions, thus, deny an analysis of the lives of peoples where magic plays a significant role, However, the ethnographers have mentioned that the theoretical dichotomies of magic/science and magic/religion do not features the real life of non-Western societies. Max Weber perceived that a distinctive feature of Western civilization is hostility to magic rooted in Judaeo-Christian religion. Sig-mund Mowinckel, Murray and Rosalie Waxes argue that magic is best comprehended, not as rite or cult, but as a world view quite different from the rational views of the world distinctive of Judaeo-Christian religions or Western science.[2] While discussing the cultures of Jungle Mahals communities, Ranabir Samaddar questions Frazerian concept of unilinear development from magic to science via religion as it denies the authenticity of the direct experiences of the colonized people. He argues that magic, religion and science remain intertwined among these communities in this region.[3]

MAGIC, MAGICIANS, BODY AND DISEASE

In general, for practical purposes, Adivasi magical practitioners may be classified as follows:

A. PRACTITIONERS OF GOOD INTENT
('WHITE' MAGICIANS)

1. Medicine Men or Healers or Folk Doctors:
   (a) Physicians (they include herbalists, exorcisers, religious healers).
   (b) Physiotherapist
2. Other Magicians: Priests, Exorcists.

B. PRACTITIONERS OF EVIL INTENT ('BLACK' MAGICIANS):
WITCHES AND SORCERERS

Adivasi Notion of Body

A closer inspection of body as a physical or cultural construct has become a scholarly inquiry. The scholarly interest in body and its various states such as texts and artefacts help us to explore the historical complexities related to human form and the relationship between physical and social body. The serious scholarly enquiry on the body is relatively new, and its incorporation into mainstream historical research is also a recent phenomenon.[4] The Adivasi notion of body and disease has been least discussed from the historical context. The aim of this article is to explore the ways in which the Adivasi communities (Oraons, Kherias, Santhals) of Jungle Mahals,[5] engage with their bodies.

Various Bodies in History

The history of the Western body was constructed in terms of a 'modern' body, a 'medieval' body, a 'classical' body, and so on. In sixteenth-century Europe, the body was perceived to be a material case for the soul, which was related with the universe in microcosmic way and located in a fractal condition. The body was viewed in the nineteenth century as a functional material mechanism. A medieval body was thought to be a microcosm which indicated the excellence of God's creation. As the modern body was described like a machine, it was conceptualized as 'bounded, interchangeable, and formed of distinct, functional parts, first via the writings of Descartes and others and anatomical dissection and, later, through new practices of discipline and spatial bounding both at home and at work'.[6] Some historians of 'the modern body' sought to find out the process of developments through which the body became ever more civilized[7] and disciplined.[8] As factories, prison and enclosures paved the way to create bounded and disciplined bodies, people could easily perceive the body as a machine. The mechanistic view of the body which was inherent in industrial discipline and the emerging medical knowledge inherent in the 'birth of the clinic'[9] became widespread throughout eighteenth and nineteenth century. In ancient Indian context, the body was generally thought be equal with the cosmos. The Tantric understanding of body, as shown by Sthaneshwar Timalsina, comprised of five essential concepts:

(i) The body of the deity is constructed with *mantras*.
(ii) As the deity emanates in the form of the *mandata*, the body of the deity is the *mandata* itself.
(iii) The human body is thought to be a temple (*deha-devagrha*).
(iv) The human body is considered to be cosmos (*pinda-brahmanda*).
(v) The body is an expression of bliss and awareness (*cidananda*).[10]

In Santhali language, *horom* means body. According to Kherwal Bintis (oral narration), Marangburu is the creator of the human being, animate and inanimate objects of earth. All human beings are the *po ponga* (generation of offspring) of Pilchu Haram and Pilchu Burhi who were regarded as the first father and mother of the human race and gradually, they expanded their *po ponga* to form the basis of human race.[11]

Men are born and all other things living or inanimate are born side by side for the fulfilment of desire and realization of life by the human being. Also happiness and sorrow to appeared on earth like a life cycle. It is reflected in a *binti*[12]:

Ot Janan lan
Dubighas janam lan;
Manmi janam lan,
Duck haun janam lan
Achur bihur janan lan
Manmi janam lan,
Raah jaung janam lan

[This song implies that the earth, plants and *durba* grass were born. Men were born as well as the elements of sorrow and sufferings followed. Silver and copper were created. Men were born as also feelings of suffering followed.]

With his protective weapon *samanam kapi*, Marangburu worked for human well-being and prosperity. Jaher Era relieves people from sorrows and suffering. According to a Santhal *binti*, Lita had eaten and drunk in a house of a human being before the purification ritual of childbirth was over. So Lita did not return home as his elder sister Jaher Era disapproved of his activity. Jaher Era was searching her brother and ultimately he was found at Jalapuri as a king of that kingdom. She requested her brother to return to their home but he refused. Lita argued that gods/goddesses have to show a tolerant attitude towards human beings. As a human being, he/she make minor mistakes and God forgave him for that.[13]

In the process from birth to manhood, every turning point of the Adivasis was marked by ceremonies and magico-religious rites which were designed to ensure safety and prosperity to the individual, family and the community. Adivasi women tattoo their arms, chest and neck below the collar bone and the legs just above the ankles. They also tattoo their feet and forehead. At the age of ten or twelve, Adivasi boys get nine cicatrices or scars raised on the dorsal aspect of the radial side of their forearms, usually left forearms. The old men claim that these marks distinguish their Adivasi fellows. They followed some rites and ceremonies in order to protect them from evil influences and supernatural dangers faced at birth and during childhood. The way one maintains one's body is the most fundamental aspect of health. Adivasi women maintain long tresses which exhibits a remarkable efficiency. A song enumerates twenty distinctly defined tresses.[14] For a long time, only men could have their hair cut. Among the medical sciences, the cutting of hair occupies a significant place in history. Therefore, it can be argued that the Adivasi bodies were considered as socio-cultural construct.

NOTION OF DISEASE

In the case of the San Community of South Africa, the supernatural potency (*n/om*), as mentioned in their cosmology, is 'unpersonified, incorporeal, immaterial, invisible and powerful' force. Lorna Marshal compared it with the features of electricity. Like electricity, supernatural potency is not visible and a powerful force and it to appeared as light, heat and kinetic energy. This force does not spread out either in the air or in the Universe. However, its presence is seen both in animate and inanimate object. The concept of supernatural potency of the Adivasis of Jungle Mahals is very similar with this concept. The Oraons belived that there were different types of *bhuts* or spirits such as household *bhut*, sept *bhuts*, village *bhuts*, village *devtas*, wandering *bhuts*, common *devtas*. The household *bhuts* were *baranda*, *chigrinod*, *panchbal* and *nasre*. The sept *bhut* was *khut nasan*. Village *bhuts* were *khunt*, *bhula* and *churil*. The village deities were Pat, Chala Pacho or Sarna Burhi. The common *devtas* were Dhartimai (the mother earth) and sun god or Singh-bonga. They considered earth both as a *devta* and as a *bhut*. The village priest dealt with both the deities and spirits of the village landscape whilst the Ojha dealt with all the mischievous spirits who were responsible for all kinds of sickness and some spirits who had been disregarded by people.[15] The tribal gods and spirits resided in the forests, hills and rivers. Thus nature became sacred to them. Every tribal village was governed by a sacred grove (*sarna/garam than*) which was a part of the original forest. Every tribal group had the concept of a sacred grove. Their deities were usually in the form of unshaped stone lumps, old woods, water bodies, etc. If anybody violated the rules and regulation of the sacred groves imposed on their social institutions, it was believed that the person would suffer from serious illness. They paid respect and were afraid of gods and ancestral spirits. It was not only a place of worship and performance but also served the socio-cultural and religious purposes.[16]

As the belief in some unnatural or super or supra-natural entity (such as ghost spirit, *jin*, etc.) by different communities was very common, the acts of *bonga* (spirits) was the key factor for the occurrence of any unbalance in the human body, i.e. disease. There were three types of *bongas*:

(i) *Singbonga* (the supreme *bonga*) people thought if they would perform their religious activities timely and properly they might lead a decent life as good human beings;
(ii) *Haparan Bongas* and *Simon Bongas*: They were regarded as the ancestral *bongas* or the benevolent spirit taking genesis after death of their ancestors. They acted as the barriers of body like skin which protected the body from outside environment;
(iii) *Bongas*: The malevolent spirits (*bongas*) were always responsible for inflicting disease.[17]

There was a general belief in most tribal societies that unmixed good or unmixed evil was not desirable in life of an individual and also in the society. When this balance was broken in an individual's life, there was disease and ill health, followed inexorably by death. Similarly when the balance was upset in society, there was a quarrel, disharmony among families and groups in the villages and lastly epidemics and calamities befell on the whole community. If an epidemic came, men and cattle started dying. The villagers deserted the entire village and migrated to a new place to avoid misery.[18]

When the Kherias observed that a draught was knocking at the door, the white magician *deonra* or *kalo* would follow a ritual. At first a *jitia-pipar* (*Ficus religiosa*) tree, possibly on the side of a rock or another higher place was chosen. In the morning, the *deonra* tied an unbleached cotton thread several times round the trunk of the tree at the height of 4 ft above the ground. Village women collected water with new earthen vessels from springs, tanks or wells, led *kalo's* wife and returned to the selected site with vessels full of water. *Kalo's* wife would first throw water over the tree from the rock. Other women would then throw water five or seven times over the tree which would fall on *kalo's* wife's head. It looked as if it were raining. *Kalo's* wife would do the same thing to the village women. After it was done they returned home and prepared food. The male members would go for the ceremonial hunt. The worship of a rain god was also common among other tribes.[19]

DIAGNOSIS AND TREATMENT

The folk doctors or *ojhas* or *mati* or *dewair* (for Oraons) followed three methods for treatment: *Bhesaja chikitsa* (herbal treatment), *mantra* treatment (hymn treatment), *daibya chikitsa* (spiritual treatment). The Kherias called the white and black magicians *deonra* and *dain bisha* respectively. Some *ojhas* treated mental illness with cures like isolation, restraint, threats and drugs.

Herbal treatment of the tribes may be subdivided into three categories: (i) Oral administration: This treatment was performed by using pills, powder and infusion. There are another kind of drugs which are used externally. (ii) Massage or physiotherapy (iii) Contact therapy: This type of treatment was adopted by hanging the medicine (root, leave, plant part, hair, nail, any other part of an animal's body, etc.) directly or in some tiny package (e.g. *maduli*) tied to cotton thread. From a folk song this type of treatment can be found:

Bandhaake saile Jwar
Kaa haan pawha ojha ghar
Bandhe debon naagalila sikad
One sajane[20]

[The song means 'My darling is suffering from insane fever. The doctor is not available now; I know that the unbeatable medicine of this fever is the root of a tree named *naagalia*.]

The eminent botanist, Valentine Ball was astonished to realize the deep knowledge of some folk doctors regarding the specific virtues of certain plants.[21] In the heat treatment method, a red hot hoe was used for heating and a thick layer of leaves of calotropis (*Akand*) is placed on the spot.[22]

Mantra chikitsa (hymn treatment) was a treatment through chanting *mantras* (hymn).[23] These are divided into four: (a) *Para*, (b) *Pasyanti*, (c) *Madhyama* and (d) *Baikhari*. The *ojhas* had created *mantras* on this type of treatment.[24]

When a man falls ill an *ojha* was called in to ascertain which spirits are the cause of illness. He comes in the evening with his winnowing fan and a handful of rice. He examines the patient first, feels his pulse, and gives him some medicine. In order to create a suitable environment, he follows some rituals and starts his *mantra* treatment. He squats cross-legged on the ground. On his lap he has the winnowing fan with some rice in it, and close at hand an unlit lamp. His left hand holds the end of the winnowing fan, and with his right hand, he stirs the rice, turning it round and round as if to mix it up well. He shuts his eyes, throws back his head, and in a low nasal voice, invokes all the local deities. Then, he chants *mantras* and incantations for a long time. During the time the house is quite silent and everyone watches and listens. Suddenly the *ojha* gets excited and bursts into lively incantations, turning his head right and left, and stirring the rice with frenzy until he falls into a trance, in which it seems to him that he is wandering about the fields, rocks and ravines of the village in search of the spirits. As he sees them, he calls each by name. When the guilty spirits shake the winnowing fan, he lights his lamp to make sure that he has discovered the right spirits. This ritual is known as *ras-batti-kar na*. When the sick man gets all right after his first attempt, he asks for a fowl which he sacrifices to the spirits. When other people of the house also get sick he concludes that the spirit has taken possession of the house and would not leave without being driven by force. This ritual is called *niskari* which is an expensive business.[25]

The physiotherapist followed the acupuncture method of treatment with red hot sickle.[26] The methods like massage therapy with specific oil on regular basis are used. In the case of wrenches or sprains, women experts are very popular.

METHODS OF COLLECTION OF MEDICINIAL PLANTS

According to the tribal belief, the efficacy of the medicine would automatically be reduced, if the *ojhas* did not follow the rules for collection of medicinal plants properly. They followed some rules. As the plants were supposed to take rest or sleep after sunset and before sunrise the *ojhas* should not disturb them by harvesting then. The Adivasis used to uproot some herbs at one breath. Accordingly, it the concentrated will force of the ojha. During the period of harvest, the horopathist prefers to collect the exposed roots only near the canal. They cut with a single stroke in the absence of any person. The *ojhas* collect some rare drugs in early morning even before attending nature's call so that the work can be executed in absence of any person. The medicine men has to debark from a tree at one breath after cutting a branch from bottom to top, i.e. in the upward direction. The shadow should not fall on the plant during the time of digging a part. This method (i.e. digging on one side only) keeps half of the root intact. The medicine men went on an annual herb exploration. It was done after scattering the seeds of plants. Without damaging or tapping the trees, gum was collected from the trees. During the rainy seasons, plants were kept free from extraction.[27]

PROCESS OF DRUG PREPARATION

Generally, medicines are taken on empty stomach. However, there are some exceptions. Some ingredients, i.e. honey, rock salt, sugar candy, black pepper, long-pepper, rice washed water, strong *mahua* (*Madhuca longifolia*) liquor, etc., are administered with the medicines.[28] Colour matching is very important for enhancing the effectiveness of medicine. Combination of different parts of the same plants is believed to be more effective than the single one. The medicine men prepare the products in the form of pills. In case of contraception, they advise the tribal women to use the pills at a specific period; i.e. just at the end of menstruation period. It is quite true that these medicines were quite potent in inhibiting the implantation of the ovum for a certain period. The fertility of ovum can be revived (restored) through some other pills made using other ingredients in some cases.[29] Some beliefs within the tribe have persisted regarding the species of particular plants. Roots are more effective than shoots of a plant. The size of the root is very important, i.e. the thicker it is, the superior the quality of the medicine. Quality of latex is regarded as a quality of medicine. Different alternative herbal medicines are applied for different persons with different receptivity to different medicines.[30]

HEALING FACTORS

The application of medicines should be in a proper way. Self-confidence of the healer is the key factor for proper treatment. Full faith of the patient in his healer also is very important. The blessing of the God is very important. The medicine men recall him (the God) during extraction of plants, during preparation and administration of the herbal medicine. The common belief is that the goddess *manasa* controls the snakes and if she is pleased snakebite can be avoided. *Manasa* (*Exphorbia nerifolia*) plant was/or is still worshipped by different tribes. This species is generally planted in the courtyards of houses to prevent entry of snakes into their houses.[31]

The Adivasis had rich knowledge of taxonomy which enriched the indigenous system of knowledge about practice of medicine, pharmacy and pharmacology. The rules for collection of plants signify the conservation of the species of medicinal plants. It indicates their need based extraction to keep the herbal resources ever sustained in nature. They warn themselves by their proverb:

Baday khanem ran/Bañkhan bir sahan.[32]

Any plant can be used as a medicine because each has some curing potential, however if the user does not know it, he must use it merely as fuel being deprived of the health service that could be provided by the plant.

CONCLUSION

Adivasis lead a community life and their notion of body and disease is social, cultural and community centered. The human body is related to the surrounding environment, as well as spirits. Their bodies are not confined and disciplined like machines but related to the eco-cosmic world. In all human societies, it is true that the 'body is always a source of experience and something that is conceptualized in a specific way, there are different ontologies of the body'. Communities perceive different things about the body in their own way. When the balance between the good and evil spirits breaks down in individual life, there is disease and ill health and in the case of Adivasi society there is disharmony. With the colonial intervention in the Adivasi landscape, the environments, their bodies and their medicinal system are also contested.

ACKNOWLEDGEMENT

I express my sincre gratitute to Professor Sajal Nag, Department of History, Assam University, for his valuable comments on the earlier draft of the paper and his kind support.

NOTES

1. The word 'Adivasi' means original inhabitant. For details, see an excellent study (Rycroft 2014) on assertion of Adivasis as indigenous peoples in India. Recently scholars (Rycroft 2014) do not italicize the word in order to normalize its use. See D.J. Rycroft, 'Looking beyond the Present: The Historical Dynamics of Adivasi (Indigenous and Tribal) Assertions in India', *Journal of Adivasi and Indigenous Studies*, I (1). (Online), 2014, 1.
2. For the entire debate see Wax, Murray and Rosalie, 'The Notion of Magic', *Current Anthropology*, 4, no. 5, 1963, pp. 495-518.
3. Ranbir Samaddar, *Memory, Identity, Power*, The Politics in the Jungle Mahals (West Bengal) 1890-1950, Hydrabad: Orient Longman, 1998, p. 214.
4. T. Sarah and K. Fisher, 'Introduction', *The Routledge History of Sex and the Body, 1500 to the Present*. New York: Routledge, 2013.
5. In, 1805, according to the Regulation XVIII, a new district named Jungle Mahals was created in Bengal Presidency consisting of twenty-three parganas (means the present Purulia district and parts of Birbhum, Bardhaman, Bunkura and Medinipur). For details of its concept and administrative geography see Suchibrata Sen, *The Santals of Jungle Mahals.*, Calcutta: Ratna Publisher, 1994, pp. 18-22.

6. Oliver J.T. Harris and J. Robb, 'Multiple Ontologies and the Problem of the Body in History', *American Anthropologist*, 114(4), 2012, pp. 668-9.
7. Norbert Elias, *The Civilising Process: The History of Manners*, tr. E. Jephcott, Oxford: Basil Blackwell, 1978.
8. Michel Foucault, *Discipline and Punish: The Birth of the Prison*, New York: Vintage Books, 1977.
9. Michel Foucault, *The Birth of the Clinic: Archaeology of Medical Perception*, London: Tavistock, 1973.
10. S. Timalsina, 'Reconstructing the Tantric Body: Elements of the Symbolism of Body in the Monistic Kaula and Trika Tantric Traditions', *International Journal of Hindu Studies*, 2012, 16, 1, p. 8.
11. Nityananda Hembrom, *Austric Civilization of India: Pre-Vedic Kherwal-Santal Civilization*, Published by Dr Bangali Kisku and Dr Meenakhi Kisku, New Delhi, p. 54.
12. Ibid., pp. 54, 59.
13. Ibid., p. 54.
14. Ibid., p. 54.
15. M.P. Dehon, 'Religion and Customs of the Uraons', *Memoirs* 1, Asiatic Society of Bengal, 1907, p. 138.
16. P.P. Mahato, *Bharater Adivasi O Dalita Samaj*, Calcutta: Sujan Publication, 1995, p. 16.
17. P.P. Hembrom and A.K. Goel, 'Horopathy: Ethnomedicine of Mundas', *Ethnobotany*, vol. 17, 2005, pp. 89-95.
18. P.P. Mahato, *Bharater Adivasi O Dalita Samaj*, 1995, op. cit., pp. 16, 89-95.
19. S.C., Roy, *The Kherias.* vol. 2, 1937, pp. 88-9.
20. Adikanta Mahanta, 2007, 'Ecological Ideologies in Tribal Folklore of Eastern India', In *Forest, Government and Tribe*, ed. C.K. Patty, New Delhi: Concept Publisher, p. 75.
21. V. Ball, 'Notes on the Flora on Manbhum', *Journal of the Asiatic Society of Bengal*, No. 3, 1868, pp. 121-2.
22. P.P. Hembrom and A.K. Goel, op. cit., 2005, pp. 89-95.
23. Adikanta Mahanta, op. cit., 2007, p. 75.
24. Ibid., p. 75. Four stages of articulation of sound. An animate being make sound either howling or zwingling human too. Pronouncement of sound through vocal organ according to linguistic is a composite factor. Reference to the objective appearance through sense organs are tremendously shuttle. Traditionally, the above psychophysical process is divided into four consecutive stages, i.e. (i) *para* (ii) Pasyanti (iii) Madhyama (iv) Vackhari.
25. M.P. Dehon, op. cit., 1907, pp. 141-9.

26. P.P. Hembrom and A.K. Goel, op. cit., vol. 17, pp. 89-95.
27. Ibid., pp. 89-95. Oral history of tribal medicine collected from Sri Bhutnath Mandi (Vill. Jaganathdi, P.O. Pabra, Dist Purulia, 6 June 2008), a Santhal medicine man, practised indigenous medicine. He has profound knowledge in this regard. He got it from his ancestors. He lamented for its deterioration, Village Gaganathdi, P.O. Pabra, Dist Purulia, 6 June 2008. Mahato, N.K. *Sorrow Songs of Woods: Adivasi-Nature Relationship in the Anthropocene in Manbhun*, New Delhi: Primus, 2020, p. 75.
28. Adikanta Mahanta, 'Ecological Ideologies in Tribal Folklore of Eastern India'. In *Forest, Government and Tribe*, ed. Patty, C.K. Concept Publisher, New Delhi, 2007, p. 75.
29. Oral history of tribal medicine collected from Smt. Nehari Baidya who belongs to Bediya community. She has rich knowledge in this respect. Vill. & Post Khairipihira, Purulia Disritct, 11 June 2006. I have also got some information from some tribal women of this locality.
30. Oral history of tribal medicine collected from Sri Bhutnath Mandi.
31. Oral history of tribal medicine collected from Sri Bhutnath Mandi, & Oral history of tribal medicine collected from Sri Bangshi Mahato who also practised indigenous medicine. Besides, some women of my village gave me some information in this regard. Vill. Boykara, P.O. Tara, Dist. Purulia, 11 November 2006.
32. The Santhali proverb was collected by the author from Late Surja Hansda, Vill. Chatarpada, P.O. Chandri, Midnapur (W).

CHAPTER 17

Satanic Cult among the Christian Tribes of the North-East India

PHOIBI LALNIROPUI TUOLOR

INTRODUCTION

Scholars often use words like 'satanic', 'ritual' and 'occult' interchangeably. No attempt will be made in this article to define satanism precisely. However, it is learnt that, for some individuals, any religious belief system other than their own is termed as 'satanic'. From a Christian perspective, the word 'satanism' had been used to describe the power of evil in the world. In this context, any act which is wrong, especially those which are particularly cruel, bizarre or repulsive can be termed as satanic in nature. As such it is difficult to define satanism as it is to define any other complex spiritual belief system.

Judeo Christian theology generally believes that there are only two powerful supernatural forces in the world: God and Satan. They regard the non-believers as satanists, as they believe that those who do not worship their God and hold their beliefs must be worshipping satan. According to them all other religions different from their own are forms of satanism. Satanism is a broad group of social movement comprizing of diverse ideological and philosophical beliefs. Their shared features include symbolic association with or admiration for satan, whom satanists see as a liberating figure. It was estimated that there were 50,000 satanists in 1990. There may be as many as one hundred thousand satanists in the world.[1]

SATANIC PRACTICES IN THE NORTH-EAST INDIA

The satanic cult is reported to be practised mostly in Christian dominated states of north-east India, i.e. Mizoram, Nagaland, Meghalaya and Christian-dominated areas of Manipur. The followers of the satanic cult are teenagers, mostly drug addicts, who do not want to obey the rules and norms of the Church, and they are basically against the Church. They are known by different names in different places like followers of the 'Dark of Prince' in Mizoram, 'Black Bull' or 'Awakening the Horror' in Nagaland, '*Achik Underground Cult, Dark Star* and *Outlawz*' in Meghalaya. The followers include both male and female, they usually gather in the cemeteries late at night to operate the practice wearing black T-Shirts. According to reports the 'satanic rituals' includes unlawful, even unnatural sex, incest and taking of psychotropic drugs.[2] They did it to attain supernatural powers and perform miracles. Most of them offered their own blood by cutting their wrist, whereas some offered chicken's blood.[3]

According to reports there are various ways and methods to join the satanic cult or satanism. The contract is initiated on mutual accord between the person and Satan, solemnized by a cut. It can be done in diverse ways. Three prominent methods found in Nagaland are: first, the person has to cut himself/herself and pour his/her own blood in places where the devil tells him/her to. Second, the devil shows certain symbols with meaning to be tattooed on the body. This is known as the tattoo covenant. Third, the devil demands the person to sign on certain things and spell certain demonic statement. Once the contract is finalized, the devil assigns certain demons to the satanist according to desire or demand. The demons work for the satanist. The satanist uses the demons in the form of spell, charm and power. There are also ranks and clans in satanism. The prominent clans in Nagaland are werewolf and vampire. The demons mentioned are different from the ones seen in media and are in spiritual form.[4]

Statistical reports from the Christian dominated north-east states had shown that, since 2011 the satanic cult followers had increased to a great extent. In Mizoram according to the General Census 2011, the total population of the state was 10,91,014 of which 86.97 per cent are Christians and 661 persons claimed to be without any religion. Such groups of people were found in different parts of the state such as 209 in Champhai district, 208 in Mamit district, 114 in Aizawl district, 39 in Serchhip and Saiha districts, 32 in Lawngtlai, 14 in Lunglei and 6 in Kolasib.[5] In 2012 according to the investigation made by Rev. L.H. Rawsea, the then faculty member of the Aizawl Theological College, it was estimated that about 300 youths were involved in satanic cult in Mizoram.[6] In Churachanpur town of Manipur according to reports in 2011, it was estimated that 500 to 700 people were involved in active satanic practice including 180 women. In Kohima alone, which is capital of Nagaland, Vatican's Fides new agency in 2013 reported that there are more than 3,000 young worshippers of satan.[7] In 2014 to prevent satan worship in Meghalaya, five alleged 'devil worshippers' were arrested and later released from Tura, the headquarter of West Garo Hills, Meghalaya.[8] Dr Jova Marak, an activist for counselling such youth, states that such groups existed in Tura and Williamnagar town and were using social media sites such as Facebook and Twitter to expand their network but the actual strength of satanic followers is not easy to ascertain.[9]

According to FBI Report on 'Satanic ritual abuse' prepared by Kenneth V. Lanning, Supervisory Special Agent Behavioural Science Unit National Centre for the Analysis of Violent Crime, the satanic or occult activity most often linked to law enforcement problems are as below:[10] (a) Vandalism; (b) Desecration of churches and cemeteries; (c) Thefts from churches and cemeteries; (d) Teenage gangs; (e) Animal mutilations; (f) Teenage suicide; (g) Child abuse; (h) Kidnapping; (i) Murder and human sacrifice.

MIZORAM

Such incidences have been reported in Mizoram as published in *The Hindu* on 18 June 2000, where a group of high school students were seen late at night inside a cemetery huddled together in a circle, holding hands and chanting invocations to satan. In the centre of the circle was placed the skull of a monkey with the inscription *Natas Si Dog*, which in reverse reads 'God is Satan'. While performing the ritual, the worshippers offered their blood to the 'fallen angel' by slashing their wrists one after the other.[11] The 'fallen angel' referred here must be the Biblical fallen angel, Lucifer. Again in 2006, Aizawl's local weekly magazines published a report that five youths were caught filming themselves nude inside a non-functional United Pentecostal Church (UPC) on the outskirts of Aizawl, a Christian majority town.[12] The incident provides a clear evidence of the prevalence of the satanic cult among the Mizo youth.

According to reliable sources, in the year 2013, Mr. Lalrinmawia of Champhai district, Mizoram was arrested by Bawngkawn and Vaivakawn police when he identified himself as a worshipper of satan and also a swindler. On being interrogated, he confessed before the police as to how he became a satanist or worshipper of satan. According to his testimony, he was once a Christian counsellor and a true believer of Jesus Christ, but while he was working as a counsellor, he was tempted by the disciple of satan named 'Belfatas' to follow him. When Lalrinmawia refused to the offer, the disciple of satan started to torture him and that compelled the latter to follow Satan. The disciple of Satan, according to him was a handsome and well built bodied man that is incomparable in the world. He also revealed the names of two disciples of Satan namely 'Belfatas' and 'Rainmen' who used to appear in flesh. While Belfatas is active among drug addicts, Rainmen is active among singers, he added. Sources informed that Lalrinmawia worshipped the much powerful and mightier kind of Satan than the evil worshipped by the majority of Mizo youths. Lalrinmawia further confessed that they had a group of satanic followers in Mizoram called 'Dark of Prince' comprising around ten members including both male and female. They usually worshipped Satan and practised the cult specifically on first Wednesday of every month.[13]

MANIPUR

Such incidents have also been reported in Manipur since 2007 when the Satanic-worshipping sect was accused of killing two ten-year- old school children namely, Muheni Martin and Hriini

Hubert in Manipur's Senapati district. The incident took place when on 14 December 2006, the children were abducted and in the next year on 27 March 2007 their bodies were found in a gorge. A day after the bodies of the children were recovered, the angry mob had set fire to the house of one of the suspects in the case and amid the debris they discovered a wooden sculpture of a head with the mark '666' on the forehead which is attributed to the antichrist in the Bible.[14]

According to the local news agency, on 28 August 2010, Satan worshippers were reported in Manipur state when at least ten people were detained by a rebel group at Rengkai village in Churachandpur district of Manipur for allegedly 'worshipping Satan'. They used to allegedly congregate at cemetery and riverbank at night to perform their rituals.[15]

According to sources, in Manipur the satanic group is led by three key leaders among whom one is from Paite community, one is from Hmar community, and one is a non-tribal (Vai). The leaders are no doubt brought up in a Christian family and one of the members was a son of a pastor, who took the initiative of spreading messages through internet against Jesus Christ. Reports also mentioned that, he gets financial assistance from some satanic worshippers abroad in his satanic evangelism. The report further states that this group would often meet on a particular hill beyond the Muolvaiphei village, known as Cherep Tlang by the local people, on a full moon night where they would perform their satanic rituals. The worship ritual includes the following steps such as lighting of candles with a goat head in the middle and they would use animal blood as sacrifice to satan. The participants performed the rituals completely naked, intoxicated themselves with drugs or dendrite and had sex freely. Reports were also found of such moments of worship held inside a church as an act of defiance to Jesus Christ.[16]

NAGALAND

Similar cases have also been reported from Nagaland since 2013, amid intense speculations, a membership form of a group called 'Awakening the Horror' was made available to Newmai News Network by a church pastor in Dimapur as recently as in first week of July 2013. According to sources, to become a member of this group, one had to submit the membership form; the members of 'Awakening the Horror' would support each other and fight jointly in case any member was attacked by anyone. The members would meet at midnight once a week at a place in Chumukedima in the outskirt of Dimapur.[17]

According to Rev. Wati Longkumer, director of the Nagaland Missionary Movement, some of the Christian youth who have renounced Satan worship have confessed that they performed their rituals after midnight at the Kohima War Cemetery and other locations, wearing black T-shirts and were called by their new nicknames. They named their group as the 'Black Bulls' and invited youngsters to join their congregation.[18]

MEGHALAYA

In the state of Meghalaya too, instances of Satan worship as well as practice of the occult has been reported. In the month of April 2014 in Garo Hills, residents of some areas of Tura have reported sightings of people practising satan worship. The residents witnessed a few youngsters dancing to satanic tunes in the middle of the night giving rise to the fear that voodoo practice might be back in the region.[19]

To curb the practice of satanic or cult worship, reports were prepared by some organizations and through such reports; it was found that there were several youths in Tura and Williamnagar who were engaged in such worship. The first incidence of such cult worship was first reported from Matchakolgre locality in Tura, following which a vigilance committee was formed. No doubt some of the satan worshippers had renounced such worship and had confessed their involvements and ways of ritual performance. Different Satanic groups were formed such as the A'chik underground cult on Facebook, Dark Star, Outlawz and ETR. The graffiti on the walls in different locality stand testimony of this practice.[20]

Again on June 2014, five alleged 'devil worshippers' were arrested and later, released from Tura, the headquarters of the West Garo Hills. All the boys were high school students and had satanic images tattooed on their bodies and they also had unique parallel lines etched across their stomachs.[21]

On 19 July 2014, the *Telegraph* had reported that a group of youngsters of Lumshyiap locality in Meghalaya had spotted a statue of Jesus Christ with an inverted cross at the verandah of a Catholic church located in a cemetery. The area falls under the St Peter and Paul Parish, Pynthorumkhrah. The window panes of the church were broken most probably in order to remove the statue.[22]

SYMBOLS AND SIGNS

In all the cases in north-east India the satanist used various symbols and signs which denoted Satan, to whom they offered sacrifices and regarded as their god, who delivered them from their sorrows and sufferings. The followers of satan used the symbols while performing the satanic rituals and also made tattoos of such symbols on their body. Such symbols and signs were also painted on the walls, the graffiti on the walls in different locality stand testimony of this practice. The following are the symbols and signs along with their meanings compiled by Pastor Billy Bissell. Pastor Bissell served as a Chaplain and Ritualistic Crime Consultant for the Police Department in Muskogee, Oklahoma.

Inverted Pentagram: Symbolizes the morning star, a name Satan has taken. It is used in witchcraft and occult rituals to conjure up evil spirits. Satanists use it two points up and pagans use it one point up. Any way it is used to symbolizes evil. It does not matter if two points are up or one. It does not matter if it has a circle around it. It is still a symbol of satan.

Baphomet: It is unique to satanism. A demonic deity and symbolic of satan. The symbol is used as jewelry such as rings, necklaces and earrings, etc. It is also now being used by the masons. It can be seen on their buildings and the emblems they put on their vehicles to identify each other.

Now it is also being used by the free masons. It can be seen on their buildings and the emblems they put on their vehicles to identify them.

Pentagram: It is a symbol used in witchcraft. Represents the elements, earth, wind, fire and water with the spirit surrounding them.

Hexagram: It is one of the most potent symbols used in the working of the powers of darkness. Used to work magic. Satanism takes and misuses Christian symbols. It is satanic when used in an occult setting with a circle around it.

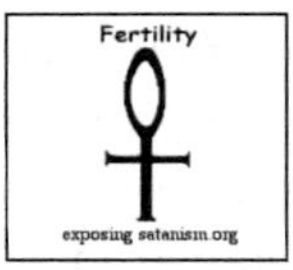

Ankh: It symbolizes fertility rites and the building up of lust within a person. A spirit of lust is the power of this union of male/female representations. Also called the Long Life Seal.

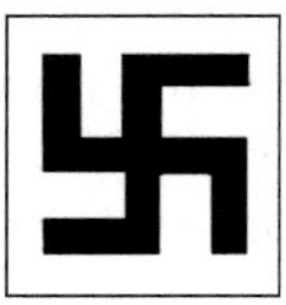

Svastika or Sun Wheel: It is an ancient religious symbol used long before Hitler came to power. It was used in Hindu Buddhist rituals inscriptions, Celtic monuments and Greek coins. In sun god worship, it is supposed to represent the sun's course in the heavens.

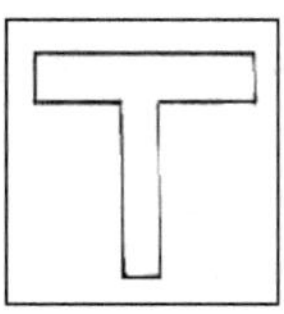

Tau Cross: It is a symbol of the god Mathras of the Persians and the Aryans of India. To them, Mathras was an 'angel of light' or the 'heavenly light'. It is used in modern masonry under the symbol of the T square.

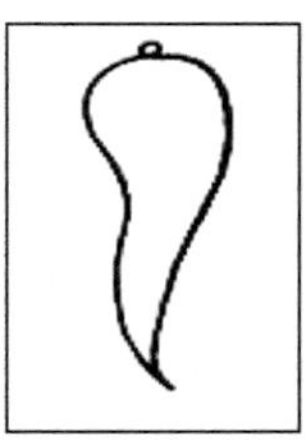

Italian Horn: There are other names Unicorn horn and Leprechaun Staff. Introduced by the Lord Druids of Scotland and Ireland. It is associated with good luck and good fortune. It is also used to ward off 'Maluka' or the 'Evil Eye'. It also means Satan will take care of your finances.

All seeing Eye: It is believed to be the eye of Lucifer and those who claim control of it have control of world finances. Used in divination. Hexes, curses, psychic control and all corruption are worked through this emblem. This one is a symbol of the Illuminati. Look at U.S. currency.

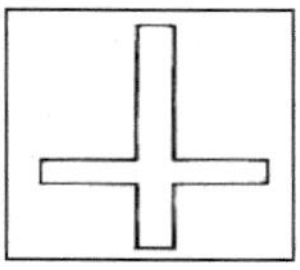

Upside Down Cross: It symbolizes mockery and rejection of Jesus. Necklaces with this emblem are worn by many satanists. It can be seen on rock singers and their album covers.

Zodiac: It is used in satanic and occult worship. Baal is considered as a Christian demon and the first Principal king of Hell. It is often mentioned in the Old Testament Bible as a pagan idol associated with the evil goddess Ashtaroth. Whereas Lucifer is the Satan himself. Beside this symbol, horoscope signs are also included.

Goat Head: It is the horned goat, goat of Mendes, Baphomet, god of the witches, the scapegoat. It's a satanist's way of mocking Jesus as the 'Lamb' who died for our sins.

Cross of Nero or Peace Sign: It is another sign that mocks the cross of Jesus. Also known as 'The Dead Man Rune'. It appears on the tombstones of some of Hitler's SS troops.

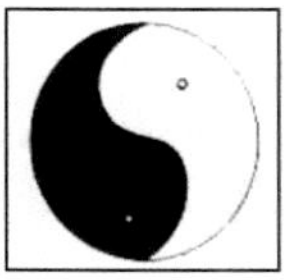

Yin-Yang: In Chinese philosophy, these are two great opposite principles or forces on whose interplay everything depends. Yang is male, light and positive; Yin is female, dark and negative.

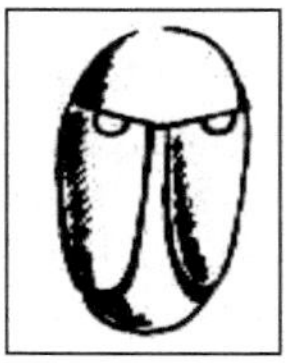

Scarab Beetle: It is the dung beetle which is the Egyptian symbol of reincarnation. It is also a symbol of Beelzebub, Lord of the flies (Satan). Worn by occultists to show that they have power. It is considered a source of protection.

Satanic 'S': It represents a lightning bolt that means 'Destroyer'. In mythology, it was the weapon of Zeus. It is worn to have power over others. It was also worn by the feared SS of the Nazi Germany.

Satanic Cross: It is an upside down question mark that questions God. Within the occult it is the representation of the three crown princes: Satan, Belial and Leviathan. It symbolizes complete power under Lucifer.

Udjat or All Seeing Eye: It is one of few symbols referring to Lucifer (king of hell), whom it is thought will pass the final judgement. Below the eye is a tear because he mourns for those outside his influence.

Star and Crescent: It represents the moon goddess Diana and the 'son of the morning', the name of Lucifer (*Isaiah* 14:12). Witchcraft uses it the way shown and satanism turns it in the opposite direction.

Anarchy: It means to abolish all laws. In other words 'do what thou wilt' the law of satanists. Used by Punk rockers and Heavy Metal followers. Also used in the cover page of Noan Chomsky's book on Anarchism.

Horned God: It represents the horned god of witchcraft. Pan or Cernunnos. Note the thumb under the fingers and given by the right hand.

Horned Hand: This is the sign of recognition between those in the occult. When pointed at someone it is meant to place a curse. Note the thumb over the fingers and given by the left hand.

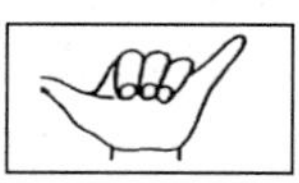

Witch Sign or Moon Sign: It is used to salute the rising moon. Also used by surfers and football teams.

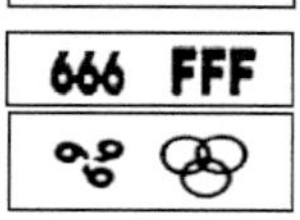

666 - The number of man. It is the mark of the beast in the book of Revelation, the final chapter of New Testament.

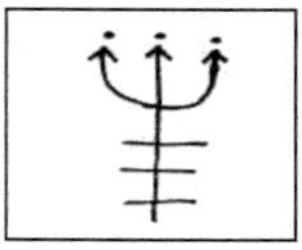

Bad Company: It indicates that she is tied to the temple of Psychic Youth.

Anti Justice: The Roman symbol for justice was an axe upright. Being upside down it represents anti-justice or rebellion. Feminists use a double axe upright as a symbol of ancient matriarchy.

Black Mass Indicator: It indicates a black mass has taken or will take place. It mocks the Roman Catholic mass. Holy items are defiled and the Lord's Prayer is recited backwards.

Church of Satan: It was founded by Anton LaVey in 1966.

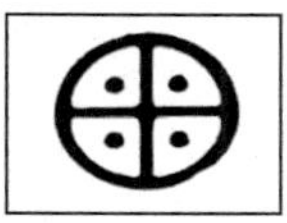

Holy Earth: It is a symbol for mother earth. It also appears as a Hopi medicine wheel and Norse sun symbol.

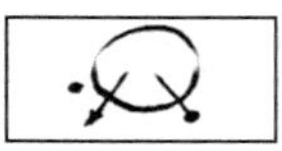

Seal of the Left Hand Path: It indicates black magic and the path to Satan.

Labyrinth: Labyrinth was an elaborate, confusing structure of Crete (island in Greece) that symbolizes the path of initiation. It is a maze design with complex branching multicursal puzzle with choices of path and direction.

Spiral: It is an ancient Goddess symbol of universal pattern of growth in nature. A variation with three lines was used by some to represent the number of the beast 666.

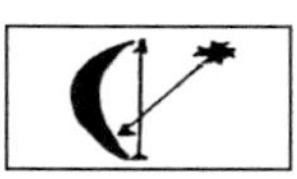

Blood Ritual Symbol: It represents animal and human sacrifices.

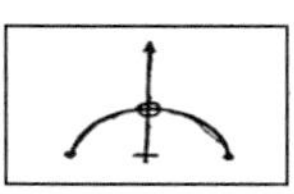

Sexual Ritual Symbol: It is used to indicate the place and purpose.

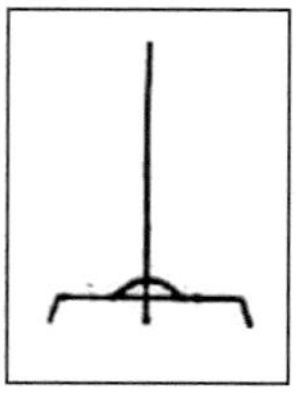

Inverted Cross of Satanic Justice: If found carved in the chest of a victim, it means the person was a traitor. The vertical line represents man's presence. The horizontal line indicates eternity past and future. The arch represents the world and being inverted is mockery of God.

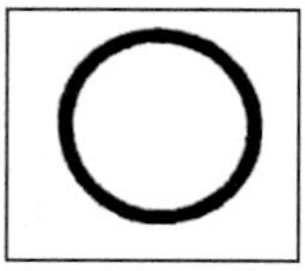

Ritual Circle: It has different meanings for different groups, protection from evil, symbolic of life cycles or completeness. It is nine feet across with a smaller one inside and perhaps a pentagram drawn inside.

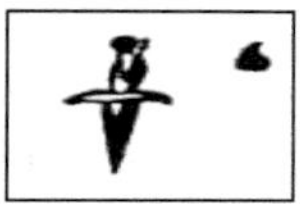

Sword of Power: It may be seen upright or upside down with a drop of blood. It is used by some satanists to represent light and darkness.

Talisman or Amulet: It is believed to have magical powers. It usually has a drawing or writing with the name or image of a deity.

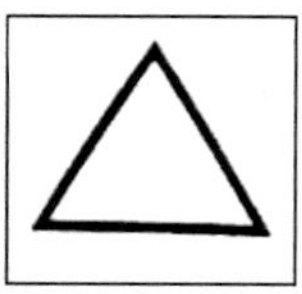

Thaumaturgic Triangle: It is used for magical purposes in casting of spells and the summoning of demons. It is found near ritual sites. It is believed to be the door through which the demon will be called.

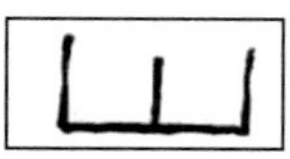

Trident: It is a symbol of enforcement among occult groups. There are many variations.

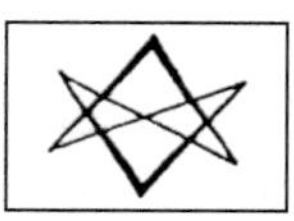

Unincursive Hexagram: It was designed by Aleister Crowley as the symbol of his Order of the Silver Star, Astrum Argentum or AA.

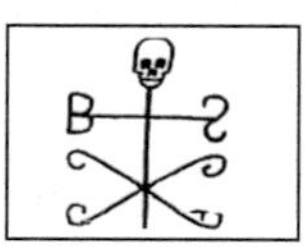

Veve: Thse are designs used in Voudoun to summon the various Loa or spirit deities. Symbol for Baron Samadi, Lord of the graveyard and death.

Figures: These symbols were compiled by Pastor Billy Bissell. Pastor Bissell served as a Chaplain and Ritualistic Crime Consultant for the Police Department in Muskogee, Oklahoma.[23]

THE CAUSE

After proper investigation it has been found that every satanist has a personal reason behind his or her involvement in such a morbid trend.

First, the family crisis, being unloved, abused and rejected in family is one main cause. Second, their hankering for supernatural fantasy as an impact of ghoulish creatures shown on certain animated shows on television and power games in gadgets. Third, a desire of devilish delights are sought for a diabolical favour. These favours can range from money, fame, power to anything.[24] However, it is mainly because of the Church which ostracizes the drug addicts or alcoholics, adulterer, murderer as it regards such persons as sinners. According to the Bible, a person should not commit adultery (*Exodus* 20:14), 'You shall not murder' (*Deuteronomy* 5:17), 'should not get drunk on wine' (*Ephesians* 5:18). Following these factors, the church ostracize a person and after excommunication, the relationship between the former member and the church naturally changes. Some denominations use passages such as 1 *Timothy* 1:20[25] as justification for shunning any member of their group. As being cast out from the congregation, he is utterly ignored. This happens even to family members who have been expelled. Parents will no longer communicate with their children, with their own biological brother and sisters or even with their own spouse. This results in the breaking up of families. Though such actions are not condoned by the Bible, the church ostracized a person officially in order to bring the sinner to repentance. Since the sinner is being shunned by the church members and families, he being invited by the satanic, groups, allows the devil to solve his problem and in return sells his soul to satan.

According to Biaksiama, a Christian scholar of Mizoram, the Western pop culture and singers influenced the youths into Satanism as some pop singers in Western countries offered themselves to satan in order to get fame and money.[26]

Spiritual Leaders' Conference on 'Satanism and Demonic Activities' was held at Bethel Counselling Centre, Lower Lanka held during 21 and 22 November 2011 and the main purpose of the conference was to discuss and consult the Church on the matter of satanic activities in Churanchanpur, Manipur. According to the report of the Conference, one of the main reasons why young people are so easily attracted to satanic worship is their financial greed. Through the report it was quite clear that how easily the satanic followers satisfied their financial greed by using satanic power. For instance, if they needed money, they would walk in the street and passersby would randomly and unknowingly drop their wallets before them. Another reason was that they would satisfy their physical desire, as they could easily attract the opposite sex towards them by using satanic power. And once they had their prey they could hypnotize them and do whatever they want with them. The report also mentioned that a boy who was recently converted from satanism was bold enough to stand before the gathering at the Conference and shared his experience. The boy revealed his unpleasant past and explained the reasons as to why he accepted satanism. During his childhood his parents divorced and his father remarried and they both were always drunk. Due to all his past experiences he felt so lost and hopeless in this world and out of desperation he decided to follow Satan in 2005.[27]

PREVENTIVE MEASURES AGAINST SATANIC CULTS

In order to quell the rapid growth of satanism, the church leaders, parents and social workers in the Christian-dominated state of Mizoram, Nagaland, Meghalaya and also the district of Churachanpur, Manipur had actively involved in organizing different programmes such as prayers, crusades and counselling. According to a report a 'Transformation Crusade' was held at Khuochiezie local ground in Kohima from 24-30 April 2013 to thwart the purported rise in the number of Satan worshippers with the theme 'Arise and shine'. After reports were found that several teenagers had taken up devil worship, churches across Nagaland also gave special times to prayers so that the supposed satan worshippers are done away with.[28] In April, church groups in the state organized crusades to rescue youngsters from satan worship. The Roman Catholic Church in Nagaland expressed shock to learn about the phenomenon and the church worked with the Protestant groups to counter it.[29]

The state and district administrators also played a very important role in order to prevent the youths from performing such practices. There are reports from the East Khasi Hills District Administration over the growing instances of devil worship, where the administration had imposed Section 144 CrPC in the entire district prohibiting devil worship or satan worship in any form, desecration of graves and vandalism of sacred symbols, movement of youth at cemeteries very late in the night without any justification, defacing the walls with graffiti and gang fights and unauthorized bike races at night. Interestingly, there is no provision in the Indian Penal Code (IPC) against any one who practises evil worship but the police can take action against anyone who indulges in unlawful activities while worshipping evil. East Khasi Hills administration gave order to the law enforcers to keep vigil in secluded areas like cemeteries to keep an eye on those who are perpetrating such desecrating acts. To prevent youths from getting into such acts, the Meghalaya police conducted counselling classes for youth in schools and colleges in the state capital and other areas within the East Khasi Hills to conduct similar classes.[30] However, aware of the rise of Devil worshipper, various groups including church bodies stepped in to control this menace.

Although churches do conduct various programmes for the youth, but those who are indulging in such acts would never turn up for them. Fr Ioanis Warpakma, parish priest of the St Peter & Paul Parish said, 'Until we are able to identify and reach out to those youths, we have to undertake measures to prevent others from becoming victims of such acts. We need to carry out more awareness drives among youths.'[31]

CONCLUSION

Thus, the Christian dominated states of north-east India witnesses a 'social menace' due to satanic cult and it could lead to a plethora of' social evils' in the near future if proper steps are not taken. The main targets of this cult are the young boys and girls who are mostly drug addicts or alcoholic, desperate children who are victimized by family crises; desire for money, fame and power. As they could not strike a rapport with the norms of the church, they find the alternative easier way to solve their problem and chose the devil's path. They become followers of Satan and enemy of the church, act against the church and the teachings of Christ. Desecration of cemeteries and venerated symbols, cutting of wrists or making tattoo marks on the body parts, adultery, etc., is against the norms and teaching of the church. Therefore, the satanic cult can be regarded as a movement against the church by those who could not follow the norms and laws of the church. It can also be said that the satanic cult is a counter attack on the rigid and conventional norms of the church. It is anti-Christ, and anti-church in nature.

NOTES

1. Wikipedia, the free encyclopedia, file:///C:/Users/Windows%207/Downloads/Setanic%20related/Satanism%20%20Wikipedia,%20the%20free%20encyclopedia.html, Retrieved on 9 October 2014.
2. News Item in *Hindustan Times,* Delhi, 18 January 2007.
3. Sanga, Zodin, 'Bible Burnt in Mizoram: Satanic?', *Aizawl,* 14 May 2012, https://dontshutupnepal.wordpress.com/2012/05/14/bibles-burnt-in-mizoram-satanic, Retrieved on 11 October 2014.
4. Ziitso, Mezhiisevi Mark, 'Satanism in Nagaland: Putting it into Perspective', in *Morung Express,* file:///C:/Users/Windows%207/Downloads/Setanic%20related/The%20Morung%20Express%20% 20Nagaland% 20Latest%20&%20Breaking%20News,%20Northeast%20&%20India%20News%20-%20Sata, Retrieved on 8 October 2014.
5. Songate, Rev. Lalroseim, 'Mizoram Religious Statistics: Possible Threat', in http://ecchurch.co.in/ecblog, 18 December 2011, Retrieved on 10 October 2014.
6. Sanga, Zodin, op. cit.
7. *Religion News Service,* 19 July 2013 and also see *News. VA* (Official Vatican Network) and fides.org for more details. Retrieved on 13 October 2014.
8. 'Move to Prevent Satan worship in Meghalaya', *The Times of India,* Guwahati, 15 July 2014. Retrieved on 28 October 2014.

9. 'The Cult Graffiti on the Wall of Tura', *Tura*, 21 april file:///C:/Users/Windows%207/Downloads/Setanic%20related/Meghalaya%20online%20news%20and%20Tourism%20website.html. Retrieved on 3 November 2014.
10. Lewis, James R, 'Satanism Today: An Encyclopedia of Religion, Folklore, and Popular Culture', Oxford, England, 2001. Retrieved on 3 October 2014.
11. 'The "Satan" Worship in Miroram Worries Church', *The Hindu*, Online edition of India's National Newspaper, Aizawl, Monday, 19 June 2000. Retrieved 8 March 2014.
12. 'Caught Nude Inside Curch', *TNN*, 8 December 2006. Retrieved 9 March 2014.
13. 'Mizo Police Nabs Self Proclaimed Satan Worshipper', *Hueiyen News Service*/ NNN, HYPERLINK 'mailto:web@thenortheasttoday.in' web@ thenorth easttoday.in,Aizawl, 22 September 2013. Retrieved on 10 March 2014.
14. 'Devil Cult Twist to Child Killing-3 kg Sculpture of a Head found in Suspects Home Triggers Speculation', *The Telegraph*, Imphal, 5 April 2007. Retrieved on 8 March 2014.
15. Hueien New Services, Rengkai (Ccpur), 28 August 2010. Retrieved on 10 March 2014.
16. Songate, 'Satanism in Churachanpur: Is it Real?', in Pathien Thucha, 25 November 2011, file:///C:/Users/Windows%207/Downloads/Setanic%20related/Satanism%20in%20 Churachandpur% 20%20Is%20It%20Real%20%20(English%20Version)%20%20%20Pathien%20Thucha.html. Retrieved on 11 March 2014.
17. Watkins, Jon, 'Signs and Symbols of Satanism', 17 December 2016, https://www.exposingsatanism.org/signs-and-symbols-of-satanism/ Retrieved on 10 June 2014.
18. Arora, Vishal, 'Satan Worship Worries Christians in Northeast India', The Washington post, 8 July 2013. https://www.washingtonpost.com/national/on-faith/satan-worship-worries-christians-in-northeast-india/2013/07/08/ee71f8f4-e7f9-11e2-818e-aa29e855f3ab_story.html. Retrieved on 10 March 2014.
19. *Meghalaya Times*, 'Satanic Worshippers Appear in Garo Hills Periphery', HYPERLINK 'http://www.Meghalayatimes.com'www. Meghalayatimes.com. Retrieved on 3 November 2014.
20. 'The Cult Graffiti on the Wall of Tura',Tura, 21 April file:///C:/Users/Windows%207/Downloads/Setanic%20related/Meghalaya%20online%20news%20and%20Tourism%20website.html. Retrieved on 3 November 2014.

21. 'Move to Prevent Satan Worship in Meghalaya', *Times of India*, Shillong, 15 July 2014 file:///C:/Users/Windows%207/Downloads/Setanic%20 related/Move%20to%20prevent%20Satan%20worship%20in%20 Meghalaya%20-%20The%20Times %20of%20India.html. Retrieved on 3 November 2014.
22. The Telegraph, Calcutta, Monday, 21 July 2014. file:///C:/Users/ Windows%207/Downloads/Setanic%20related/Crackdown%20on% 20%E2%80%98devil%20worship%E2%80%99.html#.VFjZ8 CKUefs. Retrieved on 28 October 2014.
23. Watkins, Jon, 'Signs and Symbols of Satanism', 17 December 2016, https:// www.exposingsatanism.org/signs-and-symbols-of-satanism. Retrieved on 10 June 2014.
24. Ziitso, Mezhiisevi Mark, 'Satanism in Nagaland: Putting it into Perspective' in Morung Express. file:///C:/Users/Windows%207/Downloads/ Setanic%20related/The%20Morung%20Express%20%20Nagaland% 20Latest%20&%20Breaking%20News,%20Northeast%20&%20India%20 News%20-%20Sata. Retrieved on 8 October 2014.
25 Ibid.
26. Sanga, Zodin, op. cit.
27. Songate, 'Satanism in Churachanpur: Is it Real?', in *Pathien Thucha*, 25 November 2011. file:///C:/Users/Windows%207/Downloads/Setanic% 20related/Satanism%20in%20Churachandpur%20%20Is% 20It% 20Real%20%20(English%20Version)%20%20%20Pathien%20 Thucha.html. Retrieved on 11 March 2014.
28. *Newmai News Network*/DIMAPUR, 15 July.
29. Sharon Hill, *Doubtful News*, 10 July 2013.
30. 'Crack down on devil worship', *The Telegraph*, Calcutta, Monday, 21 July 2014. file:///C:/Users/Windows%207/Downloads/Setanic%20related/ Crackdown%20on%20%E2%80%98devil%20worship%E2%80%99.html #.VFiXFyKUefs
31. 'Crack down on devil worship', *The Telegrah*, Calcutta, Monday, 21 July 2014. file:///C:/Users/Windows%207/Downloads/Setanic%20related/ Crackdown%20on%20%E2%80%98devil%20worship%E2%80%99.html#. VFiXFyKUefs

CHAPTER 18

Sylvan Spirits and Cultural Practices in Assam

RAJIB HANDIQUE

LOCATING THE STUDY ON SYLVAN SPIRITS

The question whether sylvan spirits can be considered as part of the occult is worth considering. The occult is a broad category in which varied beliefs and practices are generally included, those which normally don't fit into religion or science. According to H.P. Blavatsky,

> Occultism is based on the knowledge of the ultimate essence of all things in the Kingdoms of Nature—such as minerals, plants and animals—hence of things pertaining to the realm of material nature, however invisible that essence may be, and howsoever much it has hitherto eluded the grasp of Science. . . .[1]

According to Rudolph Steiner,[2]

> Occult science desires to free the natural-scientific method and its principle of research from their special application that limits them, in their own sphere, to the relationship and process of sensory facts, but, at the same time, it wants to retain their way of thinking and other characteristics. It desires to speak about the non-sensory in the same way natural science speaks about the sensory . . . occult science wishes to consider the employment of mental activity upon nature as a kind of self-education of the soul and to apply what it has thus acquired to the realms of the non-sensory.

A study or analysis on the sylvan spirits, which relate to spirits that dwell in forests, trees or groves may, therefore, be considered under the category of occultism.

Concurrently, one may also consider some of the beliefs and practices related to the trees, groves and forests, including their dominance by spirits with the myth-making process humans have all along been engaged with since pre-historic times. Human beings are myth-making creatures and at the same time they are also meaning-seeking creatures.[3] Religion and mythology are products of the faculty of human imagination. However, imagination is also the faculty that has enabled scientists to bring new knowledge to light and invent new and newer technology to cater to human needs.[4] In all probability, people thought gods, humans, animals and nature were inextricably bound together and subject to the same laws and composed of the same divine substance. As stated by Karen Armstrong, perhaps 'There was initially no ontological gulf between the world of the gods and the world of the men and women. . . . Mythology was, therefore, designed to help us to cope with the problematic human predicament. It helped people to find their place in their world and their true orientation.'[5] The world of gods and spirits or the world of myths and rites are all products of the human world of imagination as it interacted and responded to the vagaries of life and nature throughout the course of human history.

Thus, 'supersensible knowledge' of the past relating to the sylvan spirits may be understood better at the intersections of both occultism and mythology. As already stated, Rudolf Steiner has held the attainment of 'supersensible knowledge' as one of the objectives of any study on occultism. He tries to delve into the spiritual world of human beings, which is undoubtedly a historical phenomenon, and tries to link the same to the external non-sensory world. He emphasized that one must consider the attitude of the soul when it elaborates science and that sense-manifestation is also an essential thing as a person generally does not become aware that a certain attitude of the human soul has been employed only with regard to the manifestation of the senses. It is possible, however, to rise above this arbitrary self-limitation and, apart from special application, consider the characteristics of scientific activity. Steiner concludes that, 'This is the basis for our designating as "scientific" the knowledge of a non-sensory world-content. The human power of thought wishes to occupy itself with this latter world-content just as it occupies itself, in the other case, with the world-content of natural science.'[6]

ASSAM AND THE SYLVAN SPIRITS

Assam has always been known for her natural resources. Apart from the forests and the rivers, this area is resplendent with a large variety of life forms. The tropical humid forests coupled with the altitudinal variations have helped in creating a habitat mosaic of sorts in this north-eastern part of India. The north-east in India is part of the Indo-Malayan realm, with one of the richest bio-diverse ecosystems in the world. Today, it is also regarded famously as one of the bio-diversity hotspots.

The bio-diversity of the region has also helped in developing and supporting cultural diversity. The habitat mosaic has helped in creating different eco-zones, where people have lived and interacted for ages. This, in turn, has helped to develop different cultures and belief systems many of which are actually intimately based on the natural resource base of the eco-zones. The culinary traditions of the different indigenous communities of north-eastern India are often differentiated by the use of different herbs and plants. Likewise, even in religious ceremonies, offerings are made of things that reflect the availability of unique varieties of forest or natural produce. The occult practices too are rooted in the ecology. Parts of the belief system of communities, therefore, are invariably linked with the ecology.

The use of particular varieties of plants and animals in sacrificial offerings or the worship of particular variety of plant or animal species are all part of a belief system that took centuries to develop. Therefore, when one talks of a belief system relating to the forests or nature per se, one has to take into consideration their development in the *longue duree.* Such belief systems develop as part of the geo-history and operate as such. Fernand Braudel famously stated that 'Events were like froth on the waves of history', meaning that there were larger time frames on which the event rested. He stressed the importance of slow changing geographic factors, like the constraints placed by the natural environment upon human production and communication. In the first volume of *The Mediterranean and the Mediterranean World in the Age of Philip II*, he described the folklore of the mountain dwellers that 'reveals primitive credulity', where sorcerers, witchcraft, primitive magic and black masses were the flowerings of an ancient cultural subconscious.[7] Belief systems based on ecology are, therefore, not simple events, but a process tied to a larger realm of geo-history.

A documentation of the various aspects related to the belief system concerning demons and spirits was done by Benudhar Rajkhowa in his work *Assamese Demonology* in 1905. W.J. Reid, the noted British bureaucrat, while writing the *Introduction* to the book stated, 'The book is a faithful record of popular beliefs in Assam in all their original quaintness. And for such a task, it would not be easy to find any one better qualified than the author.'[8]

Trees came to be revered in the Brahmaputra Valley as in other parts of the world. The benefits from trees notwithstanding, over a period of time, trees or forests came to be considered as sacred. Worshipping trees is a feature of many communities in South Asia. In the north-east too, such practices evolved and drew sustenance. There were forests like the sacred groves where plants within a space are revered and worshipped. This reverence for a sacred space is very popular among the Khasis of Meghalaya. On the other hand, there were trees that were worshipped individually, like the *peepul* (*Ficus religiosa*), *sam* (*Artocarpus chaplasha*), etc. This reverence for the trees was perhaps buttressed by the prevailing value system.

Like all other countries, Assam has her indigenous ghosts.[9] The spirits might be divided into four territorial classes, viz., subterranean, terrestrial, aerial and celestial.[10] The largest number of spirits are included under the 'terrestrial' category, which is again subdivided into (a) aqueous, (b) sylvan, and (c) household.[11]

There were two spirits that were always considered as sylvan spirits, i.e. spirits that lived on trees and plants in Assam and those were the Chaman and Bura-Dangoria. Chaman is a spirit known for its taciturnity. The name *chaman* is derived from the *cham* (*sam – Artocarpus chaplasha*) tree, its usual place of living. It also lives in big trees like *nahor* (*Mesua ferrea*) in deep forests. When a man cuts a branch of a tree, or passes urine under it, he is at once possessed. When possessed by this spirit, a man loses all power of speech. It is, therefore, necessary to propitiate the spirit before anything is done to such big trees.[12]

On the other hand, of all the spirits that were in popular circulation, Bura-Dangoria was the one most religiously disposed. Those who have 'seen' him describe the Bura-Dangoria as a tall person wearing a *dhoti* with a headgear that gave him an imposing look of a wise old man. It is believed that, the *Bura-Dangoria* attends all religious assemblies among men. Nobody can fell a tree haunted by Bura-Dangoria without propitiating him. The offenders are scourged with bodily ailments. Sometimes, it so happens that the tree which is cut without propitiating Bura-Dangoria cannot be moved no matter how much of force is applied.[13]

There were also other spirits that had natural dwelling places. The *Alakhani* is a female spirit that lived in the midst of a mango grove under a plant like a mushroom. This plant is about eight inches high and called '*Alakhani Bah*' in Assamese or the cell of *Alakhani*. It is believed that there is also a male form of the *Alakhani* and may be considered as an imp. But it is the female form of this spirit that is frolicsome and is believed to possess man whom she happens to come across. The *Dot* is also believed to live in the midst of bamboo groves though it also resides in tanks, channels, morasses and out of the way places overgrown with watery plants.[14]

The knowledge of these spirits infested the popular imagination of the people. They were also a part of the folklore of Assam. Stories based on such demons (ghosts) were written by several noted writers including Lakshminath Bezbarua.[15] The fear of these spirits regulated the ways of life of the people. There were also elaborate rituals and incantations that were popularly applied to rid oneself of the unwanted afflictions from these spirits. The symptoms that marked the afflictions were also popularly known.[16] Some communities used to hold ceremonies offering prayers to the Habi Dangoria (lord of the forests). Normally, in such a ceremony, unmarried young males participate where a chicken is sacrificed, and a sombre feast is held.[17]

Throughout the pre-colonial history, people have lived in symbiotic relation with the forests. The forests have been providers of the much-needed supplies for human existence. Prior to the coming of the British, Assam had a civilization that reflected a symbiotic man-nature relationship. Perhaps, it conformed to that phase of civilizational relationship, where man was considered as a steward of nature.

The coming of the British colonial rule marked a watershed in the ecological history of Assam.[18] The colonial intervention by the British along with their extractive imperial practices changed the man-nature relations in north-eastern India. The ideology of the imperialists of human mastery over nature and the idea of subjecting nature to the service of mankind became widely accepted.

Forests in Assam were voraciously used up for meeting the many ends of the British imperialists. It was a period of progress marked by degradation of the forests through activities perpetrated by the tea planters as well as the forest department. Amidst the change in the social perception of nature, there are old customary practices that still reminded mankind of the reverence with which nature was regarded in this part of the country. The British commercialized the forests and, in a way, put them up for sale to earn revenue. There are colonial records that showed that in some cases, an amount of money used to be kept apart for performing certain rites during the timber cutting operations of the forest department. The reports of the forest department did not elaborate on the procedure of such rituals. However, one may aptly conclude that the rituals might have been undertaken to propitiate the spirits in the trees marked for felling or the forest as a whole.

Thus, the reverence to the forests remained. The reverential behaviour of the people towards the forests is reflected in many ways. As a forest official, Raghu Nath Chowdhury writes,

> During L.P. School days in my village, I maintained a small nursery of Kadam seedlings which I collected from shady places. We had house hold servants whom we treated to be our family members. I called one of them as 'Ahina Kaka' (He was Ahina Deka). I noticed that Ahina Kaka while transplanting a seedling or felling a tree or climbing it for lopping branches always bowed his head to honour sounding '*Ram Ram*'.[19]

It is interesting to note that such realities in pre-colonial, colonial or even post-colonial Assam have not been adequately documented. The British who were so adept in documenting the colonized people in all their myriad ways, however hardly ever wrote on these practices which are so popular among the masses. Perhaps, there was the apprehension of giving legitimacy to something weird or unscientific when the colonized world was sought to be imbued with scientific temperament and understanding with the efforts of the European colonizers. But the fact remained that superstitions or superstitious practices are also a historical reality.

A FIELD VIEW FROM THE TWENTY-FIRST CENTURY

Trees continued to be worshipped and it is a common sight in towns and cities to find barricading of trees sometimes with basic structure of bricks and cement, with coloured threads draping the entire trunk of the worshipped tree. Such worship of trees in towns and cities might not be always done with reverential regard to sylvan spirits, whereas there are more possibilities of such efforts being carried on with clear commercial intent mixed with some religiosity and ritualism.

However, the reverential treatment of trees with the aim of propitiating the sylvan spirits are still carried on in many places in Assam. Two examples are included herein to highlight the continuity of the old belief system. During the course of fieldwork conducted in various areas of the Brahmaputra Valley on a topic related to ecology and society, one was amazed by the continuum of such reverential worship. What was true of a comparatively advanced village like Balek near Pasighat was also true for an institution of higher education like the Dibrugarh University.[20]

Balek is a developed village near the town of Pasighat in eastern Arunachal Pradesh. The village followed significant customs and traditions handed down from earlier generations, in spite of adaptation of many aspects of modern lifestyle. The village has ear-marked a tree for worship following their tradition. It was informed that as the earlier tree was old and dying, another tree was marked out for worshipping, ensuring continuity of the practice (Figure 18.1).

Figure 18.1: A tree-worshipping temple at Balek Basti (village), Pasighat, Arunachal Pradesh. Photo: Rajib Handique (2012)

At Dibrugarh University (a public university established in 1965), one of the wings of the building of the Department of Petroleum Technology could not be constructed as there was none to cut the tree that stood on the way of its expansion (Figure 18.2). The popular belief accepted it as the abode of Burha Dangoria, a sylvan spirit. A temple developed there with the *peepal* tree (*Ficus religiosa* or sacred fig, a specie native to the Indian subcontinent and Indochina) as the reigning deity. It was significant as the belief system stood in the way of construction of a building in no less than a university and that too relating to a department in one of the most advanced fields of research and learning.

The worship of trees is based firmly on the belief that some spirit resides in them and it would cause harm to them if they are damaged or cut. Thus, the super sensible knowledge of the unknown is a reality even in the twenty-first century. They are a part of the cultural life and practice of a society, whose traditional moorings are being slowly eroded.

Figure 18.2: A tree-worshipping temple adjacent to the Department of Petroleum Technology, Dibrugarh University.
Photo: Rajib Handique (2011)

CONCLUSION

It is true that humans long back looked upon natural elements with spiritual or supernatural lens due to lack of any scientific understanding. The beliefs that developed through such engagement with the sylvan world got entrenched in time. If history is to be looked upon as a total study of human society, the belief systems including the ones like the sylvan spirits in Assam needs to be mainstreamed and studied. It would help us move forward from a paradigm of knowing to that of understanding such historical phenomena. Such beliefs play an important role in conservation of the environment. Trees like the banyan or peepul form the habitat of a large variety of life forms that includes birds of various kinds. The unseen spirits supposedly dwelling in the sylvan abode appear to be playing an important role in conservation of the environment in the twenty-first-century world.

NOTES

1. Helena Petrovna Blavatsky, *Collected Writings*, vol. IX, Theosophical Publishing House, Wheaton, Illinois, 1974, p. 252.
2. Rudolf Steiner, *An Outline of Occult Science*, Berlin, 1925, sourced from: http://bookfi.net/dl/286853/b33c52. Accessed on 2 August 2020 at 1127 hrs, p. 18.
3. Karen Armstrong, *A Short History of Myth,* Penguin Books, New Delhi, 2005, p. 1.
4. Ibid.
5. Ibid.
6. Rudolf Steiner, *An Outline of Occult Science*, Berlin, 1925, sourced from: http://bookfi.net/dl/286853/b33c52. Accessed on 2 August 2020 at 1127 hrs, p. 18.
7. Fernand Braudel, *The Mediterranean and the Mediterranean World in the Age of Philip II*, vol. I, translated from French by Sian Reynolds, pdf version sourced from http://bookfi.net/dl/1125846/5ca348, Accessed on 2 August 2020 at 1745 hrs., p. 37.
8. Benudhar Rajkhowa, *Assamese Demonology,* Printed at and Published by Patrika Paras, Calcutta, 1905. Sourced from: https://archive.org/details/AssameseDemonology/page/n11/mode/2up Accessed on 2 August 2020 at 0937 hrs., Introduction.
9. Ibid.
10. Ibid.
11. Ibid.
12. Ibid.
13. Ibid.
14. Ibid.
15. An excerpt from *Patmugi* a short story by Lakshminath Bezbarua (1864-1938) translated from Assamese into English by Sunil Kumar Barthakur, would exemplify the popular beliefs regarding sylvan spirits. 'You did a nice thing' said Alatabai 'to climb the tree in the midday, of all times. All kinds of ghosts and sprits, the gods of the land and the gods of the water come out at this hour and play about amorously.' Sourced from https://indianreview.in/fiction/patmugi-by-lakshminath-bezbaruah-assamese-short-story/. Accessed on 2 August 2020 at 1137 hrs.
16. Benudhar Rajkhowa, *Assamese Demonology,* Printed at and Published by Patrika Paras, Calcutta, 1905. Sourced from: https://archive.org/details/AssameseDemonology/page/n11/mode/2up Accessed on 2 August 2020 at 0937 hrs., Introduction.

17. The practice is mainly prevalent in Upper Assam area. The author was a witness to one such ceremony in Dibrugarh where bachelors participated with offerings to the forest spirit. The offerings included a chicken. However, such ceremonies are diminishing with increasing urbanisation.
18. Rajib Handique, *British Forest Policy in Assam,* Concept Publishing Company, New Delhi, 2004, p.154.
19. Chowdhury, Raghu Nath, *The concept of Eco-ethics and Eco-Dharma and preservation of wild-life and Forests* in The Rhino, vol. IV, October, 1998, pp. 34-8. Kadam (*Neolamarckia cadamba*) tree. The tree is grown as an ornamental plant and for timber and paper-making. Kadam also features in Indian religions and mythologies.
20. The fieldwork was conducted as part of a Major Research Project under University Grants Commission on *Society and Ecology in Post-Colonial Assam with Special Reference to Upper Assam* during 2011-13.

PART IV

WITCHCRAFT AND WITCH HUNTING

CHAPTER 19

Witchcraft Viewed through the Legal Lens in Jharkhand: A Study of Witchcraft Practices and the Anti-Witchcraft Law in Jharkhand

BASHABI GUPTA

Who is a 'Witch' and what is her 'craft' are a questions that has coloured various contexts amongst the tribal communities in Jharkhand. All the 32 tribes living in this state have stories about witches along with the practices associated with their craft. Though in most cases they are the embodiment of evil, in some instances they are also known as healers of diseases and also have the power to keep the villages or 'hatu's safe. Identification of who or what is a witch and what is her craft, is something that was an integral part of the tribal lore in the pre-colonial and colonial era, seem to be lost today. The dominant discourse in the current era in witchcraft and its practise in Jharkhand is of course one of violence against a perceived witch. This research focuses on the incidence of creating or branding of women as witches in the light of the anti-witchcraft law that has been passed in seven Indian states to stop persecution of women in this particular manner taking the example of Jharkhand. This study looks at the conditions under which women are branded as witches along with understanding the impact of the implementation of the anti-witchcraft law to help the affected women. This research suggests that there is usually a complex background of female economic subjugation, sexual exploitation, and the persecution of widows and independent, vocal women who dare to exercise their rights to inheritance and property and to their own self.

I

WHO IS A WITCH AND WHAT IS HER CRAFT: PERCEPTIONS AND UNDERSTANDINGS OF THE TRIBAL COMMUNITIES OF JHARKHAND

When discussing the idea and concept of witches and witchcraft, it needs to be kept in mind that, this is a culturally specific expression. The world of witches, spirits and *ojhas* (witch doctors and medicine men) is a vivacious and reflective one in the tribal cosmology in Jharkhand. Witches are also known as *mati*, *sokha*, *jan guru* amongst the different tribal communities in Jharkhand, though the most common moniker is the *dayan*. Behringer provides a necessary and useful comparative scope beyond the geographical and cultural limits of Christian Europe, intending to examine witchcraft as a universal phenomenon. Thinking of witchcraft not as diabolism but as 'a generic term for all kinds of evil magic and sorcery, as perceived by contemporaries', he writes, 'transforms our understanding of witchcraft so that it is no longer a Western European aberration, but something easily compared to sorcery or harmful magic as it manifests itself and is feared all over the world'. This more generic definition does indeed clear a path for transposing the European term 'witch' into other contexts and allows for a wider field for comparative studies. The concept of witchcraft in the western European context focuses on the satanic overlays and devil worship. As Richard Kieckhefer argues, 'different mythologies of witchcraft functioned differently in different circumstances'. Keeping track of what particular mythologies animated witchcraft related fear and persecution in one society as opposed to another and under what circumstances mythologies were imported imposed or reflected indigenous belief, is critically important in understanding why witch trials took particular forms in particular places.[1] Amongst the tribal communities, it is the considerations of material tangible harm and anxieties that matter for witchcraft and fear of the witches' power.

Witches are most commonly envisioned as women, who have exceptional powers over humans, animals and even natural forces. They are usually held in fear. Belief in *dayans/dans/churails* (witches) or *bongas* (spirits) occupies a central place in *adivasi* cosmology and moral economy. According to Bodding, 'There is no genuine Santhal who does not believe in witches'.[2] The Santhals oral lore of Reak Katha records. 'Witchcraft is the great trouble with us Santhals. Because of witchcraft, people in the village become enemies, doors of relatives is shut, father and sons quarrel, brothers are separated, husband and wife are divorced and in the country people kill each other.'[3] While accepting that the practice was common to many countries, Valentine Ball noted that conditions in the tribal heartland were particularly unique, 'It is a peculiarity here that the belief (of witchcraft) was so thorough, that even those who are accused of being witches or sorcerers do not deny the impeachment but accept the position readily with all its pains and penalties.'[4] Thus, belief in witches and witchcraft is ingrained in their traditions, belief systems and is still considered to pose a considerable threat to the societal fabric of the tribal communities.

Roy speaks of an Oraon saying that the world is as full of disembodied spirits 'as a tree is full of leaves'.[5] It is significant to note here, that witchcraft and witches as an idea exists both for evil and good in the tribal cosmology. The tribal religions seeks and the central idea behind the *adivasi* religious system, therefore, was to seek a pact with the most powerful and helpful deities who would enable them to conquer the evil. Troisi (1979) mentions that the evil powers had to be gotten rid of through exorcism or magic. There is, thus, difference between white or benevolent magic that is beneficial and black magic which is harmful or evil that harms. The *ojha* is the person, who overturns the impact of the black magic bringing amelioration from the harm. This person in most situations is a man who is a priest or a medicine man and occupies a prestigious position in the social fabric. In contrast, the person performing the harmful magic, is almost universally a woman who is practised in the dark arts and is, thus, known as a *dayan*. A male who is considered a *dayan* is a also feared immensely within the tribal village society. The *ojha* seeks to expose and counteract the anti-social activities of witches and the evil influence of the impersonal spirits. Fear of witches is an inherent facet of the belief in witches and witchcraft, as they are were feared as inexplicable people endowed with supernatural or extra-normal powers. The witches become witches primarily by the supposition of having 'intercourse with the *bongas*, which gives them the power of killing people by eating their entrails and also of causing fevers, murrain in cattle and other kinds of evil'.[6] They then become empowered to kill either directly or by 'setting (up) the *bongas*'. The *bongas*, in turn may bring destruction and death either by themselves or through agents.[7] The tribal communities believe that, witches eat people and induce illness such as cholera, small-pox, etc. They are also responsible for destroying crops, killing cattle and causing all round general harm. The *dayans* were, in fact, human manifestations of the 'evil-eye' or 'evil-mouth'[8] and could cause harm accordingly; if they cast an 'evil-eyes' at a person, the victim suffered stomach problems, headaches, fever, etc. If they uttered 'harmful' lines, while looking at somebody, the person was sure to suffer a fatal disease.[9] The tribal people intertwine their ideas of witches and witchcraft intricately with sickness and disease, which are caused by the working of witchcraft and healing. The killing of the witch is thus the personification of firstly a cleaning act, second, the ultimate victory of good over evil, and thirdly by offering the evil vanquished witches' blood as an offering to the good and just white magic being practised. Wilkinson noted that the Kols believed in three causes that led to sickness—witchcraft, angry *bongas* or the spirit of someone who had died. While there was a remedy for angry *bongas* and ancestor spirits who could be appeased by sacrifices— first of fowls, then goats, and if these two did not work then bullocks and buffaloes were offered—there was none for the witches, who had to be removed.[10] Dalton extends the argument to include animals as well, 'All diseases in men or animals (are) attributed to one of two causes, the wrath of some evil spirit who has to be appeased, or to the spell of some witch or sorcerer who should be destroyed or driven out of (the) land'.[11] The evidence that witchcraft has been an integral part of the tribal medicine system is provided by Bodding (1986),[12] who enumerated a fairly elaborate system of root medicines and herbs. The fieldwork amongst the Chota Nagpur tribes show that, their world of 'medicine' is a complex one consisting of sacrifices, *mantras* (incantations), divinations, and amulets provided by the medicine man or the *ojha*. If the ailing person does not heal from whatever medicine is prescribed, the medicine man is called and he responds with his armoury of traditional roots and herbs which would then magically cure the patient. Bodding notes that, '. . . it is not strange that a suspicion is always present that witches may be at work when people fall ill and do not recover.'[13] Man writes of the tribal communities attitude towards the witches that 'no reasoning with them, nor ridicule can dissuade them of their belief in witches, and of the necessity of their being at once murdered'.[14]

II

WITCHES AND LOOSE WOMEN: MODES OF VIOLENCE AND PERSECUTION

Reports of witch hunting, that is violence against a woman and driving her out of the village in the least and killing her the maximum penalty, is reported in the Indian newspapers. The persecution of women accused of witchcraft is usually seen as being linked with local superstitions, so that any study requires a sensitive approach 'without hurting the pride and sentiments of the local population' and creating a 'tribal-non-tribal divide'. However, a significant number of cases in Jharkhand have been among non-tribals, so the problem is not exclusive to tribals. This is a method by which women can be dominated and oppressed per se. The belief that superstition and illiteracy are the main causes of witchcraft-related persecution is also debatable. The case studies presented below suggest that, there is usually a complex background of economic subjugation of the woman, sexual exploitation and the persecution of widows and independent women who are vocal. As in the case of *sati*, victimizing women as witches can be seen as the height of patriarchal suppression, which devalues and undermines a woman in society, and 'keeps her in a property less and resourceless state'.[15] Women are an easy target, because they are more involved in everyday activities, like the collection of firewood. For example, the forest department guards often catch them when they are walking through the forests, and accuse them of planning to collect forest products. They also come in for sexual harassment from the guards. Thus, women have reason to feel angry with the forest department, though such anger has to be suppressed. This represents a partial picture of different aspects of everyday repression. Quite often, the male perpetrators and other female onlookers keep quiet about the entire episode. The women keep quiet, because there is always a fear that they might also be thus branded and subjected to continued violence. The men keep quiet as this silence emboldens them to commit more such crimes and also hide their wrongs. So it benefits them to be silent. This reveals the strength of the social sanction which forms a tight web of consent and silence which traps the victim of violence and protects its perpetrators. In each of these cases, social sanction and agreement prevent the women from gaining any form of support and assistance from the villagers. During the interviews with the women members of the village community and various witch doctors in West Singhbhum, Palamau, Gumla and Dhanbad, it was evident that the belief in evil spirits (including witchcraft) is part of a villager's life. The men believed that killing a woman suspected of practising witchcraft cleansed society and served his community. Villagers attribute a range of unpleasant happenings to witchcraft: accidents, unexplained deaths, chronic and incurable diseases, epidemics, crop failure, failure of a woman to have sons and death of livestock, among other things. It is, therefore, not difficult to instigate villagers against a particular woman by claiming that she is responsible for some misfortune. However, villagers would not translate their beliefs into action unless certain prominent people approved of them doing so, and gave permission for violence. This is because, where the belief is real, there is a genuine fear that the 'witch' would harm anyone who ventured close to her. This is well, illustrated in an interview with women from in West Singhbhum, Dhanbad, Gumla, Giridih and Hazaribagh. Discussing witchcraft, the women (many of whom belong to a women's group associated with literacy programmes) expressed fear about a spinster, who lived alone and whom everyone suspected of being a witch. This woman had been attacked by the villagers at the instigation of a few local men, but the police intervened, and the attacks stopped. On further investigation, it was discovered that the instigators had managed to extort some property from the woman and so were probably allowing the matter to rest. The villagers, however, genuinely believe that the woman is a witch and have boycotted her since they fear her evil powers. They want her to leave, but without the headman's sanction they cannot take any action against her. The key issue, then, concerns certain powerful people in the community who exploit the villagers' superstitious belief in persecuting women as witches. That initial push ultimately leads to a drastic crime. The conspiracy of silence, and sanctioned violence in the case of witchcraft-related crimes have major implications for property ownership and control of that said property by women. The most difficult aspect of development involves encountering the belief system of a society, especially when this is part of the ethos and culture of the community. A tribal political party member reacted sharply to proposed legislation against witchcraft since he felt that this would 'aggravate tribal sentiment against non-tribals'. Hence, even the police find it a highly sensitive issue; few if any, at all comprehend the complexity of the issue and the range of factors it encompasses. In regions where witchcraft-related crimes are common, a woman dare not protest or oppose the social system, for fear of being labelled a witch. The case illustrations clearly reveal that persecuting women as witches is pre-planned and systematically perpetrated. The main motive is to ensure that women remain inferior in status to men and that they have no control over resources or decision making. Other motives, which are usually part and parcel of this, are for material gain (such as wresting property from the woman by conveniently labelling her a witch), existing family feuds, and sexual exploitation.

Violence against women is a clear indication of their degraded social status and vulnerability and witchcraft related crimes show this. Kelkar and Nathan (1991) argue that '. . . we cannot infer the low-status of women from witch-hunting, for witch-hunting is prevalent where women have a relatively high status, and that it reflects an attack on the existing status of women.' This argument is legitimate to the extent that women who have attempted to assert themselves in a male dominated society, women who have resisted sexual advances from powerful men and women who are widows with land rights, or widows with daughters or wives of the men who are fighting land disputes on land owned, are amongst the most probable victims of witch hunting. In other words, it is usually women who have in some way threatened men's superior position in society and those who own land as property who come under attack. Thus, witch hunting discourages any attempt by women to assert themselves and ensures that they maintain their inferior position in society. Regions where witch hunting is common are also areas where women are denied participation in village council meetings, and have no decision making power regarding village matters, such as deciding wages for labour. All these decisions are made by men and result in discrimination against women. In addition, women face violence frequently, usually in the form of assault by their husbands. Given their lack of social security, net and marginalized livelihood scenario, the village headmen, i.e. *manki* and the priest, i.e. *pahan* and the traditional administration system allows the headman unilateral power in deciding village affairs and settling disputes. Incidentally, the village *manki* and the *pahan* are hereditary positions and they wield immense power in the access to and distribution of common property resources. It has also been noted that due to the private property in land ideals operating within the overarching nontribal administration, who have little knowledge about the common property resources and their ownership and usurfructuary rights of many, over land that used to belong to the village common have been registered in the name of the *manki* in the colonial period. This was further sanctioned legally in the new settlement surveys that were conducted in Jharkhand in 1961-2 in Paschimi Singhbhum, and 1975-6 in Dhanbad. These surveys made these common areas of land over to be the individually owned private property to the *mankis* and the *pahans*. In January 1995, a report from the Bhuria Committee accepted the community 'as the basic unit of the system of self-governance in tribal areas'. The report further suggested that all resolutions of disputes, day-to-day administration, investigation, and adjudication of all matters should be managed by the village community. Thus, on the one hand, the report hopes to promote control over natural resources and usufruct rights over forest produce, while on the other, it accepts a non-democratic, gender-biased, and partisan system of administration, which will legitimize a village headman's power and subject women to further subjugation.

III

THE ANTI-WITCHCRAFT LAWS IN JHARKHAND

The Prevention of the Witch (*daain*) Practices Act was passed in then undivided Bihar assembly in 1999, and was adopted by the Jharkhand State Assembly in 2002. A witch is defined in it as a person who practises sorcery, a sorcerer or sorceress, one having supernatural powers in the natural world, especially to work evil spirits or the devil; formerly used for men, women and children, now generally restricted to women; an ugly, malignant old woman; a hag; a bewitching or fascinating woman or girl or a crone. It states that the practice of witchcraft is not a real one and that no woman can be tortured or oppressed under the presumption that she is a witch or indulges in witchcraft. The word *dayan* means a woman, who has been identified as a witch by someone else having the power or intention of harming any person through the art of black magic, cast an evil eye or chant *mantras*. It is assumed that she would harm other person/persons, or the community at large in some manner. The aforementioned Act has the following provisions:

- The Identifier is a person who initially identifies or takes the initiative in identifying another person as a witch or *dayan* or who otherwise abets, instigates or facilitates such an identification in any manner by deliberate action, manner, words, etc., for causing harm to the person and his/her safety, security and reputation of whom he identifies as a witch.
- The *ojha* or witch doctor means a person, who claims himself to have a capacity to attain control over a witch whether he be known by the name of the *guni* or *shekha* or *ojha*, etc.

- The penalties imposed on the people include the identifier with imprisonment for a term that may extend for three months or with a fine of Rs. 1,000 or both.
- Damages for causing harm to any person by torture both physical and mental by identifying her as a witch, whether deliberately or otherwise shall be punished with imprisonment for a term which may extend to 6 months or a fine of Rs. 2,000 or both. The damage claim may also be settled by a judge or jury on successful proof provided by the plaintiff. Whoever does any act of healing or curing any woman said to be a witch or causing harm or torturing any woman for curing will also attract a punishment of Rs. 2,000 or one year of imprisonment.
- Abetments, conspiracies, aids, instigations in the identification of the *dayan* is to be punished with imprisonment for a term that may extend to three months or a fine of Rs. 1,000 or both.

All these crimes are cognizable and non-bailable in nature. These laws are also to be read in conjunction with other laws regarding murder and torture, abduction and imprisonment as defined under the Indian Penal Code.

In most cases that come to the courts of law, there is a murder charge along with those of wrongful confinement/imprisonment, assault, sexual offence, etc., in addition to those of witchcraft.

Hereafter, one can refer to three case laws where this law was applied. The first one is case no Criminal Appeal No. 204 of 1996 (R) decided on 4 November 2003, Rasika Champia *vs.* State of Bihar/Jharkhand. In this case, the wife of Udai Champia, an employee of the Gua mines was murdered by his neighbour Rasika Champia. The incident that caused this murder was that in the evening, their other neighbours Ramai Champia, who was the son of the accused Lodro Champia was ill and ailing and two men Mata Champia and Birsingh Deogam had been called for *jhad-phook* and *pujapath* to cure him. This event was witnessed by many people of the locality. After the ceremonies were over, the deceased woman Suramani Champia was identified by them as the person, who had practised witchcraft on the ill-child. All the three men, then, told the other people gathered there that unless she was finished she would cause harm to the whole village. Upon hearing this, Rasika Champia seized a *pharsi* or a *tanga* and attacked her. This assault with the sharp weapon caused her death. The husband when he came back, was informed of all these occurrences by his children, who were witness to the whole series of events. During the trial, it came to be known that there was some land related dispute between the two families. In this case, the people were charged for murder, assault under section 302/120B IPC and under the prevention of the Witch Practices Act. The perpetrators were punished with rigorous imprisonment for life. This appeal was upheld even in the appellate courts of Judges Hari Shankar Prasad and Amareshwar Sahay.

The second success story was that of Sushil Murmu *vs.* State of Jharkhand Crl Appeal No. 947 with Crl Appeal No. 874 of 2002 decided on 12 December 2003 in the court of Judges Doraiswamy Raju and Arijit Pasayat. This was a case where death sentence was awarded to the perpetrators of child sacrifice in the name of sacrifice for personal gain by appellant.

The third case is that of Panchu Majhi *vs.* State of Bihar/Jharkhand, Crl Appeal No. 275 of 1990 decided on 4 October 2001 in the court of Justice B.N.P. Singh. Here, the appellant was the wife of the deceased person who had been killed by the assault of several persons. This case saw the acquittal of the accused as the prosecution failed to establish its case and there were gaps in the investigation as well as the prosecution process in the court. No charge sheet was filed in the case, the investigating officer did not testify, and it was found that the parties involved in the crime were already fighting other cases regarding land occupation and ownership rights against the deceased and his wife. Thus, this case was dismissed as the prosecution failed to establish its case and the court did not rule out false implication of persons involved.

The law in Jharkhand has been restricted to district court rooms and able lawyers. Yes, it has not been applied in a widespread manner and the state government has also not held any advocacy or dissemination work on the said law. Very few cases are filed under this law and no case was filed under this law exclusively. Yet, the number of women, who have been displaced and dispossessed grows with each passing day. Thus, this law needs more strong sections and enhanced capacity as only then it will be used widely and effectively.

NOTES

1. Valerie A., Kivelson, 'Lethal Convictions: The Power of a Satanic Paradigm in Russian and European Witch Trials in Magic', *Ritual and Witchcraft*, vol. 6, no. 1, Summer, 2011, pp. 34-61, University of Pennsylvania Press, DOI: 10.1353/mrw.2011.0014.
2. P.O. Bodding, *Studies in Santal Medicine and Connected Folklore*, Calcutta: Asiatic Society, 1986, p. 38.
3. P.O. Bodding, *Horkoren Mare Hapramko Reak Katha: The Traditions and Institutions of the Santhals*, New Delhi: Bahumukhi Prakashan, 1994. The first version of this Santhal text was published in 1887 by L.O. Skrefsrud and was translated with notes and additions by P.O. Bodding in 1942.
4. Valentine, Ball, *Tribal and Peasant Life in Nineteenth Century India*, Delhi: Usha Publications, 1985, (originally published in 1880).
5. S.C. Roy, 'Magic and Witchcraft in Chhota-Nagpur', in *Man in India*, vol. 33, no. 3, 1984 (reproduced from a paper originally written in 1914): *Oraon Religion and Customs*, Delhi: Gyan Publishing House, Delhi, 1985.
6. E.G. Man, *Sonthalia and the Sonthals*, Delhi: Mittal Publications, 1983, (originally published in 1867), p. 152.
7. J. Troisi, *Tribal Religion: Religious Beliefs and Practices among the Santals*, New Delhi: Manohar, 1979, p. 402.
8. S.C. Roy, 'Magic and Witchcraft in Chhota-Nagpur', in *Man in India*, vol. 33, no. 3 (reproduced from a paper originally written in 1914); *Oraon Religion and Customs*, Delhi: Gyan Publishing House, 1985 (originally published in 1928), p. 257.
9. Raut, pp. 401-3.
10. *Singhbhum Old Records*, p. 271.
11. E.T. Dalton, *Descriptive Ethnology of Bengal*, Calcutta: Firma K.L. Mukhopadhyaya, 1872.
12. P.O. Bodding, *Studies in Santal Medicine and Connected Folklore*, Calcutta: Asiatic Society, 1986 (originally published in 1925).
13. Ibid.
14. E.G. Man, *Sonthalia and the Sonthals*, Delhi: Mittal Publications, 1983 (originally published in 1867), p. 152.
15. Shiney Varghese, 'Resistance, and Development: A Case Study from Dangs', *Development in Practice*, vol. 3, no. 1, February 1993, pp. 3-15.

REFERENCES

Archer, W.G., 'Santal Treatment of Witchcraft', in J. Troisi (ed.), *The Santals: Readings in Tribal Life*, vol. I: *Religion and Magic*, New Delhi: Indian Social Institute, 1979.

——, *Tribal Law and Justice: A Report on the Santals*, New Delhi: Concept Publishing Company, 1984.

Ball, Valentine, *Tribal and Peasant Life in Nineteenth Century India*, Delhi: Usha Publications, 1985 (originally published in 1880).

Behringer, Wolfgang, 'Witches and Witch-Hunts: A Global History', *Themes in History*, Polity Press, 4; Midelfort, 'Witch Craze', 2000.

——, 'Climate Change and Witch-Hunting: The Impact of the Little Ice Age on Mentalities, Climate Change', in 43, no.1 (online at www.springerlink.com/content/n128666646273840/); and his Witches and Witch-Hunts, pp. 51-88; 158-62, 1999.

Bhadra, G., 'Four Rebels of Eighteen Fifty Seven', in Ranajit Guha (ed), *Subaltern Studies IV*, New Delhi: Oxford University Press, 1985.

Bodding, P.O., *Studies in Santal Medicine and Connected Folklore*, Calcutta: Asiatic Society, 1986 (originally published in 1925).

——, *Horkoren Mare Hapramko Reak Katha: The Traditions and Institutions of the Santhals*, New Delhi: Bahumukhi Prakashan, 1994, the first version of this Santhal text was published in 1887 by L.O. Skrefsrud and was translated with notes and additions by P.O. Bodding in 1942.

Chaudhuri, S.B., *Civil Rebellion in the Indian Mutinies, 1857-59*, Calcutta: The World Press, 1957.

Crooke, W., *The Popular Religion and Folk-lore of Northern India*, Delhi: Munshiram Manoharlal, 1969 (originally published in 1896).

Dalton, E.T., *Descriptive Ethnology of Bengal*, Calcutta: K.L. Mukhopadhyaya, 1872.

Kieckhefer, 'Mythologies of Witchcraft in the Fifteenth Century', 1980.

Man, E.G., *Sonthalia and the Sonthals*, Delhi: Mittal Publications, 1983 (originally published in 1867).

Prasad, 'Witchcraft among the Santhals of Mayurbhanj', in J. Troisi (ed.), *The Santals: Readings in Tribal Life*, vol. I, *Religion and Magic*, New Delhi: Indian Social Institute, 1979, the article was originally published in *Adivasi*, vol. 8, no. 4.

Ray, Rajat Kanta, *The Felt Community: Commonality and Mentality before the Emergence of Indian Nationalism*, Delhi: Oxford University Press, 2003.

Roy Choudhury, P.C., *Bihar District Gazetteers: Singhbhum*, Patna: Superintendent, Secretariat Press, (1959): 1857 in Bihar (Chhotanagpur and Santhal Parganas), Gazetteer's Revision Section, Revenue Department, Patna.

Roy, S.C., 'Magic and Witchcraft in Chhota Nagpur', in *Man in India*, vol. 33, No. 3 (reproduced from a paper originally written in 1914) (1985): Oraon Religion and Customs, Gyan Publishing House, Delhi (originally published in 1928).

Troisi, J., *Tribal Religion: Religious Beliefs and Practices among the Santals*, New Delhi: Manohar, 1979.

CHAPTER 20

Witchcraft: Power Relations and Totemism of the Bodos

DINA SWARGIARI

INTRODUCTION

Witchcraft has evolved as a concept and changed into different forms over the years and in different cultural contexts. The belief in witchcraft, carried over from generation to generation continues to hold sway over the minds of people even in the twenty-first century. A witch is understood to be someone, who possesses magical powers and conjuring capabilities; the practices carried out by the witch are called witchcraft. Witchcraft involves the tapping of supernatural powers through prayers, petitions and rituals. Witches are believed to use plants, herbs, hair, pieces of cloth, nails, spit and indulge in destructive activities. They are believed to possess powers that can cure people of their illness, and who can also use these powers to harm others. They are believed to frequently visit burial places and often prepare their concoction from the ashes of the dead. They are regarded as harmful for society, so in most cases they are hunted down, socially excluded, displaced, severely punished or killed, a process which is popularly known as witch hunting. In fact, it was legally sanctioned in countries like France, Germany, Norway, Russia, Netherlands and Switzerland from the 1300s and legal witch hunting continued in Europe till the eighteenth century.[1] After the enlightenment period, witch hunting has been regarded as an illegal accusation and violation of human rights, but it is still practised in the current twenty-first century in some parts of India.

In India, though not legally permitted today, finding out witches is an established process for most of the villages or tribes who still continue with this practice. In contemporary times, the practice of witch hunting is more prominent among the people living in rural areas. Evidences from the National Crime Record Bureau has made it clear that, in India, each year 200 women are killed as witches in rural India. During the year 2000-2001, there were 253 cases of witch hunting, and in 2008-12, more than 768 women have been murdered for allegedly practising witchcraft. The report consists of the registered witch hunting cases in Andhra Pradesh, Assam, Bihar, Chhattisgarh, Gujarat, Jharkhand, Karnataka, Madhya Pradesh, Maharashtra, Odisha, Rajasthan and West Bengal. Here, middle-aged and elderly single women in tribal, as well as non-tribal areas are branded as witches and they suffer social stigma, displacement, economic boycott, torture and murder. This is prominent mostly among the tribals living in rural areas.[2] The traditional belief that the person, who practises witchcraft, causes harm to his or her community through abuse of magical power has existed for millennia. This social evil has raised its ugly head in Assam following recent incidents of killing of innocent people in the name of witch hunting. The lack of scientific understanding results in loss of life and damage of properties of a large number of innocent people. Taking the traditional and religious belief in witchcraft for granted, some powerful people of the village find it easy to brand anyone as 'witch' by spreading constructed evidence among the folks. The condition of the victimized person also reveals their marginalized status and tells us about an inherent power structure and power-politics at work which leads to such social problem as witch hunting. In Assam, the practice of witch hunting is prevalent mostly among the Adivasis, the Bodos, Mishings and Rabhas living in districts like rural Kamrup, Goalpara, Kokrajhar, Chirang, Baksa, Udalguri, Sonitpur, Jorhat, Lakhimpur, Dhemaji and Karbi Anglong. The current study is based on the Bodos living in Kokrajhar and Udalguri districts of Assam, which are taken as field area.

BODOS AND TOTEMISM

The word 'Bodo' denotes both the language and the community and is pronounced with a high tone on the second syllable. The Bodos (pronounced Bo-ros) represent one of the largest of the 18 ethnic sub-groups within the Kachari group, first classified in the nineteenth century. The Bodos have settled in most areas of the north-east and in some parts of Nepal. They are an ethnic and linguistic community and early settlers of Assam in the north-east. In feature and general appearance, the Bodos are very close to the Mongolian races and this would seem to point to Tibet and China as the original home of the race. The Bodos are recognized as a plains tribe in the Sixth Schedule of the Indian Constitution. Udalguri and Kokrajhar are considered as the nerve centres of the Bodo area in Assam. The culture of the Bodo people of India is influenced by the land, where they currently live in. For a long time, Bodos have been farmers, with a strong tradition of fishing, rearing poultry, piggery and cultivation of silkworm, growing rice, jute, mustard and corn and betel nuts. They are primarily a patriarchal and a patrilineal society. They observe religious and seasonal festivals. Bodo society is based on totemistic clannish division. They have beliefs and faiths regarding certain objects of nature which they accept as their own. There is a clannish division of Bodo society like *mosahary* (the tiger folk), here, 'mosa' means tiger and 'ary' means 'folk'. Similarly there are other clans like Owary (bamboo folk), Swargiary (heaven folk), Boisomuthiary (earth folk), Daimary (water folk), Goyary (arecanut folk), Hajoary (hill folk), etc. based on their totem. Thus, it can be seen that the common last names of the members of Bodo community are Owary, Swargiary, Brahma, Boro, Mohilary, Basumatary, Dwimary, Goyary, Khakhlary, Mosahary, Narzary, Iswary, Chamframary, Hajowary and so on which are always related to natural objects.[3] Traditionally, the Bodos were followers of the Bathou Religion. However, through the ages, a large number of Bodos have converted to other institutionalized religions like Hinduism, Christianity and Islam, etc. In recent decades, they have been influenced by social reforms under Brahma Dharma, Assamese Sarania, Islam, and the spread of Christianity.

Today, there are Bodos who follow Bathou, and there are a sizeable number of followers of Christianity and followers of Brahmo Samaj. The Bathou religion incorporates rites, rituals, social norms, ethics and philosophy of the Bodos. P.C. Bhattacharjee opined that the supreme God of the Bodos, Bathoubrai (In Bodo language *Ba* = five, *thou* = deep, *bwrai* = old man and *burwi* = old women) also known as Shivbarwi (Shiva in Hindu) has created the universe with the help of his wife Shivburwi. The *sijou* plant (*Euphorbia splenden*) is taken as the symbol of God for worship and so, this plant is planted in their altar as an emblem of supreme God. 'Bathou' as a religion is based on the 'philosophy of five' or 'the principle of five'. Their philosophy states *sijoua siriba, bathoua bandoba*, which means that the *sijou* tree has five spines and Bathou has five ties. Five is a significant number in the Bathou religion, which denotes the five spiritual elements, viz. *ong, hring, khling, fwt* and *che*, they are respectively–soil, air, water, fire and sky. Bathou always believes in five principles. The believers are of the opinion that, though Bathou the creator is not visible, He can be realized by his five elements or virtues. Those five elements have been tied into five bond unions or principles. A clean surface near the home or courtyard is considered as an ideal place for worship where a *sijou* is planted. Usually, a pair of arecanut called *goi* and betel leaf called *pathwi* is used as an offering there. On some occasions, the offering for Bathou includes rice, milk and sugar. Kherai, the biggest festival of the Bodos represents the theosophical, ethical and religious perspective of their life. It is observed by praying to *Obonglaori* (Almighty) for the well-being of the villagers and society as a whole. Though they worship eighteen other gods or goddesses, *Modai Daodai*, their belief centres mainly on the Supreme Being, almighty Shivbwrai or Bathoubwrai. During the Kherai festival, the *ojha* (traditional healer and spiritual leader) plays the primary role of chanting *mantras* for praying to God and forwarding necessary instructions for the purposes. The *douri* (priest) assists him in activities related to divinity and rituals. The *doudini* (female dancer who gets possessed by spirits) is not only a dancing oracle during the Kherai featival of the Bodos. She also turns into another form of divinity who advises the villagers with her newly acquired power of foretelling. All of them perform according to a certain code of discipline concerning the sanctity and purity of Kherai Puja.[4]

POWER OF BODO WOMEN

Like most societies, The Bodo Community is patriarchal. According to Anil Boro, 'The domestic life of the Bodos follows the patriarchal family pattern. The male member of the family is the head of the family and the owner of the family but of course the female members of the family are never kept under suppression and excessive male domination'.[5] However, Bodo women do have the liberty to work. The household work like cooking, maintaining cleanliness in the house, providing food for each and every member of the family and so on are done by the women. Moreover, extra work for additional income such as rearing of pigs, hens, goat and ducks is done by women and the produce of the kitchen garden owned by her in the house is often used as she wishes. So, the division of work between husband and wife in a Bodo family is based on the necessity and physical capability to support family life. The *Dongkha Haba* (*Dong* means possess, *kha* means ever or already) is a traditional widow remarriage system which has the significance of ensuring dignity and sanctity of the Bodo women. There is no bar in getting married to a widow. Even a widower or unmarried young man can enter into such a marriage through mutual understanding of guardians concerned and the villagers. Bodo women have right to participate in the decision making of village council, *Gamini Affat. Ishing* (a room of mother house called *Noma No* with an altar of *Bathou Bwrai* and *Mainao*), and *Bakhri*, which means granary are exclusively under the care and control of Bodo women.[6]

RELIGIOUS BELIEF SYSTEM

It is generally seen that belief in the existence of supernatural powers is very often a corollary to the belief in religion. One takes recourse to magic when religion fails to produce desired results. Unpredictable natural events, inadequate health facilities and calamitous situations lead to the belief in supernatural forces. The control of supernatural forces by means of compulsive formulae is known as magic. Magic is practised and cannot be separated fully from the worship of gods. While the gods are moved by prayer, and they are petitioned for general well-being, magic is always used with reference to specific problems. Magic is an integral part of tribal religion and its importance is equally noteworthy in the case of Bodo traditional religion. The chants of the *douris* the oracles of the *doudini*, and the different performative feats during the religious festivals particularly Kherai as mentioned above, are important aspects of the ritual. Almost all the performances in this ritualistic religious festival are in the active magical circumstances. Particularly, as the *Doudini* while performing the ritual, gets possessed by the spirit of different gods, she is a possessed being with supernatural powers. Her words of prophesy and actions of supernatural performance puts the outcome in such a way that the folk believe and live according to the *doudini's* credibility. This practice is in fact, a community reliance that holds the status of ritualistic religious magic which can never be defined as witchcraft.

It is important to note that in the cultural milieu of Assam, the traditional belief in witchcraft is prevalent in many communities. According to Initial name Brahma, in most tribal communities of Assam, religion and magic are often taken together and regarded as complementary to each other.[7] For instance, in the Bodo community of Assam, *dayan* or witch is believed to possess a special spirit of animals that perform services for them. They are, thereby, considered harmful to the society as it is believed that they can bring harm, illness and diseases to people. The suspected person is hunted down, physically tortured, driven out of villages, socially excluded and in some cases even killed on the alleged charge of being a witch and practising witchcraft. New forms of wealth and inequality, rapid growth of individualism and enmity increased social tensions among the Bodo community, are explicable in terms of occult power or witchcraft. Montague Summers argues that 'Witchcraft was inextricably mixed with politics'. The *Malleus Maleficarum*, published in 1484 by Heinrich Kramer and James Sprenger, two of the inquisition's foremost prosecutors and both

Dominican monks, pieced together a patchwork of the many political, religious and personal anxieties associated with the concept of the witch in the late fifteenth century.[8]

More than the occult practices like witchcraft, sorcery and magic, the witch hunts are practised increasingly in the Bodo community. When one looks back to the history of witch hunting in the Western countries, it is easy to understand that during the 1560s–1600s, The French wars of religion between Protestants and Roman Catholics divided France and encouraged witch hunting.[9] Prior to the process of Christianization, metaphysical powers were understood as ambiguous terms. With the spread of Zionism, however, 'good' and 'evil' were increasingly constructed in binary opposition. And witchcraft came to be identified only with the 'evil' side of this polarity. Contextual evidence of insiders such as dreams, divination, mysterious events and confessions could be sufficient for accusations of witchcraft even in situations where no social tensions were present.[10]

POWER RELATIONS AND TRIBAL SOCIETY

Witch hunting attracts more attention than the craft itself. The traditional belief in witchcraft is most common among poor rural communities with little access to education and health services, and so, having more and longstanding practice of witch hunting. Among the Bodos, when an individual gets sick or harm befalls the community, the blame falls not upon a virus or a disease affecting crop, but an alleged witch. The *ojha*, who works as a local/village medicine man plays a crucial role in this context. Witch hunting cases most often reveal that the marginalization of the alleged witches start with the discourse of the *ojha's* pointing out the diseases as the work of witch. The alleged witches are blamed and the process of accusation takes its course. The version of the victim (witch) of witch hunting is powerless compared to that of the group of people in the community who stand against her. As Foucault said, an individual is powerless compared to institutions, groups or the state.

Witch hunting has a high incidence among certain tribes like the Bodos and Adivasis of Assam. Illiteracy, poverty and lack of access to health care are definitely contributing towards perpetuating the scourge. The situation is extremely disquieting. A grim reminder is the fact that even in the millennium, when scientific knowledge is breaking new grounds, many of our societies have not been able to put their dark, primitive days behind, with ignorance and superstition throttling rational thinking and fuelling mass frenzy. In this backdrop, the recent gruesome killings of some innocent men and women, mostly elderly couples, on the alleged charge of being witches and practising witchcraft, thereby, inducing harm, disease, illness to some persons in certain Bodo and Adivasi areas of Assam are not only diabolic, but inhuman as well. Among the Bodo community, the belief in witchcraft first originated due to polygamy. The conflicts among co-wives and their resentment led to the intention of harming others out of envy, hate, selfishness, power and wrath.

In the article, 'The Idea of "Evil" among the Bodos: Text and Context', Anjali Daimary discusses the Bodo Adivasi practice of witch hunting and the resultant murder of poor women among them. According to her, it is believed that remedy of a disease caused by an evil spirit or black magic can be cured only by the *ojha* (traditional medicine man) or *kaviraj* (shaman), who has the power to drive away the evil spirit. It is a belief that a disease caused by black magic can only be countered or cured by counter magic. The *dayan* (witch) and the *ojha* are, therefore, constitutive of the everyday life, health, sickness, cure and the culture of indigenous medicinal knowledge of the Bodos. The *dayan* is seen as the propitiator of that evil. The majority of the Bodos believe that one requires an *ojha* to identify a *dayan*, but the irony is that, as case studies reveal, the *kaviraj* is no different from *dayan* and often uses his privileged position as the medicine man to marginalize and subordinate the *dayan*, associating her with all that is evil. This establishes a hierarchy of actors that functions in accordance with the contexts of need and belief in Bodo society. And also, Daimari says that, it would not be an over-statement to say that evil arises from a hierarchical social order, and when the order fails to deliver, it attempts to sustain its legitimacy by those practices that have an evil effect. Daimari's exploration of the conflict between *dayan* and *ojha* and the marginalization of the former by the latter brings out this not so easily understandable mechanism of authority and legitimization within the Bodo social hierarchy.[11]

POWER RELATIONS AND GENDER

The *Malleus Maleficarum* (a medieval treatise on witches) stated, 'All witchcraft arises from lust, which in women is insatiable'. Witches' lust was supposedly for the devil, echoing the story of Eve and it was believed that the devil could easily seduce women to join him. This explained why most of the accused witches were female. In the book *Counterfeiting God: James VI (I) and the Politics of Demonologie*, Fischlin Daniel says that the history of witchcraft is the history, in part, of male anxieties about their own empowerment, sexual or otherwise. But, it is also the history of women's oppression as gendered political subjects constructed by patriarchy, and as subjects who posed in their demonized collectivity particular threats to male empowerment. There is a substantial, though often unrecognized connection, between sexual empowerment and political empowerment and, as Deborah Willis has noted, 'To varying degrees and with varying emphases, elite discourse about the witch was concerned with promoting a new religious orthodoxy and maintaining political order and social hierarchy'. In most of the incidents or cases, accusations are made because it is believed that, the witch gains subversive power not only through her ability to dismember, but also through her control over the choice of the male member. She also has the power of critique, her comment regarding the parish priest being an obvious anti-clerical dig at the widespread corruption of the clergy, and thus an attack on a form of religious hierarchy.[12] A similar kind of marginalization of the subordinate section of the society is seen in the Bodo Society.

In rural Assam, the *ojha*, a traditional medicine man also known as the *kabiraj*, is revered for his supposed skills at countering black magic. According to traditional Bodo folklore, the medicine man learns his skills. Witches, however, are said to be born with their powers. This is a convenient distinction in what are typically patriarchal communities. It is rare to find a female *ojha*. 'When a woman practices traditional medicines, it is considered to be something evil',[13] Denial of sexual favour, for instance, can also be a strong motivating factor behind witch hunts. Tradition, thus, becomes a shield and justification for violence against women. While one section of the community is absolutely convinced that witch hunting is good, there is another section that uses this tradition for their own benefit. However, it remains a fact that generally everyone does believe in the power of witchcraft. Witch hunting is a powerful emotion that can drive a crowd to a state of mass frenzy. In most cases, the prevailing atmosphere after a 'successful' witch hunt is one of joyous triumph over evil. There is no doubt in the minds of the believers that the 'hunt' is necessary to wipe out evil.[14] Diane Purkiss in her book, *The Witch in History: Early Modern and Twentieth-century Representations*, examines the way early modern villagers, and especially women, themselves fashioned stories about the figure of the witch, stories which helped to define their identities. She argues that the witch is not solely or simply the creation of patriarchy, but that women also invested heavily in the figure as a fantasy, which allowed them to express and manage otherwise unspeakable fears and desires, centring on the question of motherhood and children. Purkiss looks at the presentation of the witch on the early modern stage. She examines the way in which these village stories were taken up and reshaped by early modern dramatists, who turned them into spectacular stage shows and interpretative challenges leading to moral homilies; the effect was to give the witch public meaning in defining the place of the stage and the notion of good order in the political and social realms. She also examines the way the women accused of witchcraft used the opportunity of supernatural agency and confession to shape an identity for themselves, which represented a compromise between their understanding of the world and the categories developed by more educated people.[15] Witch hunting practices have exploited women and their empowerment. Women are branded as witches very easily and the beliefs of witchcraft are very fast to spread among the womenfolk themselves through gossip and groupings. So, the issue of witch hunting seems to be a gendered, moreover, a feminist issue.

CONCLUSION

There is a deep-rooted traditional belief in witchcraft, that are connected to witch hunting practice among the Bodos. In reality, the witch hunter wishes to punish the victim for a perceived transgression, such as refusing sexual advances, enmity, property dispute or challenging an authority figure. But, by taking the advantage of the traditional and strong belief on witchcraft, the hunters brand someone as a witch and she is handed over to the villagers who spread constructed evidence and narratives regarding her. The villagers are not aware that the selfish motive of the hunters is always there behind it. Almost all the narratives about the witch remain unquestioned because the villager regards all of them as true. P.O. Bodding (1986) mentioned, 'There is no genuine Santal who does not believe in witches'.[16] This statement is equally applicable for the Bodos of Assam. 'Bathou' the totemistic religion of the Bodos asserts the credibility of the *doudini.* And it is necessary to note that the folk believe and live according to the *doudini's* prophecy and action. It is made clear here that the practice is in fact, a community prop that holds the status of ritualistic religious magic which can never be defined as witchcraft.

The members of the whole village or community are in one way or the other involved in the accusation of the victims of witch hunting. The *ojha* points out the diseases as the work of witches and this plays a major role in strengthening the belief in witchcraft. In fact, it is rare to find a female *ojha*, whereas there are more female witches. But, the irony is that it is not only the male section of the society who accuses the witch for practising witchcraft. There is not always marginalization, domination or discrimination of women by men but also the deep and strong belief in witchcraft, which both men and women spread while in interaction with the people not necessarily confined to the members of their own village. Subjectivities from different people get connected to each others' beliefs as a result of which the evidence, either real or constructed extend and become popular narratives among the people. The spread of such narratives occurs, due to lack of information among the folks who are mostly illiterate and find it hard to adopt to the changing aspects of science and technologies.

NOTES

1. William E. Burns, *Witch Hunts in Europe and America: An Encyclopedia*, London: Greenwood Press, 1959, p. xxi.
2. Joya Chakraborty, Anjuman Borah, 'Witch hunting in Assam: Strategising Alternative Media for Women Empowerment and Overcoming Superstition', *Journal of North East India Studies*, 3.2(2013), pp. 15-24.
3. Nirjay Kumar Brahma, 'A Study of Folk Wisdom of the Bodos', *Sunoasis Writers Network*, Retrieved 15 October 2011.
4. Nirjay Kumar Brahma, 'A Study of Folk Wisdom of the Bodos', *Sunoasis Writers Network*, Retrieved 15 October 2011.
5. Anil Boro, *Folk Literature of the Boros*, Guwahati: Adhunik Prakashan, 2001, p. 9.
6. Nirjay Kumar Brahma, 'A Study of Folk Wisdom of the Bodos', *Sunoasis Writers Network*, Retrieved 15 October 2011.
7. Kameswar Brahma, *A Study of Socio Religious Beliefs Practices and Ceremonies of the Bodos*, Calcutta: Punthi Pustak, 1992, p. 145.
8. Daniel Fischlin, ' "Counterfeiting God": James VI(I) and the Politics of "Demonologie" ' (1597), *The Journal of Narrative Technique* 26.1 (1996), p. 1.
9. Brian A. Pavlac, *Witch hunts in the Western World: Persecution and Punishment from the Inquisition through the Salem Trials*, Connecticut Westport, London: Greenwood, 2009, p. XV.
10. Isak Niehaus, Mohlala Eliazaar and Kally, *Witchcraft, Power and Politics: Exploring the Occult in the South African Lowveld*, London: Pluto Press, 2001.
11. Anjali Daimary, 'The Idea of "Evil" among the Bodos: Text and Context', in *Construction of Evil in North East India: Myth, Narrative and Discourse*, ed. Prasanjit Biswas and C. Joshua Thomas, New Delhi: SAGE publications, 2012.
12. Daniel Fischlin, ' "Counterfeiting God": James VI(I) and the Politics of "Demonologie" ' (1597), *The Journal of Narrative Technique* 26.1 (1996), pp. 1-29.
13. Anjali Daimary, 'The Idea of "Evil" among the Bodos: Text and Context', *Construction of Evil in North East India: Myth, Narrative and Discourse*, ed. Prasanjit Biswas and C. Joshua Thomas, New Delhi: Sage publications, 2012.
14. Debarshi Prasad Nath, 'Assam's Tale of Witch-hunting and Indigeneity', *Economic & Political Weekly* XLIX. 37 (2014), pp. 54-60.

15. Diane Purkiss, *The Witch in History: Early Modern and Twentieth-century Representations*, 1996.
16. Shashank Sinha, 'Witch-Hunts, Adivasis, and the Uprising in Chhotanagpur', *Economic & Political Weekly*, 42.19 (2007), pp. 1672-6. Accessed on 28 March 2013, p. 1673.

CHAPTER 21

Notions of Witchcraft among the Khamtis of Arunachal Pradesh

TAGE HABUNG &
RANJEETA MANNOW

INTRODUCTION

In all human societies, people distinguish between naturally caused illness and illness caused supposedly by the supernatural. It has been said that naturally caused categories of diseases are treated by natural means, while the treatment of supernaturally caused illness lies in the realm of magico-religious healing. In simple societies the theories of magico-religious healing reflect a faith and belief, which can be called as elements of *nonsequitur* that cannot be explained scientifically. In such societies a number of deities, spirit and humans are often associated with disease and the treatment of such a disease is done accordingly. The concept of 'witchcraft' is one which had always been taken as one of the worst stereotypical, virulent, and extremely negative images in most people's minds. The term 'witchcraft' seems to be derived from the old English word 'wicca' which means 'female magician'. Witchcraft is the supernatural action of witches, a term commonly used to describe people, usually women, supposed to have dealings with the evil spirits.[1] Conceptualizing witchcraft, Max Weber (1970) defined it as a type of technology used to tap supernatural power and direct it toward specific empirical ends. Anthropological studies of witchcraft document its widespread association with magic and religion and it was Evans-Pritchard, who made the first detailed study of witchcraft. He made detailed study of witchcraft, as a belief and the way it is practised among the Zande of the Sudan-Congo border in 1926-30.[2] In his study, Evans-Pritchard found that among the Zande tribes, most of the misfortunes are generally attributed to witchcraft. He analyses the Zande belief system which emphasized the fact that it is an entirely logical way of explaining events.

In most of the societies 'witchcraft' is seen as a belief in the supernatural power, that is inborn in some people that enable them to work evil. Witches, men or women can harm simply by thinking evil thought or by casting the evil eye. Thus, witches are always viewed negatively. They are universally considered as anti-social in human society. The witches are seen as weird persons who embody all feared and negative aspects of a culture. Witches undergo secret trainings to acquire more powers and control the spiritual realms. To acquire more powers, witches propitiate their main deity and other evil spirits. They also perform elaborate rites at cremation ground during dark nights to attain more powers. Once the witch has mastered these things she has to kill her own child or any member of the family. After the completion of the training, witches perform the magical *mantra* of witchery on a tree and if that tree dies within a few days, it indicates that the person has mastered the art of witchcraft. Witches secretly indulge in these activities at dark nights.

Witchcraft is also related to the evil eye,[3] the belief that malign power may be projected through direct gaze. The power is involuntary, stimulated by negative emotions, especially envy, and can cause misfortune, sickness, and even death. Among the tribal communities belief in witchcraft and related practices were deeply soaked in traditional customary ideas and ingrained in their folklore/tales. Such beliefs and practices could be noticed in many societies of Arunachal Pradesh. The Khamtis are tribal communities of Arunachal Pradesh among whom belief and practice of witchcraft can be noticed. In this article, an attempt will be made to understand the belief and practice of witchcraft through popular folk-tales of the Khamtis and draw a logical conclusion about these secret cultural practice. For this, both the secondary and primary data accessed to substantiate this study and logical conclusion had been collected.

Secondary data had been collected from books, journals and e-source while primary had data been collected from the Khamti inhabited area which had been interpreted with historical approach.

LOCATING STUDY AREA

Arunachal Pradesh is a homeland of 26 different tribal communities who live in different geo-cultural set up with different socio-cultural behaviour. Each tribal community is characterized by its own belief system that takes roots from its cultural identity. From the geo-cultural point of view the state can be divided into three zones, viz., western, central and eastern. The Khamtis, the subject of study in this article, are settled in the eastern part of the region. They are a branch of the Tai-Shan group inhabiting the regions of Southeast Asia, Myanmar and south China. They are said to originally belong to the Shan state of upper Myanmar, near Mongmorang which was the capital of the kingdom of Pong.

The word Khamti, is derived from two words *kham* and *ti*. In local language, *kham* stands for 'gold' while the *ti* stands for 'region'. Hence, Khamti means 'land of gold'. They shifted to the Irrawaddy Valley and established the Bor Khamti kingdom. The Burmese king annexed Bor-khamti kingdom in the middle of eighteenth century, thereafter they entered India in 1751.[4] Entering India, they finally settled on the banks of Tengapani River. At present the Khamtis are settled in Lohit, Changlang in Arunachal Pradesh and the Narayanpur area in Assam.

The Khamtis practise Buddhism as they belong to the Theravada sect of Buddhism. But elements of Hinduized practices can be also noticed among them. They have adopted a script of Shan origin know as *Lik Tai* for their language and have a rich literature consisting of *Pitakas, Ramayanas*, historical chronicles on law, social and political conditions, tantric *mantras*, etc. They used the script to make communication and invitations of marriages, festivals, funerals and official documents. Their mother tongue is Khamti, which belong to the broad branch of Siamese-Chinese linguistic group. The Khamtis believe in the existence of God and follow the teaching of Lord Buddha to attain *nirvana* or salvation. As such, the religious life of Khamtis is deeply influenced by the Buddhist ethics and morality. To them, Lord Buddha is a great moral preceptor and an embodiment of love and pity, truth and righteousness. In their daily prayer they seek his blessing for the welfare of the family and the society as a whole. Beside religious practice, they also have the secret culture of belief in witchcraft and related practice which is the area of study in this article.

BELIEF IN WITCHCRAFT AND RELATED PRACTICES AMONG THE KHAMTIS

Belief in witchcraft and related practice is generally rooted in traditional customary ideas, whereby societies form categories and order the universe around them. As such, they are not only intertwined with every aspect of societies, thought, and language, but also provide coherent and systematic means to influence the world in which man lives. For the anthropologists, such belief systems provide essential material for the understanding of the metaphysics of traditional and non-Western societies. They may also lead to a better understanding of the structural aspects of customary thoughts of a given society. So as far as the religious belief system of Khamtis is concerned, they are very 'superstitious'. In order to protect themselves against bad luck, charms and amulets are popular among the people. Some people tie holy thread around the body or wear it as a necklace while others have tattoos on their body which they call *Aang*.[5] The *yantras* endow the wearer with supernatural protection, love, health and wealth in order to bring luck and provided these *Yantras (Aang)* are also put up in the entrances of houses, commercial building, vehicles, granaries, etc. These practices clearly reflect that they adhere deeply to the traditional belief system. Their adherences to the traditional belief system can be gauged from following practices:

1. *Auspicious dates*: Auspicious dates are selected for fixing dates for weddings, on the eve of starting construction of a house or purchasing property, for setting up any business, etc.
2. *Auspicious colour*: They believe in the concept of a lucky colour for every person according to his or her day of birth.

3. *Lucky number*: They believe in deviation techniques which are often used to predict number before buying a lottery ticket.
4. *Cutting one's hair or finger nails*: They believe that cutting hair and finger nails on one's birthday and Saturday will bring bad health condition to that person. People are very conscious of this especially when it comes to children.
5. *Rainbow*: A rainbow is held in high regard and it is important to avoid pointing at it because one would lose one's finger.[6]

The Khamtis also believe in deities, sprits and ghosts. The people believe that they can protect themselves from spirits and ghosts by wearing a holy thread and making tattoos on their body made by monks and priests. Apart from these, the secret culture of belief in witchcraft and related practices is widely prevalent in Khamti society. There is a strong belief in potent powers of a witch, which is thought to produce great misfortunes and disease. They are considered a great threat to whole society and looked upon with fear and suspicion. But there is a dearth of literature to explain how belief and practices of witchcraft began among the Khamtis. Moreover, people avoid a discussion on the matters of belief in witchcraft and related practices. No one clearly gives information about how it has been practised or whether it is still practised in society.

ORIGIN OF WITCHCRAFT AND RELATED PRACTICES IN KHAMTI SOCIETY

The prevalent oral traditions and folk-tale of the Khamtis says that, the origin of belief in witchcraft and related practices among them can be traced to their settlement on the bank of the River Irrawaddy in upper Myanmar. When they settled on the bank of Irrawaddy, there was a kingdom known as Takasu which was ruled by a ruler known as Chow Khonokham. One day, the king went hunting near the bank of the river and he found a gold-coloured flower flowing in the water. He thought that one day these flowers would turn into a pure/real gold. That thought made him very happy as well as jealous thinking what if the tree were growing in another kingdom as well. The king ordered his soldier to find the 'gold' tree locally known as *tonkham*. Here *ton* refers to tree, while *kham* means gold. The soldiers started searching for the 'gold' tree by following the river route. After some days the soldier found the tree growing on the bank of Irrawaddy. They found that the gold tree also grew in another kingdom which was ruled by a Khamti *mangsa* (prince) named Maantret. The soldiers came back to their kingdom and informed the king about the 'gold' tree and the ruler of that kingdom. After getting the information, the king was very surprised to know that the ruler of that kingdom was his own brother.[7] The king thought that in future his brother's kingdom would become rich very from that 'gold' tree.

Chow Khonokham could not digest the truth and therefore, he summoned some experts of his kingdom to discuss this matter. After a long discussion, the jealous king ordered his men to make an artificial bird from bamboo and cane. The bird, named Kanka was brought to life with the help of black magic. The king deliberately made this big magic bird and made it living through black magic to destroy the 'gold' tree in his brother's kingdom. The bird flew towards the tree and made his home there. He flew to the villages in the daytime and sat on the gold tree at night. As time passed, the bird felt hungry and flew to the nearby area in search of food but didn't found anything to eat. Out of hunger he caught the children who were playing in the nearby place and ate them. This news spread like fire in the kingdom, the people were very sad and angry with that bird, and they wanted to kill it. The king Chow Maantret was informed about this, he ordered the people to kill the big bird who ate the children of his kingdom. The bird was too big to be killed by one single person. Consequently, the king summoned the four strongest and courageous men of his kingdom namely Chow Kam Yaa-Yaa, Chow Kam Yaa-Yung, Chow Kam Vihi and Chow Kam Paha and asked them to kill the bird. The four men made a plan to burn down the tree and started collecting coal for purpose. They set the tree on fire with coal and other materials as a result of which the bird flew away due to heat and smoke. Thereafter the bird sat on the mountain near the kingdom. Finally the men cut-down the tree in order to prevent the bird from sitting on it. The trunk of the gold tree was of diamonds and the flowers were of gold. Consequently, the tree was thrown into the River Irrawaddy.

After that, the bird had no choice but sit on the nearby mountain. The people made a big trap from buffalo skin, they considered buffalo skin very strong material compared to other animal skins, to catch the bird. The people left a pig near the trap and they were getting ready to attack when the bird came down to catch the pray. The plan of the people was successful and bird was caught in the trap. Once the bird was trapped, the people shot arrows into the heart of the bird and it died. As soon as it died, the people of the kingdom whose children had been eaten by bird started eating the flesh of the bird to avenge the death of their loved ones. After some days, the people who had eaten the flesh of the bird became witchas and started eating human flesh as well. It was believed that since the bird was a magic one, that had eaten human flesh, those who ate the flash of bird indirectly ate the flash of their loves ones. From that incident some people in that kingdom became witches.

The king was very sad to know that some people of his kingdom had become witches by accident. The king organized a witch hunting drive to remove witches from his kingdom. All the people from that area were examined; the marked people were tied to heavy stones and thrown into the river. The people who were drowning in the water were identified as witches and the king ordered to kill them.[8] All the witches were eliminated and the kingdom lived peacefully. But it is believed that some witches left this art to their children and grandchildren from which witchcraft again spread in society.

NOTIONS OF WITCHCRAFT AND TABOO PRACTICES

As in any other society, the Khamtis feared the witches as mysterious creatures imbued with phenomenal power. It is believed that the witches are supposed to have intercourse with the devil, which gives them the power of killing people by eating their entrails and also of causing fevers, (murrain) diseases in cattle and other kinds of evil.[9] Interacting with some elders in society gives some idea about their beliefs and practices. An elderly member of the society said that the witches practise their art during night, when all the people are asleep. They can transform their body into another living thing during the practice of their arts. They do this in order to keep their identity a secret from the people. Sometime, they transform their face into that of another person only to hide their own identities. Generally witchcraft is practised both by men and women but old women are said to be more common to practise witchcraft.[10] As per the oral tradition, witches have to eat the flesh of their first-born child. They can trap the soul of a man and eat the soulless body or human flesh by transforming the flesh into another flesh, like fish, chicken, pig, etc., and keep normal people in illusion by replacing the body of that person from log, bamboo, pumpkin, etc., and finally the man dies, when the witch completes eating his/her. The witches kill the person who knows about them to protect their identities and prevent social humiliation. The people believe that those who come in the grip of witches can be healed by priests and monks, who perform the ritual of good spirits. The witches are very active when someone dies, so people are very scared to stay in the house of a dead person. In case, if a person is affected with the magical spell of witch, persons take help from local priest known as *chowpachang*, mostly the monks.[11] As in any other society, the witches have never enjoyed a good reputation in the Khamti society. Witches are thought to be up to no good, interested in wreaking havoc and bringing misery to others.

The Khamtis firmly believe that witchcraft is an art which can be learned from a witch parent or gifted from witch parents to their children. It has been said that during migration to India in 1751, a few witches came along with them but the number went on increasing as they taught their art to their neighbours and relatives. They say that some people practise witchcraft for various reason and the most important of these are

(a) to protect themselves from spirits and ghosts, which happen to dwell in different places,
(b) for entertainment and showing their power to other people,
(c) for taking revenge on their enemy,
(d) to preserve the art form from generation to generation, etc.[12]

The elders of the society say that the witch has supernatural power; if someone talks about them, they come to know of it. People are still scared to talk about witches and do not have the courage to disclose the practice of witchcraft in society. That is perhaps the reason, why the Khamtis do not discuss witchcraft in their society which is a big hindrance for understanding witchcraft among the Khamtis. One has also been told by some elderly persons of society that practices of witchcraft had increased drastically in the early years of the nineteenth century and it was very well known among the people. The witches started to teach their art to their neighbour and relatives. The witches had to kill human being in course of practice as result of which there was an increase in the number of deaths in the early years of nineteenth century. This created fear among the people. A taboo started developing in the society in which people started believing that washing ones hair after 12 noon would attract the witch to take their name and soul while practising their art at night. They also believe that looking at a mirror during night would encouraged the witch to see ones face while practising. The weaknesses of the people encouraged the witch to flourish in their art. It has been said that, in early nineteenth century the witches started practising their art openly, but no one had the courage to talk or point a finger at the witch.[13] The people are afraid of darkness to avoid contact with the witch. It is believed that generally the witch becomes active, where people gather to celebrate festivals or a ceremony. The witches are very active when someone dies, so people are scared to stay in the house of a dead person.[14]

DISCUSSION AND CONCLUSION

The preceding discussion provokes a lot of questions. The most important question, which pertains to the notions of witchcraft among the Khamtis is whether—belief in witchcraft and practising it really existed or not. What is so unusual about the increase of such practices in the early years of the nineteenth century and rise of the death toll? If practices of witches caused the rise of death in nineteenth century, then why were such practices made open in nineteenth century? If at all the witchcraft practices existed, then reasons for their increase making it as an open art in nineteenth century can be attribute to two factors. After entering India, the Khamtis found suitable land for settlement in the areas of present Lohit and Changlang districts of Arunachal. Later they extended they territory in Narayanpur in Assam in about 1797-1800.[15] During the early part of the nineteenth century, the Burmese invaded Assam a number of times and became the rulers. The Khamtis were now afraid that the Burmese king would again annex their land like they did the Bor-Khamti kingdom in the middle of eighteenth century. Considering these factors, the Khamtis perhaps made witchcraft an open art during the early nineteenth century. This assumption is also affirmed by a popular belief according to which they say that witchcraft was practised in their society for taking revenge upon their enemy. Moreover, during this period there was a lot of difference or conflict between the Singphos and the Khamtis for territorial domination over Lohit and Changlang areas. For the defence of their people, the witchcraft practices among the Khamtis were made an open art which might have increased the rise in witchcraft practices in nineteenth century.

It is also possible that witchcraft might not have existed in reality among the Khamtis and the notion was socially constructed and popularized so that outsiders and neighbouring communities could be afraid of them. By spreading the notion of black magic in the form of witchcraft they could protect their territory from invasion. Otherwise, how is it possible that though they have been practising this tradition for more than 200 years, there is no proper information or case in record in this regard. Moreover, it has been said that the practice of witchcraft had declined drastically since 1985 in Khamti society. If it had been practised till 1985, there should be some witness of this practice but unfortunately there are no witnesses who could throw light on these practices.

It is also possible that this practice prevailed and is still prevalent among them and that is why they refused to give any information in this matter. It has already been observed that as per the beliefs prevailing among them, the witch had supernatural powers; if someone talked about them, they came to know about it and would harm those who disclosed their identities. But before coming to any conclusion one has to ascertain about the belief in witchcraft and practices among the Khamtis and this is a modest beginning in understand the same.

NOTES

1. P. C. Joshi, Sonia Kaushal, Shashi Katewa and Oinam Hemlata Devi, *Witchcraft Beliefs and Practices among Oraons in Studies of Tribes and Tribals*, 4(2), New Delhi Kamla-Raj Enterprises, 2006, pp. 145-9.
2. Lucy Mair, *An Introduction to Social Anthropology*, New York: Oxford University Press 2nd edn., 1972, p. 245.
3. Ibid.
4. Lila Gogoi, *The Tai Khamtis of the North-East*, Delhi: Omsons Publication, 1990.
5. From interview with Chow Yaa Mannow on 2-3 September 2014. He is 60 yrs old and native of Nampoong village.
6. From interview with Chow Lohani Mannow on 9 September 2014. He is 58 yrs old and native of Nanamkhampti village.
7. From interview with Chow Yaa Mannow on 2-3 September 2014. He is 60 yrs old and native of Nampoong village.
8. Ibid.
9. Ibid.
10. From interview with Chow Lukeow Munglang on 15 September 2014. He is 72 years old and native of Lathow village.
11. From interview with Chow Lohani Mannow on 9 September 2014. He is 58 yrs old and native of Nanamkhampti village.
12. From interview with Chow Lukeow Munglang on 15 September 2014. He is 72 years old and native of Lathow village.
13. Ibid.
14. From interview with Chow Yaa Mannow on 2-3 September 2014. He is 60 yrs old and native of Nampoong village.
15. M.L.Bose, *History of Arunachal Pradesh*, New Delhi: Concept Publication, 1997, p. 88.

REFERENCES

Bose, M.L., *History of Arunachal Pradesh*, New Delhi: Concept Publication, 1997.

Ellen Guiley, Rosmary, *The Encyclopedia of Witches, Witchcraft and Wicca* (3rd edn.), New York: Infobase Publication, 1997.

Farook, Ayesha and Ashraf K. Kayani, 'Prevalence of Superstitions and other Supernaturals in Rural Punjab: A Sociological Perspective', in *A Research Journal of South Asian Studies*, vol. 27, no. 2, July-December 2012, pp. 335-44.

Gogoi, Lila, *The Tai-Khamtis of the North-East*, Delhi: Omsons Publication, 1990.

Joshi, P.C., S. Kaushal, S. Katewa and O.H. Devi, *Witchcraft Beliefs and Practices among Oraons*, New Delhi: Kamla-Raj Enterprises, 2006.

Mair, Lucy, *An Introduction to Social Anthropology*, 2nd edn., New York: Oxford University Press,1972.

P. Chireau, Yvonne, *Black Magic: Religion and the African American Conjuring Tradition*, London: University of California Press, 2003.

CHAPTER 22

Society, Belief and Practice: Witchcraft and Witch Hunting in Assam

JAHNABI GOGOI NATH

The practice of witchcraft and witch hunting has often been reported from among some of the tribal communities of Assam like many other such communities in the country. In the case of Assam, the practice is largely reported from among the Bodos, Rabhas, Tiwas, the tea-garden communities—the *adivasis,* and from among the Misings. The practice of witchcraft and witch hunting has been variously interpreted by different scholars. To some, it has been a gender question—a male struggle for establishing domination over women who exercise ritual knowledge for all practical purposes, or a woman's resistance against the growing hegemony of men,[1] while to others it was a religious clash—a clash between the marginalized beliefs of the tribal communities against the organized religions,[2] while some others treat it as a kind of struggle between the rich and the poor or between the forest-based and urban communities.[3] It is even believed that in witchcraft, there is the element of ancient system of medicine and treatment, and the process of witch hunting is an attempt on the part of men to professionalize it, taking it from the hands of women.[4] Whatever be the actual reason for its origin, the practice is universal, and in Assam also, it has a reasonably remote beginning. In the present article, an attempt has been made to investigate the origin of the practice among the Bodos of Assam, the nature and impact of the craft on society. It is, therefore, an attempt to study the nature and extent of the practice in the state with particular reference to the Bodos. While doing so one must say that the study has been largely based on the paper reports, and no empirical study has been made.

WITCHCRAFT: ORIGIN AND DEVELOPMENT IN ASSAM

The word *daini* or *dayan* is the local form for the word *witch*. It is stated that this word has come from the Indo-Aryan word *dakini*.[5] According to Philip Rowson, the original meaning of the word *dakini* can be traced in the Tantra. In Tantric Buddhism *dakini* means the female personification of a stage of wisdom.[6] A popular image of the Hindu Goddess Kali is found to be associated with many other images, such as Shiva, her consort, and Dakini and Yogini her two associates. Thus, the word *daini* or *dayan* has its root in the Indo-Aryan language, and therefore, it should be noted that the word was originally foreign to the Bodos. As pointed out by a scholar, unlike tribes like the Santhal and the Bhils, the Bodos have no words for 'witch' in their own language. [7] This fact may lead one to believe that they borrowed the idea and the institution of witchcraft from their neighbours, most probably from the Hindu castes.[8] In support of such a view, we may refer to Dalton who stated that in the Chota Nagpur area along with the tribes, witchcraft was practised by women of true Aryan blood; even Brahmans were sometimes accused of witchcraft. He quotes Major Roughsedge, who wrote in the year 1818, that a Brahman woman was denounced as a witch and tried, and having escaped in the ordeal by water she was found to be a witch and, her nose was cut-off.[9] In this connection Indibar Deuri, a scholar from Assam has stated that the Bodos might have developed the idea of *daini* or *dayan* from their contact with the Santhals who used to migrate to Assam since the second half of the nineteenth century, and also suspected that their contact with the culture of the Mayang region in Nagaon, a place known for magic and sorcery, in the British period and other Assamese people might have created the concept of *daini*.[10] He further argued that the idea of witchcraft and witch hunt was therefore, never known to them till about the close of the nineteenth century.[11] He is of the opinion that in no record about the Bodos since the days of Hodgson's Essay on the Koch, the Bodo and the Dhimal Tribes (1847) till 1947, there is any information about witchcraft and witch hunting among the tribe.[12] His statement, however, is not substantiated by empirical evidence. One knows for certain that E.T. Dalton, while collecting data in Assam for his Tribal History (first published in 1872) in the early part of the nineteenth century, has clearly recorded the practice of witchcraft and witch hunt among the Bodos of Assam.[13] Bhaben Narzi, a scholar of the Bodo Kachari history and culture, mentions a witch popular among the Bodos, called Than Thin Daini and has noted that witchcraft was prevalent among the Bodos since early times. He wrote:

> The Bodos term the *mantras* that can cause evil to someone as *jadu*, i.e., magic. A man who practised magic was called *dainagourang*, and who this created evil was called *daina*. Once there was the practice of doing magic among the Bodo Kacharis to harm the enemies. However, the practice has now ceased to exist except on rare occasions.[14]

Incantation, magic, sorcery, and witchcraft have been very old practices in human society all over the world. Evidence of such practices in India are found since in the days of the *Atharvaveda*, or even earlier.[15] It was, undoubtedly, an accompaniment of the process of magic which the primitive men largelt depended upon.[16] According to W.H. Davenport Adams, the objective of a magician or witch is to know the hidden world, gratify his material greed, create conditions favourable for him and, finally, to satisfy his malice against his fellows.[17] In Assam, the emergence of the Mother Goddess in the form of Kamakhya and her manifestations in different forms and their personfication, and men's belief in various magico-religious agricultural practices are some of the significant developments in the social formation process of the state in early times. Thus, it may be presumed that the practice in Assam was of much remote origin. In the medieval times too, magic, sorcery and withcraft have been extensively recorded in literature of the land and outside. For example, while referring to the witchcraft practised by a class of women in Goalpara and Khuntaghat area in the sixteenth and seventeenth century, Mughal historian Mirza Nathan has recorded very interesting incidents. He says that:

The place of (Khuntaghat) is notorious for magic and sorcery. Thus, if a man takes by force a fowl from a *ryot* and the *ryot* comes to the judge for redress, if that person is refused justice, then the complainant by means of his magic and sorcery could make the accused produce the voice of a fowl from inside his stomach and this prove the falsity of the protestations of the accused. If a bailiff of the judge stays at a village in connection with the work of the *Dihidar* and the *Pattadar* (the tendure holder or the revenue farmer), and if in a state of drunkenness demanded fish with violence in the evening or at midnight when no fresh fish was available, and persisted in his demand by torturing the *ryots*, they would bring some leaves of a mango tree or (another tree whose name reads like *lashura*), and breathe on these leaves some words of magic and sorcery. These leaves would forthwith turn into a kind of small fish. When these fishes were cooked by him in a state of drunkenness, they turned into blood. As soon as they were eaten by the bailiff, he died.[18]

It is interesting to note that as a place of magic and sorcery the land of Kamarupa was well-known all over the country.[19] The belief in the Mother Goddess Kamakhya and her other manifestations, such as Kali, and her two associates—*Dakini* and *Yogini* are interesting in this regard. It is believed that the man engaged to sacrifice a human being before the Goddess Dikkaravasini *alias* Kechaikhati *alias* Tamreshwari, was supposed to be possessed by a witch before he propitiated the Goddess by his act.[20] The Vaishnavite literature of the period refer to the occult practices done by men in the villages where some persons created illness while some others pretended to cure it by application of *mantra*.[21] It is to be noted that everywhere most preceptors of neo-Vaishanavism came into conflict with those occult and magical practitioners, and called them sinful (*papi*), wicked (*durachar*), devils (*pisach*), etc.[22] This explains how the early beliefs in magic and witchcraft consequently came into clashes with the organized religious beliefs of the land. Even in later times the practice continued and remained popular among some sections of society. Reference to what was called *indrajal vidya* (magic and witchcraft) in Assam has been found in the literature left by the Sikh Guru Teg Bahadur, who visisted Assam during Ram Singha's invasion of the state in 1667-71.[23] In the nineteenth-century, Gunaviram Barua has recorded that women in Assam were well-known for witchcraft (*ku-kriya*) and incantation and for causing evil to society.[24] There are references in Assamese folklore and literature to women healers who had the knowledge of herbal medicine. The words *adudi* (portion) and *bejini* (medicine women) are found in Assamese folk-songs as well as oral narratives. In the ballads of Phulkonwar and Manikonwar medicine women called *bejini* who were sometimes engaged even by kings and members of the aristocracy to treat some ailments related to pregnancy and abortion are mentioned.[25]

The practice of medicine by women was once a widely practised culture in Assam. It would be mentioned that in medieval Europe when men began to acquire knowledge of medicine, they started to persecute women, who practised medicine and exercised a strong power over women and men in order to establish man's control over society.[26] The same situation prevailed in Assam also as a result of changing economic and religious situation. As a result, the culture of women's suppression by men gradually emerged and it took the form of popularizing notions like witch and witch hunting. Interestingly, in the context of globalization witchcraft and witch hunting is common among the more economically weak and educationally backward societies. To understand this new trend in witchcraft and witch hunting, it will require a systematic and in-depth study of its sociological and economic aspects, which however is not the subject of this article.

The suppression of women healers and dealers in magical potions is part of the struggle for suppression of witch craft. However, witch hunting is not just related to stamping out witchcraft and its practices alone. The area of medicine that is still the preserve particularly of old women in such societies, and who are most likely to be denounced as witches, is that of contraception and abortion. By way of preventing women from their control over child bearing capacities, men opened the way for strengthening their control over maintenance of the patrilineal line.[27]

The practice of witchcraft and witch hunting is found not only in India, they are universal all over the globe among the tribal, backward or peasant societies.[28] The practice was widely prevalent in Europe in the middle ages.[29] According to Trevor-Roper, people believed that there were witches who were associated with the 'casting of spells, the making of storms, converse with spirits, sympathetic magic'.[30] Mary Douglas in this regard has stated that the

> The term witchcraft was used loosely in Tudor and Stuart England, and was at one time or another applied to virtually every kind of magical activity or ritual operation that worked by occult method. Village diviners who foretold the future or who tracked down lost property were often called 'witches'; so were the wise women, who healed the sick by charms or prayers. Contemporary scientists whose operations baffled the ignorant were sometimes suspected as witchcraft. Here, the term witchcraft meant the employment (or presumed employment) of some supernatural means of doing harm to other people in a way that was generally disapproved of by the mass of society. A witch was thus a person of either sex (but in belief and practice more often female) who could mysteriously injure or kill other people. She could also molest farm animals.[31]

But what is more important in this case is that it involves witch hunting, a process by which some members of a community practising witchcraft attack some others of the same community for practising it considering that all evils in the society have been created by the witches.[32]

WITCH HUNTING

In a society where witchcraft is treated as a religious and cultural practice, every calamity, man-made or natural, are attributed to witchcraft; hence, a person who is suspected to be a witch, and who is normally a woman, is held responsible for all such calamities occurring in the society. Dev Nathan and others who have extensive works to their credit on the Santhal community, have stated that every 'woman live under the threat of being declared a witch. At times of crisis, like epidemics, all the women of a village could be attacked as witches'.[33] They further stated that in the village of Mahagama in Orissa, 'All the villagers (*sic*) became desperate and seeing no other remedy they beat all the women in the village and made them drink human excreta'.[34] While writing about the witch hunting practice of the Bodos of Assam, Dalton also in a similar tune, has recorded as follows:

In often happens that sickness or other misfortune is ascribed to the spells of witchcraft rather than to the wrath of the deity, and then three *ojhas* are summoned. With whose aid, and that of a cane freely applied, the elders endeavour to extort from the witch a confession of the fact and her motives, and if condemned, she is expelled from the district. A natural desire to get rid of troublesome and ugly old women was perhaps the origin of this custom.[35]

In the case of the Ho tribe of Jharkhand, Dalton gives a more clear picture about the act of witch hunt:

All disease in men or animals is attributed to one of two causes, the wrath of some evil spirit who has to be appeased, or to the spell of some witch or sorcerer, who should be destroyed or driven out of the land. In the latter case a *Sokha* or witch-finder, is employed to divine who has cast the spell, and various modes of divination are resorted to.[36]

The attempt at finding out a witch is an established process every village of the tribe has this practice. In a genuinely empirical study, Dev Nathan, Govind Kelkar and Yu Xiaogang have stated as follows the process of witch hunt among the Santhal community, which stands as almost an example in case of all tribal communities practising the craft: While women's participation in rituals became evil, men alone could be the witch finders. The *ojhas, deoras* and the *jan-gurus* perform this function with a combination of divining and knowledge in the contradictions existing in the village. Discussions with the witch finders in the Maranghada region of Ranchi and with Santhal women in Giridih and other districts showed that the witch finders through their questions and other means (investigation by assistants), gathered information from the complainants. The identification of the witch is then based on the information gathered. Initially the names of the witches are not mentioned. The complainants are left to make their own inferences. All this makes it very easy to identify the person whom the villagers (men) want to get rid off as the witch. Usually, the whole village knows beforehand who the woman to be named a witch, is. The various tensions in the village and the identity of those women who are without support are both well-known.[37]

In the first stage, a woman named as a witch may be fined, asked to 'behave' herself and otherwise threatened. Repetition of deaths due to diseases that can not be identified, or other tragedies in the village, which are certain to occur in a not too long a period of time, are then the occasion when the *ojha* may name the woman who is the witch. By this time, there is already a consensus in the village that a particular woman is a witch. Recurrence of usual tragedies is taken as proof that the witch is unrelenting. The woman may then be either driven out of the village or killed.[38]

Dev Nathan and others have further mentioned that 'police figure for one district of India (Malda) found that at least 46 persons had been killed as witches as late as in the period 1950-80. These were only those cases that came to the notice of the police and that too in a period when the phenomenon was on a lower scale than in the nineteenth century.'[39] Recording the belief of the Warlis tribe of Maharastra on witchcraft, Indra Munshi has stated as follows:

Bhutalis are believed to possess special powers by which they can instantly put a person to death or cause illness. As one political activist observed, when there is an illness, or death among human beings or cattle, widespread crop diseases or failure, the *bhutali* is held responsible. In such a situation the villagers go to the *bhagat (ojha)* to identify the cause of the calamity. . . . If the situation does not improve, the *bhagat* goes ahead with the task of identifying the *bhutali.* Through a variety of rituals like *dan herne* (reading the message in grains of rice), diva *herne* (identifying the witch in the light of a lamp), *diva herne* (identifying the witch in the light of a lamp), the *vati chalavne* (using a cup which moves and identifies the witch), the *bhagat* tries to find the witch. The *bhagat* who identifies the witch is usually not from the same village. Through a careful questioning, he can locate women who are socially weak and vulnerable, quarrelsome, destitute with poor family support, midwives, and so on. He gives a vague description of the women who caused harm.

The next step is to find to woman. The men of the village call for an identification parade. Women are sometimes made to stand on a hot pan as the Warli believe a witch's feet do not burn. At other times, the witch is simply pointed out by some one. Another way is that all the women who fit the description are beaten till some one confesses to the crime. Once the witch or witches are identified, the whole village goes through the ritual of exorcising her. The woman is beaten, sometimes to death. No one, not even close relatives, protect her from the attacks, for fear of being accused as an accomplice. A survivor in most cases leaves the village. If the woman dies, she is buried rather than burnt, and the villagers give no information regarding the death to the police.[40]

While there is an idea of witch hunting among some of the known tribes of India, there is no lack of examples of witch hunt among the tribes of Assam too, such as the Bodos, although no proper and systematic study has yet been done on the practice since at least a century ago when in the late nineteenth century Dalton recorded this practice among the community. It should be noted that the method of detecting and punishing the witch in the Bodo society does not differ much materially from what the practice has been among the Santhal or the Warli societies in other parts of India, and for that matter, any society of the country. Thus it is not the witchcraft, but the process of witch hunting that now attracts more attention than the craft itself.

Now, as against the European evidence as stated earlier, it is not known for certain as to the time when the practice of witch hunting first emerged in Assam. It has been noticed among a number of tribes, such as the Bodos, since at least the mid-nineteenth century. If Dalton is to be believed, however, it was by then (middle of the nineteenth century, 1866) a well established practice among the Bodos of Assam. In his Preface to *Tribal History of Eastern India* (earlier *Descriptive Ethnology of Bengal*) he has stated that he collected his materials from 'all available sources of information', and that he 'probably had more opportunities of observing various races and tribes, especially those usually called Aborigines, than have been conceded to any other officer now in the service'.[41] Following Dalton, a few others, such as W.G. Archer, Bodding and Hoffman, all Christian missionaries, make mention of the practice in the land in the late nineteenth and early twentieth century although the practice of witch hunting was perhaps not much widespread during that time.

The practice of witch hunting has still been reported from among the Bodos, Rabhas, Santhals and a few other communities. Thus, it is a living practice and is a continuum of an old religious and cultural practice of the tribes. The publication of news on witch hunting in the newspapers during the last half century points to this fact. It is to be noted that although in a few cases a witch could also be a man, in most cases they were women. People in such societies believe that the women earn the craft through a secret procedure and apply their craft for causing diseases and death in a village. In this connection, Bhaben Narzi has stated,

> The Bodos believe in a wonderful *daini* called *Than Thin Diani* who through her utmost desire obtain a supernatural power to do harm to the living beings. She is popular among the Rabhas as well as the Bodo-Kacharis of Goalpara. Women in the main learn the *mantras* of the *daini.* These women (or men) then do harm to anybody who would not satisfy her by offering all that is desired by the (*Than Thin Daini*) witch. As a matter of fact, people of the villages punish such a woman (or a man on some cases) thinking (him/)her to be the *daini* herself in various ways including putting his/her mouth to fire, or by cutting the nose, or by banishing (him/) her from the village.[42]

The notion of a witch and her craft has undergone significant changes during the last few decades since Bhaben Narzi's work, first published in 1966. At present, normally a woman is suspected by the neighbours to be the personification of a witch and the force behind all evils in the community. When such a suspicion falls upon her, people of the village (normally men) find her out through some specified devices and then punish her.

RECONSTRUCTING THE HISTORY INCIDENTS OF WITCH HUNTING IN ASSAM

As mentioned above, even today witch hunting in Assam has been widely reported, particularly among some tribal societies. News about occurrences of *daini* among the Bodos and a few other tribes in lower Assam, particularly those in Kokrajhar, Bongaigaon, Goalpara, Darrang, Sunitpur and Nalbari are frequently published in the newspapers and periodicals. In the year 2001 a Bodo woman named Dakharsri Baglari in the Odalguri area within the Darrang district was killed by the villagers along with her old father-in-law on the suspicion that she was a witch.[43] One Jonali Rabha in the Barjara village under Lakhipur Police Station of the Goalpara district was similarly given a verdict by the village council to be penalized suspecting her to be a witch and making her responsible for the death of a man of fifty-five years of age.[44] In the same year, in Kokrajhar in lower Assam, another Bodo woman called Angao Musahary was killed by the villagers along with a man on a similar ground.[45] Similarly, Pramilarani Basumatary, a Bodo woman, living in a village on the Assam-Arunachal border near Biswanath, was killed by the villagers on the ground that a girl of the village died due to the woman's witchcraft.[46] On another occasion a couple of the same community in Kokrajhar was killed by the villagers on the ground that they declined to confess that they were witches as accused by the villagers.[47] In the same year it was reported that a Bodo woman called Sabitry Hajowari, was burnt alive on the ground that she was declared a witch who caused the death of a girl in the same village.[48]

In 2002 there were four cases reported in *The Telegraph* and *The Assam Tribune*.[49] In the first case a couple was killed, while in the second case a woman was killed on the suspicion of practising witchcraft. A man called Kandle Hembrom in Kokrajhar was killed, as he was suspected of sheltering a *daini*.[50] During the same year, a woman called Mainamati Ghatowar of the Kakodonga Tea Estate in Upper Assam was put to hot iron test for the death of a child as it was suspected that the death was caused by her.[51]

In 2003 things did not improve much. In that year, in an upper Assam village called Jagroban Gaon a woman called Jaimati Robidas, 70 years of age was physically tortured and forced to eat human excreta and banished from her village. She was held responsible for the death of a number of children in the village of the Santhals.[52] In the same year another such incident took place in the Madhuting Tea garden in upper Assam, where a woman was tortured physically and forced to eat human excreta.[53]

In the year 2004, a woman called Moni Hemrom was killed on the ground of being suspected to be a witch.[54] Two other men along with a woman were killed on the Assam-Bhutan border at Bagcha on the same ground.[55] It was reported that this incident was actually planned in connection with the possession of waste lands.[56]

In the year 2005, in the village called Gobha, a Tiwa couple was killed by the villagers suspecting their involvement in witchcraft.[57] In the same year in the Biswanath subdivision in a village called Samukjuli a couple was killed by the villagers, because they treated the people with indigenous medicine and did not allow them to go to doctors.[58] In Kokrajhar two women in the village called Jharbari within the Sirang district were killed suspected of having practised witchcraft.[59] In the month of June 2005 a couple was killed in the Kathalguri village under Bismuri Police Station in Kokrajhar district on the suspicion of practising witchcraft.[60] A Bodo man was killed on the suspicion of being a witch in the Pub Kamardaicha village under Patacharkuchi Police Station on the Indo-Bhutan border.[61]

Similar incidents have continued to take place among the Bodos, the *adivasis* and many other tribal communities in Assam during the last decade. One of the recent developments is noted among the Mising tribe of upper Assam. It is significant to note that witchcraft and witch hunting was rarely reported from among the Misings till the last few years when sporadic reports about them began to be published from all over the state. One such incident took place in 2014 in a remote Mising village of Majuli near Jengraimukh, in which a man in the guise of an *ojha* created terror among the villagers when with his pretended power of a medicine and magic, he began to accuse people to be either socially harmful or label as *daini* and hunted. It was found that not only the illiterate section of the Misings, but also the highly educated section among them endorsed the activities of the *daini* and thus, allowed the *daini* on committing atrocities upon the selected families of the village and its neighbourhood. Interesting aspect of this case was that, instead of the villagers, mainly men, accusing someone, mainly a woman, to be a *daini*, the person himself impersonated as a *daini*—a possessed man and accused someone to be socially evil. This shows that personal or some other interests may also rest under the belief and practice of witchcraft besides its standing as a religious tradition. On the other had, it may be said that the belief and tradition of witch and witch hunting has taken a new turn along with change of power-structure in a given society.

It appears from what has been discussed above that the overall objectives behind calling a woman a witch and witch hunting that have been a long tradition among many communities of Assam, was to gain and exercise more power by someone against some others who lost it. It has been noted that attacks by villagers, led mostly by men, on the 'witches' have always resulted in the destruction of life of innocent men and women. Branded as practitioners of witchcraft, the *dainis* are the targets of violence.

It has been observed that witchcraft and witch hunting as a belief is largely common among the tribal and economically and educationally backward communities and almost all witches were from among women. In most cases, the ulterior motive behind witch hunting has been found to be economic-obtaining ownership of property, especially land and satisfying professional jealousy of men against women who handle power, to treat diseases in the society. In that sense witch hunting can be considered as an attempt to change the existing social order and the power-structure based on sexual differences. Ratna Bharali, in one of her studies has noted that, although in some case the number of victims may be almost equal in terms of sexes, the apparent calculation does not expose the truth. While women victims were all individual targets of the hunters, most of the males were either children accompanying a victimized mother or members of a family which was victimized.[62]

Witchcraft has, sometimes, been explained as a protest method of the tribal society against the growing impact of organized religion on it in the process of social transformation from tribe to caste, or from tribe to an organized and developed society. This contention finds support in the evidence of the religious history of medieval Assam, when most believers in Tantric Buddhism came into conflict with the preceptors of neo-Vaishnavism. It is recorded that Shankara Deva and many of his follower preceptors condemned them and tried to marginalize them to push them to the periphery.[63] It is not unreasonable to believe that in the process of detribalization and early Brahmanization, members of the tribal communities of Assam, particularly the Bodos, who played a historic role in the state formation process in the early Brahmaputra Valley,[64] acquired the culture of patriarchy, thereby slowly becoming accustomed to the property ownership right for men.[65] But due to a number of reasons, women retained in their hands much of the economic power through their old medicinal practice or through their relationship to the production systems. The system of having economic power with women, but socio-political authority resting with men consequently failed to cope with the changing economic systems, particularly in the colonial period and afterwards when capitalist economy came up to control the entire society. The growing tendency of witchcraft and witch hunting during the last few decades, justifies this fact. It may be suspected that the growing desire to acquire property in men's mind in a tribal and economically backward society strengthened the process of witch hunting which is a major and immediate way of obtaining land and property. It is pointed out that 'when widows do have a substantial right to land (a life interest as opposed to a maintenance right or even more so opposed to living on charity) that may become the targets of a witch hunt. It is here, where women generally have considerable authority in society that it would be necessary to attack them as source of all evil in order to establish the full authority of men. Where women's authority has been destroyed or reduced, such a continued attack would then not be necessary.'[66] Among the incidents mentioned in the present article, there are a few very clear cases where the reason was economic and property ownership. All other hypothesis, such as marginalization of tribal religion, process of male attempt to establish dominance over women, the gender question-women's protest against men's domination, or vice versa, or protest of forest communities against deforestation[67] can be explained in this light.

NOTES

1. Jeffrey Burton Russell, *Witchcraft in Middle Ages,* Ithaca, 1972, pp. 2f; Govind Kelkar and Dev Nathan, *Gender and Tribe,* New Delhi, 1991, pp. 98ff; Aparna Mahanata, 'Daini Hatya: Eta Samajtattvik Bisleshan', in Paramanand Majumdar, ed., *Daini, Jyotish aru Alaukik, Sikitsa,* Guwahati, 2002, pp. 11ff.

2. Mary Douglas, *Purity and Danger,* London, 1996, p. 102; I.M. Lewis, *Religion in Context: Cults and Cherisma,* Cambridge 1996, p. 65.
3. Marvin Harris states that the 'principal result of the witch hunt system (apart from the charred bodies) was that the poor came to believe that they were being victrimized by witches and devils instead of princes and popes. . . . It was the magic bullet of society's privileged and powerful classes' See *Cannibals and Kings: The Origins o Culture,* New York, 1977, pp. 237 ff; also Aparna Mahanta, loc. cit, p. 14.
4. Samar Bosu Mallick, 'Gender Relations and Witches Among the Indigenous Communities of Jharkand, India', in *Gender Technology and Development,* New Delhi: Sage Publication, 4 (3), 2000, p. 353; Dev Nathan and others, 'Women as Witches and Keepers of Demons: Cross Cultural Analysis of Struggles to Change Gender Relations', *Economic and Political Weekly,* 31 October 1998, p. 59.
5. S.K. Chatterjee, *Origin and Development of Bengali Language,* Calcutta: Calcutta University Press, 1970, p. 308.
6. *Art of Tantra,* 1978, Philip Rawson, London, 1978, p. 210.
7. Anjali Daimari, a scholar of the Bodos has noted that there are no written records so far found to try to trace the origin of witchcraft and witch hunting among the Bodos. Neither are there references to them in their early oral traditions. Cf. Debarshi Prasad Nath, 'Assam's Tale of Witch-Hunting and Indignity', *EPW,* XLIX, no. 37, 2014, p. 56.
8. S. Bosu Mallik, 'Gender Relations and Witches Among the Indigenous Communities of Jharkhand, India', in *Gender Technology and Development,* New Delhi: Sage Publication, 4(3), 2000, p. 346.
9. Cf. E.T. Dalton, *Tribal History of Eastern India,* 1872, original title *Descriptive Ethnology of Bengal,* Reprint, New Delhi, p. 200.
10. Indibar Deori, 'Daini : Asamar Janagosthi', in Paramananda Majumdar ed., *Daini, Jyotish Aru Alaukik Sikitsa,* Guwahati, 2002, pp. 23ff.
11. Ibid., p. 29.
12. Ibid., p. 27.
13. E.T. Dalton, p. 86.
14. Cf. *Boro-Kachariri Samaj aru Sanskriti,* op.cit, pp. 237f.
15. D.P. Chattopadhyaya, *Lokayata,* 4th edn., Calcutta, 1978, pp. 620f.
16. Ibid.
17. Witch, Warlock and Magician, vol. II, London, 1889, p. 203.
18. Mirza Nathan, *Baharistan-I-Ghaybi,* ed. and tr. M.I. Borah, vol. I, p. 132.
19. S.K. Bhuyan, *Studies in the History of Assam,* Gauhati, 1965, pp. 74ff.
20. As reported to the present author by the people of the Sadiya region in

Upper Assam and belief of the people of the Chutiya community of Assam who once ruled a part of Upper Assam with the head quarters at Sadiya.

21. R.M. Nath, ed., *Background of Assamese Culture*, 2nd print, Guwahati, 1978, pp. 47f.
22. M. Neog, Sankaradeva and His Times-Early History of Vaisnava Faith and Movement in Assam, Guwahati, 1998, pp. 88f.
23. B. Kakati, *Purani Kamrupar Dharmar Dhara,* in *Banikanta Rachanawali,* Guwaharti, 1991, pp. 204ff.
24. *Assam Buranji*, reprint, Guwahati, 1972, p. 203.
25. In a ballad called *Manikonwarar Geet* (collected & ed. B.P. Chaliha, Guwahati, 2005, pp. 210(ff) the queen is said to have requested a woman medicine practitioner—*bejini* to secretly abort her having unable to bear paid of pregnancy at the old age. The *bejini,* however, is said to have refused to abide on fear of being killed by the king. Maheswar Neog has stated that the ballad speaks of the age of the Ahom rule in Assam. See *Maheswar Neog Rachanawali,* vol. I, Dibrugarh, 1986, p. 388.
26. Mary Douglas, *Purity and Danger*, op. cit., p. 102.
27. Indra Munshi, 'Women and Forest: A study of the Warlis of Western India', in *Gender, Technology and Development,* 5(2), New Delhi, 2001, p. 187.
28. M. Winternitz, *History of Indian Literature*, reprint, Delhi, 1990, vol. I, p. 128.
29. Cf. Dev Nathan et al., 'Women as Witches and Keepers of Demons', in *Economic and Political Weekly*, October, 1998, p. 58.
30. H.R. Terevor-Roper, *The European Witch Craze of the Sixteenth and Seventeenth Centuries and Other Essays,* New York, 1967, p. 91.
31. Mary Douglas (ed.) Witchcraft Confessions and Accusations, London, 1970, p. 48.
32. Ibid.
33. Dev Nathan et. al., p. 61.
34. Cf. W.G. Archer, *The Hill of Flutes: Love, Life and Poetry in Tribal India,* London, 1974, p. 303; Dev Nathan et al., p. 61.
35. Dalton, op. cit., p. 86.
36. E.T. Dalton, pp. 86, 199.
37. Dev Nathan et al., p. 61.
38. Ibid.
39. Ibid., p. 58.
40. 'Women and Forest : A study of the Warlis of Western India', in *Gender, Technology and Development*, vol. 5, no. 2, 2001, New Delhi, 2001, p. 182ff.

41. E.T. Dalton, op. cit., p. ii.
42. Bhaben Narzi, *Baro Kacharir Samaj aru Sanskriti,* 3rd edn., Guwahati, 1985, pp. 243f.
43. Ibid.
44. *Amar Asam,* 7 May 2001.
45. Ibid., 8 February 2001.
46. Ibid., 29 June 2001.
47. Ibid., 18 August 2001.
48. Ibid., 24 August 2001.
49. *The Telegraph,* 2 October 2002.
50. Ibid., 24 October 2001.
51. *Amar Asam,* 29 December 2002.
52. Ibid., 28 June 2002.
53. Ibid., 26 July 2003.
54. Ibid., 29 April 2004.
55. *Amar Asam,* 9 November 2004.
56. Ibid.
57. *The Sentinel,* 12 June 2005.
58. *Amar Assam,* 15 March 2005.
59. *The Sentinel,* 27 April 2005.
60. Ibid., 12 June 2005.
61. Ibid.
62. 'Witch Hunting needs Serious Concern', in *Bibungthi,* vol. I, pt.ii, 2011, pp. 26f; cf. Debarshi Prasad Nath, 'Assam's Tale of Witch Hunting and Indignity' in *EPW,* vol. XLIX, no. 37, p. 57.
63. *Gurucharit Katha,* ed., M. Neog, Guwahati, 1982, pp. 38, 308.
64. The Bodos have a system of keeping a young boy for a girl at the house of the girl called *gharjonwai rakha.* The *Gharjonwai,* however, is not entitled to the ownership of the property which the girl inherits from her parents. They also have a system called *dhoka* or *dangkha* whereby a widow marries a man and keeps him with her at her home. This man, however, does not become the rightful owner of the property which the woman possesses from the side of her former husband. (See Narzi, op. cit., pp. 87ff). It appears that this proprietary right of women has been a cause of witch-hunt among the Bodo society.
65. Govind Kelkar and Dev Nathan, op.cit., p. 100.
66. Ibid.
67. See fn. no.1; Aparna Mahanta, 'Daini Hatya: Eta Samajtatvik Bisleshan', in Paramanad Majumdar, ed., op. cit., pp. 11ff.

CHAPTER 23

The Enchanted Community: *Kaose* and *Doi* (Witchcraft) among the Kukis of North-East India

JANGKHOMANG GUITE

In 2014, when I was on a holiday at home, I came across one very disturbing or rather tormenting video clip of *kaotom* circulating across social networking. It was difficult to say how many people had actually viewed the clip. But the fact that I got this clip from an aged man who was not conversant to, and has the least interest in social networking convinced me that the clip in fact had a wide circulation. Very soon, I came to know that this clip had gone viral across the land, at least among the Kukis, in the north-east and other cyber cities of India. I came to learn soon that similar clips of *kaotom* had, now and then, circulated in the social media in recent times. Society was also often flooded with stories of what they called *kaotom*. It was in the midst of such criss-crossing rumour wire that I also learned certain underground outfits killing some people accused of *kaotom*. When I heard all these, I was deeply appalled by the new development that reminded me of history. At times I asked myself whether history was repeating itself. I thought it was not good. This episode struck me not only because of the sympathy I had regarding the accused persons, but more importantly by the growing trend of instances such as this which had the potential to break the very social fabric of Kuki society. This particular episode had already disturbed the peace and tranquillity of the local society. Strong views had already been expressed by different sections of the population. The public mind had been poisoned with fears and hatred for group of people who had traditionally been condemned as *kaose*. We had been trying hard to weave together some scattered pieces of historical evidence to understand the subject and are on the verge of reaching the conclusion that the existence of *kaose* and *doi* in Kuki society was merely in the social mind. They were social constructs specific to a particular time and space and had nothing to do with the reality.

Considering the damning impact, the said episode would have wrought to the shivering minds of the thousands, of the possible mental dissociation it would have brought in their thought, one eventually decided that some inventory should be taken to see what really conspired in the darkness of the 'great conspiracy'. While it had devastated the minds of thousands so that the chance of winning them was diminishing fast, one thought that the electrifying episode had at the same time opened up a new vista for academic discourse especially because it opened up the minds of thousands who had till then considered this as an 'unsayable' (*seingeilou*) thing in the society. To the Kukis, *kaose* was always a 'secret subject'. It was a subject every Kuki knew which everyone pretends to forget. It was a subject everyone learned secretly from childhood days, which everyone preferred to keep 'as a secret'. This is the subject, which one would call the greatest conspiracy of silence in Kuki history, which the episode had, for a moment, challenged, if not punctured.

Before I come to some of the findings in this study on the episode and another one which occurred a little before this one, I would like to share my childhood experience. This ancient ideas had permanent impact in the mind of every Kuki, a fact not overstated. When in junior school I had a very close friend. Those few years of our friendship was one of the best times I ever had in my life. There, no one cared or talked about clan, family, community, or nation matter that children are concerned with today. No one talked about rank, hierarchy, wealth and so on. It was just a true life. On many occasions, one had food together in his house, then in my house. Now and then, we spent the evening or the night together—shared stories, folklore and so on. Now and then, there were visits to the jungle for fishing, bird hunting, collecting bamboo shoots and so on. Now and then, we played games, kerosene (*thao-po*) was carried for pocket money. That was just a beautiful world. Yet, one very very bad afternoon, another friend of mine said something that devastated me. It was a great shock. It was a shock of a different kind which one would prefer to call a mental quake that saddened the remaning years in that school. He said 'secretly' that my close friend was *akiseite* (lit. 'what we said'). He said the 'unsayable' and one knew what he had said. I knew such 'unsayable' stories much earlier, but I had not known or seen anyone until I was told that my own friend was one of them.

It is a rule among the Kukis that, you can never ask a person accused of *kaose* whether s/he is one of them. Therefore, I started enquiring from other people. Surprisingly, the answer was positive; everyone seemed to know it. Some had even said that my friend's family was one of the most 'active' one (*alaangte/akhohte*) and hence most feared one. It was literally devastating. Every Kuki had had the psychological fear of *kaose* from childhood days. The children were indeed frightened with such stories. I was fall of fear, panic, and terror. That was one of the saddest days in my life. From that day onwards, I was not even able to face my friend. Kukis believed that *kaose* can read people's mind; it is said that they knew what was being thought about them, not to speak of the ill that is spoken of them. Hence, I always thought that my friend knew what I was thinking about him. That gave me uneasiness every time I met him. The life together with him after that was so uncomfortable that I never had a single day of happiness. I felt like I was in hell, in the frying pan. I was literally besieged and tormented every single day. Sometimes, I felt I should cut-off my friendship but I was afraid because I believed that he would immediately strike me down if I did that. But that was not the most serious point I had in mind. The truth was that, I could not just forget my childhood friend, who until that time was so close to me as if we were brothers.

When I think of this today, I feel very sorry for my friend, and for my own ignorance. But at the same time, I was not odd; my behaviour was what it really was, and is, in Kuki society. That was the pain, the suffering and torment that every Kuki felt in their mind; the non-*kaose* (who felt 'atheng' or clean) in the presence of *kaose* (who were condemned to be 'aboh' or polluted) and the latter among the former. Definitely, my friend did not know what I had in mind. He was completely unaware of my body language, not to speak of what we had talked to others about him. To him, things were usual, normal until we departed and went to different schools. My own silent conspiracy tormented me for a good many years which otherwise would have been the happiest years. This is the irony that every Kuki who would eventually realize one day that what they had in mind was imagined nothing more. It was just a mindcraft, a hostage to ancient belief, the state of mind that keep them conspiring against their brothers for none of their folly, none of their real being. Some might have had this experience earlier, many might just heard about it. But the fact is, when everyone knew about *kaose* they preferred to remain silent, a silence which was of course studded with fear and hatred.

OF SAVAGE MODERN MEN: TWO ELECTRIFYING EPISODES

Coming back to that electrifying episode, I took two of my students and a few other associates to take a ground inventory. That field trip made me realize that the belief in *kaose* is still overwhelming and deep rooted in our society. We spent the first two days in finding out who were the people accused, attacked and involved in the horrifying clip. We were told initially that the scene had taken place somewhere in Tuibuong in Churachandpur district, Manipur. We literally took the clip from door-to-door in and around Tuibuong. Tuibuong youth leaders were helpful. Everyone told us that they had also seen the clip but were not aware of the details of the incident. Eventually, on the second day, we were lucky enough to find out where the tragic incident had taken place that led us further. But what astonished me during these two days of search was that, if a random survey is to be taken, the following conclusion can be easily arrived at. Most persons were aware of the video clip(s). They all felt terrible after seeing it. Some women told us that what they had taken to be a notion a story, till this time, it had proved to be true. A very nervous woman told us:

'Although I used to hear about it, I did not believe it before, now I see that *kaose* really exist'. She went on saying '*kaose* are really horrible, I am really afraid now. The society should do something to stop this silent killing.' This woman was concerned about the safety of her children. The clip shows the alleged *kaose* woman 'revealing' that all the children who died recently in her village were 'devoured' by her. That was the message that frightened thousands of women who felt insecure and agitated. The innocent children were also similarly traumatized and tormented after seeing the clip. An old man protested, 'What are the *gollhangho* [lit. youth, meaning militants] doing, how could they let this thing happen'. There were also people who protested against the circulation of the clip on social media. They felt that this is a usual thing going on in our society, but putting up in social media is something they considered 'unethical' because it tormented people's mind, because it broke the silence of what was supposed to be 'unsayable'. They wanted that whatever happened should happen behind the closed door recalling the ancient principle of 'unsayableness' (*seingailou*) to the root.

After getting sufficient information, we went up to the village where the accused and victim lived. After travelling for a little more than an hour we reached the village. When we asked the villagers about the woman who was accused of the black art, they looked stunned and nervous. Initially, they told us that they were not there, probably they were suspicious of our intention. When we told that we were researchers and there was no bad design behind it, they hesitatingly told us that she had gone to the *jhum* field and would be back in the evening. They told that her house was at the corner of the village. We saw her house and it was locked. Since we could not wait till the evening, we decided to go to the *jhum* field. There in the thatched *jhum* house we finally found her with her daughter, grandchildren and two sons-in-law. She was an aged lady, thin, poor, and humble. We told her our purpose of visit and started inquiring about the clip. She broke down and told us the whole story behind the accusation made against her. She claimed that her own son, the son of her husband's first wife, was the main person behind the conspiracy.

Her story went this way. She was the second wife of her husband who had a son from his first wife. This boy had stayed away in another village in his mother-in-law's house (apute) since his childhood days indicating the childhood trauma under a step-mother. Later, he got married to one of the girls from his father's village but continued to live in his mother-in-law's village. His father and stepmother were living in the former village for more than twenty years. The husband died a year back. Until this time, no single accusation had been levelled in the village. The conspiracy began immediately after her husband died. After the conspiracy was made public and viral, her elder brother, who was also a chief of another village, came to her village and declared that their family had never been accused of being *kaose* in the past. They were instead the clan or the family which was considered as *thenchilahnate* (provider of clean spouse) by everyone. Her brother took the matter to the village chief who promised that he would do anything to remove the 'false' accusation made. But this never came about, and will perhaps never materialize because we learnt from them later that they were fully in favour of the accusation.

We also talked to one of her daughters and her husband and another man close to them. They all told us about the hard times they were going through in the village where people did not even look at them, not to speak of talking to them, as if a glance at them would likely cause sickness or death. Every one avoided passing their house (her married daughter's family also stayed with her). She told us that she used to be an active member of the church women's society. But after this, none of the women would come to her house, not to mention of an association with her, nor was she invited for the regular women fellowship and family prayer groups. In fact, the social environment was so hostile that it forced them to lead a secluded life. They said they were even ashamed of going to the church or any other public gatherings in the village. Of course, no one asked them to leave the village as in olden days, but the way the whole village community treated her family, amounted to putting a pressure on them to move away from the village. The kind of social ostracism and hatred shown toward *kaose* was, therefore, clearly visible.

Perhaps, the chief's family was also part of the conspiracy because the man who played a central role in the brutal scene of exorcism or 'seized' (*nodoh* or *kaomat*) was the brother of that village chief. That gory scene in the clip was performed in his house under his direction. In the clip, he was seen to have told the same woman that he had 'seized' (*mat*) her with other three sickly persons or 'victims' earlier when she had committed the same brutality on them as in this clip. What a savage men he was? It should be noted that this man was a deeply religious (Christian) person. He was the Secretary of that village church. The morning we met him we had to wait for him for a while. He came from the 'prayer-mountain' where he had gone out the previous night for a whole-night prayer. He proudly claimed that had done a 'good job'. But he did not realize that he had committed a great crime against humanity, first towards the sick persons and then to the woman he had implicated again and again as *kaose*. Certainly, such brutal acts against sickly people cannot be spared under human rights law: torture was one that attracts punishment under any legal framework.

This chief's family and the majority of the villagers belong to the same clan. The husband of the accused woman also belonged to the chief's clan but she did not. The conspiracy, she said, was that her step son wanted to come back to his father's village after her husband died and wanted to own the house as per his customary entitlement as the eldest son. But for this to happen, his step mother would have to leave that house and most importantly, that village. Hence, she asserted that it was a well-planned out conspiracy against her. Interestingly, the alleged victim of *kaose* shown in the electrifying clip was the elder sister of her step son's wife. This connection made the claim of the accused woman very strong. Therefore, we went to the alleged victim. She told us that she had been suffering from occasional stomach ache 'for a long time' for which she had been consulting a few doctors. She was on medication. She was also suffering from asthma.

That day while going to the Lamka for a consultation with the doctor, she had stayed at the house of the chief's brother just mentioned. This man seemed to have invited the (in)famous, and popularly known in Lamka area as, '*kao* doctor'. This '*kao* doctor' first offered her some liquid (about half a tea cup) before prayer. He also used two sticks which he called *lhagao chemjam* (angel's sword) as if they were his sthethoscope. With these sticks, he punched the abdomen where his patient had felt the most pain. This woman told us that the moment, she consumed the liquid she became unconscious and went in a state of trance (*manga banga lhajenjen*). She said that she could hear what other people asked her as in a dream (*mangjejen*), but could not remember whatever she had said. She said that her stomach ache was immediately healed or relieved after she was conscious but she felt the pain on her skin over which the '*kao* doctor' had hit with his *lhagao chamjam.* But she also told us that after sometime her original pain continued and her ailment was not cured. When we met her she was on her usual medication.

We then went to the '*kao* doctor' who told us that he was 'used by' (*manchah*) Christian angels (*lhagaotheng*) who told him to use two branches of certain common garden plant as *lhagao chemjam* (angel's sword) and certain liquid made of the same plant to cure any ailments. The liquid was made by a simple method. The upper skin of a branch of the said plant was removed and then dipped (for about half-an-hour) into a cup of water so that the bitter white fluid of the plant mixed with the water. We tasted the water; it was stingingly bitter. This liquid was given to the sick and it was so powerful that it immediately sent him/her into a trance. The fact that hundreds of people, from across Manipur and outside, had flown into his house for treating different ailments show the effectiveness of the liquid. Truly, many received, according to him, a 'miraculous' cure. It appears that the plant contains a very strong medicinal value which still needs to be studied in a laboratory. We have had a case of person being cured from diabetes after taking the liquid.

But the problem with this '*kao* doctor' was that he was also a strong believer in *kaose* and what he called *lhagao boh* (malevolent spirit) or *doi* (black magic or wizardry). So anyone who came to him was declared as 'possessed' by either of the above black art. Whenever an ailment was related to stomach or abdomen, he would invariably pronounce *kaobol* or *kaotom* (devoured by *kaose*). What a savage! He proudly claimed that the angels had given him the 'power to see' (*hettheina*) who was actually 'devoured' by *kaose*. He even claimed that he could identify, who was *kaose* by looking at the eyes. He also claimed proudly that he was able to 'cure' more than a hundred cases of *kaotom* in recent times. But when he declared this with pride, he did not realize that he was as savage and inhuman as those who had invited him. This innocent '*kao* doctor' did not realize that when he claimed with pride of the 'success', he actually indicated the fact that he was responsible for gaining popularity of the belief in *kaose* in recent times. This was particularly because he mindlessly indulged in savage method of exorcising *kaotom* such as declaring many of medically sick persons as *kaobol*, needlessly questioning several things of his patient who was falling in a trance such as the identity of *kaose* (which is actually an act of putting certain names in the mouth of the person, who was in a trance and who normally responded with 'yes' or 'no'. When we told him that *kaose* do not exist in reality and he had actually committed a serious crime by defaming and devastating many innocent people, he defended himself devilishly by saying that he did not ask any questions of the sick but those who had invited him did that. Interestingly, he agreed to abide by the suggestion not to ask any more question of the sick in future.

The second case was of similar but more savage kind. Two sick persons were taken to one house, and in the same savage manner, they were forced to pronounce certain names, one to a father and another to his daughter, through application of torture, terror and intimidation. The village authority was equally intolerant and enchanted. It invited the family which was accused as *kaose* and without giving any opportunity to defend themselves, ordered them to immediately leave the village the same night. They were threatened of public outrage if they failed to abide by the order. We met the family, who were forced to leave that village and lived in the outskirts of another village not very far from the previous one. The story we uncovered was that the daughter of this family, a beautiful, spiritual, and active member of the village church, had another female friend from the same village. There was a handsome gentleman, who fell in love with this young woman whom her friend had also apparently liked. One day, the former (her friend) told the gentleman that his girl-friend was *akiseite* (pronounced *kaose*) so that she could win him for herself. The gentleman did not take it seriously, probably he thought that is a safe idea. When he met his girl-friend he had casually, jokingly, told her of the accusation. Accusing someone as *kaose* is a serious defamation charge among the Kukis. The friendship eventually broke down not only between the two friends, but between the two families. This went on for a while which eventually ended up in the electrifying incident, where she and her father were implicated to be *kaose* and their eventual expulsion from the village. Certainly, this was nothing more than a sinister design by the accuser, who wanted to prove to the people that what she had said was true. Otherwise, such an accusation being a serious defamation charge, public wrath could backfire on them. It was but a spiteful act on the part of the accusers, who had not yet realized that they were still under an ancient skill though the world they lived in was a world filled with science and reason.

The relationship was such that this unfortunate family belonged to a clan other than the prevailing clan (chiefly clan) of the village. They were what is known locally as *phungchaga* (lit. orphan clan, meaning different clan of the village). The accuser's family also belonged to another clan, but maternally related to the prevailing clan of the village. In fact, her brother was an influential person in that village. The family of the accused had no history or precedence of any accusation earlier. This was the first time, they were accused in their family history, both from the side of the mother and father. Therefore, they took the matter to their *phungpi* (lit. clan head, meaning clan organization) so that the wrong accusation could be corrected through the clan (*phung*) to clan level. Here also, we can see the kind of hostile social pressure put on this hapless family. The girl told us that she stopped going out of the house, not to speak of going to the church. The kind of social boycott that befell on the family was so tormenting that it completely devastated them to the point they would never recover again. In fact, the whole episode of exorcism was farcical, taking the people to the age of savagery. Guns were pointed against the sick, they were tortured to say what they actually did not want to say and so on. Our cross-examination of the clip with the reality was unmatched. The tormenting scene in the clip also shows clearly that the two names of the accused were literally put into the mouth of the sick persons.

Certain significant conclusions can be drawn from the above two cases. First, it was the product of a local or neighbourhood tension, say, between a son and unkind step mother or between two friends in love with a handsome gentleman. Second, it proved that the accused were implicated for the first time in their family history. In other words, both the accused families had no precedence of such accusation in their family genealogy in the past. Third, both the families belonged to *khochaga* (the other minority clan) in their village. Fourth, both the accused were innocent women. In the first case there was one more significant thing: she was an aged, widow, poor, and humble. Fifth, the accusers belonged to the dominant and chiefly clan who had certain sinister designs of defaming the family of the accused. Sixth, in both the cases, the chiefly clan was unsympathetic to the plight of the accused; no justice was provided to them as in the olden days despite the case being a serious defamation. This was probably because the chief's family had nothing to lose, politically and socially, the fate that would certainly be reversed had it happened to any of their clan members or someone related to them. Seventh, the kind of social ostracism shown to the families of the accused clearly indicated that the idea of *kaose* is still very much alive and strong in the Kuki society.

Eighth, the Kuki church is equally apathetic to the idea of *kaose.* It can even be said that the church, instead of destroying such a concept, promoted the idea of *kaose* as one of its newly acquired concept of *lhagao boh* (unwanted spirit, an evil and hence sin). Declaring *kaose* as *chonse* (sinner) would bring a serious social implication in the future. The fact that an active church member or persons who were deeply religious or who even took the name of God and Christ, say, the '*kao* doctor' for instance, were involved in the dark conspiracy is a case that proves the position of the Kuki churches on the subject. Ninth, and more seriously, the existence of a concept like *kaose* in a society lacking any protection against defamation of the kind, is a serious social problem which had the potential of breaking the social fabric. This is especially so in a society which is undergoing rapid change, with spiraling social evils and so on. Thus, if an anti-social attitude towards the so-called *lou-ne* (drug addicts) produced Satanists (followers of Satan), the proliferating cases of defamation as *kaose* and its accompanying concept of them as sinners, unfit to 'enter heaven', then very soon large numbers of the Kuki population would be dragged to the Satanist followers. From the trend of defamation charges since recent times, we can say that in not very near future the Kuki society is going to have more *kaose* than the non-*kaose* (the *atheng*). Tenth, and most importantly, the two cases prove strongly that *kaose* is a social construct, an ancient concept, which can be used by anyone for anyone whom s/he wanted to defame. In other words, *kaose*, as the two cases show, did not exist in reality; it was through accusation, and the lack of power to defend oneself against such defamation, that a certain family was eventually condemned and known as *kaose*, nothing more. Let us see what *kaose* and *doi* was, and how society responded them, in the past.

DEFINING *KAOSE* AND *DOI*

Very often, there was an ambiguity in our understanding of *kaose* and *doi* which are of different categories under the generic *athenglou* (unclean or polluted, meaning 'evil') in Kuki society. *Kaose* is understood in different terms among their relatives in Chin Hills and Lushai Hills. For instance, the Lushais called it *khawhring* and the Lakhers called it *ahmaw*. Truly, there is no equivalent English term to define *kaose* or *khawhring* or *ahmaw*. Hutton (1980: 155), for instance, translated *kaose* as 'vampire'. Carey called it the 'evil eye'. Shakespear avoided giving an English term. Parry (1988: 462-3) pointed out the inaccuracy of existing English terms to define the belief. He said, 'It is impossible to translate the term accurately; it approximates to the evil eye, but is not exactly the same'. He felt that it is 'a sort of vampire soul'. J.H. Hutton (1980: 155) defined *kaose* as a person 'who can so project their astral bodies as to enter into those they wish to and devour their internal organs, particularly the liver and heart'. This definition seems accurate as it recognized the presence of an 'astral bodies' or spirits in a person, which s/he has the 'power' to project to those people they wish to attack. Yet, his understanding of the term 'devour' on 'their internal organs', that is feeding greedily on the vital organs, seems wrongly applied that led him to translate *kaose* as 'vampire'. Certainly, *kaose* is not a vampire and as far as the local understanding of them is concerned, they did not eat or feed on the vital organs of the people they attacked. Instead, it is said that *kaose* either *le* (lick), *pe* (bite) or *tom* (lit. cover, meaning overwhelm/engulf) which did not eat but tormented the internal organs of the victims. For clarity, we see similar beliefs in other tribes that came under similar cultural area of what is commonly known as Kuki-Chin cultural world.

Thus, a similar belief was recorded in Lushai Hills and Chin Hills. In Lushai Hills, John Shakespear recorded among the Lushais what they called *khawhring* which is an equivalent of *kaose.* Like *kaose,* he defined *khawhring* as an external body residing in a women (remember, it's only in women unlike *kaose* which can dwell in both men and women). He recorded that 'Khawhring lives in certain women, whence it issues forth from time to time and takes possession of another woman, who, falling into a trance, speaks with the voice of the original hostess of the Khawhring' (Shakespear 1983: 111). *Kaotom* (engulfed by *kaose*) is also similarly understood like this among the Kukis. Among the Lakhers, N.E. Parry (193: 462) also recorded a similar belief which they called *Ahmaw*: 'A person is said to be *Ahmaw* when his spirit has the power of entering into another person's body and causing severe stomach ache'. Thus, *kaose, khawhring, ahmaw* and so on are different terms used by different Kuki-Chin tribes to mean the same sort of belief that defined an external body or spirit which resides inside a human body who had the power to use this spirit to enter another person's body generally for certain negative reasons.

The reasons for the attack were said to be many and varied, but they can be reduced to one word: envy. It was said that *kaose* attacked a person mostly, if not exclusively, out of envy. Parry (1931: 462) lucidly put this down,

The belief is that a person who is *ahmaw* is always of an envious nature, and when he sees anyone else possessed of clothes or other property that he would like himself, he becomes very envious, and sends his spirit into the body of the person whose property he envies and at once cause the most violent stomach ache, which on occasions is believed to have resulted in death. An *ahmaw,* in fact, is a sort of vampire soul, which, on seeing any one prosperous and happy, tries to get hold of the property of the person he envies by entering his body and making him ill, in the hope that the sick man will then make offerings to him.

To these, food should be added as a central theme of envy among the Kukis and Lushais. Besides, it was also said that an attack could take place due to insult or humiliation. Since people used the invisible spirit to enter the body of others in order to satisfy their 'envy', *kaose* also comes under the category of black, negative or evil arts.

The Kuki-Chin cultural world also had another set of the black arts locally known as *doi* (Kuki) or *dawi* (Lushai) or *deu* (Lakher). *Doi* is further divided into two: positive (white) and negative (black) magic. While the positive *doi* (commonly known as *indoi* among Kukis) was exclusive to the practice of an institutionalized priesthood called *Thempu* or *Puithiem*, the negative *doi* was a practice akin to English witchcraft and wizardry or often given a generic term black magic. While the former used the method of *kithoi* (healing), the later used *kibol* (doi-a-bol, witchery, or wiz-ardry). Parry (2009: 18)) said that '*Dawi* is magic and a *Dawithiam* is a wizard'. He differentiated between *khawhring* (*kaose*) and *dawi* (*doi*) as: 'A *Khawhringnei* is a person who is possessed of an evil eye, while a *Dawithiam* is an active wizard'. Shakespear defined *dawi* as 'witchcraft'. The difference can also be seen from the method of attacking a person. *Kaose* sent its spirit inside the body and caused torment, *doithem* used certain 'poison' to attack its victim through food or a certain spirit for the same purpose. Ambiguity arises mostly from the fact that both used certain spirits to attack their victim. This ambiguity is even more complicated by the way society responded to the so-called black or evil arts. We can see that both the beliefs were clubbed together under the rubric of *athenglou* (unclean or unwanted) practice that the society struggled to stamp out over the ages. Besides most tribes/clans, sometimes villages felt its rival group both as *kaose* and *doithem.* Thus, Chins felt that all Lushais were both wizards and evil eyed people, a single glance from whom was supposed to cause sickness. This association of the two, *kaose* and *doi*, together as an anti-social combination or having to do with the whole tribe should not, however, confuse us from the fact that the same culture informed us of a clean divide between the two sets of negative elements in the society.

The difference can also be seen from its later development. When *doi* (both positive and negative) was successfully stamped out by the society over a period of time, *kaose* remained intact and at time vibrant. This not only indicates why *kaose* is a different set of belief system, but also that it requires a separate and different treatment from *doi.* Broadly, *doi* is a *practice* or an 'art' that requires a determined training under an able teacher. Whereas, *kaose* is a *concept* that does not require training and teacher; it lives inside the body of certain persons and is passed on through generations along the blood line. The person may refuse to use that power but does not lack that power which s/he can use anytime. The death of *thempu* or *doikungpu*, however, marked the end of his art unless he passed the knowledge on, through training, to someone else. *Kaose* is understood to be a sort of spirit and it can proliferate like virus through the bloodline and the heirs, if not controlled. Thus, great care was taken in the past, and of course still in the present, that *kaose* do not spread. Besides other discriminatory practices, an in-built mechanism in the institution of marriage such as the *neite* or *putechanu kijuon* was enforced and a strict prohibition on sharing of *samthi* (comb) and *nam* (cane-plaited band for carrying load in basket) with certain persons was pronounced. One can also see from the origin myths of the two, which also clearly shows a different origin.

MYTHICAL ORIGIN OF *KAOSE* AND *DOI*

Different Kuki-Chin groups had different narratives on the origin of *kaose.* At least two important narratives are available among the Kukis. The first is was related to a very old tradition which took place not very long after they came out from Noimang (Khul). Legend has it that Santhuh was the first known *kaose* among the Kukis. Pu Chonghtu cut the neck of Santhuh for swallowing up, in one gulp, the bridal-meat called *sachan* or *sahap* of his eldest son Thanpi's bride Seichin of Vanlaite. Somehow the decapitated neck was rejoined again by a mysterious creature called *chilchitenupa*. With a shorter neck, Santhuh was transformed into a gibbon (*guldu*). Since then, *guldu* was prohibited for human consumption due to the fear that the *kaose* spirit might enter their body. Those who had eaten *guldu* against the social injunction therefore became *kaose*. The second narrative said that when the Kukis were in present Chin Hills, they came across a talking *mithun* called *Sielpao* (being possessed by *kaose*). One day Kipgen and Chongloi killed this *mithun* and ate the meat. After they had eaten the meat *kaose* entered their body (Haokip 2011: 23-35).

Among the Lushais, the origin of *khawhring* (or *kaose*) is slightly different from the Kuki version. Shakespear (1983: 111-12) recorded one translated account of the Lushais in this respect. He wrote:

> Wild boars have Khawhring. Once a man shot a wild boar while out hunting. On his return home, they cooked the flesh. Some of the fat got on the hand of his sister, who rubbed her head, and the wild boar's Khawhring just passed into her. On the next day, without any provocation, she entered another girl. She took entire possession of her. People said to her, 'Where are you going to?' She replied, 'It is the wild boar my brother shot'. 'Well, what do you want?' they said. 'If you will give me eggs I will go away', she replied. They gave her eggs and she went.

From the above account it is clear that *kaose* first entered and resided the human body through a consumption of certain meat possessed by *kao* (say, gibbon or *mithun* among the Kukis) and through the hair after the application of boar's fat on the head. They enter the other person's body out of envy, in this case, for eggs, that is, the food of other they crave for themselves.

As far as the origin myth of *doi* (black magic) or wizardry among the Kukis is concerned, it is generally believed that they all learned the art from the Koms, one of the Kuki tribes. Another legend narrates that Pu Hangsai, the lionman, was the source of such black magic which Pu Galngam had from him. Hangsai also appears in the Lushai legends. The story of the origin of 'black magic' or what Shakespear has called 'witchcraft *dawi*' among the Lushai is, however, well established. Shakespear noted that 'the Lushais are firm believers in witchcraft'. He recorded:

Dawi witchcraft was known to Pathian. Vahrika also was something like Pathian. Vahrika had a separate water supply, and Pathian's daughter was always disturbing it. Vahrika said, 'What can it be? and lay an ambush. Pathian's daughter came, and he caught her and was going to kill her. But she said 'Don't kill me; I will teach you magic'. So she taught him, and Vahrika taught it all to Keichalla, Lalruanga and Hrangsai-puia. Then, Lalruanga went to court Zangkaki, and Zangkaki, who was a friend of Pathian's daughter, bewitched Lalruanga, who has forgotten his 'dawi bur' (magic gourd), and he said to Chaichim (the mouse), 'Go and fetch my dawi bur which I put in my basket'. So the mouse went to fetch the dawi bur and got it, but the Tuiruang (Barak) river rose very high. The mouse took the dawi bur in his mouth and started to swim over the river. The dawi bur was washed away by the river till it stuck in the fish trap of the Thlangom tribe, who said, 'What is this?' The dawi bur was singing like anything. The Thlangoms broke it open. No sooner had they opened it than they each acquired knowledge of magic. Then the Thlangoms were chanting the magic song. Some Mizo (natives of these Hills) who were passing through the village also heard the song of those who knew magic. The Mizo saw a man eating rice. 'May you be bewitched!' they said. They bewitched him in his rice eating, and for a year after whenever he ate cooked rice it changed into dry uncooked rice, and it swelled inside him till his stomach could not hold it and he died. Thus, the Mizo learnt about magic. Nowadays also there is magic, but those who knew it won't teach it without payment.

The crucial point here is '*dawi* witchcraft' came from Pathen's daughter. The art was passed on to humans which eventually fell, of course accidentally, in the hands of Lhangum clans. When the Lhangums (Kukis) were chanting the 'magic song', the Lushais learned it from them. The name of 'Hrangsai-puia' is significant; he is also closely associated with Kuki legends as the powerful lionman and the friend (*jol*) of Galngam, the legendary warrior of the Kukis who learned the art of magic from Hangsai (Hrangsai-puia). The legendary personalities in Kuki-Chin cultural world, such as Vahrika, Keichalla, Lalruanga, and Hrangsaipuia all belonged to the supernatural world 'something like Pathian' who were associated with human beings.

'AS THEY SAID': CHARACTERS OF *KAOSE* AND *DOI*

We have noted that *kaose*, *khawhring* or *ahmaw* are different terms used by different Kuki-Chin tribes, which mean a person who can so project or has the power to issue forth from time to time his/her astral bodies or spirit as to enter into or take possession of another person's body or those they wish to and devour [*pat* or bite] their internal organs, who, getting a severe stomach ache and falling into a trance, speaks with the voice of the original hostess (Hutton 1980: 155; Shakespear 1983: 111; Parry 1988: 462). We have also noted that the primary reason for their attack is 'envy'. They are always of 'an envious nature', who envy the delicious food and wealth of the others that they themselves did not have. It is significant to note that 'envy' is something which the stateless societies in the Kuki-Chin world wanted to stamp out in their society indicating the importance given to equality of all and freedom from any kind of envy which they considered was the source of social tension.

Hutton (1980: 155) also noted: 'Some Thado say that if a man is suffering from the attacks of a vampire, and his hair be cut off, it will be found, when he is recovered of the diseases, that his hair is intact and that of the vampire has been cut'. In Lushai Hills, Shakespear (1983: 112) also noted another significant character of *khawhring*. His informant had told him that 'presently all those who borrowed the *hnam* (a plaited cane band for carrying loads) of the girl with the Khawhring also got possessed'. This means, one can get *khawhring* (*kaose*) through the hair, that is, by sharing *nam* (cane-plaited band) and comb (*samthi*) with them. This is the main reason why tradition has strongly forbidden the sharing of *nam* and *samthi* with other people, especially with unknown persons. Shakespear (Ibid.) was also told by his informant of another channel through which *khawhring* can pass on from one to another. 'If one with a Khawhring has a daughter', his informant told him, 'the child is always possessed, so no one wants to marry a person with a Khawhring'. This means that *khawhring* is hereditary; it passes on from mother to daughter through the bloodline. This means that the male, husband and sons, were immune to *khawhring*. The idea of the hereditary factor is also shared by the belief among the Kukis and Lakhers, except that this hereditary character was not only from mother to daughters, but also to the sons and the spirit possessed even her husband. Among the Kukis, it continues to be the standing belief that a man who married a woman who is known as *kaose* also got possessed after they got the first son. But a woman, who married a man reputed to be *kaose* got possessed the moment she entered his house after marriage.

In Lushai Hills, Shakespear also noted another interesting case. He said that the Lushais believed that the *khawhring* girls sometimes 'walk in their sleep and go and lick up urine, as the metna do, under the zawlbuk, and that when starting forth on those expeditions their feet and hands shine as if they were coated with phosphorous. . . . This state is called "Thlahzung"' (1983: 112). This belief is also shared by the Kukis, who said that the *kaose* used to walk during the night in the form of fire-balls (*kao-mei,* 'ghost-fire'). According to the Kukis, such fire-ball are of two kinds. One is what they called *kao-mei* or 'ghost-fire'. Hutton identified *kao-mei* as 'the Will o' the wisp, as it consists in small pale moving fires and is regarded as harmless to human beings'.[1] Kukis also identify another fire-ball known to be *gam-kao* or 'jungle-ghost', which is dangerous to human beings. Hutton again noted: 'It appears in the night in the form of a much more powerful light, single and concentrated, but with some movement, as it swells and subsides'. Hutton (1980: 155) noted that his Kuki informant:

> . . . watched one in the jungle near Kohima; one was seen by a woman of Thenjol in 1916 or thereabouts, when she left her house at night. It was in the top of the tree and she ran back to her house in terror, fastened the door, and fainted. She recovered enough to tell her husband what she had seen, but was smitten with violent diarrhoea and vomiting and was dead by morning.

In the Chin Hills, there seem no clear distinction between an attack by 'evil eye' (*kaose*) and 'wizard' (*doithem*). People simply felt that a 'single glance' of those persons, whom they considered as possessing the evil eye or wizards 'is sufficient to bewitched them and who are capable of causing lizards to enter the body, balls of string to form in the stomach'. Carey & Tuck (2008: 200) noted of the Chins belief as,

> All ailments which are not understood are considered to be either the work of a spirit or a wizard, and all internal complications are thought to be due to the presence of a foreign body, which has been introduced in some mystic manner, and which most often takes the form of balls of hair or string, lizards, and rats.

From the above historical narratives, we may add some important characteristics assigned to the *kaose* in the present day. Apart from those characters of *kaose* noted above such as it is hereditary (parents to children), permanent (cannot be removed from those persons), contagious (sharing of comb and *nam*) and envious (always envying others goods and delicious food), one may add others here. We have seen that the victims of *kaose* usually experienced severe stomach ache and went into a state of 'trance', which come close to psychological or medical state of dissociative disorder particularly that of dissociative amnesia.[2] It is also said that the physical body of the *kaose* and the victim lies in coma, saliva oozing from the mouth and remains virtually in an unconscious state. Another belief said that distance is not a matter for the ferocious spirit to unleash an attack as it can traverse against time and space in the atmospheric zones. *Kaose* is also said to possess an astral ear. There is a saying *gun in akhen louleh kaose ten mithusei aja thei jiuve* (unless separated by Gun River the *kaose* could hear people who had spoken ill of them), meaning only a river can prevent the *kaose* from hearing what is said.

It is also said that a young suitor can know a *kaose* maiden whose beauty enhanced as the night gets older. It is also said that the third son or daughter of a family is immune to possession by *kaose.* It is not only hair, but any body parts of the victim that is cut-off or injured will appear in the *kaose* body but not in the victim after s/he recovers. *Kaose* that resides in a person dies when the host *kaose* died or vice versa. *Kaose,* it is again said, usually attack the weak (like children, women, or elderly) or sickly person whom they can win over. This means that *kaose* had to literally fight hard to enter a person's body and possess it and hence they avoid a healthy and strong person as they are, it is again said, not able to win them. The characteristics of *kaose* can go on indefinitely so much that the mental world of the Kukis is studded with fear and hate against them. The same is true of *doi*. This expressed itself in the form of societal responses to *kaose* or *doi*, the point that will now be taken up.

FEAR, HATE AND VENGEANCE: CRIMINALIZATION OF *KAOSE* AND *DOI*

The belief in *kaose* and *doi* was universal in the Kuki-Chin world. Shakespear (1983: 111), for instance, noted that the 'Lushais are firm believers in witchcraft' and 'the belief in Khawhring is universal'. Carey and Tuck (2008: 200) also noted that the 'Chins fully believe in witchcraft and the power of the evil eye'. As they came under the 'evil' category of the society, the struggle to stamp out *kaose* and *doi* was also one that is historical. No one can say for sure when it began and how exactly it took a shape. Nevertheless, *kaose* and *doi* had certainly assumed a position as one of the most dreaded 'evil' practices in the past just as it was the 'most disgusting people'. Hutton (1980: 155), for instance, noted that among the Thadou Kukis,

> Thado live in great dread of vampires, kaushi. . . . So great is their fear of persons reputed to have this power that *they will not as a rule on any account mention the name of a person as being a kaushi* for fear that if the vampire came to hear of it he would start to devour the person who had spoken ill of him. (emphasis mine).

Parry (1988: 463) also noted that, among the Lakhers '*Ahmaw* is greatly feared, and to accuse any one of being *ahmaw* is very serious defamation. The fine for falsely accusing any one of being *ahmaw* is a cow *mithun* or 60 rupees'. Among the Lushais, if a man accused another of being a wizard or *khawhringnei* and is unable to prove it he was liable to a fine of Rs. 40 (Parry 2009: 18). In the

Chin Hills, Carey and Tuck (2008: 200) also noted an extreme case in which the Chins believe that a 'single glance' by the so-called wizards or evil eye was 'sufficient to bewitch them'. They felt that the wizards or the evil eye 'are capable of causing lizards to enter the body, balls of string to form in the stomach, and to inflict any and all those afflictions which are *the evil gifts of the spirits*'. In this context of fear and terror, *kaose* and *doi* represents the 'evil gifts of the spirits' to human being and hence, became a constant neighbourhood nightmare. They had constantly haunted and tormented the minds of people over the ages as if they are criminals lurking all around for a prey.

It was under such circumstances of 'dread', 'fear', and 'terror' that societal response to *kaose* and *doi* needs to be situated. We have noted that 'envy' was central to the cause of their attack and it was this 'envy' that a non-state society was most biased against. Thus, the very association of *kaose* and *doi* with 'envy' turned the social temperature against them into what I would call 'hate'. A combination of fear and hate determined social action against the *kaose* and *doithem.* It was within this fear and hate paradigm that vengeance against the 'evil gifts of the spirits' and methods employed to get rid of them may be seen from a different social context. Among the Lakhers, people were so terrified by *ahmaw* that appeasement was apparently the norm. Among the Kukis, methods of both appeasement and violence were combined to deal with them. Violence dominated the response against the black art among the Lushais and the Chins. Let some of the historical evidences on these aspects of social response be discussed.

Among the Kukis, it has been seen that people were so scared that 'they will not as a rule on any account mention the name of a person as being a *kaose*' (Hutton 1980: 155). Even muttering the name of a person accused of *kaose* was extremely fearful. Keeping the secret 'within the wall' does not, however, foreclose their hatred for the *kaose.* Within the opaqueness and calm of the societal conspiracy of silence was an open domain of manoeuvering their mobility, their attack and their everyday life. A strong regime of vigilance, well-known to everyone, was therefore in place. One obvious area of regimented manoeuvering system was the institutionalization of the fear in the custom of marriage. The fear of them, aversion to avoid being one of them, was so strong that all possible measures were taken to avoid any marriage relationship with them. An inbuilt mechanism, the institutionalized fear in the marriage custom, was the system popularly known as *pute-chanu kijon.* The idea was to have a 'clean' (*atheng*) or 'known' partner and to avoid any nuptial relationship with a person related to *kaose.* It was also noted how sharing of *samthi* (comb) and *nam* (cane-plaited band for carrying load in basket) was strictly prohibited in the society as a measure to avoid the proliferation of *kaose* through the hairs.

In Lushai Hills, a similar hatred was shown toward the *khawhringnei.* Shakespear noted that 'no one wants to marry a person with a Khawhring' and no one would 'let a person possessed by a Khawhring enter [their] houses'. If a *khawhring* 'sits on the bed of a true Lushei she will certainly be fined a metna'. To avoid marrying them, to prevent them from entering their house, and to fine them if they sit on their bed, were indeed a more extreme form of social ostracism taking us to the level of the notion of 'untouchability' in Brahmanical social system. No wonder, Shakespear (1983: 111-12) was told by his Lushai informants that those 'possessed of Khawhring are *most disgusting people,* and before the foreigners came *they were always killed*'. Seeing them as 'most disgusting people' and 'killing' them always, if found was an extreme case of hatred that takes the subject close to the 'witch-hunting' pogrom in early modern Europe. Among the Lakhers, Parry (1988: 463) also noted the similar tenor of societal hatred towards the *ahmaw,* 'Any one who is *ahmaw* is unclean; and if a woman is believed to be *ahmaw,* nobody will marry her'. In Chin Hills, those who possess the power of 'evil eye' (*khawhring* or *kaose*) were not even looked at because the mere sight of them was considered 'sufficient to cause sickness and distress' (Carey & Tuck 2008: 200). Therefore, they avoided seeing those people accused of the evil eye or considered wizards. And worst, they wouldn't let those accused to enter their village, or as among the Lushais, killed them whenever they found them in their midst. This point will be dealt with shortly.

The contour of social responses to *kaose* can also be seen from the way they dealt with *kaotom* (those possessed/attacked). Among the Kukis, *kaose* was usually first appeased by offering what s/he wanted (or enived) from the victim. Rituals like *Saguojuon-kithoina* and *Sa-phephou* were performed. Offering ranging from food, clothes to certain property might be given so that *kaose* would spare the victim. But when such appeasement was refused, violence would invariably follow. The first step toward this violence was known as *kao-mat* (to catch), which means to hold the *kaose* tightly so that s/he would not run away. Certain methods were deployed such as *thoulen-khukhum* (holding under nets), holding by the toes, and so on. The identity of the *kaose* was invariably asked so that s/he could be attacked at his/her house, if possible. An application of pain was a means to force the *kaose* to 'reveal' (*kiphong*) or to 'leave' (*alha*) the victim. This process could go along with offering/appeasement. In the extreme situation, certain items such as the horn (say, *sasan-ki*) would be use 'to kill' the *kaose*. This violent step may involve killing of *kaose* in his/her house or through certain application of pains. As the latter could cause the death of the victim such extreme application of pain/torture was normally avoided.

In the absence of *thempu* to perform the necessary ritual, this violent measure was usually the first step after most Kukis had become Christian. But this was not the normal practice in olden days when every village had their *thempu* to do the necessary exorcism (*nodoh*). An extreme step prescribed in the olden days was known as *khengsumlhah*. It was a ritual performed by the *thempu* in which the spirit of the *kaose* was 'called upon' (*kou*) to an appointed place, that is, a hole impression (of a sharpened stump of certain tree call *khengthing*) on the ground like the *sum* (mortar). When the spirit came in the form of some insects to the appointed place to eat certain food items placed there, a fatal blow was given by *thempu's* assistant with the sharpened stump. The stump was then put into the ground and then covered with earth so that it was not visible to anyone. *Khengsumlhah* was considered to be an infallible cure for *kaotom*. It led to the death of the *kaose* and hence the cure.

The Lakher method was predominantly appeasement. When one was attacked by *ahmaw*, Parry mentioned four stages of ritual; each stage would be followed by the next if the *ahmaw* refuse to leave. In the first stage, little meat, rice, salt, chilies, beer, tobacco, nicotine water, bananas and other edibles were placed in a gourd spoon on which the victim spat. The spoon was put on the threshold of the house for a while and then placed at the foot of the house ladder. If the *ahmaw* refused to leave, the second step followed, in which a fowl was sacrificed and cut into half. The half with the head was cooked and with some gravy, salt and rice was placed on the plate on which the victim again spat as before. After putting it on the threshold for a while, it was taken outside the village fence.

If the *ahmaw* still refused to leave, the third step was performed in which small pig was killed and singed, again cut into half. The half with the head was set aside and placed in the verandah. The other half was cooked and put on the plate. In the meantime, clothes, ornaments, and property were collected. Two plates, one with cooked meat and the other with raw meat, were taken to the victim who spat again on them. They were, then, put on the threshold for a while, after which they were taken outside the village fence. The clothes and other things were taken back while the plates were abandoned there. If the *ahmaw* still refused the fourth and last step followed in which a little blood was drawn from the big toe of one of those present, smeared on a bit of stick and offered to the *ahmaw*. The patient licked some of the blood on the stick and the following incantation was made: 'O, *ahmaw*! We have offered you everything you want, and still you are not satisfied, so now we offer you human blood, which is what you most desire'. This was said to be an infallible cure for stomach ache caused by an *ahmaw*, and was the only Lakher sacrifice, in which human blood was used.[3]

In the Lushai Hills, it has been seen from its origin story that appeasement was also one method of exorcism against *khawhring* attack. It has been seen that people asked her certain questions. When they knew that she wanted eggs, they gave her eggs and 'she went away'. This is a familiar method common to all Kuki-Chin tribes. Shakespear also noted one account of violent method employed against *khawhring* among the Lushais. He remarked:

A missionary described to me a weird scene of excitement which he once saw, the object being to exorcise a Khawhring which had possessed a girl. Amid a turmoil of shouting, drum-beating, and firing of guns the spirits was ordered to quit its temporary abode and return whence it came (1983: 111-12).

Shouting, drum-beating, and firing of guns were means to scare the *khawhring* so that she 'quit' her temporary abode. Thus, a combination of force and blandishment method is used by most tribes against the *kaose* attack.

How was *doi* or witchcraft or wizardry (*doi-a-kibol*) dealt with then? One can see similar societal fear and hatred toward this 'evil' art as well. One has no account to show how the society had reacted to the black art among the Kukis. But, again, the tenor of their opposition to it can be gleaned from the cases of Lushai Hills. Shakespear, for instance, noted that in 1897 three whole families were 'massacred' because it was thought that they were 'bewitching' a very old chieftainess. 'The livers of the wizards were cut out and portions carried to the sufferer', remarked Shakespear, 'but unfortunately, she died before being able to taste them and thus prove the efficacy of the remedy'. The Lushais believed that the consumption of the liver of the wizard was the best remedy for any wizardry (Shakespear 1983: 109). McCall also cited one case in the village of chief Liankhama Sailo in about 1850. This village, Zawlnghak, had about 1,000 houses of which there were 150 houses of the Rangte (Gangte) clan. One day, Liankhma's 'most brave young man', Thangvuka, had a dream in which he saw Keitawna and on this very night his house was filled with smoke and mist of an unprecedented kind. Keitawna belonged to Gangte clan and had the reputation of being a *dawithem* or sorcerer. Hence, Thangvuka became 'so disturbed with the obvious implications of this dream' that he eventually killed Keitawna. He cut out Keitawna's liver and ate a little of it. His objective was, McCall remarked, 'to neutralize the effect of any evil words which Keitawna may have uttered against Thangvuka's welfare'.

Shortly after that, McCall went on narrating, 'all the Rangtes appeared before the chief in fury and in a spirit of revenge against Thangvuka'. They demanded from the chief 'to decide whether he wished the friendship of all the Rangtes or whether he preferred to lose them all that he should keep Thangvuka'. To their surprise, the chief decided in favour of Thangvuka and 'ordered that they should not kill Thangvuka'. With this reply, he noted:

> All the Rangtes packed up their families and chattels and made off to Manipur State swearing eternal enmity with one and all of Liankhama's villagers in perpetuity—a situation which persisted, resulting in the mutual taking of heads until peace was enforced by the arrival of the British Government (McCall 2003: 71-2).

McCall also cited another case in which Liankara and Kanglova, two brothers of Dokhuma Sailo, chief of Chawntleng, were suffering from phthisis [tuberculosis]. They suspected that certain men of their village were the cause, casting a spell through sorcery. These men had been previously known, while they were under the influence of Zu, to have threatened others by claiming to possess supernatural power. The chief decided that the 'accused should be killed'. Therefore, Leta, Leta's mother, Buka and Vungbakira were all killed while the fifth Laikuala fled to Hnachang village where, however, he was at once killed, as the Hnachang chief was related to Dokhuma and knew the circumstances. The sick brothers were given pieces of dead men's livers and 'were eventually cured, while all the villagers drank of the blood as a prophylactic against any further spread of the dread disease which had, they believed, originated in the evil works of the sorcerers' (McCall 2003: 72-3).

The subject of witchcraft had harassed the society so much that the British administration was often dragged to a disquieting 'law and order' problem. Thus, since from the inception, the colonial administrators initiated a certain line of policy to tackle the recurring problems in local society infested with the idea of witchcraft and sorcery. McCall, for instance, noted that 'on occasions when *a stir* was being caused by the presence of a suspected sorcerer' the district administrators used to order that the chief should not issue any 'sanction of murder'. But 'in order to relieve the people in their present very real anxieties he would give the suspected sorcerer twenty-four hours in which to make himself scarce, the man, or woman, being ordered to seek shelter in a village over a hundred mile or so distant'. Meaning: expelling them from such a village in order to avoid any 'murder' of them by the enraged/charged crowd that would cause a greater embarrassment to the administration.

McCall (2003: 72-3) went on record to say,: 'It is admitted that not every society similarly situated would have been willing to condone this merciful settlement [wizards family] and the murder of the five victims detailed above may mark the true feelings of the people'. Truly, 'murder' or death was the result of the fatal wrath against the 'merciful' wizards and *kaose.* Indeed, that marked 'the true feelings of the people' against the 'evil' (*athenglou*) practice. 'So strong was the feeling about these wizards', Shakespear (1983: 109) also remarked, 'that four or five households of their relatives had to be given a special and isolated site, as no village would receive them'. Parry (1983: 18) also noted that,

> *Dawi* is magic and a *Dawithiam* is a wizard. In the old days, if a man accused another of being wizard, he would probably have been murdered by the person he accused. If a man could clearly be shown to be a wizard, no chief would allow him into his village and he would have had nowhere to live.

The feeling of hatred against them was so great that many of them, having been boycotted by the society, were forcibly dragged toward Christianity, when the missionaries accepted them. It is evident that some of the early Christians in Lushai Hills were those who had been boycotted by the society as *khawhringnei* or wizards.[4] They constituted the early population of the 'Christian villages'. Evidence also suggested that this belief had also been utilized by some chief as a tool to expel some well-to-do families in the village. Parry (2009: 18), for instance, remarked, 'In the old days chiefs were given to accusing well-to-do people of being *Dawithiam* or *Khawhringnei* as then they could turn them out of their villages and confiscate their property'.

One can see similar response from the people of Chin Hills. Here, people hardly differentiated between *kaose* and witchcraft; both are equally feared and hated. Carey and Tuck, for instance, noted that the Chins have begged their permission 'to shoot individuals who have the misfortune to be pronounced wizards'. When they were told that British 'do not admit of the spilling of blood except when blood has been intentionally spilled', the Chins replied that the customs of the British 'are most unjust and protect the wizard who is allowed to practice his uncanny occupation in peace and who kills people right and left, but, because he spills no blood, we take no notice'. This means that, as in Lushai Hills, death was the societal response to anyone who is declared wizard or possessing the evil eye. If not to kill them was considered 'unjust', then killing them was consider to be the 'just' way to deal with them. What is even more interesting in the Chin's notion of witchcraft and evil eye was that accusation was not restricted to individuals alone; they also believed that the all members of a certain tribe or community were wizards and had the evil eye so that they took all measures 'not to see' them or mingle with them in any manner. This is also shared by other tribes but less intensely than among the Chins. This latter point will be dealt with shortly.

Thus, one can see that *kaose* and *doi* had really become a nightmare to the local society in the past. They were feared and hated as if they were criminals. This was translated into a mixture of collective societal response ranging from the refusal to let them enter into the house or village, preventing their gaze, refusal to arrange nuptial relationship with them, debar them from cultural and ritual events to killing them. Whenever they were caught in their alleged attack on other persons, they were either appeased by being offered something or subjected to violent methods even to the point of death, expulsion from the village, and so on. In other words, a combination of force and blandishment method was used to deal with *kaose* and *doithem.*

MYTH OR REALITY: UNDERSTANDING *KAOSE* AND *DOI*

The pertinent question then is—how is one going to understand these historical accounts of *kaose* and *doi*? Did they really exist or was it a mere social construct? Several studies on witchcraft around the world show that it was neither an 'art' nor a 'practice'. It was merely a 'social construct', whose reality lies in societal urge for supernatural explanations of worldly ailments. Studies on European witchcraft show that such ideas gained popularity since the late sixteenth and early seventeenth century. Certain factors were found to be responsible for the upsurge in the idea of witchcraft such as the intense religious (Christian) awakening of the sixteenth century and an exposure to frequent famine, plague, poverty and crime. The new religious fevour sharpened the idea of the devil's intervention in human affairs. Certain people were thought to be entering into a 'compact' with the former and received super-natural power to enable them to practise black magic and commit secret killing. The increasing human calamities due to famine, plague, poverty and crime lend support to such religious idea as society was still lacking science and medicine to define such recurring calamities. Hence, there was an intense craving for supernatural explanations and cures for personal or community disasters.

Interesting cases were excavated from the social experiences. The accusers and accused generally knew each other well and were usually neighbours who had quarrelled. Often trouble started when someone begged for food. In France and Switzerland, beggars who were denied charity were likely to accuse their ungenerous neighbours of witchcraft. In England, beggars who were denied charity or rejected by neighbours were blamed for local calamities and charged with witchcraft. In both the cases, witchcraft was the product of the breakdown of neigbourhood relationship when people were desperately poor and hungry. In other words, witchcraft was the result of a neighbourhood tension. In this, women were the usual victims for some familiar reasons. They were thought to be spiritually weaker (as in the Adam and Eve story in the Bible) so that demonology was conceived of in explicitly sexual terms—female witches fornicating with the devil for favour. Women identified as witches were generally socially objectionable persons (old, humble, ugly and poor). They were generally convicted of witchcraft mainly due to the inhuman torture procedure applied during interrogation in which they were forced to say 'yes'. To the rich and higher class witch hunting was politically and socially safe as they were hardly implicated, so witch hunting went on and caused havoc in the lives of several thousands of the weak, the poor and the hapless.

Thus, one can see that intense religious awakening, an exposure to the wrath of nature, the growing neighbourhood and social tensions, and gender disparity have all played a pivotal role in the proliferation of the idea of witchcraft in early modern Europe. In conceptualizing European witchcraft, Eva Pocs (1999), for instance, identified three varieties of witches in popular belief, 'neighbourhood witch' or 'social witch', 'magical' or 'sorcerer' witch, and 'supernatural' or 'night' witch. 'Neighbourhood witches' were the product of neighbourhood tensions, and found only in self-sufficient serf village communities where the inhabitants relied largely on each other. Such accusations followed the breakdown of some social norms and exchange. Claims of 'sorcerer' witches and 'supernatural' witches could arise out of social tensions, but not exclusively. 'Sorcerer' witches were persons who had, through magic, increased their fortune to the perceived detriment of a neighbouring household. Due to neighbourly or community rivalries and the ambiguity between positive and negative magic, such individuals could be labelled as witches. The 'supernatural' witch had nothing to do with communal conflict, but expressed tensions between the human and supernatural worlds and in Eastern and Southeastern Europe such supernatural witches became an ideology explaining calamities that befell entire communities. It is from the context of this European background that we may be able to know more clearly about the cases in the Kuki-Chin world. A brief discussion on the social and political background, therefore, becomes pertinent.

SOCIAL AND POLITICAL BACKGROUND

With such burgeoning knowledge on witchcraft, the question is—where do we put *kaose* or *doi* of Kuki-Chin cultural world in the historical context? It would be too early to give a concrete answer to the pertinent question that we put to ourselves as to whether *kaose* is a myth or reality. Nevertheless, situating the belief in historical context would certainly generate some dividends toward that end. First, although we have certain reference of a very old tradition (Santhuh *kaose* or *guldu* origin of *kaose*) what becomes a more common genre among the Kukis was the *selpaothei* origin of *kaose* which traced its landscape of memory in the Chin Hills. The emptiness of *kaose* in any other older traditions, be it folklore, folk tales, legends, myths and so on, makes the *selpao* tradition even more significant. The Lushei tradition of *dawi* origin also lends support to the *selpao* tradition. The Lushai tradition placed River Barak (Tuilong) from where the art of black magic had eventually fallen into the hands of human beings (the Lhangum Kukis) from where Lushais also learned it. Such origin stories may appear 'absurd' in the eyes of scientific history, but something was certain here. They pointed out that the idea of *doi* and *kaose* gained popularity when the Kukis lived in a particular geographical space called Chin Hills.

The traditions should be taken as a topographical metaphor in which a cartographic recollection of the past had a significant social dimension of the 'art' in question. It is a well-established fact in history that the so-called 'new Kukis' (Chin, Kuki and Mizo) escaped to the Chin Hills from Burma plain in about thirteenth and fourteenth centuries. Although the advance groups (mostly 'old Kuki groups') might have gone there many centuries before. The advance party of the 'new' groups might have already reached Barak River corridor somewhere in the fifteenth and sixteenth century, because it was during this time that Tripura court chronicles had a mention of the Kukis who had close relationship with that kingdom.[5] If *kaose* and *doi* traditions trace its origin to the period around this time, it certainly gained its popularity in the eighteenth century in a situation when the Kuki-Chin world witnessed one of the most stressing social and political turmoil in their history.[6]

In about the middle of eighteenth century, the Chins got firearms made in the west from Burma through the trade channel. This had provided them with an edge over other communities who had been till then living together with them in a geographical space at the centre of present Chin Hills although their population spread out sparsely till part of the present Mizoram and Manipur hills. Thus, by breaking the balance of power at the core of their world, the Chins began to follow a policy of war and conquest over other tribes/clans. The Hakas, Falams and Suktes emerged dominant over the present Chin Hills, whereas the Lushais, Thadous and other tribes had to either submit before the new conquerors or migrate to other places. The Lushais migrated to the Lushai Hills in about 1810 and very soon built-up their hegemony over the whole Hills, subjugating or expelling those tribes/clans who lived there. This situation of internecine warfare, deaths, subjugation, absorption and criss-crossing flights and migration strongly shattered the social and cultural landscape of the Kuki-Chin world. From each tribe/clan to another or often from one village to another, everyone seems to have been at war and contestation.

Unlike in the calm of their earlier settlements, each village now consisted of a mixture of different clans and tribes. The village community was generally divided into the ruler and ruled or the dominant/prevailing chiefly clan and the subjugated/absorbed clans. William McCulloch (1980: 58), for instance, aptly noted this changing social composition in the Kuki villages:

> Since their expulsion from their own hills, the different tribes have become *mixed up together* in villages situated in positions selected with reference to convenience of cultivation . . . a popular chief is sure seen by accessions from less favoured ones to become large, but its inhabitants will remain in it is *uncertain*, for the *ties* by which they were held together in their native hills have been *rudely broken*, that they have scarcely existence, and any whim may lead them to another village. (emphasis mine)

This situation was even more markedly noticeable in the Lushai Hills and the Chin Hills where there were good numbers of large villages sprouting up by the additional number of subjugated population consisted of mixed clans. The Haka population, for instance, consisting of almost entirely the 'Chiefs and slaves', the chiefs being drawn together by the need of controlling their 'powerful dependents' (Carey & Tuck 2008: 202 & 204). Falam was divided into six quarters under six 'Elders' and Haka into several quarters under different chiefs. Interestingly, there was a 'royal' quarter called 'Boto quarter' in Falam where the five council men lived with their retinues (Carey & Tuck 2008: 149-50). The Lushai Hills, a large village, which contained mixed population, was divided into several quarters or *veng* generally inhabited by people of the same clan, each having its *zawlbuk* (bachelor's dormitory) (Shakespear 1983: 20).

One can now well imagine the social situation in such villages where rulers and subjugated population lived together. Truly, the concentration of a large number of 'mixed' populations in such villages had indeed 'rudely broken' the earlier 'ties by which they were held together in their native hills'. These 'broken' social ties were not only the source of political 'uncertainties' to the prevailing chiefly clans but also the root of conflict and neighbourhood tensions in the village. With warfare, death, subjugation, displacement and flight becoming regular phenomena through the eighteenth and nineteenth centuries, scarcity and poverty, and hence, many unwanted social elements such as the poor, orphans, widows, destitute, and so on, also escalated in the society. The overwhelming neighbourhood tensions, social conflicts, and community disengagements eventually produced a situation where each of them, individually and in groups, suspected the others, especially the weak and minorities, for all mischievous acts whenever any personal or community disaster fell upon them. The increasing human calamities due to warfare, deaths, poverty, diseases, crime and the lack of science and medicines to explain, define, and cure such calamities led to an intense craving for supernatural explanations and cures. Thus, all sicknesses and human calamities that befell individuals and the community, were considered to be due to interventions of the spirits. Carey and Tuck, for instance noted, 'The people fully believe that spirits seize and maltreat them, and when a man explains that he has been knocked down and badly mauled by a spirit, no one can convince him otherwise, though we put the occurrence down to fainting and other kinds of fits' (2008: 198). The village *thempu* or *puithiem* (wise men or medicine men, as they were known and who claimed to understand what the spirit wants) would be invariably consulted for the cures. The role of supernatural power was not only highly suspected for human disasters but was often sought after as a social therapy by way of appeasement through a *thempu.* In a worst case scenario, certain people such as *kaose* and *doithem* were believed to have the power to control some supernatural powers. Thus, whenever a certain disaster took place in the society certain people would not only be suspected but also be accused for the calamity. The accused people became *kaose* or *doithem* in the local society and if the accusation was proved they would invariably be punished. Therefore, it is within such distressing social and political circumstances that the gaining popularity of black magic or witchcraft (*doi*) and *kaose* or evil eye must be best situated.

The gaining momentum in the belief in *kaose* and *doi* generated an interesting social dimension on the subject. The number of *kaose* and *doithem* increased when the society was undergoing crisis not because more and more people became one of them but because the society had produced more and more of them out of social tensions within the village society as well as between two or more villages, clans and tribes. Here, politics and power relations played a vital role. At one level, the neighbourhood tensions in the village led to the accusation of, and the criminalization of the weak, the poor, and the hapless innocent individuals as being in control of the spirits to cause harm on the dominant and powerful. At another level, conflict between villages, clans, or tribes also ended up in accusing each other for all the disasters that befell their community. This led to criminalizing each other as *kaose* or *doithem.* As in the village society, such accusation between villages, clans, and tribes also took the direction in which the powerful tribe accused the weaker tribe. Thus, in both the cases such accusations were closely related to power and social relation in a nutshell. These form of defaming, criminalizing and labelling the weaker 'others' as *kaose* or *doithem* by the more powerful persons, clans or tribes merely on political and social ground is what one called the politics of defamation, the point one shall now come to.

POLITICS OF DEFAMATION: *KAOSE* AND *DOI* AS PRODUCT OF NEIGHBOURHOOD TENSION

A few historical accounts suggested that the growing popularity of the belief in *kaose* and *doi* (when the society was undergoing crisis) was the product of neighbourhood tension in the village society. The intense belief in the idea of black magic and *kaose* due to the growing tensions in the society transformed them to be a neighbourhood nightmare. This nightmare had haunted both the one and the many, the rulers and the ruled, the powerful and the weak, so that whenever disaster fell on anyone they invariably turned towards some supernatural power as the cause and also for the solution. As it was believed that such supernatural powers had been under the control of certain persons called *kaose* and *doithem*, whenever personal or community disaster occurred certain people would be eventually accused for the plot. Yet, interestingly the evidence suggested that the idea of *kaose* and *doi* had been rampantly employed as an effective instrument of social control and oppression by the powerful, the haves, and the one, against the weak, the poor and minority clans/tribes. Evidence suggested that the powerful chiefs or members of the prevailing clan in the village often used this social rhetoric as a handy tool to criminalize, punish and oppress the weak and minority clans (*khochaga*) in the village.

Thus, the Lushai chiefs were said to have condemned certain well-to-do people in their village as *dawithiem* or *khawhringnei* so that they could expel them from the village and, according to Lushai custom, take possession of their properties. Similarly, the weaker and marginal clan(s) in the village (the *phungchaga*) would always be the victims of the wrath of the members of the dominant clan(s). Whenever any disaster fell on any or all members of the dominant clan, these 'merciful' clan(s) would not only be suspected but also, in most cases, accused of using black magic or sorcery against them. Thus, one sees that the minority Gangte clan of Zawlnghak village were 'reputed' to be wizards, not because they possessed such a black art but because they were accused of having it. A strange happening in a house or dreaming of one of them was sufficient evidence to proclaim them as wizards. Such a declaration was invariably followed by murdering one of them and then an expulsion from the village. One also sees that whenever any incurable sickness befell members of the dominant or chiefly clan, the weaker and poorer family or clans would normally be blamed for the cause through wizardry. Thus, an attack of tuberculosis on two of the chief's brothers led to the barbaric murder of five members of a poor family whose livers were eaten and blood were drunk by the whole village. And, the illness of an aged chieftainess in 1897 led to the massacre of three whole families who were suspected of 'bewitching' her and their livers were cut out and portions carried to the victim.

On the other hand, it has also been seen that certain persons who belonged to the poorer class or of the minority clan could use the social rhetoric of *aoi* or *kaose* to defend themselves from any tyrannical control of the powerful. Certain persons who were accused of being wizards had threatened others of possessing supernatural power that eventually led to their death in the hands of the intolerant powerful class. One can see that before the gory massacre of five members of the family took place, these persons were seen to have 'threatened' other people against their possession of supernatural power. In this sense, the public rhetorical space on the notion of black magic or *kaose* was often utilized by the weak and powerless in the village community as an instrument to warn or threaten the dominant and powerful class not to take them lightly. It could be a means to evade any tyrannical dealing of the chiefly clan.

Besides, if certain wizards were 'reputed' magicians before they were murdered, it is also possible to think that they could have been popular magicians or wizards in the local society for some good reasons such as in healing certain ailments. Otherwise, they would have been killed a long time back. They were murdered now mainly because the powerful might have been envious of their popularity in the local society or of their gaining wealth. The fact that the whole Gangte clan members rose up in protest against the murder of their kinsman Keitawna have shown that the latter was either not a wizard at all or that he could be a popular magician who served the local society for some positive reasons. In this context, it was not on a mere suspicion that he had been murdered by a young warrior but it could have been a sinister design by the chiefly clan to eliminate him in the local society. The protection given by the chief to the murderer, his most powerful warrior and his acceptance of Gangte migration to Manipur (which was normally disliked by most chiefs) lends support to this argument. Thus, one can see that *kaose* and witchcraft were the product of local and neighbourhood tensions and closely related to social and power relation in the village society. The breakdown of traditional ties among different social groups (tribal, clans, families or individual) and the dominance of tense social relationship among them, eventually produced more and more of what was consider to be witchcraft and *kaose*.

The fact that it was only women that the *khawhring* could possess is again significant. This takes one to the important subject of gender that dominated the notion of European witchcraft. Thus, it was women who were at the receiving end of the male-dominated patriarchal society. The fact that *khawhring* could be only women shows that the 'evils' of the society could be performed only by women. If any woman was known as *khawhring* (or *ahmaw* or *kaose*), then 'no one wants to marry' them, no one would let them enter their houses, they would 'certainly be fined a metna' if she sat on the bed of someone, and worst 'they were always killed'. They were said to be the 'most disgusting people' in the society as the witches of early modern Europe. Thus, the patriarchal society saw women as the 'weaker' section of society and hence was vulnerable to having relationship with supernatural powers in order to put herself on an equal footing with the men. The male dominated societal angar over the *khawhring* was therefore the male act against ambitious women. In this way, unfortunate and hapless women were often criminalized and accused of being *khawhring* or *kaose* whenever some human calamities were experienced by certain members of the society.

POLITICS OF DEFAMATION: *KAOSE* AND *DOI* AS PRODUCT OF COMMUNITY CONFLICTS

Evidence also suggested that the growing popularity of *kaose* and *doi* were also largely the product of social or community tensions. The inter- and intra-tribal warfare and conflict across the hills, as noted earlier, generated a strong sense of hatred towards each other. This resulted in labelling each other as wizards or *kaose* to defame and criminalize them as the 'most disgusting people' in the society. What was significant in this politics of defamation among different tribes/clans is that it followed a certain unique pattern. The political relationship between different tribes was apparently central to this pattern. One can see that it was always the powerful tribe who accused the weaker tribe(s) as wizards and *kaose* or casting the evil eye. But interestingly, such accusation was hardly reciprocated by the latter tribe. Instead, the latter tribe would declare that they were not wizards or had the evil eye but passed on the bug of defamation to the tribes who were weaker than them or whom they considered as inferior to them. This would be repeated by the latter tribe/clan in the same manner. Thus, the accusation went on, following a particular direction based on the power matrix across the hills until it dovetailed and proliferated among the mixed population of the village *vengs* (colony). It was in this mixed colony where one saw that such accusation had become fashionable as a social therapy to sickness believed to be caused by malevolent spirits and was mainly directed towards the innocent *khochaga* or *phung-chaga* (the weak, the poor, the minority clans, and the women).

At the pan-tribal level, one has already noted the power grid and political matrix across the Kuki-Chin world where the Chins (Hakas, Falams and Suktes) and Pois (of Lushai Hills) had emerged victorious over other tribes like Yahows, Siyins, Lushais, Thadous and so on. The Lushais, in their turn defeated the Thadous and other 'old Kuki tribes' of Lushai Hills. The Thadous were successful in establishing themselves as the paramount power over many of the Naga tribes in the present hills of Manipur. One can see that the politics of defamation more or less followed this matrix of power relationship. To understand this power matrix, it would be proper to begin with the way in which the plain dwellers of Burma thought about the people living in the margins of the valley, in the Chin Hills. To the 'civilized' and powerful Shans/Burmese population of Burma plains, the Chins who lived in the margins of the valley were infamously known as 'necromancers' and 'sorcerers' whose mere glance was thought to have caused sickness and even death.[7] But, such an accusation was flatly denied by the Chins. The Chins, although they strongly believed in 'witchcraft' and 'evil eye', would instead declare that they did not practise or possess the 'evil' art but said that all the other tribes around them such as the Siyins, Yahows, and many of the Lushais were proficient with it. Carey and Tuck (2008: 200), for instance, noted this clearly:

> The Chins fully believe in witchcraft and the power of the evil eye. The Hakas and independent southerners are particularly bad in this respect and consider that the Siyins, Yahows, and many of the Lushais are wizards, whose single glance is sufficient to bewitch them and who are capable of causing lizards to enter the body, balls of string to form in the stomach, and to inflict any and all those afflictions which are the evil gifts of the spirits.

Parry (1988: 465) also noted that the 'Chins also believe in witchcraft and the evil eye, especially among people belonging to other tribes'. Phayre also noted that this existed among the Lungkhes and Tseindus of Arakan (Chins/Pois by Lushais) declaring that 'We do not practice witchcraft, but other people around us do'.[8] Such charges of defamation had been firmly grounded in the minds of the people so much so that whenever a disaster/sickness befell anyone they would immediately blame those people they defamed and criminalized as wizards or having the evil eye. Carey and Tuck, for instance, mention an interesting case on this count. One Surgeon-Major Newland had once told them the story of a Chin who came to him and 'complained that *a rat had entered his stomach at the glance of a Yahow* and he went to hospital quite prepared to die'. This man was given 'an emetic and reported in the morning that he had vomitted up the rat in the night and he then went home happy and cured' (Carey and Tuck 2008: 200). Shakespear (1983: 110) also noted another interesting case when he, with Captain Hall, forced their way to Haka in 1890 to join General Symons. He said that 'the chiefs of that village [Haka] besought the General not to allow any of our Lushai followers to go within sight of it, lest they should, by merely looking at it cause *fearful misfortunes*'. Carey and Tuck (2008: 200) also mention another similar case in 1893.

In 1893, when a Lushai officer came to Haka to take over the mules, he was accompanied by Lushai coolies, who strolled down to the village to chat; their approach was marked by *a stampede of the women*, who fled to the fields or hid in the houses and who afterwards explained that the mere sight of one of these Lushais was sufficient to cause sickness and distress (emphasis mine).

Accusing a particular person when one falls ill just because he belongs to a particular community (say Yahows or Lushais) or preventing them from entering their village or a 'stampede' to get rid of them, when they come for a friendly 'chat', are extreme cases to show that such politics of defamation and criminalization of a community had eventually become naturalized and a cultural reality in the minds of the accusers when the accused remain innocent and clean.

Similarly, the Lakhers (Pois), who were also another powerful tribe of Lushai Hills and who had 'pressed' the Lushais northward, also considered other tribes around them in the same manner. Parry (1988: 465), for instance, noted:

> Black magic which is known as *deu* or in Savang as *thaihna,* is also much feared by the Lakhers, who say that though *there are no magicians in the Lakher country,* there are many among the Tlaikopa (Lushais), Tikupa (Tipperahs), Takangpa (Chakmas) and Kalaspa (Mughs). In consequence, the Lakhers are very careful of their behavior when travelling among these peoples. (emphasis mine)

Parry also noted one interesting case, where he found the Lakhers acting in a similar fashion, as we see in the Chin Hills, against the Lushais. He remarked:

> When I first took some of the Lakher chiefs into Aijal they absolutely refused to go into any of the villages we passed through on the way, or to go and dine or drink with any of the Lushai chiefs, though they received several invitations, as they were afraid of being enchanted. They believe that the magicians put some substance, possibly an insect or a small stone, into food or drink, and that this eats the internal organs and so causes death. (Parry 1988: 465) (emphasis mine)

Absolute refusal to enter the Lushai's villages or 'to go and dine or drink' with them despite receiving several kind 'invitations', is again another extreme case of how criminalization of a particular tribe had become a social realism. Thus, in the Chins and Lakher's world view, the Lushais were undoubtedly known as the infamous wizards and sorcerers.

But surprisingly, such accusations were never reciprocated by the Lushais. Instead, they passed on the bug of defamation to other tribes whom they considered as inferior or weaker to them and exonerated themselves from such charges of defamation by declaring that they did not practice witchcraft and magic. Thus, the Lushais declared that there was no witchcraft or wizards among them but said that the tribes to the north of them were 'very proficient'. Parry (1988: 465), for instance, noted that the 'Lushais in the same way say that though there are no Lushai magicians there are many among the Thados'. Shakespear (1983: 110) also noted clearly how the bug of defamation was passed on from Chins to Lushais and then to other smaller tribes: 'The Lushais maintain that the tribes to the north of them, such as Paihte, Bete &c., are very proficient at witchcraft, while the Chins consider the Lushais such experts at the craft'.

It has already been noted how the Lushai tradition claimed that they learned the art of witchcraft from the Lhangum (Kuki) clans indicating the fact that it was not they, but the Kukis who were proficient in the art. True to the matrix of the politics of defamation, the Thadou-Kukis would not, again, reciprocate with relation to the Lushais but pass on the bug to the weaker tribes like Koms whom they claimed as proficient in the black art. The Thadous were particularly bad in considering all the Nagas as *kaose,* a defamation that is extreme in their world view. Hence, the defamation went on and on. Parry (1988: 465, fn. 1) remarked at this prevailing politics of defamation in the Kuki-Chin world lucidly, 'All the Lushai Kuki tribes seem to be fond of accusing their neighbours of practising wizardry and witchcraft, while maintaining that they themselves are guiltless of these practices'. Considering the damaging consequences of being labelled as witchcraft and *kaose*, every tribe would do anything to show that they were 'guiltless of the practices'. Hence, passing on the bug to other tribes was one strategy for the same reason.

The matter being a serious charge of defamation, such accusation between different tribes/clans/villages, at times, caused warfare and bloodshed. This happened in a situation, when accusation took place between two tribes/clans/villages, who were equally powerful or who considerd themselves on the same plank in the power matrix. The Suktes, who were mainly responsible for pushing the Thadou-Kukis toward the north from Chin Hills and who were victorious by conquering most of the Kuki villages up to the valley of Manipur, for instance, accused the latter as *kaose* and wizards. But this had caused heavy bloodshed between the two tribes. It was said that the Kukis could not take the charge of defamation lightly and responded with attacks on the Suktes (also known as Kamhows). This was popularly known among them as *Suhte gal* that centred primarily on the question of such defamation charges. Carey and Tuck noted one interesting case of how the Chins felt about the Kukis. During their political tour in the Chins Hills they found 'some tall stone pillars still standing' on the original site of the Chassad Kukis (or Taksatte by the Chins). But, when they asked the Chins about the pillars 'they were silent, or said they did not know'. But afterwards, a friendly Chin 'quietly whispered' and told them, 'Those stones at Taksat were set up by the spirits: but do not tell anyone that I have told you so, as the spirits would be avenged on me if they hear that I have done so' (Carey & Tuck 2008: 199). Even after the Chassads left their original sites, the Chins were still in great fear of the spirits which were worshipped or under the control of the Chassads. This, in fact, was a clear case in which the politics of defamation as *kaose* and *doithem* had been so deeply ingrained in their minds that even the remains/relics of them (such as stone pillars) were still feared. The case between two equally powerful villages within the same tribe or between different clans was a similar one. Thus, in 1870, the Guites under their chief Sumkam attacked 'a Manipuri village' (possibly the village belong to the Thadous), noted Shakespear, 'to avenge a charge of being wizards [read as *kaose*]' (Shakespear 1983: 143).

The fact that certain tribes were not targeted with similar charges of defamation whereas certain other tribe/clan/village were not only targeted but also attacked for the same charge, is a significant marker to what is called the power matrix between them. One can see that an accusation on the ground of *kaose* or witchcraft had indeed amounted to declaration of war. An attack and bloodshed usually followed when such accusation was made between two equals. The fact that the weaker tribe refused to reciprocate the same charge made on them to their accuser, invariably the more powerful tribe, but simply passed on the bug to the weaker tribe was strictly in keeping with this power matrix. The fear of an attack from a more powerful tribe/clan in case of reciprocation and the safety from any such attack from the weaker tribe when accused, led to what is known of the politics of defamation. In other words, such politics of defamation was politically and socially secure to them. It was politically safe because it prevented an attack or bloodshed from both the powerful and weaker tribe/clan/village. Socially, it saved the accusing tribe/community from the charge of wizardry or *kaose* as if the bug was passing on to the weaker tribe/clan while they remained 'guiltless'.

But more importantly, the politics of defamation was also politically and socially motivated. Politically, because the charge of defamation was motivated mainly by political/community conflicts between two or more tribes/clans/villages. In labelling the 'enemy' tribes/clans/villages with such a powerful instrument of defamation the accuser wanted to show that they were a more powerful and dominant tribe than the accused. It was something like a slap on the face of the defeated tribe, a criminalization of the worst kind, so that they would never rise again to prominence. Sequel to the first, it was also motivated socially because the accuser felt that they were at the higher level of the civilizational ladder. To declare the enemy tribe as unwanted or evil people (*athenglou*) was not only a means to proclaim oneself as 'clean' and 'guiltless' (*atheng*) but also a civilizational tool to pronounce the 'others' as crude, coarse and uncouth. To proclaim someone as 'uncivilized' is a means to proclaim oneself as cultured and civilized. Thus, to the Burmese, the Chins were 'necromancers' and 'sorcerers' because they were, in their opinion, uncultured people who lived beyond the pale of civilization. To a civilized people, 'necromancers' and 'sorcerers' were ways of terming 'others' as 'savage', 'barbarians' and 'uncivilized hordes'. In this context, such a charge of defamation was actually motivated civilizationally. It was largely within this civilizationally framed charge that the politics of defamation need to be located.

For instance, the politically victorious Haka and Falam Chins felt that other tribes around them were uncivilized and uncultured. Vumson (1986: 5), for instance, noted that the Hakas, in their 'arrogant social posture' above the others, understood or used the generic term 'Zo' to mean their relatively 'uncultured' and 'uncultivated' people of southern Haka division. This 'arrogant social posture' towards the other tribes was therefore central to the politics of defamation. Thus when the Chins accused the Lushais, Yahows, Siyins, Thadous and so on of being infamous wizards and having the evil eye whose 'single glance is sufficient to bewitched them and who are capable of causing lizards to enter the body, balls of string to form in the stomach', they actually meant to defame them as uncultured and uncivilized people. This was simply a means to 'cleanse' themselves of the bug of defamation caused to them by the plain dwellers as well as to proclaim themselves as an advanced, cultured and civilized people over and above other tribes. The same attitude was shared by all tribes towards their politically inferior tribes such as Lushais to Thadous, Paites, Bete and so on and Thadous to Koms, Nagas, etc. Thus, from such politics of defamation on the ground of *kaose* and *doi* one can clearly see how the civilizational notion of the plain dwellers (the state people) had eventually climbed the hills among the tribes (the non-state people). In this, political relation between different tribes was central. Therefore, the passing of the defamation bug from one tribe to another was indeed the passing of the cultural notion of things in history instead of being the existence of something in reality.

KAOSE AND *DOI* AS A SOCIAL CONSTRUCT

It is too early to go for any hard line conclusion from the historical tour into the dark world of *kaose* and *doi*. The little evidence that is put up here still runs the hazard of counter opinion from the century old belief and character of the black art. None the less, the few materials that we could ponder upon suggested, in clear terms, certain definite ideas on the subject for further investigation and sustained debate. One can see that the belief in *kaose* and *doi* proliferated and stayed on in the society as a privileged cultural/civilizational tool of the powerful against the weak, as an instrument of control and domination by the dominant community on the hapless poor, minority clans and women. In other words, it was merely the product of social and political tensions between different and warring tribes/clans/villages/individuals. Lacking reason, science, and medicine, all ailments were traditionally believed to be caused by the interventions of supernatural powers such as malevolent spirits. But the new idea (that probably gained ground when they were in the Chin Hills) that some of these 'spirits' were under human control made things worse than anticipated. *Doithem* (variously known as magician, wizard, sorcerer, witchcraft, etc.) and *kaose* (variously known as vampire, evil eye, witchcraft, etc.) were two powerful human figures that emerged powerfully in Kuki-Chin world view. The growing tensions between different social groups across this country in the eighteenth and nineteenth centuries provided a fertile breeding ground or a congenial social and political atmosphere for the growth of numbers of accused *doithem* and *kaose.*

In this context, *kaose* and *doi* were merely a social construct which had become popular as an effective and powerful instrument of defamation by the powerful vis-à-vis the weak. Accusing someone as the 'most disgusting people' in the society was merely a political and social tool not only to defame the 'enemy' as uncultured and uncultivated, but also to cleanse oneself from the bug or the 'guilt' of similar defamation charge made on them by more powerful neighbours. This idea percolated at the level of tension-ridden village community where it was found that the powerful and chiefly clan(s) used it as a weapon to kill, to expel from the village, to devastate, to control, or to oppress the innocent minority clan members (*phungchaga*), the weak, the poor, and the hapless women (*khochaga*). Sometimes, it was used to control the properties of certain well-to-do people in the village but the bug was used predominantly against the 'weak'. On the other hand, the weak also sometime proclaimed as having the power to control the supernatural 'spirits' (which they never had in reality but merely taking advantage of the social rhetoric on black magic), and threatened the intolerant dominant clans/community of the village to keep away from any untoward tyranny against them.

If it is a social construct, and that everyone proclaimed that they never had such power in reality, then, how was it that *kaose* and *doi* stayed on in the society? This is especially so with the case of *kaose* among the Kukis. What is interesting about the politics of the charge of defamation was that once a person or community was accused, nothing could stop the accuser from believing in what they had declared it to be true. This was despite a strong presence of social mechanism to check on false accusation, say, a fine of Rs. 40 (among the Lushais) or Rs. 60 (Lakhers) or one mithun (Lakhers and Kukis). But the fact remains that the effectiveness of such control mechanism depended upon who accused whom. Normally, when a case of defamation came up in a village the matter was decided at the chief's court. But the problem with this system of justice was that there was no individual or mechanism to check the chief's decision. It would be false to say that the chief followed certain inviolable rules in the justice delivery system. The truth is that when the accusation was made by the chief himself or by his family members against the poor and the weak members (*khochaga*) of the village community or by his clan members against minority clan members (*phungchaga*), the chief invariably sided in favour of the former.

The irony is that once the chief decided (as the final arbiter) the matter in favour of his own men, the matter ended there and there was no higher court for the accused to relieve himself from the injustice. The chief's decision, howsoever bad it might have been, was considered as final and the truth was said to be finally established among the village community. To go against the chief was a serious challenge to his authority. Among the Thadou-Kukis the grand council of the clan heads (*pipa* or *phung-upa*) could check such injustice but that was hardly sought after considering the difficult geographical or political terrain of the time from where such help might come. Hence, the poor and the weak had to withstand the worst of such injustice done to them without any chance of succour. The matter stayed there and from generation to generation, those families, who were once accused and declared (out of social or political spite) as wizards or *kaose* would continue to be known by the people to be that, openly or secretly. This point will be taken up shortly.

The village society had at least the chief court to decide a case of accusation, no matter to what extent it could provide justice to all. At least, the chiefly clans or powerful people could get justice if accusation was made against them, unless it was from the chief himself. But think about the politics of defamation between two or more rival and warring tribes. In such a case, the hill society as a whole lacked any common court of arbiter where such charges could be settled. Such accusation between tribes (say, by stronger tribe towards weaker tribe as one sees it) remained unattended. In certain cases, it has been seen that bloodshed took place between the two tribes/clans/villages, due to such a charge of defamation. In both the cases, the matter ended with the spiteful accusation and hence, it stayed on so much so that the accusing tribe would eventually act in a hostile manner towards the accused while the latter would continue to feign ignorance. There was a stampede among the women of Haka when some Lushai coolie strolled down the street, ignorant of the accusation, for a talk. Similarly, Lakher chiefs had 'absolutely refused' to enter Lushai villages or have food and drink together with them when the Lushei chiefs, feigning ignorance, kindly 'invited' them to their houses. Thus, what was purely political in character now turned into social and cultural reality. The Chin women (and men) had not realized that they were similarly accused and thus, treated by the Burmese, when they visited the plain and that the latter's behaviour was a mere civilizational gesture to the people they thought were uncultured and uncultivated. It was this civilizational thinking, which centred on social and political relationship between two or more communities, which perpetuated the belief on *kaose* and witchcraft in history and in society.

When such power matrix had been broken between different tribes with the coming of colonialism and when the 'uncultured' tribe exalted in the new colonial world orders, the idea of such a politics of defamation had died out just as the belief had also gradually waned. If such an accusation ever arises again, the society would now be provided with an overarching colonial administration to arbitrate the matter and provide justice. Truly, if justice based on science and reason is to be given in each case, tribe to tribe or individual to individual, there is no way to prove that certain tribe or individual is *kaose* or wizard in the first place. The belief lingered on even during the colonial period but it had lost its killer instinct as in the past. Already in the 1920s, Parry informed of *khawhring*: 'Nowadays, most people are not afraid of *Khawhringnei* and do not worry about them but the belief still lingers on'. On sorcery/witchcraft or *doi* he informed, 'Although the belief in magic is gradually dying out it still exists especially in the more backward villages and cases frequently arise fairly in which a man complains that some one has accused him of being a *Dawithiam*' (Parry, 2009: 18). It has been noted that when such cases arose in the village, the British administration immediately intervened, prohibited the chief to any order of persecution, ordered the accused families to migrate to other places where the administration had at times created new village for them and thus, resolved the problem. It has also been noted that it was this section of the socially ostracized population, who had embraced Christianity and become one of the early Christians who took up the mission to spread the new religion across the hills. This new mission would surely have not only destroyed a fearful image they had carried before to those accusers but also demolished the very idea of witchcraft and *khawhring* that did not really exist. Thus, the belief eventually died out in the Lushai Hills in time and in parts of the Chin Hills where a similar development had taken place.

But the same belief lingered on among the Kukis. It is difficult to say for sure, why it has been so. Yet certain factors may be considered as crucial. Perhaps, the foremost reason for the continuing popularity of the notion of *kaose* among the Kukis may be located in its very principle of 'unsayableness' (*seingailou*), which was called the conspiracy of silence. Contrary to this principle, in Lushai and Chin Hills it has been that the social response was broadly open and direct. We have seen that the *khawhring* and wizards were openly confronted by the society. They were socially boycotted openly—denying marriage, preventing them from entering other houses, fine for sitting on the bed of others, or denying them a normal life in society. Or, they might immediately be murdered or expelled from the village and find nowhere to live or be refused an entry into the village to keep them out of sight. This 'openness' brought the matter to the fore. Under such a situation, the accused got the opportunity to sue in the court (chief or colonial) and hence appropriate 'justice' given accordingly such as killing them, expulsion from village or exonerating from the defamation. Such justice hardly came about among the Kukis, due to the 'opaqueness' of social response or where the story of *kaose* remained a 'secret affair'. People were secretly 'notified' through the darkness of a 'secret' family conversation by the society. Under the carpet of small talk and across the subterranean world, people were not given to open confrontation with *kaose* unless they were 'caught' in the 'evil' act. Thus, when everyone knew who the *kaose* were among them, no one 'as a rule' spoke of them in the open for fear that they might be overheard by the latter. This is what was called the conspiracy of silence, which was central to the continuing importance of *kaose*. Therefore, a brief discussion on this aspect of silence among the Kukis has becomes pertinent.

A search for historical or ethnographical accounts on *kaose* from research materials it was a surprise to see that there was nothing that could provide any substantial story on it. It was especially surprising to see that the official ethnographers of Kukis like William Shaw and John Shakespear were completely in the dark on the subject. It was only J.H. Hutton, whose academic excellence and in-depth understanding of the tribal world was able to add a few lines in the appendix of Shaw's monograph. This remains, perhaps, the only account one has so far to ponder over on the subject which was so engrained in the mind of every Kuki. In fact, this should not surprise one much mainly because the fear of being heard by the *kaose* compelled everyone to shut up his or her mouth. Hence, there is no historical account of *kaose* available for in-depth analysis.

In other words, the orthodoxy about the 'rule' or the principle of 'unsayable' or 'undiscussable' on the subject of *kaose* created a situation, where an 'outsider' found the paucity of knowledge on the subject common to everyone. But surprisingly enough, this was, and is, not so much the case with an 'insider', who learned the story of *kaose* behind the safety of a closed door and in the subterranean veil of family conversation. Indeed, the ideal of 'unsayableness' makes Kukis virtually a silent community whose knowledge about *kaose* was communicated as information passed among members of a secret society. This silence was, perhaps, the longest surviving 'conspiracy' in the history of the Kuki, whereby people maintained collective silence about something of which each one of them was personally aware. This state of thing is what Zerubavel (2006) called 'conspiracy of silence'.

Ironically, this conspiracy of silence was murkier even to the accused. Most of them did not even know that they had been labelled as *kaose* by the society of which everyone was aware. Even when they heard it from some *muhchuh* (outspoken) they would truthfully deny that they were not *kaose.* But that did not help as the protest was not reciprocated by the hostile and silent community who simply felt that the denial was 'obvious' (*asei dinga lha*). Since the accusation, spread through the subtle string of the 'secret' family conversation and within the rumour-mongering subterranean world, there was no way in which the accused could find any justice in the chief's court or elsewhere. Even if he found the accusers, it was even more difficult to prove before the chief court that he was not a *kaose* just as it was difficult for the chief to decide if he was positive or not. The matter became worse when the accused belonged to the poor section, was a widow and powerless and the accuser was powerful and a member of the clan.

Thus, the story of defamation charge went on and on under the carpet and without the chance of recall. A situation, therefore, was reached when the hostile society remained silent regarding the accusation, even when the *kaose* themselves denied that they never knew about any accusation. Such a 'co-denial' was unmistakably a social phenomenon that involved mutual avoidance. But the irony was that, such a situation of co-denial eventually produced an 'open-secret' identity of a section of the population, who had become not a member of the society but a 'unsayable' person outside the society. Thus, within the notion of 'unsayableness' and in the subterranean world of the Kuki conspiracy of silence, certain myths (such as the *selpaotheinete* or *kaobelpote*) or certain 'un-recallable' old accusations had continued to haunt, truncate and devastate the lives of certain clans, villages, families or thousands of innocent Kukis even till today. Thus, while the familiar belief such as *khawhring* and *ahmaw* had died out in Lushai Hills a long time ago, the Kuki society was and is still haunted by the ancient spell of the politics of defamation.

Besides, Christianity has often been said to be a powerful factor that ends *khawhring* and *doi* in the Lushai Hills. Here the church, particularly under the Western missionaries, took keen interest on the subject. It was, as they said, successful in exorcising (*nodoh*) the 'spirit' from the accused *khawhring* and won over the minds of the people. This had provided them the first fertile ground for conversion among this 'merciful' population. As the *khawhring* converts were the early batch of the so-called 'Christian soldiers' (*Christa sepai*), it was possible that their influence over the subject was tremendous and hence its eventual evaporation from the minds of the people. But the same church did not have a similar impact among the Kukis. Here, it was found that church did not take any particular policy on the subject nor was it keen to abolish it. This was particularly for the same reason noted above. The belief or practice had gone so 'underground' within the subterranean world of social conspiracy of silence that the Western missionary, just as the district officers, were not able to find the subject demanding church action. Thus, if the openness against the *khawhring* provided a good ground for the church to intervene and demolish it, the 'opaqueness' of or the principle of 'undiscussableness' of *kaose* prevented any meaningful interventions from the church as the state. Hence, *kaose* neither appeared as an anti-Christ practice nor as a 'law and order problem'. This is similar to the case in the present Kuki church. Therefore, *kaose* stayed on under the gripping garb of the Kuki conspiracy of silence over the ages and is still alive.

The above discussion takes one to some clean thought. Taken from the point of its origin, the belief in it and practices from the point of social responses to the so-called black art, seen from the prism of politics and in the context of power and social relations in the hills, what eventually emerges clearly is the fact that the belief in *kaose* and *doi* remain as a 'belief' rather than a reality. It was, and, is a social construct over a period of time that spread and concretized as an instrument of the powerful against the weak, nothing more. Seen from this prism of power the belief is far from real. From the existential standpoint, the belief is studded with myths and mythologies, whims and whimsical allegories, farces and farcical stories, believing the unbelievable fiction, and so on, which science and reason would find being uncomfortable bed fellows with.

WHY DO WE NEED TO STUDY *KAOSE* NOW?: A MISSIVE TO KUKI READERS

The historical injustices and certain alarming recent happenings over few of the Kukis prompted one to write this small piece in order to open up a debate so that the balloon of silence could be punctured for a meaningful resolution on the subject. This silence, as has been noted, will take one nowhere. It was not the *kaose* but the conspiracy of silence about the *kaose* that enchanted the Kuki community for this long. Unless this silence is broken and the subterranean conspiracy is brought overground, in the open, and before a proper social forum there will not be any justice to a section of Kuki population who had endured unwarranted charge of defamation over the centuries. This historical injustice is now compounded by the alarming growth of such charges of defamation since the 1990s when the Kukis experienced another phase of political and social turmoil. More and more number of charges of accusation have come up and many cases were the first time in their family history. The two cases referred to above, were the tip of an iceberg of such charges which had taken place in recent times. The '*kao* doctor' mentioned above also claimed with pride that he alone was able to 'cure' more than a hundred cases of *kaobol*, indicating that the belief had grown in an alarming proportion again. In places like Moreh where thousands of displaced Kukis (in the wake of the Naga ethnic cleansing programme) were settled, the mind of the people had already been 'engulfed' or 'besieged' by the fear of *kaose* and *doi* so much so that accusations and hatred of certain families or persons had studded the everyday chores of the enchanted population.

Unlike in Lushai Hills, the Kuki Churches have taken hardly any serious note of the subject. Truly, it provided equality to all, including the *kaose*. Truly, it was also able to destroy most of the traditional rituals and ceremonies where *kaose* found no equality with others. Pastors may preach repeatedly against any discrimination on the ground of *kaose*. Yet the church failed to take any proactive step on the question of *kaose*. Apparently, it was also restrained by the social principle of 'unsayableness' about *kaose*. Its silence, in fact, led the church to accept the 'norms' silently. Worst, its silence on *kaose* on the one hand and its forefront principle of 'war' against 'Satan' and other malevolent spirits (*thilha* or *lhagaoboh*) in the society inadvertently and silently brought *kaose* under the latter category. It tended to consider *kaose* in the way witchcraft was considered by the church of early modern Europe. This was most visible in its conflicting injunction of people accused of *kaose*. On the one hand, the Kuki church maintained that all *kaose* were members of the church and could attain salvation. On the other hand, it deplored *kaotom* (possessing the other or entering another body to torment or kill) and declared it as a 'sin' to do so. This meant that the church condemned the act of *kaose* but endorsed the existence of *kaose* in the society. In other words, the church accepted that *kaose* existed in Kuki society quietly and silently and its aim was not to destroy it but to control it from attacking people. This is but surrender to the myth of ancient belief in *kaose* and an expression of defeat.

The Kuki church silently accepted defeat before what it considered *lhagaoboh* or sin particularly on certain ground. It silently accepted that certain medical problems are *kaobol* (an attack by *kaose*) and vehemently deplored that such *kaobol* was a diabolical act (*dai-bol* or *kholai-lang bol*). Thus, what was socially condemned as *athenglou* now became *chonset* (sin) in the church. Recent cases of *kaobol* involved church leaders, elders, or people who took the name of Christ to 'expel' or 'exorcise' (*nodoh*) the *kaose* from the victim's body. There is even a person who is popularly known as '*kao* doctor' who was a devoted Christian and claimed that he was anointed by the angels (*lhagaotheng*) to 'heal' (*damsah*) people possessed by 'spirits' (*lhagaoboh*) and *kaose*. When asked whether *kaose* is *lhagaoboh*, he promptly answered 'Yes, *kaose* is *lhagaoboh*'. Thus, the social concept of *kaose* intrudes in the church definition of diabolical works. In this context, the Kuki church lacked any definition of *kaose* or simply silently accepted that it is a diabolical conspiracy against Christianity. It was under such circumstances that the belief in *kaose* 'stay-on' among the Kukis even after the celebration of a hundred years of Christianity. This is again unfortunate.

Today the *kaose* live a normal life in a village community, as if they are normal people in the eyes of an outsider. Most village chief have stopped discriminating them in the village affairs on the ground of being *kaose*. But the truth is that no one forgets them as *kaose* and the diabolical conspiracy against them is as alive as it used to be in the past. Besides, the rapid decline of what one would call the traditional 'shields' against *kaose* such as the cross-cousin marriage (the *pute-chanu kijuon*) could not prevent one from thinking about, not to mention of believing in, the *kaose*. Discrimination on the ground of sharing a comb, in communal feasting, and inter-clan or family interactions, and so on, had subsided or gone. But this could not prevent one from thinking about *kaose*. Broadly, *kaose*, as an ancient idyllic, instead of dying out, continues to remain well entrenched and deep rooted in our time. One glaring example of this can be seen when a person chooses his/her life partner. Young people may stop asking this question of their partner, but their parents would not. In a most devilishly language parents may ask: *itobang mi hinao vem*? (what kind of family/people are they? are they clean or unclean?), the language, however ambiguous it might have been, was however easily knowable to their children. Or a secret mission is always an optional in the conspiracy. If they found the partner's family in state of even *sei-a theng sei-a boh* they would do anything to prevent the marital alliance.

The worst thing is, even today many young men and women consciously avoid those people, who are accused as *kaose* or have any blood relationship with *kaose*, for a lover or partner. *Kaose* are silently condemned to remain outside the corridor of the charmed circle of usual matrimonial selections. They have been silently rejected, boycotted, and ostracized as in the past. They continue to remain in a society, not as a person and family even when they think they live as a person and family, incomplete and mutilated when they are complete as much as we are. In a way they are living a 'bare life' having no identity other than how they are secretly known by the larger public. When they thought they are part and parcel of the community, the community actually denied them any membership; their identity is a mere 'unsayable' which is not even a being. But the pertinent question is—How long are we going to remain silent and let our own brothers and sisters remain as unsayable, undiscussable persons? How long are we going to say *sei ngailou ahi*? (it is unsayable). How long are we going to keep this 'conspiracy of silence' concealed? Unless we are able to puncture this balloon of silence, *kaose* will remain alive and vibrant in the society. Instead of ending, it will continue to proliferate in the society and we should be warned that this has got the potential to break the social fabric in a big way.

The objective is to start puncturing this balloon of silence and see how this 'conspiracy of silence' could be taken up for intellectual debate and discussion. This is seen as a necessary step toward the emancipation of one's brothers and sisters from being a hostage of an ancient spell on two grounds.

- First, the belief in *kaose* cannot be buried away even in the face of an overarching dominance of the church, the chiefs and the declining customary practices of discrimination against them because it relies on a *concept* rather than *practice*, an *idea* rather than an *art*, a *belief* rather than *fact*, a *thought* rather than a *science*, and finally a *myth* rather than something *real*.
- Second, since a *concept* can be destroyed or demolished only by a counter concept, the role of intellectuals to find out the way how this concept could be demolished becomes necessary. For that, the truth about *kaose* should first be established.

This article is not only to point out what had happened in the past but more importantly to state that what had happened in the past says that *kaose* never existed in reality, it was just a social construct, it was a mere civilizational tool in the hands of the powerful to defame, criminalize and devastate the weak. It was the product of social, political or neighbourhood tensions. The victims of *kaose* were actually attacked not by *kaose* or spirit, but they were actually suffering from a psychological disorder particularly that of dissociative amnesia caused by constant state of mental stress and trauma which in most cases were caused by certain diseases like tuberculosis, malaria, stomach ache and so on which medical science can dignose clearly and which medicine can surely cure.

Those people, who are still influenced by those ancient spells should be warned, that if *kaose* really existed they should first accept that they are also one of them on two grounds. First, if a mere accusation makes someone a *kaose*, history has it that all the Kukis (particularly the 'Thadous') had once been accused as *kaose* and *doithem* by both the Lushais and the Chins. They have been hated as if a single glance from them would cause sickness and misfortune. Such accusation stayed on and it has not gone so that in the past some blood has been spilled. The same pattern was repeated within the tribe, clan, or village level in which the weak, the poor, and the hapless section of the population have often been accused whenever some disaster befell the powerful and chiefly clans/class. History has it that such accusation was nothing, but a mere politics of defamation and was merely an expression of the civilizational notion of the powerful against the weak, produced in the context of social and political tensions between different tribes/clans/villages. Certain people became *kaose* merely, because they were not able to defend or find justice due to the overwhelming power of the accusers. *Kaose* exist merely because of that, nothing more. Therefore, if you accept that the *kaose* really exist than you should accept that you are *kaose* as well as those who had once been accused by the Lushais and Chins and who had not been able to do anything about the charge of defamation. As the politics of defamation shows, once bitten is always bitten. Hence, you have been bitten and bitten now; there is no escape.

Second, if you still think that you are safe from such politics of defamation, you still think that you are *kaose* because you are in no way safe from it. Consider the cases in which one, as the theory of *kaose* says, can become *kaose*. There are two ways a person could become *kaose*: blood-line (marriage) and through the hair. You are not married to a person who is accused as *kaose* or are not the children of one of them, but please recall your past and ask yourself: have you, your parents, grandparents, at anytime, shared a comb (*samthi*) or a *nam* (cane plaited hair band for carrying goods) with other persons who could have been *kaose*? Have any one of them ever visited a hairdresser for a haircut where all the so-called *kaose* have also had their hair cut some time? It is hard to believe in today's world that one's parents and grandparents had never visited a barber's parlour a single time in their life or never shared combs with any other persons. This is especially true for those people living in urban centres, but equally true also for those living in the village whose life was closely connected to the urban centres. Those who believe in the *kaose* must think about this seriously. If you had a history of that, make sure or accept that one is one of the *kaose* because it was from such a hairdresser's or sharing of combs with others that the spirit of *kaose* had already entered your body and resided there. You had the power to command now. What remains is that you just have to give a command and torment people. Can you do that? If you can, accept that *kaose* exist. If you cannot, then reconsider your belief in the *kaose* and start saying that *kaose* do not exist in reality, instead of lingering in your thought with the ancient farcical spell of barbarism, savagery and primitive memory. This is the new world of science and reason.

THE ROAD AHEAD

If the *kaose* is historically incomprehensible, other sciences (social and medical) must buy more time to show that it is a social construct and one that is a medical subject. They need to, one by one, deconstruct what would be called the theories of *kaose* through meticulous research and dedication. Until that is done, it would not be possible to convince the mesmerized mind of the thousands, whose belief in the *kaose* was built on the deep foundation of the seven layers of the earth (*leitho-thosagi*) and secured inside the seven layers of the 'iron gate' (*thihpi-thosagi*), to put it mataphorically.

NOTES

1. 'Will-o'-the-wisp' is 'a dim, flickering light seen hovering at night on marshy ground, thought to result from the combustion of natural gases'. For different ancient ideas on this, see https://en.wikipedia.org/wiki/Will-o%27-the-wisp (accessed on 17 May 2016).
2. It is mainly caused by a traumatic or stressful event. Currently 'trance and possession' disorder came under the generic dissociative disorder, which is purely of psychological causation and can also be due to brain damage.
3. For this ritual see Parry, *The Lakhers*, pp. 463-4.
4. I am thankful to David Vumlallian Zou for bringing this to my knowledge. Of course more missionary accounts on this 'evil' practice can add more insight and it is up to future researchers to find out more from those missionary accounts.
5. See *Rajmalah* (the Royal Chronicles of Tripura Kingdom).
6. For detail discussion on this crisis situation see Jangkhomang Guite, 'Civilisation and its malcontents: The politics of Kuki raid in nineteenth century Northeast India', *The Indian Economic and Social History Review*, 48, 3 (2011), pp. 339-76.
7. See, for instance, Fr. Sangermano, *A Description of Burmese Empire: Compiled Chiefly from Burmese Documents*, tr. W. Tandy, London, 1966, 1833, p. 43.
8. As quoted in Parry, *Lakhers*, p. 465, fn. 1.

REFERENCES

Carey, B.S. & H.N. Tuck, *The Chin Hills: A History of the People, our Dealings with Them, Their Customs and Manners and a Gazetteer of Their Country*, Aizawl: TRI, (1894), 2008.

Guite, Jangkhomang, 'Civilisation and Its Malcontents: The Politics of Kuki Raid in Nineteenth Century Northeast India', *The Indian Economic and Social History Review*, 48(3), 2011, pp. 339-76.

Haokip, P., 'Belief in Malevolent Spirit "Inn-Kaose" in Traditional Religious System of Chin-Kuki: A Descriptive Analysis', *Journal of North East India Studies*, 1(1), 2011, pp. 23-35.

Hutton, John N., 'Notes' on 'Vampire' in William Shaw, *Notes on the Thadou Kukis*, Delhi: Spectrum, (1928), 1980.

McCall, A.G., *Lushai Chrysalis*, Aizawl: TRI, (1949), 2003.

McCulloch, William, *An Account of the Valley of Manipore and of the Hill Tribes*, Delhi, (1859), 1980.

Parry, N.E., *A Monograph on Lushai Customs & Ceremonies*, Aizawl: TRI, (1928), 2009.

Parry, N.E., *The Lakhers*, Delhi: Omsons, (1931), 1988.

Pocs, Eva, *Between the Living and the Dead: A perspective on Witches and Seers in the Early Modern Age*, Budapest: Central European University Press, 1999.

Sangermano, Fr., *A Description of Burmese Empire: Compiled Chiefly from Burmese Documents*, tr. W. Tandy, London, (1833), 1966.

Shakespear, John, *The Lushei Kuki Clans*, Delhi: Cultural Publishing House, (1912), 1983.

Vumson, *Zo History*, Aizawl, 1986.

Zerubavel, Eviatar, *The Elephant in the Room: Silence and Denial in Everyday Life*, New York: Oxford University Press, 2006.

CHAPTER 24

Witchcraft, Witch Hunting, Gender and Property Relationship

NIKITA SHANDILYA

If one believes in witches and witchcraft, it is very obvious that they believe in the existence of evil and other supernatural forms of power. People have divided it into good and bad power. The constant fear of things beyond the comprehension of people led to their superstitions. Fear makes a person act so dangerously that to get rid of it they do something without any logical understanding or in the right state of mind. This fear is actually in the mind, mostly when one is insecure about oneself, weak, lonely or guilty.[1] Evil and the other superstitious beliefs have their roots in myths which are never true. The folklores, which are sometimes misinterpreted or exaggerated for the state of fun or interest take a different shape with time and situation.[2] The fear of facing problems by oneself or his near and dear ones facing it makes one helpless. This instigates them to follow such beliefs and rituals attached to it and they are bound to follow the code of conduct that society has made up irrespective of one's likes or deslikes. But when traditional ideas related to evil gets attached to religion, people fear them more. They agree to it so as not to offend the supernatural powers, which actually gets transmitted from one generation to the other. Thus, the wheel keeps moving and the rituals and practices are performed blindly without being questioned.

What is evil? The answer varies from person to person, because for different people and communities evil has different meanings and definitions. For some, it is related to colours, weather, food, certain directions, which are even forbidden in some religion, even the menstrual cycle of a women. The women in all cultures are burdened for being evil which is not a present-day problem but has been there from the beginning of humanity. Eve was blamed as an evil, as she forced Adam to commit sin. It is mostly seen that evil, impure magic and bad spells are always linked to women as they have become the easiest target for man in particular and society in general. If one looks at any community, women from all sections of the society have been victimized and accused of being a witch or something evil. The difference is that some do not hide it and some accept it submissively.[3] Evil started to take roots as people believed in superstations and women began to be considered as the figurative form of evil.

When it comes to customary laws and rituals it has been observed that the women are restricted from taking part in them. The events are believed to become impure if women participate as they are not allowed to perform the rituals which are assigned only to men. Folklore, myths and even literature have not spared women, mostly portraying them as the worshipper of evil power. In non-literate or semi-literate tribal societies, folklore has central importance: whether in the form of songs, riddles, proverbs, myths, stories and legends, they form an integral part of the tribal socio-cultural milieu.[4] The women are made to believe not only by society and men but also by the other women like mother (to her daughter) and mother-in-law (to her daughter-in-law) that they are impure and have no rights or position in the society among men, who are believed to be more learned and stronger than them. The oppression of the women starts with the family. They are burdened with all the customs and rituals they have to follow. The prestige and the social status of the family is to be taken care of by the women in the house, irrespective of what the men do, even if they commit a crime. A man's power and strength is always celebrated and he is taught to boast of his manhood. In tribal societies, war and display of physical strength is still given much importance and celebrated in many community functions which also have a major role to play in witch-hunting. Age-old traditions like these have actually made the youth more aggressive and violent. Witch hunting has become the best forum for such youth to display their strength and power among other people, who make them feel superior and it has also helped such youth to terrorize the weak in the community.[5] Sometimes because of such practices women suffer from frustration, inferiority as they do not receive the rightful position and status they should have. Their voice is suppressed in every way and they start believing themselves impure and evil due to emotional insecurities they go through, which actually leads to mental disturbance and instability in them.

CASE STUDY 1

Victim: Ainu Boro, age 26; Village: Binyakhata, Kokrajhar District

The victim had married against the will of her own parents. Her husband was from the Bodo community and she belonged to a Hindu community. She ran away from her house with Pradwp Boro and came to her in-laws' house. Initially, she was accepted in the groom's house after a community feast was given to the people. But slowly she was forbidden by her mother-in-law and sister-in-law from attending community functions and other religious ceremonies of the Bodo community. When anything bad happened in the family or she forgot to clean the courtyard before her husband left for work, she was taunted that a bad omen had taken shelter in their house and eaten up the family's happiness and possessed their son, her husband. The neighbours started cursing her and even her shadow was not allowed in their house. The sister-in-law took this opportunity and cursed the victim. If she forgot to do some household work, she would say that the victim had distracted her. Out of jealousy she wanted her to suffer and be scolded by the elders in the house. She was made to stay alone and not treated properly. Her husband did not defend her and an *ojha* was brought who asked the boy to get rid of her, as by doing so, he could bring back peace in his house. The boy disowned her saying that she was a witch, who had actually brought unhappiness to the house. It was because he had offended the ancestors by marrying outside the caste that he had to suffer and now, by marrying a Bodo girl from his own community, he would be spared and happiness would return to the family. The victim was tortured and she accepted that she was evil and impure and left the house. At present, she works as a maid in the town and wishes never to go back to her own family or village out of fear.

The gender difference is so strong that it has already developed a pre-conceived notion among the people about who needs to do what and who needs to suffer the most. Gender differences should not only be seen with regard to tradition, customs and rituals. It is also used to emphasize how the political and social milieu has actually tangled both the sexes and how women or any marginalized group is made a victim out of it. Witch hunting is one of the major examples where gender plays an important role and it has transformed from witch hunting to women hunting in reality.[6] The gender analysis has actually opened up significant potentialities in knowing the history and the social sciences.[7] In the discourse of social history with more emphasis the marginalized section of the society like the tribes, women's history occasionally finds a place. Culture and tradition along with social customs have never freed women but have actually clutched them more tightly than letting them enjoy their freedom and space. Freedom of women was always scary and made the man insecure. The changing socio-economic and political affiliation of society with time has also changed, specially the contours of gender relationship in these sections of society, where oppression was suffered by men and women alike, from precolonial to post-colonial times. In such a situation and condition, the man is surrounded by a crisis which give vent to his frustration. He takes out his frustration upon the women or the weak which become his easy target. He can then celebrate the manhood he is taught about. He takes pride in and gets satisfaction or has a feeling of achievement when he sees someone weaker than him suffer and plead in front of him. The analysis of gender and its role in witchcraft and witch hunting needs to be understood with intense care and in broader light by not only focussing on the female but on the man too.

The notion of evil and superstition varies from community to community and within the community, it sometimes differs from person to person. The Bodo community believes in both evil and good power. The concept of witch (*daini*) came to them at a much later stage. Earlier, evil for them was related to spirits and other supernatural powers which could not be seen. If there was a misfortune or problem, they would offer their prayers and perform rituals to please these powers which they believed resided in the big old tree of the village or deep in the forest.[8] Later, they started to relate evil with *daini* (witch) and started being violent to control the evil. Earlier, they only offered prayers and offerings, but now not only the victim was ostracized from the village, but tortured and even murdered. They related bad or evil power with *daini* (witch) and good is related with the *ojha* (priest), who was earlier the medicine man and the most learned man in the community. He is now believed to have the power to counter spell to the evil and can bring back peace and harmony into the community. If one looks closer, evil is always related to women and the *ojhas* are mostly men who have now become witch finders more than a priest. The Bodo earlier related evil with diseases, crop failure, or sudden change in weather and to avoid such calamities, religious ceremonies were held yearly, but such practices have changed with time and people now demand an instant solution which they believe would be given by the *ojha* and out of fear and jealousy people have turned the evil to be the *daini* (witch) in the village.[9]

The social construction of the Bodo women in their community was not so marginalized and oppressed as it has now turned out to be. If one looks at the social description of women by Rev. Sidney Endley, the Bodo women have been given a very respectable and important position. They also shared economic as well as social sphere in the society, from paddy cultivation to gathering of valuable herbs from the forest and selling them in the market and earning for their family. The forest was the major place for the women. They were experts in the resources of the forest as compared to their male partners, who would ideally spend their time drinking or some time hunting. These medicines were earlier supplied to the *ojhas* (medicine men) of the community by the women of the villages. But after the enclosure movement, when the forest was taken from these people, the women were left idle in their household. Earlier, even in the folklores there was the mention of the female *ojha.* A woman can become one if she is capable of it. During the late nineteenth century, there was a thick line drawn between the differences between men and women, which have actually complicated the understanding and the reason behind gender differences. Folklores such as *Haynamuli* in 1985, written by Monoronjan Lahary shows the protagonist as the female *ojha* (medicine woman), who was humiliated as her medicine failed and did not satisfy the landlord's family, due to which, she and her daughters too paid a price and later died of poverty. She is still represented as the divine spirit in the *kherai puja* of the Bodos known as the *Deoudini.*

There was not a complete absence of male witches, but they mostly believed in more women learning witchcraft than men. The women were now seen as persons who could possess the evil powers. Earlier, the evil was believed to be in animals, birds and other objects which were not auspicious for the Bodo community and regarded as a bad omen or sign, like the old banyan tree of the village. People and small children were forbidden to sleep under it and women specially during their menstrual cycle must avoid crossing such huge trees. If they ever came out of their houses, they should not comb their hair in the courtyard of the house.[10] Now if any one broke such rules of social conducts, people assume that the woman is evil because she is not following the code of conduct. Movement of women were more restricted and their actions were under surveillance, they were even restricted to go into the forest and were supposed to return home before sunset.

CASE STUDY 2

Victim: Praffulla Basumatary and his Wife, Occupation: Retired Principal of Udalguri College

The victim says that his wife fell into the trap of his brother's daughter and people who were already jealous of them, instigated the other villagers against them. People were easily convinced that the professor's wife was a witch. His brother's daughter who was studying in Mumbai came home during her vacations. She started to fall sick after a week and one day she told her neighbour that her aunt was evil and she had dreamt that she wanted to kill her. It was even said that she worshipped something in the night and because of her weakness she could not see it properly. Praffulla Basumatary's wife was an outspoken woman and many persons in the village did not like her as she was not very social and did not attend village functions. People were always jealous of their prosperity and happiness specially their relatives, as both their children were well settled. One night, there was a fight between the brothers and the professor's wife scolded the girl harshly. The next morning the news spread like wildfire in the village, that she was the witch who was trying to kill her brother-in-law's daughter as she had come to know about her secrets. People surrounded her house and started insulting her and tried to harm her and when her husband tried to defend her he too was called a *daina* (witch). He was not even allowed to enter college after that! Both were mentally harassed and tortured. They were frequently threatened and were asked to leave the village by his brother's friends and, at last, out of fear, they had to leave their ancestral property and went away from the village. Even his children were not spared. An *ojha* was brought from the nearby village, who was a Santhal. He too declared that the house where they had lived must be demolished for the welfare of the village and certified the wife a witch, as she was making the girl more sick and weak. After all this, the principal left his village and settled at another place away from his own village. His property in the village is now completely occupied by his brother and the girl who was sick. She was actually in a relationship with a boy in Mumbai and lived with him. The aunt had come to know about it and she used her sickness as a means to help herself get rid of her. Later, the girl was detected with jaundice and fever and after that she went back to Mumbai.

Such beliefs have made people so blind that they have forgotten to use their own sense of what is right and what is wrong. During their crisis or mostly out of frustration people start being judgemental and already form some pre-determined view about the other based on some false assumptions. Even after realization, external pressure and guilt binds people to let crimes like witch hunt happen even against their wishes. It is also witnessed by the elderly people of the village and the village chiefs. The youth want an immediate solution and because of their aggression and restlessness, the incident such as a witch hunt turns to be very violent and many crimes takes place in the name of witch hunting, overnight. Even before punishment can be assigned to the victim by the community and its elders, murders happen overnight in the name of witch hunting.[11] Sometimes even the judgements are manipulated and biased where people in power and position take the opportunity to do what they want. During such situations people seek their own benefit and wish to establish their own political influence.

CASE STUDY 3

The victim is a widow of 50-8 years, who was living with her adopted son. She served the village as a midwife for many years. She owned one *bigha* of land, two goats and the house in which she was living. The house she lived in was in the interior of Chirang district named Rupi. The place was affected mostly by diseases and natural calamities and was very under developed. Small children were mostly sick. One night, a few people came to her place and surrounded the house and declared her a witch. When asked what she had done, they said that one of the children who was sick, had dreamt that an old lady with terrifying looks was trying to eat up all the chickens in the village and had shouted in her dreams that woman should be killed. There was also news earlier that the victim used to go to the forest alone at night. Her adopted son did not even defend her, as he was afraid of being killed by the villagers. The youth demanded that the woman should be beaten up which would oblige her to tell the truth. The elders of the village asked the boys and other people to wait till morning and a decision would then be taken. The victim refused to leave the village and in anger cursed everyone. The next day one of the men, who wanted her out of the village fell from the tree and broke his leg. His wife created a scene and all the people assembled and the people tortured her killed one of her goats and said it was a sacrifice to the evil and beat her so badly, that she could not walk and was crippled.

After the incident she was given shelter in a house but they too were threatened by the other people. Eventually the woman had to evacuate her house which now she knows was occupied by the youth for their own purpose.

Witchcraft and witch hunting have taken a very nasty form with time. The more society is developing, the more complicated and complex such crimes are getting. People are going back to such thoughts and practices. Hostility and fury of the people have made them more vulnerable. It is not only seen among the illiterate and poor people but also among the educated and economically stable people in the urban areas. It is the mentality of the people which is getting more prone to evil with time. It has been said that, mostly with time and progress people become more calm and stable. However, it has been seen that people have become more vulnerable in the matter of witch hunting, compared to earlier times. Earlier, if any person was suspected to be a practitioner of witchcraft, he/she was asked to live in a hut in a corner of the village near a flowing river. He or she would not be allowed to have any social contact with the people.[12] The village headman would keep a check on the person and if the people felt that he was no longer dangerous to the community, he was brought back to the village and allowed to lead a normal life. But at present, it has become an event and a way to demonstrate one's power over the accused. Here, the crime is committed with the consent of all the people in the village which actually encourages the others to do the same. It is more of a gender oriented crime than a belief or practice. Women are physically assaulted and even raped. The victims are made to do such heinous things that it is even impossible to think. They are made to eat human excreta, drink urine and do many more such things. Such violation does not stop with the victim but continues from generation to generation, life is made miserable for the family, who defend such crime.[13]

CASE STUDY 4

A widow in the Chirang district accused of being a witch because the neighbour's child died, after she visited their house. She stayed with her son, who was a carpenter. The people started talking about her and rumours were spread, but she was able to defend herself. Everything was normal until a day, when because of some community festival that was held in the village, the woman's brother's son came to stay with them and attended the festival. That very night he did not come back home after the function and in the morning he was found dead. After investigation by the police, three men were taken in custody. According to them, they did the right thing by killing the boy as he was related to the witch. They were drunk and said that they had only beaten up the boy but did not kill him.

Such incidents aroused fear among other people about having relations with the victim and thus the victim never received any support from people. Sometimes, women were seen as enemies of other women. Witch hunting has been used as a way to take out ones frustration, anger and gain superiority over the other. Man has always tried to establish his superiority over woman. They seek to portray and establish their manhood by subjugating women. Men have not only turned out to be the enemy of women but women have also not missed the opportunity to make other women feel inferior and weak in whichever way possible. Position and power have corrupted people so much that it now hardly matters to anyone to think before causing harm to their near and dear ones. Self-interest and self-benefit have taken the place of community welfare.[14]

CASE STUDY 5

The victim was a resident of Gosaigoan, Kokrajhar. She was an old lady in her 80s, who was rescued by Pratibha Brahma, who runs an NGO and employs the women specially those who were victims of witch hunting, in her weaving loom. The victim was staying with her daughter-in-law and her son stayed away, as he was working in some firm as daily wage earner. The daughter-in-law did not have good relations with her mother-in-law, as she blamed her for not being able to stay in the town with her son. She ill-treated her and the old lady lived in a very minimal way one could think of. The daughter-in-law was not conceiving and told people and her family members that it was the old woman who was the cause of it. She also claimed that the old woman did not want her to conceive so that she could look after her. She also told people that she could not sleep because of fear, that the old woman would sleep and sit beside her and chant some spells. It was very easy for her to convince people because the old woman and her appearance suited her description. She stayed untidy and dressed shabbily as she could not take care of herself due to old age. The son too was convinced by his wife and her family members forced him to get rid of his mother. People started discussing her and she was left alone in a small hut for a week. Her condition became worse as she could hardly eat or see anything. One night people decided to burn the hut when one woman from the village informed Pratibha Brahma who rescued the old woman from her hopless condition. She started asking numerous questions and the daughter-in-law felt that she was trapped and was scared of legal prosecution so she accepted that she was the actual culprit, who made up such stories so that the old woman could go away and she could shift with her husband and inherit the property which the old woman owned. People started accusing the daughter-in-law, but still they do not stay together. The old woman was moved to an old age home where she is being taken care of.

CASE STUDY 6

Devini was the youngest daughter-in-law of the family. She was loved and liked by all. She also belonged to a economically stable family. She had all the characteristics and features which were desired by a Bodo family in their daughter-in-law. Everyone was pleased and the groom's family also got many gifts from the bride's family. Everything was fine, but after a few months problems started with her sister-in-law. The victim did not have a good relation with her husband. One day, she found her sister-in-law and her husband in a very compromising situation, which is strictly forbidden in the Bodo community. Relations with elder sister-in-law are not warranted as she is seen as a mother figure. After that, when she shouted and called people, she was physically tortured by her husband and beaten up by her sister-in-law. She was threatened by her sister-in-law that, if she said anything about them, they would tell people that she was a witch and was making up such stories which were actually sinful. After a few months, her mother-in-law died, so the victim was now more scared to oppose her sister-in-law and she started doing whatever she was asked to do. She was suffering from mental torture. When people slowly suspected the illegal relationship of the sister-in-law and the victim's husband, both of them started deputing her as a *daini* (witch) and even the brother-in-law remained silent and did nothing to save the self-respect of the family though he was well aware of his wife's guilt. He kept drinking, continuously and was beaten up by other people when he abused his wife and brother. One day he was found dead and according to the victim, it was her husband who had killed him because of the property he owned as the elder son. When the administration investigated the murder, her husband said that it was his wife who was a witch. She had killed their mother and the brother too and the whole village was with him and the police too did not investigate much and the innocent girl was beaten and humiliated till she accepted she was the witch after that she was asked to leave the village.

It has been seen that the victims were young girls who could be physically exploited, widows who were helpless and inherited the property of their husband and the old, who becomes a burden for the family. The *jou* (local brew) too led to victimization as when a person was over drunk and, out of anger or sometimes not in his/her senses, said he was the *daina* (witch) he too was not spared. In such situations, people took advantage to settle their age-old scores and take revenge by murdering their enemies in the name of witch hunting. Even, if it is found that in a house the *jou* (local rice beer) gets spoilt after fermentation, it is blamed on the person who makes it because, according to their custom, they believe that if a person has evil thoughts in their mind while making the brew, it gets spoilt. Only a person with a clean heart and mind can make the best local brew. There are many incidents, where friends have attacked those close to them, while drunk, and said that they did such things because the other one had confessed of being a witch and later, they realized that they did it because they were drunk.

CASE STUDY 7

Feswali Brahma was a 28 year old, who was not married and so, her father and two brothers were worried. She lived with them and sometimes stayed in her maternal uncle's place with her grandmother. Her mother had died long back and she had one sister-in-law. The latter hated and disliked her, as she was dependent on her husband. She wanted to get rid of her and the best way was to find a groom for her. Every time a family and a groom come to see her, she was rejected. Once a family came with betel nuts and local brew to fix the marriage, but they went away in the middle, making some excuses. The girl also owned some share of land given to her by her father and a weaving loom which was not liked by the sister-in-law. The rice beer she made also did not turn out to be great in taste. Her sister-in-law was literally mad with her and kept abusing her the whole time. Even her brothers did not like her for sitting at home and inheriting the property. The victim too was frustrated and angered with her condition and kept fighting with her neighbours and slowly everyone started avoiding her. A neighbour's child passed away because of high fever. The local medicine too failed in healing the girl and all the sacred thread that the *ojha* gave did not work. The local people started questioning the *ojha*, but he was saved because of the daughter-in-law, who instigated people that it was the witch in the village, who was bringing hard luck to everyone and the *ojha* took the opportunity and said that it was none other than Feswali and asked people to hand her to him. The sister-in-law at once brought her to him and asked the quack to take her, where she was sexually exploited by the *ojha*. After the incident, the second brother got married and the people believed happiness has returned to the village as the evil was in the control of the *ojha*.

There are many such instances. If one meets a victim, he/she will realize how a woman is blackmailed and objectified by society, which encourages the quacks to exploit the helpless and manipulate other people. The foresightedness of the common people has actually disappeared or they do not intend to see much. The social norms have tangled the weak so badly, that it has become almost impossible for the marginalized to help one from not being exploited by people in power. The *ojhas* who were actually the learned men in the community, did not practise their traditional herbal medicines as it had almost become impossible for them to collect the herbs medicines from the forest, as it was mostly known by the women. Moreover, people demand miracles rather than medicines which they are unable to do and so their place has been taken by quacks, who performs their practices in the name of *ojhas.* They have actually shifted their profession to being witch hunters in the villages, creating illusion among people by casting magical spells in the name of controlling the evil in the society. The society has made him so strong that, he can even threaten the women specially if they so against him and keep exploiting them in the name of religion. People are even ready to be exploited.[15] Not only this, but the *ojhas* also have the support of the accuser, who plots against the victim to brand an innocent person a witch. They are, nowadays, staying in the nearby villages, where they hide their real identity.[16] They have their own sources and agents spread in the targeted village, where people are emotional and socially unstable due to crisis and deprivation. These quacks are seen in areas, which suffer from natural calamities. It has become a way of earning a living by exploiting people. Along with the instigators, it is found that the accusers are also close to the victim. Mostly, land and property issues have taken a different turn in the accusation related to witchcraft and witch hunting. Earlier, land and property was not that important as everything was community based and progress was aimed at community welfare.

CASE STUDY 8

The victim was of the age group 40-50 and was a widow who lived with her two sons near her husband's house. She inherited two *bighas* of land, one cow and a wooden cart. She also owned a few betel nut trees planted in her husband's house. After the death of her husband she got one *bigha* of land too. Initially the younger brother refused to give and his wife too had bad relations with the widow, which made her stay separately. The problem worsened after the sister gave birth to a premature baby girl and the day she went to see the baby it died that very night. People started to talk about the widow and did not welcome her presence on happy occasions. After few days, her eldest brother-in-law's eldest daughter ran away with a boy outside their caste and the victim was blamed for that as the girl would frequently visit her aunt. After all these incidents, the victim was abused and forbidden to come to their house or even take the share of their betel nut trees. After three months her youngest son died due to fever and the people started believing in the rumours spread by the victim's family of her being the witch. Everything she did was because of the greed to have all the property herself. It was also believed that she had sacrificed her younger son to please the evil spirits, and she would visit the cremation ground alone at night. Finally, a meeting was held where before she arrived, local brew was served to all the people by her husband's family so that the villagers could easily be manipulated and the youth were completely out of their senses and started abusing her even before the meeting started. The woman was humiliated and beaten up to death until her eldest son somehow escaped and informed the police but before he could reach she was strangled to death and was found naked and lying there dead. Seeing this, the son ran away from the village as he was scared to stay alone.

CASE STUDY 9

Here, the victims were two brothers who were both ostracized by the village which believed them to be practitioners of witchcraft and both were believed to be the *dainas* of the village. Everything started in the community feast and both were drunk. There was a fight regarding some old issue related to land. Out of aggression, one cursed the other to die and the others just watched the fight. One of the men in the group shouted that both the brothers knew black magic. One of the brothers kept staring at another person and that person fainted and everyone started hitting the brothers. The next day both the brothers went to the police, which was miles away from their village. The administration cooperated and came along with a doctor and organized a meeting against the blind belief regarding witchcraft and witch hunting. They asked them to do away with such belief system, and warned the villagers not to trouble the brothers. The doctors asked them to consume less of the local alcohol, which was actually creating health problem to them and unbalanced mind which instigated them to commit crimes.

Superstition is not actually what leads to the cases of witch hunting but it has a solid base if one analyses it.[17] Witch hunting is seen mostly during the twentieth century in Bodo area, especially during the initial days of demand for Bodoland. It was used as a way to demonstrate their power and hostility towards the government and a way of expressing their anger and differences from the other community. But these killings have never been recorded or any justice given to the people who suffered in the name of witch hunting. There was no proper investigation, as it was defended by the people who did not want anyone to interfere in their religious practices or question their rituals and belief system. The belief in superstition has actually saved many criminals who commit crimes in the name of religion even today. There is a lack of awareness on such social crimes in these areas.[18] The people have such less faith in the system of governance that others have taken the opportunity to spread more disturbance and fear among the common people, there is very little essence of brotherhood among the people left.[19] The areas, where such crimes still prevail in the name of witch hunting are those areas which have been stricken with unemployment, deprivation of development and insurgency too, which is actually a political turmoil tangled along with other problems which are intentionally unnoticed by the people in power. These areas act as a buffer zone between the people in resistance against the established government. These disturbed zones are used politically by the government and the people to manipulate the common men who are used as objects to fulfil their motives of self-interest.[20]

CASE STUDY 10

The victim is from Chirang district originally, but has now settled in Bongaigoan. She, and her husband barely survived. According to the victim, there was a community feast going on. The region is always troubled with militancy and insurgency problem. Young boys are abducted in the name of insurgency by militants so the women in the village are scared regarding their young boys and husbands and such a situation also gives rise to new forms of religion and rituals in the village where the women follow all kinds of religious practices and offerings that has been told to them.[21] The prayers would take place mainly at night and which made the environment very unsafe for the women as there would be teasing specially by the militants. It was a full-moon night and the victim was returning home after the religious ceremony. On the way, she was raped and dragged to the forest. She said there were more than two men, who raped her and she could not understand their language. The next day her husband found her and he was still mentally disturbed as the victim says. The victim's uncle reported the matter to the police but the youth of the village particularly, a few of them, did not let them investigate much and threatened both that, if they filed a complaint or the police comes to the village again, they would be thrown out of the village and branded as witches. The victim was at last given protection by the Mahila Samiti, which works under supervision of Birubala Rabha, the witch hunting crusader.

According to some victims, the clash between militants and Insurgents in the BTAD area has cost them with their lives and the women no longer feel safe. Sometimes, the local people dress like the insurgents and rape them, physically abusing them and their family. The militants, who are there for them supposedly for their protection, make the situation worse for them at times. Whenever they protest against such nuisance, the voices are suppressed by their own people who get financial support from the people in power. They do not want such things to come out and the most outspoken women are threatened of being accused of witchcraft and for such situations even the *ojhas* are bought off to plot against an innocent woman branded as a witch so that the people believe the whole drama made up by the ones in power.[22] The situations in these areas are so sensitive and politically influenced, that it becomes dangerous even for the one who defends such crimes. A person does not even think twice before taking a life in the name of witch hunting.[23] Witch hunting has a very deep root where not only property, land and the other customary laws provokes one to commit such a crime but also ambitious, learned women are not spared by the most educated and progressive society in the name of witch hunting. It has actually nothing to do with belief or evil but people do it out of jealousy, insecurity and greed. The people need employment rather than being idle in life because being idle leads to such impulsive thoughts and frustration out of jealousy regarding the prosperity of others.[25] Many times it is seen that during elections there would be a sudden rise of rumours of a sage coming to the village who can tell one's fortune and future. He stays in the village temple in isolation and keeps chanting *mantras* which can also heal a sick person without seeing him and rumours of his power and spells are discussed so that people from distant villages come to worship him. Slowly he starts taking interest in the welfare of the village and manipulates everyone to cast their votes for a specific person he names for the well-being of the community and by doing such things, he manipulates the people and earns money from the people who appoint him for their political agenda.

CASE STUDY 11

The victim is a girl of 18 years. She was frequently unwell and her parents took her to the doctors in town travelling many miles from her house. At last, when the girl did not recover, they left the medication completely and went to the *ojha* in the nearby village. She and her parents were asked to convert to Vaishnavism by the *ojha*. She became a prime figure in the village where people started bringing gifts for her as they believed God (*Aai*) resided in her. She started having dreams and narrated to people what God wanted from them and in the meanwhile the *ojha* too became famous along with her and was called Narayan Baba by the people. But one day the girl vomitted and blood was seen in it by her friends and they were scared and ran away. People also saw her eating non-vegetarian food and one of her aunts said that evil had now taken control over her and it was due to her that her friend would have high fever, especially after sunset. She was now hated by the same people who worshipped her as God. She was abused as a witch now and out of fear her parents sent her to stay with her maternal uncle in the town though her aunt was not willing to keep her at first. Her father is presently working hard to build a house in the other village so that he can bring his daughter to stay with them. The mother is still scared that something might happen to them if the people again became mad and lose their mind. The victim's family cannot even go to the police because once the police leave their house, they would be again disturbed by the villagers. They were scared of the police finding their fault, so to avoid such thing they have confined themselves to their house and workplace.

CASE STUDY 12

The victim was a converted Christian. He lived in Suribari of Kokrajhar district. He had converted because during his bad times when his sick wife needed medical assistance he asked for financial help but no one came forward and advised him to go to the *ojha*, but he was totally against it. In the meantime, he was helped by a priest who ran a missionary school in the town and not only did he help his sick wife to be treated properly, but also employed and sheltered them. He was very much influenced and touched by the kind act of the priest. Nobody was happy in the village with his conversion. He was now not welcomed at the community functions and religious occasions. The youth in the village, specially the local political party was very much against his presence in the village and threatened him to leave the village, as they believed he was an impure soul now. A man from the village was found dead and there were frequent mishaps. Slowly, the people started abusing him and even hit him, whenever he was alone, branding him and his wife, as witches who were now impure and wanted to make the other people impure by influencing them to convert. His house was destroyed and his wife was physically abused by a few men. He and his wife have left the village, with his house and the plot of land being occupied by his brother's son.

The word *daini* (witch) has become a weapon in the hands of those wanting to trouble people and fulfil their personal grudges. It is seen that many a times the victim gives up defending herself and agrees to be called a witch or whatever evil the people relate to her, out of fear and frustration. Earlier, there were some victims who agreed to be so that they would get some social attention and offerings such as food and clothes as they were worshipped to please the evil in them or animals such as black cock are sacrificed in their name.[26] A false assumption on knowing *dainibidya* (witchcraft) sometime for fun even becomes serious, as it costs the life of an innocent. Witchcraft has also turned out to be a business, where one can see many forms of gods emerging overnight. It has actually turned out to be a flourishing money making way out in such troubled and disturbed areas. Many such people are punished by the local youth, who in the name of religion exploit and loot people. The women of the age of 40-60 are easy targets of being branded as witches because of their unusual behaviour, specially at the time of menopause, when she has hormonal imbalance and people in the rural areas are unaware of such changes in them are easily convinced that they are 'possessed' by evil or a witch. Sometimes, women are also termed impure because of many changes one goes through. So, medical assistance and awareness on such issues need to be gender oriented, so that both the sexes are well aware of it, rather than being scared or afraid of the changing attitude and behaviour of one.

CASE STUDY 13

The victim was sexually abused for many days by the *ojha*. The victim was a widow, who was branded a witch by her own brothers to get hold of the property her husband had left for her and the plot of land she got from her own father. She was first taken to her own house after her husband's death and was later tortured by her sisters-in-law. Though, she was ready to give away everything she had, still she was taken to the *ojha* and blackmailed by him. It was said that, if she refused to have sexual relation, she would be declared a witch. The victim was found in a very bad condition by the youth organization which rescues victims who are socially, physically abused. The girl, later, committed suicide.

According to Pratibha Brahma, who put her own life in danger and rescued many victims, the main problem lies with the Bodo people themselves, who are still very gullible and believe everything so easily that it becomes easy for other people to exploit them. They also have the problem of easily getting aggressive at any matter, may be because of the long deprivation they faced and the crisis they are surrounded by. By doing all, these things they might succeed in keeping themselves alive and bring themselves to notice. But, she also says that whatever the reason may be of being described as dangerous or primitive by people, a great number of victims in the Bodo community have got justice either from the administration or through the various active NGOs working in these areas, where the government bodies refuse to come as people have preconceived notions regarding the marginalized people and their culture. Myths and beliefs continue to grip Indian society leading to irrational thought and actions. In the recent times, Assam is experiencing an increased number of instances of people resorting to behaviours, which is illogical and dangerous. It is based on beliefs in the existence of some unseen or magical powers concentrated in the hands of some individuals, who can cause harm to others.[27] The folklore which have also given women a negative stature is also a reason for such gender oriented crimes and rituals in a society that have to be followed. History has also celebrated his story and painted her story behind the veils, where she needs to be covered most of the time to protect the people being possessed by her spells which have always remained unknown to the world of man. The period when the Brahma religion was starting to be preached and women and men were mostly taught and encouraged on work ethics, crime caused by women's spells were less because people were made to think rationally and logically about their actions and decisions. Witch hunting should not be made on the pretext of words such as faith, beliefs and superstitions. It has never been their culture or practice, but is made such during these progressive times, where people use such derogatory ways to achieve their goals. Though witchcraft and witch hunting is seen mostly as a gender oriented crime, incident such as the one in Thaigarguri village which is 50 km away from Kokrajhar town has proved that out of anger and frustration people can do anything to better their situation.[28] In this incident five heads were chopped off in the name of witch hunting and the culprits were not even sorry for their deeds as they believed that they had committed this heinous crime for betterment and welfare of the people, as the village had been suffering for quite a long time. At present, the village headman name Samarendra Narzary, who actually gave the orders for the murder of the innocent people in the name of witch hunting, works against such crime as he was able to realize that his action took away the lives of four men and one woman in an inhuman manner. There are many people who have now become crusaders, who were earlier victims of witchcraft and witch hunting or accusers, for whom innocent lives were taken away only on mere suspicion and false assumption.

NOTES

1. Sameshwar Narzary, Interviewed, 22 January 2017, Kokrajhar, Assam.
2. Sonjiy Buglary, Interviewed, 17 March 2017, Udalguri, Assam.
3. Chitrelekha Das, Interviewed, 24 February 2017, Guwahati.
4. Shasank Shekhar Sinha, 'Restless Mothers and Turbulent Daughters Situating Tribes' in *Gender studies*, New Delhi: Stree Publication, 2005, p. 35.
5. Sumandra Narzary, Interviewed, 7 March, Chirang, Assam.
6. Chitrelekha Das, Interviewed, 24 February 2017, Guwahati.
7. Shasank Shekar Sinha, 'Restless Mothers and Turbulent Daughters Situating Tribes' in *Gender Studies*, New Delhi: Stree Publication, 2005, p. 21.
8. Praffula Basumatary, Interviewed, 4 February 2017, Udalguri, Assam.
9. Raju Narzary, Interviewed, 22 January 2017, Kokrajhar, Assam.
10. Victim X, Interviewed, 26 January 2017, Kokrajhar, Assam.
11. Deepen Bodo, Interviewed, 3 February 2017, Udalguri, Assam.
12. Mada Ram Brahma, Interviewed, 6 and 9 February 2017, Kokrajhar, Assam.
13. Preetam Choudhury Brahma, Interviewed, 21 January 2017, Kokrajhar, Assam.
14. Romen Boro, Interviewed, 4 March 2017, Udalguri, Assam.

15. Praffula Basumatary, Interviewed, 4 February 2017, Udalguri, Assam.
16. Sonjit Basumatary, Interviewed, 5 February 2017, Udalguri, Assam.
17. Prtibha Brahma, Interviewed, 22 January 2017, Kokrajhar, Assam.
18. Preetam Choudhury Brahma, Interviewed, 21 January 2017, Kokrajhar, Assam.
19. Raju Narzary, Interviewed, 22 January 2017, Kokrajhar, Assam.
20. Jinny, Interviewed, 2 March 2017, Chirang, Assam.
21. Sumandra Narzary, Interviewed, 7 March, Chirang, Assam.
22. Pratibha Brahma, Interviewed, 22 January, Kokrajhar, Assam.
23. Deepen Boro, Interviewed, 3 February 2017, Udalguri, Assam.
24. Raju Narjary, Interviewed, 22 January 2017, Kokrajhar, Assam.
25. Deepen Boro, Interviewed, 3 February 2017, Udalguri, Assam.
26. Prafulla Basumatary, Interviewed, 4 February 2017, Udalguri, Assam.
27. *Witch hunting in Assam: A Report*, OKD Institute of Social Change and Development, Guwahati, 2015, p. 1.
28. Preetam Choudhury Brahma, Interviewed, 21 January 2017, Kokrajhar, Assam.

CHAPTER 25

Women as Witches, Women as Homo Sacer: A Study of Contemporary Witch Hunting

OBJA BORAH HAZARIKA

Witch hunting has been prevalent in varying degrees all over the world throughout history in diverse forms. Although, outlawed by law in most countries, the practice of witch hunting continues without much interference on the part of the law, the state, and the educated to alter and prevent it. In many parts of India, witch hunting continues to be reported. Assam reports witch hunting incidents almost on a daily basis. Despite advocacy against superstitious beliefs, which are believed mainly to underlie the witch hunting incidents, such violation of rights of people who are victimized as witches, who happen mostly to be female, continue unabated. Continuance of witch hunting is, thus, a stark reminder of the level of pernicious practices which continue to mar society. It is also a marker of the abysmal level of education and awareness prevailing in several parts of the country. The poor level of sociocultural evolution and appalling level of human rights protection available to the victims can also be gauged through the incessant witch hunting cases.

This article will attempt to make a theoretical analysis of the phenomenon from the perspective of the concept of '*homo sacer*, itself once referred, in ancient Rome, to a person excommunicated from society, removed from the safeguards offered to its normal members so that his biological life subsequently could be taken by anyone with impunity', provided by Giorgio Agamben. The study will be conducted with an objective to examine how 'witch hunting' produces 'witches' as *Homo Sacer* in today's society which in turn leads to a situation where the victims are devoid of human rights, legal rights or any other rights which are deemed basic or fundamental for living in a meaningful and fruitful way. The societal, cultural, religious, and economic reasons, which underlie the creation of the 'witch' as *Homo Sacer* will be explored in order to provide a theoretical understanding of the phenomenon of creating 'women' as 'witches', which in turn leads to 'witches' being situated beyond the reach of law, which in turn makes them *homo sacer*, and how that may imply that 'women' are *homo sacer* in such societies. This article is thus grounded in a post-modernist framework provided by Agamben and is rooted, both in 'Human Rights' and 'Feminist' discourse.

INTRODUCTION

There are several attributes given to witchcraft in human history, for instance witchcraft has historically been employed to bring about 'the death of some obnoxious person, or to awaken the passion of love in those who are the objects of desire, or to call up the dead, or to bring calamity or impotence upon enemies, rivals and fancied oppressors'.[1] Ronald Hutton has identified five characteristics generally shared by those, who believe in witches and witchcraft across different cultures and time periods:

(a) witches use non-physical means to cause misfortune or injury to others;
(b) harm is usually caused to neighbours or kin rather than strangers;
(c) strong social disapproval follows, in part because of the element of secrecy and in part because their motives are not wealth or prestige, but malice and spite;
(d) witches work within long-standing traditions, rather than in one-time only contexts; and
(e) other humans can resist witches through persuasion, non-physical means (counter magic), or deterrence including corporal punishment, exile, fines or execution.[2]

Along with the existence of a belief in witchcraft, there has also existed witch hunting in human history, prevalent over many countries throughout the ages. Witch hunting implies killing or hurting of the so-called 'witch' mostly by members of the community. There are reports of various treatments meted out to witches by the attackers; most of these aims to cause injury and hurt. It has been noted that:

> . . . helpless 'witches' are hounded and punished by being stripped naked, paraded around the villages, their hair is burnt off or their heads tonsured, their faces blackened, their noses cut off, their teeth pulled out (they are supposedly defanged) so that they can no longer curse, they are whipped, they are branded, sometimes, they are forced to eat human excreta and finally, they are put to death (the victim is hanged, impaled, hacked, lynched or buried alive).[3]

Where these women are left to live, they are considered '. . . inauspicious and malevolent, socially ostracized and forced to forego their livelihood. Where they don't end up losing their life, they are made to lose their mental balance.'[4] Sometime, if the witch is not killed, the family will be socially confined and will be boycotted by the whole village and the community. This will result in loss of livelihood and movement will be restricted. This may also cause forced migration or displacement and may cause illegal trafficking too.[5]

The killing of accused witches continues to be reported from countries like Indonesia, Sri Lanka, India, Burundi, Uganda, Cambodia, Papua New Guinea, Ghana, United Republic of Tanzania, South Africa, Angola, Mali, Democratic Republic of Congo, Nigeria, Nepal, etc.[6] Earlier, it was prevalent in Europe and America as well. Until the thirteenth century, the belief that there was such a thing as a witch was considered by church officials to be superstitious nonsense (Nelson 1975).[7] However, witch hunting became a norm in the following centuries. During the period from 1400 to 1700, an estimated 5,00,000 to one million people were burned as witches in Europe (Ruether, 1975).[8] In Reformation Europe, it was overwhelmingly women who were tried as witches. In 1484 Pope Innocent VIII issued a bill making witchcraft a form of heresy and empowering inquisitors to eradicate this cancer from Christendom. *The Malleus Maleficarum* (The Witches' Hammer) by Jakob Sprenger and Henry Kramer became a classic statement of misogynism, as it articulated the reasons why women were witches.[9] The authors claimed, that the term female came from the word *femina*, which meant 'lacking in faith'. The basic premise of the Malleus was that witches are pawns of the devil and that the devil recruits his agents through carnal lust. As they put it in the Malleus, 'All witchcraft comes from carnal lust, which in women is insatiable'. In fact, the inquisitors taught that witches ride broomsticks at night to 'black Masses', in which they fornicate with the devil and feast on roasted children (Nelson, 1975).[10]

WITCH HUNTING IN INDIA

Witch hunting is practised in some form or the other in different parts of India, but mostly concentrated in the areas (states/UTs) of Andhra Pradesh, Assam, Bihar, Chhattisgarh, Gujarat, Jharkhand, Karnataka, Madhya Pradesh, Maharashtra, Orissa, Rajasthan and West Bengal. Mostly, '. . . middle aged and elderly single women in tribal as well as non-tribal communities are orchestrated as witches, leading to social stigma, displacement, economic boycott, torture and even murder.'[11] Even men are sometimes labelled as witches. According to the National Crime Record Bureau between 2008 and 2012, more than 768 women have been murdered for allegedly practising witchcraft. The rate of conviction in cases of crime against women is the lowest in India (26.9 per cent), when compared to other crimes and adding to this crisis is the fact that there is no specific law in India to fight witch hunting. Witch hunting cases are currently registered under Sections 302 (murder), 320 (grievous hurt), 351(assault), 354 (assault or criminal force to women with intent to outrage their modesty), 364(a) (kidnapping for ransom) and 503 (criminal intimidation).[12] There are three states in India, which have laws against witch hunting: Bihar was the first state in India to pass the Prevention of Witch (Dayan) Practices Act of 1999. This was followed by the Anti-Witchcraft Act in 2001 passed in Jharkhand along with the 2005-2006

Chhattisgarh and Rajasthan laws. There is no such law in Assam which passed The Assam Witch Hunting (Prohibition, Prevention and Protection) Act, 2015 which received the assent of the President on 13 June 2018. Except, a project called Project Prahari by the Assam Police, there is no legal measure to curb this crime. This project too is not a continuous action.[13]

WITCH HUNTING IN NORTH-EAST INDIA

In the north-eastern region of India, which is home to diverse indigenous communities, the practice of witch hunting is prominent. The practice is more prominent, though not limited to, the Rabha, Hajong, Mishing, Bodo and the Adivasi and tea community in Assam.[14] Witch hunting is still very common in districts of Goalpara, Kokrajhar, Chirang, Baska, Sonitpur, Udalguri, Tinsukia, Dhemaji, etc., of Assam. According to available statistics, 81 cases of witch-hunting were reported in the state between 2006 and 2010.[15] The method in identifying and then punishing the 'witch' follows a similar pattern in most of the cases reported. At first instance,

> . . . the witch is called a 'daini' in local parlance and believed to cause ailment to people, destroy crops and other livestock etc. She is usually identified by an 'ojha', 'bez' or 'deodhani' (all names for witch doctors) and either banished from the community or killed. Sometimes, the designated family of the witch is levied a hefty fine by the community leaders, by which she may be pardoned of her ill deeds/intentions against the fellow villagers.[16]

In addition, the belongings and the properties of the woman is taken away by the people.[17]

CAUSES OF WITCH HUNTING

Some contend that witch hunting aims to rob the woman of her property. Sometimes, it is also directed as punishment for turning down sexual advances or even to settle any grouse that some person with a say in village politics might nurse against that woman. Those who seek to rob the woman may be her own family. But in situations where the woman is unprotected, i.e. she is a widow or a single woman, there's no shortage of people eyeing her land. Witch-hunters (or property-hunters), irrespective of being family members or outsiders, often use the services of *ojhas* or 'witch-doctors' to further their cause. In many rural communities with limited or no access to health care, these *ojhas* become powerful figures. Police investigation has found, in many cases, that the local *ojha* has accepted a bribe to name a woman as a witch.[18] An accusation of witchcraft can be the result of a land conflict or of economic rivalries and competitions, or it can mask the refusal to support family or community members that are seen as a drain on its resources, or can be a device to justify the enclosures of communal lands.[19] There is another reason, which has been forwarded to explain resurgence of witch hunting in Africa which can be applied to India and Assam's witch hunts as well. In this view, argued by most contemporary anthropological studies, it is stated that witch hunts are not a legacy of the past, but a response to the social crisis that globalization and neo-liberal restructuring economies of Asia and Africa, especially India have produced.

Justus Ogemboo in *Contemporary Witch-hunting in Gusii, Southwestern Kenya* (2006: 111ff.),[20] argues that structural adjustment programmes and trade liberalization have so destabilized African (and Asian) communities, and undermined their reproductive system and thrown households into such 'deprivation and despair' which people are not able to comprehend, that many people have come to believe that they are the victims of evil conspiracies, carried out by supernatural means.[21] He points out that, after Kenya (and in the same fashion, India) 'adjusted' its economy, which led to unemployment and currency devaluation, so that basic commodities became unavailable, state-subsidies to basic services, like education, health, public transport, were gutted. In short, millions of people, in rural and urban areas, found themselves unable to provide for their families and communities and without any hope for the future. This led to rising mortality rates, especially among children, due to the collapse of the healthcare system, growing malnutrition, and the spread of AIDS, contributed to suspicions of foul play leading to a situation, where some who were the source of all these ill happenings were targeted as witches. Ogembo argues that the persecution of witches was further instigated by the proliferation of fundamentalist sects, re-injecting into religion the fear of the devil, and by the appearance of self-defined 'traditional healers', exploiting people's inability to pay hospital fees and hiding their incompetence behind appeals to the supernatural.[22]

AGAMBEN AND WITCH HUNTING IN ASSAM AND ELSEWHERE

This article attempts to understand the modern-day phenomena of witch hunting in Assam, and elsewhere, as the continuance of *homo sacer*, 'bare life', 'biopower' and 'state of exception', as used by Agamben to describe life in Western democracies or in concentration camps where the sovereign or the government has control, not only over the territory but over the bodies of the people as well. The term '. . . *homo sacer* itself once referred, in ancient Rome, to a person excommunicated from society, removed from the safeguards offered to its normal members so that his biological life subsequently could be taken by anyone with impunity.'[23] The state of exception in ancient Rome was created when '. . . normal political rights and legal safeguards were stripped away, so that the *homo sacer* was reduced to the mere naked, or bare, life of a human being alive only in a biological but not in any political sense, since he has none of the usual rights of a member of society.'[24] Agamben, however, says that such conditions exist today, when citizens of democratic or modern-day governments also lose control of their own bodies, manifested in biometric deposits or concentration camps depending on the intensity of government control. Thus, no one is free, everyone is at the risk of becoming *homo sacer* at the will of the government. Even those with safe citizenship status can at any moment become *homo sacer*, for example, under Emergency Law between 1975-7 in India, when fundamental liberties were suspended and right to political life was taken away in one swipe. Agamben insists that democratic states of the West are built on the mechanism that produced *homo sacer*, and are not fundamentally different from that, which enabled Hitler's concentration camps.

Agamben insists that for 'those safely holding membership in present-day Western societies, how the built-in threat of their own exclusion from its protections and their acquiescence in this order of things (such as the acceptance of government and corpocratic surveillance; the—black prisons? and Guantánamo as a permanent state of exception) is the foundational mechanism of power in these modern states.'[25] Agamben's device of using ancient Roman law of *homo sacer* and Foucault's concept of state control over peoples bodies—bio-power, to explain today's state control over the population, helps one examine the phenomena of witch hunting in Assam and elsewhere. For the accused witch, banishment marks an entry into a state of exception—which is a concept in the legal theory of Carl Schmitt, which indicates a situation which is similar to a state of emergency, but based in the sovereign's ability to transcend the rule of law in the name of public good. Following banishment, the witch becomes reduced to bare life and violent closures to witchcraft related insecurities become legitimate, in a fashion similar to what happened to *homo sacer* in ancient Rome and the inmates in the concentration camps and those in Abu Ghraib—who are outside the law and can be killed without the killer being accountable for the act, thereby stripping them of any rights whatsoever and depositing them in a state of exception. The state of exception is a space devoid of law. When community chiefs and family elders or *ojhas* expel the witch from the community, they suspend the general norm of community orientation, very akin to what the sovereign does to inmates in the concentration camps or what Hitler did to the Jews.

Under normal circumstances, a person belongs to both the community and the family. Membership in a village means that one is entitled to social, cultural, religious and community support, help and protection. However, on being proved a witch, when the witch is banished, she no longer enjoys this protection. The witch instead becomes a security challenge for the village from whom the villagers need to be find protection and thus, she is reduced to being a *homo sacer* and banned or made to go into the state of exception. She becomes excluded from the moral community in a very physical manner and deprived of her human rights by being banished from the village and the protection, thus far given to her is lifted. In this condition, everybody might legitimately expose her to violence thus challenging her material security and the integrity of her body. She might be tortured and subjected to other human rights abuses. Because the witch is a dangerous person, it becomes both legitimate and necessary to eliminate her, either physically by killing her or geographically by driving her away from her home town. Because of the dangerousness of the witch, she becomes stripped of her rights and reduced to bare life. This implies that labelling somebody a witch legitimizes a politicization of human life, a bio-politicization of the body of the witch. When a chief or a family elder decides upon the banishment of the witch, they draw an outer limit of the moral community and make a distinction between valuable and non-valuable life. In other words, the moral community comes into being by excluding somebody and thereby creating the boundaries of the community The one who is banned is abandoned by law, exposed and threatened. Her life can be lived only on the mercy of others and the others can kill her without regret or accountability.

Being cast out of the community means that her life is meaningless. When the witch is banished, she goes from being in a position of qualified life to bare life. The banished witch, is thus, a figure akin to Agamben's *homo sacer.* The cases of violence analysed below indicate that, like *homo sacer*, the witch occupies a zone of indistinction between life and death, human and animal. Through banishment the witch becomes bereft of her bios. 'Those who are captured in the sovereign ban and stripped of all legal status, find themselves, by the same act, banned from the political community. In this way, the sovereign decides which lives will be recognised as belonging to the community of political beings and which will be classified only in terms of biological fact. The basis of this distinction is addressed by Agamben with recourse to the two terms used by the Greeks to distinguish between forms of life: *zoe*, 'natural reproductive life' confined to the private sphere, and *bios*, 'a qualified form of life', political life'—Donoghue, A. 2. July 2015. Sovereign Exception: Notes on the Thought of Giorgio Agamben. Critical Legal Thinking. https://criticallegalthinking.com/2015/07/02/

sovereign-exception-notes-on-the-thought-of-giorgio-agamben/ The witch can be treated in an inhuman and degrading manner because she is not regarded as human. She can be 'hounded and punished by being stripped naked, paraded around the villages, their hair is burnt off or their heads tonsured, their faces blackened, their noses cut-off, their teeth pulled out (they are supposedly defanged) so that they can no longer curse, they are whipped, they are branded, sometimes, they are forced to eat human excreta and finally, they are put to death (the victim is hanged, impaled, hacked, lynched or buried alive)'[26] without any accountability to law. Additionally, everybody might subject the witch to violence. According to Agamben, the one who is banned is somebody, who may be considered as dead and whom everybody may legitimately harm. Through expulsion from the village community, the witch suffers social death. *Homo sacer* is thus somebody towards whom everybody can act as sovereigns, not just the government. Everybody might decide the fate of the witch/*homo sacer*. It is a figure that might be killed with moral impunity. After banishment, the imposition of the state of exception with regards to the witch, authorities and commoners become entangled. Every member of the community might begin to act as sovereigns towards the witch, performing violent acts that further constitute the accused witch as the embodiment of the existential threat of spiritual attacks. The witch falls victim to community violence. Although, the witch hunts of today seem to fall perfectly into the *homo sacer* category provided and used by Agamben, it is noteworthy to mention that in Agamben's analysis, he only laments the doings of the state or a leader like Hitler as policing the bodies of his people, but in the witch hunting cases, it is the locals, who can act as the sovereigns even before the witch is declared to be a witch, in witch hunting, the locals are the sovereigns who decide on the fate of the hunted, making her *homo sacer*. In this light, it can also be argued that dowry deaths, dowry persecution and some other evils in which a person is rendered without political life and is ill-treated even by their own family is rendered as a *homo sacer* by the family, which in turn becomes the sovereign. In all these cases, it signals a miserable lack of natural justice or human rights prevalent in today's society. It is also to be noted that since most witches since antiquity have been women, it is a feminist issue as well. Women's rights and bodily control has been the topic of many debates, both political and academic. From merely fighting for women's socio-political rights, the debate has been enlarged to include the control of women over her body. As shown earlier, one of the causes underlying witch hunting is the fact that women are seen as a burden, as a contender for family property, strong willed women are seen as a threat to patriarchal norms, and some have even opined that women whose skills as mid-wives and having knowledge of herbs were seen as a threat to men's domination, with a view to prevent such independence among women. The witch theory was used to nip all such developments. History is replete with torturous treatments meted out to women in the form of Sati, female genital mutilation, etc., all on the basis of some ill-conceived socio-religious-cultural viewpoints. Witch hunting, though admittedly not confined to women, is another such drudgery faced by women. It has been established earlier in the article that witches are *homo sacer*, and now it is seen that witches are mostly women, it is safe to opine that in such circumstances women are *homo sacer* (at least more than the men) in Assam, and wherever else witch hunting or any such practices prevail where the community or common man becomes the sovereign with the power of destroying another's life by declaring that, she is a witch and thereby, strip her of her village security, protection and community life and expose her to life as a non-entity, who can be killed without accountability.

The practice of witch hunting constitutes an extreme form of violence against women. The state should adopt appropriate measures to eliminate the practice of witch hunting, prosecute and punish those involved and provide for rehabilitation of, and compensation to, victimized women. Creating public awareness of forms of violence against women rooted in custom as an infringement of women's human rights should be taken up by NGOs, and the state as well. Project Prahari of Assam Police Department is a project aimed to prevent witch hunts. Organizations like AMSS, AIDWA, Some Sah Mozdur Santha, ABSU, WinG, All Bodo Women Justice Forum Assam Network, etc., have been trying to stamp out this evil practice. Though accused women can take help from legal system, but they are unable to do that because of displacement, loss of livelihood, lack of community and family support. It is more like a social, rather than criminal issue. Still, the issue is not considered as that of human right violation. Proper education, health facilities, especially in rural/remote areas, will enable the issue to be tackled properly.[27] If the argument about the family or the village, as the new sovereigns deciding the fate of hapless women by blaming them as witches is pursued it can be noted that dangerous social collapse is in the offing. It is a manifestation of banal beliefs and practises, which are being followed by people. Human life and rights are being rapidly undone by the fact that villages, quacks, sorcerers and local thugs are amassing power over other peoples bodies in their own hands and a phenomena of a state of exception within a state of exception is being created.

NOTES

1. Field research by AMSS Report written by Anjuman Ara Begum, Assam Mahila Samata Society (Mahila Samakhya) Assam, 2010.
2. Ronald Hutton, 'Anthropological and Historical Approaches to Witchcraft: Potential for a New Collaboration?', *Historical Journal*, 2004.
3. Rakesh K. Singh, 'Witch-Hunting: Alive and Kicking', *16 Women's Link*, vol. 17, no. 1.
4. Ibid.
5. Field research by AMSS Report written by Anjuman Ara Begum, Assam Mahila Samata Society (Mahila Samakhya) Assam, 2010.
6. Ibid.
7. Mary Nelson, 'Why Witches Were Women', in Jo Freeman. Palo Alto, ed., *Women: A Feminist Perspective.*, CA: Mayfield, 1975, pp. 335-50.
8. Rosemary Radford Ruether, *New Woman, New Earth*, New York: Seabury Press, 1975.
9. Keith A. Roberts and David Yamane, *Religion in Sociological Perspective,* http://www.sagepub.com/rsp5e/study/resources/82986_11pe_3.pdf
10. Mary Nelson, op. cit., 1975, pp. 335-50.
11. Joya Chakraborty, Anjuman Borah, 'Witch Hunting in Assam: Strategising Alternative Media for Women Empowerment and Overcoming Super-

stition', *Journal of North East India Studies*, vol. 3(2), July-December 2013, pp. 15-24.
12. Ibid.
13. Field research by AMSS Report written by Anjuman Ara Begum, Assam Mahila Samata Society, (Mahila Samakhya) Assam, 2010.
14. Joya Chakraborty and Anjuman Borah, op. cit., 2013, pp. 15-24.
15. Field research by AMSS Report written by Anjuman Ara Begum, Assam Mahila Samata Society (Mahila Samakhya) Assam, 2010.
16. Joya Chakraborty, Anjuman Borah, op. cit., 2013, pp. 15-24.
17. Field research by AMSS written by Anjuman Ara Begum, Assam Mahila Samata Society, (Mahila Samakhya) Assam, 2010.
18. Rakesh Singh, op. cit.
19. Silvia Federici, 'Witch-Hunting, Globalization, and Feminist Solidarity in Africa Today', *The Commoner.* New York, 2008.
20. Ogembo, Justus M., *Contemporary Witch-hunting in Gusii, Southwestern Kenya*, Lewinston: The Edwin Mellen Press, 2006.
21. Ibid.
22. Ibid.
23. 'Outlaws, Barbarians, Slaves Critical Reflections on Agamben's homo *sacer*' *Journal of Ethnographic Theory* 2(1), pp. 161-80.
24. Ibid.
25. Ibid.
26. Rakesh Singh, op. cit.
27. Field research by AMSS written by Anjuman Ara Begum, Assam Mahila Samata Society, (Mahila Samakhya) Assam, 2010.

CHAPTER 26

Witchcraft Practices in the Plantations of Upper Assam: A Case of the Santhals

OLYMPIA KURMI AND
SARAH HILALY

INTRODUCTION

The indigenous societies in India can be categorized on the basis of their habitat, their belief systems and the level of their encounters with organized religion. There are very few societies where indigenous practices are not mediated by the organized religion. In the north-east, three of the hill states have Christianity as the core of the belief system with layers of indigenous traditions subsumed within it, while one state has an indigenous belief system competing with Christianity. The indigenous communities of western and central India have been incorporated within the fold of Hinduism. While some of their deities have been subsumed within the Hindu pantheon, a substantial layer of indigenous beliefs remain at its core. This dimension is apparent in the religious practices of the santhals and important indigenous communities of those who inhabit the colonial regions of Chota Nagpur, particularly the space of the Santhal Parganas. The Santhals are one of the groups of Austro-Asiatics inhabiting the central and eastern part of India in the State of Jharkhand. Other cognate tribes belonging to this group are the Mundas, Hos, Kharias, Savaras (inhabit Orissa and Andhra Pradesh) and also the hunter-gatherers Birhors. Their origin and migration stories allude to their journey from Yunnan through the north-east of

India to their present location. The entire group were united as Kherwars, before they separated into individual tribes.[1] In terms of livelihood, the Birhors were hunter gatherers, while the other Austro-Asiatic tribes were all agriculturists incorporating a supplementary activity of gathering wild food. As regards specific forms of agri-cultural evolution, the Mundas farm terraced fields, carrying out wet-rice cultivation, while the Santhals practised the slash and burn or swidden agriculture of neolithic lineage. They are well-known for their expertise in clearing forest and turning it into arable land.[2]

The Santhals have been incorporated into the dominant Hindu society and the norms of social stratification. Their production system has also shifted away from community ownership of land and forest, yet some vestiges of it still remain. Their belief system rests on the belief that all diseases to both men and animals are attributed to either the wrath of evil spirits to be appeased or the spell of some witch or sorcerer, who should be destroyed or driven out of the land. They have a different set of rituals for the village collectively and for the family. In this space, only men can relate to the family spirits through prayer and partake of the sacrificed animal. Women are completely excluded from participating both in family and village rituals. They are not permitted access to the family spirits, nor are woman permitted to enter the inner shrine. They can neither sacrifice nor witness the process. The family spirits (*abge bonga* and *orak bonga*) of the clan and the family are passed on from father to son. The ritual specialists too are men.[3] Such a marginal position of woman is contingent to their not being ritually assigned full membership of the clan. Entry into the sacred groves are prohibited as also in the main dance of the agricultural festival.[4]

Within the Santhali cosmology, centrality is accorded to their belief in *dayans/dans/churails* (witches) or *bongas* (spirits) 'There is no genuine Santal', wrote Bodding, 'who does not believe in witches' (1986: 38).[5] This is posited within the belief that human beings can be intimate with and control evil spirits. Both men and woman can within this system bring harm and even kill their kin, as well as their fellow villagers. As women are ritually inferior in the society, any visible sign of them being in close contact with the *bongas* would be treated as a witch and persecuted. Ritual specialists belonging to certain Hindu castes would generally play the role of an exorciser, which is a pointer to the hybrid cultural evolution, which renders women marginalized and the sole gender identified as keeper of evil. It is to be noted at this point of the discourse that neither the Santhal, nor the Bhil have words for 'witch' in their own languages.[6]

The Santhal myth of the origin of witchcraft ascribes it to the struggle between the genders, and in Santhal society as a whole. According to a version in circulation, is that the women came to know that the men had approached Maran Buru to teach them something. The women got the men drunk, dressed up in their attire and tricked Maran Buru into teaching them. Maran Buru then taught them the incantations and gave them the power of eating men. The next day when the men came, Maran Buru realized that he had been tricked by the women. He then made the men 'expert in the art of witch-finding'.[7] So this myth introduces the idea of trickery, which gives the woman power that draws one into the idea of illegimate knowledge which they actually have no access to. The entitlement of men to such knowledge renders their authority supreme. Hunting witches, therefore, is a process of re-establishing social order with men at the centre of it. Women are denied access to priesthood, as it is presumed that they would turn to witches and misuse power.[8] The threat of being declared a witch and persecuted is thought to be a deterrent to non-conformist or deviance from established norms. It is during occasions of social crises in terms of epidemics or social tensions, due to conflicts that woman in the villages are targeted, persecuted inhumanly and even killed. Particularly, the life interest of widows in their husbands land is one of the key causes of persecution. This is because many Santhal woman can gather and sell forest produce and have exclusive rights over their income. This narrative has provided a background of the Santhal social milleu in their native habitat and their cultural evolution.

This article deals with the Santhals who have been uprooted from their traditional habitat, displaced and traumatized under conditions of colonial rule. The universe of study would be the Santhals who live within and outside the plantations of Assam, where they were brought in as indentured labour along with other groups from eastern and central India. In addition, it was the Santhal experiment of 1880, which encouraged their movement into the forest villages of Goalpara for extraction of timber. Living in a milieu uprooted from their habitat, they continue to follow many aspects of their traditional culture.

THE HABITAT AND PEOPLE

The State of Assam lies between 22° 19' north to 28° 16' north latitudes and 89° 42' east and 97° 12' east longitudes. Falling under three natural divisions, it comprises of the two river valleys of the Brahmaputra and the Barak. The intervening range of the North Cachar and Karbi Hills separate the two valleys. On its north it is girdled by the Himalayan state of Arunachal Pradesh, home to a multitude of tribes. On its east lies, Nagaland, Manipur with Mizoram and Tripura to its south. Its demography is characterized by tribes living, both in the hills and plains and castes speaking both in Bengali and Assamese languages.

In the medieval period, the states of the Ahoms and Dimasas existed as distinct spaces within the geography of Assam. The current territoriality of Assam is the result of colonial intervention. With the advent of the British in 1826, in the aftermath of the First Anglo-Burmese War, the state under the Ahoms passed to British occupation. After a lapse of two years in 1828, the administrative division of Lower Assam (Kamrup Darrang and Goalpara districts) was annexed to the colonial state. Upper Assam (Sibsagar and Lakhimpur districts) was restored to the Ahom ruler Purander Singha. In 1838, Upper Assam was resumed and annexed to British territory on grounds of mis-governance. The latent cause was, however, the fateful discovery of tea and its successful manufacture in 1837.

Consequent to the manufacture of tea in 1836, the Government of Bengal approved the scheme and gave Assam, the first set of wasteland rules. The wasteland rules were revised in 1854. These rules permitted only Europeans to avail such concessions instituted Assam's plantation regime. This industry was labour intensive and hence there had to be a constant supply of labour. The myth of the Chinese as the 'ideal tea-grower', led the British to induce their migration into the plantations till 1843. Then, the tea plantations came to be served by local inhabitants mainly Kacharis and Nagas. Resistance from these populations to intensive work and the expansion of the plantation industry resulted in a demand for labour.

From 1859 onwards, labourers from central and eastern Indian highlands and forests were imported for the tea plantations in large numbers. These indentured labour were brought in and regulated through the labour acts. The first Labour Act was passed in 1863, seeking to regulate the transport of labourers emigrating to Assam Valley, as well as their recruitment through *arkattis* (licensed recruiters). An Amendment Act of 1870 in the form of the *sardari* system of recruitment was also recognized. According to the Bengal Administrative Report for 1867-8, 22,800 were imported laboures and only 11,633 were local labourers. By 1880s, immigration of plantation labourers took place on an extensive scale.

The designation 'Upper Assam' was an administrative division in colonial Assam comprising of the undivided Lakhimpur and Sibsagar districts in the upper reaches of the Brahmaputra Valley. The other divisions are: Lower Assam, North Assam and Hills and Barak Valley. The division is under the jurisdiction of a Commissioner, stationed at Jorhat. In the aftermath of India's Independence, districts falling under Upper Assam are Dhemaji, Dibrugarh, Lakhimpur, Golaghat, Jorhat, Sibsagar and Tinsukia. An extended list of the region also includes the districts of Sonitpur, Karbi Anglong & Nagaon. The Upper Assam region is the most productive region in the state, which is rich in natural resources like coal, oil and natural gas as well as tea plantations.

The tea labour communities, constitute the oldest amongst Assam's immigrant groups. They were recruited by the British tea planters from present-day Jharkhand, Chhattisgarh, Bihar, Andhra Pradesh, Orissa, Uttar Pradesh and West Bengal, between 1861 until the early twentieth century, to work as indentured labourers in tea plantations in Assam, spread over the districts of western Assam, Morigaon, Nagaon, Sonitpur and Darrang in middle Assam, Golaghat, Jorhat, Sibsagar, Dibrugarh and Tinsukhia in eastern or upper

Assam, North Cachar and Karbi Anglong districts in southern Assam and the Barak Valley. Belonging to the indigenous groups such as Santhals, Mundas, Oraons, Kharias, Gonds, Khonds, Kisang and Nagesias, they settled down in Assam at the end of the contract period. During the colonial period, some left the tea plantations to settle in the surrounding agricultural lands before the expiry of the contract. The latter came to be known as time-expired or ex-tea coolies' who lived in villages neighbouring the tea estate, providing casual labour depending on seasonal demand. The present-day population of the tea labour community in the state is estimated to be 20 per cent of the population of the state, which according to a conservative estimate comes to six million. Despite their numerical strength and long history in Assam stretching more than a century, they remain 'outsiders' without the tribal status, as has been accorded to them in their place of origin, and are deprived of benefits availed by the other backward castes. Among the plantation workers, Santhals would constitute about three lakh out of the total tea tribes.

PRACTICE OF WITCHCRAFT AMONG SANTHALS

The belief system of the Santhals in their new space of habitation since the nineteenth century follows the same trajectory as amongst their kin in the Chota Nagpur region. The Santhals are one of the aboriginal tribes of India and were brought by the British in the latter half of the nineteenth century along with other tribes to the tea plantations of Assam to work as indentured labourers. They have retained their unique identity, traditional practices, rites and rituals in Assam. They practise their own religion and system of worship known as *sarna*. It is a form of nature worship wherein the Supreme deity is Marang Buru (God of Mountains) and Thakurjibi, who is believed to be the creator of the universe. The creator, however, does not feature in the numerous festivals, rites and rituals of the Santhals except his name being invoked on certain occasions. Uprooted from the original homeland, the Santhals in Assam, have over the course of time, become more Hinduized than their Jharkhandi and Oriya counterparts. They have adopted numerous Hindu practices while striving to maintain their own. A substantial section of the population have also adopted Christianity in certain parts of the state.

The key role in the religious rituals is played by their priests. The priest who is highly revered and performs the life cycle rituals is the *naikekhili*, who comes from the Murmu/Hembrom clan of the Santhals. He is the main priest and performs the rituals at his own private place of worship. In his absence, the *puja* can be performed by *naike* (also priest), who can substitute the main priest only if the *naikekhili* is not available. However, to be chosen as a *naike*, it is believed that he should be possessed by the *gosain* (Marang Buru). To ascertain, whether he is really possessed by the deity or not, he has to undergo certain tests. He is generally beaten with a *charchari* (a form of whip made from thatch), and if he is possessed by the deity, the whip either breaks or bends. This system of selection of *naikes* is dying out and generally people are selected as *naikes*, if they belong to the appropriate clan and are knowledgeable in these matters of the spirit. Within the traditional belief system there is no scope of worship of idols. In festivals such as *Baha* that signify the onset of spring. The *naikekhili* has to perform the *puja* under a grove of *sal* trees with the presence of the *majhi* (village head), *jog majhi* (*majhi's* assistant), and *godet* (helper). Only after the *naikekhili* performs this *puja* in the common place of worship, others in the village are allowed to perform the same at their homes. In this *puja*, the Marang Buru is invoked with an offering of wine and a sacrifice of either a white cock or white goat is made. In Upper Assam, steps were taken to abolish animal sacrifices and currently fruits and flowers are offered to the deity instead. The *naikekhilis* and *naikes* do not participate in magical practices. Their services are required at the time of festivals, and other life cycle rituals.

Like their counterparts in Jharkhand, the Santhals, among the tea tribes of Assam have a rich history of magical practices. Their belief in the magical world remains strong even today and irregularities in health, wealth and prosperity are believed to be the handiwork of someone, who has intentionally harmed them through the use of black magic. A clear distinction is made between white magic and black magic. While white magic is done to remove the ill-effects of black magic, to perform exorcism, to cure the sick, to resolve problems in domestic life or work, black magic is done to harm someone with the intent to cause illness, loss of property and also to kill. However, it is interesting to note that the person who is knowledgeable in white magic might also be skilled in black magic. Among the Santhals, the medicine man or the practitioner of witchcraft is called *ojha*, who is conversant with both the arts. The knowledge of magic or witchcraft is attained through rigorous training and practice and passed on by an *ojha* to a person of his choice. This choice is made by carefully selecting a disciple, who is seen to be worthy of receiving such secret and powerful knowledge. Knowledge might not be passed on even to kin, if that person is deemed to be unworthy or seen as incapable of mastering the art. It is also worthwhile to mention that this knowledge is highly protected, not disclosed even to family members and passed on by the *ojha* only when he is old or infirm.

Magical powers are also attained by certain people who can be termed as witches or magical practitioners. There are also instances of couples being witches and practising such magical rituals. They would go into the most secluded part of forests to participate in the highly secret rites and rituals that give them their power. Such power can be attained by offering sacrifices and invoking the main deities or spirits like Rangkeni, Baghut, Churkin (malevolent spirit/witch), etc. While each of these deities is not necessarily evil, the power attained through deviantly manipulating them can be used for harming others. Some of the Santhals have gone on to compare Marang Buru with the Hindu God Shiva and Rangkeni with the Hindu Goddess Kali and much like a Tantric gains his power, the *ojha* or witch can gain power. While spirits and deities are benevolent and their blessing is sought for the happiness, prosperity and health by the Santhals, they can be invoked to attain special powers which can be used either for good or evil. Santhals have numerous deities and spirits whose powers can be used alternatively for good and evil. Spirits are called *bongas*. *Apge bonga* is a house spirit and protects the house of a Santhal. Certain rituals are performed to appease the house spirit for protection and peace at home.

Another spirit called *baghut* (tiger spirit) is a very violent one and its power can be used to harm someone. The most important deity, however, in the Santhal magical world is Rangkeni (compared to Goddess Kali), whose power is the strongest among all spirits and deities. Black magic practitioners generally invoke this Goddess to obtain power, to curse or harm someone. It is believed that the harm done through this magic is most effective and mostly irreversible. This Goddess is easily appeased and the power granted by the Goddess is very potent. Another lesser spirit which grants power is Churkin, which literally translates into a witch. Churkins are less powerful compared to other spirits/deities. Marang Buru, the supreme deity of the Santhals is a benevolent god and does not bestow evil powers. However, his powers/blessings can be used by an *ojha* to alleviate the sufferings of an individual affected by black magic. Lay people cannot perform secret magical rites, since it requires greater practice, skill and expertise in magic. However, if a common person is selected by a *guru*, that person can learn it. A person is selected by the existing practitioner, who has to pass on the knowledge before he/she dies. Otherwise, his whole family will be cursed and eliminated by the deity/spirit from which he draws his powers. The selected one can be any random person, who might be a son or daughter or relatives or any random person having the requisite qualities.

These magical practices of the Santhal tribe are quite ancient and have been preserved even now. However, it is interesting to note that the Santhals in Kokrajhar and surrounding areas have been more stringent in retaining their age-old customs, rituals and beliefs than their counterparts located in upper Assam. The Santhals of Upper Assam have either become more Hinduized or Christianized and have also become more intermingled with other tribes and castes in the area. As such, theirs is a more relaxed outlook and in fact, the younger generations do not follow the Sarna religion rigidly, only elements of it in life-cycle rituals and do not blindly believe the magical and healing abilities of *ojhas*, witches and shaman, etc. *Ojhas* are respected members of the society and their help is required in alleviating the ill effects of black magic, ill health, etc. However, it is worthwhile to mention that these *ojhas* can dabble in black magic themselves and their services are sought to harm someone as well. A Santhal can seek help from *ojhas* belonging to other tribes too.

Whenever some harm befalls an individual or his family, it is generally believed that it is the handiwork of a black magic practitioner/witch. Even some educated Santhals persist in believing the powers of black magic. Though the belief in black magic is quite common, people do not have a clear understanding of who has actually done it. Conjectures are made regarding the identity of the black magic practitioner and people blame anyone who seems suspicious. However, the *ojha* is a well-known figure in the community as he provides his healing and has problem solving abilities to help others. In certain cases, he helps to identify who is a witch or black magic practitioner by citing some of their specific traits or characteristics.

There are no specific characteristics or symptoms by which the practitioners of witchcraft can be identified. People generally assume that a person may be a practitioner because of his or her looks such as being ugly, hunchbacked, emanating foul smell, etc., or someone who has threatened them in some way or someone who stays in isolation and is anti-social in behaviour. The physical characteristics of a person who practises witchcraft varies according to people's perception. A person with a violent temper and prone to threatening people, or one who is easily offended and does not engage in social interactions is suspected of participating in these practices. The Santhals believe that the practitioners might be envious of their health, wealth, beauty, etc., and have targeted them out of spite and jealousy. They may even blame members of their family for the cause of their misery. Identification can also be made with the help of an *ojha*, who would give certain specific details about the perpetrator. It is generally clues regarding their appearance, their traits or the location where the witch/practitioner lives. Priests cannot help to identify those who practice such craft.

It is seen that the belief in black magic and the harm caused by it is more at an individual level than village level in the Santhal populated areas in Upper Assam. Harm can range from ill-health, loss of property, hindrances in someone's career, obstacles in someone's marriage, death, etc. At village level, harm can be in the form of an epidemic like cholera, diarrhoea, blood dysentery, etc. Women are generally deemed to be associated with the practice, though both genders engage in these practices. It is a mere supposition that the power comes more easily to women than man. But, men are more powerful if they attain magical power. Hence, male practitioners are more feared.

There are ways to protect oneself from the harms of black magic. Devotion and regular worship of the supreme deity helps in warding off such evil attacks. If that doesn't help, the services of *ojhas* are sought whose mastery over such art helps in dispelling their ill effects. People are sometimes falsely accused of practising witchcraft. Such accusations are based on conjectures and speculations. The reasons for such false accusations can be a continuing dispute, grudge or petty jealousy. Women are generally accused of practising black magic, but persecution resulting in death is very rare in Upper Assam. Persecution or punishment of people or witch hunt is not common amongst Santhals in Upper Assam. This might be attributed to the fact that proper identification of the offending party is very hard. If someone is suspected of engaging in these arts and causing harm, the help of *ojhas* is sought to punish the culprit.

Persecution/witch hunt is very rare, though there have been few incidents, which generally went unreported. However, if such a hunt is organized, the victims generally tend to be women, who are either widows or those deemed to be fallen women. The most extreme form of punishment—which is also very rare—would be beating up the offending party by the members of the family of the aggrieved party or a group or a village mob. Other forms of recriminations include counter retaliatory measures through the *ojha*. In the rarest of cases where persecution results in death or driving the accused person away from the village, it might be related to custody of land or other property.

Witchcraft is a dying tradition amongst the Santhals of Upper Assam. Growing education and awareness amongst them has contributed immensely towards eradicating these practices. Also, it is seen that certain elements of these arts have been lost as they have been passed from one generation to the other and the newer generations are not as strict as their elders in observing the many rules and strictures required of them while practising these arts. The art requires constant and rigorous practice which might take a toll on the health of the practitioner. Though these practices are dying out, some elements of it still survive amongst them. If all medical help to an ailing person doesn't cure his affliction or ill health, the help of *ojhas* is sought still. No notable effort has been made by anyone to raise an awareness against these issues like Birubala Rabha among the Rabhas, where witch hunt is very rampant. The church, growing awareness and modern education are some facilitator of change amongst the people. Certain tribal organizations are also instrumental in bringing awareness to the people.

NOTES

1. Dev Nathan, Govind Kelkar and Yu Xiaogang, 'Women as Witches and Keepers of Demons: Cross-Cultural Analysis of Struggles to Change Gender Relations', *Economic and Political Weekly*, vol. 33, no. 44, 31 October-6 November 1998), p. WS59.
2. Ibid.
3. Ibid.
4. Shashank Sinha, 'Witch-Hunts, Adivasis, and the Uprising in Chhotanagpur', *Economic and Political Weekly*, vol. 42, no. 19, 1-18 May 2007, p. 1673.
5. Ibid.
6. Samar Bosu Mullick, 'Gender Relations and Witches among the Indigenous Communities of Jharkhand', *Gender Technology and Development*, 2000, 4, p. 346.
7. Dev Nathan, Govind Kelkar and Yu Xiaogang, op. cit.
8. Ibid.

CHAPTER 27

Magic and Witchcraft (*Dawi*) among the Mizos

ROHMINGMAWII

This article attempts to highlight the traditional knowledge about magic and witchcraft among the Mizosas told in folk narratives as well as those practiced earlier in the 'pre-Christian' era. One says 'pre-Christian' specifically because, as elsewhere, the scenario changed after the people embraced Christianity. Christianity was introduced to Mizoram (then known as 'Lushai Hills') with the arrival of the pioneer missionaries in 1894, and the colonial rule was officially established in 1890. As people began to embrace Christianity, the practice of magic and witchcraft was found incompatible with the Christian belief that facilitated its gradual disappearance. At the beginning of their rule, the colonial officials had to deal with cases related to the practice of magic and witchcraft but the growth of Christianity in Mizoram has a concurrent effect on the disappearance of this 'evil' practice which was considered to belong to their 'dark' past.

In theoretical discussion, magic and religion are often grouped together as there are some common qualities between them.[1] Evans-Pritchard found that 'magic is an integral part of religion and culture', and used to explain the unexplainable phenomenon, and thus relevant in preparing a meaningful world for the Azande.[2] Sir James Frazer in his book, *The Golden Bough (1890)* proposed an evolutionary scheme of magic, religion, and science where 'magic preceded religion because, according to Frazer, the former was logically more simple' and so on. This was followed by Sigmund

Freud.[3] But the post-modern scholarship challenged the western evolutionary conception of magic, religion, and science, thereby paving way for more sensitive treatment of magic.[4]

DAWITHIAM AND THE PRACTICE OF *DAWI*

Among the Mizos in the earlier period, the people who were able to channelize or connect with the external (supernatural) power were known as *dawithiam* (magicians/wizards/witches) and *zawlnei* (diviners/prophets/dreamers). The folktales and folk narrative contain accounts of magic/witchcraft/sorcery *(dawi)* and *dawithiam* but there are limited and scanty written references about it. It is difficult to differentiate between magic and witchcraft in these narratives because the Mizos used only a single term '*dawi*' and '*dawithiam*' for the practice and practitioner of this art respectively. Thus, in the case of the Mizos, it is not possible to strictly follow the pattern of studies conducted in other communities.

The Mizos believed that certain tribes were more experts in the art of *dawi*. Some sub-tribes, like Hmar and Vaiphei were considered to be expert magicians. The famous legendary wizards, Lalruanga, Hrangsaipuia, and Zangkaki all belonged to Hmar tribe. It was believed that these Hmar tribes had inherited the chants and art of magic and were experts at *dawi*. Vaiphei and other clans in Manipur were also considered to be good magicians and practicing magic widely.[5] It is difficult to establish historical relevance as to why certain clans were connected with the art of magic. They also believed that the neighbouring people (*vai*) were good at the art of magic.[6]

There are different narratives about the source of *dawi* (magic/witchcraft). According to legend, the famous legendary wizard, Lalruanga was said to have acquired the art of magic from the heavenly being, Vanhrika whom he captured for tampering with his catch in his traps. To save himself, Vanhrika taught Lalruanga the art of *dawi*. Lalruanga was depicted as a special person who was able to foretell the weather even when he was inside the womb. And as the legend goes, that magic was passed on to the plain people (known as *vai*) when Lalruanga's magic box was carried away to the plains by the river to the hands of the *vais* who learned magic from it.[7] In other oral traditions, the art of magic was said to have been passed on from one *dawithiam* to another and it is said that the apprentice should be a person of high quality, which was in some cases tested through the counting of grains of rice. Another qualification is that the apprentice should be a trusted person whom the magician trusted not to use the magic against him.[8] Among the Mizos, the practice of *dawi* was mostly associated with men though diviners were mainly women. Even the folk tales about *dawithiam* are dominated by names of men—like Lalruanga, Hrangsaipuia, Huatungamtawna, etc., although there was a reference of a woman *dawithiam* named Zangkaki.[9]

In Mizo practice, *dawi* was performed in two ways—one is only through words (chanting), and the other is by giving something to eat. Those who could bewitch only through chanting were considered to be expert magicians. The Superintendent of the Lushai Hills, A.G. McCall noted,

> The Lushais [Mizos] themselves do not seem to have been addicted to sorcery on a wide scale as a sort of black magic cult. They were rather victimised by members of other clans within their midst who might at times make a bold bid for power by this means. One method by which such sorcerers might cause death was to create the image of the victim and by weird incantations sing a song of sorcery in the hope of causing death by the sorcerer touching that part of the image he wished as the seat of pain. But such an elaborate procedure was not the only one adopted by sorcerers.[10]

Generally, a person's effigy was made by beeswax and as the wizard would chant over it, the figure would fall to the ground and the targeted person would die, instantly or later. A lock of hair or comb was also connected with *dawi*. If they had a dream of swallowing a comb or lock of hair, or even a hairy animal skin, it would surely mean that somebody had cast a spell on them. It was also believed that putting a small piece of *kelhnamtur* between the nails and dropping it secretly in someone's food was casting a spell and they would suffer from some chronic or wasting disease.[11] It was believed that when a person was bewitched, a bone, a tiger's fang, a lock of hair, or a feather/fur were deposited inside his stomach and that object grew and caused chronic stomach ache which would not be cured and eventually, he/she would die.

The practice of witchcraft or *dawi* was very real to the Mizos, and they were scared of those who were believed to have a destructive magical power. To protect themselves from a magical spell, the men in the drinking bout normally sipped a small amount and spat it out, and also left a small amount in the cup. When a housefly dived in their cup of rice beer, they took it as a sign that they were impenetrable to any magical spell.[12] Strangers with unkempt hair or displeasing appearance were generally considered to be *dawithiam* and were objects of fear. Such guests were often well-treated by their hosts out of fear. There were instances where such strangers were killed as they were suspected of being *dawithiam.*[13] The people tried to get rid of those they suspected of *dawithiam* from their community. This may be partly because the counter-magic was very expensive, and not many people were able to perform.

It was believed that eating the liver of a *dawithiam* was a cure for a magical spell, and it would also protect them from any such attacks in the future. Therefore, when *dawithiam* were killed, their liver was extracted and shared in small pieces among the people to protect themselves from any magical spell.[14] The Nagas, on the other hand, believed that the witches ate the internal organs like the liver, heart, lungs, etc. of their victims.[15] When some Mizo chiefs were compelled to accompany the Superintendent to Manipur, they were very scared of *dawi* from the Hmars and many of their followers returned home. The few men who dared to complete the tour were rewarded with exemption from forced labour (coolie) for a lifetime. To protect themselves from *dawi,* they collected the soil at the entrance of the village, made a small ball out of it, and swallowed it without water.[16]

COUNTER-MAGIC (*DAWI SUT*)

It was believed that the only way of recovery from *dawi* was through counter-magic (*dawisut*).[17] One way to counter the magic is to eat the liver of the person who bewitches them. Another way is through performing a counter-magic procedure called *khangpuizam* or *mubuvial.*[18] Counter-magicians were found mainly among the priests (particularly *Sadawt*)[19] but not all the *Sadawt* had this power. Khupvunga Hmar, chief Vuta's *Sadawt* was a famous witch-doctor who had the reputation of healing the sick and undoing *dawi*. It was the duty of the *Sadawt* to detect the cause of illness and prescribe the course of treatment, mostly in the form of sacrifices of fowls and other domesticated animals. Sickness was largely attributed to the evil spirits, and these sacrifices were meant to appease the spirits that caused it. Sickness as a result of *dawi* was also within the range of the *Sadawt* function though not all *Sadawt* were capable of attending the case.

The counter-magicians were few, as they needed to have a stronger power compared to the *dawithiam* who bewitched the person. It is said that if the person did not have a stronger power, there was a chance that he himself would be counterattacked and even die. For this reason, many magicians tried to avoid the request to counter the magic by demanding a high price for their service, or if the victim was still able to manage the cost, they would stealthily run away.[20] Thus, unless and until they knew the strength of the spell, counter-magicians did not like to perform counter-magic.[21]

The technique of counter-magic was a treasured art and was not simply passed on to others. It was a complicated procedure that required many items and the chanting was also lengthy which was done with careful preparation. The procedure and the items used by counter-magicians were diverse among the performers. One author opines that counter-magic is the most complex form of *inthawi* (generally translated as a sacrifice)[22] while another author opines that in the process of counter-magic, good or evil spirits were not involved but it was purely between the *dawithiam* and the counter-magician, and the performance should also be seen as a fight between two powers, different from other religious rituals.[23] Though the procedure might not be part of the religious functions of the priests, they were often the persons who were sought after to help the people out of the magical spell.

When counter-magic was performed, they raised poles (*uingul*) around the house of the sick person, and a thick woody creeper (*kawihrui*) connected these poles. The poles were also covered by this plant, a reed was also planted against each pole, they also collected some weeds (*hlo-rual*), like *sakeingho, khum, lemthilte, sialinuchhu* and various kinds of *ai* (the name of a root, supposed to have magic properties, used by sorcerers; the name of a small plant) like *ailaidum*, *aithin*, *dizung*, etc. They also made clay figures of the *dawithiam*, the counter-magician, and another figure to be placed outside. The priest (counter-magician) should wear a brand-new cloth, a turban, and put on the wings of an eagle and an owl.[24] It was believed that if the wizard attacked the counter-magician, he would fly above him like the eagle, and he was brave like the owl.[25] The priest and his team then carried a chicken, a pig, a goat, and a dog and followed the beam of the house. The priest threw away the chicken at the back of the house, the pig on one side, the goat on the other side, and the dog in front of the house. He then killed the dog and the other animals, put away the *serh*, and cooked the rest of the meat. The sick man was made to drink the blood of the dog while it was warm with a spoon; he had to break the spoon after finishing it. The person was then made to sleep facing the front door, and the woody creepy plant was tied to his toe which was tied again to the pole outside. The priest then gathered his collection of weeds, took a sip of rice beer, and spat at the person while fanning him with the weeds. He cut the roots (*ai*) on the forehead of the person, dipped them in the water, and made him drink it. After that, he went outside and danced with the pole on his shoulder without holding it. The dog's bladder and the figure of the wizard were placed at the pit, he broke the bladder and broke the clay figure, and put the pole over it. He would then place his own figure at the side of the pole. After that, they would start the feast. But the priest should not eat anything, he should go home with one of his followers after the feast was over, kill a chicken at the doorpost, place the blood on the doorpost, and entered the house with his follower, and the procedure was over.[26] It was a complex procedure that lasted the whole day. It is said that when such counter-magic was performed, a mist would be seen to cover the house and its surroundings.

There were only very few people who could perform counter-magic and therefore, unlike the normal religious performance where only the clan's priest performed for their specific clan, in the case of counter-magic, they shared the priest who knew the art.[27]

DAWITHIAMRAWT (MASS KILLING OF *DAWITHIAM*)

The chiefs often ordered the death penalty to those who were suspected to be *dawithiam.*[28] The victims were from the weaker section, like old men, old women, and young boys. This was probably a common practice among other tribal groups as well. Pritchard also observed that among the Azande, those citizens who 'make themselves a nuisance to their neighbours and those who are weak are most likely to be accused of witchcraft' and the richer and more powerful members of the society were hardly accused.[29] However, the accused among the Mizos were not necessarily the bad citizens. It seems that in some cases, jealousy was also the reason for accusing someone of *dawithiam*. The charge of *dawithiam was* hardly brought for a fair trial for they were eliminated at the earliest chance. Thus, the accusation of *dawithiam* was sometimes a chance to revenge on their rivals, which was as bad, or even worse, as the *dawi* itself.

A Vaiphei by tribe, Lunhmingthanga was a strong and brave man in the village of Chawngthleng. He was accused of being a *dawithiam.* He was tricked and killed by the order of the chief. His tribe, the Vaipheis then became the target of villagers as they were suspected of acquiring the art of *dawi.* They ran away from the village but they were pursued and killed. One of the groups pleaded for their life and gave themselves to be their slaves, claiming they did not know the art of magic, but the villagers replied that they did not dare to keep *dawithiam* as slaves. They were all killed and their raw liver was eaten by the chasers. (Mrs. Hualrochhingi and Mrs. Lalkeuvi of Chhipphir, eyewitnesses, gave an account of this event.) This happened around 1885.[30]

The incident of mass killing of *dawithiam* (known as *dawithiamrawt*) happened not only at Chawngthleng (Dokhuma was the chief) but we know from oral tradition that it also happened at Hmuizawl (Kalkhama's village), Lungleng (Dokapa's village), Thingsai (Lallianhleia's village), Khuangthing and Muallianpui.[31] The clans, particularly of the Hmars and Vaipheis, who were a minority in the village, were targeted and killed.[32]

In the early part of the colonial rule, the chiefs of the villages of

Thingsai, Khuangthing, and Muallianpui decided to kill those who were suspected to be *dawithiam,* most of which were from the Pakhup of Fanai clan. The chiefs of these villages acted together on an appointed night to kill the suspect *dawithiam.* Among those who were killed were an old man, an old woman, and a few young men. At midnight, the villagers broke into their houses, killed them, and extracted their liver, obviously for consumption as protection from *dawi.*[33] The slaying was followed by a celebration with rice beer at the village square and the executioners were adorned with *chhawn,* a piece of ornament entitled only to the brave men who killed enemies in defense of the village. There were some accused *dawithiam* who escaped the massacre. The incident reached the knowledge of the government. The four ringleaders, Dokapa, chief of Lungleng, Lallianhleia of Thingsai, Thanghleia, and Mehbawka and his brother were imprisoned. Four of them died in prison; Lallianhleia was released in 1906 after five years in prison. After this incident, Lungleng village disintegrated, and villagers from Muallianpui also migrated to Lungphun village.[34]

Superintendent A.G. McCall recorded the case of Keitawna, a Rangte clan from Manipur. He had a reputation of being a *dawithiam.* Thangvuka, a brave young man of chief Liankhama saw Keitawna in his dream, and on that very night, 'his house was filled with smoke and mist of an unprecedented kind' that disturbed Thangvuka who strongly believed that he was bewitched by Keitawna. It was said that Keitawna's method of practicing sorcery was to call upon his victim at a drinking bout, insert a tiny portion of poison between his nail, and hand over the rice-beer mug to his victim, and the victim became an easy prey in his hand. So, Thangvuka killed Keitawna and ate a little of his liver 'to neutralise the effect of any evil words which Keitawna may have uttered against Thangvuka's welfare.' The Rangte clan were very offended and decided to return to Manipur and continued to be hostile against Liankhama's village.[35]

After the colonial rule, the first Superintendent Col. J. Shakespear did not allow murder for the case of suspicion of *dawithiam*and gave the suspect a chance to seek shelter in a distant village and thus reduced the cases of such murder.[36]

CONCLUSION

Among the Mizos, *dawi* or black magic was mostly associated with sickness or health-related aspects and even with death. Chronic diseases, especially stomach ache, was considered to be the manifestation of a person bewitched by someone, the reason could be serious hostility or enmity. The counter-magic was associated with blood while magic was associated with sickness and death. General misfortunes were not necessarily connected with black-magic, rather, it was believed to be in the hands of God. If a person meets good fortune, they used to say, 'His god is good.' If they faced misfortunes they consulted a diviner who would prescribe a treatment. [37]

Society, in general, feared black magic and magicians, and if anybody was found to be a *dawithiam* or suspected to be so, they were put to death and their liver was eaten to protect themselves from the magical spell. Some clans were believed to be experts in the art of magic; the persons who knew the art of *dawi* were generally considered of high intelligence. *Sadawt* (priests) were considered to be well-versed in countering magic though there were not many who practiced it.

While some earlier scholars under the influence of the writing of Christian missionaries tend to group all magical practices as related to the indigenous religion, the relationship between religious practices and *dawi* is still a subject of debate. A scholar like James Dokhuma identifies counter-magic performance as part of a religious sacrifice but Rev. Zairema maintains that the rituals performed for magical acts or counter-magic are different from religious rituals though it is translated as *inthawi* (sacrifice) in all the earlier writings.

One of the most important functions of *Sadawt* was to treat illness, and *dawi* was also considered one of the causes of illness which was treated by some *Sadawt* by performing counter-magic. The scientific knowledge of health and its related issues after the colonial rule and the belief in Christianity gradually changed the outlook of Mizo community, and the treatment of sickness was also replaced by modern medicine. As a small tablet could eradicate sickness, the Mizos believed that there must be some magic spell in it, hence the name *damdawi* (*dam* means healing/healed, *dawi* means magic). They believed in the magical power of *damdawi* so much that they expected to get healed instantly, or by simply keeping the tablet in their pocket or under their pillow.[38] McCall believes that 'the very personality of the British government meant in itself an end to all sorcery' and that the Superintendent only intervened to relieve the anxiety of the people.[39] The practice of *dawi* in the form of black magic was pushed to the back and disappeared from the popular Mizo culture over a long time.

NOTES

1. J.W.G.W. (1939). 'Reviewed Work: *Witchcraft, Oracles and Magic among the Azande* by E.E. Evans-Pritchard, C.G. Seligman' in *Sudan Notes and Records*, 22(2), pp. 285-291. Retrieved 9 August 2020, from http://www.jstor.org/stable/41716340.
2. https://www.britannica.com/topic/magic-supernatural-phenomenon/Sociological-theories. Retrieved 9 August 2020.
3. Ibid.
4. Ibid.
5. C. Lianthanga, *Hmanlai Mizo Nun,* Mizoram Publication Board, Aizawl, 1999, p. 178; L. Sanglura, 'Lalhleia Sailo Chanchin' in *Mizo Lalte Chanchin*, Tribal Research Institute, Govt. of Mizoram, 2012, p. 59.
6. Rev. Zairema, *Pi Pute Biak Hi*, Zorun Community, Aizawl, 2009, p. 94; *Mizo Thawnthu*, Tribal Research Institute, Department of Art and Culture, 1992 (3rd Rep. 2008), p. 94.
7. Mizo Folktale, told by Rualthankhuma to the author, (1991).
8. James Dokhuma, *Hmanlai Mizo Kalphung*, Aizawl: Hmingthanpuii, 1992, (2nd ed. 2008).
9. C. Lianthanga, op. cit., p. 178.
10. A.G. McCall, *The LushaiChrysallis,* Tribal Research Institute, Govt of Mizoram, Aizawl, 1978, p. 71.
11. C. Lianthanga, op.cit., p. 178.
12. Ibid.
13. Ibid.
14. Ibid., p. 179; Rev. Zairema, op. cit., p. 94; *Mizo Thawnthu,* op. cit., p. 94.
15. A. WatiLongchar, *The Tribal Religious Traditions in North East India: An Introduction,* Published by Author, Eastern Theological College, Jorhat,

Assam, 1991 (revised 2000), p. 80. He clearly distinguished between magic and witchcraft.

16. L. Sanglura, 'Lalhleia Sailo Chanchin' in *Mizo LalteChanchin,* Tribal Research Institute, Department of Art and Culture, Govt. of Mizoram, 2012, p.59.
17. James Dokhuma, op. cit., p. 89.
18. C. Lianthanga, op. cit., p. 179.
19. There were two kinds of priests- *Bawlpu* and *Sadawt. Bawlpu* was involved largely with village rites while *Sadawt* functioned like witch-doctors.
20. Rev. Zairema, op. cit., p. 94.
21. James Dokhuma, op. cit., p. 93.
22. Ibid.
23. Rev. Zairema, op.cit., pp. 90-3, 95-7.
24. Ibid, p. 96, James Dokhuma, op. cit., p. 90.
25. James Dokhuma, Ibid., p. 94.
26. Rev. Zairema, op. cit., pp. 90-3, 95-7.
27. James Dokhuma, op. cit., p. 93.
28. C. Lianthanga, op. cit., p. 178.
29. E.E. Evans-Pritchard, *Witchcraft Oracles and Magic among the Azandes,* New York: Oxford University Press, 1976 (rep.), p. 52.
30. C. Lianthanga, op. cit., pp. 179-80.
31. Ibid; B. Lalthangliana, *Mizo Chanchin (A Short Account and Easy Reference of Mizo History)*, Author, 2009, p. 82.
32. C. Lianthanga, ibid.
33. The families collected the dead bodies at Thingsai and buried them in the same grave which is still there today. B. Lalthangliana, op.cit., pp. 82-3.
34. B. Lalthangliana, Ibid. The villagers had the liberty to remain with the chief or migrate to another chief, which was an important means of check and balance to the authority of the chief in the traditional political system.
35. A.G. McCall, op. cit., pp. 71-2; 'LiankhamaZawlnghak Lal Chanchin' in *Mizo LalteChanchin,* pp. 294-5.
36. A.G. McCall, Ibid., p. 73.
37. C. Lianthanga, op. cit., p. 7.
38. *Reports by Missionaries of Baptist Missionary Society, 1901-1938,* comp. the Mizoram Gospel Centenary Committee (Baptist Church of Mizoram, Serkawn, 1993), p. 56, 79; Zairema, *God's Miracle in Mizoram:A Glimpse of Christian Work among Head-Hunters,* Aizawl: Synod Press &Bookroom, 1978, p. 25.
39. A.G. McCall, op. cit., p. 73.

CHAPTER 28

Practice of Witchcraft among the Adis of Arunachal Pradesh

SARAH HILALY

INTRODUCTION

Indigenous traditions are based on an awareness of the integral and whole relationship between the planes of the symbolic and material life. In their everyday practices, there does not exist a distinction between the cosmological ideas and ritual practices embedded in their religion. The term, 'lifeways', encapsulates the holistic context in which the traditional environmental knowledge remains a dominant strand in the cosmologies of indigenous peoples. Cosmologies or oral narratives help to transmit the world view of the people by describing the web of human activities occurring within the powerful spirit world of the local bioregion. The context is made comprehensible through enacting rituals of the key myths of creation, origin and migration and revolves around the activities of the cultural hero and his life experiences. Religion is, therefore, constituted not merely as a system of beliefs and ritual practices, but is intrinsically entwined with their forms of subsistence, kinship, language, governance, and landscape.[1]

In most of the indigenous societies, the early myths allude to a series of circumstances, which lead to the creation of the universe. The process of creation is generally characterized by chaos and disruptions followed by orderliness. The creator is a key figure who recedes into the background, as life forms like plants, animals and spirits begin to inhabit the space. Humans too inhabit this mythical space, wherein they coexist with other life forms interacting and at times in conflict. The emergence of the first man segregated from the spirit world marks the final segregation of physical realm from the spiritual, though not at the level of ontology. The first human or cultural hero emerges, his triumphs, struggles and his human frailties are exemplified through the myths, which shows how reality came into existence. The cosmology endeavours to provide a code, through which society should strive 'equilibrium between peoples and between peoples and the other part of the environment, and between peoples and gods'.[2]

A few benevolent spirits inhabit the symbolic world, believed to influence people's health, ensure success of a clan, ensure a bountiful harvest, fertility of cattle, and create harmony within the community. There is however, an array of spirits with malevolent attributes including ancestral spirits, especially emanating from the souls of people dying unnatural deaths, who are considered responsible for the sudden disruptions of everyday life. In the face of unexpected events like accident, sickness, death or being lost in the wilderness, rituals which serve as the main vehicle for the expression of beliefs and feelings are conducted, ultimately seeking to balance and adjust the relationship between human and supernatural beings with most being healing rituals. The ritual specialists play a key role in this intervention with the spirits and negotiating with them on behalf of the humans. The myths, which are enacted and re-enacted in the form of ritual chanting, codify rules, which in turn help people to understand what kind of behaviour is expected of them, or disallowed, in order to maintain a sense of belonging to their own culture. It acts as a medium for self-awareness and awareness of others encoding therein the morality of a particular culture. Therefore, indigenous religion is a cultural system that has to be preserved and transmitted.

In addition to the action of the spirits, many traumas and tragedies, which remain irresolvable by ritual interventions, are attributed to black magic, evil eye, witchcraft, and confrontation with demons or possession.[3] Witchcraft is an all-pervasive belief within the indigenous belief systems and institutionalized religions across the world. It is the same set of spirits, who are cultivated for benefit of the society, are also invoked individually by both ordinary men and woman extolling its deviant qualities to acquire power. Such powers can be cultivated either through inheritance or learning. Through this acquired power, they seek to destroy their enemies. In many indigenous societies, the ritual specialists are capable by the mediation of their corpus of knowledge to eliminate the effects of such aberrant practices. However, the divination capability of the ritual specialists makes them play a key role in identifying the practitioners of witchcraft in the event of an absence of protective rituals within the community.

MEANING AND DISCOURSE ON WITCHCRAFT IN INDIGENOUS SOCIETIES

At the outset, it is essential to identify the meanings that have been evolved by scholars ranging from anthropologists to historians, to define the practice of witchcraft. Ronald Hutton, on his reading of multiple studies pertaining both to the anthropological and historical studies, broadly identifies five characteristics according to which witches all across cultures can be classified.[4] The first defines a person who uses non-physical means to cause misfortune or injury to other humans. This is explicable through the categories used by English-speakers in describing them as 'uncanny', 'mystical', or 'supernatural'. The second category comprises of those persons who work towards harming neighbours or kin rather than strangers, so that she or he is a threat to other members of his or her community.[5] The third abiding characteristic of the witch figure is that she or he earns general social disapproval usually of a very strong kind, in the context of having violated normative behaviour on two particular traits. Secrecy is the norm within which a witch operates, as the intended victim is unaware of the impending harm, until it has been executed. The harm caused by the witch emanates not from the desire to acquire greater wealth or prestige, but from motives of malice and spite. The fourth characteristic is the belief that the appearance of a witch figure is not an isolated and unique event. They generally work within the framework of a tradition and are possessed either of or by powers using techniques in circulation in the societies or introduced into it from outside. They are not freak occurrences within the natural order of things rather created by inheritance, training or initiation.[6] The fifth characteristic is that their fellow humans can resist them and worldwide this resistance takes three different forms though they are not exclusive. One is to persuade or force the witch to divest herself or himself permanently of his or her special powers, or to heal the harm that has been caused and to desist from causing more.[7] The broad contours of the outlined definitions are indicative that witchcraft represents the evil inherent in the universe, which manifests itself through humans, who act as vessels of transmission due to certain attributes inherent in their nature. The other dimension is that it embodies all that is selfish, vindictive, and anti-social within human communities, epitomizing treachery and disharmony in societies that strive for unity and neighbourliness.[8]

Studies on witchcraft have long dominated the discourse in anthropology, particularly the British social anthropologists who worked in Africa since the early decades of the twentieth century. In his classic work, *Witchcraft, Oracles and Magic among the Azande*, the anthropologist E.E. Evans-Pritchard describes the beliefs and practices of the African tribe, the Azande.[9] According to the Azande belief system, various misfortunes encountered in daily life may be attributed to the action of witches. Other anthropologists of the Manchester School explored the social dynamics of witchcraft suspicions and accusations in Africa.[10] Influential anthropological studies like that of Peter Gescheire (1997), argued that witchcraft was a mechanism for coping with stress and uncertainties introduced by late capitalism. Comaroff and Comaroff argue that while on one hand it helps to enrich some, it disempowers others.[11] Early scholars like S.F. Nadel who compares four African societies, argues that witchcraft studies needs to contextualize their social relationships in order to extract deeper meaning of how this institution functions under conditions of stress and contradictions.[12] Similar views have been expressed by Mary Douglas (1999) and Ajay Skaria (1997) on the play of kinship in witchcraft practices.

These studies feed into the corpus of studies taken up by historians, who drew ethnographic parallels in order to explore similar beliefs in the English past. The knowledge developed by the pioneers who analysed practices of witchcraft in African societies, Pritchard and Marwick began to include in their corpus, studies on early modern witch trials in Europe. Rodney Needham argued that comparitivism within anthropology, could lead to an evolution of an image of the witch, based on experiences both from Africa and Europe.[13] While a handful of historians in the 1970s attempted to study witchcraft in Africa and Europe within the same frame of reference, it was weakened by the questions raised by Hildred Geertz. Her argument was on the premise that comparison of general categories of witchcraft across continents and time was rather difficult. Rather, she insisted and called for the recognition of cultural particularity in such studies. Since the mid-1980s historians cross-referenced data between different parts of Europe and English colonies in America, which enriched such studies. Later studies witnessed the abandonment of the idea of a universal category to define the history of witchcraft through the lens of a global model.

In practice, however, in all indigenous societies, there occurs a wide variation in the process of identification of the witch. There are also societies according to Ronald Hutton, where all the ills confronting humans are attributable to spirits, rather than a belief that humans could initiate non-physical harm.[14] Yet the communities who had neighbours with similar social, economic and cosmological backgrounds did not develop the belief in witches.[15] Studies revealed that the gender of the witch is not a static image among the indigenous societies across Africa and Asia, where either men or women could be identified as witches, though the dominant figure in Europe were women who were indiscriminately hunted.[16] The strategy of dealing with witches ranged from the use of exorcising techniques, to persuading them to abandon the craft totally or in the severest case, of witch-hunt taken up at the behest of the entire community or by families of victims. The victims of witchcraft could generally be members of affinal families, with stray references to agnatic families as victims surface.

The external defining characteristics of a witch in some societies would be elderly and domineering woman, married, widowed or single. Physical deformities rendered a woman suspect, while forceful and articulate woman were branded and those considered trouble-some and quarrelsome were also under the scanner. Women displaying special qualities like intelligence and beauty were likely to be declared a witch. In the backdrop of these assessments of the tradition of witchcraft, I would like to foreground my study of magical practices among the Adis of Arunachal Pradesh. Since the practice of witchcraft constitutes an aberration and is practised in secrecy, the identities of the informants who have provided essential data for the study, are not being named.

THE HABITAT, PEOPLE AND MYTHS OF ORIGIN

Arunachal Pradesh is a state that straddles the north-eastern extremity of India and is essentially a constituent of the Eastern Himalayas. It is surrounded by international borders along its east with Bhutan, in its north with Tibet and a small section of China and Myanmar on its west. The valley of the Brahmaputra skirts its south. Home to multitudes of tribes and sub-tribes, it represents a cultural mosaic of diverse groups with linguistic and cultural variations populating the geographical space. Influences of the neighbouring polities of Tibet and Assam are marked in the realm of religion and culture. Groups whose culture and religion is predominantly shamanistic animism inhabit the central zone of the state.

The Adis who form the universe of this study constitute a major ethnic group in Arunachal Pradesh and occupy the central zone of the state. They inhabit the lower sections of Lower Dibang Valley District, Upper Siang, East Siang and Eastern portion of the West Siang district of Arunachal Pradesh. The Adi is a generic term used for the Padam-Minyong and the Gallong appellation along with a conglomerate of sub-tribes.[17] Among them the Minyongs and Padams who constitute the core of the study, inhabit East Siang district on both the banks of the river. The East Siang district is a wild mountainous area of 4,005 sq. km situated approximately between 27° 43° and 29° 20° North latitudes and 94° 42° and 95° 35° East latitudes.[18]

Based on the rich repository of oral tradition of the Adis in the Abang, their belief system alludes to creation myth where the earth is created out of nothingness Keyum. Sedi-Melo is the creator of the earth. Donyi-Polo the benevolent god sustains moral order of the living beings and lower deities. Five generations following Sedi-Melo, Pedong-Nane (rain Goddess) was born. She bore thousands of children, which manifested as living spirits, animals and Doni-Tani the first human. He is considered as the progenitor of all tribes inhabiting the central region of Arunachal Pradesh. After creating Doni-Tani (human beings) Pedong-Nane disappeared. It is in this corpus of myths that all the objects important for human existence can trace their origin. The first sacrificial animal was Limir-Sobi or Limur Sobo a cosmic Mithun (Bos frontalis) which was sacrificed by the first group of people called the Engo-Takar or Doni-Dongor. From the dismembered parts of this cosmic animal, which was broadcast, particularly flesh and hair-emanated objects like grass, shrubs and trees where non-human life forms lived and sustained. Goddess Kine-Nane provided the knowledge of the first cultivated crops. In order that birds and rodents do not destroy the cultivated crops, Engo-Takar, sacrificed a mythical Mithun Kumgum-Sobo. The dismembered parts of this animal transformed into fruit bearing roots and plants as sustenance for birds and rodents, which saved grain from destruction.[19]

It is the activities of Doni-Tani since his birth that gave humankind all its attributes like colour, speech and melodious voice. During his infant years, his crying could not be stopped by any means, hence his parents displayed natural toys like red leaves of a tree to pacify him. It was only when he was handed the wooden sword and knife that the crying stopped. These are construed as first instance of human knowledge of the significance of these implements in their everyday lives. All activities of humankind were henceforth to be defined by the training which Doni-Tani received from his father and other experienced elders. He also on occasion was trained how to negotiate with spirits by his elders and receive protection. Most of the religious rituals dedicated to spirits find their roots in Doni-Tani's life experiences. The various restrictions enjoined on society in everyday life are again attributed to the mistakes committed by Doni-Tani during his lifetime. The life cycles rituals and particularly the funerary rituals stem from the rituals performed for Doni-Tani's mother.[20]

The primary spirits, which are appeased, are many, among whom the prominent are Gumin Soyin (village spirit), Kine Nane (spirit of paddy) and Sisi Moyi (spirit of jungle).[21] The Padam-Minyong ritual specialist is called a Miri. He performs all religious rituals and rites enjoined in their moral code to try and sustain equilibrium within society. He maintains balance by acting as an intermediary between the spiritual world and the human world. He performs the divination to ascertain the potency of the ritual chants, the abangs and offers the prescribed sacrifices revealed through divination seeking blessings of the spirit on behalf of the people. The Miris can be divided into categories, depending on the specialized rituals they perform and are spiritually gifted as their bodies are inhabited by the spirit ancestor. Their position is, therefore, neither hereditary, nor elective as their qualities are inborn.

However, there is an alternate space, where the same spirits are not appeased in accordance with the set codes, rather their deviant aspects are cultivated. Hence, it is not the priest who draws power from the spirits, rather ordinary people involve themselves in cultivating such practices. Such practices are foregrounded outside the ambit of the sacred relationship between the priest and the spirit. Rather priests in most of the cases act as diviners to ascertain the identity of persons involved in the aberrant practice, which harms mankind. They also try to free the people from the ill effects of both spirit possession as well as acts of blackmagic/witchcraft. This article seeks to examine whether such practices exist among the Adis and the notions and attitudes of the society towards such practices.

BELIEF AND PRACTICE OF WITCHCRAFT AMONG THE ADIS

Adis believe in magical practices.[22] Among the Padams, Adis who comprise of the universe of study, a clear distinction is made between white magic and black magic. The magical practices like *mogum, donyi tato* and *gonamrinam* fall under the category of white magic and other magic like *pyonam, morumokeng* and *oksik* is grouped under black magic. White magic is essentially meant for service to the community, hence, considered beneficial for the prosperity and well-being of the society. Black magic is performed to bring harm to an individual and for society at large.

The popular myth, which maintains the distinction between white magic and black magic in Adi society, is traced back to the roots of humanity represented by Doni-Tani. This myth manifests that Doni-Tani descended from the Pedong Nane, who did not come alone but the spirits descended concurrently from the same mother. Some of the spirits who evolved were Banji Banmang (bloodthirsty spirits), Epom-Robo (jungle spirits), etc., to name a few. Except for Doni-Tani, all other spirits descended along with him are considered evil or wicked. Hence, it is believed that there was a clash between the wicked spirits and Doni-Tani, which led to the partition of their respective realms of existence. Thereafter, while the spirits could view humans, the humans could not, except through the mediation of the ritual specialist. Therefore, the prevailing belief is that all the black magic can be related to wicked spirits and on the contrary, all white magic is linked with Doni-Tani and his activities.

The identity of performer of white magic need not to be hidden since it can be performed publicly. However, the identification of the performer of black magic is based on assumption and circumstantial evidence. The dream interpretation usually helps in identifying the perpetrator; however, their absolute identification always remains vague even with the help of a priest.

Usually the priest does not take part in the magical practices except for *tagong* and *oksik*. Both the white magic practices and the black magic ones can be performed by any ordinary folk, therefore the intervention of the priest in performance of such magic is not solicited. While knowledge regarding white magic is circulated well in advance and can be performed in public, black magic practices remain hidden and considered an aberrant activity in the society. As all the spirits invoked for both white and black magic descend from the Pedong-Nane, it is a common belief that if a person encounters *takangappun [takang* (plant), *appun* (flower)] in a jungle and keeps it with him/her, they attain some supernatural powers. This is because the *takang* blooms rarely. Hence, it is believed that whosoever sees the blooming of this plant are no ordinary people.

Skills acquired for the occult can be both hereditary and acquired. In the event of it being hereditary, the power or magic is passed down through generations. In case it is acquired, a power can be acquired intentionally by coming under the influence of some wicked spirit without his/her knowledge. In both cases, the possessor of such power becomes captive to the wicked spirits. Accordingly, he/she has to fulfil the demands of the wicked spirit even though it might go against the grain of the inherent character of the person. Hence, to escape from such gruesomeness, the possessors often try to find solace in the present day by taking refuge in other religions like Christianity. In the context of the specific gender who become such practitioners, it has been observed that women are much more prone to it than men.

Another belief related to the attainment of power or magic is through obtaining a shiny object from the python. Pythons are perceived to be in possession of power, which helps them to create an illusion for their prey. Such power is visible in the form of a shiny object lying on the back of python, while it is either sleeping or resting. It is believed that if anyone can secure the object, which is representative of the power of python, the person can create any kind of illusion on whomsoever they want to harm. However, trying to obtain such power is taking a very big risk, as dealing with a giant python at times could become fatal.

In addition to the python, birds like the eagle and owl are considered to have a vision, which can foresee the future or even visualize extraordinary events. Hence, the possession of an eagle's or owl's eye is also considered to be a source of power. Therefore, there is a desire to posses such objects in order to carry out the hidden traits of the trade considered aberrant, is quite strong. The harm caused, varies according to the intention of the witch ranging from moderate ailments to loss of life, loss of property, causing mental imbalance, and living a deserted life, etc.

The chants used for the practice of the occult appear to be very difficult to comprehend though it is possible to state the ways in which they are practised. Based on the limited data that has been shared by the informants during collection of data in fieldwork, some of the important practices pertaining to both the white and black magic can be outlined as follows:

(a) *Mogum*: This is considered white magic, and is generally performed during the cultivation season when the rain fails to arrive. Therefore, it is performed to summon rain. Common people who have experience regarding the processes involved can perform this ritual. In the event of the ritual performance going wrong, it can adversely affect the health of the performer, or else can bring in heavy storm and thunder instead of just the rain. Through a simple procedure, the performers chant, though the challenging part is the chanting of the appropriate words that usher the magical spell. The ritual includes a component wherein the horn of a buffalo is half buried vertically in the centre of the river. The performance does not enjoin mass participation, nor is it accompanied by taboos. There is no particular day chosen for the performance of such rituals for magic.

(b) *Tagong*: *Tagong* is a remedial activity aimed at removing a fish-bone getting stuck in the throat which results in difficulty during swallowing. Only an expert in this field performs such remedial ritual. The magician or the priest would massage gently on the neck while chanting his/her magical words and simultaneously take out the bone stuck in the throat without causing any pain to the sufferer. Through *tagong* it is attempted to purify the blood of a person infected by the poison called *emo* (aconite, generally used on tips of arrows). The expert or the priests remove the poison from the blood by sucking it out.

(c) *Donyi Tato*: The purpose of *donyi tato* is exactly the opposite of *mogum*. Even in terms of ritual performance, *mogum* and *donyi tato* greatly differ from each other. *Donyi tato* is performed to summon the sun to appear in times, when continuous rains hinder the activities of daily subsistence like cultivation of paddy field. This particular practice is done only after the village council or *kebang* provide approval. Unlike the *mogum, donyi tato* witnesses mass participation by the male members of the society in its performance. Women are not permitted to participate in the performance and the entire village under the stricture of a taboo is prohibited from carrying out activities for subsistence like weaving, collecting firewood, performing agricultural related activities, hunting, etc. The process for the ritual begins with all the male members gathering at the village dormitory called *musup*, to prepare objects like *pobang* (a net like craft made of bamboo) and gather leaves of *tuduk* tree. While making this object, some members would go to catch a chicken or a hen of red colour from any household within the village. This requirement for a red coloured hen is, as it appears to resemble the red hue at dawn and dusk, which in turn seeks to please the sun god. In the afternoon, the head of the hen is chopped off, fastened to the top of 5-7 ft long bamboo along with *pobang* and *tuduk*, and placed at the roof of the *musup*. All the members would in unison shout out, pleading that the sun god accepts their sacrifices and listen to their grievances, seeking to attract the attention of *donyi* 'sun'. Soon thereafter, the weather would change, when the rains would stop and the people are allowed to resume their usual activities from the next day.

(d) *Gonamrinnam*: *Gonamrinnam* is more of a sacrificial ritual, which is performed in order to keep away any one with an eye who could hinder a person's progress. One who is capable of creating hindrance is called the *gona-rinna* and the process of hindering adopted by such a person is *gonamrinnam*. The hinderer may usher in bad luck, bad spirit, and bad wishes for people in the village. Hence, it is performed whenever a person ventures out for achievement of specific goals like ensuring success during hunting of animals, fishing, trade, and currently even before going out for a job interview, etc. The performance can be done in advance or just prior to departure particularly when a person comprehends obstruction from unseen quarters. The ritual process is simple and can be undertaken by anyone who finds disturbance or obstruction in his/her achievements.

Those who seek success in their hunting or fishing expeditions usually make an offering of egg, meat, wine, rice, etc., to keep away the *gona-rinna*. Whoever ventures for the tradition trade or modern livelihood activities like business or job, etc., may simply make a request to *gona-rinna* to leave them alone.

According to a belief, the castrator of the village is prohibited from venturing freely as his presence might cause hindrance in hunting, fishing or other trades. As he usually castrates domestic animals, it is believed that the *gona-rinna* hovers over him after he performs castration. He is not permitted to join a group going out for successful trades as his *gona-rinna* may prevent the group from achieving their motives.

(e) *Moru mokeng*: *Moru mokeng* is regarded as the most harmful witchcraft among all the forms of black magic. This magic is practised either to harm or kill the enemy. In this form of witchcraft, any belonging of the victim like clothes, hair, etc., is buried under the earth with a spell cast over it. The victims of such witchcraft will gradually become weaker and engulfed by illness unidentifiable through divination of the deities. If the buried material can be dug out in appropriate time, the life of the victim can be saved or else sooner or later the victim succumbs to death. *Moru mokeng* can be performed by anyone who specializes in aberrant practices. However, it is a risky proposition for the performer too, as a failed performance can have a reverse effect on the performer. The failure of the *moru mokeng* can be due to two prime reasons, in the event of the victims *aid alo* (courage of the soul) being stronger than that of the performer and, in the event of the buried material being traced out before the motive of the performer takes effect.

(f) *Oksik*: *Oksik* is another form of black magic witnessed in Adi society, whrein it can only be performed by those who possess *oksik uyu* (bad spirit). Both men and women can possess this spirit. The persons possessed by such a spirit are believed to be bloodthirsty and harm or even kill humans for their blood and soul. Whenever this spirit gets attracted towards a person, it ensures that it would be certain to achieve its goal of control over people. Usually, the villagers have a sense of who among them is possessed by such spirit. Hence, they avoid consuming any food item before them, lest the spirit of *oksik uyu* is attracted toward such objects. Its attraction can bring in ailments like stomach ache, losing consciousness for a while, or sudden unexplained illness, etc. Such a spirit generally is attracted to all edible objects. The spirit can take hold of a person magically and miraculously by creating illusions.

(g) *Pyonam*: In this practice of witchcraft an illusion is created over a large number of persons that is the *pyonam* (stealing). The Adis believe in two types of *pyonam*. One kind is the *uyu ager* which is usually the handiwork of a bad spirit, which induces the urge on a person to steal under its spell. The other practice of *pyoperung pyonam* refers to the proclivity of consciously stealing without any interference from the bad spirit. According to the prevalent belief system, the person stealing with intention can be easily apprehended, while catching the thief driven by the spirit becomes difficult. The person driven by the bad spirit and forced to steal objects, can do so even if the nature of person involved is not inclined towards such aberrant acts.

It is generally believed that the best way to protect oneself from being a victim of witchcraft is to try and consciously avoid persons perceived to be in possession of such power. It is usually advisable not to annoy a witch or keep any resentment against him/her. If, at all, the witch hinders anyone, the first step is to perform sacrificial rituals. The affected person and his family perform the sacrificial ritual by offering egg, local wine, meat or animals in order to please the evil spirit.

In the event that such acts of sorcery severely affect village life, village elders summon then the family presumed to be practitioners of witchcraft or even the village council called *kebang* which takes initiative to negotiate and handle the issue. The *kebang* would find the best way out of the imbroglio with the mediation of a priest. This is because all contradictions and complications in Adi society is usually tackled and handled by the *kebang*. The priest and elders would be summoned to investigate into the matter. If the joint action yields result, the council would summon the perpetrator issuing sufficient warning to the perpetrator to stop his/her mischievous actions. If the accused continues to persist with his witchcraft practices, the person would be apprehended and kept as captive by confining his/her feet between a wooden log often chained too. The person is also confined in isolation in a small hut.

CONCLUSION

With the disruption of village life due to out-migration for livelihood, they no longer remain the only space for daily existence. Despite adopting alien religious beliefs and the norms of modern medicine, this fear of the unknown persists at a primordial level. Instead of performing white magic, currently they rely more on more scientific notions of explanation. Yet, whenever modern medicine fails to offer solutions to ailments, the essential belief in black magic is invoked as intensely as it was in early Adi society.

Since the onslaught of modern education, which does not help in retaining oral traditions and newer forms of religion too, knowledge of older traditions has become a dying breed of knowledge. A minor attempt to document such practices though aberrant, yet essential to their world view helps in retaining such knowledge for posterity.

The symptom in a person affected by witchcraft is not obvious. It can be identified only with the help of the community priest by performing some rituals.

However, the identification of the performer of black magic is based on assumption and circumstantial evidence. The dream interpretation usually helps in identifying the perpetrator; however, their absolute identification always remains vague even with the help of priest.

Traditionally, it is believed that the witchcraft performers, have a *modii* (a regular time period of their performance). Whenever, they realize their time or *modii* has arrived, they isolate themselves and exercise paranormal activities while chanting magical words in a semiconscious state. Their *modii* generally occurs during the waning of the moon. However, it is unpredictable sometimes and can occur even at an odd time like during day time when people are around which lead to suspicion among the onlookers.

The harm is in accordance to the witch's intention. It ranges from moderate ailment to loss of life. Some have acute property loss, mental imbalance, deserted life, etc. Both can indulge in such activity, however, woman are much more susceptible than man.

The performers of white magic are considered normal human and one need not to distance himself/herself from such practitioner. However, one needs to be more way of black magic performers as they can cause harm even without much resentment. Hence, such practitioner is considered to be abysmal and is feared by people and society.

NOTES

1. John A. Grim, 'Indigenous Traditions and Ecology', *The Forum on Religion and Ecology at Yale*, originally published in *Earth Ethics* 10, no.1, Fall 1998, http://fore.research.yale.edu/religion/indigenous/
2. K. Powers William, 'Cosmology and the Reinvention of Culture: the Lakota Case', in *The Canadian Journal of Native Studies* VII, 2, 1987, p. 166.
3. Ülo Valk, 'Eyes of Legend: Thoughts about Genres of Belief', *Indian Folklife*, no. 25, January 2007, p. 12.
4. Ronald Hutton, 'Anthropological and Historical Approaches to Witchcraft: Potential for a New Collaboration?', *The Historical Journal*, vol. 47, no. 2 June, 2004, p. 421.
5. Ibid., p. 422.
6. Ibid., p. 423.
7. Ibid.
8. Ibid.
9. E.E. Evans-Pritchard, *Witchcraft, Oracles, and Magic Among the Azande*, Abridged Edition, Oxford: Clarendon Press, 1976.
10. The key figures in this scholarship are: Max G. Marwick; (1965), *Sorcery in Its Social Setting: A Study of the Northern Rhodesian Cewa*, Manchester: University of Manchester Press; John Middleton (1960), *Lugbara Religion: Ritual and Authority among an East African People*, London: Oxford University Press; John Middleton (1963), 'Witchcraft and Sorcery in Lugbara', in *Witchcraft and Sorcery in East Africa*, ed., John Middleton and

E.H. Winter, pp. 257-75, London: Routledge and Kegan Paul; J. Clyde Mitchell (1956), *The Yao Village: A Study in the Social Structure of a Malawian People*, Manchester: University of Manchester Press; Victor Turner (1957), *Schism and Continuity in an African Society: A Study of Ndembu Village Life*, Manchester: Manchester University Press.

11. Cf., Nandini Sundar, 'Divining Evil: The State and Witchcraft in Bastar' in *Gender Technology and Development*, 2001, 5, p. 431.
12. S.F. Nadel, 'Witchcraft in Four African Societies: An Essay in Comparison', *American Anthropologist*, New Series, vol. 54, no. 1, January-March 1952, pp. 18-29.
13. Ronald Hutton, 'Anthropological and Historical Approaches to Witchcraft: Potential for a New Collaboration?', *The Historical Journal*, vol. 47, no. 2 June, 2004, p. 414.
14. Ibid., p. 424.
15. The Andaman Islanders of the Indian Ocean, the Korongo of the Sudan, the Tallensi of Ghana, the Gurage of Ethiopia, the Mbuti of the Congo basin, the Fijians, the hill tribes of Uttar Pradesh, and the Ngaing, Mae Enga, Manus, and Daribi of New Guinea did not at all believe in witches. Ronald Hutton, 'Anthropological and Historical Approaches to Witchcraft: Potential for a New Collaboration?', *The Historical Journal*, vol. 47, no. 2 June, 2004, p. 424.
16. In India, various studies among the tribes of eastern and central India reveal different gender dimensions in witchcraft. Among the inhabitants of Chota Nagpur the Santhals, (shifting cultivators), Mundas, Hos, implicate woman as witches. Witch hunting is predominant practice among Santhals while cognate tribes like Kodaku and Hill Korwa do not believe in witchcraft, nor do the matrilineal Birhor and Erenda Munda. In Bastar incidence of witch-hunt is limited. According to Elwin Muria, men could be classified as witches, while in southern Bastar stories of woman witches circulate. Among the Dangs in Mewar and Gujarat, magical aggression is attributed to a male witch who is many ways is an aberrant priest, while the woman witch or female vampire could assume animal forms.
17. The Gallongs known as the Duba Abors in the British records have constituted them into Galos as a separate tribe in the 2011 through constitutional correction.
18. Tuting Borang, 'Funerary Rites of Adis: A Case Study of Padam Minyongs', Unpublished MPhil Dissertation, 2012, p. 35.
19. Tahan Mize, 'Animal Sacrifices in Adi-Religious Ceremonies', in *Diigok-Roli* (The Call of the Dawn): Solong-Gidii Magazine, 2010, vol. V , Itanagar, pp. 29-31.

20. Katon Borang, 'The Evolution of Mankind', *Donyi: A House Journal of the Donyi-Polo Study Circle*, vol. 1, no.1, January 1998, Itanagar, pp. 12-15.
21. Tuting Borang, 'Funerary Rites of Adis: A Case Study of Padam-Minyongs', Unpublished MPhil Dissertation, 2012, p. 11.
22. Fieldwork for this study has been carried out in Padam villages like Ayeng and Kiyit under Mebo circle of East Siang district. Data has also been generated from Dambuk village in Dambuk circle of Lower Dibang Valley district. As the practices of witchcraft does exist, the names of the informants are being kept under cover.

CHAPTER 29

Practice of Witchcraft among the Rabhas of Assam

BARNALI SHARMA

Witchcraft is believed to be the 'practices of a witch or witches, especially the use of magic or sorcery; the exercise of supernatural power supposed to be possessed by a person in league with the devil or evil spirits'.[1] However, the terms magic and sorcery; how to access this supernatural power; who these witches are, etc., are baffling with no concrete definitions. Its indentification is beyond one's simple understanding of the concepts of binary opposites: night and day, life and death, good and evil, human and beast. Scholars define, 'witches as the "other" and yet they are also "us". Witches are living projections of feelings that defy easy rationalization or reconciliation: amity and enmity, compassion and cruelty, self-confidence and fear.'[2] The human nature of acting by emotion occupies the centre stage in witchcraft. It is a human occupation engaging with an unseen world. Witchcraft hovers, it is invisible but powerful and persistent. It is essentially a mysterious occult phenomenon closely associated with religious believes and practices of a society.

In the *Dictionary of Anthropology*[3], a witch has been defined as a person, often a woman, who has supernatural powers to cause evil. They can look into the future, escape harm, transform themselves and accomplish almost everything desired. Witchcraft is a religion that respects mother nature, and she is neither completely positive nor completely negative. This is the reason why some people believe in the existence of witches and credit them with the possession of the most wholesome power. A witch is neither a spirit nor a ghost, but a human being who has acquired extraordinary powers. A witch has a magical rod, a concealed birth mark or other sign of her individuality, while still being associated with the power of darkness.

But every belief has a origin, a purpose and develops in some social, political and psychological situation. In fact, witchcraft is a worldwide phenomenon. The belief in witchcraft and its practice seems to have existed in different countries and societies across the world. In every religious belief the concept of evil is ingrained deeply. The Bible has a lot of references to witchcraft and strong condemnations of such practices are enjoined.[4] In Christianity, also in Indianism and Islam, sorcery came to be associated with heresy and apostasy. In Europe (especially in Central Europe), in the late medieval and early modern period, fear of witchcraft gripped church leaders who led intensive witch hunts. History reveals that it was a period of transition. Rise of Protestantism, the social and demographic destabilization caused by the Black Death, the transition from feudalism to capitalism, were some important incidents of the period. The manual entitled *Malleus Maeficarum* is an outline to identify witches who were mostly women, to persecute and punish them after trial. Federicci Sylvia in *Caliban and the Witch* had delved into the issue discussing that the birth of the proletariat required a war against women, inaugurating a new sexual pact and a new patriarchial era: the patriarchy of the wage. Women were branded as witches as it was a question of disciplining the women's body. In the beginning of the seventeenth century, the first male mid-wives began to appear and within a century, obstretics came under state control.[5] The sixteenth and seventeenth centuries were the heyday of mercantilism, the period marked the beginning of demographic recording (of birth, death and marriages), of census taking, and the formalization of demography itself as the first 'state science'. It is a clear proof of the strategic importance that controlling population movements was acquiring in the political circles that instigated witch hunt.[6]

In an agrarian society, witchcraft assumes a different dimension. Conflict resolution was expected by supernatural intervention plausible by access to the spirits. E. Evans Pritschard, working among the Azande tribe in Sudan defines witchcraft as, '. . . an ability to perpetuate evil that derives from an intrinsic quality of the evil doer that is not deliberately acquired. It is purely a psychic act.'[7] To M.G. Marwick, '. . . the power of witchcraft is believed to have been derieved from mystical inheritance. They are slaves of addiction and aberrations, bizarre people, sometimes tragic figures.'[8] This is true among the oppressed communities in agrarian societies, who go to a witch doctor to detect witchcraft activity or application of magic and sorcery responsible for their misfortune and sickness.[9] Witches are, hence, seen as peculiar people who embody all the feared and negative aspects of a culture. Belief in witchcraft can, therefore, be said to be culture based.

In India, the occult art too has its roots in antiquity.[10] R.S. Saletore in the book *Indian Witchcraft* has delved into the issue citing references from the *Atharvaveda* (often described as the earliest book of Indian priestly magic), Brahmanas, etc. References of havoc caused by demons and *pishachas*, or evil forces along with instances of divination, propiation of inimical powers by various means are found in *Rigveda*, and other Vedic texts.[11] Such beliefs persisted even in Buddhism and Jainism, as the Buddhist and Jaina monks were given staves to shield themselves against demons (*rakshasas*) and ghosts (*pishachas*). The *Yakshinis*, said to share many of the characteristics of witches are commemorated in Buddhist folklore.[12] *Yogini*, *Dakini*, *Asurani* are believed to have been associated with sorcery. The witch *daini* or *dakini*, known in mythology as an *asrapa* (blood sucker), was an imp or fiend, attending on Kali, an eater of human flesh, the source of her power. In south India, Kali is believed to descend on a man who has drunk goat's blood. In folklore, witches frequent burning grounds and cemeteries, penetrate anything on earth, open or cover the skies, restore the dead to life, set water on fire, change stones into wax, separate lovers, transform heroes or heroines into any form they like, control the weather, cause storm and tempests, appear lovely at first, roam naked in the graveyards and change shapes whenever they please. When 'off-duty', they behave like normal people.[13] A person's name, image, hair and his footprints were believed to be interconnected so as to serve the purpose of injuring him.[14] The witches (*dakinis*) were well-versed in Tantric lore and esoteric rituals.[15]

However, certain beliefs associated with the practice of witchcraft are common in all cultural practices. For instances, notions of cannibalism, practising in the dead of a new moon and full moon night, the ability to roam around, while the physical body is present in the house, associating the colour black with evil and the power of the 'evil eye' in bringing misfortune to the community are associated with witchcraft. Generally, most of the witches are old, poor, women who are widowed, infertile, possess ugly features, or old and unprotected. Socially ostracized women are usually targeted. In many cultures, the medico-religious practitioner is also considered a practitioner of magic and witchcraft. The amount of knowledge of curing by a *shaman* in culture is recognized by the culture as possible danger. The basic attitude is that if one can cure a disease then they may also cause a disease.[16] To undo the wrongs there exist witch doctors and these are generally men; thereby, making clear the notions of patriarchy and power relations clear, with men occupying the supreme position in these belief system. It is the fear of the unknown, which pushes one to resort to such practices and hence can be associated with superstition. Such practices exist even in the present time among marginalized societies and many ethnic communities. Witches, therefore, were and are cultural hybrids, blending learned and popular traditions. Neither of these traditions translated directly into practice, partly because each was inconsistent in itself. Modulation in meaning occurs whenever distinctions are forced: the elite ignore folk magic or extirpate it as blasphemy; the common people regard magicians as helpful healers or horrible hags.[17]

In this context, the article will look into the practice of witchcraft prevalent among the Rabha community in Assam. The Rabhas are among one of the aboriginal settlers of Assam and belong to the Tibeto-Burman linguistic stock. The majority of the Rabhas inhabit the undivided Goalpara, Kamarupa, Darrang districts in Assam and the Garo hill districts of Meghalaya. Besides the Rabhas are also found scattered in Nowgaon, Sibsagar, Karbi Anglong, Dibrugarh, North Lakhimpur and Cachar districts in Assam, parts of Meghalaya as well as districts of Purulia, West Dinajpur and the 24 Parganas in West Bengal.

Among the Rabhas, there exists a strong tradition of witchcraft; deeply embedded in their social system connecting it with religious beliefs. Reference to such practice is found in the *Baharistan-i-Ghaibi* written by Allauddin Ishfani alias Mirza Nathan, a Mughal general who had accompanied the Mughal army during the Ahom Mughal conflict in the early part of the seventeenth century. It states,

> Muhammad Zaman Tabrizi, who was appointed as a *Karori* (revenue officer) in the pargana of Khuntaghat (which falls in the present Goalpara and is a Rabha dominated area) was a victim of such witchcraft. The incident has been stated as follows: Muhammad Zaman was a hot tempered man and he began to oppress the ryots and seize their beautiful girls and boys. This place is notorious for magic and sorcery. Thus, if a man takes by force a fowl from a ryot and the ryot comes to the judge for redress and if that person is refused justice then the complainant by means of his magic and sorcery could make the accused produce the voice of a fowl from inside his stomach and thus proves the falsity of the protestations of the accused. If a bailiff of the judge stayed at a village in connection with the work of the *Dihidar* or the *Pattadar* (the tenure holder or the revenue farmer) and if in a state of drunkenness he demanded fish with violence in the evening or midnight when no fish was available, and persisted on his demand by torturing the ryots, then they would bring some leaves of mango tree or another tree whose name reads like *lahsura* and breathe on this leaves some words of magic or sorcery. These leaves would forthwith turn into a kind of small fish. When these fish were cooked by him in a state of drunkenness, they turned into blood. As soon as they were eaten by the bailiff, he died.[18]

Even Muhammad Zaman was bewitched by some person, that for two or three days he used to produce sounds of beast like dogs, cats or other animals of that class, following which he died.[19]

There are also numerous folk tale, folklores on witchcraft which has made the belief more strong in the minds of the people. One such tale is that of the *Kekra Khowa Rani*. The story goes as follows: in an earlier generation of the Zamindari of Mechpara Pargana, One Thanaram had a daughter in law from the Rabha Community. She was a simple village girl, extremely beautiful filled with fun and frolic, which attracted the attention of the feudal lord in one of his inspection tours around the area. Paying a bride price (*a poon sika rup kesa taka*) he married her and brought her to his house. But, she was unable to adjust to the new environment—the language and culture was unfamiliar to her. Her physical and mental health deteriorated and she yearned to return to her mother's house. For her satisfaction she was brought to her mother's house accompanied by the royal attendants. Here, the royal servants were surprised to see her devouring smoked crabs (known as *kekra* in the Rabha dialect). Henceforth, she came to be known as *Kekra Khowa Rani.* To place her in the context of the article, she was a soft-hearted woman, compassionate towards unfortunate women who were branded as witches (*daini*, in local term) and excommunicated from the society. Therefore, she established a rehabilation camp at *Bagnai.*[20] The inmates here reorted to begging and some even worked as day wagers. There is a belief among the Rabhas even today that such people should be given alms handsomely. If the spirits in them are satisfied, they will never cause harm.[21] It is, therefore, clear that in the earlier days they were not killed as they are done today.

Evaluating the above two incidents brings forth the history and culture of the place. The first is a question of resistance to foreign invasion. The second speaks of the food habits of the ethnic community which was disapproved by the elite section. The belief in the existence of spirits is not specifically a tribal concept. It was in vogue among the caste Hindus also. Late nineteenth-century colonial officials had set up an opposition between 'castes' and 'tribes' It was a cardinal item of faith among officials that the tribes of India were very different from its castes, both racially and in terms of their social structure. Tribal social structure was believed to be more egalitarian; tribes were thought to be isolated from the mainstream of Indian life and were felt to possess a 'spirit of independence' lacking among the castes. In the colonial discourses, witch-killings were considered to be practised principally by the tribes, and uncommon in caste societies.[22]

Benudhar Rajkowa in a treatise written in 1904 mentions the existence of evil and good in the social belief system in Assam.

Saturday and Tuesday were considered inauspicious as the knowledge of the evil influences of Saturn and Mars were ingrained in people's mind, along with the belief of good and evil omens associating birds and animals.[23] Existence of spirits, some of whom were benign, malign or indifferent, were well accepted. It is, however, a striking fact that the generality of the Assamese spirits are malignant.[24] Here, the author has distinguished the spirits into four categories—subterranean, terrestrial, aerial, celestial. But the largest number of spirits known to Assamese are terrestrial. They may be either male or female. But terms like, *phisayani*, *daini* existing today are terms specific to women. The word *daini* is derived from Sanskrit *dakini*, an attendant of Goddess Kali. She is a female spirit, a cannibal, 'her greediness being at the highest tension her mouth waters and the lower lip protrudes as soon as she happens to see a man in front'.[25] This idea of a witch is carried forth to this day. This must be due to the influence of Hinduism on their animistic belief system.

Being essentially animists, the Rabhas believed that supernatural beings abide in all objects animate and inanimate. This belief '. . . has been the characteristic of practically all primitive people and has been regarded by some scholars as the earliest forerunner of what we call religion'.[26] They are highly superstitious and assign all misfortune and disease as the work of the different deities, who should be appeased by sacrifice and rituals. According to them, the spirits are benevolent and malevolent. They have their separately assigned residence in a distinct province and exercise their power within their limitations. The spirits are invisible to the normal eye and may be manipulated to assume any form. It is the spirit in every object that wills and acts and so really count. It has no form of its own and so the Rabhas have never tried to form their images.[27]

Regarding the deities which in their local dialect are known as *bai* or *dai*, the Rabhas believe, the benevolent deities always help the people and control the various natural objects. They are worshipped annually by the villagers for the general well-being—for good health, good crops, prosperity and happiness.

BENEVOLENT DEITIES WITH THEIR FUNCTIONS

Name of the Deities	Function of the Deities
Langa	The deity of lives
Rise Bai	Chief Household deity
Khokchi	Deity of agriculture
Hasang	Another deity of agriculture
Rantak	Deity of house
Manasa	Deity of snakes
Kali	Deity of lives
Kachai Khati	Most powerful deity of all
Bhagavati	Deity of small pox

On the other hand, the main aim of the malevolent deities is to cause harm to people and bring misfortune to them. They believe the malevolent deities are controllers of disease and pain. So, to keep away disease these deities are invoked individually. The following table gives a list of malevolent deities or spirits of the Rabhas with the names of disease caused by them.

MALEVOLENT DEITIES OF THE RABHAS

Name of the Deities	Disease
Baima Bai	Abortion, stomach pain in pregnancy
Tikkar Bai	Stomach ache , headache etc
Bangra Bai	Body wound
Bisayali Bai	Rheumatism
Budha Bai	Post Natal Complicacies
Hudum Bai	Pain in joints of the body
Jakhani Bai	Crying child
Jakua bai	Body pain
Khisan Bai	Various eye diseases
Kama hachu Bai	Leprosy
Kuber Bai	Dyspepsia
Khusami Bai	Fever in the evening
Lambing Bai	Continuous ill health
Maira Bai	Headache
Rambang Bai	Epilepsy among the children
Singra Bai	Fever

It is believed that that a witch is malevolent. The belief and practice of witchcraft is most widely spread among the Rabhas, particularly in the Kamarupa and Goalpara districts of Assam. Witchcraft originally meant the work of a female sorcerer among the Rabhas. The person who exercises witchcraft may be male or female and is a public figure of fame and repute, while in other cases he may be notorious. A sorcerer might include the use of material objects and medicines to invoke supernatural malevolence.

The Rabhas believe that a man or woman can convert himself or herself into a demon or witch with magical power. In Rabha language, a witch is called Tikkar Bai or *daini.* A female person practising witchcraft is locally called *daini* or *bhutuni* and in case of a male they call him *daina* or *bhutia.* Sometimes they are locally called *daini bidya* or *bhutia bidya* or *bhutuni bidya.* According to the Rabhas, the Tikkar Bai or *daini* (witch) is actually a demon, to be produced from human beings. According to Rajen Rabha, they believe that a man or woman could convert himself or herself into a witch. By dint of magical power, the head can be cut-off from his or her neck. They believe that he or she (only head) walks with the help of his or her tongue and moves very fast hither and thither. A witch can also climb up the trees to eat jackfruit, mango, banana, etc. They are believed to have the power to fly and to move from place to place at high speed. They believe the witche, or *daini* are active mainly at night. The witches perform most of their deeds at night and their usual way of movement is flying while the body lies in apparent sleep. The spirit of witch, flies with flapping its wings like a bat. They believe that a witch or *daini* can see things in complete darkness as clearly as in the daytime and watch things happening far away and can see god, ghost and other supernatural beings that are invisible to common mortals. A witch or *daini* can instantly transform himself or herself into cat, bat, dog, bird, insect or any other animal of its choice.

If the witch wishes, he/she can cause various diseases in the body of the enimies by force of his/her jugglery. The Tikkar Bai or *daini* or witch is a male or female spirit and can do harm, when manipulated by some expert person who lives in the neighbourhood within their own community. Often, the person attacked by a Tikkar Bai or witch or *daini* become unconscious and lies as a dead body. The symptom of attack of a Tikkar Bai or *daini* is fever or severe pain in the stomach and the patient lies senseless. After that, the *ojha* or some experienced person covers up the body of the sick man with fishing net and ties up the little fingers of hands and feet and joins the fingers with unboiled raw threads by uttering magical chants so that the power of *daini* goes from the physical body of the patient. After that, the *ojha* places the leaves of *nag dangra* (*Pteris vittata*) trees and a little quantity of dung of a pig in front of the patient. The patient becomes restless. At that time, the *ojha* asks the name and address of the patient considering her as a Tikkar Bai or *daini* (witch). The witch is bound to confess her real identity and reveal her enmity with the patient. The nature of a *daini* is that she never reveals her own identity at first, rather she blames others. During that time, the voice of the patient also changes into the voice of the *daini*. The *ojha* does not leave her. He pierces the body of the patient with the teeth of a hog until she gives her identity. At last, she reveals her real identity, cries loudly for her ignorance, she offers lame excuses for her fault, and requests him to allow her to leave the body of the patient. She is compelled to swear that she would make a noise or break a tree in the household compound as a sign of leaving. After swearing this, as soon as the *daini* or witch departs from that place, the patient is cured completely for a while.[28]

BELIEFS ABOUT THE WITCHES

Some general beliefs about the witch among the Rabhas are as follows[29]:

1. Generally, the man or woman who practise witchcraft can never see eye-to-eye with other people.
2. Witches cannot sit on the *pira* (small wooden stool), which is made of only one piece of wood. If he or she sits on it, his/her hips get stuck to it.
3. Witches can see a person's heart like an image through a glass.
4. If the witch is in a sitting or standing position and someone nails

the shadow on its head, it cannot move from that particular place where he/she is sitting or standing.

5. Even when the witch sleeps at night, the head which looks like a fireball goes in search of victims.
6. Witches change themselves into animals like cat, dog, bat, etc., and go in search of victims.
7. The witch bewitches and kills her own child or relative if she fails to get other victims.
8. The *mantra* (spell) of witchcraft consists of only six words. If these words are remembered at night, the witch can wander around separating her head from her neck by magical powers.
9. Witches are active at night.
10. The victims are invariably members of their own village or relatives.

ACTIVITIES OF THE WITCHES

The witches are mainly women, widows, poor, infertile and sometimes men also who bewitch people and animals.[30] They perform various activities during the day, while at night they gather in small groups or sometimes alone visiting one homestead after another carrying out wicked practices. Before a man or woman is admitted to the group of witches, he or she has to prove that she had caused the death of close relatives, preferably her own child.

The witches use things collected from multiple sources to prepare medicines. At the dead of night she applies special medicines on the targeted victim. The witch collects clothes, hair or other things used by the victim. Mixed with other things these are buried at the entrance of the victim's house or in the campus. Gradually, the victim falls ill as believed by the people. It is quite similar to the idea of black magic. A witch may be considered a magician or sorcerer according to the type of work he or she does.

The witches may perform other destructive activities. They might not kill a man entirely on their own initiative rather invoke the dangerous spirits to cause diseases. Usually, the medicine men or healers invoke the spiritual world for help in curing the sick. Evil witches misuse this power for their own ends rather than for the benefit of others.

A witch tries to obtain an object connected with the person, whom he or she wants to harm, such as hair, nails, clothes, etc. He or she goes to burial place and puts the objects into a grave where there is a body or the ashes of a body and curses it. The witches may make an effigy of the victim's body, making it as thin as a skeleton or deforming its hands. It is believed the condition of the person deteriorates along with the condition of the effigy.

DIVISION OF WITCHES

Among the Rabhas, witches are divided into many types according to their activities. Some of them are malevolent and some benevolent. According to Shri Biswanath Rabha Tara of Bamungdanga village of Maldhara area of Goalpara district, witches are divided into six main divisions. According to their characteristic features these are[31]:

Sanibari manbatang, Mangalbari manbatang, Narami manbatang, Mirami manbatang, Dantray manbatang, Sintray manbatang.

Besides these the witches are again divided into eight divisions according to their activities. These are:

Fungisakay (*sai khaiti*—ash devourer)
Raysak saleka Kaya (*kalpat saleka*—licking palm leaves)
Ramini Bai (*alibatt pujita ba bate pothe dharota*—waits at the entrance)
Tikam Fakay (*china mostak*—appears to be familiar)
Kaya Tikkar (*nara rupi daini*—like a human being)
Ki Tikkar (general *daini*)
Bai (*kali rupi daini*)
May Tikkar (*lakhimi daini*)

All these are together known as *tikkar sung* or *maha daini.*

The Rabhas believe that a witch is a demon and he or she is manifested in human beings. They believe a witch can cut-off his/her throat by magical power at night and the head moves around on her tongue. They can also fly with magical power with the help of their hair.[32] Witchcraft is a continuous process among the Rabhas. The knowledge is passed on from the mother to the daughter from the time 'she learns to wear clothes' (meaning from a very early age. However, others who volunteer to acquire the knowledge can do so by undergoing training under an expert. While talking with Upen Rabha Hakasam.[33] One came across a very interesting piece of information, which emphasizes the patriarchial attitude of the society. All rituals in the Rabha society are conducted by the members of the four clans Pam (*mantra path*), Teng Tong (*dhulia*), Sursung (perform *puja*) and Rungdung (*prasad* making). They believe the male members of the *pam gotra* are intelligent and have excelled in many ways but they consider that women of that *gotra* use their intelligence for evil purpose.

Another important aspect connected with witch hunting is the role of the diviner who in their estimation can forecast and warn against any impending danger. Publicly organized divination is very common among the Rabhas. The Rabhas have female diviner (*deodhanis*), female religious dancers who perform shamanistic dances and make pronouncements in a state of trance on the occasion of Marai Puja. Often the priests themselves perform the functions of foretelling the future with the help of omens and auguries. When a person is sick for a prolonged period, a diviner or *ojha* or *ojhane* (also called a *pujari*) is called from a nearby village. The *ojha* first declares without seeing the sick man or woman that the person is in the grip of witch or *daini.* After that, the diviner starts the process of divination to discover the disease and gives some clue about the witch who is responsible for it. After the declaration, the villagers hold a meeting and decide that the named person is a *daini* or witch. Based on suspicion and superstition the villagers physically harass, torture and sometimes kill the witch. Most of the woman are punished by cutting off their hair because the Rabhas think that the head flies with the help of her long hair by dint of her magical power and cause harm to her enemy at night. The norm of killing a witch is to behead her/him. Today, there has been an increase in witch hunting which to a great extent is used as an excuse to fulfil their ulterior motives. They behead their enemy to substantiate it as a case of witch hunting. Here comes the politics of identification. The traditionally ingrained belief is taken advantage of by the people in the community with vested interests especially *ojhas* for gaining power over the people and their livelihood. Some common cause of convicting one as witch are illness, property dispute, damage of crops, sudden death of domesticated animal, cultural differentiation, strained relation with neighbours, mishap in marriage, rice beer offering, widow or widower, food poisoning, ugly features, etc. With scientific reasoning one can conclude that these faults cannot be the outcome of machination of any person or spirit (as it is believed to be). Thus, myths and beliefs continue to grip the society impeding rational thinking and actions.

Another aspect which needs emphasis is the fact that though the Rabhas have gradually embraced Hinduism, they still have deep faith in their traditional nature worship.[34] It is the belief that man must live in harmony with nature. If a person falls ill, it is believed to be the outcome of violating the balance between human beings and nature. On the one hand, it has the genesis of environment friendly beliefs and movements, but on the other, these concepts lead to a belief in sorcery, black magic, evil spirits and so on. In recent times, forces of cultural homogenization and ethnic revivalism too has been a determining factor in the rise of witch hunt practices among the ethnic communities. Of the Rabha dominated areas, some villages of Goalpara which were ideologically Left dominated from a distant past, under the leadership of Bishnu Prasad Rabha, a revolutionary political figure of Assam belonging to the revolutionary Communist Party of India (RCPI) and a few more influential communist leaders, during the fifties and sixties of the twentieth century, there was not a single case of *daini* or with hunt as the villagers could recall.[35] But, it has crept into the society now in the past three/four decades. Perhaps the assertion of belief in the *daini* has come also as a revivalist tendency under the sway of the idea of autonomous identity of the ethnic community, as distinct socio-cultural entity.

Therefore, the superstructure of belief systems, rituals and customs, the idea of their collective identities have situated the community within certain constraints and promises leading to intended or unintended consequences of their actions.

NOTES

1. Malcolm Gaskill, *Witchcraft: A Very Short Introduction*, Oxford University Press, New York, 2010, p. 1.
2. Ibid., p. 2.
3. E.B. Tylor, *Dictionary of Anthropology*, W.R. Goyal Publishers and Distributors, Delhi, 1990.
4. Christopher, Lakra *Witch Hunting and Gender Exclusion*, Indian Social Institute, New Delhi, Xavier Publications, Ranchi, 2017, p. 12.
5. Silvia Federici, *Caliban and The Witch,* Phoneme Publishers and Distributors, Delhi, 2013, p. 184.
6. Michael J. Cullen, *The Statistical Movement in Early Victorian Britain: The Foundations of Empirical Social Research,* cited in Silvia Federici, *Caliban and The Witch*, Phoneme Publishers and Distributors, Delhi, 2013, pp. 181-2.
7. E. Evans Pritchard, *Witchcraft in Africa*, cited in Douglas Mary (ed), *Witchcraft, Confessions and Accusations*, Tavistock Publications, London, 1970. p. xxiii.
8. M.G. Marwick, 'The Social Context of Cewa Witch Beliefs', *Africa* 22(2): 120-35, (3): 215-33, cited in Lakra Christopher, *Witch Hunting and Gender Exclusion*, Indian Social Institute, New Delhi, Xavier Publications, Ranchi, 2017, 1952, p. 15.
9. Christopher Lakra, *Witch Hunting and Gender Exclusion,* Indian Social Institute, New Delhi, Xavier Publications, Ranchi, 2017, p. 15.
10. R.S. Saletore, *Indian Witchcraft*, Abhinav Publications, New Delhi, 1981, p. 4.
11. Ibid., p. 61.
12. Ibid., p. 58.
13. Ibid., p. 120.
14. Ibid., p. 3.
15. Ibid., p. 122.
16. H.W. Haggard, *Devils, Drugs and Doctors*, New York and London, Harper and Brothers, 1929, pp. 501-5.
17. Malcolm Gaskill, op. cit., p. 27.
18. Nathan Mirza, *Baharistan-i-Ghaibi*, tr. M.I. Borah, vol. 1, para 306, p. 273.
19. Ibid., vol. 1, para 307, p. 274.
20. Upen Rabha Hakasam, 2013, *Bhasa Sahitya Shrasta Drasta Aru Samaj Nirmata,* Aak Bak, Guwahati, 2013, p. 401.
21. Interview with Prof. Upen Rabha Hakasam. Presently a Professor in the

Department of Assamese, Guwahati University on 15 September 2015. He has worked extensively on tribal cultural history and practices and has a number of books to his credit.

22. Ajay Skaria, 'Women, Witchcraft and Gratuitous Violence', in *Colonial Western India, Past & Present*, no. 155 (May 1997), pp. 109-41.
23. Prafulladutta Goswami (ed.), *Assamese Popular Superstitions and Assamese Demonology*, Gauhati University. Press , Guwahati, 1973, p. 23.
24. Ibid., p. 119.
25. Ibid., p. 190.
26. Smith Marrion, *Survey of Social Science*, Houghton Mifflin Co. Massachusetts, 1945, p. 285.
27. Rabha Rajen, *The Rabhas*, ABILAC, Guwahati, 2002, p. 186.
28. Ibid., p. 207-8.
29. Mahananda Das, Witchcraft Among the Rabhas of Kamrup and Goalpara Districts of Assam, Unpublished Thesis Gauhati University, 2012, p. 43.
30. Upen Rabha Hakasam, *Rabha Loka Sanskriti*, Asom Prakashan Parishad, Guwahati, 2003, pp. 112-19.
31. Cited in Ibid., p. 46.
32. Ibid.
33. Interview with Prof. Upen Rabha Hakasam, on 15 September 2014.
34. Upen Rabha Hakasam, *Rabha Loka Sanskriti*, 2003, p. 20.
35. *Witch-Hunting in Assam: A Report*, prepared by OKD Institute of Social Change and Development, Guwahati, Under the aegis of Assam Police, November 2015.

CHAPTER 30

Contextualizing Witch Hunting Practices in Assam

DEBARSHI PRASAD NATH

Witch hunting rests on the idea of witchcraft and black magic. Practices of witch hunting have been prevalent in Assam for a long time now. Scholars such as E.T. Dalton had pointed out to the prevalence of witch hunting in nineteenth-century Assam. Though the practice has been in vogue for a long time, it has recently seen a revival of sorts with its spread to communities which were not generally known to follow it. For a long time, it was considered to be a 'tribal' issue, an issue therefore, that the mainstream could afford to ignore. Gradually, the practice of this ritual has begun to spread across communities.

Cultural contact can lead to the reification of differences and cynical retreats into celebration of what each group regards as distinctively its own (Krupat 1992: 15). It has been argued elsewhere that, nationalist aspiration and violence characterizes the ethnic identity politics of Assam. 'Communities can respond to complex transitions in diverse ways. If the state is seen as opposed to the interests of a community then its edicts are not reliable; in fact they have to be opposed to keep alive the nationalist aspirations of a community' (Nath 2014: 59). One preserves, guards, and celebrates that in which one finds reason to take pride or that which reinforces one's sense of self as imagined—or would like to be. One may find utility in a historical event or individual as a symbol at one time but not at another. A similar view is expressed by Gretchen who says, 'We preserve, guard, and celebrate that in which we find reason to take pride or that which reinforces our sense of ourselves as we imagine we are—or would like to be. We may find utility in a historical event or individual as a symbol at one time but not at another.'

Once upon a time there was a belief that, the process of modernization initiated by the British in the post-colonial world would make 'dirty' things like witchcraft disappear as they apparently did in Europe earlier. However, as time has proved, this was not to be. People rely on their cultural memory to feed their ideas into new circumstances. There is never any abandonment of all ideas from the past. Witchcraft and witch hunt in contemporary Assam have become a prominent way of coping with the very 'modernity' that was supposed to have done away with them.

Belief in witches and witchcraft tend to exist in the background of community affairs in the societies where such ideas are held. Mary (a fictitious name) belongs to the *Adivasi* community of Assam. She lives in the Napaam area of the Sonitpur district. She and her mother work as domestic help in the Tezpur University Campus. Mary's mother occasionally played the role of an *ojha*, a traditional healer for members of her community. Belief in witchcraft is a part of the social set-up and if not in broad daylight, it flourishes in the shadows, in the dark 'underworld', fed by gossip and rumour. During such periods, belief in witches and witchcraft is kept alive by rumour sparked by jealousy and resentment. However, like Sigmund Freud's 'unconscious' it waits for the opportune moment and emerges into the public sphere only in times of anxiety such as the actual sickness or death of someone in a neighbouring family.

It was quite obvious from the interactions with Mary's mother that, she actually took pride in the fact that people approached her with requests for curing their ailments and solving their problems. But the *ojha* always walks on a tightrope. It does not take a long while for people to turn against each other in a general atmosphere of mistrust and suspicion. When the reasons for the general hardship and adversities of life of people like Mary and her mother and others in the community are not apparent, people strive desperately to locate an enemy, a visible one on whom they can take out all their pent up frustration. In a society besotted with identity politics, a society in which class solidarity has long crumbled and where gender solidarity was never allowed to materialize, the best response to get out of the anxiety of these problems is to evoke a pristine past on the basis of a shared cultural memory.

On one occasion, some of Mary's neighbours fell ill. They suspected Mary's mother of foul play. Mary's mother tried to argue that she was in no way responsible for the maladies that afflicted them. However, one night the villagers gathered near Mary's house and barged into her house with sticks and knives to threaten her mother with dire consequences if the spell that she had apparently cast on the neighbouring family was not immediately revoked. Interestingly, Mary's village is inhabited by *Adivasis*, Assamese, Nepalese and Bengali Muslims. The perpetrators of violence informed Mary's mother that she would be put to trial by the villagers on charges of being a witch. It was also decided by the perpetrators that only the members, who belonged to their community would be allowed to attend the meeting. Mary later talked about her attempt to persuade them about the need and logic of inviting members of other communities. But this was not granted as it was apparently an 'internal' matter of the community that needed to be sorted out within it. The only discourse that has acceptability in this context is the discourse of indigeneity. For once, the timely intervention of the police helped to avert what seemed at one point of time to be an imminent disaster.

Shashank Sinha in 'Witch-Hunts, Adivasis, and the Uprising in Chhotanagpur' notes a sudden surge in 'witch-hunting' practice during 1857-8, a practice that the British had banned for its obvious barbarity. As Sinha argues, witch-hunts actually symbolized an attack on the new laws and edicts issued by the 'enemy'. They were a local response to the varied resistance that the British faced across north India:

> Effectively combining both gender and anti-colonial tensions, witch-hunts were systematically incorporated into the mobilisation strategies of the anti-colonial *Adivasi* movements in Chhotanagpur. (2007: 1675)

There is indeed no doubt that considering the kind of frenzied passion that witch hunts can trigger off, it could have been a very potent weapon for ethnic mobilization.

Shashank Sinha's reading of witch hunting practices of the *Adivasis* of Chota Nagpur area during the 1857 uprising does provide a new perspective for understanding the resurgence of such practices among the *Adivasis* of Assam in the twentieth century. The *Adivasis* migrated to Assam in the nineteenth century and once they settled down here they lost touch with their homeland. Fernandes, Pereira and Khatso have stated the prevalence of the matriarchal system in *Adivasi* society. Once they switched over to the patriarchal system, the woman's role decreased in all spheres and it resulted in the deterioration of her status (2007: 117). A study of the 1920s mentioned most tea garden *Adivasis* as followers of the tribal Sarna religion (2007: 141). There were signs of Sarna among them even in the 1980s. However, gradually Christianity and Hinduism took over.

Today, the Adivasis have begun a process of retracing their lineage back to Jharkhand as the starting point for reclaiming their identity. The problem is not uncomplicated for as Fernandes, Pereira and Khatso point out, very few *Adivasis* are left with memories of their customary law (2007: 104). In order to revive their cultural past they have gone back to handicraft items from Jharkhand. The *Adivasis* have tried to link their cultural past 'to a customary law which they have lost to a great extent because of their isolation in the regimented work structure of the tea gardens' (Fernandes, Pereira and Khatso 2007: 104).

In the process of 'integration' and 'assimilation' with institutionalised religions, many ethnic communities have internalized a deep-seated fear and suspicion of woman. Thus, 'traditional' patriarchal prejudices (which did exist in spite of the existence of matriarchal systems in some societies) combine with an internalized sense of male authority to produce a dangerous concoction in so far as women are concerned. Patriarchal religious values, indigenous as well as acquired, combine to strengthen the stereotypes of women as jealous, vindictive and secretive and more inclined towards witchcraft. The fact that women are in charge of the reproduction of their families magnifies men's fear of their powers.

Being politically correct about social and customary practices of the north-east has become such an imperative that ideas of equality and justice have taken a backseat. This explains why this grossest violation of human rights in Assam has not received the kind of attention that it deserves.

CONCLUSION

Witch hunting practices in Assam can, on the one hand, be seen as a fallout of the tremendous pressure that globalization has exerted on land resources. Globalization has led to the shrinking of land resources of indigenous communities. Land resources are shrinking at a rate never witnessed before, thus striking at the very root of the social fabric of ethnic communities. If one looks at the cases of witch hunting that have been reported in the state of Assam in the last two decades, the group that appears to be the most vulnerable is people with landed property. Land grabbing on the pretext of witch hunting is therefore becoming very common. Second, the perceived threat of globalization has led to ethnic mobilization, insisting on a revival of traditional practices and customs. The revival of some of these practices may also be seen as a defiance of the new cultural order imposed by globalization. Moreover, the increasing involvement of global players in the health sector has unfortunately widened the chasm between communities, who have access to modern health care in the towns and cities and those who are left in the lurch in rural areas. Incidents of witch hunting tend to rise during periods of political and social instability. Third, in the context of the ethnic assertion movements of the north-east, revival of indigenous knowledge needs to be seen against the background of reclamation of traditional ways of life. Moreover, in an increasingly 'competitive' world there is a great deal of pressure on traditional healers to deliver. The distrust of Western medicine that has been encouraged by various schools of thought in the name of reclaiming non-empirical ethnoscience and proposing alternative modernities has done irreparable harm to communities living in the 'margins' such as the *Adivasis* of Assam.

Many communities around the world today foresee the nightmarish scenario of cultural homogenization, with diverse national cultures giving way to a world dominated by Western values and symbols. It is also true that, while traditions are restrictive in certain respects, they can also be a way of ensuring freedom and identity-assertion in a society beset with insurgency, consumerism and identity politics. But to retain traditional customs and practices only to prove that these are still useful in the local contexts would be a hazardous proposition. There is obviously no doubt about the fact that some traditional values and practices can be liberating, but it is also a fact that there is a lot in it that clash with universal values of human rights. Ironically, the fight for economic equality is fought in a cultural terrain. The divorce of culture from economics being complete, token protests in the name of indigenous culture is all that one is seemingly left with.

REFERENCES

Adams, Gretchen A., 2000, 'Mysteries, Memories, and Metaphors: The Salem Witchcraft Trials in the American Imagination', *The Proceedings of the American Antiquarian Society, 1880-2008*, vol. 110, part 2.

Dalton, E.T., 1960, *Descriptive Ethnology of Bengal*, Calcutta: Bengal Government Press.

Fernandes, Walter, Melville Pereira and Vizalenu Khatso, 2007, *Customary Laws in North East India: Impact on Women*, New Delhi: National Commission for Women. URL: www.ncw.nic.in/pdfReports/Customary%20Law.pdf. Accessed on 24 February 2012.

Krupat, Arnold, 1992, *Ethnocriticism: Ethnography History Literature*, Berkeley, Los Angeles and Oxford: University of California Press.

Nath, Debarshi Prasad, 2014, 'Assam's Tale of Witch Hunting and Indigeneity', *Economic & Political Weekly*, vol. XLIX, no. 54.

Sinha, Shashank, 2007, 'Witch-Hunts, Adivasis, and the Uprising in Chhotanagpur', *Economic & Political Weekly*, 42(19): 1672-6, viewed on 21 February 2012, http://www.jstor.org/ stable/4419566.

Contributors

Archana Barua, Professor & Head, Department of Philosophy, Assam Don Bosco University, Sonapur, Gauhati.

Assaduzzaman, Assistant Professor, BBB College, Morigaon, Assam.

Barnali Sharma, Associate Professor, Department of History, Gauhati University.

Bashabi Gupta, Associate Professor, Department of Geography, Miranda House, University of Delhi, Delhi.

Chandan Kumar Sarma, Associate Professor and Head, Department of History, Dibrugarh University.

Debarshi Prasad Nath, Professor and Head, Department of Cultural Studies, Tezpur University, Assam.

D.L. Haokip, Assistant Professor, Department of History, Gauhati University.

Dina Swargiari, Research Scholar, Tezpur University.

Edward Gait, former ICS and author of *History of Assam* (1905).

E.K. Santha, Assistant Professor, SRM University, Sikkim.

Hermina B. Lakiang, Assistant Professor and Head of History Department, Bissau College, Shillong.

Jahnabi Gogoi Nath, Professor and Head, Department of History, Dibrugarh University.

J.H. Hutton, formerly of Indian Civil Service and chair of William Wyse Professor of Social Anthropology at the University of Cambridge.

Jangkhomang Guite, is Associate Professor at Department of History, Manipur University, Imphal.

JAE-EUN SHIN, Research Fellow, Research Institute for Languages and Cultures of Asia and Africa, Tokyo University of Foreign Studies.

KYNPHAM SING NONGKYNRIH, Professor, Department of History, North Eastern Hill University, Shillong.

M. PARWEZ, Professor, Centre for Advanced Studies in History, Aligarh Muslim University.

MAHENDRA PRASAD GURUNG, Research Scholar, Department of Mass Communications, Sikkim University.

NIKITA SHANDILYA, Research Scholar, Department of History, Assam University, Diphu.

NIRMAL KUMAR MAHATO, Associate Professor, Department of History, Vidyasagar University, Medinipur, West Bengal.

OBJA BORAH HAZARIKA, Assistant Professor Department of Political Science, Dibrugarh University.

OLYMPIA KURMI, Assistant Professor, Department of Commerce, Rajiv Gandhi University.

PHOIBI LALNIROPUI TUOLOR, Assistant Professor, Department of History, Handique Girls College, Guwahati.

RAJIB HANDIQUE, Professor and Head, Department of History, Gauhati University.

RANJEETA MANNOW, Assistant Professor in Economics, Donyi Polo Government College, Kamki, Arunachal Pradesh.

ROHMINGMAWII, Assistant Professor, Department of History, Pachhunga University College, Aizawl.

SARAH HILALY, Professor, Department of History, Rajiv Gandhi University.

TAGE HABUNG, Assistant Professor in History, Government College Doimukh, Arunachal Pradesh.

TEJIMALA GURUNG NAG, Professor, Department of History, North Eastern Hill University, Shillong.

TINGLEINAM THAGIEW, Research Scholar, Department of History, Assam University, Silchar.

VANDANA GOSWAMI, Independent Researcher.